"The Law
of the Spirit"

Studies in Biblical Literature

Hemchand Gossai
General Editor

Vol. 86

PETER LANG
New York • Washington, D.C./Baltimore • Bern
Frankfurt am Main • Berlin • Brussels • Vienna • Oxford

John A. Bertone

"The Law
of the Spirit"

Experience of the Spirit
and Displacement
of the Law in Romans 8:1–16

PETER LANG
New York • Washington, D.C./Baltimore • Bern
Frankfurt am Main • Berlin • Brussels • Vienna • Oxford

Library of Congress Cataloging-in-Publication Data

Bertone, John Anthony.
"The law of the Spirit": experience of the Spirit and displacement
of the law in Romans 8:1–16 / John A. Bertone.
p. cm. — (Studies in biblical literature; v. 86)
Includes bibliographical references and index.
1. Bible. N.T. Romans VIII, 1–16—Criticism, interpretation, etc.
2. Letter and spirit antithesis (Pauline doctrine). I. Title. II. Series.
BS2665.52.B47   227'.106—dc22   2005006763
ISBN 978-0-8204-7853-1
ISSN 1089-0645

Bibliographic information published by **Die Deutsche Bibliothek**.
Die Deutsche Bibliothek lists this publication in the "Deutsche
Nationalbibliografie"; detailed bibliographic data is available
on the Internet at http://dnb.ddb.de/.

The paper in this book meets the guidelines for permanence and durability
of the Committee on Production Guidelines for Book Longevity
of the Council of Library Resources.

Printed in Germany

Table of Contents

PART ONE
Pauline Antecedents: Spirit and Law in Ethical Renewal and Jewish Eschatology

PART TWO
The Spirit Displaces the Law as the Principle of New Life: Romans 7–8

PART THREE
Conconance Between the New Era of the Spirit and Judaism's Covenantal Nomism

Editor's Preface

More than ever the horizons in biblical literature are being expanded beyond that which is immediately imagined; important new methodological, theological, and hermeneutical directions are being explored, often resulting in significant contributions to the world of biblical scholarship. It is an exciting time for the academy as engagement in biblical studies continues to be heightened.

This series seeks to make available to scholars and institutions, scholarship of a high order, and which will make a significant contribution to the ongoing biblical discourse. This series includes established and innovative directions, covering general and particular areas in biblical study. For every volume considered for this series, we explore the question as to whether the study will push the horizons of biblical scholarship. The answer must be *yes* for inclusion.

In this volume John Bertone examines in two significant parts Jewish eschatology and the role of the Spirit in covenant renewal within the context of Second Temple Judaism, together with Paul's understanding of the Spirit and the Law. While the author acknowledges Paul's familiarity and understanding of the role of the Spirit in covenant renewal within the context of Second Temple Judaism, he argues in a compelling and systematic way that Paul's understanding and employment of this idea is radically different. Indeed, Bertone submits that there is a tangible tension and dissonance between Paul and Second Temple Judaism's understanding of the role of the Spirit. This study proposes a manner of reading Paul in relation to Jewish eschatology and Second Temple Judaism that must be reckoned with. Agree or not, here is a study that scholars will find instructive and sophisticated.

The horizon has been expanded.

Hemchand Gossai
Series Editor

Author's Preface

This research was originally written as a Ph.D. dissertation at the University of St. Michael's College (University of Toronto). My interest in Romans 7–8 began in my teenage years and persisted during my post-graduate studies where I had the opportunity to engage in a more critical reading of this text. I quickly recognized that Paul was attempting to communicate something profound. His understanding of the relationship between Christ, the Spirit, and the Law and their respective roles hit at the very core of his convictional world. However, at the same time, I wondered why Paul intentionally chose to express his thoughts using vague and obscure language (e.g., "the law of my mind," "the law of sin," "the law of the Spirit of life in Christ Jesus"). I also began to question why, on the one hand, he went to great lengths to show the disparity between the Spirit and Law, but then, on the other hand, in the very same context, he attempted to mask this and show how the Spirit's role was harmonious with that of the Law. I soon discovered that both the ambiguous language and the textual tensions were not limited to his explication of the relationship between the Spirit and the Law in Romans 7–8. They surfaced in most of Paul's other letters as well, when he addressed the Mosaic Law and its relationship to a variety of subjects. It appeared then, what transpired in Romans 7–8 was part of a larger and more complex issue. This means that the tensions cannot be explained by the situational context of the letter alone (i.e., Paul was responding to accusations that he was advocating an antinomian point of view).

My research led me to explore E.P. Sanders' influential study, *Paul and Palestinian Judaism* and Gordon Fee's book, *God's Empowering Presence*. Fee challenged me to look at Paul's understanding of the Law via his pneumatology. In further consultation with other sources, I discovered that there was a common tendency to read Paul's pneumatology through a Christological lens. This was particularly true of Romans 8, even though the Christocentric participatory language was used sparingly in this chapter. In addition, I found that these textual tensions between the Spirit and the Law were either explained away as Paul's two-sided perspective of the Law or, when the tensions were recognized for what they were, they were said to be expressive of Paul's straightforward contradictions on the Law.

My interpretation of Romans 7–8 attempts to be sensitive to Paul's pneumatological statements, emphasizing how his understanding of the experience of the Spirit makes its own unique contribution to the question of the place and purpose of the Law for believers. At the same time, with the use of Leon Festinger's, Cognitive Dissonance Theory, I suggest an alternate way of interpreting the textual tensions. My hope is that this study would make a contribution to the ongoing discussion of Paul and the Law.

I would like to express my appreciation to the numerous people who enabled me to write this book. Without their support and direction this study could not have been possible. First of all, I am especially thankful to have had the privilege of working under the direction of Dr. Terence L. Donaldson, Lord and Lady Coggan Professor of New Testament Studies at Wycliffe College, a man who demonstrates comprehensiveness of learning and enthusiasm for the study of the New Testament. His friendship and patience in challenging and correcting my course of research were evident throughout the composition of this study. On more than one occasion when I faced the daunting task of trying to understand the complexities of one of the most controversial passages in Pauline literature and was ready to abandon this investigation for a subject with fewer complications, he helped me see the light at the end of the tunnel. His example of responsible biblical scholarship has left an indelible mark upon my life; ἀνὴρ...δυνατὸς ὢν ἐν ταῖς γραφαῖς (Acts 18:24).

I am grateful to Professors Ann Jervis (Wycliffe College) and Michael Steinhauser (Director for Advanced Degree Studies, Toronto School of Theology), who have read this study in its entirety and have interacted with it in critical and constructive ways. Professor Stephen Westerholm of McMaster University provided a thorough analysis, which sharpened my thinking in many areas.

I wish to thank Ms. Phyllis Korper (Senior Acquisitions Editor of Peter Lang Publishing) and Professor Hemchand Gossai (Series Editor) for accepting this work for publication in their Studies in Biblical Literature series. Ms. Maria Amoroso also provided helpful assistance in the production of the book.

My deepest thanks go to my parents, who lightened the financial load in various ways throughout the duration of my research. They first taught me about the importance of the Christian faith and the indispensable role of the Spirit in my life. Over thirty years ago medical science was dumbfounded when my younger brother, who was diagnosed with a severe case of Meningitis and given little hope of becoming well, suddenly experienced a full recovery. *Emitte Spiritum tuum, et creabuntur.*

Most of all, my wife Beth Joy was truly an inspiration of joy for me in this period of study and provided loving companionship. She put her own aspirations of education on hold so I could complete this study. Her support has been unwavering, even though she did not fully understand the relevance of my research. Our three children Christian, Justin, and Lauren have enriched our lives in unique ways. I've often heard my children say to others, "Daddy is writing his book," not knowing what was involved, but then they quickly added, "And we're going to Disney World when it is done." They make life fun. *Io vi amo a tutti.*

John A. Bertone
Niagara Falls, Ontario
February 9, 2005

Abbreviations

Periodicals, Serials, and Reference Works

AB	Anchor Bible
ABR	*Australian Biblical Review*
AnBib	Analecta biblica
AGJU	Arbeiten zur Geschichte des antiken Judentums und des Urchristentums
ALS	Applied Logic Series
BBB	Bonner biblische Beiträge
BDAG	Bauer, W., F.W. Danker, W.F. Arndt, and F.W. Gingrich. *Greek-English Lexicon of the New Testament and Other Early Christian Literature*. 3rd ed. Chicago, 2000.
BDB	Brown, F., S.R. Driver, and C.A. Briggs. *A Hebrew and English Lexicon of the Old Testament*. Oxford, 1907.
BDF	Blass, F., A. Debrunner, and R.W. Funk. *A Greek Grammar of the New Testament and Other Early Christian Literature*. Chicago, 1961.
BevT	Beiträge zur evangelischen Theologie
BHT	Beiträge zur historischen Theologie
Bijdr	*Bijdragen: Tijdschift voor filosofie en theologie*
BJRL	*Bulletin of the John Rylands University Library of Manchester*
BNTC	Black's New Testament Commentaries
BST	Bible Speaks Today
BTB	*Biblical Theology Bulletin*
BU	Biblische Untersuchungen
BZNW	Beihefte zur Zeitschrift für die neutestamentliche Wissenschaft
CBQ	*Catholic Biblical Quarterly*
CCS	Cambridge Classical Studies
EBC	The Expositor's Bible Commentary

EDNT	*Exegetical Dictionary of the New Testament.* Edited by H. Balz, G. Schneider. ET. Grand Rapids, 1990–1993
EKKNT	Evangelisch-katholischer Kommentar zum Neuen Testament
ETL	*Ephemerides theologicae lovanienses*
EvT	*Evangelische Theologie*
ExpTim	*Expository Times*
FRLANT	Forschungen zur Religion und Literatur des Alten und Neuen Testaments
HBT	*Horizons in Biblical Theology*
HNT	Handbuch zum Neuen Testament
HNTC	Harper's New Testament Commentaries
HTKNT	Herders theologischer Kommentar zum Neuen Testament
HTR	*Harvard Theological Review*
ICC	International Critical Commentary
Int	*Interpretation*
ISBE	*International Standard Bible Encyclopedia.* Edited by G.W. Bromiley. 4 vols. Grand Rapids, 1979–1988
JASP	*Journal of Abnormal and Social Psychology*
JBL	*Journal of Biblical Literature*
JETS	*Journal of the Evangelical Theological Society*
JJS	*Journal of Jewish Studies*
JPT	*Journal of Pentecostal Theology*
JPTSup	Journal of Pentecostal Theology: Supplement Series
JQR	*Jewish Quarterly Review*
JR	*Journal of Religion*
JSNT	*Journal for the Study of the New Testament*
JSNTSup	Journal for the Study of the New Testament: Supplement Series
JSOTSup	Journal for the Study of the Old Testament: Supplement Series
JSSR	*Journal for the Scientific Study of Religion*
JTS	*Journal of Theological Studies*
LCL	Loeb Classical Library
LD	Lectio divina
LS	*Louvain Studies*
NAC	New American Commentary
NCB	New Century Bible
Neot	*Neotestamentica*
NIBCNT	New International Biblical Commentary on the New Testament

NICNT	New International Commentary on the New Testament
NICOT	New International Commentary on the Old Testament
NIDNTT	*New International Dictionary of New Testament Theology.* Edited by C. Brown. 4 vols. Grand Rapids, 1975–1985
NIGNT	New International Greek Testament Commentary
NovT	*Novum Testamentum*
NovTSup	Novum Testamentum Supplements
NRTh	*La nouvelle revue thevologique*
NTS	*New Testament Studies*
Numen	*Numen: International Review for the History of Religions*
OTP	*Old Testament Pseudepidgrapha.* Edited by J.H. Charlesworth. 2 vols. New York, 1983.
PA	Philosophia Antiqua
PR	*Psychological Review*
RB	*Revue biblique*
RevExp	*Review and Expositor*
RevQ	*Revue de Qumran*
SBEC	Studies in Bible and Early Christianity
SBF	Studium Biblicum Franciscanum
SBM	Stuttgarter biblische Monographien
SBT	Studies in Biblical Theology
Scr	*Scripture*
SEÅ	*Svensk exegetisk årsbok*
SJT	*Scottish Journal of Theology*
Semeia	*Semeia*
SNTSMS	Society for New Testament Studies Monograph Series
SP	Sacra Pagina
SR	*Studies in Religion*
SSS	Semitic Study Series
ST	*Studia theologica*
Str-B	Strack, H.L., and P. Billerbeck. *Kommentary zum Neuen Testament aus Talmud und Midrasch.* 6 vols. Munich. 1922–61
SUNT	Studien zur Umwelt des Neuen Testaments
TDNT	*Theological Dictionary of the New Testament.* Edited by G. Kittel and G. Friedrich. Translated by G.W. Bromiley. 10 vols. Grand Rapids, 1964–1976
TJ	*Trinity Journal*
TNTC	Tyndale New Testamnt Commentaries
TOTC	Tyndale Old Testament Commentaries

TPINTC	TPI New Testament Commentaries
TZ	*Theologische Zeitschrift*
UNT	Untersuchungen zum Neuen Testament
VoxEv	*Vox evangelica*
VT	*Vetus Testamentum*
WBC	Word Biblical Commentary
WUNT	Wissenschaftliche Untersuchungen zum Neuen Testament
ZAW	*Zeitschrift für die alttestamentliche Wissenschaft*
ZTK	*Zeitschrift für Theologie und Kirche*

Hebrew Bible/ Old Testament

OT- Old Testament
MT- Masoretic Text

Gen.	Genesis	Song	Song of Songs
Exod.	Exodus	Isa.	Isaiah
Lev.	Leviticus	Jer.	Jeremiah
Num.	Numbers	Lam.	Lamentations
Deut.	Deuteronomy	Ezek.	Ezekiel
Josh.	Joshua	Dan.	Daniel
Judg.	Judges	Hos.	Hosea
Ruth	Ruth	Joel	Joel
1-2 Sam.	1-2 Samuel	Amos	Amos
1-2 Ki.	1-2 Kings	Obad.	Obadiah
1-2 Chron.	1-2 Chronicles	Jonah	Jonah
Ezra	Ezra	Mic.	Micah
Neh.	Nehemiah	Nah.	Nahum
Esther	Esther	Hab.	Habakkuk
Job	Job	Zeph.	Zephaniah
Ps.	Psalms	Hag.	Haggai
Prov.	Proverbs	Zech.	Zechariah
Eccl.(Qoh)	Ecclesiastes (Qoheleth)	Mal.	Malachi

New Testament

NT-New Testament

| Matt. | Matthew | Lk. | Luke |
| Mk. | Mark | Jn. | John |

Acts	Acts	Tit.	Titus
Rom.	Romans	Phlm.	Philemon
1–2 Cor.	1–2 Corinthians	Heb.	Hebrews
Gal.	Galatians	James	James
Eph.	Ephesians	1–2 Pet.	1–2 Peter
Phil.	Philippians	1–2–3 Jn.	1–2–3 John
Col.	Colossians	Jude	Jude
1–2 Thess.	1–2 Thessalonians	Rev.	Revelation
1–2 Tim.	1–2 Timothy		

Apocrypha and Septuagint

LXX- Septuagint

Bar.	Baruch	Jdt.	Judith
Add. Dan.	Additions to Daniel	1–2 Macc.	1–2 Maccabees
Pr. Azar.	Prayer of Azariah	3–4 Macc.	3–4 Maccabees
Bel.	Bel and the Dragon	Pr. Man.	Prayer of Manasseh
Sg. Three	Song of Three Young Men	Ps. 51	Psalm 51
Sus.	Susanna	Sir.	Sirach/Ecclesiasticus
1–2 Esd.	1–2 Esdras	Tob.	Tobit
Add. Esth.	Additions to Esther	Wis.	Wisdom of Solomon
Ep. Jer.	Epistle of Jeremiah		

Dead Sea Scrolls

CD	Cairo Genizah (*Damascus Document*)	1QS	*Serek Hayahad* or *Rule of the Community*
DSS	Dead Sea Scrolls	1QpHab	*Pesher Habakkuk*
1QH	*Hodayot* or *Thanksgiving Hymns*	1Q21	*T. Lev* (Aramaic)
		1Q34	Liturgy Prayers
		4Q213–214	Leviticus (Aramaic)
		4Q215	*T. Naph.*
		4Q504	*Dibre Hame'orot* or *Words of the Luminaries*
1QM	*Milhamah* or *War Scroll*	4Q538	*T. Jud.* (Aramaic)
p	Pesher (e.g., 1QpHab)	11QMelch	*Melchizedek* text from Qumran cave 11

Q   Qumran
1Q, 2Q   Numbered caves of Qumran, followed by abbreviation of book

Old Testament Pseudepigrapha

Aristob.	Aristobulus	T. Ash.	Testament of Asher
As. Mos.	Assumption of Moses	T. Benj.	Testament of Benjamin
2 Bar.	2 Baruch	T. Dan.	Testament of Daniel
3 Bar.	3 Baruch	T. Gad	Testament of Gad
4 Bar.	4 Baruch	T. Iss.	Testament of Issachar
1 En.	1 Enoch	T. Jos.	Testament of Joseph
2 En.	2 Enoch	T. Jud.	Testament of Judah
3 En.	3 Enoch	T. Levi	Testament of Levi
4 Ezra	4 Ezra	T. Naph.	Testament of Naphtali
Jan. Jam.	James and Jambres	T. Reub.	Testament of Reuben
Jos. Asen.	Joseph and Aseneth	T. Sim.	Testament of Simeon
Jub.	Jubilees	T. Zeb.	Testament of Zebulun
3 Macc.	3 Maccabees	T. Abr.	Testament of Abraham
4 Macc.	4 Maccabees	T. Isaac	Testament of Isaac
5 Macc.	5 Maccabees	T. Jac.	Testament of Jacob
Odes Sol.	Odes of Solomon	T. Adam	Testament of Adam
Pr. Jac.	Prayer of Jacob	T. Job	Testament of Job
Pr. Jos.	Prayer of Joseph	T. Mos.	Testament of Moses
Pr. Man.	Prayer of Manasseh	T. Sol.	Testament of Solomon
Pr. Mos.	Prayer of Moses		
Ps.-Philo	Pseudo-Philo		
Pss. Sol.	Psalms of Solomon		
Sib. Or.	Sibylline Oracles		

Philo

Abr.	De Abrahamo	Leg. All.	Legum allegoriae I,II,III
Cher.	De cherubim	Legat.	Legatio ad Gaium
Conf.	De confusione linguarum	Migr.	De migratione Abrahami
Congr.	De congressu eruditionis Gratia	Mos.	De vita Mosis I,II
		Mut.	De mutatione nominum
Decal.	De decalogo	Op.	De opificio mundi
Det.	Quod deterius potiori insidari soleat	Plant.	De plantatione
		Post.	De posteritate Caini

Ebr.	De ebrietate	Praem.	De praemiis et poenis
Fug.	De fuga et inventione	Quaest.in	Quaestiones et solutiones
Gig.	De gigantibus	Gn.	in Genesin I,II,III,IV
Jos.	De Iosepho	Quis Her.	Quis rerum divinarum heres sit
Quod Deus	Quod Deus sit immutabilis	Spec.Leg.	De specialibus legibus I, II,III,IV
Som.	De somniis I,II	Virt.	De virtutibus

Josephus

Ag. Ap.	Against Apion	Life	The Life
Ant.	Jewish Antiquities	War	Jewish War

Rabbinic Works

Deut. Rab.	Deuteronomy Rabbah
Gen. Rab.	Genesis Rabbah
m. Abot	Mishnah Avot
m. Sanh.	Mishnah Sanhedrin
m.Qidd.	Mishnah Qiddushin
m.Giṭ.	Mishnah Giṭṭin
Midr. Ps.	Midrash Psalm
Qidd.	Qiddushin
Sanh.	Sanhedrin
S. Eli. R.	Seder Eliyahu Rabbah
Sipra Lev.	Sifra Leviticus
Tg. Neof.	Targum Neofiti
Tg. Onq.	Targum Onqelos
Tg. Ps.-J	Targum Pseudo-Jonathan
Tg. Yer.	Targum Yerusalmi
tr. Yad.	Tractate Yadayim
Tos.	Tosepta Qiddushin

Greek and Latin Works

Leg.	Leges- Laws (Plato)
Praep. Evang.	Praeparatio evangelica- Preparation for the Gospel (Eusebius)
Resp.	Respublica- Republic (Plato)

Bible Versions

ASV	American Standard Version
JB	Jerusalem Bible
KJV	King James Version
NAB	New American Bible
NASB	New American Standard Bible
NIV	New International Version
NKJV	New King James Version
NRSV	New Revised Standard Version
REB	Revised English Bible
RSV	Revised Standard Version

Introduction

Contradiction is not a sign of falsity, nor the lack of contradiction a sign of truth.

Blaise Pascal

When you encounter difficulties and contradictions, do not break them, but bend them with gentleness and time.

Saint Frances de Sales

1. Spirit and Law in Romans 8:1–16: The Presence of Two Tensions

1.1 Textual Tension: Continuity or Discontinuity Between Spirit and Law?

Many interpreters extol Rom. 8 as "the inner sanctuary within the cathedral of Christian faith; the tree of life in the midst of the Garden of Eden; the highest peak in a range of mountains."[1] The importance of Rom. 8 has long been recognized; some regard it as the climax of Pauline soteriology in the letter and thus a summary of the preceding arguments.[2] Yet at the same time, Rom. 8:1-

---

[1] See Douglas J. Moo, who lists some of the rich metaphors used by previous interpreters to describe Romans 8 (*The Epistle to the Romans* NICNT [Grand Rapids: William B. Eerdmans Publishing Company, 1996], p. 467).

[2] "It (*Rom. 8*) forms a certain peak in Paul's whole discussion, because it seeks to bring out the reality of the new aeon and of the new life that human beings can now lead in union with Christ and through his Spirit" (J.A. Fitzmyer, *Romans: A New Translation with Introduction and Commentary* AB 33 [New York: Doubleday, 1993], p. 481); "This section (*Rom. 8:1-30*), therefore, climaxes the soteriological dimension of the argument that began in 1:18..." (Gordon D. Fee, *God's Empowering Presence: The Holy Spirit in the Letters of Paul* [Peabody, Mass.:

16 has proven to be a matter of unresolved controversy for New Testament specialists. The focal point of this controversy is a persistent conundrum in Pauline scholarship: Paul's view of the Law.[3] In a cursory reading, v. 4 appears to stand in perplexing tension with what precedes. More specifically, the tension has to do with the relationship between νόμος and πνεῦμα.[4] Prior to this, they are set in opposition to each other, especially in Rom. 7:6 ("But now we have been discharged from the Law...so that we may serve in newness of the Spirit and not in oldness of letter") and 8:2 ("...the Spirit of life in Christ Jesus has set you free from the Law of sin and death"). These statements seem to suggest a discontinuity between the Law and the Spirit. But in Rom. 8:4 ("the righteous requirement of the Law has been fulfilled in us...who walk according to the Spirit") and probably within the phrase, "the law of the Spirit" in 8:2[5] as well, they appear conjoined, operating in a more harmonious

---

Hendrickson Publishers, Inc., 1994], p. 516); "For that chapter (*Rom.* 8) is not only Paul's most sustained exposition of the work of the Spirit; it also forms the climax to Paul's exposition of the gospel in Romans 1-8" (James D.G. Dunn, "Spirit Speech: Reflections on Romans 8:12-27" in *Romans and the People of God: Essays in Honor of Gordon D. Fee on the Occasion of His 65th Birthday* [ed. Sven K. Soderlund and N.T. Wright; Grand Rapids: William B. Eerdmans Publishing Company, 1999]), pp. 82-91, quote taken from p. 82.

[3] The use of νόμος in Paul is not uniform: it can refer to the legislation of the Sinaitic covenant (Rom. 2:20, 23, 25-27; 13:8, 10), the Pentateuch as a whole (Gal. 4:21), both to the Prophetic Writings and the Pentateuch (Rom. 3:21; 9:31; 11:8-10), to the whole of the OT (1 Cor. 14:21; Rom. 3:19), and it can be used figuratively with a corresponding genitive or word of explanation (Rom. 7:21-23; 8:2) (see W. Gutbrod and H. Kleinknecht, "νόμος," *TDNT*, Vol.IV, pp. 1022-91, esp. pp. 1070-1). In what follows in this investigation, except within a direct quotation where all attempts are made to maintain the integrity of the author's wording, a capitalized reference to "Law" refers to the legislation of the Sinaitic covenant (e.g., Rom. 2:20, 23; 7:7; 13:8, 10), not to the OT or even the Pentateuch, but to specific legislation connected with the covenant on Sinai recorded in the Pentateuch.

[4] The use of πνεῦμα figures prominently in Rom. 8. It occurs 31 times in Paul's correspondence to the Romans, and out of these, there are 21 occurrences in chap. 8 alone (vv. 2, 4, 5 [2x], 6, 9 [3x], 10, 11 [2x], 13, 14, 15 [2x], 16 [2x], 23, 26 [2x], 27). Even more telling is that out of the 21 times it is used in chap. 8, 17 occur in vv.1-16. Νόμος is used 5 times in Rom. 8 (vv. 2 [2x], 3, 4, 7) and in all of its occurrences it is either directly or indirectly brought into association with πνεῦμα.

[5] In the following section (2. Current Trends in the Interpretation of Rom. 8:1-16 from the "New Perspective") the various interpretations of νόμος in Rom. 8:2 will be addressed and also the manner in which they are brought into association with the statements Paul makes in Rom. 7:1-6 and 8:4, regarding the relationship between the Spirit and Law.

manner.[6] Furthermore, Rom. 8:2,4 is in tension not only with what precedes but also with what follows in the chapter itself. Once Law and Spirit have been correlated in Rom. 8:2,4, the Law falls away and there is no statement advocating its obedience. The only operative agent at work in the moral life of the Christian is the Spirit (e.g., the Spirit is the source of "life" ["the *Spirit* of *life*," v.2; "the mind of the *Spirit* is *life*," v. 6; "the *Spirit* is *life*," v. 10; "But if the *Spirit*...dwells in you...the one who raised Christ from the dead will also give *life*...on account of his *Spirit* who lives in you," v.11; "but if by the *Spirit* you put to death the practices of the body, you will *live*," v.13]).[7] It is only in Rom. 8:2,4, that Paul attempts to align Law and Spirit; prior to this in 7:1-6 they are set against one another and after this in 8:5-16, the Spirit alone is in view and believers' existence is described without reference to the Law whatsoever. However, in Rom. 8:2,4, the Spirit and Law are linked in a congruent way. Therefore, Rom. 8:2,4 is anomalous.

1.2 External Tension Between Paul's Convictions on the Spirit's Relationship to the Law and Jewish Eschatology

This section of Romans presents a second tension, specifically between Paul's statements in Rom. 7:6 and 8:2, where Law observance is said to be a negligible part of believers' existence, and Jewish eschatological expectation. It was anticipated that the Spirit would be instrumental in the creation of a new covenant relationship and a new disposition within Israel, enabling her to observe the Law.[8] Even though Second Temple Judaism expected a concordant relationship between the Spirit and the Law,[9] and Paul had the

---

[6] If νόμος is linked *indirectly* with the Law in the phrase "the law of the Spirit of life in Christ Jesus," then the tension is present within Rom. 8:2 itself with the words that follow: "has set you free from the Law of sin and death." Paul previously describes the Law and its association with "sin and death" in Rom. 7:10-11.

[7] Paul's description of the life-giving Spirit in Rom. 8:2, 6, 10, 11, 13 is no doubt an intentional move on his part emphasizing the Spirit's role as counterpart to Law obedience (cf. Lev. 18:5; Deut. 4:1; 5:33; 6:24-25; 8:1; 30:15-18; Ezek. 18:1 cf. vv. 9, 21; 20:11 cf. 13, 21; Neh. 9:29, where Law observance is said to result in "life"). Within close proximity to Rom. 8, Paul himself affirms the idea that the intended goal of the Law was "life" in Rom. 7:10 ("...and the commandment [*of the Law*] which was intended for *life*...") but never takes this up in Rom. 8:1-16, where he describes the new epoch inaugurated with Christ's redemptive work.

[8] Jer. 31 (38 LXX): 31-34; Ezek. 11:19, 20; 36:26- 37:14.

[9] See for example, Wis. 1:5,7,9; 7:22-8:1; 9:17-18; Philo *Gig.* 55 cf. 26-27; *Jub.* 1:22-25; *T. Sim.* 4:4; *T. Jud.* 20:1-5; *T. Benj.* 8:1-3; *T. Lev.* 2:3; 1QH IV, 1, 25-26 (cf. 4Q504.5); V,19; VI, 12-

importance of the Law etched within his thinking from his youth, he still advocated discontinuity between the role of the Spirit and the role of the Law in believers' lives and thus abandoned a fundamental component of Jewish eschatological expectation. Indeed, Pauline scholarship has continually grappled with the issue of how a Jew like Paul[10] could bear such non-Jewish sentiments toward the Law.

The tension Paul creates in Rom. 8:1-16 on his discourse between the Spirit and Law is not an isolated problem involving only the Spirit, but characterizes his explication of the Law as a whole. The complications of continuity and discontinuity have long been recognized within the Pauline corpus. As D.E.H. Whiteley succinctly and candidly puts it, "St. Paul's statements about the Law would appear to be in flat contradiction with each other."[11] Paul's statements about the Law have often been the topic of protracted scholarly debate. They are complicated by the fact that the various contexts in which they are found do not revolve around one subject alone. On the contrary, these statements combine a variety of themes that address the Law's relationship to believers, non-believers, Jews and Gentiles. For example, on the one hand Paul makes the following positive comments on the Law: the Law is said to be an advantage of the Jews in that they have "been entrusted with the very words of God" (Rom. 3:2 cf. 9:4); the believer's "faith does not nullify the Law" rather, it "establishes or upholds it" (Rom. 3:31); "the Law has become our tutor to lead us to Christ"(Gal. 3:24).[12] These statements affirm the Law and communicate a positive role for the Law in the believer's life. However, at the same time they are in tension with Paul's depreciatory comments on the Law elsewhere. For example, the Law is said to lead to condemnation (2 Cor. 3:9); Law leads to death (2 Cor. 3:6; Gal. 2:19; Rom.

13, 25; VIII, 10-15; XV, 6-8; XX, 11, 12; 1QS X,11; 1QS IV, 21 (citations from the DSS are from Geza Vermes, *The Complete Dead Sea Scrolls in English*, Fourth Edition [New York: Penguin Books, 1997]).

[10] See Rom. 3:9; 1 Cor. 9:20; Gal. 1:13,14; 2:15, where Paul considers himself Jewish in the fullest sense of the word and 2 Cor. 11:22, where he goes so far as to boast of his Jewish pedigree.

[11] D.E.H. Whiteley, *The Theology of St. Paul* Second Edition (Oxford: Basil Blackwell, 1974), p. 76.

[12] Paul makes other statements affirming the Law in different contexts: "Is the Law sin? May it never be"(Rom. 7:7); "the Law is holy, and the commandment is holy and righteous and good"(Rom. 7:12); "did that which is good [Law] become death for me? May it never be"(Rom. 7:13); "For the one who loves another has fulfilled the Law" (Rom. 13:8); "For the whole Law is fulfilled in a single commandment" (Gal. 5:14).

7:5,9); those who promote the Law belong to "the mutilation" (Phil. 3:2) and are enemies of Christ (Gal. 5:12); with the coming of Christ the time of the Law has come to an end (Rom. 10:4; Gal. 5:18, 23).[13] These statements emphasize discontinuity between the role of the Law in the former era and its role in the present for believers. Therefore, the tension in Rom. 8:1-16 is indicative of Paul's statements about the Law elsewhere. They are difficult to reconcile with each other, and concomitantly, the statements advocating discontinuity of the Law are at odds with Judaism and Paul's Jewish past.

2. Current Trends in the Interpretation of Romans 8:1-16 from the "New Perspective"

2.1 The "New Perspective": Law Obedience and the Maintenance of Covenant Status

In his book, *Jüdische Theologie auf Grund des Talmud und verwandter Schriften*,[14] Ferdinand Weber espoused the view that "legalism" was the primary goal depicted in rabbinic writings.[15] Relationship with God was mediated through the Law on a strict economic basis. If the commandments were followed, payment was granted as reward. Conversely, punishment was incurred for failing to perform them. Eternal life or eternal punishment was based upon the number of merits and demerits that belonged to each person.[16] Although Weber's work was directly related to what the rabbis believed, New Testament scholars frequently used it as a summary of Jewish religion during the time of Jesus and Paul.[17]

---

[13] See some of the other pejorative comments Paul makes concerning the Law: Paul claims the Law brings knowledge of sin (Rom. 3:20; 7:7-12); it was "added so that the trespass might increase" (Rom. 5:20); to be under the Law is to be "kept in custody" (Gal. 3:23; 4:1); the Law means one is a descendant of Hagar (slavery) rather than of Sarah (freedom) (Gal. 4:21-31).

[14] Second Edition, (ed. Franz Delitzsch and George Schnedermann; Leipzig: Dörffling Franke, 1897).

[15] Weber included an analysis of the targums, midrashic writings, Mishna, Tosepta and the Talmuds (*Ibid.*, pp. xv-xxxiv).

[16] *Ibid.*, pp. 48, 279, 292, 334-36.

[17] See the influential commentary by William Sanday and Arthur C. Headlam, *A Critical and Exegetical Commentary on the Epistle to the Romans*, Fifth Edition, ICC (Edinburgh: T and T Clark, 1906), pp. 137-8. The commentary itself was reprinted seventeen times from 1895-1952.

Claude G. Montefiore and George Foot Moore launched a mounted effort
in protest of Weber's ideas. Montefiore claimed that Rabbinic Judaism did not
promote the idea of self-righteous Jews who could earn their way to heaven via
meritorious works. The Law was not a burden but a benefit and delight.[18]
Good intention to perform the Law was just as important as actions.[19] A good
and gracious God was ready to forgive the offending party and if good deeds
did not exceed the evil ones on judgment day, God would graciously forgive
the sinner.[20] Moore pointed out the methodological errors in Weber's
analysis. Weber's choice of sources were dubious in that they were quotations
from rabbinic sources which he found in old Christian apologetic works on
Judaism,[21] which demonstrated a missionary motive.[22]

The decisive verdict against Weber's views came in the publication of E.P.
Sanders' seminal work, *Paul and Palestinian Judaism: A Comparison of Patterns of
Religion.*[23] Significant progress has been made by the promotion of the new
perspective on Paul, initiated by Sanders and carried on by others,[24] which has
helped to place the discussion of Paul and the Law in a more appropriate
framework within Judaism. Sanders' work left an indelible mark upon the
manner in which Pauline scholarship approaches the study of the Jewish Law.
He successfully verified the work of Montefiore and Moore by examining
rabbinic literature, the Dead Sea Scrolls, the Apocrypha and the
Pseudepigrapha, which represented Jewish literature from about 200 BCE to
200 CE. Sanders claimed that Jewish literature in this period demonstrated a
pattern of religion that he called "covenantal nomism." "Covenantal nomism"
consists of 8 components (as follows): 1. God chose Israel and, 2. has given the

---

[18] C.G. Montefiore, "Rabbinic Judaism and the Epistles of Paul," *JQR* 13 (1900-1901), 161-
217, esp. 174-5.

[19] *Ibid.*, p. 176.

[20] *Ibid.*, p. 178.

[21] G.F. Moore, "Christian Writers on Judaism," *HTR* 14 (1921), 197-254, esp. 231-33.

[22] *Ibid.*, pp. 228-31.

[23] Philadelphia: Fortress Press, 1977.

[24] For example, James D.G. Dunn states, "A fresh assessment of Paul and of Romans in
particular has been made possible and necessary by the new perspective on Paul provided by
E.P. Sanders" (*Romans 1-8*, WBC 38A [Dallas: Word Books, 1988], pp. lxiv-lxv); "The role of
the law, both within the Judaism against which Paul was reacting and within the new
perspective on Paul, has not as yet been properly perceived. In what follows I will therefore
attempt briefly to 'set the scene' for an understanding of this important integrating strand of the
letter" (*Ibid.*, p. lxvii).

Law; 3. the Law implies both God's promise to maintain the election; and, 4. the requirement to obey; 5. God rewards obedience and punishes transgression; 6. the Law provides for means of atonement, and atonement results in, 7. maintenance or re-establishment of the covenantal relationship; 8. all those who are maintained in the covenant by obedience, atonement and God's mercy belong to the group which will be saved.[25] The covenant and the relationship God chose to enter into with Israel were based upon his free act of grace. God's grace also provided a means of atonement and opportunity for repentance when his people transgressed.[26] Law obedience provides for the maintenance or re-establishment of the relationship. Therefore, salvation is not secured through meritorious observance of the Law.[27] This investigation will work within this general framework of the new perspective.

2.2 A Christological Solution that Precedes Plight: Paul's Contradictory Thoughts on the Law

Sanders' book had a sweeping impact that changed the characterization of Judaism and concomitantly plunged Pauline scholarship into a quandary. This new perspective raised the need for re-examining the nature of Paul's criticism of Judaism, particularly the role of the Law within the covenant relationship. Sanders' own response to this dilemma is that Paul did not misunderstand Judaism and he did not disparage the Law because it was oriented to works of pious achievement.[28] Rather, Paul had an exclusivist soteriology; if God sent Christ to save, then righteousness could not be by the Law (Gal. 2:21; 3:21). The chronological logic of Paul's thought originated in the conviction that

---

[25] *Paul and Palestinian Judaism*, p. 422.

[26] "Election and ultimately salvation are considered to be by God's mercy rather than human achievement" (*Ibid.*, p. 422). While ready to acknowledge that Palestinian Judaism was a religion centered on God's grace, mercy, and forgiveness, some took issue with Sanders' assessment of the evidence, particularly with respect to the Qumran covenanters. Qumran viewed the proper keeping of the Law as a means of salvation that distinguished the sect from other Jews (see reviews of *Paul and Palestinian Judaism* by N.A. Dahl, *RelSRev* 4 [1978], 153-8, esp. 155; G.B. Caird, *JTS* 29 [1978], 538-43, esp. 540; W. Horbury, *ExpTim* 89 [1977-78], 116-18, esp. 116).

[27] See *Paul and Palestinian Judaism*, pp. 1-59, for Sanders' description of the misrepresentation of Judaism within the influential works of modern New Testament scholarship.

[28] "Our analysis of Rabbinic and other Palestinian Jewish literature did not reveal the kind of religion best characterized as legalistic works-righteousness. But more important for the present point is the observation that in any case that charge is not the heart of Paul's critique" (*Ibid.*, p. 550).

Christ was the Savior of the world and that salvation occurred when one participated in Christ. If God acted in Christ to save the world, it must follow that the Law could not have been God's means of salvation. The Law, even though given by God, has the function of consigning everyone to sin in order that everyone might be saved by God's grace in Christ. Thus, Sanders characterizes Paul's thought as proceeding from "solution" to "plight."[29]

The decisive point at which Paul came to see Christ and the Law as antithetical was his Damascus experience. It was through this experience that Christ displaced the Law as the center of his convictional world. Using Phil. 3:4-11 and Gal. 1:16 as foundational texts, Sanders posits the idea that Paul's conversion/call experience was the moment when righteousness by Law and righteousness by faith in Christ were posed as mutually exclusive alternatives. He states:

> Thus we come to the following train of experience and thought: God revealed his son to Paul and called him to be apostle to the Gentiles. Christ is not only the Jewish messiah, he is savior and Lord of the universe. If salvation is by Christ and is intended for Gentile as well as Jew, it is not by the Jewish law *in any case*, no matter how well it is done, and without regard to one's interior attitude. Salvation is by faith in Christ, and the law does not rest on faith.[30]

Within the new perspective, there have emerged different ways of accounting for the internal textual tensions Paul creates in his explication of the Law. Heikki Räisänen and Sanders are content to leave the tension unresolved, claiming Paul's statements on the Law are contradictory. Räisänen contends that Paul's thoughts on the Law lacked consistency and misrepresented Judaism because he drove "a wedge between law and grace, limiting 'grace' to the Christ event."[31] Sanders claims that Paul's statements on the Law are entirely dependent upon the contingencies he is addressing. When he is discussing the requirement essential for membership in the people

---

[29] Ibid., pp. 474-502; see also the comments in Sanders' other book, *Paul, the Law, and the Jewish People* (Philadelphia: Fortress Press, 1983), p. 47.

[30] Ibid., p.152. See also p. 151, where Sanders quotes Georg Eichholz who states, "the encounter with Christ has for Paul the consequence that Christ becomes *the middle of his theology*, just as previously the Torah must have been the middle of his theology" (Georg Eichholz, *Die Theologie des Paulus im Umriss* [Neukirchen-Vluyn: Neukirchener Verlag, 1972], pp. 224f.).

[31] *Paul and the Law*, Second Edition, WUNT, no. 29 (Tübingen: J.C.B. Mohr, 1987), p. 187; see also pp. 199-202; "The 'Law' of Faith and the Spirit," in *Jesus, Paul and Torah: Collected Essays* Translations from the German by David E. Orton, JSNT no. 43 (Sheffield: JSOT Press, 1992), p. 67.

of God, there is "flat opposition between faith and law."[32] However, when questions of behaviour are addressed, his answers had "a logic of their own…There is no systematic explanation of how those who have died to the law obey it."[33]

Sanders interprets νόμος in the phrase ὁ νόμος τοῦ πνεύματος τῆς ζωῆς ἐν Χριστῷ Ἰησοῦ in Rom. 8:2 not as a reference to the Mosaic Law but as a linguistic move on Paul's part emphasizing a new "law," a move that intimates the abolition of the Mosaic Law.[34] Νόμος is a wordplay predicated upon its application in Rom. 7:22-23 and 25b, used figuratively, signifying something close to "custom, rule, principle, or norm."[35] Sanders advances the argument that Paul created a tension in Rom. 8:1-4 between the idea that Christians are not under the Law at all (vv. 1, 2) and the idea that those in Christ fulfill the

---

[32] *Paul, the Law and the Jewish People*, p. 114.

[33] *Ibid.*, p. 114.

[34] The use of νόμος in the phrase "*law* of the Spirit of life" is a "play on the word *nomos*," which indicates that "Christians are not under the law at all— they have died to the law, not just to part of it and not just to the law as perverted by pride, but to the law as such" (*Ibid.*, pp. 98-9); Räisänen says "law" in Rom. 8:2 must be interpreted metaphorically. It is a word play that begins in Rom. 7:21-25. Rom. 8:2 supports "the conclusion that Paul often speaks of the actual abolition of the Torah" (*Paul and the Law*, p. 52).

[35] BDAG, p. 677; Sanders, *Paul, the Law, and the Jewish People*, p. 15, note 26 and p. 98; Räisänen says "law" refers to something close to "order" but also that the meaning is controlled by the qualifying genitives (*Paul and the Law*, 1987], p.52; see also in his "Das 'Gesetz des Glaubens' [Röm 3:27] und das 'Gesetz des Geistes' [Röm 8:2]," *NTS* 26 [1979/80], 101-17); "power, inner principle, binding authority" (Douglas Moo, *Romans 1-8*, The Wycliffe Exegetical Commentary [Chicago: Moody Press, 1991], p. 507); "Paul is using the word 'law' metaphorically, to denote exercised power, authority, control…" (C.E.B. Cranfield, *The Epistle to the Romans*, ICC Vol. 1 [Edinburgh: T & T Clark Limited, 1975], p. 364); Ernst Käsemann explains νόμος and its association with the Spirit as "the Spirit himself in the ruling function in the sphere of Christ" (*Commentary on Romans* [trans. Geoffrey W. Bromiley; Grand Rapids: William B. Eerdmans Publishing Company, 1980], pp. 215-6).

Contrary to the above interpretations, it is most likely that Paul did not intend νόμος in the phrase ὁ νόμος τοῦ πνεύματος to be interpreted as "custom, rule, principle, or norm." In Rom. 8:2 νόμος probably did not have any substantive meaning of its own except to identify an *indirect* relationship with the Mosaic Law. If Paul did not want to allude to the Mosaic Law he could have said simply: "The Spirit of life in Christ Jesus has set you free from sin and death." The discussion on the use of νόμος in Rom. 8:2 will be taken up more fully in Part Two, The Spirit Displaces the Law as the Principle of New Life: Romans 7-8.

Law (vv.3-4), and are thus required to keep it.[36] Paul still preserves certain
ethical norms, which the Law advocated, and insisted that those in the Spirit
observe its requirements (Rom. 8:4). As Sanders sees it, we cannot tell whether
or not Paul was consciously aware of this contradiction. Nevertheless, Paul
makes no effort to solve it.[37] Sanders is content to leave the tension in Rom.
8:1-4 unresolved, advancing the position that Paul's statements on the Law
are contradictory because they are driven by the broader issue of a
Christological solution that dominates his thinking, consequently leaving his
former Jewish convictions in a disjunctive state with his new Christian
convictions.

2.3 Continuity Between Jewish and Christian Convictions: Two-Sided Perspective of Law Observance

James D.G. Dunn and Frank Thielman find continuity between Paul's Jewish
and Christian convictions and explain the tensions not as contradictory
statements, but as a description of the two-sided perspective of Law observance
operating in two separate epochs: Law observance impeded by the power of sin
in the previous epoch and Law observance enabled by the new power of the
Spirit in the present epoch, inaugurated by Christ's redemptive work.[38]

---

[36] Käsemann, who asserts that Paul is promoting the abolition of the Law in Rom. 8:2, states
that Paul is taking over an existing formulation (cf. Matt. 5:17ff.) in Rom. 8:3,4. He describes
this as an anacoluthon, which disturbs the logic of the train of thought. This means that a clear
decision on Paul's meaning here is not possible. As a result, Paul "pays the price for the fact that
his argument is affected by motifs from another source." Paul is not promoting Law observance
but is emphasizing what God has done in letting Christ die (*Commentary on Romans*, p. 218).

[37] Sanders, *Paul, the Law, and the Jewish People*, pp. 98, 99, 103; Räisänen is even more extreme
than Sanders. He argues that Paul's contradictory statements on the Law in Rom. 7:1-8:4 are
intentional, indicating Paul's inability to make a clean break with the Law. These statements are
proof of his own self-contradiction. Therefore, the interpreter should not seek a consistent
position on the Law from Paul (*Paul and the Law*, pp. 199-202; "The 'Law' of Faith and the
Spirit," p. 67).

[38] Dunn, *Romans 1-8*, pp. 392-3; Frank Thielman, *From Plight to Solution: A Jewish Framework for
Understanding Paul's View of the Law in Galatians and Romans* (Leiden/ New York: E.J. Brill,
1989), p. 102. In his most recent monograph, Thielman has abandoned his interpretation that
Paul promotes observance of the Law. His new position is that the epoch of the Law has been
succeeded by "the law of Christ" but with the qualification that there is overlap between "the
law of Christ" and what the Law advocated: "The Mosaic law is no longer binding on believers.
Believers instead must conform to the teaching of Jesus, teaching that absorbs within it
elements of the Mosaic law" (*The Law and the New Testament: The Question of Continuity* [New

Dunn sees νόμος as a direct reference to the Law in Rom. 8:2. The phrase τοῦ νόμος τῆς ἁμαρτίας καὶ τοῦ θανάτου refers to the Law constricted by sin, unable to be observed by believers, resulting in death. Its counterpart is the phrase ὁ νόμος τοῦ πνεύματος τῆς ζωῆς, which refers to the Law, whose precepts are ingrained upon people's hearts by the Spirit, who also enables its obedience, and thus produces life.[39] Dunn explains Paul's negative depiction of the Law in Rom. 8:2 (τοῦ νόμος τῆς ἁμαρτίας καὶ τοῦ θανάτου) as a description written from the perspective of the former epoch, prior to Christ's redemptive work.[40] The phrase, ὁ νόμος τοῦ πνεύματος τῆς ζωῆς is a depiction of the Law's role in the present epoch, made possible because of Christ's redemptive work. Therefore, Paul sees the role of the Spirit in a manner consistent with the future expectations of Jer. 31(38 LXX):31-34 and Ezek. 36:25-27. His convictions are said to comply with a Jewish traditional continuum whose eschatological expectation included the Spirit's creation of a new disposition within Israel, enabling her to observe the Law. As a result, the words τὸ δικαίωμα τοῦ νόμου πληρωθῇ ἐν ἡμῖν τοῖς...περιπατοῦσιν κατὰ πνεῦμα in Rom. 8:4 refer to the continuity of God's purpose in the Law and through the Spirit, which evokes the sense of eschatological fulfillment of prediction or promise in the present epoch.[41] Dunn describes Paul's statements on the Law in Rom. 8:1-4 not as a contradiction but as a description of the contrast between two epochs and therefore, claims there is continuity between Paul's Jewish and Christian convictions.

York: The Crossroads Publishing Company, 1999], p. 33); "In Galatians Paul says explicitly, and in Romans he implies, that the new era has brought with it a new law, 'the law of Christ' (Gal. 6:2)...The new law, then, incorporates parts of the Mosaic Law within it, but apparently only insofar as the teaching of Jesus reaffirms their validity" (Ibid., p. 35).

[39] Dunn, Romans 1-8, pp. 392-3; See also Thielman (From Plight to Solution, p. 102) and N.T. Wright who interpret this in a similar manner (The Climax of the Covenant: Christ and the Law in Pauline Theology [Minneapolis: Fortress Press, 1991], p. 198).

[40] James D.G. Dunn, The Theology of Paul the Apostle (Grand Rapids, Michigan/Cambridge, U.K.: William B. Eerdmans Publishing Company, 1998), pp. 643-4; Thielman, From Plight to Solution, p. 89.

[41] Dunn, Romans 1-8, p. 423; Thielman, From Plight to Solution, p. 89.

2.4 Problem Definition in Relation to Previous Research

The interpretations of both Sanders and Dunn pose some significant difficulties within the context of Rom. 8. Contrary to Dunn's interpretation, Paul never promotes the idea that believers are to observe the Law. Paul attributes a life-giving function specifically to the Spirit (vv. 2, 6, 10, 11, 13) and not the Law (cf. Rom. 7:10-11). In Rom. 8, Paul underscores the comprehensive soteriological role of the Spirit, who secures relationship with God and thus makes Law observance redundant. Had Paul thought of a different level of Law-keeping in Rom. 8:2, one would have expected him to say that the Law, with the aid of the Spirit, was a source of life in the new epoch in Christ. But there is no indication of this in Rom. 8. In Rom. 8:14-16, it is the experience of the Spirit, not the Law, which provides confirmation of the believer's familial relationship with God ("the Spirit himself bears witness with our spirit that we are children of God" [Rom. 8:16]).[42]

Paul uses the verb πληροῦν in Rom. 8:4 because it is the word that best expresses a sense of continuity between the soteriological roles of Spirit and Law, without declaring that Christian behaviour is prescribed by the Law. Πληροῦν means "to make full, fill, to bring to completion that which was already begun, to complete, finish, to bring to a designed end."[43] Paul does not use the verb ποιεῖν,[44] which would have made it clear that he had Law observance in mind.[45] He consistently distinguishes between "doing" the Law's commands for those "under the Law" (Rom. 10:5; Gal. 3:10, 12; 5:3) and "fulfilling" the Law by Christians (Rom. 8:4; 13:8, 10; Gal. 5:14), who are not "under the Law" (Rom. 6:14). The "righteousness" that the Law called for but could not produce has been brought to "completion" (i.e., "is fulfilled," "is completely satisfied"[46]) in believers who conduct their lives according to the

---

[42] Ironically, Dunn makes the following comment in an earlier monograph: "Paul insists that Christianity is quintessentially a religion of Spirit rather than of law" (*Jesus and the Spirit: A Study of the Religious and Charismatic Experience of Jesus and the First Christians as Reflected in the New Testament* [Grand Rapids: William B. Eerdmans Publishing Co., 1997], p. 320).

[43] BDAG, pp. 828-9.

[44] *Ibid.*, pp. 839-42.

[45] See Stephen Westerholm's explanation of the difference between "keeping/doing" the Law and "fulfilling" the Law (*Israel's Law and the Church's Faith: Paul and His Recent Interpreters* [Grand Rapids: William B. Eerdmans Publishing Company, 1988], pp. 201-5).

[46] *Ibid.*, p. 204.

Spirit's leading.[47] The Spirit, not the Law, is the source of "righteousness." Elsewhere Paul claims that "righteousness" has nothing to do with observing the Law but is rather the result of the Spirit's work in the lives of believers.[48] Paul also makes it clear that he himself no longer lives a life in conformity with the Law (e.g., Gal. 2:15-21; 1 Cor. 9:19-22).

In his attempt to resolve the tension, however, Dunn does not sufficiently account for the soteriological emphasis on the Spirit and the disappearance of the Law in Rom. 8:5-16. Nowhere in Rom. 8 does Paul encourage believers to observe the Law because this will result in life. The reason for this is that Paul sees no continuing role for the Law in the life of the Christian, since the Spirit stands alone as the principle of new life.

Thus Dunn's attempt to smooth out Sanders' reading of Rom. 8:1-4 is not successful. The tension between Rom. 8:2, 4 and its context remains. At the same time, however, Sanders' reading fails to take into account two significant features of the passage. The first has to do with the significance of the Spirit in Rom. 8:1-16. Sanders places too much emphasis on Paul's understanding of this experience as a single experience of Christ rather than an ongoing experience of the Spirit.[49] Sanders associates Pauline pneumatology so closely

---

[47] See Leander Keck, who states that in Rom. 8:4, Paul communicates the idea that the Spirit accomplishes "the right intent of the law- life" ("The Law and 'The Law of Sin and Death,'" in *The Divine Helmsman* [ed. J.L. Crenshaw and S. Sandmel; New York: KTAV, 1980], p. 51).

[48] See Rom. 12:1-15:13, where Paul speaks of "fulfilling" the Law (13:8), which has nothing to do with observing external requirements of the Law but has everything to do with "righteousness, peace, and joy in the Holy Spirit" (14:17).

[49] This is no doubt a current trend in contemporary Pauline scholarship. Previous studies have focused extensively on Paul's Christophany at Damascus (1 Cor. 9:1; 15:8; Gal. 1:12; Phil. 3:4-11) and claim that this decisive experience provided the impetus for a reversal of values from a Law-centered to a Christ-centered paradigm. It was at this point in time that the idea of a suffering and dying Messiah was a contradiction and therefore an affront to Torah (Deut. 21:22-23) which sets up the antithesis in Paul's mind between Jesus as the Jewish Messiah, and Law (See James D.G. Dunn, "'A Light to the Gentiles': The Significance of the Damascus Road Christophany for Paul," in *The Glory of Christ in the New Testament* [ed. L.D. Hurst and N.T. Wright; Oxford: Clarendon Press, 1987], pp. 251-66, see esp. pp. 264-65; J. Christiaan Beker, *Paul the Apostle: The Triumph of God in Life and Thought* [Philadelphia: Fortress Press, 1980], pp. 185-86; F. F. Bruce, *Paul, Apostle of the Heart Set Free* [Grand Rapids: Eerdmans, 1977], pp. 70-1). Others claim that Christ and the Law represented mutually exclusive boundary markers and thus rival ways of determining the community of salvation (T.L. Donaldson, *Paul and the Gentiles: Remapping the Apostle's Convictional World* [Minneapolis: Fortress Press, 1997], pp.172-3; U. Wilkens, "Die Bekehrung des Paulus als religionsgeschichtliches Problem," *Rechtfertigung als Freiheit: Paulusstudien* [Neukirchen-Vluyn: Neukirchener, 1974], pp. 11-32; Beverly Roberts

with Christology that it simply functions as a subsidiary category of Christology, which consequently fuses pneumatology with Christology and makes them identical in function. Pauline pneumatology is read through a Christological lens, blurring the distinction between the two. This is clearly apparent when he discusses Rom. 8:1-4.[50] For example, Sanders states, "Its (*Law*) requirement is just, in itself its aims aright. But the requirement is fulfilled only *in Christ (Rom. 8.4)* (emphasis added), and the aim, life, is accomplished *only in Christ (Rom. 7.10; 8.1-4)* (emphasis added)."[51] Granted, all that Paul says in Rom. 8 is predicated upon Christ's redemptive work (vv. 1-3) but the Christocentric participatory language is used sparingly in Rom. 8:1-16.[52] Paul's concern and description is concentrated upon the believer's experience of the Spirit, which is distinct and separate from his Christology. There is no indication that Christ fulfilled the Law's requirement since Rom. 8:4 clearly says that it is fulfilled ἐν ἡμῖν τοῖς...περιπατοῦσιν κατὰ πνεῦμα.[53] This is conclusive proof that Paul intended a pneumatological emphasis in the phrase ὁ νόμος τοῦ πνεύματος τῆς ζωῆς ἐν Χριστῷ Ἰησοῦ (v.2),[54] which he takes up in the rest of Rom. 8. The Spirit is not to be

---

Gaventa, *From Darkness to Light: Aspects of Conversion in the New Testament* [Philadelphia: Fortress Press, 1986], p. 39; Martin Dibelius, *Paul* [ed. W.G. Kümmel; trans. F. Clarke; Philadelphia: Westminster Press, 1953], pp. 47-51; W. D. Davies, *Invitation to the New Testament* [Garden City, NY: Doubleday & Co., 1966], pp. 260-3; M.S. Enslin, *Reapproaching Paul* [Philadelphia: Westminster Press, 1972], pp. 56-57).

[50] See pp. 466-8 in his *Paul and Palestinian Judaism*, where Sanders discusses Rom. 8:2 in the context of salvation through Christocentric participation and the Spirit is brought in simply as an expression of this theme.

[51] *Ibid.*, p. 497.

[52] The Christocentric participationist terms, which Sanders believes to be the key to unlocking the essence of Pauline soteriology, are few in Rom. 8:1-16 (see vv. 1-2 ["in Christ Jesus"]).

[53] This is the reason why Paul writes that the Spirit is resident within the believer (οἰκεῖ ἐν ὑμῖν) in Rom. 8:9, 11.

[54] Similar to Sanders, Räisänen fuses pneumatology with Christology and assumes that Christocentric participation mentioned in Rom. 8:1,2, is the point of emphasis in all that follows. For example, he states, "Paul assumes within the framework of his theological theory first, that the law cannot be fulfilled apart from the *union with Christ* (emphasis added) and secondly, that the Christians fulfill what is required by the law (Gal. 5:14ff.; Rom 13:8-10; *Rom.* 8:4 [emphasis added] cf. 2:29)" (*Paul and the Law*, p. 113). However, in Rom. 8:4, Paul uses the passive voice πληρωθῇ, because he wants to underscore the idea that the Spirit is the external active agent that achieves the intended goal of "righteousness"; it is not specifically "union with Christ" or the "Christian" as Räisänen claims in the above statement (See John Ziesler who states, "...the passive reflecting the fact that Paul is talking not about what believers do, but

subsumed under Christology. Paul makes a distinction between the redemptive work of Christ in the past[55] and the ongoing work of the Spirit in the present[56] that displaces the function of the Law.

In this connection, it is important to note the centrality of the Spirit in Paul's depiction of the "in Christ" reality in Rom. 8, where Paul underscores tangible experiences of the Spirit in the lives of believers: "walking according to the Spirit"(v. 4), "the mindset of the Spirit" (v. 6), "you are ...in the Spirit" (v.9), "the Spirit (of God/ the one who raised Christ from the dead) dwells in you" (vv. 9, 11), "if by the Spirit you put to death..." (v. 13), "for those who are being led[57] by the Spirit..." (v.14), "Spirit of adoption, by whom we cry out ..." (v.15), "the same Spirit testifies with our spirit..." (v. 16). In all of these statements, the Spirit is described as an experienced and present reality. Furthermore, in vv. 13-16, a shift takes place; Paul switches from second to first person plural forms,[58] indicating that Paul includes himself in this description of believers' experience(s) of the Spirit.

Rom. 8:14-16 is significant in this context because it is the linchpin to everything Paul has claimed of the Spirit thus far in Rom. 8:1-16. It is the climactic conclusion to Rom. 8:1-16, and in particular, Paul's explication of the phrase ὁ νόμος τοῦ πνεύματος τῆς ζωῆς in v.2. In vv. 14-16, Paul expresses the charismatic awareness of familial relationship, which is the mark

---

about what is done in and through them by the Spirit" [*Paul's Letter to the Romans* TPINTC (London: SCM Press, 1989/ Philadelphia: Trinity Press International, 1989), p. 208]).

[55] It is no coincidence that when Paul speaks of Christ's redemptive work he uses the aorist tense: "God, having sent his own Son...*condemned* (κατέκρινεν) sin" (v.3).

[56] When Paul speaks of the work of the Spirit he uses the present tense: "the Spirit of God *lives* (οἰκεῖ) in you" (v.9), "the Spirit...*lives* (οἰκεῖ) in you" (v.11), "by the Spirit...*you put to death* (θανατοῦτε)" (v.13), "for all who *are led* (ἄγονται) by the Spirit" (v.14), "the Spirit...*by whom we cry out* (κράζομεν)" (v.15), "the Spirit *testifies with* (συμμαρτυρεῖ) our spirit" (v.16). In Rom. 8:34, Paul states that God raised Christ and is currently at "the right hand of God." However, the Spirit is presently at work in believers' lives.

[57] "Being led by the Spirit" is a variant of "walking according to the Spirit" (v.4), "the mindset of the Spirit" (v. 6), "in the Spirit" (v. 9). In Rom. 8:13, Paul depicts Christian behaviour as an integrated balance between yielding to the deeply felt inward compulsions of the Spirit and human effort ("If *by the Spirit, you* put to death the practices of the body, you will live").

[58] Paul uses the second person plural verb form in the phrases, "if by the Spirit...*you put to death* (θανατοῦτε) the practices of the body, *you will live* (ζήσεσθε)" (v.13) and "*you received* (ἐλάβετε) the Spirit of adoption" (v. 15). However, in v. 15 he writes, "the Spirit of adoption by whom *we cry out* (κράζομεν)" and in v.16, "the Spirit testifies with *our* (ἡμῶν) spirit that *we are* (ἐσμέν) children of God."

of the Spirit and also the distinctive character of Christian experience.[59] He writes, "The Spirit himself testifies with our spirit that we are children of God" (Rom. 8:16). Furthermore, this experience began at the inception of Christian life and continues from that point into the present.[60] Paul explains that the experience of familial relationship is inextricable with displaying behaviour befitting that relationship (vv. 12-14, cf. Paul's definition of "walking according to the Spirit" in vv. 4-9).[61] Therefore, what is in tension with Paul's convictions regarding the Law is not simply his convictions about Christ but more specifically, Paul's convictions about both Christ and the Spirit. This suggests the possibility that the "train of experience and thought"[62] that Sanders has proposed for Paul should be revised to include Paul's ongoing experience of the Spirit.

If Paul advocates the idea that the Spirit displaces the Law in Rom. 8:1-16, the second tension between Paul and Jewish eschatological expectation comes fully to the forefront. The new perspective has not yet addressed this tension in a satisfactory manner. Sanders sees no continuity at all between Paul's Jewish past and his Christian present; they are "just ships passing in the night."[63] He depicts Paul as jumping in an arbitrary manner from covenantal nomism into Christianity. Dunn claims that Sanders did not adequately explore the extent to which Paul explicated his pattern of religion in relation to Judaism's covenantal nomism and, instead, became fixated upon the differences between Paul and Judaism. As a result, "the Lutheran Paul has

---

[59] Dunn, *Jesus and the Spirit*, p. 319.

[60] In Rom. 8:15, the use of the aorist tense verb in the phrase, ἐλάβετε πνεῦμα υἱοθεσίας is juxtaposed with the present tense verb in following phrase, ἐν ᾧ κράζομεν, indicating a decisive moment in the past when the Spirit was received, and from that moment, the Spirit is continually experienced through the inspirational cry of sonship.

[61] With the use of ὅσοι γὰρ πνεύματι in v. 14, Paul links the experience of "sonship" with v.13, πνεύματι τὰς πράξεις τοῦ σώματος θανατοῦτε. Sanders posits a bifurcation in Paul's view of the Law as it relates to membership within the family of God and Christian ethics; i.e., the Law and Christ are mutually exclusive alternatives when it comes to securing membership within God's family but when it comes to Christian ethics, the Law is to be observed, since it still continues to function as the basis for Christian behaviour (see above). This distinction between membership within the family and God and Christian ethics is erroneous in light of Rom. 8:4-16, where Paul maintains that relationship with God and Christian ethics are both the work of the Spirit and not the Law.

[62] See the long quote above from Sanders, *Paul, the Law, and the Jewish People*, p. 152.

[63] This is the characterization coined by William Horbury in his review of Sanders,' "*Paul and Palestinian Judaism*," *ExpTim* 89 (1977-78), 116.

been replaced by an idiosyncratic Paul who in arbitrary and irrational manner turns his face against the glory and greatness of Judaism's covenant theology and abandons Judaism simply because it is not Christianity."[64]

But this brings us to a second aspect of the text that Sanders has overlooked—Paul's tendency to describe the role of the Spirit using terms and concepts drawn from Judaism's covenant relationship.[65] In fact, Rom. 8:1-16 is replete with covenantal concepts that are brought into direct association with the Spirit. In Rom. 8:2, Paul describes the work of the Spirit using the phrase "the *law* of the Spirit of life" and in 8:4, he claims that the work of the Spirit within believers "fulfills the righteous requirement of the Law." In Rom. 8:5-16, Paul associates the Spirit with covenantal concepts previously associated with Law observance. For example, Paul describes the Spirit as imparting "life" (Rom. 8:6, 10, 11, 13). In Judaism the purpose of the Law was to bring "life" (Lev. 18:5; Deut. 4:1; 5:33; 6:24-25; 8:1; 30:15-18; Ezek. 18:1 cf. vv. 9, 21; 20:11 cf. 13, 21; Neh. 9:29 cf. Rom. 7:10 ["...and the commandment (*of the Law*) which was intended for life..."]).[66] The Spirit is the source of "righteousness" (Rom. 8:4),[67] "peace" with God (Rom. 8:6 cf. v.7),[68] and is the means by which familial relationship with God is secured (i.e., "sonship" [Rom. 8:14], "children" [Rom. 8:16, 17]).[69] In Second Temple Judaism Israel's status as "son of God" is grounded in the Law by obeying it.[70] Therefore, contrary to Sanders, Paul has not completely abandoned Judaism's

---

[64] James D.G. Dunn, "The New Perspective on Paul," in *Jesus, Paul and the Law: Studies in Mark and Galatians* (Louisville, Kentucky: Westminster/ John Knox Press, 1990), pp. 183-214, quote taken from p. 187.

[65] See for example, 1 Cor. 6:11 ("you were justified...by the Spirit"); 2 Cor. 3:6 ("a new covenant...of the Spirit"); Gal. 3:14 ("the promise of the Spirit"); 4:24 ("two covenants" cf. v. 29 "according to the Spirit"); Rom. 2:29 ("circumcision of the heart by the Spirit"); 14:17 ("the righteousness and peace and joy in the Holy Spirit"); Phil. 3:3 ("the circumcision...by the Spirit of God").

[66] In Second Temple Judaism, Law observance is said to result in "life" (Bar. 3:9 cf. 4:1; Sir. 17:11,12; *m. Abot* 6:7; *Pss. Sol.* 14:2).

[67] See Deut. 4:1; 5:1; 29 times it is said in Ps. 119 that righteous behaviour is called for by the Law.

[68] See Num. 25:12; Sir. 45:24; Ezek. 34:25; 37:26; Isa. 54:10; Mal. 2:5, where reference is made to the "covenant of peace" and those who entered this covenant were to observe the Law (Sir. 45:3, 5, 17; Mal. 3:6; Ezek. 36:27; 37:24).

[69] See Exod. 4:22; Jer. 3:19; 31:9; Hos. 11:1.

[70] *Jub.* 1:24f.; Sir 4:10 cf. vv. 1-9; Wis. 2:13 cf. v.12, 16-18; *T. Jud.* 24:3.

conception of the covenant relationship, since he depicts the Spirit's role using terms and concepts that were central to it.

In Rom. 8:1-16, even though Paul posits the Spirit rather than the Law as the principle of life in the new era, he still describes the Spirit's work using the language of Judaism's covenant relationship. There is a very real sense in which Paul perceives a disjunction between his Christian present and Jewish past, in particular, his convictions on the role of the Spirit in the present are incompatible with his convictions on the role of the Law, which he inherited from his Jewish past. Yet at the same time, he attempts to negotiate the logical tensions between the two by describing common characteristics between them. In what follows in this investigation, we shall attempt to give an explanation of this phenomenon in the text by employing a theory within the field of study known as social psychology.

3. The Aims of This Study

In Rom. 8:1-16, Paul exhibits two tensions. The first tension is internal, between Rom. 8:2,4, where the Spirit and Law are conjoined and complementary, and its surrounding context, where the Spirit and Law are set in opposition (Rom. 7:6 cf. 8:2 ["...the Spirit of life in Christ Jesus has set you free from the Law of sin and death"]) or where the Law is eclipsed by the Spirit (Rom. 8:5-16). Paul reflects his viewpoint more clearly in the context; i.e., the Spirit has displaced the Law as the principle of life for the believer. Such a displacement is also evident in Paul's description of his own pattern of life. But this brings a second tension to light, between Paul's view of the Spirit and Law, and Jewish eschatology, which expected Spirit and Law to co-exist in a harmonious manner.

This study will contribute to the understanding of these tensions in three ways. First, with Sanders, this study will argue that the best way to understand the tension in Paul's discourse about the Law is to posit a new set of convictions and a new perspective on Judaism, which have resulted from Paul's transformative experience. But against Sanders, Paul's conception of the Law explicated in Rom. 8 is not simply the result of a one-time Damascus experience described in Christocentric language, but is also the result of Paul's ongoing experience of the Spirit described in pneumacentric language. Thus, Paul's "train of experience and thought" must include his ongoing experience of the Spirit in order to make sense of the dynamics of Rom. 8.

Second, the phenomenon observed in Rom. 8:2,4, where Paul aligns Spirit and Law, is part of a larger phenomenon apparent in Rom. 8:5-16, where Paul consistently describes the role of the Spirit using terms and concepts drawn from Judaism's covenantal nomism. This trend stands in contrast with Paul's more fundamental conviction, that the Spirit has displaced the Law as the principle of life for the believer.

Third, this study will propose that Cognitive Dissonance Theory will elucidate and provide an understanding of the phenomenon apparent in the text. In Paul's Jewish upbringing, the Law functioned as the necessary means of sustaining covenantal relationship with God. But after Damascus, Paul experienced a relationship with God through the mediating work of the Spirit apart from Law observance. As a result, according to Cognitive Dissonance Theory, Paul perceived two cognitions in dissonant relationship. To reduce this dissonance, he establishes "cognitive overlap" by describing the work of the Spirit using distinct terminology characteristic of Judaism's covenantal nomism. Also, by influencing believers (i.e., Paul's social group that included both Jewish and Gentile believers) in Rome to understand and apprehend his cognition that the Spirit has displaced the need for Law observance, he attempts to obtain social support and validation. Paul's dissonance between Spirit and Law would be significantly reduced if believers in Rome acquiesce and he gains adherents. Since this theory involves the application of a particular interpretive method, it will be addressed in the following section, 4. Methodological Considerations (4.3 Application of Cognitive Dissonance Theory).

4. Methodological Considerations

4.1 Setting the Limits: Rom. 8:1-16

This investigation will be an expositional study on Paul's description of the relationship between the Spirit and Law in Rom. 8:1-16. Most agree that Rom. 8:1-30 divides itself nicely into two self-contained units: vv. 1-17 and vv. 18-30. Some divide vv.1-30 either within v.17 itself, where Paul concludes on a triumphant note (i.e., the believers' status as heirs of God and joint heirs of Christ),[71] or following v.17, after Paul has introduced the between being heirs and the themes of present suffering and future glorification.[72] However, Paul's description of the relationship between Spirit and Law converge in Rom. 8:1-16. The use of πνεῦμα occurs 21 times in Rom. 8, and 17 of these occur in vv.1-16 (vv. 2, 4, 5 [2x], 6, 9 [3x], 10, 11 [2x], 13, 14, 15 [2x], 16 [2x]). Νόμος is used 5 times in Rom. 8, in vv. 2-7 (vv. 2 [2x], 3, 4, 7), forming either a direct or indirect relationship with πνεῦμα. Furthermore, within the confines of Rom. 8:5-16, Paul associates the Spirit with covenantal concepts previously associated with Law observance in Second Temple Judaism and the themes broached in vv. 17ff have little bearing on what Paul says with respect to the Law. Since the purpose of this study is to examine the intersection between Spirit and Law, and the themes in v.17ff are tangential to this task,[73] the focus of this investigation will be limited to Rom. 8:1-16.

4.2 Paul's Pneumatological Reflection Set in a Jewish Covenantal Framework

Paul makes positive references to his Jewish ancestral traditions (Rom. 3:9; 1 Cor. 9:20; 2 Cor. 11:22; Gal. 1:13, 14; 2:15) and discloses his knowledge of Jewish new covenant expectation (Jer. 38 [LXX]: 31-34; Ezek. 36:25-27) in Gal. 4:23-29, Rom. 2:29, 7:6, and more directly in 2 Cor. 3:1-18.[74] Also, he employs traditional covenantal terms and concepts in Rom. 8:1-16 to describe the role of the Spirit. This indicates that there is formative influence in his

---

[71] For example, J. Christiaan Beker notes the antithesis in Rom. 8 between the new domain described in vv. 1-17a and the sharp dissonant note of v. 17b, which opens a section of the church in the world and its suffering (vv. 17b-30), almost contradicting what has gone before in vv. 1-17a ("Suffering and Triumph in Paul's Letter to the Romans," *HBT* 2 [1985], 105-19)

[72] See Fitzmyer, *Romans*, p. 505, who states, "Paul finished his discussion in the last paragraph (*vv. 1-17*) with the mention of suffering. Now (*vv. 18ff.*) he passes from that stage, realizing that such suffering in this life has its counterpart in the incomparable glory awaited by those who so suffer"; Dunn notes how Paul "so often uses his concluding thought (*Rom. 8:17*) to provide a bridge to the next stage of his reflection (*vv. 18-30 cf. Rom. 5:20-21*)" (*Romans 1-8*, p. 447). Thus, the idea that believers are children and heirs entails both suffering and future glorification, which Paul takes up in vv.18-30.

[73] The four references to the Spirit in Rom. 8:23, 26 (2x), 27 are specifically related to the themes of present suffering and expectation of future redemption introduced in v. 17 and do not relate to Paul's discussion on the Law in vv. 2-7.

[74] Fee, *God's Empowering Presence*, p. 812, footnote 18.

thinking from both Ancient and Second Temple Judaism and that Paul's pneumatological reflection occurs within a Jewish covenantal framework. These facts warrant more extensive inquiry into the prevailing Jewish thoughts on new covenant expectation and moral and ethical renewal, taking particular note of the relationship between Spirit and Law. By surveying information from a wide range of Jewish literature (i.e., Diaspora Literature, Palestinian Literature, Dead Sea Scrolls) we will be in a better position to understand contemporary first century CE Jewish religious thinking on these subjects. This information, in turn, will enable us to see how Paul's ideas described in Rom. 8:1-16 compare to prevalent Jewish notions on the Spirit and Law. This study intends to treat Ancient and Second Temple Judaism, and Paul's thoughts expressed in Rom. 8:1-16, independently, each on their own terms. This is a conscious effort designed to avoid the extremes of presenting Paul's thoughts as the quintessential expression of Judaism or, at the other end, to treat Paul's ideas in complete isolation from Second Temple Judaism. Furthermore, the disjunctions between Paul and Second Temple Judaism will assist us to appreciate the reasons why Paul exhibits a persistent drive to reduce the tensions between his Christian and Jewish convictions, such as the one he demonstrates in Rom. 8:1-16.

4.3 Application of Cognitive Dissonance Theory

4.3.1 Spirit and Law: Conflict Within Paul's Convictional World. The continuity/discontinuity interplay between Spirit and Law in Rom. 8:1-16 has been erroneously dismissed as being prompted by nothing more than the situational context in which Paul finds himself with respect to the believers in Rome. It is argued that even though Paul emphasizes a "no-Law" position, it was expedient for him to demonstrate a sense of continuity between the Law and the Spirit by using terms such as πληροῦν in Rom. 8:4 because he had gained a reputation of being anti-Law.[75] Consequently, he was engaged in a

---

[75] F.F. Bruce states, "One reason for his setting this full statement before them may have been his awareness that his message was being misrepresented by his opponents in various places; he seizes the opportunity to set the record straight" (pp. 14-5); cf. "Paul's gospel is thus fully absolved from the charge of antinomianism," (p. 55) (*Romans* TNTC [Leicester, England: Inter-Varsity Press/ Grand Rapids, MI: William B. Eerdmans Publishing Company, 1985]); see also Victor P. Furnish, *Theology and Ethics in Paul* (Nashville: Abingdon, 1968), pp. 99-106; Neil Elliot, *The Rhetoric of Romans: Argumentative Constraint and Strategy and Paul's Diaologue with Judaism* JSNTSup 45 (Sheffield: JSOT Press, 1990), pp. 97-8.

polemical argument against the charge of antinomianism leveled against him: "The use of the term πληρωθῆ at this point in Paul's argument (*Rom.* 8:4) is very strategic and crucial...[he] has been accused of teaching antinomianism due to his law free gospel...Paul makes use of the word πληρωθῆ very deliberately. He does so for polemic reason (*sic*)."[76] In Rom. 6:1 it is assumed that a "no-Law" position would lead to unrighteousness, but actually the problem is that those under the Law are not able to do what the Law demands (Rom.7:14-24). In reality it is those who are not under the Law's constraints that ultimately fulfill the righteous requirement of the Law through Christ and the Spirit (Rom. 8:2-3).[77] In this view Paul intentionally uses the term "fulfill" because it was ambiguous. By saying that Christians "fulfill" the Law, Paul claims that they alone can fully satisfy the real intention of the Law. At the same time, the term "fulfill" speaks to the objection that the requirements set forth in the Law have not been "done," even though he never intended that Christian behaviour was meant to conform to the Law.[78]

But it appears that there is more transpiring in Rom. 8 than simply Pauline polemics. The character of the language Paul uses in Rom. 8:1-16 does not indicate that he was too heavily preoccupied with battling the claims of being against the Jewish Law, even though there is a slight indication that the content of his gospel message had spread and been misrepresented (e.g. "Let us do evil that good may come," [Rom. 3:8][79]). Paul does not use the invective he does in his other written correspondence where he is clearly defending his

---

[76] Keith D. Bienert, "The Apostle Paul's View of the Law According to Romans 8.1-17," (doct. diss., São Leopoldo, 2001), pp.75-6; "8:1-4 is intended as the climax of his apology of the law" (Räisänen, *Paul and the Law*, p. 67; see also p. 144).

[77] *Ibid.*, pp.75-6.

[78] "For Paul it is important to say that Christians 'fulfill' the whole law, and thus to claim that their conduct (and theirs alone) fully satisfies the 'real' purport of the law in its entirety, while allowing the ambiguity of the term to blunt the force of objection that certain individual requirements (with which, Paul would maintain, Christian behavior was never meant to conform) have not been 'done.'" Compare with the statement, "The paradox is deliberate; it is hardly the expression of unresolved tensions in Paul's thought" (Westerholm, *Israel's Law and the Church's Faith*, quote taken from p. 205; see also pp. 201-3; "On Fulfilling the Whole Law [Gal. 5.14]," *SEA* 51 [1985-87], 229-37, esp. 235). The above statements indicate that Westerholm believes Paul's language of "fulfilling the Law" in Rom. 8:4 is the result of the interchange in Paul's argument against the Jews that they have transgressed the Law and his counterclaim that only Christians fulfill the Law; it is not an indication of a tension within Paul's own convictional world between Spirit and Law.

[79] Moo, *The Epistle to the Romans*, p. 21.

theological convictions against the onslaughts of his opponents (e.g. "For you gladly put up with fools, since you are 'so wise'" [2 Cor. 11:19]; "You foolish Galatians, who has bewitched you..." [Gal. 3:1]).[80]

Paul's polemical purpose seems secondary to the more immediate concern of his letter. He has never been in Rome and most likely was not acquainted with the believers there (cf. Rom. 1:10 where Paul writes, "in my prayers, always asking that I might somehow now at last succeed by God's will to come to you" [see also vv. 13-15]). In Rom. 15:23-31, he reveals his impending plans: he looks forward to coming to the Christian community in Rome via his travels to Spain (vv.23-24, 28) but must first carry a collection to the poor in Jerusalem that he has gathered among the believers in Macedonia and Achaia (vv.25-26), he is also aware that he may encounter some opposition in Jerusalem from two groups ("unbelievers in Judea" and believers themselves who may misunderstand his intentions) (v. 31) and therefore, he asks for the support of the Romans themselves for prayers that his Jerusalem trip would be successful (v.30).

In his correspondence with the believers in Rome, Paul lays out an extensive treatment of his understanding of the gospel, containing didactic material that echoes themes and phrases from his earlier writings (1 Thess., Gal., Phil., 1 and 2 Cor.).[81] His main concern is clear. His purpose in the letter was to introduce himself by way of communicating the components of his gospel message[82] and through this, gain the backing of the Roman congregations for his future plans.[83] In the process of conveying the intricacies of his gospel message, he was reflecting on the various subjects addressed in

---

[80] See Fitzmyer who states, "For one thing that Romans is not is a polemical or apologetic writing. It is, for example, quite different from Galatians, which treats much of the same doctrine, but is clearly polemical" (*Romans*, p. 73).

[81] See G. Bornkamm, "The Letter to the Romans as Paul's Last Will and Testament," *ABR* 11 (1963-64), 2-14 reprinted in K.P. Donfried (ed.), *The Romans Debate: Revised and Expanded Edition* (Peabody, Mass.: Hendrickson, 1991), pp. 16-28, especially pp. 25-27; Fitzmyer lists 3 pages of echoes of themes and phrases from Paul's earlier letters (*Romans*, pp. 71-3).

[82] "[A] letter of recommendation which Paul has written on his own behalf...The topic of the letter is...this gospel" (H. Koester, *History and Literature of Early Christianity: Introduction to the New Testament* Vol. 2 [Philadelphia: Fortress Press, 1982], p. 140); "So far, however, he (*Paul*) was unknown to it (*congregation in Rome*) personally and had to introduce himself officially" (Käsemann, *Commentary on Romans*, p.3).

[83] Ulrich Wilckens, "Über Abassungszweck und Aufbau des Römerbriefs," in *Rechtfertigung als Freiheit*, 110-70, especially, 127-139, 167 (Neukirchen-Vluyn: Neukirchener Verlag, 1974).

his previous preaching and correspondence.[84] This is particularly the case with respect to the Law and Spirit in Rom. 8:1-16.[85]

When one compares the type of discourse in Rom. 8:1-16 with the other Pauline epistles, the continuity/discontinuity interplay with respect to the Law seems to be Paul's consistent practice throughout his letters, regardless of the historical circumstances he was addressing in his correspondence at the time.[86] In addition, Paul customarily describes the Spirit's role with covenantal concepts previously associated with Law observance.[87] Often these associations between the Spirit and covenant are unprecedented and most are *non sequitur* jumps in the logic of Paul's argumentation.[88] Both the consistent presence of a continuity/discontinuity interplay and Paul's inclination to describe the Spirit's role within the framework of Judaism's covenant relationship indicate that these are most likely his method of negotiating a conflict within his personal convictional world. The idea of Paul's previous commitment to observe the Law, particularly knowing that it had been given by God to the Jews (Rom. 3:2) and that it was necessary to maintain covenantal status with God (Rom. 7:10-11; 10:5), was a lingering thought even in light of his newly acquired convictions formed by his experience of Christ and the Spirit.

---

[84] "Echoes of themes and phrases from earlier Pauline writings...reveal(s) that Paul has been reflecting on his own preaching of the gospel ...in his ministry in Asia, Macedonia, and Achaia" (Fitzmyer, *Romans*, p. 71).

[85] For example, Rom. 7:25; 8:1-2 (through Christ/ Spirit one is freed from the Law, sin, and death) demonstrates some parallel to 1 Cor. 15:57; 2 Cor. 3:17; Gal. 5:18. Also Rom. 8:14-15 (those who are led by the Spirit; adoptive sonship, "Abba, Father") is comparable to Gal. 4:5-6.

[86] See footnotes 12 and 13 above and related discussion.

[87] See footnote 65.

[88] For example, in Rom. 2:29, "circumcision of the heart" is a phrase used in Ancient Judaism in the context of Israel's covenant relationship with Yahweh (Deut. 10:16; 30:6; Jer. 4:4; 9:25,26). But its relationship to the words, "in the Spirit not letter" is not self-explanatory. There is no explicit reference made in Ancient and Second Temple Judaism to the relationship between "circumcision of the heart" and the "Spirit." It is also an atypical Jewish sentiment to posit an antithesis between "letter" and "Spirit" (see also Rom. 7:6 cf. Jer. 31:31-34; Ezek. 36:26-27). Furthermore, the mention of the Spirit in Rom. 2:29 is somewhat incidental to the argument and is brought in so offhandedly here in its context. In vv.25-29, the emphasis is on the value of circumcision for those who observe the Law and the relationship this has to the status of being a "Jew." It is not until Rom. 5:5 that Paul takes up this idea of the Spirit again. This corresponds to Daniel Patte's method of locating convictions "'in the cracks, in what is odd in the argument, in what does not contribute to the unfolding of the argument or even hinder it" (*Paul's Faith and the Power of the Gospel: A Structural Introduction to the Pauline Letters* [Philadelphia: Fortress Press, 1983], pp. 39-40).

In his correspondence with the Romans, Paul's intention was to communicate the fundamentals of his gospel message by reflecting on the content of his preaching in the past. In this process we notice that the tension between the Law and the Spirit, and more fundamentally the tension between his Jewish past and his Christian present, are recurring phenomena. This suggests that the interchange between Spirit and Law is the result of Paul's attempt at reducing the conflicts and tensions within his own convictional world and not primarily to provide a rebuttal to the accusation of supporting an antinomianism point of view. The textual tensions in Rom. 8:1-16 are not entirely the result of the external exigencies of his pastoral ministry, though these may have provided him with the stimulus to work out the implications of his basic convictions. Therefore, the adoption of a method that places too much emphasis on the contextual situation, where Paul responds to a particular set of circumstances in his ministry, will be insufficient to account for the dynamics that exist in his description of the relationship between the Spirit and Law. While it is necessary to note the interrelatedness between contextual and convictional levels, it would be methodologically erroneous to blur the distinctions between them. Accordingly, it is essential that we employ an interpretive method that properly addresses the situational context of Paul's correspondence with Rome and, at the same time, takes into consideration behavioural patterns for an individual who encounters disjunctions within his personal belief system. In the following section, we shall explore the suitability of Cognitive Dissonance Theory.

4.3.2 Cognitive Dissonance Theory and the Tensions in Rom. 8:1-16. Leon Festinger first propounded Cognitive Dissonance Theory in the 1950's.[89] The application of this theory has been diverse; it has been used to analyze the behaviour of maze running rats,[90] the development of values in children,[91] the impact hunger has on college students,[92] and to determine the proselytizing

---

[89] This was first published by Leon Festinger, *A Theory of Cognitive Dissonance* (Evanston: Row, Peterson and Company, 1957) and later reissued under the same title by Stanford University Press, Stanford, CA in 1962.

[90] D.H. Lawrence and L. Festinger, *Deterrents and Reinforcement* (Stanford: Stanford University Press, 1962).

[91] E. Aronson and J.M. Carlsmith, "Effect of the Severity of Threat on the Valuation of Forbidden Behavior," *JASP* 66 (1963), 584-88.

[92] M.L. Brehm, K.W. Back, and M.D. Bogdonoff, "A Physiological Effect of Cognitive Dissonance under Stress and Deprivation," *JASP* 69 (1964), 303-10.

behaviour of religious zealots.[93] The theory attempts to explain problems arising in post-decision making circumstances, in particular, when individuals have made firm commitments to beliefs, called "cognitions," and the expectations associated with these beliefs are inconsistent with reality and experience. This gives rise to the experience of dissonance and the need to reduce it. Festinger proposes that individuals faced with such circumstances exhibit a drive to bring all cognitive elements into a consistent relation with one another, that is, there is a drive that seeks to resolve dissonance and restore a sense of equilibrium. The more cognitive elements correspond between the different alternatives, the less the resulting dissonance. One manner of achieving this is to establish "cognitive overlap" between alternatives, that is, to take elements corresponding to each of the alternatives and put them in a context where they lead to the same end result. Another major vehicle for reducing dissonance is to search for social validation regarding one's cognitions within one's own social group. The larger the number of people one knows who agree with a given belief, the less the magnitude of dissonance. This means that influencing others within the social group to form a consensus that coincides with one's beliefs can significantly reduce cognitive dissonance.[94]

The concern with consistency between expectation and experience makes Cognitive Dissonance Theory eminently suitable as a heuristic tool to provide an explanation for both the internal textual tensions in Rom. 8:1-16 and the external tension between Paul's native Jewish convictions and his Christian convictions. Festinger's theory provides a suggestive way of accounting for the dynamics of Rom. 8:1-16: Paul's description of his pre-Damascus commitment to Law observance ("much more a zealot for the traditions of my ancestors" [Gal. 1:14] cf. "being blameless according to the righteousness which is in the Law" [Phil. 3:6]) and his knowledge of Jewish eschatological

---

[93] L. Festinger, H. Riecken, and S. Schachter, *When Prophecy Fails* (Minneapolis: University of Minnesota Press, 1956).

[94] Leon Festinger, *A Theory of Cognitive Dissonance*; for a concise definition of Cognitive Dissonance Theory see p. 31 and for the various components of the theory mentioned above see the following: the drive to reduce dissonance, pp. 9, 18; the influence of reality/experience on cognitions, pp. 10-11, 24-25, 27; logical inconsistencies between cognitions, p. 14; cognitive overlap, pp. 45-46; the reduction of dissonance by acquiring social validation, pp. 177, 179, 182, 185, 188-91, 200.

tradition that advocated a harmonious relationship between Spirit and Law;[95] the disequilibrium between the Spirit and Law, i.e., the inconsistency between his cognitions on the Law and the cognitions formed by his experience of the Spirit (Rom. 7:6; 8:2 cf. Gal. 5:18); his drive to quell the tensions between the Spirit and Law by establishing consonance between them (e.g., in Rom. 8, "the *law* of the Spirit," v.2; "the righteous requirement of the Law may be fulfilled in us...who walk according to the Spirit," v.4; the description of the role of the Spirit using terms and concepts that were fundamental to Judaism's covenantal nomism); and his attempt to influence the believers in Rome to affirm his cognition that the Spirit accomplishes what the Law intended to do, that is, give life.

4.3.3 Criticisms and Developments. Since its first publication in the 1950's, Cognitive Dissonance Theory has been the stimulus for a prodigious amount of research.[96] Some of this includes criticisms of the theory itself. The theory states that when two cognitions are in a state of tension because there is a

---

[95] There are allusions to the eschatological promises of Jer. 38 (LXX):31-34 and Ezek. 36:25-27 in Gal. 4:23-29; Rom. 2:29, 7:6, and more directly in 2 Cor. 3:1-18. The mention of "two covenants" in Gal. 4:24 and its association with v. 29 ("according to the Spirit") alludes to the new covenant promise of Jeremiah read in conjunction with Ezekiel. Rom. 2:29 combines the idea of "circumcised hearts" with the "Spirit" and thus recalls Deut. 30:6 and the promise of the new covenant. Paul's argument in 2 Cor. 3 corresponds to Jeremiah in that it associates the idea of writing on "hearts" (v.3) with the distinctive phrase "new covenant" (v. 6), which is combined only in Jeremiah in the OT (Jer. 38 [LXX]: 31, 33) (Richard B. Hays, *Echoes of Scripture in the Letters of Paul* [New Haven: Yale University Press, 1989], p. 128; Wright, *The Climax of the Covenant*, note 7). Also, the contrast between "stony tablets" and "tablets of fleshly hearts" (v.3) in association with the Spirit (vv. 3, 6), no doubt recalls the distinction between "heart of stone" and "heart of flesh" and the work of the Spirit in Ezek 11:19-20; 36:26-27. Paul suspends his normal negative use of σάρξ (see for example, Rom. 6:19; 7:5, 18, 25; 8:3, 6; 1 Cor. 15:50; 2 Cor. 4:11; 7:5; 12:7-9; Gal. 2:20; 3:3; 4:13-14; 5:16-17 cf. vv. 19-23; Phil. 3:3) for the positive reference to ἐν πλαξὶν καρδίαις σαρκίναις (v. 3), paralleled in Ezek. 11:19; 36:26 (Dunn, *The Theology of Paul the Apostle*, p. 147, footnote 103). He has re-interpreted the tradition in a unique way by assimilating "heart of stone" to "tablets of stone" and thus connected it with the Mosaic Law (Ralph P. Martin, *2 Corinthians* WBC 40 [Waco, TX: Word Books, Publisher, 1986], p. 52).

[96] The notoriety of Festinger's Cognitive Dissonance Theory has been compared to that of Thomas Kuhn's, *The Structure of Scientific Revolutions*, Second Edition (Chicago: University of Chicago Press, 1970). In fact, the two theoretical approaches have been combined (E.L. McDonagh, "Attitude Changes and Paradigm Shifts: Social Psychological Foundations of the Kuhnian Thesis," SSS 6 [1976], 51-76).

discrepancy between belief and experience, there will be a drive to resolve this and achieve consistency. Critics argue it is often the case that most people live with conflicting cognitions and do not attempt to alleviate any dissonance they experience. David A. Snow and Richard Machalek claim that social scientists should not assume that those who hold unconventional beliefs consistently face the problem of reconciling discrepancies between belief and experience, since many belief systems do not require consistent and frequent confirmatory evidence. Confirming evidence may simply go unacknowledged.[97]

Conflicts and tensions may be ubiquitous and can be counteracted by more powerful drives. For example, dissonance can have great utility in that people learn from their experiences. In such cases the reduction or resolution of dissonance would entail the loss of learning potential.[98] It is possible to explain the supposed disconfirmation of belief in terms of its faulty understanding of the original commitment and therefore maintain that the expectation has not yet been disconfirmed. It would be difficult to see how natural misunderstanding of a previous commitment is to be separated from dissonant reduction forms of explanations.[99] Critics contend that in order for the Cognitive Dissonance model to work there must be a clear indication that a dissonant relationship exists between conflicting cognitions and also that there is an effort to reduce this tension.

Even though Festinger's Cognitive Dissonance Theory has been used extensively within biblical scholarship,[100] this model has been criticized for

---

[97] David A. Snow and Richard Machalek, "On the Presumed Fragility of Unconventional Beliefs," *JSSR* 21 (1982), 15–26, esp. 22–3.

[98] "Man cannot live by consonance alone" (Elliot Aronson, "Dissonance Theory: Progress and Problems" in *Theories of Cognitive Consistency: A Sourcebook*, [ed. Robert P. Abelson *et al.*; Chicago: Rand McNally and Company, 1968], pp. 5–27, quote taken from p. 26); see also Robert P. Carroll, *When Prophecy Failed: Cognitive Dissonance in the Prophetic Traditions of the Old Testament* (New York: The Seabury Press, 1979), p. 104.

[99] R. Brown, *Social Psychology* (Glencoe, Illinois: The Free Press, 1965), p. 595; see also his assessment of Cognitive Dissonance Theory on pp. 601–4.

[100] See, for example, Carroll, *When Prophecy Failed*; "Prophecy, Dissonance and Jeremiah XXVI," *Transactions of the Glasgow University Oriental Society* 25 (1976), 12–23; "Ancient Israelite Prophecy and Dissonance Theory," *Numen* 24 (1977), 135–51; J.G. Gager, *Kingdom and Community: The Social World of Early Christianity* (Englewood Cliffs: Prentice-Hall, 1975), esp. pp. 37–49; H. Jackson, "The Resurrection Belief of the Earliest Church: A Response to the Failure of Prophecy?," *JR* 55 (1975), 414–25; U. Wernik, "Frustrated Beliefs and Early Christianity," *Numen* 22 (1975), 96–130; see also John J. Collins, who uses Festinger's Theory of Cognitive Dissonance to explain the tension Diaspora Jews experienced between their Jewish traditions

being used anachronistically. It is argued that employing a theory generated from contemporary North American experiences to explain something in the first century Mediterranean world seems incongruous and is highly suspect.[101] In the social context of the first century Mediterranean world in which the early Christian movement was set, the world permeated with dissonance and inconsistency.[102] Rather than any attempt to resolve cognitive dissonance resulting from the disconfirmation of beliefs, Bruce J. Malina argues it was precisely the dissonance itself along with "normative inconsistencies" typical of early Christian movement groups that halted the progress of extremists' tendencies (e.g., murder-suicide, destruction by local governmental forces, violence, confrontation with opposing forces) and the possible annihilation of the movement. Normative dissonance provided opportunity for self-directed change and management of group loyalty. This accounted for the survival of the Jesus movement, even in the wake of the death of its focal figure and the dispersal of its core membership.[103]

When used as an explanatory model for biblical interpretation, Cognitive Dissonance Theory has been criticized for utilizing a modern Western conception of the individual self that is not shared cross-culturally, particularly in the first century Mediterranean culture. The primary difference between the two cultures is that in the modern Western world the individual is *idiocentric*, that is, the individual self is set apart from one's own social context as free and autonomous. But, in the non-Western and ancient world, the individual is *allocentric*, that is, the individual self is identified only within the society and social group of which one is a part; when you know someone's family or

---

that encouraged separation from Gentiles on the one hand, yet on the other hand, found Hellenism to be an admirable way of life in which to participate (*Between Athens and Jerusalem* [New York: Crossroad, 1983]).

[101] Gager uses Festinger's theory to explain the persistence of the early Christian movement even in the wake of the death of its leader, Jesus. He argues that when group members (early Christian group) find that the belief system to which they have committed themselves has been disconfirmed, their reaction is to bring new members into their group (to proselytize) (*Kingdom and Community*, pp. 20f., esp. p. 40). Gager's use of Festinger's theory has been reviewed in Bruce J. Malina's "Jesus as Charismatic Leader?" *BTB* 14 (1984), 55–62.

[102] See Ramsay MacMullen, *Roman Social Relations: 50 B.C. to A.D. 284* (New Haven, CT: Yale University Press, 1974); Keith Hopkins, *Conquerors and Slaves* Sociological Studies in Romans History, Vol. 1 (Cambridge, UK: Cambridge University Press, 1978).

[103] Bruce J. Malina, "Normative Dissonance and Christian Origins," *Semeia* 35 (1986), 35–59, esp. 35–39.

ethnic origin, you know all you need to know about them.[104] Festinger's Cognitive Dissonance Theory claims there is psychological discomfort within individuals who encounter two cognitions in dissonant relationship, which incites introspective analysis and the need to reduce the experience of dissonance. Some social scientists have retorted, contending that behaviour centred on the notions of the self is incongruent with the allocentric conception of self, characteristic of the individual who lives in the first century Mediterranean context. Malina states, "They (ancient people) knew or cared little about psychological development, psychological motivations and introspective analyses."[105]

It may be generally true that the first century Mediterranean world tolerated inconsistencies and, even in some cases, the dissonance itself accounted for the survival of various groups. However, in this case, Paul did not exhibit tolerant behaviour, enduring the inconsistencies between Christ/Spirit and Law, and not taking any active steps to alleviate these inconsistencies. Furthermore, he was not willing to stand by and conform to the managing pressures of other contemporary Jews who advocated the importance of the Jewish Law. Paul exhibited a headlong pursuit in convincing his contemporaries of his belief that Law observance was detrimental to faith in Christ and was redundant in light of the Spirit's role. For example, in Gal. 2:11-21, Paul openly censured Peter for reverting to living by the stipulations set forth in the Jewish Law. Paul demonstrates a firm commitment to the gospel message that allowed no room for discussion. He

---

[104] See Marcel Mauss, "A Category of the Human Mind: The Notion of Personhood; the Notion of Self," in The Category of the Person: Anthropology, Philosophy, History (ed. M. Carrithers, S. Collins, and S. Lukes; trans. W.D. Halls; Cambridge: Cambridge University Press, 1985), pp. 1-25, esp. pp. 19-22; Harry C. Triandis, "The Self and Social Behaviour in Differing Cultural Contexts," PR 98 (1989), 506-20; Bruce Malina, "The Individual and the Community-Personality in the Social World of Early Christianity," BTB 9 (1979), 126-38; Bruce Malina, "Is There a Circum-Mediterranean Person? Looking for Stereotypes," BTB 22 (1992), 66-87; Bruce J. Malina and Jerome H. Neyrey, "First Century Personality: Dyadic, not Individual," in The Social World of Luke-Acts (ed. Jerome H. Neyrey; Peabody, MA: Hendrickson Publishers, 1991), pp. 67-96.

[105] Malina, "The Individual and the Community," 131; see also his "Normative Dissonance and Christian Origins," 38, where he specifically names Festinger's theory for being an inappropriate model to analyze the behaviour of people within the first century Mediterranean culture because individuals in this era and culture had an "anti-introspective, dyadic personality."

declares an overt disparity between himself and other Jews regarding his convictions on the Law.[106]

Paul consistently took active steps to alleviate the dissonance between Christ/Spirit and the Law, even though he never succeeded in resolving it altogether.[107] There is no evidence to suggest that he engaged in this because it provided him with great utility; i.e., it was a learning process for him. His Jewish ancestral traditions had clearly delineated the importance of the Law and set in place definitive expectations regarding the relationship between the Spirit and Law. There is no indication that Paul misunderstood these traditions. Paul's letter to the Roman believers represented his own mature understanding of the Gospel (Rom. 1.16-17) and was most likely written in the latter part of his missionary career. This letter represented Paul's more developed thought, written to a church that was not his own founding, under congenial circumstances with time for careful reflection and composition.[108] Even in these circumstances Paul displays a similar drive, comparable to his previous letters, to show equilibrium between Christ/Spirit and the Law, even though the two were perceived to be in a dissonant relationship.

The focus of Cognitive Dissonance Theory has often been misplaced. Its emphasis is not exclusively on the individual and the psychological discomfort a person experiences when he encounters disequilibrium between two cognitions. Rather, Cognitive Dissonance Theory is concerned mainly with an analysis of the behavioural patterns involved in restoring consistency within the group setting. This theory properly belongs to the field of study called "social psychology," which interprets behavioural patterns within a given social setting.[109] It is devoted to determining principles of congruity, consistency, and

---

[106] For example, in Gal. 2:4-6, Paul states: "some false brothers had infiltrated to spy on the freedom we have in Christ Jesus" (v. 4), "we did not give in to them for a moment" (v.5), "as for those who seem to be important- whatever they were makes no difference to me...those ones added nothing to my message" (v.6). See also Gal. 1:6-10 for a demonstration of Paul's unequivocal resolve to maintain the integrity of the gospel message.

[107] See discussion above and footnotes 12 and 13 that demonstrate Paul's regular effort in demonstrating a dissonant/consonant relationship between Christ/Spirit and the Law.

[108] It is the nature and timing of Paul's correspondence to the believers in Rome that made it a suitable tool to discover the mature convictions of the Apostle. Dunn describes it "as a kind of template on which to construct our own statement of Paul's theology" (*The Theology of Paul the Apostle*, pp. 25-6).

[109] See Festinger's Ch. 8 entitled, "The Role of Social Support: Theory" (*A Theory of Cognitive Dissonance*, pp. 177-202). Ironically, Malina and Neyrey criticize Festinger's Cognitive

balance in one's society and one's social group. Social psychology is "about the mesh between the self and society."[110] In allocentric societies, like the first century Mediterranean context out of which Paul spoke, it is not that self-interests did not matter but that self-interests are interpreted in relationship to in-groups, groups of people who believe they share a common bond and purpose.[111] In this case Paul's "in-group" was fictive (e.g., "household of faith," [Gal. 6:10] cf. Mark 3:31–35, where members addressed one another as "sister" or "brother")[112]; it was comprised of both Jewish and Gentile believers of whom the Roman believers were a part and who all shared the common experience of the Spirit.[113] This indicates that the nature of Paul's communication in Rom. 8 was not simply to engage in an introspective analysis on the tensions between the Spirit and Law for the sake of alleviating personal psychological discomfort and venting his frustrations. It was more than this; Paul strove to gain the support for his cognitions from the fictive group whom he valued and of which he was a part.

Leon Festinger's model of Cognitive Dissonance is an appropriate explanatory tool that will assist us in elucidating both the internal and external tensions Paul exhibits in his explication of the relationship between the Spirit and Law in Rom. 8:1–16. Since this theory belongs under the taxonomy of social psychology, it has the potential to take into account both the specific

---

Dissonance Theory for being used anachronistically, yet they advocate the necessity of employing "social psychology" as the appropriate perspective in which to interpret ancient first century Mediterranean culture ("This book studies persons in society, and so its dominant perspective is that of sociology and anthropology; the focus is what is called *social psychology*" [*Portraits of Paul: An Archaeology of Ancient Personality* (Louisville, KY: Westminster John Knox Press, 1996), p.10]).

[110] William A. Gamson, "The Social Psychology of Collective Action" in *Frontiers in Social Management Theory* (ed. Aldon D. Morris and Carol McClurg Mueller; New Haven, Conn.: Yale University Press, 1992), pp. 53–76, quote taken from p. 53.

[111] "The self ...can be related to a group the way a hand is related to the person whose hand it is...[this] conception is found in collectivist cultures, where the self overlaps with a group, such as family or tribe" (Harry C. Triandis, "Cross-Cultural Studies of Individualism and Collectivism" in *Cross-Cultural Perspectives* [ed. John J. Berman; Lincoln, Nebr.: University of Nebraska Press, 1990], pp. 41–133, quote taken from p. 78).

[112] Malina and Neyrey, *Portraits of Paul*, p. 160.

[113] See Rom. 8:15–16, where Paul uses the first person plural to describe the common experience of the Spirit among believers: "the Spirit of adoption by whom *we cry out* (κράζομεν)" (v.15) and "the Spirit testifies with *our* (ἡμῶν) spirit that *we are* (ἐσμέν) children of God" (v.16) cf. "fellowship of the Spirit" (Phil. 2:1).

situational context from which Paul's correspondence with the Roman believers was written and the broader cultural context of the first century Mediterranean world from which Paul spoke.

PART ONE

Pauline Antecedents: Spirit and Law in Ethical Renewal and Jewish Eschatology

Introduction

New Testament scholarship today would affirm, "Paul was a Jew."[1] He was born and brought up a Jew and never ceased to be a Jew.[2] It is no coincidence that within his written correspondence Paul never refers to himself as Χριστιανός,[3] and even when he speaks of his encounter with Christ, he refers to it only as a calling and commissioning, and not as a conversion.[4] The important corollary for this investigation is that Paul who thought through his convictions on the Spirit did so within a Jewish framework.[5] Indeed, it has long been recognized that Judaism provided the conceptual framework for the early Christian community's pneumatological reflection. Friedrich Büchsel states, "Denn das Denken der Urgemeinde, auch der Geistgedanke der Urgemeinde, war am Alten Testament und der jüdischen Überlieferung orientiert."[6] It is for this reason that our inquiry into Paul's pneumatology

---

[1] Albert Schweitzer, *The Mysticism of Paul the Apostle* (New York: Seabury, 1968); W.D. Davies, *Paul and Rabbinic Judaism* (London: SPCK, 1948); Hans-Joachim Schoeps, *Paul: The Theology of the Apostle in Light of Jewish Religious History* (Philadelphia: Westminster, 1961).

[2] See Rom. 11:1 ("an Israelite, of the seed of Abraham, of the tribe of Benjamin"); Phil. 3:5 ("circumcised the eighth day, of the nation of Israel, of the tribe of Benjamin, a Hebrew of Hebrews, as to the Law, a Pharisee").

[3] See Acts 11:26; 26:28; 1 Pet. 4:16.

[4] See Gal 1:15-16; 1 Cor. 9:1, 16, 19-27; 15:8-11 and related discussions in John Knox, *Chapters in a Life of Paul* (London: A. & C. Black, 1954), p. 117; Johannes Munck, *Paul and the Salvation of Mankind* (London: SCM, 1959), pp. 11-35; Krister Stendahl, *Paul Among Jews and Gentiles* (Philadelphia: Fortress Press, 1976), pp. 7-12.

[5] See related discussion above in the "Introduction" for the point that Paul consistently explicates the Spirit's role using terms and concepts characteristic of Judaism's covenantal nomism.

[6] Friedrich Büchsel, *Der Geist Gottes im Neuen Testament* (Gütersloh: C. Bertelsmann, 1926), p. 240; see also pp. 200-1, 239-40, 252; "Coming to Paul himself we notice first that the Apostle explicitly links the Christian possession of the Spirit to the Old Testament eschatological

begins with a survey of how the various pneumatological perspectives were related to the observance of the Torah within the configuration of the Jewish covenant in Second Temple Judaism.

Since the Jewish eschatological expectation of the new covenant and Israel's ethical renewal was firmly established upon the promises of Ancient Judaism and subsequently taken up in Second Temple Judaism, I have organized the sources in Part One (Pauline Antecedents: Spirit and Law in Ethical Renewal and Jewish Eschatology) into two main groups: Ancient Judaism and Second Temple Judaism. In order to appreciate the diversity within Second Temple Judaism, I have further divided this grouping into three sub-sections: Diaspora literature, Palestinian literature, and Qumran literature. While Diaspora and Palestinian Judaism can be distinguished on the basis of language and geography, there has been a growing recognition that Palestinian Judaism had undergone profound Hellenization by the second century B.C.E.[7] This should help to remind us that the lines of demarcation between Diaspora and Palestinian literature cannot be pressed too firmly. The

---

promise" (Geerhardus Vos, "The Eschatological Aspect of the Pauline Conception of the Spirit," *Biblical and Theological Studies*, Members of the Faculty of Princeton Theological Seminary [New York: Charles Scribner's Sons, 1912], pp. 211-59, quote taken from p. 224); for more modern expressions of the same idea see James D.G. Dunn, *Baptism in the Holy Spirit: A Re-examination of the New Testament Teaching on the Gift of the Spirit in Relation to Pentecostalism Today* (London: SCM Press, 1970). He writes, "Implicit here, therefore, is the thought of the Spirit as the new covenant fulfillment of the ancient covenant promise. The gift of the Spirit is now the means whereby men enter into the blessing of Abraham,"(p. 47); "In Romans, when Paul speaks of the Spirit, he does not understand *pneuma* as in the Hellenistic world of his time...but rather as an apocalyptic manifestation of the endtime, as in the OT...Consequently, when Paul uses *pneuma*, he takes over much of the OT idea of 'the Spirit of God'" (Fitzmyer, *Romans*, p. 124); "There can be little question that Paul considered his understanding of the Spirit to flow directly out of the Old Testament" (Fee, *God's Empowering Presence*, p. 904); Paul was a Jewish rabbi "whose conviction that Jesus was the Messiah assured him of the dawning of the eschatological age in which the Spirit of God was to act in a new way" (Clark H. Pinnock, "The Concept of the Spirit in the Epistles of Paul," [Ph.D. dissertation, University of Manchester, 1963], pp. iv-v); see also Robert P. Menzies, who traces the pneumatological traditions of the early Christian community back to Intertestamental Judaism (*The Development of Early Christian Pneumatology With Special Reference to Luke-Acts* JSNTSup 54 [Sheffield: JSOT Press, 1991], pp. 52-112).

[7] David E. Aune, *Prophecy in Early Christianity and the Ancient Mediterranean World* (Grand Rapids: William B. Eerdmans Publishing Company, 1983), p. 16; Davies, *Paul and Rabbinic Judaism*, pp. 1-16; M. Hengel, *Judaism and Hellenism: Studies in their Encounter in Palestine During the Early Hellenistic Period*, Vol. 1, (trans. J. Bowden; London: SCM Press, 1974), p. 312.

Qumran community deserves separate analysis since it qualifies as a "sect" in Second Temple Judaism. While the Pharisees and Sadducees in Jewish society attempted to influence other Jews by their beliefs, they did not understand membership within their respective groups to have special theological or eschatological significance. In contrast, the Essenes at Qumran considered membership in their community to be exclusive and have eschatological significance; they were the Community of the New Covenant and through initiation and obedience thought of themselves as the elect ones.

CHAPTER ONE

Ancient Judaism[1]

There is little doubt that Paul was vigorously engaged in the reappropriation of Israel's Scriptures to such an extent that he insistently sought to show how his theological convictions were firmly grounded in the witness of Israel's Scriptures. Of the 89 OT quotations in the Pauline letters, 51 occur in Romans alone.[2] This is striking since Paul's letter to the Romans constitutes only about a third of the authentic Pauline corpus. Even though there is no explicit quotation from the OT to be found in Rom. 8:1-16, such heavy concentration of scriptural quotation in the rest of his correspondence is a sure indication that Paul's thoughts were, to a significant degree, informed by God's word to Israel. Furthermore, Peter Stuhlmacher demonstrates how in Rom. 8 the Apostle combines early Jewish messianic and wisdom tradition founded upon the OT (2 Sam. 7:14; Ps. 2:7; 89:28; Is. 11:2; 61:1f; Prov. 8:22). These are related to the promise of an "arrangement" from God with respect to the Law (Jer. 31:31-34; Ezek. 36:27) to form a new unified Christian whole.[3] For these reasons, it is indispensable that we engage in a survey of the Spirit's relationship to Israel's ethical life in Ancient Judaism, particularly as it related to Law observance. By doing this we will be isolating one of the main influences upon Paul's thought in his composition of Rom. 8:1-16 and, at the

---

[1] There is no special treatment given to the Septuagint (LXX) under its own heading in "Diaspora Literature" because the LXX was fairly consistent with the MT regarding its translation of those passages associated with Jewish eschatology and ethical renewal.

[2] Dietrich-Alex Koch, *Die Schrift als Zeuge des Evangeliums: Untersuchungen zur Verwendung und zum Verständnis der Schrift bei Paulus* BHT 69 (Tübingen: J.C.B. Mohr [Paul Siebeck], 1986), pp. 21-24; this count does not include the 6 quotations found in Ephesians and the Pastorals, which are not considered to be part of the authentic Pauline corpus by most NT scholars.

[3] Peter Stuhlmacher, *Paul's Letter to the Romans: A Commentary* (trans. Scott J. Hafemann; Louisville: Westminster/ John Knox Press, 1994), pp. 117-18.

same time, be in keeping with Paul's propensity towards a dialectical intercourse with Israel's "holy texts."

The Hebrew term רוּחַ occurs 378 times in the OT[4] with various meanings.[5] There are general uses of the word רוּחַ in the Hebrew Scriptures: breath (Ps. 33:6; Is. 11:4; Job. 4:15; Hos. 12:2), the principle that gives life to the body (Gen. 6:17; 7:15; Hab. 2:19), the seat of emotions, intellectual functions and attitude of will (2 Ki. 19:7; Job 32:8; Ex. 35:21). But it is also used to denote the effective power of God (Ezek. 1:12, 20; Num. 11:25, 29): the divine power which creates life (Ezek. 37:9, 10; Ps. 104:30); the divine power which gives mental abilities (Exod. 31:3; 35:31; Micah 3:8); the divine power which fashions moral powers (Is. 32:15; Hag. 2:5; Ezek. 39:29; Zech. 4:6; 6:8; Ps. 51:11); God's saving power (Is. 4:4; 32:15; 63:11; Neh. 9:20).[6] In the LXX translators normally use πνεῦμα to translate the Hebrew רוּחַ. Of the 378 occurrences of רוּחַ in the Hebrew OT, 277 appear in the LXX as πνεῦμα.[7] When the OT came to be translated into Greek, however, the translators demonstrated a tendency not to use πνεῦμα for human emotions, inclination, thought or determination.[8] Instead, terms such as θυμός and ψυχή were used when indicating human thought or determination (e.g. Gen. 41:8; Exod. 35:21; Eccl. 7:11; Job 15:13; 6:4; Zech. 6:8; Ezek 39:29).[9] The Hebrew use of רוּחַ and its association with God influenced the concept of πνεῦμα. Πνεῦμα in Greek usage was normally applied only to the concepts of wind, breath and life but the translators of the LXX added a new dimension to the use of πνεῦμα in that it became associated with the effective power of God.[10]

---

[4] BDB, pp. 924–26.

[5] Friedrich Baumgärtel, "Spirit in the OT/ Judaism," *TDNT* Vol. VI, pp. 359–68, esp. pp. 360–63.

[6] *Ibid.*, pp. 360–63.

[7] See Marie E. Isaacs, *The Concept of the Spirit: A Study of Pneuma in Hellenistic Judaism and its Bearing on the New Testament*, Heythrop Monographs 1 (London: Heythrop College, 1976), p.10.

[8] E. Best notes how the use of πνεῦμα referring to the spirit of humans virtually disappears in Josephus and Philo. This is an extension of a tendency already found in the LXX ("The Use and Non-use of Pneuma by Josephus," *NovT* 3 [1959], 218–25).

[9] *Ibid.*, p. 11. However, there are exceptions to this general tendency. The LXX uses πνεῦμα to translate רוּח for human emotion and thought in Judg. 9:23; 8:3; Eccl. 7:8; Num. 5:14; Deut. 2:30.

[10] *Ibid.*, p. 17; see also W.R. Shoemaker, "The Use of *Ruach* in the Old Testament and *Pneuma* in the New Testament: a lexicographical study," *JBL* 23 (1904), 13–67. There is an indication

This investigation will be limited to the use of רוּחַ/πνεῦμα referring to the Spirit of God, and in particular, the Spirit's role in ethical renewal. In certain places the distinction between the Spirit of God and human spirit cannot be made; God was the creator of all humans and thus רוּחַ becomes a linking term, which refers to both God's Spirit and human life in its dependence upon God (Deut. 34:9; 2 Kgs. 19:7; Ps. 51:10; Isa. 61:3; Ezek. 18:31).[11] Presupposed in the OT is the idea of the Spirit as God's dynamic presence among his people transforming, creating anew, and empowering Israel to live faithfully within the covenant relationship (Judg. 3:7-11; 11:27-29; Ps. 51:10-11; Isa. 42:1, etc).[12] This survey will include both a general discussion of the Spirit's relationship to Israel's religious life in non-eschatological contexts and a more particular survey of the eschatological dimension of OT pneumatology as it relates to the Mosaic Law.

1. The Spirit, Ethical Renewal, and the Law in Non-Eschatological Contexts

In Ancient Judaism there are only sparse references to the relationship between the Spirit and ethics in non-eschatological texts. For example, in the context of Num. 11:17, 25-26, 29, where Moses appoints seventy elders to assist him in his obligations to lead Israel, it is said that the Spirit was bestowed upon the seventy elders and they prophesied. But the content of the prophecy is not given and no further comment is made on the effects this had upon their leadership capabilities. It is implicit that these 70 leaders continued to assist Moses in the administration of the covenant people. The prophetic

---

that only Stoicism applied πνεῦμα to God (Posidonius described God as πνεῦμα in Stobaeus, *Eclogae* 1.1.).

[11] Commenting on Ps. 51:10-11, Alasdair I.C. Heron states, "It is a moot point whether the second use of *ruach* here should be translated as 'Spirit' or 'spirit,' as God's own *ruach* or the *ruach* of man which he renews. The two senses are so intimately bound up together...*ruach* even as applied to man has an implicit reference to God as man's creator and sustainer; thus it becomes a linking term, which refers both to God and the human life in its dependence upon God" (*The Holy Spirit* [Philadelphia: Westminster Press, 1987], p. 7).

[12] W. Hildebrandt, *An Old Testament Theology of the Spirit of God* (Peabody, MA: Hendrickson, 1995), p. 18; Lloyd Neve, *The Spirit of God in the Old Testament* (Tokyo: Seibunsha, 1972), pp. 7-11.

utterance simply served as a convincing proof of this.[13] In a similar fashion, Mosaic leadership is carried on in Joshua "in whom is the רוּחַ/ πνεῦμα" (Num. 27:18). This was the power given by God, which quickens moral and religious life patterned on the life of Moses.[14] In particular, this power was given to effect the proper daily administration of the Law, which was necessary to maintain fellowship with God.[15] Ironically, the Book of Deuteronomy, which functions as an exhortation and homiletical exposition of the Law given by Moses, makes only passing references to the Spirit. For example, Deuteronomy is concerned about the office of a prophet (18:15-22) but makes no specific mention of the prophet's association with the Law. In Deut. 34:9, Joshua "was filled with the Spirit of wisdom (מָלֵא רוּחַ חָכְמָה)... and the children of Israel obeyed him and they did as the Lord had commanded Moses." This is only a vague indication of the Spirit's relationship with the Law.

In the Book of Judges, the cyclical pattern of oppression followed by liberation is evident.[16] There is consistent alternation between the humiliation through oppression when Israel sinned against God, and the deliverance from the power of her enemies through a Spirit-anointed leader.[17] The overall character of the book can be described as "Deuteronomic," that is, its religious perspectives reflect the distinctive covenantal theology of Deuteronomy[18];

---

[13] "But we are not to infer from the fact, that the prophesying was not repeated, that the Spirit therefore departed from them after this one extraordinary manifestation. This miraculous manifestation of the Spirit was simply to give to the whole nation the visible proof that God had endowed them with His Spirit, as helpers of Moses..." (C.F. Keil and F. Delitzsch, *The Pentateuch: Three Volumes in One*, Vol. 1, Book III, [trans. James Martin; Grand Rapids: William B. Eerdman's Publishing Company, 1985], pp. 70-71).

[14] *Ibid.*, p. 215.

[15] See Num. 28:1ff., which follows hard on the heels of Joshua's commissioning as successor to Moses. Moses is required to oversee the proper sacrificial offerings as stipulated in the Law.

[16] "Then the Israelites did what was evil in the sight of the Lord...he (Lord) gave them over to plunderers..." (Judg. 2:11-14) cf. "Then the Lord raised up judges, who delivered them out of the power of those who plundered them...Whenever the Lord raised up judges for them, the Lord was with the judge, and he delivered them from the hand of their enemies..." (Judg. 2:16-18); compare also with Judg. 3:7,9; 3:12, 15; 4:1-3, 23-24.

[17] William J. Dumbrell, *The Faith of Israel: Its Expression in the Books of the Old Testament* (Grand Rapids: Baker Book House, 1988), p. 70.

[18] See Deut. 11:1-8, 18-20, where Israel is commanded to observe the Law; blessings result when Israel keeps the Law (11:13-15, 22-25, 27) and curses, if she disobeys (11:28). This is comparable to the oppression-liberation cycle in the Book of Judges.

chaos was a natural consequence of Israel's failure to maintain covenantal faithfulness, but order and blessings were restored when the people renewed their commitment to God.[19] In Judg. 3:7-11, Othniel is raised up as a judge and "the Spirit of the Lord came upon him (וַתְּהִי עָלָיו רוּחַ יְהוָה, v.10)."[20] Israel had broken the Law ("did evil... forgetting the Lord their God and worshipping the Baals and the Asherahs," v.7 [cf. Exod. 20:4-6]). It would be erroneous to interpret the Spirit's role here as simply the power that envelops or covers a human being to perform miraculous deeds or to prophesy. The judges were not only military leaders who conquered the enemy but also rulers who advocated the proper administration of the Law; e.g., they would dispose of the idolatrous practices.[21] Othniel's appointment as a judge in Israel is simultaneous with the conferral of the Spirit (v.10). As a result of his leadership, the "land had rest for forty years" (v.11). In the OT "rest in the land" was considered a soteriological concept representing God's salvific intervention and restored covenant relationship (e.g., Josh. 21:43-44; Deut. 26:1-9).[22]

This pattern of leadership is reflected in Gideon,[23] Jephthah,[24] and in Israel's archetypical leader, David. In 1 Sam. 16:13, it is said that "the Spirit of the Lord (רוּחַ יְהוָה) came mightily upon David from that day forward." It is explicit here that the Spirit was not some momentary occurrence but was a consistent reality in David's life and the necessary requirement for his effective

---

[19] Peter C. Craigie, *The Old Testament: Its Background, Growth and Content* (Burlington, ON: Welch Publishing Company Inc., 1986), pp. 133-34.

[20] Cf. "the Spirit of Jehovah came upon him" (Judg. 11:29; 1 Sam. 19:20, 23; 2 Chron. 20:14; Num. 24:2); "the Spirit of Jehovah clothed the man" (Judg. 6:34; 1 Chron. 12:18; 2 Chron. 24:20).

[21] See Judg. 2:16-20, which gives a paradigmatic summary of the function of the judges; see especially vv.19-20, which states that the major responsibility of the judges was to rid the land of idolatry and thus restore covenant relationship with Yahweh; for secondary sources see Matthias Wenk, *Community-Forming Power: The Socio-Ethical Role of the Spirit in Luke Acts*, JPT Sup 19 (Sheffield: Sheffield Academic Press, 2000), pp. 62-63; C.F. Keil and F. Delitzsch, *Joshua, Judges, Ruth, I and II Samuel: Two Volumes in One* Vol. 2, Book I, (trans. James Martin; Grand Rapids: William B. Eerdmans Publishing Company, 1985), pp. 293-94.

[22] W. Brueggemann, *The Land: Place as Gift, Promise and Challenge in Biblical Faith* (Philadelphia: Fortress Press, 1977), pp. 45-53; Gerhard von Rad, *Old Testament Theology* Vol 1 (New York: Harper and Row, 1965), pp. 296-305.

[23] "The Spirit of the Lord took possession of Gideon" (Judg. 6:34).

[24] "The Spirit of the Lord came upon Jephthah" (Judg. 11:29).

leadership.[25] The Spirit empowered David to lead Israel in the time when her enemies oppressed her[26] in order to bring her into possession of the "land."[27] Israel received the blessings of land and liberation from her enemies through her Spirit-anointed leaders. But even more than this, it was the distinct work of the Spirit that had a profound effect upon her relationship with Yahweh. Israel experienced forgiveness and a renewed sense of Torah obedience.[28]

The penitential Psalms 51 and 143 each depict the Spirit as the agent of moral and covenant renewal. The verb כּוּן, used in Ps. 51:12, usually means "to be set up, established, fixed" as a house upon pillars (Judg. 16:26, 29), or can be used metaphorically of a temple mount (Isa. 2:2; Mic. 4:1), or of the firmness of the earth (Ps. 93:1; 96:10).[29] Here in Ps. 51, however, the word is to be interpreted in a moral sense, "to be directed in right ways" (cf. Prov. 4:26; Ps. 119:5). It makes a positive association with "a clean heart," which suggests fidelity to the covenant union with Yahweh (Ps. 5:10; 78:37; 119:5).[30] In Ps. 51:13, the psalmist petitions Yahweh, "Cast me not out from your presence, and do not take your Holy Spirit from me." The mention of Yahweh's "presence" (פָּנֶיךָ) evokes the tradition of Exod. 33, where Yahweh, in response to Moses' prayer, agreed to accompany the Israelites with his "presence." In Ps. 51:13 as in Exod. 33 and Isa. 63:9-11, Yahweh's "presence," which is equivalent to the "Holy Spirit," had a salvific function. The psalmist implores Yahweh not to remove his "Holy Spirit" since this is the key agent of renewal and salvation that sustains him in the covenantal relationship (cf. "renew a steadfast spirit within me" [v. 10], "restore to me the joy of salvation and grant me a willing spirit to sustain me" [v.12]).

In Ps. 143, clinging to the idea of Yahweh's covenant faithfulness ("in your faithfulness" [v.1]), the psalmist recognizes his inabilities and helplessness (vv.

---

[25] The words, "from that day forward" (וָמָעְלָה הַהוּא מֵהַיּוֹם/ ἀπὸ τῆς ἡμέρας ἐκείνης καὶ ἐπάνω) in 1 Sam. 16:13 confirms that the Spirit was a consistent experience in David's life from that moment onward; "The passage implies a 'perpetual attribute,' not just a sporadic occurrence" (Hildebrandt, An Old Testament Theology of the Spirit of God, p. 126).

[26] See 1 Sam. 17; 23; 30.

[27] See 2 Sam. 21:14; 24:25, where God heeded the "supplications for the land."

[28] Hildebrandt, An Old Testament Theology of the Spirit of God, pp. 39-41.

[29] BDB, pp. 465-67.

[30] It is no coincidence that the psalm itself is replete with terms and concepts characteristic of the description of Yahweh's covenantal relationship with Israel (e.g., כְּחַסְדֶּךָ [v. 3], תִּצְדַּק [v. 6], etc.) (George T. Montague, The Holy Spirit: Growth of a Biblical Tradition [New York: Paulist Press, 1976], p. 75).

4, 7), and calls out for God's mercy (v. 1). He requests assistance from Yahweh's "good Spirit" (רוּחֲךָ טוֹבָה [v. 10]) for guidance to accomplish God's will ("show me the way in which I should walk" [v.8]/ "teach me to do your will" [v. 10]). This appears to have close connection with Ezek. 36:25-27, where the prophet foresees a time when God's Spirit would bring transformation to Israel and empower her to live according to God's will expressed in the Mosaic Law.[31]

Even though the word בְּרִית is never used in Micah, fidelity to the Mosaic covenant is unmistakably the basis for the condemnation of idolatry (1:5-7 cf. Exod. 20:3-6) and the social crimes of his day (2:2; 3:1-3, 9-12; 6:8 cf. Exod. 23:1-9). As part of his censure of the false prophets in 2:11 and 3:5-8, Micah declares his own identity as a prophet who has the Spirit of the Lord: "But I, however, am filled with the power of the Spirit of the Yahweh (אֶת רוּחַ יְהוָה), with justice and might to declare to Jacob his transgressions and to Israel, his sins," (3:8). The word "justice" (מִשְׁפָּט) covers a wide range of meaning from "judgment, attribute of being just, ordinance, decision of the judge in a case of law, one's right, custom."[32] In the OT the term is frequently used to represent, in a crystallized sense, the societal code of ethics in the Mosaic Law.[33] This was true of the prophets, who viewed מִשְׁפָּט as the fulfillment of God's will expressed in the Law (cf. Jer. 5:28; 7:5; Isa. 1:17).[34] In the words אֶת רוּחַ יְהוָה, the Hebrew particle אֶת conveys the concept of assistance or direct agency (cf. Gen. 4:1; Judg. 8:7; Esth. 9:29; Job 26:4).[35] This indicates a clear relationship between the Spirit and the Mosaic Law. The Spirit inspires the prophet to pronounce judgment upon the people, and this judgment finds its basis in the Mosaic Law.

---

[31] See below for a detailed discussion of the Spirit's role in Ezek. 36:25-27.

[32] BDB, pp. 1048-49.

[33] See for example, Exod. 24:3 (the NIV translates the word מִשְׁפָּט here as "laws"); 23:4-5; Lev. 5:10; Deut. 24:17-22.

[34] Thomas E. McComiskey, "Micah," EBC Vol. 7 (Grand Rapids: Zondervan Publishing House, 1985), pp. 418-19.

[35] R.J. Williams, Hebrew Syntax: An Outline (Toronto: University of Toronto Press, 1967), p. 61.

2. Ezekiel Envisions a New Covenant-Era of the Spirit: Ezek.36:25–37:14 (11:19–20)

Ezek. 36:16–31 is an oracle presupposing an exiled Israel in dire straits, where the loss of her homeland could function as a strike against the efficacy of Yahweh who had originally led them out of Egypt and into the promised land.[36] This is the reason why vv. 22, 23, 32, attempt to make clear that Yahweh will now act "for the sake of my holy name." The prophet demonstrates how Yahweh is justified because of what he promises for the future.[37] Pre-exilic Israel had fallen into disobedience and had broken away from the covenant agreement, which granted her special relationship with Yahweh (Ezek. 44:7). Now, Ezekiel comes to the stark realization that Israel was innately incapable of obeying the Torah.[38] Therefore, it is no surprise when the prophet questions the present effectiveness of the "covenant" and the inability of God's people to keep Yahweh's commands. Ezek. 36 (cf. 11:19, 20[39]) foretells a time of the infusion of Yahweh's Spirit in human hearts that results in unprecedented Torah obedience. The prophet's prediction is not isolated, but is similar to the "new covenant" teaching of Jeremiah, except for the focus on the Spirit.[40] Jeremiah incorporated the idea of a בְּרִית חֲדָשָׁה (38

---

[36] See particularly Ezek. 20:5ff., where Yahweh rehearses his promise made to Moses on Mt. Horeb in Exod. 3:6ff. and later to the Israelites when they reach Mt. Sinai in Exod. 19:3ff.

[37] Joseph Blenkinsopp states, "The taunt addressed to the deportees, that Yahweh had proved powerless to prevent the deportation, illustrates the urgency of coming up with a theological explanation" (*Ezekiel* Interpretation [Louisville: John Knox Press, 1990], p. 165).

[38] Ezek. 2:3ff; 15 cf. Jer. 13:23.

[39] The reference to the renewal of Israel's heart and its association with Torah obedience in Ezek. 11:19–20 automatically links this passage with Ezek. 36:25–27; 37:1–14 and thereby implies that God will accomplish this by putting his Spirit within Israel (Ezek. 36:27).

[40] The parallels between Jeremiah and Ezekiel are striking: Jeremiah proclaims a "new covenant" (31:31) cf. Ezekiel also looked for a "covenant of peace" (34:24; 36:26–28) and a "new heart and a new spirit" (11:19, 20; 36:26) as the security and guarantee of a new messianic era; Ezekiel looked back to the covenant which Israel had broken (16:59) as did Jeremiah (31:32); cf. Rabbinical literature (e.g. *Midr. on Song of Solomon* 2; *Midr. Tanhuma Exod. Foll.* 114). It is often said that Jer. 31:31–34 and Ezek. 36:25–27 are to be read together ("Although Ezekiel does not use the term 'new covenant' as Jeremiah did [Jer 31:31], covenant renewal is implicit from the language used in vs. 28 [*Ezek. 36*]: 'You shall be my people, and I will be your God" [Montague, *The Holy Spirit*, p. 47]; see also R. Bultmann, "Weissagung und Erfüllung," *ST* 2 [1949], 21–44 and later published in *ZTK* 47 [1950], 360–83; Douglas Rawlinson Jones, *Jeremiah* NCB [Grand

[LXX]:31, διαθήκη καινή) where Yahweh will inscribe the Torah in his people's hearts, and thus, the Torah will be received and honoured to become the motive and power of mind and will (Jer. 31:31-34).[41]

Ezekiel's "newness" and renewal is demonstrated first in 36:25, when Yahweh will sprinkle the house of Israel (זרק; LXX, ῥανῶ) with clean water, which is figurative and represents a ritual act of cultic purification, as in Ps. 51:4, 9 (i.e., spiritual purification from idolatry).[42] But even more telling is that it signals the external removal of an old phase of existence and the beginning of a new one, where the two phases are mutually exclusive.[43] Thinking in linear time, it is the abjuration of the past, which is characterized as disorderly and idolatrous, and the beginning of the new, which is characterized as the period of fresh start. Secondly, concomitant with external newness must be internal transformation. This is described in v. 26, where the לֵב חָדָשׁ (LXX, καρδίαν καινήν) and רוּחַ חֲדָשָׁה (LXX, πνεῦμα καινόν) replace לֵב הָאֶבֶן (LXX, τὴν καρδίαν τὴν λιθίνην). This corresponds to the assurance of Jer. 31:33 ("I will put my Law within them and write it on their hearts"). At the centre of Jeremiah's new covenant relationship is the תּוֹרָה (v. 33, LXX uses the plural νόμους).[44] The prophet is not promulgating new content within Torah, but he is explicitly contrasting the new covenant relationship with the old in relation to the manner in which Israel receives it (נָתַתִּי אֶת־תּוֹרָתִי בְּקִרְבָּם וְעַל־לִבָּם אֶכְתֲּבֶנָּה cf. διδοὺς δώσω νόμους μου εἰς τὴν διάνοιαν αὐτῶν, καὶ ἐπὶ καρδίας αὐτῶν γράψω αὐτούς).[45] Up

---

Rapids: William B. Eerdmans Publishing Co., 1992], p. 400; G.A. Cooke, *A Critical and Exegetical Commentary on The Book of Ezekiel* ICC [Edinburgh: T & T Clark, 1936], pp. 391-92).

[41] See Ellen Juhl Christiansen who notes that Jeremiah's promise of a "new covenant" does not signify a change in the content of the Law but the manner in which it is transmitted (*The Covenant in Judaism and Paul: A Study of Ritual Boundaries as Identity Markers* [Leiden/ New York/ Köln: E.J. Brill, 1995], pp. 57-58).

[42] Cf. also with Zech. 13:1; Is. 4:4, where mention is made of "the fountain opened for sin and impurity."

[43] See Walter Zimmerli who states, "The act is understood as a ritual introductory act which is intended to remove the old uncleanness..." (*Ezekiel* Vol. 2, Hermeneia, [trans. James D. Martin; Philadelphia: Fortress Press, 1983], p. 249).

[44] The LXX use of the plural νόμους for the singular תּוֹרָה indicates that the translators did not conceive of the Torah in an abstract sense as a revelation of the general will of God (Scott J. Hafemann, *Paul, Moses and the History of Israel: The Letter/Spirit Contrast and the Argument from Scripture in 2 Corinthians 3* WUNT 81 [Tübingen: J.C.B. Mohr (Paul Siebeck), 1995], p. 132).

[45] Christoph Leven claims that the Law functions as the concretization of the covenant theology and is applied to Israel's history in the light of the breaking of that covenant. Therefore, the

to this point the Torah had been an external requirement. It was written by
God on two stone tablets and given to Moses for conveyance to the people
(Exod. 31:18; Deut. 4:13; 5:22; 10:1-4). But in the future it would be within
them (בְּקִרְבָּם וְעַל־ לִבָּם). The words קֶרֶב and לֵב can be considered
synonymous expressions.[46] This is Jeremiah's way of speaking of a change in
inward disposition.[47] From לֵב comes planning and volition (Jer. 7:31; 23:20)
and religious and moral conduct; it is in the לֵב where one finds impetus to
serve Yahweh (1 Sam. 12:20; Jer. 32:40; Prov. 7:3; Is. 51:7).[48] The use of εἰς
τὴν διάνοιαν ("in the mind") in the LXX corresponds to the OT use of the
"heart" as representing one's intellect and rational functions.[49] The
stipulations of the Torah no longer simply comprise an external written code
but they are to be received and honoured and become the motive and power
of mind and will.[50] The heart represents the place of understanding (Deut.

---

promise of Jer. 31:31-34 is to bring the Law back to its original purpose, namely, to restore the
relationship of Israel and Judah to Yahweh, which has been destroyed (*Die Verheissung des neuen
Bundes in ihrem theologiegeschichtlichen Zusammenhang ausgelegt* FRLANT 137 [Göttingen:
Vandenhoeck & Ruprecht, 1985], p. 132).

[46] See Prov. 14:33; Ps. 39:4; 55:5; 109:22; Lam. 1:20 where קֶרֶב and לֵב are used together.

[47] לֵב refers to the "inner man, mind, will" and קֶרֶב to "inward part, seat of thought and
emotion" (BDB, p. 524 and p. 899 respectively).

[48] See Friedrich Baumgärtel, "καρδία - לֵב, לֵבָב in the OT," *TDNT*, Vol. III, pp. 605-7, esp.
pp. 606-7.

[49] G. Harder, "Reason, Mind, Understanding," *NIDNTT*, Vol. 3, (ed. Colin Brown; Grand
Rapids: Zondervan Publishing House, 1986), pp. 122-30, esp. pp. 124-5; Hans Walter Wolff
demonstrates that the "heart" represents one's driving desires and longings and is the inward
place where one's vital decisions of the will are made (*Anthropologie des Alten Testaments*, Fifth
Edition [Munich: Chr. Kaiser Verlag, 1990], pp. 43-46, 51-54).

[50] Jones, *Jeremiah*, p. 401; "It is the notion of internalization; the stipulations and content of
divine torah will be internalized in the minds of the people" (Robert P. Carroll, *From Chaos to
Covenant: Use of Prophecy in the Book of Jeremiah* [London: SCM Press Ltd., 1981], p. 218); "He
(Yahweh) will set his *law* within them and write it on their hearts, that is, on their minds and
wills" (J.A. Thompson, *The Book of Jeremiah* NICOT [Grand Rapids: William B. Eerdmans
Publishing Co., 1980], p. 581); "God himself will graciously bring about the necessary change in
his people's inner nature so that their past failure to obey his laws will be replaced by both the
will and the ability to do so" (Ernest W. Nicholson, *The Book of the Prophet Jeremiah: Chapters
26-52* [Cambridge: Cambridge University Press, 1975], p. 71). William L. Holladay claims that
the meaning "within them" and "on their heart" (v.33) goes in two directions. They appear to
be ambiguous. קֶרֶב ("interior") is used in Jer. 6:1 referring to the interior of the city and
"hearts" is used in parallelism with "altars" (17:1). "Interior" and "heart" suggest the city within
the land and the temple within the city. As a result, one may conclude that "within them" and

29:3; Jer. 23:16) and conscious decisions of the will (Jer. 17:9-10). This means that in contrast to the conflict that now exists between God's commandments and the desires of one's heart, under the new covenant there will be perfect harmony between God's Law and inward impulses and will.[51] The Torah will be obeyed willingly and not grudgingly.

The covenant described in Jer. 31:31 is qualified as "new" because there is a very real sense in which there is discontinuity with the one instituted at Sinai. This is emphasized by the adverbs לֹא כַבְּרִית (v. 32 cf. οὐ κατὰ τὴν διαθήκην) and לֹא עוֹד (twice in v. 34; Jer. 30:8; 31:12, 40; note the strong negation in v. 34 [38 LXX], οὐ μή) and the words, הֵפֵרוּ אֶת־ בְּרִיתִי (38:32, αὐτοὶ οὐκ ἐνέμειναν ἐν τῇ διαθήκῃ μου). The word "new" in Jer. 31:31 associated with the covenant, corresponds to the לֵב חָדָשׁ (LXX, καρδίαν καινήν) and רוּחַ חֲדָשָׁה (LXX, πνεῦμα καινόν) in Ezek. 36:26, which is associated with the לֵב בָּשָׂר (LXX, καρδίαν σαρκίνην). In the OT "flesh" is not regarded as something evil or as the peculiar place in which sin dwells.[52] Here in Ezek. 36:26, it expresses the whole inner attitude of yearning after God.[53] In the OT a "stone" heart represented a "perverse and hard heart" that was disobedient to God's commandments.[54] Therefore, in light of the emphasis on obedience in close proximity (v. 27), Ezekiel most likely means that in the "newness" there is removal of a perverse heart that results in disobedience; this is replaced by the "new heart," "new spirit," and "heart of flesh," which results in Torah obedience.

But how is such radical redirection to be achieved, since more than one prophet has recognized that Israel was inherently incapable of keeping

"on their heart" refers to the renewal of worship in the temple. Holladay also advocates the more common meaning, contrasting exterior written Law associated with insincere obedience (cf. 12:2b) and the interior intentionality of will, where people will be able to obey the Torah freely and gladly (Jeremiah Vol. 2, Hermeneia [Minneapolis: Fortress Press, 1989], p. 198).

[51] See Helga Weippert, who argues that God writing the Torah on hearts in the new covenant relationship indicates such a complete change of person that one may speak of a new creation ("Das Wort vom Neuen Bund in Jeremia xxxi 31-34," VT 29 [1979], 336-51, esp. 347)

[52] See BDB, p. 142 for the various meanings: "of the body (of humans)," "male organ of generation (euphemism)," "kindred, blood-relations," "man over against God as frail or erring," "all living beings."

[53] Friedrich Baumgärtel, "Flesh in the Old Testament," TDNT Vol. VII, pp. 105-8, esp. p. 107.

[54] See Ezek. 11:19-20, where the removal of the "heart of stone" results in obeying God's "statutes" and "ordinances" (cf. Zech. 7:12); a similar thought occurs later in rabbinic literature, where "stone" is considered one of the seven names of "evil inclination" with respect to lack of obedience (b. Sukk. 52a); see also the meaning "perverse, hard heart" (אָבֵן, BDB, pp. 6-7)

covenant Law? The third unique contribution Ezekiel makes with respect to this new covenant relationship is found in Ezek. 36:27. This goes beyond Jer. 31 in that it uniquely presents an objective force which makes Yahweh an active participant in Israel's new phase of obedience to his covenant. The words, "And I will put my Spirit within you" (בְּקִרְבְּכֶם אֶתֵּן אֶת־רוּחִי וְ/ Καὶ τὸ πνεῦμα μου δώσω ἐν ὑμῖν) encapsulate the means by which this is achieved. It is precisely the infusion of Yahweh's Spirit in the human heart that brings new and unique strength for this obedience.[55]

In Ezek. 36:27, רוּחַ/ πνεῦμα is the power which fashions ethical behaviour. More specifically, it is the power that results in obedience to Yahweh's commandments: "And I will put my Spirit within you and make it that (MT, אֶת־אֲשֶׁר וְעָשִׂיתִי[56]/ LXX, καὶ ποιήσω ἵνα ...πορεύησθε[57]) you will walk in my statutes; and you shall keep my judgments, and do them." In v. 27, the term חֹק (LXX, δικαίωμα) refers to codes of conduct[58] and is often used interchangeably with "commandment," "torah," (2 Kgs 17:37; 2 Chron. 19:10).[59] Likewise, מִשְׁפָּט (LXX, κρίμα) is used to refer to individual stipulations within the Torah.[60] Because Yahweh places his Spirit within Israel, she will be equipped to follow the statutes and ordinances of the Torah. The verb עשׂה means "to do, perform"[61] (cf. LXX, ποιεῖν)[62] and הלך is used figuratively to mean "live ('walk')-of moral and religious life"[63] and both have the same connotation of "doing, performing/living" with respect to the

---

[55] This idea was already expressed in Ezek. 11:20 but there was no specific reference to the Spirit of God.

[56] The presence of אֶת with the verb עשׂה means to "do something in relation with" (BDB, p. 794). In Ezek. 36:27, אֶת is used to refer to "doing" in the sense of keeping/ performing (עשׂה) "statutes" (בְּחֻקַּי) and "judgments" (מִשְׁפָּטַי). It is the Spirit that enables this.

[57] The word ποιήσω is written in the future tense and is used in a causative sense, "I will cause you to walk" (F.C. Conybeare and St. George Stock, Grammar of Septuagint Greek: With Selected Readings, Vocabularies, and Updated Indexes [Peabody, MA: Hendrickson, 1995], p.76; see also BDAG, p.840). In Ezek. 36:27, it is the prerequisite placing of the Spirit within individuals that causes one to "walk" in the "ordinances" and "keep" the "judgments."

[58] Lev. 10:11; Num. 30:17; Deut. 4:6; 6:24; 16:12; Ps. 119:5.

[59] For חֹק see BDB, p. 349; for δικαίωμα see TDNT Vol.II, pp. 219-23, esp. p.220.

[60] BDB, p. 1048, where the term מִשְׁפָּט is in association with Levitical laws (Lev. 5:10; 9:16; 1 Chron. 15:13; 24:19; 2 Chron. 8:14); divine law in general (Jer. 8:7).

[61] Ibid., p. 793.

[62] BDAG, p. 839.

[63] Ibid., p. 234.

Torah.[64] The unique idea being espoused here is that there is unprecedented Torah obedience now possible with the new infusion of the Spirit.

Previously there have been allusions to the Spirit of God in the earliest writings of the Hebrew Scriptures. However, with the realization of Israel's failure and incapability to keep covenant agreement, beginning with Ezekiel, there is unprecedented and consistent attestation to the divine Spirit as the agent of inner transformation.[65] The Spirit was the principal feature in the coming age.[66] For Ezekiel, it is uniquely the "Spirit" that functions as the means by which obedience to the Torah takes place and subsequently, also the means by which ratification of the new covenant is achieved. Even though Jer. 31:31-34 makes no mention of the Spirit, vv. 33-34 are comparable to Ezek. 36:27 in that both passages advocate Torah obedience as the central component of the new covenant relationship. The "Spirit" which leads to this radically different basis for relationship was, in effect, the indication that a new dispensation had dawned.[67]

Ezek. 37:1-14 can be divided into two sections: vv. 1-10 is the vision[68] and vv. 11-14 is the interpretation of that vision. In vv. 1-10, the description of desiccated bones is suggestive of a field that had witnessed combat and slaughter. At the word of the Lord, the prophet commands the bones to live. The bones come together, flesh appears upon them, but the only thing that remained was animation, which would be accomplished by God's Spirit/breath (רוּחַ [LXX, πνεῦμα] vv. 8-10). It is clear that the narrative is held together by this key term.[69] In the OT the words רוּחַ and נְשָׁמָה both

---

[64] See the use of עשׂה in Deut. 16:12; 30:8, Num. 15:39 and הלך in Ezek. 5:6-7; 11:12, 20; 18:9, 17; 20:13, 16, 19, 21; Lev. 26:3; 1 Ki. 6:12; Jer. 44:10, 23.

[65] See Ezek. 39:29; Isa. 44:3; 59:21; Joel 2:28, 29.

[66] See Ezek. 37:14; 39:29; Is. 42:1; 44:3; 59:21; Hag. 2:5; Joel 3:1-2.

[67] Blenkinsopp, Ezekiel, p. 168.

[68] The recurring narrative phrase, "the hand of Yahweh was on me" indicates a state of trance in which a vision was experienced (cf. Ezek. 3:22; 8:1; 37:1; 40:1) (see J. Hehn, "Zum Problem des Geistes im Alten Orient und im Alten Testament," ZAW 43 [1925], 210-25, esp. 224).

[69] In Ezek. 37:1-14, רוּחַ is used in vv.5, 6, 8, 9 (4x), 10, 14; "To be sure, Yahweh's Spirit plays a key role (vv. 5, 6, 10), just as it does in other scenes of restoration where the inner transformation of Israel is described, under the image of a new heart [Ezek. 11:19; 36:26-27]" (Christopher R. Seitz, "Expository Articles: Ezekiel 37:1-14," Inter 46 [Jan., 1992], 53-56, quote taken from 53).

refer to the principle of physical life. This is the manner in which רוּחַ is used here in vv. 1-10.[70]

In the interpretation of the vision, this corresponds to the words, "And I will put my Spirit within you" (וְנָתַתִּי רוּחִי בָכֶם/ Καὶ δώσω πνεῦμα μου εἰς ὑμᾶς) in v.14. However, in v. 14, the use of the word רוּחִי (cf. LXX, πνεῦμά μου) with the first person possessive ending clearly denotes the work of the Spirit of Yahweh and is suggestive of more than simply the breath of life functioning to revive dead corpses.[71] This means that one must think beyond this to the promise of the Spirit in 36:27 (cf. 39:29) by which inner transformation of the people takes place. In this sense, Ezek. 37:1-14 comes close to what was said in 36:25-27. The metaphor of dry bones is expressive of physical and spiritual debility[72] and occurs frequently in poetry.[73] The language in Ezek. 37:11 comes close to Prov. 17:22 ("A cheerful heart enlivens the body but a downcast spirit dries up the bones"). The idea of dried bones in metaphorical terms refers to fading hope of recovery. This loss of hope was described in Ezek. 19:5 ("her hope was lost"). The bones that the prophet saw refer to "the whole house of Israel" (v.11). In the events of 722/21 and 597 B.C.E., Israel was pushed into disaster and defeat to the point of death (587 B.C.E.).

In order to prevent the old history of disaster in the land from repeating, the Spirit of Yahweh (רוּחִי/ LXX, πνεῦμα μου) would bring revivification[74] but also inner transformation to the house of Israel. In this sense there is correlation to what was said in 36:16ff. In 36:28a, the words, "Then you shall dwell in the land that I gave to your ancestors," are a direct result from

---

[70] For רוּחַ in the sense of the "breath of life" see Jer. 10:14; 51:17; Eccl. 3:19, 21; Gen. 6:17; 7:15 and נְשָׁמָה used with the same meaning see Job 33:4; 34:14; 37:10; Gen. 2:7 (Baumgärtel, "Spirit in the OT," pp. 360, 362).

[71] "Of course my spirit is not the same as the breath (or spirit) of v. 9" (Cooke, The Book of Ezekiel, p. 400); "On the basis of the vision one thinks in the first instance of the newly bestowed spirit of life in v.9. But it is remarkable that the reference here is explicitly to 'my spirit' (רוּחִי), i.e., the spirit of Yahweh, which the language of the רוּחַ -statement in the vision has studiously avoided" (Zimmerli, Ezekiel Vol. 2, p. 263).

[72] "A metaphor meaning, we are utterly dispirited. High spirits and good cheer are figured as moist, oily, or sappy bones..." (Moshe Greenberg, Ezekiel 21-37: A New Translation with Introduction and Commentary AB [New York: Doubleday, 1997], p. 745).

[73] See Is. 66:14; Job 21:24; Ps. 31:10; Prov. 17:22.

[74] There is no doubt that Ezek. 37:1-14, with the images of unburied dead bones and the opening of graves, envisions the restoration and regathering of the defeated house of Israel.

Yahweh's Spirit being placed within Israel (v. 26). The "heart of flesh" will enable walking in the statutes and observance of Yahweh's ordinances. In other words, possession of the land presumes the new disposition of Israel created by the Spirit of Yahweh. This is the idea communicated in Ezek. 37:1-14 and paralleled in 36:16-28; Yahweh's Spirit is placed within Israel and results in new life (וִחְיִיתֶם) and placement in the land of possession.[75] In order to emphasize the surety of this future, a statement expressing divine assertion is included: "Then you will know that I the Lord have spoken, and I have done it, declares the Lord" (v.14).[76] Ezek. 37:1-14 expresses the event of regathering and restoration of the politically defeated Israel concomitant with the inner transformation that takes place within her.[77]

In Ezek. 36-37, the prophet sets in place the view that God is in control of history and its various phases. It speaks of the Spirit of Yahweh dwelling in the midst of his people and being the distinctive characteristic of the new covenant community of Israel. The gift of the Spirit of Yahweh was the foundational feature in the hopes of the coming age (cf. Ezek. 39:29; Is. 42:1; 44:3; 59:21; Hag. 2:5; Joel 3:1, 2).[78] Yahweh's Spirit will bring about a new disposition in Israel in that it will enable her to obey the Torah. Since God must demonstrate fidelity to his promises, the appropriation of the new covenant expectation to subsequent generations remains a real possibility.

3. The Eschatological Spirit as the Agent of Ethical and Covenant Renewal: Various Texts

In addition to the new covenant promises envisioned in Jer. 31 (38 LXX):31-34 and Ezek. 36:25-27 (ll:19-20); 37:1-14, various passages in the OT

---

[75] Regarding Ezek. 37:1-14, Leslie C. Allen states, "The following of the promise with an assurance of dwelling or settling in the land both in 36:28 and here confirms that an echo of 36:27 is intended" (*Ezekiel 20-48*, Vol. 29 WBC [Dallas: Word Books, Publisher, 1990], p. 187).

[76] Cf. Ezek. 36:16, "I the Lord have spoken, and I will do it."

[77] In its original intended meaning the primary purpose of the vision of the valley of dry bones and their revivification is not with the bodily resurrection of individuals (see Wilhelm Neuss, *Das Buch Ezechiel in Theologie und Kunst bis zum Ende des XII. Jahrhunderts: Beiträge zur Geschichte des Alten Mönchtumus und des Benediktinerordens 1-2* [Münster: Aschendorff, 1912], pp. 50, 56ff., 71).

[78] Cooke, *A Critical and Exegetical Commentary on the Book of Ezekiel*, p. 392.

identify the Spirit as the agent of ethical and covenant renewal in the future promises of Israel's restoration; the Spirit is to be the means by which Israel is empowered to conform to a Torah-based ethic. Isaiah's message of hope and comfort includes a promise of God's intervention in the future (Isa. 40:1-14). God's creative power is associated with his רוּחַ (Isa. 40:13). The LXX translates this as "mind" (νοῦν) as it does in passages like 1 Chron. 28:12 and Ezek. 20:32.[79] However, here in Isa. 40, the context emphasizes God's רוּחַ as *Spiritus creator* not as the internal "mind of the Lord."[80] The Jews in Babylon were in the midst of a polytheistic environment. In Isa. 40:18ff., the prophet commences his attack on idolatry and the iniquitous practices of the exiled Jews. This recalls the Sinaitic covenant that denounces idolatry (Exod. 20:4-5). Consequently, the prophet communicates a message of future help and restoration (Isa. 41:1-20), which is reminiscent of Israel's privileged status as God's covenant people.[81] The Spirit will achieve comprehensive social renewal and form a community that confesses Yahweh's name (Isa. 44:1-5).[82] Thus, Isa. 40:13; 44:3 describe covenantal and ethical renewal accomplished by the eschatological Spirit.[83]

---

[79] For a proponent of this translation see R.N. Whybray, *The Heavenly Counsellor in Isaiah XI. 13-14* (Cambridge: Cambridge University Press, 1971), pp. 10-13.

[80] Geoffrey W. Crogan, *Isaiah, Jeremiah, Lamentations, Ezekiel* EBC Vol. 6 (Grand Rapids: Zondervan Publishing House, 1986), p. 245. See also the disparity in meanings between the NRSV and NIV. The NRSV translates this as "the spirit of the Lord" versus the NIV, which interprets it as "the mind of the Lord" (Isa. 40:13).

[81] See the assertion "I am the Lord, your God" (Isa. 41:13), which is reminiscent of the opening of the Decalogue (Exod. 20:2); in Isa. 41:14 the use of גֹּאֵל recalls Exod. 6:6; 15:13; the use of "the Holy One of Israel" in Isa. 41:16 indicates the special relationship God has with Israel (cf. Exod. 3:13-15).

[82] Claus Westermann, *Isaiah 40-66: A Commentary* (trans. David M.G. Stalker; Philadelphia: Westminster Press, 1969), p. 137.

[83] In addition to Isa. 40:13; 44:3, there are two other implicit references to the Spirit as the agent of ethical renewal. In Isa. 4:4, there is reference made to the Lord "cleansing the bloodstains from Jerusalem by *a spirit* of judgement and *a spirit* of fire." In the context (Isa. 3:1-4:1) we read that Israel's sins arouse God's anger and induce his judgement upon them. But subsequently, he will restore and cleanse Israel by a רוּחַ of judgment and fire. It is possible to interpret this reference to the "spirit" as God's Spirit. Also, in Isa. 63:10, the words, "they rebelled and grieved his Holy Spirit" most likely make an association to Israel's resistance to the leadership of the Spirit-endowed leader (cf. Num. 11:11, 17) and in this sense they are said to "grieve his Holy Spirit" (Wenk, *Community-Forming Power*, pp. 63-4).

In a cursory reading, the book of Joel does not appear to describe the eschatological age[84] in Jewish covenantal language and in particular, it appears that the promise in the future, "I will pour my Spirit on all people" (אֶשְׁפּוֹךְ אֶת רוּחִי עַל־ כָּל־ בָּשָׂר / ἐκχεῶ ἀπὸ πνεύματός μου ἐπὶ πᾶσαν σάρκα) in Joel 3:1 makes little association with the Jewish Torah.[85] However, upon closer reading, it becomes clear that this pronouncement is set within a Jewish covenantal context. Similar to Zephaniah (2:1-3), Joel summons the people to repentance and acknowledges his own moral failures (Joel 2:12f). The call of the prophet culls a parallel from the traditions of Jewish history regarding their present experience of "locusts" and "drought" (Joel 1:4-12), which are implicitly regarded as God's chastisement for breach of covenant (cf. Deut. 28:23f., 38; Amos 4:7-9). Conversely, rain and good crops are an indication of covenant blessing (cf. Lev. 26:4ff.; Deut. 28:11f.).[86] In Joel 2:21-23, the prophet calls his audience to anticipate the future blessings of the Lord. The mention of rain coincides with the covenant promise in Deut. 11:13-15 and Lev. 26:3,4.[87] In the Leviticus passage, obedience ("if you walk in my statutes") is the prerequisite for the "rains" and a fruitful harvest. The words, לִצְדָקָה (lit., "according to righteousness") in Joel 2:23 refer to "the claims of the covenant, according to the norm of fellowship" and indicate that the mention of "rain" represents "a token of covenant harmony."[88]

In Joel 3:1, the prophet predicts the Spirit as the agent of covenant renewal, which is comparable to Isa. 32:15; 40:13; 44:3 (cf. Jer. 31 [38]:31-34; Ezek. 36:25-27; 37:1-14).[89] The verb שָׁפַךְ / ἐκχεῶ is equivalent to the use

---

[84] The theme that dominates the book of Joel and gives it cohesion is יוֹם/ יְהוָה ἡ ἡμέρα Κυρίου (Joel 1:15; 2:1, 11, 31; 3:14). This was a Jewish eschatological notion that referred to a time when Yahweh would finally intervene in the world to establish his sovereignty (Isa. 2:6-22; Amos 5:18-20; Zeph. 1,2).

[85] P. van Imschoot notes that the prophetic announcement in Joel 3:1 makes no reference to the Spirit's role in fashioning morals/ethics: "Ici les effects de l'esprit sont d'ordre purement psychique; rien ne permet de leur attribuer une portée morale" ("L'Esprit de Jahvé et l'alliance nouvelle dans l'Ancien Testament," *ETL* 13 [1936], 201-26, quote taken from 212-13).

[86] Leslie C. Allen, *The Books of Joel, Obadiah, Jonah and Micah* NICOT (Grand Rapids: William B. Eerdmans Publishing Company, 1976), p.37.

[87] Deut. 11's mention of "grass" and Lev. 26's mention of "fruit" parallel Joel 2.

[88] Allen, *The Books of Joel, Obadiah, Jonah and Micah*, p. 93 and footnote 29.

[89] See A. Kerrigan, who recognizes that Joel 3:1-5 does not limit the Spirit's manifestations to prophecy, visions, and dreams but contemplates the advent of a period in which everybody will enjoy receiving communications directly from God in a way similar to that described in Jer.

of יָצַק and עָרָה[90] in Isa. 44:3 and 32:15 respectively, and denotes the same idea of "pouring out." H.W. Wolff argues that בָשָׂר in Joel 3:1 does not simply mean "body." Instead, it signifies both the physical and especially the ethical frailty ("Hinfälligkeit") of the people,[91] since the context implies the need for repentance (Joel 1:13-14; 2:12-13). Therefore, Joel envisions the Spirit's work in forming a renewed society that obeys the Jewish Torah and makes no distinction on the basis of status; i.e., the Spirit will be "poured out" upon slaves, young men and women (Joel 3:1-5).[92]

In Zech. 3:1-10, the prophet has a vision of Israel's restoration as a priestly nation; in particular, Joshua will govern the house of God (vv. 6-7). In a subsequent vision meant to encourage the two leaders Joshua and Zerubbabel, Yahweh identifies the source by which this was to be accomplished[93]: לֹא בְחַיִל וְלֹא בְכֹחַ כִּי אִם־ בְּרוּחִי אָמַר יְהוָה צְבָאוֹת /Ούκ ἐν δυνάμει μεγάλη, οὐδὲ ἐν ἰσχύι, ἀλλὰ ἐν πνεύματί μου, λέγει Κύριος παντοκράτωρ (Zech. 4:6). An effusion of the Spirit was to induce a response of "grace and supplication" (Zech. 12:10).[94] It is possible that the use of the verb שָׁפַךְ connotes the same eschatological outpouring of the Spirit as in Joel 3:1, since the identical verb is used.[95] The use of בַּיּוֹם הַהוּא in the immediate context (Zech. 12:11; 13:1, 2, 4) with the use of the *waw* consecutive perfect ("And I will pour out..." [12:10]) confirm the idea that the prophet understood this to be an eschatological phenomenon.[96] It will be a time of

---

31:31-34 and Ezek. 36:26ff. ("The 'Sensus Plenior' of Joel III, 1-5 in Act., II, 14-36," in *SP* Volumen Alterum [Paris: Gabalda, 1959], pp. 295-313, see esp. p. 312).

[90] See BDB, p. 427 and p. 788.

[91] Wolff, *Anthropologie des Alten Testaments*, pp. 55-6. "Flesh" essentially distinguishes humans as belonging to an order of being other than that of God. Humans are fragile, creaturely, and fallible. This stands over against the Jewish idea of the perfection of Yahweh.

[92] There is good indication in *Midr. Pss.* 14:6 that the promise of Ezek. 36:25-27 is understood in terms of the Joel promise: "Neither the words of the Master nor the words of the disciple are to be fulfilled in this world, but the words of both will be fulfilled in the world-to-come: The words of the Master, 'A new heart also will I give you and ye shall keep Mine ordinances (Ezek. 36:26),' will be fulfilled; and the words of the disciple, 'I will pour out My spirit upon all flesh; and your sons and daughters shall prophesy (Joel 3:1 [2:28]),' will also be fulfilled."

[93] Kenneth L. Barker, *Daniel-Minor Prophets* Vol. 7, EBC (Grand Rapids: Zondervan Publishing House, 1985), p.629; Hildebrandt, *An Old Testament Theology of the Spirit of God*, p. 101.

[94] "The Spirit which conveys grace and calls forth supplications" (T.T. Perowne, *The Books of Haggai and Zechariah* [Cambridge: Cambridge University Press, 1886], pp. 132-3).

[95] Wenk, *Community-Forming Power*, p.60, footnote 13.

[96] See also the LXX use of the future tense ἐκχεῶ ("I will pour out").

national contrition or repentance, where the country is purged of idols and false prophets (13:2-3). Thus, the Spirit will initiate a covenant arrangement similar to the one prophesied in Jer. 31 (38 LXX):31-34 and Ezek. 26:25-27: 1. empowerment through the Spirit to obey Yahweh's Law (Jer. 31 [38 LXX]:33a; Ezek. 36:26-27 cf. Zech. 12:10; 13:2-3), 2. an intimate personal relationship and fellowship (Jer. 31 [38 LXX]:33b cf. Zech 13:9), 3. forgiveness of sins (Jer. 31 [38 LXX]: 34b; Ezek. 36:26 cf. Zech. 3:4, 9).[97]

4. Israel's Leaders, Spirit-Endowment, and the Torah

References to the Spirit-anointed leader are set in an eschatological context and are consistent with Ancient Judaism's expectation of a harmonious relationship between the Spirit and Torah. The Spirit-endowed leader was to be instrumental in promoting a renewed sense of obedience to the Mosaic Law. In Isa. 11:2, one of the characteristics of this eschatological figure is that "the Spirit of Yahweh will rest on him" (נָחָה עָלָיו רוּחַ יְהוָה cf. ἀναπαύσεται ἐπ' αὐτὸν πνεῦμα τοῦ θεοῦ [LXX]). Further description is given regarding the specific role of רוּחַ/ πνεῦμα; it is qualified as the Spirit "of wisdom (חָכְמָה) and understanding (בִּינָה)" and "of knowledge (דַּעַת) and of the fear (יִרְאַת) of the Lord." "Wisdom" and "understanding" are parallel concepts and can be used to denote understanding that leads to moral conduct.[98] In Ezr. 7:25, Ezra is said to possess a "God-given wisdom" and had the specific function of choosing judges who knew the "laws of God." As a wisdom-endowed leader, he was to "teach those who did not know them (laws)." In Ancient Judaism, "knowledge" was not merely the possession of information about God's essence; it also included knowledge of God's command and the requirement to obey it.[99] Likewise, the "fear of the Lord" refers to hearing and obeying the moral demands of Yahweh expressed in the

---

[97] See Barker who notes the parallels between Zech. 13:1 and surrounding context, and Jer. 31:31-34; Ezek. 36:25-27 (Daniel-Minor Prophets, p. 685).

[98] See Prov. 4:11; 9:9; 23:19, 24 cf. Prov. 2:3; 7:4; 9:10; note the parallelism between the two terms in Prov. 9:9-10 (Georg Fohrer, "σοφία-The Old Testament," TDNT, Vol. VII, pp. 476-96, esp. pp. 476-7).

[99] R. Bultmann, "γινώσκω, κτλ.," TDNT Vol.I, pp. 696-701, esp. p. 698; this is comparable to the prophet Jeremiah's association of "knowledge/knowing" with the acceptance of God's rule by obeying the Torah (Jer. 4:2; 9:3 cf. 12).

Mosaic Law (Deut. 4:10 cf. 4:5, 6, 8; 8:6).[100] Thus, the leader in Isa. 11:2 will acknowledge the commands of God and will execute divine judgement based upon righteousness stipulated in the Torah (Isa. 11:3b-5). He is able to perform this function because the Spirit has personally influenced his own life with the same qualities he is to restore.[101]

In the first servant song (Isa. 42:1-4), God designates his Servant to perform a threefold task: "to bring forth justice to the nations" (v.1c), to "bring forth justice in truth" (v.3c), to "establish justice in the earth" (v.4b). Intimately related to the Servant's mission is his endowment with the Spirit; it is precisely the divine רוּחַ that empowers him to accomplish his mission effectively ("I will put my Spirit upon him [נָתַתִּי רוּחִי עָלָיו] and he will bring justice to the nations," v.1).[102] The endowment of a leader (king, prophet, or judge) with the Spirit is a tradition found in the historical books (e.g., 1 Sam. 16:13; 2 Kgs. 2:9). While it is possible that reference to the Spirit was an indication of this leader's authentication, it is more likely that רוּחַ יְהוָה represented much more than this. The Spirit was a permanent endowment in order to fulfill a God-given task.[103] This coincides with what is stated in v.4 that the רוּחַ יְהוָה would equip the Servant to endure a sustained period of suffering while performing his task.[104]

---

[100] Günther Wanke, "φόβος, κτλ.," *TDNT*, Vol. IX, pp. 197-219, esp. p. 201.

[101] Israel's leaders demonstrate this common characteristic; they were Spirit-endowed and were empowered to lead the people back into covenant relationship with Yahweh. When the nation falls prey to their enemies, they cry out to God and God raises up a Spirit-anointed leader who restores covenant faithfulness among his people. In particular, the leader exercises "judgement" based upon the Jewish Torah (see Judg. 3:7-11; 6:33-35; 11:14, 27-29). Consequently, the work of the Spirit through Israel's leadership restores relationship with God and they experience forgiveness and liberation. This type of leadership appears to be patterned upon Moses (Num. 11:17 [Moses] cf. Num. 11:17, 25 [70 elders]; Num. 27:18 [Joshua]; 1 Sam. 16:13-14 [David]; Isa. 63:11-14[reference to Moses]).

[102] Wonsuk Ma, *Until the Spirit Comes: The Spirit of God in the Book of Isaiah* JSOT Supp. 271 (Sheffield: Sheffield Academic Press, 1999), p. 91; Edward J. Young, *The Book of Isaiah: The English Text, with Introduction, Exposition,and Notes* Vol. III (Grand Rapids: William B. Eerdmans Publishing Company, 1972), p. 110; G.W. Grogan, "Isaiah," *Isaiah-Ezekiel* EBC, Vol. 6 (Grand Rapids: Zondervan Publishing House, 1986), p. 255.

[103] In Isa. 11:2, 4, it is said that the Spirit of Yahweh "will rest" upon him and he will execute divine judgment; see Christopher R. North who equates Isa. 11:2 with 42:1-4 (*Isaiah 40-55* Torch Bible Commentary, Second Edition [London: SCM Press, 1964], p. 61).

[104] Ma, *Until the Spirit Comes*, p. 96.

The use of מִשְׁפָּט in Isa. 42:1-4 is associated with the Gentiles (עָלָיו cf. τοῖς ἔθνεσιν, v. 1). In deutero-Isaiah (40-55), the instances of מִשְׁפָּט with reference to the Gentiles occur in the "trial speeches" (e.g., Isa. 41:1-5, 21-29) in a juridical sense. In Isa. 41:1-5, the claim to divinity made by the gods of foreign nations (i.e., Gentiles) is declared invalid by judicial means, since Yahweh alone is God. In Isa. 42:1-4, the Servant's task would be to bring this judgement to the Gentiles who worship other gods.[105] Significant for our purpose is that the basis for this judgment is the Decalogue (cf. Exod. 20:2-5), where it is stated that exclusive worship belongs to Yahweh. Thus, the Spirit equips the Servant of Isa. 42:1-4 to execute judgment on the foreign nations who serve other gods, since Yahweh alone has the rightful claim to divinity and is to be worshipped as God as stipulated in the Mosaic Law.

Isa. 61:1-2 depicts a Spirit-anointed leader ("the Spirit of the Sovereign Lord is upon me") whose purpose was to proclaim the good news among the poor. The preposition יַעַן denotes purpose and intention ("because the Lord has anointed me to proclaim good news" יַעַן מָשַׁח יְהוָה אֹתִי לְבַשֵּׂר).[106] The series of infinitives, "to proclaim...to bind up...to declare...to declare...to comfort...to provide," which go down to the end of v. 3, set forth the purposes for which the Spirit was bestowed upon the messenger. It is through this act of proclaiming that he is to effect a new era of salvation. The juxtaposition of "year" and "day" in Isa. 61:2a indicates that no particular event is in mind, but a new era.[107] Those who benefit from the preacher's message are described as "poor," "broken-hearted," "captive," and "in prison." The use of עָנָו can be taken literally meaning "material poverty" but it can also encompass a broader meaning of "weakness and affliction,"[108] having overtones of piety (Pss. 40:17; 72:12, 14).[109] The "broken-hearted" (לְנִשְׁבְּרֵי לֵב) can have a specific reference to moral character.[110] In. Is. 57:15 a similar construction is used in reference to the mourning for sin or the destruction of Jerusalem, though even this was considered punishment for sin. "Freedom for captives" (לִשְׁבוּיִם דְּרוֹר) is related to the freedom brought by the year of jubilee.[111] The phrase "the

---

[105] Westermann, Isaiah 40-66, p.95.

[106] BDB, p. 774.

[107] Westermann, Isaiah 40-66, pp. 366-67; see also Ma, Until the Spirit Comes, p. 125.

[108] BDB, p. 776.

[109] Grogan, "Isaiah," p. 333.

[110] See Pss. 34:18,19; 51:19; 147:3; Isa. 57:15; BDB, p. 525.

[111] "The Lord has sent his servant to proclaim the jubilee year when debts are remitted and lands restored (Lev. 25:25ff.; Jer. 34:8ff.)" (Christoph Barth, God With Us: A Theological

release from darkness for the prisoners" (וְלַאֲסוּרִים פְּקַח־קוֹחַ) is translated as καὶ τυφλοῖς ἀνάβλεψιν ("and recovery of sight to the blind") in the LXX. This can be interpreted figuratively, as in a spiritual sense, i.e., being able to discern God's words and deeds.[112] The above descriptions are to be read in light of vv. 2-3 ("to comfort all who mourn"/ "provide for those who grieve"/ "to bestow a crown of beauty/ "oil of joy"/ "garment of praise"). They indicate the rejuvenation and renewal that comes by being in covenantal relationship with Yahweh.[113] The mention of being "called oaks of righteousness" confirms this. The use of צֶדֶק here designates individuals who are associated with the covenant, who in this context are described as reaping the blessings associated with it.[114]

5. Summary

In non-eschatological contexts, the Mosaic Law becomes the basis for the Spirit's role in fashioning Israel's ethical behaviour. This is particularly true in Judg. 3:7-11; 6:34; 11:29, the penitential Psalms 51 and 143, and the prophet Micah (3:8). Complementing Jeremiah's new covenant expectation (Jer. 31 [38 LXX]: 31-34), the book of Ezekiel (36:25-27 [11:19-20]; 37:1-14) envisioned Yahweh's Spirit as the agent by which Israel experiences inner transformation and is equipped to observe the moral and religious codes of conduct advocated by the Jewish Torah. Belief in the Spirit as the source for empowerment to observe the Torah had widespread attestation in Ancient Judaism. Various OT passages (e.g. Isa. 40:13; 44:33; Joel 3:1; Zech. 4:6) identify the Spirit as the basis for the formation of a Torah-based ethic and covenant renewal in the future promises of Israel's restoration. In accordance with this, Israel's leaders would be Spirit-endowed and thus enabled to fashion their own lives by the moral code of the Torah and subsequently influence others to experience a renewed sense of obedience (Isa. 11:2-5; 42:1-4; 61:1-2).

Introduction to the Old Testament [Grand Rapids: William B. Eerdmans Publishing Company, 1991], p. 347); see also the use of the phrase שְׁנַת הַדְּרוֹר in Ezek. 46:17.

[112] See Isa. 42:18; 43:8; 56:10 (Wolfgang Schrage, "τυφλός, κτλ.," *TDNT* Vol. VIII, pp. 270-94, esp. p. 281).

[113] C.F. Keil and F. Delitzsch, *Isaiah: Two Volumes in One* Vol. 7, Book I, (trans. James Martin; Grand Rapids: William B. Eerdmans Publishing Company, 1986), p. 427.

[114] "[P]eople as enjoying the righteousness of salvation" (BDB, p. 842) cf. Isa. 60:21, where the author speaks of Israel's "righteousness" and the covenantal blessing of land.

CHAPTER TWO

Second Temple Judaism

1. Diaspora Literature

The sources examined under the rubric of "Diaspora Literature" include those writings produced during the Second Temple period in regions outside of Palestine and written originally in Greek. Sources will be arranged in chronological order. In this section it is beneficial to survey texts in regions outside Palestine that explain the Spirit's influence upon God's people within the covenantal relationship and the effect the Spirit had upon observance of the Jewish Law. Our investigation will not be limited to texts that have an explicit or implicit association with the new covenant Jewish eschatological promises in Ancient Judaism (Jer. 38 [LXX]:31-34; Ezek. 36:25-27 [11:19-20]; 37:1-14). Subjects that address Jewish ethics and moral renewal, even though not set in an eschatological context, still convey important corollaries for ascertaining the relationship between Spirit and Law as perceived by Paul in Rom. 8:1-16. Even these would have the potential of exerting significant influence on the formation of eschatological convictions in first century C.E. Jewish thinking.

1.1 Wisdom of Solomon[1]

The central aim of the author of Wisdom is to encourage Jews to adhere to their traditional beliefs against the threat of apostasy within a Hellenistic

---

[1] The Wisdom of Solomon is generally dated in the 1ˢᵗ century B.C.E. but possible dates range from mid-2ⁿᵈ century B.C.E. to the mid 1ˢᵗ century C.E. (Otto Eissfeldt, *Einleitung in das Alte Testament unter Einschluss der Apokryphen und Pseudepigraphen sowie der apokryphen- und pseudepigraphenartigen Qumran-Schriften*, Fourth Edition [Tübingen: J.C.B. Mohr (Paul Siebeck), 1976], p. 815; Lester L. Grabbe, *Wisdom of Solomon* [Sheffield: Sheffield Academic Press, 1997], pp. 87-90; Ernest G. Clarke, *The Wisdom of Solomon* [London: Cambridge University Press, 1973], pp. 1-2).

environment.[2] Consequently, it places the Jewish monotheistic belief in Yahweh in dialogue with the Gentile world.[3] This means that the argument the author puts forth with respect to the Spirit's role in the covenantal relationship and its relationship to the Law must be coherent with Jewish traditional beliefs. It can be said then that the purpose within the book complies, to a certain extent, with a Jewish universal outlook.[4] The Spirit's relationship to the Law would have to be articulated in a legitimate and convincing manner in order to prove Israel's religious and ethical supremacy over prevalent competitive Hellenistic ideas.

The term διαθήκη appears only once in Wis. 18:22 but the terms νόμος[5] and ἐντολή[6] occur several times. The author of Wisdom employs the term πνεῦμα in a variety of ways. The term refers to breath or wind,[7] a permeating force that "fills the world" and holds all things together,[8] the source of physical life,[9] and finally, it is equated with wisdom. The references to πνεῦμα as wisdom shall form the basis of this analysis.

1.1.1 Spirit of Wisdom and Obeying the Law. The book of Wisdom opens with an exhortation to leaders who "judge the earth" (Wis. 1:1 cf. 6:2-12), urging them to love justice and seek the Lord in integrity of heart. This insight builds upon the OT concept of the leaders of Israel as guides and advocates of

---

[2] Scholars have been almost unanimous in arguing for Egypt as the place of composition, for various reasons; Wis. 19:13-17 makes a point of the wickedness of Egypt and Wis. 17:16 has allusions to ἀναχωρήσις ("withdrawal"), a sort of "strike" by peasants who fled to the desert or elsewhere to hide when the tax burden became too great (Grabbe, *Wisdom of Solomon*, p.90); see also David Winston, *The Wisdom of Solomon* 43 AB (New York: Doubleday, 1979), p. 63; Eissfeldt, *Einleitung*, p. 816. Reference is made to those Jews who had abandoned the Jewish faith (Wis. 2:12) and had been attracted to the cultural life of the Greeks. Consequently, the author hoped to rekindle within his audience a genuine zeal for God (chs. 1-9).

[3] References to "judges of the earth" (Wis. 1:1) and rulers of the earth in chs. 6-9 indicate that he could have also had a Gentile audience potentially in mind as well (Grabbe, *Wisdom of Solomon*, p. 91); "[The author] sought to prepare them, as well-educated Jews, to live in a Hellenistic society; to provide them religious insights, in a contemporary form, in order to establish links between their traditional faith and all the new ideas of the pagan society wherein they lived" (Clarke, *The Wisdom of Solomon*, p. 5).

[4] See Wenk, *Community-Forming Power*, p. 85.

[5] See Wis. 2:11,12; 6:4, 18; 9:5; 14:16; 16:6; 18:4,9.

[6] See Wis. 9:9; 16:6.

[7] For πνεῦμα as breath/wind see Wis. 2:3; 5:3, 11; 7:20; 11:20; 13:2; 17:18.

[8] See Wis. 1:7.

[9] See Wis. 12:1; 15:11, 16.

covenant faithfulness towards Yahweh.[10] The ruler's task is to produce δικαιοσύνη (Wis. 1:1 cf. 2 Sam. 8:15; 22:21; 1 Kgs. 3:6, 9; 10:9) and encourage the people to "seek him" (the Lord) (ζητήσατε αὐτον). In Wis. 1:4, σοφία is not the result of one's study or of experience in life, but rather, a guest who enters (εἰσελεύσεται) and comes to live (κατοικήσει). It is also claimed that she is not indifferent to the kind of dwelling she desires; sin frustrates the purpose of σοφία. There is a parallelism between v.4 and v.5, indicating that wisdom is equated with the ἅγιον πνεῦμα παιδείας.[11] The adjective ἅγιον suggests that the phrase is not to be interpreted in an anthropological sense (i.e., "a human spirit"). Instead, it is best understood as the transcendence and consecration associated with the nature of God[12] and therefore, means more than simply something one acquires through human learning or practice. The Spirit is an external force that fashions and transforms human behaviour. A cursory reading of the role of the Spirit in Wis. 1:5-7 seems to suggest that righteous behaviour is the prerequisite for receiving the Spirit and not the result of the Spirit's indwelling. Because "deceit/ unrighteousness" drives away the Spirit, the Spirit cannot be

---

[10] See Deut. 17:14-20; 2 Sam. 8:15; 22:21; 1 Kgs. 3:6, 9; 10:9 cf. with Chapter One, section 4 (Israel's Leaders, Spirit-Endowment, and the Torah) and scriptural passages cited.

[11] "Wisdom is closely related with πνεῦμα (1,6; 7,22;9,17)" (Eckhard J. Schnabel, Law and Wisdom from Ben Sira to Paul WUNT 2. Reihe 16 [Tübingen: J.C.B. Mohr (Paul Siebeck), 1985], p. 131); "Now in vs. 5 wisdom is described as the 'holy spirit of discipline'" (Montague, The Holy Spirit, p. 104); "En outre la sagesse n'est seulement un effect de l'esprit divin, elle est son équivalent" (P. van Imshoot, "Sagesse et Esprit dans l'Acien Testament," RB 47 [1938], 23-49). The structure of v. 4 demonstrates synonymous parallelism with v.5; just as "wisdom" cannot "enter" (εἰσελεύσεται) nor "reside" (κατοικήσει) in the same place as "sin" (ἁμαρτίας), so the "Holy Spirit of discipline" (ἅγιον πνεῦμα παιδείας) "will flee deceit" (φεύξεται δόλον) and cannot co-exist with "unrighteousness" (ἀδικίας).

[12] "Holy spirit is a personification of God already found in the Greek Bible (Isa. 63:10-11)" (Clarke, The Wisdom of Solomon, p. 17). See also Wis. 1:7; 9:17; 12:1, where πνεῦμα is associated with God. The book of Wisdom uses terminology which emphasizes the affinity of πνεῦμα/σοφία with God. In Wis. 7:25 wisdom is described as the vapour (ἄτμις) of God's power. This suggests a relationship between God and the vapour of his breath (πνεῦμα) (cf. Eccl. 24:3). God's wisdom/Spirit is described as his effluence (ἀπόρροια) (7:25); the reflection (ἀπαύγασμα) of the everlasting light (7:26 cf. Isa. 60:19f.); the unspotted mirror of the power of God (7:26); the image (εἰκών) of his goodness (7:26); she is light, more beautiful than the sun (7:29). The book of Wisdom also attributes the same activities to God and πνεῦμα/σοφία: wisdom is the Spirit devoted to a human's good (φιλάνθρωπον) (Wis. 1:6) as God loves all that lives (φιλόψυχε) (Wis. 11:24).

conceived as possessing ethical influence.[13] However, the context indicates something quite different than this interpretation. The concept παιδεία, which is here associated with the Spirit, carries connotations of the type of discipline related to ethical life. In the wisdom tradition, the use of παιδεία refers primarily to the discipline associated with the study of the Law (Prov. 6:23 cf. 16:22; 10:17) as the basis for human conduct.[14] As "the Spirit of discipline," the Spirit itself fosters a Torah-based ethic. In v. 6, wisdom is described as φιλάνθρωπον πνεῦμα, that is, a "Spirit that loves humans," and in this context, refers to the Spirit's role in not allowing evil to go unnoticed. In v. 7 the words, "Because the Spirit of the Lord has filled the inhabited earth (πεπλήρωκε τὴν οἰκουμένην), and he who controls all things (τὸ συνέχον τὰ πάντα) has knowledge of the voice," claim that the Spirit's omnipresence is the basis for the assertion in the preceding verses. Putting these things together, we can conclude that the Spirit's presence (or lack of it) becomes a type of judgment or rebuke for those who sin (cf. Wis. 11:20); sin in one's life frustrates the Spirit's role in nurturing acceptable behaviour. It is comparable to Isa. 63:10 where it speaks of "grieving" the Holy Spirit.[15]

This interpretation of the Spirit's ethical influence is consistent with the author's (under the pseudonymity of "Solomon") request in Wis. 7:7: "Because of this I prayed and understanding was given to me: I called upon God, and the Spirit of wisdom (πνεῦμα σοφίας) came to me." In 6:2-7:6, we learn that the author perceived himself to be in the same category with those leaders and rulers who "neither kept the Law (οὐδὲ ἐφυλάξατε νόμον), nor walked according to the purpose of God" [6:4 cf. v. 18).[16] But he prayed, and the "Spirit of wisdom" transformed him into a leader who obeyed the Law (7:22) and became "a friend of God" (7:27).

---

[13] This is the erroneous conclusion of Gunkel who tends to restrictively characterize the Spirit's work in giving revelation and wisdom but assigns the Spirit no part in the formation of ethics (Gunkel, *The Influence of the Spirit*, p. 21).

[14] Georg Bertram, "παιδεύω, κτλ.," *TDNT* Vol. V, pp. 596-625, esp. pp. 603-6.

[15] Montague, *The Holy Spirit*, pp. 104-5.

[16] See Schnabel, who asserts that the book of Wisdom seems to avoid and downplay references to the Jewish Law but concedes that possible references to the Jewish Law are made in Wis. 2:12; 6:4; 9:9; 18:4, where the ethical perspective of the Law is emphasized (*Law and Wisdom*, pp. 131-2); while Winston believes νομός in Wis. 6:4 most likely does not make an overt reference to the Mosaic Law, but rather, refers to natural principles of justice, he allows for the possibility that a number of Jewish Hellenistic writers viewed the Torah itself as an expression of natural law (*The Wisdom of Solomon*, p. 153).

In Wis. 9:13 the point of reference in the questions, "For what is *a human being* (ἄνθρωπος) that can know the will of God? Or who can think what the will of the Lord is?" is a "human being" not just the king, "Solomon."[17] The phraseology most likely stems from Isa. 40:13-14; 55:8 (cf. Prov. 30:2-4; Sir. 1:1-10; 18:1-7; 24:28-29; 1 Bar. 3:29-37) and serves to underscore the idea that there are certain innate limitations within every human being with respect to morality (9:14-16). Wisdom and the Holy Spirit are given a soteriological function in 9:17-18 in that they are the essential sources of moral and religious life.[18] Even though the Greek noun σωτήρ is not used, the verb σῴζω in 9:18 certainly indicates that the Spirit has a salvific function.[19] The Spirit (τὸ ἅγιον σου πνεῦμα, 9:17) is instrumental in "straightening the paths of those on the earth" (9:18). As Winston aptly puts it, "This verse [9:18] makes the culmination of the author's emphatic teaching in this chapter concerning man's complete dependence on God's gift of his Spirit of wisdom for the achievement of a righteous existence."[20] Put in other words, the prayer is the conclusion of the author's understanding that the Spirit of wisdom is the necessary means by which one is empowered to obey the Jewish Law and maintain covenant faithfulness.[21] The echo of Isa. 40:13-14; 55:8[22] in Wis. 9:13, the phrase διωρθώθησαν αἱ τρίβοι ("the paths were set right," Wis. 9:18 cf. Prov. 4:26; 1QH 4:31), and the author's persistent reference to "righteous"[23] living confirm this.

---

[17] Clarke, *The Wisdom of Solomon*, p. 64.

[18] G. Verbeke, *L'évolution de la doctrine du pneuma du Stoicism à S. Augustin* (Paris: Desclée de Brouwer, 1945), p. 229; J.S. Vos, *Traditionsgeschichtliche Untersuchungen zur paulinischen Pneumatologie* (Assen: Van Gorcum, 1973), p. 64.

[19] Wisdom, which is equated with the Spirit, is a mediatoral figure (8:2-9), is said to guard the first human creation (10:1), preserved Abraham blameless (10:5), saved Lot (10:6), delivered all those who served her (10:9), delivered Joseph from sin (10:13) and people from a nation of oppressors (10:15). The soteriological function of Wisdom/Spirit is one of the distinctive features of the Wisdom of Solomon (John S. Kloppenborg, "Isis and Sophia in the Book of Wisdom," *HTR* 75 [1982], 57-84, see esp. 72).

[20] Winston, *The Wisdom of Solomon*, p. 208.

[21] This is the contention of Wenk, even though he interprets Wis. 9:17-18 restrictively as "Solomon's" request for the Spirit's assistance to be the "guardian of covenant loyalty" (*Community-Forming Power*, p. 87).

[22] The phrases ἄνθρωπος γνώσεται and βουλὴν θεοῦ / θέλει ὁ Κύριος in Wis. 9:13 are parallel to the thoughts of Isa. 40:13-14; 55:8.

[23] See the references to δικαιοσύνη and its various adjectival and verbal forms in the immediate context of Wis. 9:17-18: 8:7; 9:3, 12; 10:3, 4, 5, 6, 10, etc. Gottlob Schrenk observes

1.2 *Joseph and Aseneth*[24]

The story of Joseph and Aseneth elaborates the biblical account in Gen. 41:45, where Pharaoh gives Aseneth, the daughter of Potiphera, priest of On, to Joseph for his wife. It addresses the issue of how Joseph, the model of chastity, piety, and devoted servant of Yahweh, could marry a foreign Hamitic girl, daughter of an idolatrous priest. Joseph is a Jew who worships God and lives on the bread of life and will not kiss a heathen woman who eats food offered to idols. Still Joseph prays for her conversion. In response, Aseneth destroys her idols, engages in a week of fasting and crying, and repents for her conceit and idolatry. Joseph then comes and marries her.

Even though the giving of the Law on Mount Sinai postdates the setting of the narrative, the author measures the behaviour of both Joseph and Aseneth according to the standards set by the Jewish Law.[25] He gives and reports a number of important characteristics associated with the Mosaic Law: appropriate worship ("it does not befit a man who worships God"[26] [*Jos. Asen.*

---

that "δίκαιος is the man who fulfils his duties towards God and the theocratic society, meeting God's claims in this relationship" ("δίκη, κτλ.," *TDNT* Vol. II, pp. 179–225, quote taken from p. 185).

[24] Most scholars agree that *Joseph and Aseneth* was composed in Greek by a Jewish author in Egypt and perhaps may contain some Christian interpolations (e.g., T. Holtz contends that the threefold kiss in *Joseph and Aseneth* [19:11] reflects a valentinian and mystery religions influence ["Christliche Interpolationen in 'Joseph and Aseneth,'" *NTS* 14 (1967/68), 482-97]. However, others see the kiss being influenced by Jewish sapiential tradition [D. Sänger, *Antikes Judentum und die Mysterien: Religonsgeschichtliche Untersuchungen zu Joseph und Aseneth* (Tübingen: J.C.B. Mohr (Paul Siebeck), 1980), pp. 165–7]). *Joseph and Aseneth* is most likely written between 100 B.C.E. and 117 C.E. (C. Burchard, "Joseph and Aseneth: A New Translation and Introduction," *OTP* Vol. 2, Edited by James H. Charlesworth [New York: Doubleday, 1985], pp. 181, 187; see also Edith M. Humphrey, *Joseph and Aseneth* [Sheffield: Sheffield Academic Press, 2000], pp. 28-31).

[25] Burchard makes the erroneous conclusion that the author of *Jos. Asen.* shows no interest in the Mosaic Law ("But the author could have found a way to mention these events [Exodus, the giving of the Law on Mount Sinai, and the institution of the cult] if he was interested in them...Divine life is not mediated to man through the Law...it is obtained through the right use of food, ointment, and by the avoidance of the pagan way of partaking of them"). He also draws a faulty distinction between the author's emphasis on idolatry and the transgression of the Law ("Joseph and Aseneth," pp. 190-1). The author of *Joseph and Aseneth* no doubt recognizes that the explicit mention of the Law would be an anachronistic reading of the story. But this does not mean that he completely refuses to use the Law as the basis of ethics and morality.

[26] All quotations from *Jos. Asen.* are taken from Buchard's ET of "Joseph and Aseneth," *OTP* Vol. 2, pp. 202-47.

4:8 cf. Exod. 18:21]),[27] the honeycomb (cf. Aseneth is fed a piece of supernatural honeycomb [Jos. Asen. 16:15-16]),[28] idols (Jos. Asen. 9:2; 10:12 cf. Exod. 20:4-5), God's description ("jealous and terrible God" [Jos. Asen. 11:7; 12:4 cf. Exod. 20: 5f.]), lawlessness ("lawless deed of an afflicted person" [Jos. Asen. 11:10]), commandments ("keep your commandments which you have commanded...and never transgress your ordinances" [Jos. Asen. 12:2]). This means that the author of Joseph and Aseneth introduces his knowledge of the Mosaic Law into the story even though the setting of the narrative predates the actual giving of the Law. Therefore, even though there is no explicit reference to the Mosaic Law, it still functions as the basis for ethics and morality.

In three separate passages the author refers to the Spirit as the power that transforms human beings. In Jos. Asen. 4:7, Joseph is said to be "a man powerful in wisdom and experience, and the spirit of God is upon him." Elsewhere Joseph is identified as a Spirit-endowed individual.[29] The correlation between wisdom and God's Spirit reflects Jewish traditional attributes[30] found in wisdom literature.[31] As was stated above, wisdom and the Spirit are associated with observing the Jewish Torah.[32] In the immediate context, Joseph is also described as "a man who worships God" (Jos. Asen. 4:7). Jos. Asen. uses θεοσεβής and never the term εὐσεβής.[33] Θεοσεβής is a terminus technicus to designate monotheistic worship of Yahweh that requires appropriate ethical standards.[34] What is particularly significant for our purposes is that it is used in the OT in reference to those who are especially knowledgeable of and obey the Mosaic Law.[35]

---

[27] It is no coincidence that the idea of "humans who fear God" used to depict Joseph (Jos. Asen. 4:8) is the characteristic that Jethro recommends that Moses look for in individuals who were to assist him in governing the people based upon the "ordinances of God and his Law" (Exod. 18:20 cf. vv. 21-22).

[28] Honey is regarded as a symbol for the Law (Ps. 19:9-10; 119:103; Philo, Fug., 137-139)

[29] T. Sim. 4:4; Philo, Jos. 116-7; Jub. 40:5.

[30] See Gen. 41:39 where Joseph is said to be "discerning and wise."

[31] Wis. 7:7; 8:2-9; 9:17-18.

[32] See above, under Wisdom of Solomon, particularly, "Spirit of Wisdom and Obeying the Law."

[33] See Jos. Asen. 8:5f.; 21:1; 23:9f., 12; 28:5; 29:3.

[34] Buchard, "Joseph and Aseneth," p. 206, footnote 4.2.1.m.; see also G. Bertram, who claims that θεοσεβής has a strong ethical sense to it ("θεοσεβής, θεοσέβεια," TDNT Vol. III, pp. 123-8).

[35] See for example, Exod. 18:21 (LXX), where θεοσεβεῖς is used in association with τὰ προστάγματα τοῦ θεοῦ καὶ τὸν νόμον αὐτοῦ (v.20).

In *Jos. Asen.* 8:9, Joseph prays for Aseneth's conversion: "renew her by your spirit." In this context, the Spirit's renewal is associated with "light," "life," "truth."[36] Jewish tradition associates "light" with the Torah in that its knowledge functions as the light of the world.[37] This refers not only to usual knowledge of the Torah but also its fulfillment.[38] In Second Temple Judaism, God's commandments are called the "commandments of life"[39] and the Torah is called the "Law of life."[40] The Law functions as the source of knowledge and truth.[41] This indicates that the type of Spirit-renewal the author describes here with respect to Aseneth coincides with the ethical and moral standards and functions associated with the Jewish Torah.

Jos. Asen. 19:11 reads, "And Joseph kissed Aseneth and gave her spirit of life, and he kissed her the second time and gave her spirit of wisdom, and he kissed her the third time and gave her spirit of truth." In antiquity outside of biblical literature, kissing was the means of transferring breath, conveying the soul, and the vehicle by which to attain supernatural strength.[42] In the OT, we have reference to Samuel who anoints and kisses Saul as king.[43] Later in the narrative we read that the Spirit had departed from Saul.[44] This implies that the Spirit was conveyed by Samuel to Saul through the anointing with oil and its association with the kiss.[45] There is a later rabbinic source that makes a reference to the animation of the dead bones in Ezek. 37:9 through God's breath (Spirit): "God will embrace them and kiss them and bring them into the life of the world to come."[46] Furthermore, the threefold reference to the

---

[36] "Lord God of my father Israel, the Most High, the Powerful One of Jacob, who gave *life* to all (things) and called (them) from the darkness to the *light*, and from the error to the *truth*, and from the death to the *life*; you, Lord, bless this virgin, and renew her by your spirit." (*Jos. Asen.* 8:9).

[37] A. Oepke, "λάμπω, κτλ.," *TDNT* Vol. IV, pp. 16–28, esp. 23–4.

[38] See *T. Ben* 5:3; 4 Esr. 7:97.

[39] Bar. 3:9 cf. 4:1 (see R. Bultmann, "The Concept of Life in Judaism," *TDNT* Vol. II, pp. 855–61, esp. 855).

[40] Sir. 17:11; see also m. *Abot* 6:7; *Pss. Sol.* 14:2.

[41] See Ps. 119:160 (MT) ("The sum of your word is truth; and every one of your righteous ordinances endures forever"); Ps. 19:9 ("the ordinances of the Lord are true and righteous altogether") (G. Quell, "ἀλήθεια, κτλ.," *TDNT* Vol. I, pp. 232–7, esp. 235–6).

[42] G. Stählin, "φιλέω, κτλ.," *TDNT* Vol. IX, pp. 113–71, esp. pp. 119–23.

[43] 1 Sam. 10:1.

[44] 1 Sam. 16:14.

[45] Wenk, *Community-Forming Power*, p. 96.

[46] *S. Eli. R.* 17 cf. *Odes Sol.* 28: 6–8.

Spirit's association with ζωή, σοφία, and ἀλήθεια again connects the Spirit with the function of the Jewish Law.[47] In *Jos. Asen.* 21:10-21 we have reference to the Spirit's transformative power in Aseneth's religious and ethical life.

1.3 Philo Judaeus[48]

The writings of Philo Judaeus provide an interesting contrast to those of the book Wisdom. Even though Philo is intensely proud of his Jewish heritage and faith,[49] he attempts to interpret Jewish beliefs in terms appropriate to the Hellenistic world in which the Jews of the Diaspora were living.[50] Philo could assimilate so much from Hellenism and still consider himself a Jew.[51] Consequently, his reaction to the Diaspora situation was different from that of the author of the Wisdom of Solomon, who sought to defend against the infiltration of Hellenistic syncretism.

Philo's lack of emphasis on eschatology demonstrates an individual more at home in his world.[52] There are sparse references to a futuristic eschatology. He stresses the necessity of understanding the revelation that had already been given for the present in the Mosaic Law. When reference to eschatology is

---

[47] See above for the Spirit's association with "life, wisdom, and truth" and how these related to the knowledge and observance of the Jewish Law. This makes it unlikely that this was a later Christian interpolation since precedence to the conveyance of the Spirit through a kiss is to be found in Jewish tradition (Sänger, *Antikes Judentum*, p. 207).

[48] Philo Judaeus was from Alexandria (an Egyptian city with a large Jewish Diaspora population in Greco-Roman times) and lived from about 30 B.C.E. to about 50 C.E. (Naomi G. Cohen, *Philo Judaeus: His Universe of Discourse* [New York: Peter Lang, 1995], p. 11; Samuel Sandmel, *Philo's Place in Judaism: A Study of Conceptions of Abraham in Jewish Literature* [New York: Ktav Publishing House, Inc., 1971], p.2; David M. Scholer, "An Introduction to Philo" in *The Works of Philo: Complete and Unabridged* [trans. C.D. Yonge; Peabody, MA: Hendrickson Publishers, 1993], pp. xi–xviii, esp. p. xi). All citations of Philonic texts (Greek and English) are from F.H. Colson and G.H. Whitaker, and Ralph Marcus, *Philo 10 and 2 suppl* LCL (London: Heinemann; Cambridge, MA: Harvard University Press, 1929-1962).

[49] Philo describes himself as a scholar of Moses (*Spec. Leg.* 1.345) and as one of "the disciples of Moses" (*Quis Her.* 81). In his own mind he was far removed from those described in *Conf.* 2 as "persons who cherish a dislike of the institutions of our fathers and make it their constant study to denounce and decry the Laws." Philo wrote to refute these scoffers.

[50] Philo's philosophical and historical-apologetic writings relate his concerns as an exegete of the Pentateuch of Moses within Hellenistic philosophical traditions (see Scholer, "An Introduction to Philo," pp. xii-xiii).

[51] See the discussion under the subsection entitled, "Jew or Greek?" (Ronald Williamson, *Jews in the Hellenistic World: Philo* [Cambridge: Cambridge University Press, 1989], pp. 2-5).

[52] Isaacs, *The Concept of the Spirit*, p. 24.

made, it appears to be focused around the reunion of the Exiles,[53] a time of national prosperity,[54] and the universal reign of peace for humans and nature.[55] At that time, Israel's unrepentant enemies will be punished.[56] There is no fundamental difference between the manner in which Jewish Law is to be received between the present and the future (cf. Jer. 38 [LXX]: 31–34; Ezek. 11:19–20; 36:25–27; 37:1–14). The Mosaic Law remains "firm, unshaken, immovable...[and] secure from the day when [it was] first enacted to now, and we may hope that [it] will remain for all future ages as though immortal."[57] This makes it altogether clear that Philo did not place too much emphasis on covenant renewal.

Philo uses the term πνεῦμα 151 times[58] in his extant writings, in various ways.[59] He employs the term with reference to the four elements, particularly, air,[60] the force in the universe that gives cohesion to its various parts,[61] the rational aspect of the human soul,[62] and prophetic inspiration.[63] The distinction between the rational aspect of the human soul and prophetic inspiration, at certain places, appears to be ambiguous; Philo describes common characteristics between them and, in some sense, they are coalesced with respect to their function. For example in *Leg. All.* I, 32, 36–38, he

---

[53] *Praem.* 164f.

[54] *Praem.* 168; *Mos.* II, 44.

[55] *Praem.* 79–94.

[56] *Praem.* 169; 171.

[57] Quote taken from *Mos.* II, 14; see also 144.

[58] Peder Borgen, Kare Fuglseth and Roald Skarsten, *The Philo Index: A Complete Greek Word Index of the Writings of Philo of Alexandria* (Grand Rapids: Wm. B. Eerdmans Publishing Company, 2000), p. 285; Philo uses πνευματικός 9 times and the term πνεύμων 6 times (*Ibid.*, p. 285).

[59] G. Verbeke notes four distinct uses of the word πνεῦμα in the Philonic texts (*L'évolution de la doctrine du Pneuma du Stoicisme à S. Augustin*, pp. 237–51);W. Bieder sees six uses of the term πνεῦμα in Philo: higher element of air, that which holds all matter together, the soul's essence, divine Spirit which humans acquire by inbreathing, and the prophetic Spirit ("II. πνεῦμα in Hellenistic Judaism- 1.Philo" *TDNT* Vol. VI, pp. 372–5).

[60] *Ebr.* 106; *Cher.* 111; *Gig.* 22; *Cher.* 111; *Op.* 29–30. Πνεῦμα can refer to breath (*Mos.* 1.93; *Quod Deus* 84) or to wind (*Op.* 41; *Abr.* 92). *Contra* G. Verbeke is the contention of A. Laurentin, who maintains that πνεῦμα is not air itself but rather its movement, which makes the Spirit divine presence and action ("Le pneuma dans la doctrine de Philon," *ETL* 27 [1951], 390–437, esp. 391–404, 420).

[61] *Quod Deus* 35–36.

[62] *Leg. All.* I, 32f.

[63] *Mos.* II, 40; *Gig.* 24.

describes God who "had breathed (ἐμπνεύσειεν) into it (soul) a power of real life" (I, 32 cf. "that which is inbreathed is the spirit or breath" [τὸ δὲ ἐμπνεόμενον τὸ πνεῦμα, I, 37]) and this is equivalent to God "inspiring" (I, 33 ["The question might be asked, why God deemed the earthly and body-loving mind worth of divine breath (πνεύματος θείου)..."], cf. 36, 38). Furthermore, as will be demonstrated below, Philo associates both the rational aspect of the soul and prophetic inspiration with the work of the πνεῦμα θεῖον in the process of human transformation and ethics.[64] The scope of this investigation will be limited to these two uses in Philo since they reflect the Spirit's role in character-formation and the acquisition of ethical behaviour.

1.3.1 The Spirit, Human Soul, and Virtues. Philo regarded πνεῦμα as the rational aspect of the human soul. God breathed his πνεῦμα θεῖον into every human being at creation (Gen. 2:7); it is this that differentiates humans from animals[65] and thus makes the mind (νοῦς) rational and capable of receiving knowledge of God.[66] God deemed all humans worthy of "divine inspiration" because he loved to give good things to all, thus "encouraging them to seek and participate in virtue" (προκαλούμενος αὐτοὺς εἰς μετουσίαν καὶ ζῆλον ἀρετῆς).[67] Elsewhere in Philo's writings we see that the concept of

---

[64] See *Op.* 135; *Quaest. in Gn.* I, 4,51; see secondary sources which make this observation: Wenk, *Community-Forming Power*, p. 92, footnote 29; M.M.B. Turner, *Power From On High: The Spirit in Israel's Restoration and Witness in Luke-Acts* (Sheffield: Sheffield Academic Press, 1996), p. 125; *contra* Menzies and Isaacs who advocate a firm distinction between the divine rational Spirit, which is universal and permanent, and the charismatic prophetic Spirit, which is selective and non-permanent (Menzies, *The Development of Early Christian Pneumatology*, pp. 63-7; Isaacs, *The Concept of the Spirit*, p. 38).

[65] *Spec. Leg.* IV, 123.

[66] *Leg. All.* I, 36-38; *Op.* 135; *Det.* 80-90; *Plant.* 18-22; *Congr.* 97; "C'est grâce à ce pneuma divin que nous sommes capables de connaître la nature de Dieu et que nous pouvons sortir des limites étroites de notre prison corporelle en parcourant l'étendue du ciel et de la terre par la force de notre intelligence" (Verbeke, *L'evolution de la doctrine du Pneuma*, p.242); see also J.A. Davis, *Wisdom and Spirit: An Investigation of 1 Corinthians 1.18-3.20 against the Background of Jewish Sapiential Tradition in the Greco-Roman Period* (Lanham, MD: University Press of America, 1984), p. 56; B.A. Pearson, "Hellenistic-Jewish Wisdom Speculation and Paul," in *Aspects of Wisdom in Judaism and Early Christianity* UNDCSJCA, 1(ed. R.L. Wilken; Notre Dame, IN: University of Notre Dame Press, 1975), pp. 43-66, see esp. p. 54. However, there are exceptions to this pattern in Philo in that the πνοή rather than πνεῦμα is given to humans at creation (see *Leg. All.* I, 42).

[67] *Leg. All.* I, 34.

ἀρετή is closely associated with the Jewish Law.[68] For example, Moses is described as "the living Law" (τὸν νόμον ἔμψυχον)[69] and his function as a "legislator" would be to "possess all the virtues fully and completely" (γενήσεσθαι νομοθέτη προσήκει παντελέσι καὶ ὁλοκλήροις κεχρῆσθαι ταῖς ἀρεταῖς πάσαις).[70] In the same context, four specific "virtues" are mentioned ("love of humanity, of justice, of goodness, and hatred of evil") and these are for everyone who is inspired with "a zeal for Law-making" (ὅτῳ ζῆλος εἰσέρχεται τοῦ νομοθετεῖν).[71]

What is significant is that πνεῦμα is closely related to Philo's concept of conscience. As a result, it plays a large part in his theory of ethics. Like the conscience, whose nature is to hate evil and love virtue,[72] to make humans aware of their misdeeds,[73] and to act as both accuser and judge,[74] πνεῦμα is the permanent and universal gift of God, giving aptitude in goodness and fashioning morality in all: "[God's] breathing 'into the face' is to be understood both physically and ethically."[75] It functions as "the self-dictated instinct" of the heart.[76] The πνεῦμα of wisdom "causes the streams of the pleasures to slacken"[77] and also quickens the mind towards the knowledge of God.[78] Therefore, πνεῦμα and conscience appear to be identical in function; both are instrumental in the formation of morals within human beings in general.

1.3.2 The Prophetic Spirit and Character Transformation. There is a sense in which prophetic inspiration (or the charismatic Spirit) is not the permanent possession of every human being.[79] Philo never clarifies the relationship

---

[68] See also *Decal.* 52; *Leg. All.* III, 237; *Spec. Leg.* IV, 144; in some other Jewish circles "ἀρετή approximates to δικαιοσύνη, which elsewhere is logically subordinate to it as one of the four cardinal virtues" (Otto Bauernfeind, "ἀρετή," *TDNT* Vol. I, pp. 457–61, quote taken from p. 459).

[69] *Mos.* II, 4.

[70] *Mos.* II, 8.

[71] *Mos.* II, 9.

[72] *Decal.* 87.

[73] *Virt.* 124; *Spec. Leg.* II, 49; *Det.* 23f., 146; .

[74] *Op.* 128.

[75] *Leg. All.* I, 39.

[76] *Conf.* 59.

[77] *Som.* II, 13.

[78] *Plant.* 23–24.

[79] For example, Philonic texts: "though the divine spirit may stay a while in the soul it cannot abide there" (*Gig.* 28); "He [Moses] then has ever the divine spirit at his side...but from those

between the rational aspect of the soul granted universally and the Spirit as the source of prophetic inspiration reserved for a select few.[80] When he describes the Spirit's inspiration upon select individuals, they experience physiological changes,[81] and are granted special revelations[82] and persuasiveness of speech.[83] Furthermore, Spirit inspiration has an ethical, transforming effect upon their character; i.e., they become the essence of virtue and perfection, the quintessential characters who obey the Jewish Law.[84]

For Philo, Abraham was the historical patriarch who became the archetypical Jew who came to a monotheistic worship of God.[85] His crowning praise was, "this man keeps the divine Law (τὸν θεῖον νόμον) and all the divine commandments (τὰ θεῖα προστάγματα)." He based this statement

---

others, as I have said, it quickly separates itself" (Gig. 55), see also Quaest. In Gn. I, 90; Quod. Deus 2; secondary sources: "The uniqueness of Moses, according to Philo, is evident also in Moses' prophetic gift" (John R. Levison, "Inspiration and the Divine Spirit in the Writings of Philo Judaeus," Journal for the Study of Judaism in the Persian, Hellenistic, and Roman Period 26 [1995], 271-323, quote taken from p. 309); "What is evident is that a special place is claimed for prophetic inspiration" (Isaacs, The Concept of the Spirit, p. 47); Isaacs also lists the seventy elders, Jeremiah, Abraham, and Moses as select individuals whom Philo claimed experienced prophetic inspiration (Ibid., p. 47).

[80] Menzies, The Development of Early Christian Pneumatology, p. 65, footnote 3 with A.J.M. Wedderburn, Baptism and Resurrection: Studies in Pauline Theology against Its Graeco-Roman Background WUNT 44 (Tübingen: J.C.B. Mohr, 1987), pp. 272-3; M.A. Chevallier, Souffle de dieu: Le Saint-Esprit dans le Nouveau Testament Le Point Théologique 26 (Paris: Éditions Beauchesne, 1978), p. 72.

[81] Abraham's eyes, complexion, stature, carriage, movement, and voice are changed when he is inspired by the Spirit (Virt. 217); see also the description of the beauty of Adam when God breathed into his soul (Op. 136-50); Moses' appearance was changed when he was under the influence of inspiration (Mos. I, 57; II, 272); this is comparable to the inward and external beauty typical of the Greco-Roman world (see for example Plato, Resp. 3.402D; 7.535A).

[82] "Pure knowledge" (Gig. 13f.; 22-24); wisdom to lead (Mos. II, 40); future prediction (Mos. II, 246-52).

[83] Persuasive voice (Virt. 217); hearers understood (Virt. 217).

[84] Mut. 123; Mos. I, 277; Gig. 24, 55; Fug. 186-88.

[85] "But he made...Abraham also to be typical...For Abraham, being interpreted means 'Father of a great multitude'"(Leg. All. III, 83); see also Leg. All. III, 203, 228; Abr. 273; Mut. 201; Virt. 212-219; Quis Her. 90-92; Mig. 44. Samuel Sandmel claims that Philo made a distinction between the literal Abraham who was the historical character of the simple biblical account and the allegorical Abraham who abandoned pantheistic materialism and went on to perceive the true God (Philo's Place in Judaism, pp. 96-7).

about Abraham on Gen. 26:5.[86] Philo recognized that the codified Jewish Law had not been written but, nevertheless, reads a reference to the Law into the text of Gen. 26:5 and portrays Moses praising Abraham for obeying it without flaw.[87] But not only did Abraham obey the Law but he himself was "a law and an unwritten statute."[88] Abraham was a paradigm for all proselytes and the manner in which he lived his life was regarded as the standard of virtue for all.

In *Virt.* 212-219, Philo provides a description of the process by which Abraham came to a monotheistic worship of God and how he came to be seen as one who obeyed the Law impeccably and manifested all the virtues in his life. Abraham's Chaldaean influence was considered an impediment and human reason alone was insufficient to perceive knowledge of the one true God.[89] However, under the influence of the Spirit's inspiration (τοῦ θείου πνεύματος, ὅπερ ἄνωθεν καταπνευσθέν),[90] he was transformed into another human being with noteworthy attributes:

> Indeed, they continued to treat him with a respect which subjects pay to a ruler, being awe-struck at the all-embracing greatness of his nature and its more than human perfection. For the society also which he sought was not the same as they sought, but oftener under inspiration another more august. Thus whenever he was possessed (ὁπότε κατασχεθείη), everything in him changed to something better, eyes, complexion, stature, carriage, movements, voice. For the divine spirit was breathed upon him from on high (τοῦ θείου πνεύματος, ὅπερ ἄνωθεν), made its lodging in his soul, and invested his body with singular beauty, his voice with persuasiveness, and his hearers with understanding.[91]

---

[86] *Abr.* 275: "Abraham went as the Lord commanded him...entering into the path of virtue...remembering his commandments...God is represented in another passage as saying, 'Abraham has kept all my law.'" In a manner similar to Philo, the rabbis use Gen. 26:5 to prove that Abraham observed the whole Torah (*Qidd.* 82a) or both the Torah and the words of the Scribes (*Tos. Qidd.* V).

[87] Sandmel contends that Philo refers to "the law of nature" in *Abr.* 275, most likely based upon the words τῇ φύσει σπουδάσας ὑγιαινούσαις (*Philo's Place in Judaism*, p. 141, footnote 202). But the use of the singular νόμος and the definite article in the designations τὸν θεῖον νόμον καὶ τὰ θεῖα προστάγματα indicates that this refers more specifically to the Jewish Law given by Moses superimposed into the interpretation of Gen. 26:5 by Philo. The use of the singular ὁ νόμος is not found in the LXX version of Gen. 26:5, indicating that Philo read a reference to the Jewish Law into this OT text.

[88] νόμος αὐτός ὤν καὶ θεσμὸς ἄγραφος (*Abr.* 276).

[89] *Virt.* 212-213.

[90] *Virt.* 217.

[91] *Virt.* 217.

This coincides with what is said in *Abr.* 275 (quoted above) when Philo speaks of Abraham as one who "did the divine law and the divine commands." Even though he does not explicitly mention τὸ πνεῦμα in the context, Philo states that Abraham's impetus to keep the Law came from an "untainted impulse [that] led him" (ἀνόσοις ὁρμαῖς ἐπακολουθῆσαι).[92] This makes some correlation with the idea of Spirit possession in *Virt.* 217. Abraham's virtue and "greatness of soul"[93] includes a description not only of exceptional external beauty (eyes, complexion, stature, carriage, movements, voice) but also inward beauty, the excellence of character expressed in the acquisition of virtues (greatness of nature, human perfection)[94] and obedience of the Law: "Perception of these truths and divine inspiration (ἐπιθειάσας) induced him to leave his native country...knowing that if he stayed the delusions of the polytheistic creed[95] would stay within him..."[96] Therefore, the unique characteristic of Philo's description of Abraham is the attribution of his unprecedented observance of the Law, moral transformation and virtuous perfection to the Spirit; it did not come by human striving.

This same pattern of Spirit-inspiration, which results in a dramatic transformation in character, is evident in Philo's description of the lives of Moses and the seventy elders.[97] Philo considered Moses to be king, Lawgiver and High Priest *par excellence*,[98] but also "a prophet of the highest quality."[99] Under normal circumstances, Moses could not have aspired to be the Lawgiver and Prophet that he was without divine inspiration. His human

---

[92] ὁρμή is defined as "a psychological state of strong tendency, *impulse, inclination, desire*" (BDB, p. 724); it is used in Philo to refer to the idea of pursuing, even in opposition to reason or nature (Georg Bertram, "ὁρμή, κτλ.," *TDNT*, Vol. V, pp. 467-74, esp. p. 468).

[93] *Virt.* 216.

[94] "And having gained faith, the most sure and certain of the virtues, he gained with it all the other virtues...not because of the outward state which surrounded him, mere commoner that he was, but because of his greatness of soul, for his spirit was the spirit of a king" (*Virt.* 216-17).

[95] Cf. "You shall have no other gods before me" (Exod. 20:2).

[96] This corresponds to the Greco-Roman ideal of beauty, where inward beauty complements external beauty (cf. Plato in *Resp.* 3.402D and 7.535A) (Levison, "Inspiration and the Divine Spirit," 314-5).

[97] Philo writes of Caleb (Numb. 14:24): "And Caleb himself was changed wholly and entirely; for as the scripture says, 'a new spirit was in him;' as if the dominant part in him had been changed into complete perfection; for the name Caleb, being interpreted, means 'the whole heart'" (*Mut.* 123).

[98] "Moses was the best of kings, of lawgivers and of high priests..." (*Mos.* II, 187).

[99] *Mos.* II, 188.

mind "could not have made so straight an aim[100] if there was not also the divine spirit (θεῖον πνεῦμα) guiding it to the truth itself."[101] In their "forgetfulness of the true God," the Israelites made a golden calf. It is said of Moses that he was "cut to the heart...He therefore became another man, changed both in outward appearance and mind; and, filled with the Spirit (ἐπιθειάσας), he cried: 'Who is there who has no part with this delusion nor has given to no-lords the name of lordship? Let all such come to me.'"[102] Through Spirit-inspiration, Moses became acutely cognizant of God's Law and initiated judgment upon those involved in the idolatrous act. One of the distinctive features of Moses' function as a legislator was to be able to command between "what should be done and forbid what should not be done" and as a prophet "declare by inspiration what cannot be apprehended by reason."[103] This coincides with Gig. 55, where it is said of Moses, "He then has ever the divine spirit at his side, taking the lead in every journey of righteousness." Elsewhere we read that the "spirit of Moses," which came upon the seventy elders, distinguished them from the other Israelites by uniquely guiding them into the "real truth" and "wisdom."[104] In Fug. 186, Philo again refers to the Spirit's infilling of the seventy elders but this time explicitly associated with specific virtues (187-88). The seventy elders are analogous to the seventy palm trees by the fountains, which are the fountains of instruction that lead to a virtuous life based upon the Mosaic Law (177-204).[105]

---

[100] The words εὐσκόπως εὐθυβόλησεν in Mos. II, 265, are translated as "such correct and felicitous conjectures" by C.D. Yonge (The Works of Philo, p. 515).

[101] Mos. II, 265.

[102] Mos. II, 271-2.

[103] Mos. II, 187; see also Praem. 53, 55, where Moses' office as a Lawgiver was inextricably connected with his gift of prophecy. Moses is described as a leader in the possession of piety and righteousness and as a Lawgiver and King he would discern between right and wrong. But most significant is that it was the "gift of prophecy" that was given to him "to ensure him against stumbling."

[104] Gig. 24.

[105] Philo's Fug. 177-204 makes consistent references to the Decalogue and its various application in Jewish life both in the literal and allegorical senses: e.g., Lev. 20:18 in 188-191; Lev. 18:7 in 193; Gen. 24:15 in 194-5; Gen. 14:7 in 196; Jer. 2:13 in 197-201.

1.4 Flavius Josephus[106]

Josephus claims that he was born and brought up in Jerusalem.[107] If asked about the various components of the Jewish Law, according to his own words, he would be able to repeat them all the more readily than his own name.[108] He claims that the chief priests and the leading men of Jerusalem would constantly consult him from the time he was a young man of 14 years of age.[109] Every week Jews (including Josephus) assembled to listen to a portion of the Law.[110] But surprisingly, in his biblical explication of the covenantal promises, Josephus never uses the word διαθήκη to translate the Hebrew word בְּרִית[111] because he was consciously shifting the emphasis from the covenantal land of Israel to the biblical personalities themselves and to the role of the Diaspora. It would have appeared treasonous to the Romans had he stressed Jewish possession of the land of Palestine.[112]

Josephus employs the word πνεῦμα 34 times in his extant writings,[113] referring to wind and breath,[114] but is reluctant to use the term in an anthropological sense ("human spirit").[115] When πνεῦμα refers to God, he

---

[106] Josephus' earliest writing is his account of the *Jewish War* (ca. 79-81 C.E.) (Louis H. Feldman, *Josephus's Interpretation of the Bible* [Berkeley: University of California Press, 1998], p. 132; see also Wm. Whiston, *The Complete Works of Josephus* [Grand Rapids: Kregel Publications, 1981], p. 427, footnote *). He died sometime after 100 C.E. (William S. LaSor, "Forward," *The Complete Works of Josephus*, pp. vii-xii, esp. p. vii). It is most likely that he wrote from Rome under the patronage of the Roman emperor in the wake of the disaster of the Jewish revolt of 66-74 C.E.

[107] *Life* VII-VIII. All citations from Josephus (English and Greek) are from H.J. Thackeray and R. Marcus (eds.), *Josephus with an English Translation*, 9 Vols, LCL (London: W. Heinemann, 1926-65).

[108] *Ag. Ap.* II, 178.

[109] *Life* IX.

[110] *Ag. Ap.* II, 175.

[111] See *Ant.* I, 157, which corresponds to Gen. 12:7, where the promise of the inheritance of land to Abraham's descendants is completely omitted; see also *Ant.* I, 170, which parallels Gen. 13:14-18, *Ant.* I, 184, which parallels Gen. 15:18, *Ant.* I, 193, which parallels Gen. 17:19-21 (Feldman, *Josephus's Interpretation of the Bible*, p. 154).

[112] Feldman, *Josephus's Interpretation of the Bible*, p. 154; B.H. Amaru, "Land Theology in Josephus' *Jewish Antiquities*," *JQR* 71 (1980-1), 210-29.

[113] Karl Heinrich Rengstorf, *A Complete Concordance to Flavius Josephus* Vol. III (Λ-Π) (Leiden: E.J. Brill, 1979), pp. 434-5.

[114] E.g., *Ant.* III, 291; XI, 240; XVII, 169.

[115] Josephus usually substitutes the word ψυχή with the word πνεῦμα when reference is made to "human spirit" (Best, "The Use and Non-Use of Pneuma by Josephus," 219-20).

prefers the designation τὸ θεῖον πνεῦμα[116] rather than τὸ πνεῦμα τοῦ θεοῦ.[117] It is this idea of "the divine Spirit" that concerns us in this study. Josephus always associates the "divine Spirit" with prophecy or prophets.[118] Consequently, we must look more closely at the phenomenon of prophecy or the function of a prophet to determine his thoughts on the Spirit's relationship to the Law. If Josephus describes the prophets, who are under the compulsion of the Spirit, speaking against acts that violate the various conditions set forth in the Torah, then it can be said that Josephus perceived the Spirit's function to be one of advocating a Torah-based ethic.

Louis H. Feldman cites 169 instances where Josephus deliberately introduced the word προφήτης or the verb προφητεύειν where it is not to be found in the original biblical text.[119] This makes it clear that Josephus had a fascination with the activities of the prophets and Spirit-inspiration.[120] In fact, he himself claimed to have been inspired and have the powers of prediction.[121] The prophet is actually possessed by God. For example, in Balaam's defence to Balak, he asks, "Have you reflected on the whole matter and do you think that it rests with us at all to be silent or to speak on such themes as these, when *we are possessed by the spirit of God?* For that spirit gives utterance to such language and words as it will, so that *we are all unconscious.*"[122] Josephus describes this experience as transcending human reason.[123] Prophets are individuals who are excellent not only in their speech but also in character.[124] Even though Josephus equated the return from Babylon with the cessation of prophecy (i.e,

---

[116] See Ant. IV, 108, 118; VI, 166, 222; VIII, 408; X, 239.

[117] Ant. IV, 119.

[118] See Ant. IV, 108, 118, 119; VI, 166, 222, 223; VIII, 408; X, 239.

[119] Louis H. Feldman, "Prophets and Prophecy in Josephus," JTS 41 (1990), 388-422, esp. 389-91.

[120] See Ant. IV, 329, where Josephus describes the utterances of Moses, the greatest prophet of all, as the very speech of God Himself.

[121] Josephus joined the ranks of the Pharisees, who were said to have the gift of foreknowledge (Ant. XVII, 43 cf. IV, 174-5). In addition, he looked upon himself as a latter-day Jeremiah (War V, 391-2); he noted the parallel between the prophets' prediction of the first destruction of the Temple and his own prediction of the destruction of the second Temple. Josephus also foretold that Vespasian would become emperor (War III, 400-2).

[122] Ant. IV, 119-20.

[123] Ant. VI, 223 ("Saul, losing his reason under the impulse of that mighty spirit...").

[124] Ant. VIII, 244.

the prophetic inspiration associated with the composition of biblical books),[125] he does perceive a degree of prophetic inspiration that continues during his time that coincides with the type demonstrated by the biblical prophets.[126] While it is true that Josephus never calls himself a "prophet," he did regard himself as a successor to the prophet-historians of the OT.[127]

Surprisingly, Josephus places more emphasis on prophets as historians and predictors of the future[128] than prophets as moralizers, whose primary task was to encourage the observance of the Law. This is mainly because of the historical situation; his audience preferred to have a historical account that emphasized political and military matters rather than deal with ethical issues.[129] As we shall see this does not mean that Josephus was not aware of the function of prophets as advocates of moral renewal and promoters of a Torah based-ethic.[130] In fact, Josephus stands in continuity with the attitude of Israel's prophets towards the Torah. That is, prophetic preaching recognizes not only the Torah but also its very basis; to reject the Torah is apostasy from Yahweh.[131]

In the editorial comments on 1 Kgs. 11:11, Josephus introduces a "prophet sent by God" rather than, as in the OT, God Himself, who warns King Solomon that his unlawful practices would be punished.[132] It is said by

---

[125] See *Ag. Ap.* I, 41; for secondary literature see Best, "The Use and Non-Use of Pneuma by Josephus," 224; Chevallier, *Souffle de Dieu*, p. 73, Bieder, "πνεῦμα," *TDNT* Vol. VI, p. 375.

[126] See *War* VI ("Numerous prophets [προφῆται], indeed, were at this period suborned by the tyrants to delude the people, by bidding them await help from God..."); *Ant.* I, 240-1 ("Cleodemus the prophet [ὁ προφήτης], also called Malchus...")

[127] D.E. Aune, "The Use of ΠΡΟΦΗΤΗΣ in Josephus," *JBL* 101/3 (1982), 419-21, esp. 420-1; J. Blenkinsopp, "Prophecy and Priesthood," *JJS* 25 (1974), 241-2.

[128] *Ant.* IV, 303; V, 351; VIII, 418-9; IX, 145.

[129] "Josephus alludes amazingly little to the biblical account about the prophets as moralizers, but this is presumably because his audience preferred to have his history stress political and military rather than ethical issues" (Feldman, "Prophets and Prophecy in Josephus," 395).

[130] Wenk dismisses Josephus as one who makes no contribution to the subject of the Spirit and ethical renewal, and therefore, does not address Josephus at all in his investigation (*Community-Forming Power*, p. 84). However, as we shall note below, Josephus perceived the prophets to be under the compulsion of the Spirit and promoting behaviour that complies with the precepts of the Jewish Torah.

[131] W. Gutbrod, "B. The Law in the Old Testament," (esp. "The Attitude of the Prophets towards the Law" [pp. 1039-40]) *TDNT* Vol. IV, pp. 1036-91.

[132] *Ant.* VIII, 197 cf. *Ant.* VII, 72, 294, where Josephus introduces a prophet and the OT represents God directly speaking to an individual.

Josephus that Solomon "married many [women] from foreign nations...thereby transgressing the laws of Moses who forbade marriage with persons of other races,[133] and he began to worship their gods[134] to gratify his wives and his passion for them."[135] In *Ant.* VIII, 197, the prophet's specific function was to denounce Solomon's "unlawful acts (παρανομήμασι)" and warn him that he will soon be punished for his violations of the Law ("he should not long continue in his course with impunity").

Again, in other supplements to the OT stories, Josephus on three occasions emphasizes how the prophets admonished the Jews to obey the Torah and warned that if they did not comply they would suffer the consequences. Josephus elaborates upon the story of 2 Chron. 30:1, where Hezekiah the king invites all his subjects to celebrate the festival of Unleavened Bread, which had not been observed because of the "lawless action (παρανομίας)" of the previous kings.[136] Furthermore, he invites the people to "return to their ancient custom and reverence God."[137] It is said that the "prophets" also exhorted the people in the same manner as Hezekiah and foretold what "they would suffer if they did not alter their course to one of piety toward God."[138] In response, people of the tribes of Manasseh, Zebulun and Issachar listened to the prophets and "the priest performed all things in accordance with the law"[139] and "the city also they purified of all pollution from idols."[140]

Josephus' explanation for the dissolution of the ten tribes of Israel was as follows: "To such an end (exile), then, did the Israelites come because they violated the laws and disregarded the prophets who foretold that this misfortune would overtake them if they did not cease from their impious actions."[141] With respect to the other two tribes of Israel, Josephus describes Josiah's fear of exile since they also had "transgressed against the laws of Moses" like their forefathers[142] and subsequently, consulted the prophetess

---

[133] Exod. 34:16; Deut. 7:3; 23:3.

[134] Exod. 20:4f.

[135] *Ant.* VIII, 191-2; see also 195, where Solomon is said to have "sinned and [gone] astray in the observance of the laws."

[136] *Ant.* IX, 263.

[137] *Ant.* IX, 264.

[138] *Ant.* IX, 265-6.

[139] *Ant.* IX, 270.

[140] *Ant.* IX, 273.

[141] *Ant.* IX, 281.

[142] *Ant.* X, 59.

Oolda.[143] The prophetess responded by saying that because they had violated the Law and had not repented, they would be punished, but that these calamities would be put off until after Josiah's death because he was a righteous man. When Josiah heard these words, Josiah initiated moral and spiritual renewal among the people; "he compelled them to take an oath and pledge that they would truly worship God and keep the laws of Moses."[144]

In summary, it was because of the historical circumstances that Josephus did not dwell extensively on moral and ethical issues as described in the Jewish covenants. However, this did not mean that he was ignorant of Ancient Israel's emphasis on the Spirit's work in inspiring the prophets to warn against the consequences of violating the Jewish Law. In his editorial comments on various scriptural texts Josephus indicates that through the prophet, the divine Spirit initiated a Torah-based ethic and in some instances, this led to moral and ethical renewal.

1.5 Summary

In Diaspora literature there is widespread attestation of the Spirit's role in the formation of a Torah-based ethic, and in some situations, evidence of the Spirit as the agent of covenant renewal. The Spirit is equated with wisdom (Wisdom of Solomon, *Joseph and Aseneth*, Philo), which is not acquired through learning or practice but is perceived as an external force that fashions and transforms human behaviour to comply with the Jewish Law. In the phenomenon of prophetic inspiration (Philo, Josephus), the Spirit has an ethical, transforming effect upon one's character; i.e., individuals become the essence of virtue and perfection, quintessential characters who obey the Jewish Law. Prophetic preaching recognizes not only the Torah but also its very basis that to reject the Torah is apostasy from Yahweh. The importance of abiding by the Jewish Torah is particularly evident in the stories of Joseph and Aseneth and Philo's interpretation of the life of Abraham in that even though the actual giving of the Law postdates the narrative setting of the story, the authors interpret the behaviour of the characters in the story in light of the various precepts of the Jewish Law.

---

[143] Ant. X, 60–1. This corresponds to 2 Kgs. 22:11 and 2 Chron. 34:19, where Josiah consults the prophetess Huldah.

[144] Ant. X, 63.

2. Palestinian Literature

The sources examined in this section include Jewish writings located in Palestine, most of which were originally written in a Semitic language. Similar to the previous section, this survey will be arranged in chronological order except for the last section (2.5 Israel's Leaders: Anointed with the Spirit and Advocates of the Law), which will focus upon the subject of Israel's leadership and will discuss various texts from different time periods. This survey will be restricted to those texts that specifically establish a relationship between the Spirit and Law in an eschatological context or contexts that address the Spirit as the agent of covenant and moral renewal, where the Law itself functions as the standard of behaviour. Since Paul demonstrates a proclivity towards boasting about his Jewish pedigree,[145] it is most likely that Jewish literature produced in Palestine would have exercised a significant amount of influence upon his thinking.

2.1 The Wisdom of Ben Sira[146]

Ben Sira's purpose was to bolster the faith and confidence of Jews by demonstrating that true wisdom is to be found in the inspired books of Israel.[147] A central part of Israel's literature was the Law. Consequently, he pronounced woe to those who renounced Israel's Law ("Woe to you, the ungodly, who have forsaken the Law of the Most High God [νόμον θεοῦ ὑψίστου], Sir. 41:8). Νόμος is used approximately 30 times in reference to the Mosaic Law.[148] This frequency of usage itself indicates that the Law is of particular interest to Ben Sira; it formed the very basis of his life and

---

[145] See discussion above (Introduction to Part One).

[146] The Wisdom of Ben Sira (or "Sirach") was originally written in Hebrew and later translated into Greek (see the Prologue to the Greek translation in the LXX). It was composed by Jeshua b. Eleazar b. Sira, ca. 180 B.C.E. in Jerusalem and later translated into Greek by his grandson in Alexandria after 132 B.C.E. (Patrick W. Skehan and Alexander A. DiLella, *The Wisdom of Ben Sira: A New Translation with Notes* AB Vol. 39 [New York: Doubleday, 1987], pp. 3, 8–16, 51; Schnabel, *Law and Wisdom from Ben Sira to Paul*, p. 8; G.W.E. Nickelsburg, *Jewish Literature Between the Bible and the Mishnah: A Historical and Literary Introduction* [London: SCM, 1981], pp. 55, 64).

[147] Skehan and DiLella, *The Wisdom of Ben Sira*, p. 16.

[148] E. Hatch and H.A. Redpath, *A Concordance to the Septuagint and other Greek Versions of the Old Testament (including the Apocryphal Books)* Vol. II (Oxford: Clarendon Press, 1897), p. 948.

thought.[149] The Law is associated with wisdom in that the Law is the locus of wisdom.[150] The majority of passages that correlate wisdom and Law have an ethical connotation; both wisdom and Law lead to "the fear of the Lord."[151] Piety characterizes the wise person who keeps the commandments.[152] Those who obey the commandments are said to act "wisely" and this leads to "wise" results.[153]

Interrelated with wisdom and Law is the Spirit. Sir. 39:6 reads, "If the great Lord is willing, he will be filled with the spirit of understanding (πνεύματι συνέσεως); he will pour forth words of wisdom of his own and give thanks to the Lord in prayer."[154] The term πνεύματι συνέσεως refers to the understanding that comes from the Spirit of God. The collocation of πνεῦμα with σύνεσις finds precedence in the LXX with reference to wisdom imparted by the Spirit of God.[155] Personal diligence and perseverance in study are insufficient to make the scribe truly wise; spiritual inspiration is the means by which wisdom is achieved.[156] Every human being has been created with

---

[149] Surprisingly, G. von Rad claims that "the Torah is not a subject of particular interest to Sirach" because it plays a secondary role to his wisdom teaching (*Wisdom in Israel* [trans. J.D. Martin; London: SCM, 1972], p. 247). Schnabel, on the other hand, demonstrates the importance of the Mosaic Law for Ben Sira. Ben Sira associates the Law with traditional wisdom material (Sir. 1:5, 26; 19:17, 20, 24; 24:23; 32:14-18, 22-23); i.e., the Law is the basis of the sage's thoughts when he comments on the concepts of the fear of the Lord, the destiny of humans, creation, and wisdom (*Law and Wisdom from Ben Sira to Paul*, p. 30).

[150] See Sir. 1:26; 3:22; 6:37; 15:1; 19:20; 21:11; 24:23; 33:3; 34:7ff.; see secondary source Eissfeldt, *Einleitung in das Alte Testament*, p. 811.

[151] Sir. 2:15, 16; 51:15 cf. Prol. 12-14, 29, 35-36.

[152] Sir. 15:1, 15.

[153] Sir. 24:22; 32:23; 33:2, 3; 44:20; 34:8.

[154] Another possible reference to the Spirit's role in covenant renewal is Sir. 48:12, where it is said that "Elisha was filled with his spirit" ('Ελισαιὲ ἐνεπλήσθη πνεύματος αὐτοῦ)(cf. 2 Kgs. 2:9-10). It is not certain whether this refers to Elijah's spirit or God's Spirit. If it implies a reference to God's Spirit then the following verses indicate that Elisha's ministry and miracles were a result of the Spirit of God within him (Sir. 48:14 ["He did wonders in his life, and at his death were his works marvellous."]), whose aim was to effect a renewed obedience in Israel towards the Law and thus restore faithfulness to the covenant (Sir. 48:15 ["In all of this the people did not repent, neither did they depart from their sins..."]).

[155] Exod. 31:3; Deut. 34:9; Isa. 11:2.

[156] The "spirit of understanding" is a "*gelegentliches donum superadditum*" (G. Maier, *Mensch und freier Wille: Nach den jüdischen Religionsparteien zwischen Ben Sira und Paulus* WUNT 12 [Tübingen: J.C.B. Mohr (Paul Siebeck), 1971], p. 37; see also H. Stadelmann, *Ben Sira als Schriftgelehrter: Eine Untersuchung zum Berufsbild des vormakkabäischen Sofer unter Berücksichtigung seines*

"insight of understanding (ἐπιστήμη συνέσεως)"[157] but the Lord imparts the unique "spirit of understanding" to some scribes.[158] Commenting on this verse, J.A. Davis claims that "the quest for wisdom is only brought to fulfillment and completion by entrance of a 'spirit of understanding,' that is, by an experience of divine, spiritual inspiration...the wise man is set apart for the scribe by the experience of spiritual inspiration described in Sir. 39.6."[159] The consequence of receiving the "spirit of understanding" is that the scribe is enabled to engage in a threefold activity as expressed in 39:6-8. One of these is that "he will show the wisdom of what he has learned, and will glory in the Law of the Lord's covenant (νόμῳ διαθήκης κυρίου)" (v.8). Literally, the verb is translated "he will boast (καυχήσεται) in the Law." The idea that knowledge and observance of the Law is the basis for boasting is one of the unique contributions of Ben Sira.[160] This is later echoed in rabbinical literature.[161] The Law is also closely identified with the "covenant."[162] In Sir. 24:23, βίβλος διαθήκης is equated with νόμον ὃν ἐνετείλατο Μωυσῆς. This means that the Spirit not only transforms the scribe into a sage, but this individual's wisdom is expressed in a tangible way by obeying the Law because he has acquired a renewed sense of covenantal relationship.[163] The sage is an example of one who "fears the Lord" and obeys the Law.[164] Furthermore, his transforming experience of the Spirit equips him to "teach others how to

---

Verhältnisses zu Priester-Propheten- und Weisheitslehrertum WUNT 2.6 [Tübingen: J.C.B. Mohr (Paul Siebeck), 1980], p. 234).

[157] Sir. 17:7.

[158] Note the introductory, "if the great Lord is willing (ἐὰν κύριος ὁ μέγας θελήσῃ)" in Sir. 39:6.

[159] Davis, Wisdom and Spirit, pp. 20-1.

[160] See Sir. 24:1ff, esp. v.8.

[161] R. Bultmann, "καυχάομαι, κτλ.," TDNT Vol. III, pp. 645-54, esp. p. 647.

[162] Cf. Sir. 24:23; 28:7; 38:33; 41:19; 42:2, where Law and covenant are closely associated.

[163] Wenk, Community-Forming Power, p.67; compare with Menzies, who posits a distinction between ethics associated with the normal study and practice of the Mosaic Law, and knowledge conveyed through Spirit-inspiration (The Development of Early Christian Pneumatology, p. 70). However, Sir. 39:8 read in light of 39:6 communicates the idea that one of the effects of Spirit-inspiration is character transformation that results in an acute awareness of the ethical requirements in the Mosaic Law. In other words, one should not interpret Ben Sira's conception of Spirit too restrictively as prophetic inspiration that excludes the Spirit's role in fostering Law-obedience and covenantal renewal.

[164] Sir. 2:15-16.

acquire wisdom and to glory in the Law as he does (39:8 cf. 42:2a)."[165] The Spirit is the agency by which the wise one will, in turn, nurture and foster obedience to the Mosaic Law among God's people.

2.2 *Book of Jubilees*[166]

The *Book of Jubilees* is an elaboration of the account in Exod. 24:18, where it is said that Moses spent forty days on Mount Sinai. The content of *Jubilees* focuses upon the revelation God gives to Moses of the apostasy and ultimate restoration of his people (ch.1) and the primeval history of humanity and the subsequent history of God's chosen people until the time of Moses (chs. 2-50). Eschatology plays an important role in *Jubilees*. In fact, there are three passages whose specific function is to teach matters of eschatology: 1:4b-26, 27-28; 23:14-31.[167] Of particular significance for this investigation is 1:23-25. These verses are set within a plea for God not to forsake Israel. Moses is horrified at the forecast of the exile; Israel will incur the wrath of God because she has not kept the covenant and the commandments of the Law.[168] He cries out for God to have mercy ("O Lord, my God, do not abandon your people...do not deliver them into the hand of their enemy...O Lord, let your mercy be lifted up upon your people," [*Jub.* 1:19-20]). As a result, God's reply of restoration comes in vv.23-24:

> But after this they will return to me in all uprightness and with all of (their) heart and soul. And I shall cut off the foreskin of their heart and the foreskin of the heart of their descendants. And I shall create for them a holy spirit, and shall purify them

---

[165] See Sir. 4:11-19; 6:18-37; 39:13 and Skehan and DiLella, *The Wisdom of Ben Sira*, p. 452.

[166] The author of Jubilees was a Jew who lived and composed his writing in the Hebrew language in Palestine between 161-140 B.C.E. (O.S. Wintermute, "Jubilees: A New Translation and Introduction," *OTP* Vol. II, pp. 43-45; see also J.C. VanderKam, *Textual and Historical Studies in the Book of Jubilees* Harvard Semitic Museum, Harvard Semitic Monograph 14 [Missoula, Montana: Scholars Press, 1977], p. 283). Although Hebrew was the original language of the book, there are only fragments of some twelve Greek manuscripts of Jubilees. The only complete version of the book is written in Ethiopic (J.C. VanderKam, "The Book of Jubilees," in *Outside the Old Testament* [ed. M. De Jonge; Cambridge: Cambridge University Press, 1985], p. 112; Wintermute, "Jubilees," p. 42).

[167] Gene L. Davenport, *The Eschatology of the Book of Jubilees* (Leiden: E.J. Brill, 1971), p.19.

[168] "And they will serve their gods, and they will become a scandal for them and an affliction and a torment and a snare. And they have forsaken my ordinances and my commandments and the feasts of my covenant and my Sabbaths ...and they will forget all of my laws and all of my commandments..." (*Jub.* 1:10-14 cf. 15:34).

so that they will not turn away from following me from that day and forever. And their souls will cleave to me and to all my commandments. And they will do my commandments. And I shall be a father to them, and they will be sons to me.

Regarding the Law, it is said that Israel will "cleave...to all of my commandments," because God will have created both the desire ("And I shall cut off the foreskin of their heart and the foreskin of the heart of their descendants") and the ability to keep it. This alludes to Jer. 31 (38 LXX):33,[169] where the new covenant relationship is characterized by the manner in which Israel receives the Law (נָתַתִּי אֶת־תּוֹרָתִי בְּקִרְבָּם וְעַל־לִבָּם אֶכְתֲּבֶנָּה cf. διδοὺς δώσω νόμους μου εἰς τὴν διάνοιαν αὐτῶν, καὶ ἐπὶ καρδίας αὐτῶν γράψω αὐτούς).[170] In the future the Law would be placed within them and there will be a change of inward disposition. The reference to "cut[ting] off the foreskin of their heart" in Jub. 1:23 is equivalent to Jer. 31:33, where it refers to a transformation of motives. Indeed, their motives will be transformed to the extent that they will never rebel again (Jub. 1:23-24). In addition, Jub. 1:24 picks up the theme of familial intimacy as a unique description of the renewed covenant relationship ("And I shall be a father to them, and they shall be sons to me" cf. Jer. 31:33).

Jub. 1:23 also mentions the means by which Israel is transformed within her inner disposition: "I shall create for them a holy spirit,[171] and I shall purify them." The "holy spirit" to be "created" is best understood as "the sphere of God's power for righteousness."[172] This should not be taken in an anthropological sense to denote "the human spirit," since the context makes it clear that the "spirit" spoken of in Jub. 1:23 is contrasted with "the spirit of

---

[169] See other allusions to Jer. 31 (38 LXX):31-34 in Jub. 1:15-17; 2:19-20; see Thielman (From Plight to Solution, p. 42) and Wenk (Community-Forming Power, p. 79, footnote 34) who claim Jub. 1:20-25 refers to Jer. 31; "He makes use of expressions and data familiar from Kings, Isaiah, Jeremiah, Ezekiel, and several of the twelve minor prophets" (Wintermute, "Jubilees," p. 48)

[170] Davenport notes the lack of parallel language between Jub. 1:23-24 and Jer. 31 (38 LXX):31-34; nothing is said in Jubilees about the Law being written on the heart (The Eschatology of the Book of Jubilees, p. 27). But this dissimilarity seems arbitrary in light of the corresponding meaning of "circumcised hearts" (Jub. 1:23). Davenport readily admits that "the circumcised foreskin of the heart means transformed motives" (Ibid., p. 27).

[171] The use of the adjective "holy" to describe the Spirit and the lack of a syntactical indication of possession referring to humans (e.g., "God aroused the holy spirit of a lad [emphasis added] named Daniel" [Theodotian's version of Susanna 45]) makes it probable that the author of Jubilees intended a reference to the Spirit of God.

[172] Turner, Power From on High, p. 128, footnote 32.

Beliar" (Jub. 1:20).[173] This means that the author intended "Spirit" to be interpreted in a cosmic sense opposing the spirit of Beliar in the world. Reference to the "holy Spirit" and surrounding ideas makes it clear that the author alludes to Ezek. 36:25-27. Ezek. 36:27 (MT, בְּקִרְבְּכֶם אֶתֵּן רוּחִי וְאֶת /LXX, Καὶ τὸ πνεῦμα μου δώσω ἐν ὑμῖν) presents an objective force which makes Yahweh an active participant in Israel's new phase of obedience to his covenant. It is the infusion of Yahweh's Spirit that brings new and unique strength for this obedience. Jub. 1:23 also associates the Spirit's work with purification (cf. Ezek. 36:25, where it describes "newness" and renewal when Yahweh will sprinkle them [זרק; LXX, ῥανῶ] with clean water, which is figurative and represents a ritual act of cultic purification). In summation, the author of Jubilees clings to the eschatological promises of Jer. 31 (38 LXX):31-34 conflated with Ezek. 36:25-27 to emphasize a future time when Israel will experience a transformation in her disposition by means of the Spirit, and this will result in covenant renewal and a new sense of obedience to the Law.

2.3 Testament of the Twelve Patriarchs

The Testament of the Twelve Patriarchs is composed of the final speeches of the sons of Jacob, modeled upon Jacob's last words in Gen. 49. Prior to his death, each son gathers his offspring and reflects on his life, confessing his misdeeds, offering words of exhortation to his family to avoid sins, and concluding with predictions of Israel.[174] Almost without exception the patriarchs'

---

[173] The "spirit of Beliar" came to designate a demonic power, Satan (Wintermute, "Jubilees," p. 53, footnote h).

[174] There is no consensus on the provenance, date, and compositional history of the Testament of the Twelve Patriarchs. R.H. Charles contends for Palestine as the place of writing with Hebrew as the original language, written during the reign of John Hyrcanus ca. 137-107 B.C.E., but with later Greek translations and Christian interpolations (The Apocrypha and Pseudepigrapha of the Old Testament in English Vol. II [Oxford: Clarendon Press, 1913], pp. 282ff; see also J. Becker, Untersuchungen zur Entstehungsgeschichte der Testamente der Zwölf Patriarchen [Leiden: E.J. Brill, 1970]; J.H. Ulrichsen, Die Grundschrift der Testamente der Zwölf Patriarchen: Eine Untersuchung zu Umfang, Inhalt und Eigenart der ursprünglichen Schrift Acta Universitatis Upsaliensis, Historia Religionum, 10 [Uppsala: Almqvist & Wiksell, 1991]). Others advocate an author who wrote from Syria in Greek about 150 B.C.E. but drew upon a free tradition, with Hebrew and Aramaic testaments serving as models (H.C. Kee, "Testament of the Twelve Patriarchs: A New Translation and Introduction," OTP Vol.I [New York: Doubleday, 1983], p.777-8). Still others argue for a Christian redaction in its last stage of completion ca. second century C.E. (M. de Jonge, "Christian Influence in the Testament of the Twelve Patriarchs," NovT [1960], 182-235; J. Jervell, "Ein Interpolator interpretiert: Zu der christlichen Bearbeitung der Testamente der

autobiographical comments contain moral exhortation. Therefore, ethics are one of the *Testaments'* main themes.[175] It is true that this literature presents universal virtues strongly reminiscent of a Hellenistic society[176] such as: integrity,[177] piety,[178] honesty,[179] self-control,[180] etc. But it is also evident within these writings that the basis of ethics is the Jewish Law.[181] There is evidence of the Spirit's role in the formation of a Torah-based ethic.[182] It is to this phenomenon that we now turn our attention.

Apart from Issachar and Asher, all of the *Testaments* depict Joseph's exemplary role. His life and conduct is the model of one who observes the commandments of the Jewish Law. For example, in *T.Ben.* 3:1 we read, "Now,

---

zwölf Patriarchen," in *Studien ze den Testamenten der zwölf Patriarchen* [ed. W. Eltester; Berlin: Alfred Töpelmann, 1969], pp. 30-61). However, the *Testament of the Twelve Patriarchs* deserves to be included with Palestinian literature because of its similarity to some of the Qumran writings (see links between 1Q21; 4Q213-214b whose Aramaic text parallels parts of T. *Levi* 8-9; 11-14; 4Q215 parallels T. *Naph.* 1:11-12; 4Q538 parallels T. *Jud.* 12:11-12) and its unique Jewish emphases that indicate the influence of Jewish sources: 1. emphasis on the Levitical priesthood and messianology that cannot be harmonized with the early Christian movement, 2. the dualism between God and Beliar, 3. the calendar, 4, the issue of intermarriage (E. Ferguson, *Backgrounds of Early Christianity* [Grand Rapids: Eerdmans, 1987], p. 364; M.A. Elliott, *The Survivors of Israel: A Reconsideration of the Theology of Pre-Christian Judaism* [Grand Rapids: Eerdmans, 2000], pp. 419-24, 552-55).

[175] Robert A. Kugler, *The Testaments of the Twelve Patriarchs* (Sheffield: Sheffield Academic Press, 2001), p. 17; H.W. Hollander and M. De Jonge, *The Testament of the Twelve Patriarchs: A Commentary* (Leiden: E.J. Brill, 1985), p. 41.

[176] Kee sees virtues reminiscent of Stoicism ("Jubilees," p. 779); see also Kugler who identifies the moral teaching of the *Testaments* to comply with Hellenistic (Hellenistic-Jewish and Christian) ethical norms. This is in accordance with his claim for a second century C.E. date of completion for the composition of the *Testaments* (*Testament of the Twelve Patriarchs*, pp. 17, 36-38).

[177] *T.Sim.* 4:5; *T.Lev.* 13:1; *T.Iss.* 3:2; 4:8; 5:1; 7:8; *T.Jud.* 23:5. All citations from the *Testaments* are taken from the ET of Kee, "Testament of the Twelve Patriarchs," *OTP* Vol. I, 782-828.

[178] *T. Reub.* 6:4; *T.Iss.* 7:5; *T.Lev.* 16:2.

[179] *T. Dan.* 1:3.

[180] *T.Jos.* 4:1-2; 6:7; 9:2-3; 10:2-3.

[181] See *T.Zeb.* 10:2; *T.Ben.* 3:1; *T.Iss.* 7:6f.; *T. Dan.* 5:2f.; *T. Jud.* 26:1; *T. Jos.* 19:6; see also Hollander and De Jonge who state, "For the author of the Testaments God's law consists (almost) exclusively of ethical commandments" (*The Testament of the Twelve Patriarchs*, p. 43).

[182] There are a significant number of references to the Spirit (over 80) but not all of these refer to God's Spirit (e.g., "seven spirits of deceit," "the spirit of envy," "evil spirits," "spirit of error," [*T.Reub.* 2:2-8; *T.Sim.* 3:1; 4:9; *T.Jud.* 20:1; etc.]). Reference to the Spirit in *T.Levi* 18:11-12 (cf. Matt. 18:18; Rev. 22:2, 4, 19); *T.Jud.* 24:2-3 (baptism of Jesus); *T.Ben.* 9:3 (Matt. 27:51; Mk. 15:38; Lk.23:45) reflect a Christian interpolation and will not be included in this analysis.

my children, love the Lord God of heaven and earth; keep his commandments (φυλάξατε ἐντολὰς αὐτοῦ)[183]; pattern your life after the good and pious man Joseph." In this section of the last testament (T.Ben), the author sums up all the scattered statements concerning the qualities of Joseph. His crowning achievement as a "good and pious man" was the performance of the Law; he fears and loves God and keeps the commandments.[184] In T. Sim. 4:4, it refers to Joseph as "a good man, one who had within him the spirit of God (ἔχων πνεῦμα θεοῦ ἐν αὐτῷ), and being full of compassion and mercy he did not bear ill will toward me, but loved me as well as my brothers." In this case the "goodness" of Joseph appears to be traced back to the influence of the Spirit of God.[185] The generalized statements in T.Ben 8:1-3 confirm this: "he has no pollution in his heart because upon him is resting the spirit of God (ὅτι ἀναπαύεται ἐπ' αὐτὸν τὸ πνεῦμα τοῦ θεοῦ)."[186] The use of ὅτι in causal clauses ("because upon him is resting the spirit of God") reveals the reason for the assertion in the first clause ("he has no pollution in his heart").[187] It is also significant that "goodness," which is represented in both T.Ben. 3:1 and 8:1, is the result of the Spirit's work in Joseph's life, and is directly associated with keeping the Jewish Law (cf. T.Ben. 3:1 quoted above where the expression τὸν ἀγαθὸν καὶ ὅσιον ἄνδρα is placed in association with φυλάξατε ἐντολὰς αὐτοῦ). Putting these things together we can conclude that the Spirit has significant ethical import; the Spirit induces Joseph to abide by the Law and thus, he is said to be "a good man."

T.Lev. 2:3 and T.Jud. 20:1-5 affirm the idea that the Spirit is the agent of moral behaviour. The "spirit of understanding (πνεῦμα συνέσεως)"[188] came upon Levi and assisted him in perceiving "deceit," "sin," and "injustice"

---

[183] Greek quotations are from R.H. Charles, The Greek Versions of the Testaments of the Twelve Patriarchs (Oxford: Clarendon Press, 1966).

[184] Hollander and De Jonge, The Testament of the Twelve Patriarchs, p. 43.

[185] Erik Sjöberg, "πνεῦμα, κτλ.," TDNT Vol. VI, p. 384; Turner, Power From On High, p. 126.

[186] Cf. Isa. 11:2, where the same clause καὶ ἀναπαύσεται ἐπ' αὐτὸν πνεῦμα τοῦ θεοῦ is used in the context of a positive ethical influence upon a messianic figure. However, in T.Ben. 8:1-3 there is no indication of a messianic figure.

[187] See the explanation of "reason (cause)" (R.A. Young, Intermediate New Testament Greek: A Linguistic and Exegetical Approach [Nashville, TN: Broadman and Holman Publishers, 1994], p. 190)

[188] This coincides with Jos. Asen. 4:8, where it is said, "And Joseph is a man powerful in wisdom and knowledge, and the spirit of God is upon him, and the grace of the Lord is with him."

(T.Lev. 2:3).[189] The context describes an angel who guided Levi through various visions.[190] Later in T.Lev. 9:7, Levi communicates that Isaac kept calling to him to "bring to my remembrance the Law of the Lord, just as the *angel* (emphasis added) had shown me." As preparation for his role in the priesthood, the angel emphasizes that Levi was to be thoroughly versed in the various precepts in the Jewish Law.[191] Likewise, Judah exhorts his children that there are two spirits: the spirit of truth (τὸ πνεῦμα τῆς ἀληθείας) and the spirit of error. It is said, "the spirit of truth testifies to all things and brings all accusations" (T.Jud. 20:1-5). In his closing words of summary to his children, Judah says, "Observe the whole Law of the Lord, therefore, my children."[192] In both T.Lev. 2:3 and T.Jud. 20:1-5 the emphasis is on the Spirit's role in promoting a Torah-based ethic.

2.4 *Pseudo-Philo* (Latin Title: *Liber Antiquitatum Biblicarum*)[193]

Ps.-Philo[194] is a creative retelling of the biblical stories from Adam to David (Genesis to 1 Samuel) interwoven with legendary expansions of these

---

[189] Some have drawn attention to an eleventh century manuscript "e" of the T.Lev.: "[7 Remove] far away from me, Lord, the spirit of unrighteousness and evil thought and sexual immorality, and remove arrogance from me, [8] and make known to me, Lord, the spirit of holiness (τὸ πνεῦμα τὸ ἅγιον), and give me resolution and wisdom and knowledge and strength..." (T.Lev. 2:3b, 7-8) (Translation by R.L. Webb, *John the Baptizer and Prophet: A Socio-Historical Study* [Sheffield: JSOT Press, 1991], p. 119 cf. Turner, *Power From on High*, p. 127; Wenk, *Community-Forming Power*, p. 78). Even though this is a late manuscript, R.H. Charles thinks "e" goes back to a Hebrew original (Charles, *The Apocrypha and Pseudepigrapha of the Old Testament in English*, p. 284). In this text "the Holy Spirit" is contrasted with "the spirit of unrighteousness," "evil thought, sexual immorality, and arrogance" and is associated with "wisdom and knowledge and strength." This makes it more explicit that the Spirit takes on a comprehensive role in promoting a Torah-based ethic.

[190] T.Lev. 2:6ff.

[191] "Day by day he was informing me, occupying himself with me" (T.Lev. 9:8).

[192] T.Jud. 26:1.

[193] Many believe the extant Latin version of *Pseudo-Philo* is probably a translation from a Greek version, which itself was a translation of a Hebrew original, composed in Palestine in the first century C.E., around the time of Jesus (D.J. Harrington, "Pseudo-Philo: A New Translation and Introduction," OTP Vol. 2, pp. 298-300).

[194] Ps.-Philo was not written under the name of "Philo," nor was the Latin title, *Liber Antiquitatum Biblicarum* its original title. The ascription to Philo rests on its similarity in form and content to the *Antiquities* written by Josephus; i.e., since one book of *Antiquities* was written by Josephus, this other book of *Antiquities* must have been written by Philo (D.J. Harrington,

accounts. Of central importance to the author is the Jewish Law; it is considered an eternal commandment that will not pass away.[195] Also significant is that the Deuteronomistic concept of history (sin-punishment-salvation) pervades the book,[196] where the biblical notion of covenant is the basis of relationship between God and humanity.[197] There are numerous references to the Spirit in *Ps.-Philo*[198] but two make a contribution to our investigation: 9:8 and 27:9–10.

Ps.-Philo 9:8 is set within the context of the birth of Moses. The story embellishes the account in Exod. 1–2 by describing the action of Moses' father Amram when Pharaoh ordered that all males born into Hebrew families be thrown into the Nile River. In this situation the Hebrew populace responded by setting up a decree that Hebrew males should refrain from having sexual relations with their wives until God takes action. However, Amram refuses to abide by this ruling, based on the conviction that God promised numerous progeny in the Abrahamic covenant. Consequently, God is pleased with Amram's belief and utters the following words about Moses, Amram's son, in *Ps.-Philo* 9:8:

> And I, God, will kindle for him my lamp that will abide in him, and I will show him my covenant that no one has seen. And I will reveal to him my Law and statutes and judgments, and I will burn an eternal light for him, because I thought of him in the days of old, saying, "My spirit will not be a mediator among these men forever, because they are flesh and their days will be 120 years."

These words no doubt prepare the reader for God's covenant instituted through Moses at Sinai.[199] In *Ps.-Philo* 11:1–5, central to the covenant relationship is the Law, which is said to enlighten people on how to serve God (v. 2). It is further claimed of the Law that its statues are eternal and they serve as the basis for punishment for those who do not keep them (v. 1). The words in *Ps.-Philo* 9:8, "My spirit will not be a mediator among these men forever, because they are flesh and their days will be 120 years," are reminiscent of

---

"Pseudo-Philo, *Liber Antiquitatum Biblicarum*," in *Outside the Old Testament* [ed. M. De Jonge; Cambridge: Cambridge University Press, 1985], p. 6).

[195] *Ps.-Philo* 11:5; the Law was prepared from the creation of the world (32:7) and is considered an eternal light (9:8). All references and citations are taken from the ET of Harrington's, "Pseudo-Philo," OTP Vol. 2, pp. 304–77.

[196] See *Ps.-Philo* 6:11; 27:7, 15; 45:3; 49:5.

[197] Harrington, "Pseudo-Philo," p. 301.

[198] See, for example, *Ps.-Philo* 3:2; 18:10–11; 28:6; 31:9; 32:14; 36:2; 60:1; 62:2.

[199] See *Ps.-Philo* 10:2; 11:1–5.

Gen. 6:3. The use of the possessive "my spirit" makes it clear that the author refers to the Spirit of God. In *Ps.-Philo* 3:2, the same words from Gen. 6:3 are used but are translated, "my spirit shall not *judge*[200] (emphasis added) those men forever." The MT uses the verb ידון, which is difficult to translate. It can mean "to abide in, dwell."[201] This is the manner in which the LXX understood it by using the word καταμένειν ("to stay, live"[202]) as its equivalent. A rendering of Gen. 6:3 is found in *m. Sanh.* 10:3: "The generation of the flood has no share in the world to come and they shall not stand in the judgment since it is said, 'My spirit shall not *judge* (emphasis added) with man forever.'"[203] This indicates a Jewish tradition that interpreted ידון in Gen. 6:3 "to judge" rather than "to abide in, dwell." In *Ps.-Philo* 3:2, the author understands Gen. 6:3 to indicate a contrast between the withdrawal of the Spirit from some people on the one hand, and God's covenant with Noah on the other hand.[204] Those who no longer experience the judgment of the Spirit in their life are said to have a change in status with God; they no longer experience the influence of the Spirit in convicting them of their sin, and consequently, will suffer the consequence of not sharing in the future covenant God will make with Noah.[205] Therefore, the author perceives the Spirit's role primarily in the realm of ethics.[206] In *Ps.-Philo* 9:8 the author interprets this phrase as, "my spirit will not be a *mediator*" (emphasis added). In this context the period before the new revelation of the Law at Sinai is compared with the period beginning with Moses and the Sinaitic covenant. The Spirit's role in ethics prior to the giving of the Law would be complementary to the Law's function after it had been given. Both Spirit and

---

[200] Harrington, "Pseudo-Philo," p. 306; Harrington claims *Ps-Philo* is reading the Hebrew *ydwn* as in the MT and understanding it to mean "judge" (see footnote 3b, p. 306).

[201] BDB, p. 192.

[202] BDAG, p. 522.

[203] ET from Jacob Neusner, *The Mishna: A New Translation* (London: Yale University Press, 1988).

[204] See Gen. 9:8–12 cf. *Ps.-Philo* 3:11–12.

[205] See *Ps.-Philo* 3:4 (*"The time set for all* men dwelling upon the earth has arrived, for their deeds are wicked") cf 6–7; compare with *Ps.-Philo* 18:10–11 and 60:1, where those who no longer experience the Spirit are contrasted with those who are in covenantal relationship with God.

[206] This is confirmed by the rendering of Gen. 6:3 in *Targums Neofiti* and *Pseudo-Jonathan*: "Behold I have put my spirit in the sons of man because they are flesh, and their deeds are evil" (*Neofiti*); "Did I not put my holy spirit in them that they might perform good deeds?" (*Pseudo-Jonathan*).

Law are instrumental in securing relationship with God (i.e., they both have a mediatorial function; cf. *Ps.-Philo* 11:2, "For even if men say, 'We have not known you, and so we have not served you,' therefore I will make a claim upon them because they have not learned the Law").[207] In this sense, both the Law and Spirit share in the formation of ethics. However, this is expressed negatively, by saying that the Spirit will not always be the mediator ("My spirit will not be a mediator among these men forever...").

In *Ps.-Philo* 27:9-10, we read, "Kenaz arose, and the spirit of the Lord clothed him...he was clothed with the spirit of power and was changed into another man, and he went down to the Amorite camp and began to strike them down." Israel was at a time of national crisis because they were dominated by foreign oppression, the Amorites. Furthermore, certain individuals grumbled against their leader Kenaz, claiming he sent others out to battle but he himself stayed at home.[208] As a result, Kenaz prayed that he would single-handedly be equipped to defeat the Amorites. In his request there is a call for God to act on the basis of the "covenant of the last days."[209] After he prayed he went alone into the Amorite camp. Through Kenaz the Spirit was instrumental in fulfilling the covenant promise for God to act in behalf of Israel, to save and restore her. This corresponds to the sin-punishment-salvation cycle so prominent in the Judges, where Israel's leader saved her from corporate sin and restored covenant relationship between God and his people.[210] Correspondingly, *Ps.-Philo* concludes the narrative describing Kenaz's great victory with this response from Israel, "Now we know that the Lord has decided to save his people; he does not need a great number but only holiness."[211] As his final words Kenaz summoned the people together

---

[207] Concerning *Ps.-Philo* 9:8, Wenk states, "The Spirit is in the first stage considered to be God's positive ethical influence upon people, a role that beginning with Moses is directly fulfilled by the covenant between God and his people and by the law as the content of this covenant" (*Community-Forming Power*, p. 71). However, Wenk goes too far in claiming that the Spirit's role as mediator was superseded by the role of the Law in the covenant at Sinai ("once expressed in terms of a judgment by the Spirit, once with the idea of the Spirit as a mediator, a role that *Pseudo-Philo* thought was apparently taken over later by the new covenant at Sinai, the law" [*Ibid.*, p. 71]). If this is the meaning in *Ps.-Philo* 9:8 then the author of *Pseudo-Philo* would not have depicted the Spirit's ethical influence *subsequent* to the Sinaitic covenant (cf. 27:9-10).

[208] *Ps.-Philo* 27:2.

[209] *Ps.-Philo* 27:7 cf. 26:12-13, where Kenaz remembers God's covenant with Moses.

[210] See Judges 3:7-10; 6:1, 7-10, 13-14, 33-35; 10:6-8 cf. 11:14, 27-29, 32-33.

[211] *Ps.- Philo* 27:14.

and rehearsed Israel's covenant obligations: "For you have seen all the wonders that came upon those who sinned...or how the Lord our God destroyed them because they transgressed against his covenant...stay in the paths of the Lord your God lest the Lord destroy his own inheritance."[212]

2.5 Israel's Leaders: Anointed with the Spirit and Advocates of the Law

Set within the *Similitudes of Enoch* (37-71),[213] *1 En.* 49:3 and 62:2 refer to the Messiah who is said to be anointed with the Spirit. Various names are given to this figure: "the Elect One"[214] (49:2), "the Son of Man" (62:3), "the Righteous One" (53:6), and "the Anointed One" (52:4). *1 En.* 49:3 reads, "In him dwells the spirit of wisdom, the spirit which gives thoughtfulness, the spirit of knowledge and strength, and the spirit of those who have fallen asleep in righteousness." This text is practically a verbatim reproduction of Isa. 11:2,[215] which clearly presents the Messiah as one endowed with the Spirit of God.[216] Thus, the author of *1 Enoch* intentionally borrows from Isa. 11:2 to depict this figure as one anointed with the Spirit and through this anointing as provided with the "wisdom," "knowledge," "strength," and "righteousness" necessary to function in his role as "the Elect One."[217] Likewise *1 En.* 62:2 corresponds to Isa. 11:4, where it claims that the Spirit equips "the Elect One" to rule with the "spirit of righteousness": "The Lord of the Spirits has sat down on the throne of his glory, and the spirit of righteousness has been poured out upon him. The word of his mouth will do the sinners in; and all the oppressors shall be eliminated from before his face."

---

[212] *Ps.-Philo* 28:2.

[213] The consensus of scholars at the SNTS Pseudepigrapha Seminar which met in 1978 in Tübingen and in 1978 in Paris was that the *Similitudes of Enoch* were written about the first century C.E. (E. Isaac, "1 [Ethiopic Apocalpyse of] Enoch: A New Translation and Introduction," *OTP* Vol.1, p.7).

[214] ET from E.Isaac, "1 (Ethiopic Apocalypse of) Enoch," pp. 13-89.

[215] The phrase, "the Spirit of the Lord" has been left out in *1 En.* 49:3 and the phrase "Spirit of knowledge and fear of the Lord" in Isa. 11:2 has been replaced by "spirit of those who have fallen asleep in righteousness." It is suggested that these changes reflect the intention of the author of the *Similitudes* to avoid subordinationist language (M.A. Chevallier, *L'Esprit et le Messie dans le Bas-Judaïsme et le Nouveau Testament* [Paris: Presses Universitaires de France, 1958], p. 19).

[216] Menzies, *The Development of Early Christian Pneumatology*, p. 72.

[217] *1 En.* 49:4 cf. 51:3-4.

In *1 En.* 61:11-12 "the Elect One" is enthroned and the congregation extols God charismatically "in the spirit of faith, in the spirit of wisdom and patience, in the spirit of mercy, in the spirit of justice and peace, and in the spirit of generosity." *1 Enoch* expected these qualities acquired through the Spirit to be modeled on the composite "Messiah of the Spirit" based upon Isa. 11:1-4 because they flowed like water from before him (*1 En.* 49:1).[218] As was noted above, the concept of "wisdom" is defined as understanding that leads to moral conduct and "righteousness" is associated with divine judgement based upon the Torah.[219]

Another allusion to Isa. 11:1-4 is found in the *Psalms of Solomon*,[220] where the Spirit is again depicted as the means by which the Messiah shall be endowed with special characteristics. In *Pss. Sol.* 17:37, it is said that the Messiah will be "powerful in the holy spirit ($\delta \upsilon \nu \alpha \tau \grave{o} \nu$ $\grave{\epsilon} \nu$ $\pi \nu \epsilon \acute{\upsilon} \mu \alpha \tau \iota$ $\dot{\alpha} \gamma \acute{\iota} \omega$) and wise in the counsel of understanding, with strength and righteousness."[221] The psalmist perceived the Spirit as the source of the Messiah's wisdom, strength, and righteousness. A similar reference to Isa. 11:1-4 is found in *Pss. Sol.* 18:5-8. Here the Messiah will act "in the fear of his God, in wisdom of spirit ($\grave{\epsilon} \nu$ $\sigma o \phi \acute{\iota} \alpha$ $\pi \nu \epsilon \acute{\upsilon} \mu \alpha \tau o \varsigma$), and of righteousness and of strength, to direct people in righteous acts, in the fear of God" (v.7). Evidently the psalmist thought of the Spirit in the Messiah's life as functioning to influence others as well; he was to initiate moral renewal based upon the requirements of the Jewish Law. As R.B. Wright claims, "the psalmist is a moral rigorist...[who] undoubtedly derives his notions of God's requirements from the Law."[222]

---

[218] Turner, *Power From on High*, p. 132; Wenk, *Community-Forming Power*, p. 80.

[219] See Chapter One, Ancient Judaism (4. Israel's Leaders, Spirit-Endowment, and the Torah) and the discussion on Isa. 11:1-4.

[220] The *Psalms of Solomon* can be dated from 125 B.C.E. to the early first century C.E. (R.B. Wright, "Psalms of Solomon: A New Translation and Introduction," OTP Vol. 2, p. 641).

[221] ET from Wright, "Psalms of Solomon,"pp.651-70.

[222] *Ibid.*, p. 645; see *Pss. Sol.* 10:4 and 14:1-3 for the idea of a Torah-based ethic ("The Lord is faithful to those who truly love him, to those who endure his discipline, to those who live in the righteousness of his commandments in the Law, which he has commanded for our life. The Lord's devout shall live by it forever..." [14:1-3a]); see also *Pss. Sol.* 4:8; 17:11, 1 8 for other references to the Law.

2.6 Summary

The Wisdom of Ben Sira describes the Spirit of understanding, which is associated with covenant renewal and obeying the Law. In the context of the prediction of Israel's exile, the author of *Jubilees* depicts Moses' plea for God's mercy. God's reply centres on Israel's restoration through a reiteration of the eschatological promise for covenantal renewal found in Jer. 31 (38 LXX):31-34 read in conjunction with Ezek. 36:27. Israel will experience transformation in her disposition through the Spirit and this will result in a renewed performance of the Law. The *Testaments of Benjamin* and *Simeon* affirm that Joseph's goodness was the result of the Spirit of God in his life, and they add that his goodness was concretized in the performance of the Law. In the *Testaments of Levi* and *Judah* the Spirit of understanding assisted Levi in perceiving deceit, sin, and injustice, things that were contrary to the Law. Likewise, Judah exhorts his children that the Spirit of truth exists to help discern error. *Ps.-Philo* adopts a Deuteronomistic concept of history, where the biblical notion of covenant functions as the basis of relationship between God and humanity. The Spirit's role is complementary to the Law in securing relationship with God; e.g., Kenaz was endued with the Spirit and was instrumental in God's soteriological plan to restore Israel's covenantal relationship. This, in turn, ensued in Israel's covenant renewal with God. *1 Enoch* and the *Psalms of Solomon* fashion their description of the Messiah upon Isa. 11:1-4, where Israel's leader is anointed with the Spirit to rule and judge effectively in accordance with the Jewish Law. Furthermore, the composite qualities of the Messiah were to be emulated by others as well. In sum, Palestinian literature describes the Spirit as the agent of moral renewal that conforms to a Torah-based ethic.

3. Qumran Literature

Non-biblical manuscripts from Qumran were discovered in 11 caves at the northwestern edge of the Dead Sea in close proximity to the communal settlement of Hirbet Qumran. It will be these texts that form the basis of this survey. Scholarly consensus dates the Qumran Scrolls roughly between 200 B.C.E. and 70 C.E., with a small portion of the text reaching as far back as the third century B.C.E., and the bulk of the extant material dating to the first century B.C.E.[223] Central to this sectarian community was covenant ideology.

---

[223] Geza Vermes, *The Complete Dead Sea Scrolls in English*, Fourth Edition (New York: Penguin Books, 1997), pp. 13-14; J.H. Charlesworth, "The Origin and Subsequent History of the

In particular, the Essenes considered themselves the Jewish remnant of their time, the new covenant community.[224] Since the community pledged itself to observe this alliance between God and Israel, their paramount aim was observing the precepts of the Law.[225] Initiates into the community are said to "return to the Law of Moses"[226] and the novice pledges himself to practise the whole Law with all its implications, even unto death.[227]

The use of רוּחַ appears approximately 150 times in the Qumran literature. However, it is used with diverse meanings[228]: it can refer more generally to

---

Authors of the Dead Sea Scrolls: Four Transitional Phases Among the Qumran Essenes," RevQ 10 (1980), 213-33, esp. 233.

[224] The designation בָּאֵי הַבְּרִית הַחֲדָשָׁה (CD VI, 19; VIII, 29 cf. Jer. 31:31, where it is a hapax legomenon) is applied to the Qumran community. It considered itself the "Renewed Covenant" (S. Talmon, "The Community of the Renewed Covenant: Between Judaism and Christianity," in The Community of the Renewed Covenant [ed. Eugene Ulrich and James Vanderkam; Notre Dame: University of Notre Dame Press, 1994], pp. 3-24, see esp. pp.12-13). G. Vermes claims that Qumran's covenant ideology focused upon the inner transformation of the individual Jew patterned upon Jer. 31:31-33 and Isa. 54:13 (An Introduction to the Complete Dead Sea Scrolls [Minneapolis: Fortress Press, 2000], pp. 146-7). It is no coincidence that the term בְּרִית occurs 42 times in CD, 32 times in 1QS, 27 times in 1QH, 13 times in 1QM, 7 times in 1Qsb, and in 20 further references as listed by K.G. Kuhn (Kondordanz zu den Qumrantexten [Göttingen: Vandenhoeck & Ruprecht], 1960). English translations are from Vermes, The Complete Dead Sea Scrolls in English and all Hebrew texts are from E. Lohse, Die Texte aus Qumran: Hebräisch und Deutsch mit Masoretischer Punktation, Ubersetzung, Einführung und Anmerkungen, Second Edition (München: Kösel Verlag, 1971).

[225] The Qumran community referred to itself as the "house of the Law" (CD [MS B] II, 9-14), "community of the Law" (1QS V, 2); its members are people who "observe the Torah" (1QpHab VIII, 1; XII, 5).

[226] CD XV, 9, 12; XVI, 1,2,4,5 cf. 1QS V, 9.

[227] 1QS V, 7-11; CD XV, 5-15; XVI, 8,9; 1QH VI, 17-18.

[228] For a survey of the various uses of רוּחַ see A.E. Sekki, The Meaning of Rua(c)h at Qumran SBL Dissertation Series No. 110 (Atlanta: Scholars Press, 1989); F.F. Bruce, "Holy Spirit in the Qumran Texts," The Annual of Leeds University Oriental Society 6 (1966-68), 49-55; A.A. Anderson, "The Use of 'Ruach'in 1QS, 1QH and 1QM," JSS 7 (1962), 293-303; J. Becker, Das Heil Gottes: Heils- und Sündenbegriffe in den Qumrantexten und im Neuen Testament SUNT, 3 (Göttingen: Vandenhoeck & Ruprecht, 1964); G. Johnston, "'Spirit' and 'Holy Spirit' in the Qumran Literature" in New Testament Sidelights: Essays in Honor of A.C. Purdy (ed. H.K. McArthur; Hartford, Conn.: Hartford Seminary Foundation Press, 1960), pp. 27-42; W. Foerster, "Der Heilige Geist in Spätjudentum," NTS 8 (1961-2), 117-34; F. Nötscher, "Heiligkeit in den Qumranschriften," RevQ 2 (1960), 333-44; D. Hill, Greek Words and Hebrew Meanings: Studies in the Semantics of Soteriological Terms SNTSMS 5 (Cambridge: Cambridge University Press, 1967), pp. 234-41.

wind,[229] it is used anthropologically referring to the disposition of humans,[230] angelic or demonic beings,[231] or it can refer to the Spirit of God. Even though there appears to be no clear and consistent meaning for the word רוּחַ, its frequency in the DSS demands attention. Our attention will be limited to the use of רוּחַ referring to the Spirit of God and its relationship to covenantal ideology. Because of the emphasis on covenant, Law, and Spirit, this body of literature yields some fruitful results for understanding the type of relationship the Essenes conceived of between Spirit and Law in Jewish eschatology and ethical renewal.

3.1 The Eschatological Spirit, Covenant, and the Law in the *Thanksgiving Hymns*

There are good reasons to believe that the *Thanksgiving Hymns* were the most venerated and used writings of the Qumran sect. If this was the case, the theological assertions contained within them were widespread and of utmost influence within the community.[232] P. von der Osten-Sacken's assessment is that 1QM represents the oldest tradition in Qumran pneumatology, followed by the *Hodayot*, which demonstrates a continuum with Old Testament traditions.[233]

---

[229] See 1QH IX, 10; XIV, 23; XV, 5, 23; CD VIII, 13; XIX, 25.

[230] 1QH X, 15; 1QM VII, 5; XI, 10; XIV, 7.

[231] 1QM XII, 9; XIII, 10; XV, 14; 1QH XV, 29; XVIII, 8.

[232] See A. Dupont-Sommer, *The Essene Writings From Qumran* (trans. G. Vermes; Oxford: Basil Blackwell, 1961), pp. 198–99. He suggests a possibility that in the *War Rule* some of the *Hodayot* were read by the High Priest in solemn hours immediately preceding the battle against Belial and his cohorts ("Then the High Priest shall rise, with the [Priests], his brethren, and the Levites, and all the men of the army, and he shall recite aloud the Prayer in Time of War [written in the Book] of the Rule concerning this time, and also all their Hymns," [1QM XV, 5]). It is also significant that six other manuscripts of the same collection (*War Rule*) were found in cave IV. This suggests that the procedural practices, including the reading from the *Hodayot*, are of great significance within the community.

[233] P. von der Osten-Sacken, *Gott und Belial: Traditionsgeschichtliche Untersuchungen zum Dualismus in den Texten aus Qumran* (Göttingen: Vandenhoeck & Ruprecht, 1969), pp. 165–69; see also M.O. Wise, who contends that reference to the material of the Teacher of Righteousness in the *Hodayot* represents the oldest tradition (*The Temple Scroll: Its Composition, Date, Purpose and Provenance* [Ph.D. dissertation, University of Chicago, 1988]).

All the texts discovered in the eleven caves are either biblical manuscripts themselves or works based on Scripture.[234] This is particularly true of the *Thanksgiving Hymns*, which allude to the eschatological promises made in the book of Ezekiel.[235] The author[236] viewed himself as the recipient of Yahweh's eschatological Spirit based upon the passages in Ezek. 36:25-27; 37:1-14. The peculiar form of רוּחַ אֲשֶׁר נָתַתָּה בִּי בָּרוּחַ in 1QH V, 19; VIII, 11; XX, 11, 12 is syntactically parallel to the passages in Ezek. 36:27; 37:14, where the prophet foretells a time when God will put his "Spirit" in his people. This use of the phrase has proven to be more than a stereotyped expression or customary terminology since there are distinct themes that accompany it, forming a common link with the passages in Ezekiel.[237] This indicates that the Essenes believed the future promise spoken through the prophet was actualized in

---

[234] See the comments of Geza Vermes, "The Qumran Interpretation of Scripture in its Historical Setting," *The Annual Leeds University Oriental Society*, Vol. VI, 1966-68 (ed. John McDonald; Leiden: E.J. Brill, 1969), pp. 84-97, esp. p. 86.

[235] Ironically, many believe the Qumranians said very little about the gift of the Spirit in Jewish eschatological promises: "The Qumranians believed in the Spirit as creative, sustaining, illumining, and renewing at the final judgment; yet they have remarkably little to say about the gift of the Spirit in the eschatological fulfillment of the promises" (Johnston, "'Spirit' and 'Holy Spirit' in the Qumran Literature," p. 38). See also the remarks of W.D. Davies, "Paul and the Dead Sea Scrolls: Flesh and Spirit," *The Scrolls and the New Testament* (ed. Krister Stendahl; London: SCM Press Ltd., 1957), pp. 173ff. In a more recent attempt A.E. Sekki broaches the idea that the sectarians of Qumran thought of themselves as recipients of the eschatological Spirit but remains non-committal in his position. Even after he presents substantial proof that 1QH patterns its pneumatological assertions upon the eschatological promises stated in Ezekiel, he states, "...*if* (emphasis added) the sectarians did view themselves as the recipients of Ezekiel's eschatological promise of the Spirit..." (*The Meaning of Rua(c)h at Qumran*, p. 89).

[236] Menahem Monsoor states, "In numerous instances the hymns seem to be the product of a single author whose own personal experience and feelings they vividly reflect" (*The Thanksgiving Hymns: Translated and Annotated with an Introduction* [Grand Rapids: Wm. B. Eerdmans Publishing Co., 1961], p. 45). The question of the identity of the author is equally inconclusive; some equate the author with the Teacher of Righteousness (see Joseph Coppens, "'Mystery' in the Theology of Saint Paul and its Parallels at Qumran," *Paul and the Dead Sea Scrolls* [ed. J. Murphy-O'Connor and J.H. Charlesworth; New York: Crossroads, 1990], p. 137).

[237] Holm-Nielsen offers a sound cautionary note. Even when there is a complete agreement of words or phrases between texts, it may simply be a matter of the everyday language of the time: stereotyped expressions, customary terminology, etc. These may well have originated in the OT but now are completely detached from their original meaning and the theological premises based upon them. Contextual matters will be the determinants. Passages that demonstrate accompanying thematic links between texts are sure indications of intentional dependence (*Hodayot: Psalms From Qumran*, p. 302).

their own community; they possessed the eschatological Spirit and were consequently empowered to abide by the Law.

The second[238] most frequent means of referring to God's Spirit in Qumran literature is the singular absolute use of רוּחַ, which is found in the expression בָּרוּחַ אֲשֶׁר נָתַתָּה בִּי (1QH V, 19; VIII, 11; XX, 11, 12).[239] What is intriguing about this construction is that of the Hebrew literature known to have been used at Qumran, the grammatical formation using רוּחַ in Ezek. 36:27 (רוּחִי אֶתֵּן בְּקִרְבְּכֶם) and 37:14 (וְנָתַתִּי רוּחִי בָכֶם) is syntactically parallel with the constructions found in 1QH V, 19; VIII, 11; XX, 11,12.[240] In common between the constructions in 1QH and Ezekiel is the absolute form of רוּחַ. The unqualified use (absolute form) of רוּחַ referring to Yahweh's Spirit is twice as frequent in Ezekiel as in all other OT sources combined, so that it can be said to be an Ezekielian characteristic.[241] In Qumran literature, particularly in the *Hodayot*, the author(s) most frequently used רוּחַ in construct with קוֹדְשֶׁכָה.[242] This suggests that the psalmist suspended his normal use of רוּחַ in the construct state to pattern his wording after that of Ezekiel's. Since he uses the absolute form of רוּחַ in 1QH V, 19; VIII, 11; XX, 11, 12, instead of its most common usage in the Hymns, it is most probable that he was intentionally trying to preserve the wording of Ezekiel. 1QH V, 19; VIII, 11; XX, 11, 12 all have the preposition -בְּ but with the first person pronoun suffix (בִּי, "in me"), emphasizing the personal application of the promise of God's eschatological Spirit (cf. בְּקִרְבְּכֶם ["in your inward parts"], Ezek. 36:27/ בָכֶם ["in you"], Ezek. 37:14). Ezekiel's use of the first person singular, imperfect use of the verb נתן (אֶתֵּן ["I will give"], Ezek. 36:27/ וְנָתַתִּי ["And I will give"], Ezek. 37:14), which indicated prophetic foretelling still

---

[238] The most frequent means of referring to God's Spirit in the DSS is with the singular רוּחַ in construct with the singular קוּדְשׁ plus the pronominal suffix כה /ךְ or ו referring to God (e.g., 1QS VIII, 16; 1QH IV, 26; VI, 13; VIII, 2, 3, 7, 12; XV, 6; XVII, 32; XX, 12; CD II, 12)

[239] The use of the preposition -בְּ attached to the word רוּחַ does not serve to qualify the word but simply to relate it to either previous or subsequent subjects in the sentence.

[240] Sekki recognizes this in his *The Meaning of Rua(c)h at Qumran*, p. 87. An exception to this is 2 Kgs. 19:7. While this verse contains the phrase, the content demonstrates no hint of eschatological connotation. Here, רוּחַ refers to "inner disquiet" (see Baumgärtel, "Spirit in the OT," *TDNT* Vol. VI, p. 361).

[241] See Ezek. 2:2; 3:12, 14, 24; 8:3; 11:1, 24; 36:26; 37:14; 43:5 and outside Ezekiel: Num. 27:18; Isa. 32:15 (57:16?); 1 Chron. 12:19; 2 Chron. 12:19; 2 Kgs. 19:7 (paralleled in Isa. 37:7).

[242] For example see 1QS VIII, 16; 1QH IV, 26; VI, 13; VIII, 2, 3, 7, 12; XV, 6; XVII, 32; XX, 12.

outstanding, is changed to the second person singular perfect (נָתַתָּ ["you have given"], 1QH V, 19; VIII, 11; XX, 11,12). The shift in verb tense emphasizes the present state in which God has already placed the Spirit within the psalmist. It is a completed enactment of Ezekiel's prophetic promise for the future realized in the present.

It is a consistent characteristic within the *Hodayot* not to make extended verbatim quotations from the OT but use it freely and paraphrasing the use of individual expressions.[243] A change of historical context results in an existential interpretation of Scripture. Therefore, paying attention to syntactical parallels between the Hymns and the OT can be telling; they reveal the need for investigating further correlation between the two passages in question. At this point it is safe to conclude that in all probability the psalmist deliberately patterned his wording in order to make a linguistic connection with Ezek. 36:27 and 37:14. However, in order to determine whether he wanted to make more than simply linguistic parallels, we must compare the various themes associated with the Spirit in both contexts. This is where the ultimate benefit for our survey is to be found.

The specific role of the Spirit envisioned in Ezek. 36:27 and 37:14 was to create a new disposition within Israel, which led to a renewed covenantal relationship with Yahweh, expressed in a tangible way by her obedience of the Jewish Law. This is communicated succinctly in Ezek. 36:26, 27, which reads, "And I will give you a new heart and I will put a new spirit within you; I will remove from your body the heart of stone and give you a heart of flesh. I will put my Spirit within you, and make you to follow my statues and be careful to observe my ordinances." It is precisely this main theme that is paralleled in the contexts of these hymns. This reality is the prerogative of all the members of the Qumran community. Although some of the *Hymns* express the individual thoughts of the psalmist,[244] the thoughts of 1QH V, 19; VIII, 11; XX, 11, 12 represent the common experiences of the community as a whole.[245] There is

---

[243] Holm-Nielsen, *Hodayot: Psalms From Qumran*, p. 304. He characterizes the *Hodayot's* use of the OT as a "'covert' use of Scripture...to create original poetry..." (p. 306).

[244] See particularly 1QH IX, XX, XV–XIX; these appear to refer to the experiences of the author abandoned by his friends and persecuted by his enemies (Vermes, *The Complete Dead Sea Scrolls in English*, p. 244).

[245] This deduction can be made because of the various subjects with which the work of the Spirit is associated in 1QH XX, 11, 12. The psalmist claims the manner in which one comes to "know" God is through the Spirit. Subsequent to this is a discussion on "the children of your grace" or the sectarian community as a whole and the benefits bestowed on them by God's

general consensus among scholars that the reception of the Spirit is a common experience of all; it is specifically associated with a person's entrance into the community. This is particularly true of the *Thanksgiving Hymns*.[246]

The psalmist desires to serve God with a "perfect/ whole heart" (וְלֵב שָׁלֵם) (1QH VIII, 7). The adjective "perfect/ whole" in combination with "heart" commonly connotes the idea of the "completeness/ wholeness" of the "inner person's seat of mind, inclinations, resolutions" in serving God and keeping covenant relation.[247] One's complete being is involved in serving God, which is made possible by God's Spirit (1QH VIII, 11). This thought is linked to God's covenant relationship (בְּרִיתְךָ, line 7) with his people. In 1QH VIII, 13-14, the psalmist implores God that he be made "righteous" and asks God to "[Grant me] the place [of Thy loving-kindness] which [Thou hast] chosen for them that love Thee and keep [Thy commandments, that they may stand] in Thy presence [for]ever." In 1QH XX, 19-21, 25 and V, 15-16, the psalmist compares himself with God and finds himself lacking in righteous conduct (XX, 19) to the point of not being able to understand the mysteries of God. In XX, 25, he calls himself "a fount of defilement and ignominious shame, a container of dust..." In V, 15, he considers himself "but a fabric of dust...whose counsel is nothing but uncleanness ignominious shame... and over whom the perverse spirit rules." His loathsome sinful condition may become "an object of fear forever...and an object of fright to all flesh" (V, 16). In these contexts, it is the Spirit that imparts this knowledge to the psalmist

---

initiative. One of those benefits is "they shall *know* you [God] (lines 20-22)." In lines 11, 12, it is by the Spirit that the psalmist "knows" God. Since the community experienced what "knowing" God means, it is safe to assume that God's children (those in the community) have the common experience of the Spirit. See also the *Damascus Rule* (CD) VII, 3ff., where members of the covenant community undertake that each of them will avoid all forms of uncleanness "and not defile his holy Spirit" (F.F. Bruce, "Holy Spirit in the Qumran Texts," p. 54).

[246] See 1QH VI, 12-13 cf. XIII, 18-20; XIV, 11-13; XVI, 10-12, 14-15; H.W. Kuhn has argued persuasively that 1QH VI, 13 refers to the gift of the Spirit which is granted to every member upon entrance into the Qumran community. Associated with the Spirit in the same verse is the verb to "draw near" (נגשׁ), which is a *terminus technicus* for entrance into the community (cf. 1QH VI, 17-21). (*Enderwartung und gegenwärtiges Heil: Untersuchungen zu den Gemeindeliedern von Qumran* SUNT 4 [Göttingen: Vandenhoeck & Ruprecht, 1966], pp. 131-2); see also Holm-Nielsen, *Hodayot: Psalms From Qumran*, p. 221; Johnston, "'Spirit' and 'Holy Spirit' in the Qumran Literature," pp. 27-42, 40-41; Sekki, *The Meaning of Rua(c)h at Qumran*, pp. 79-83; Menzies, *The Development of Early Christian Pneumatology*, pp. 84-86.

[247] Cf. 1 Chron. 28:9 and 29:9; see BDB, pp. 524-5, 1023-4.

and in turn, he is able to recognize his sinful condition.[248] George Johnston aptly describes the Spirit's role in the following words: "The Spirit gives moral and intellectual insight, but on the basis of the closest devotion to and study of the Mosaic Law..."[249]

These thoughts are comparable to Ezek. 36:26,27, where the idea of the "new heart" is parallel to the "new spirit" and correlates to the psalmist's notion of a complete and radical dedication to God.[250] Also in common is the idea of a new disposition that is evident in a tangible way: "you will follow my statutes" (בְּחֻקַּי תֵּלֵכוּ) and "you will be careful to keep my ordinances" (וּמִשְׁפָּטַי תִּשְׁמְרוּ וַעֲשִׂיתֶם). This is made possible because of Yahweh's Spirit (רוּחִי אֶתֵּן בְּקִרְבְּכֶם).[251] In sum, the psalmist perceived the eschatological

---

[248] 1QH XX, 11b-12; V, 18b-19.

[249] Johnston, "'Spirit' and 'Holy Spirit' in the Qumran Literature," p. 41.

[250] "God by the Spirit assures the poet of forgiveness and fellowship (1QH XVI, 11ff.)...The background of this hope is clear enough: Ezek. 36:25-27; 37:5f., 14..." (Johnston, "'Spirit' and 'Holy Spirit' in the Qumran Literature," p. 40).

[251] There is further correspondence between the contexts of 1QH V 19; VIII, 11; XX, 11, 12 and Ezek. 36:27; 37:14 that are indications the psalmist is borrowing from the eschatological promises of the Spirit spoken of in the book of Ezekiel. In 1QH VIII, 9, 11, the psalmist recognizes that the presence of God's Spirit in his life is based upon God's grace (חֶסֶד, line 9). This is commensurate with Ezek. 36:32, which attests to the fact that this new future disposition in Israel through the work of the Spirit is based upon God's sovereign act and not on Israel's merit: "I want you to know that I am not doing this for your sake, declares the Sovereign Lord. Be ashamed and be disgraced for your conduct, O house of Israel!" The psalmist requests cleansing by the Spirit (לְטַהֲרֵנִי, 1QH VIII, 12) and thereby proceeds to carry out his favour toward him (חַסְדֶּיךָ עִם עַבְדְּךָ לָעַד, 1QH VIII, 12). In Ezek. 36:33-38, the emphasis is on the need for Israel's cleansing in the future (v.33) as prerequisite for receiving Yahweh's favour. The spatial promises of the restoration of land and city are missing in the Hodayot. This is not uncommon because in later Judaism these were not taken to be literal promises of land but simply representative of eschatological life (Ps. Sol. 14:10; 1 En. 40:9; 4 Macc. 18:3) (see W. Foerster, "κληρονόμος," TDNT Vol. III, pp. 776-81). In 1QH XX, 11, 12, the Spirit is associated with ידע ("to know"). The construction בִּי נָתַתָּה אֲשֶׁר בָּרוּחַ אֵלִי יְדַעְתִּיכָה is best translated "I have known you, O God, by the Spirit you have put within me" (cf. the translation of Eduard Lohse, "habe ich dich erkannt, mein Gott, durch [emphasis added] den Geist, den du in mich gegeben hast..." [Die Texte aus Qumran, p. 159]). This indicates that the psalmist's "knowing" is through the agency of the Spirit (see the possible meanings of the preposition -בְּ in C.L. Seow's, A Grammar for Biblical Hebrew [Nashville: Abingdon Press, 1987], p. 36]). This does not connote "inspiration" (contra A.A. Anderson who states, "The holy Spirit is also the source of prophecy...Probably somewhat similar are the instances where the psalmist declares that he knows God by the Spirit which God has put within him [he cites 1QH XX, 11; V, 19 as examples] ["The Use of רוּחַ in 1QS, 1QH, and 1QM," 302]). Rather, this means, "to have

promise of the Spirit foretold in Ezekiel, actualized in the Qumran community.

Closely related to the idea of covenant renewal in the *Hodayot* is the liturgical prayer in 1Q34 II, 5-7, which speaks of the history of humanity from creation and culminating at Sinai:

> But in the time of Thy goodwill Thou didst choose for Thyself a people. Thou didst remember Thy Covenant and [granted] that they should be set apart for Thyself from among all the peoples as a holy thing. And Thou didst renew for them Thy Covenant (founded) on a glorious vision and the words of Thy Holy [Spirit], on the works of Thy hands.

The "words of Thy Holy [Spirit]" refer to the words of the Law that constitute the covenant. Not only do the words of the Spirit provide insight into the covenant, but they also are instrumental in actually establishing the covenant.[252] The Spirit is associated with God's covenant at Sinai and with the renewal of the covenant when initiates enter the Qumran community. The liturgical prayer communicates the fall of humanity at creation.[253] At Sinai God instituted a covenant, but now this covenant is renewed in the eschatological people at Qumran.[254]

The experience of the Spirit is not an occasional occurrence, limited to the time of admittance into the community. The Spirit is also instrumental in sustaining the individual in the covenant relationship. In 1QH XV, 6-7 the psalmist writes, "I thank Thee, O Lord, for Thou hast upheld me by Thy strength. Thou hast shed Thy Holy Spirit upon me that I may not stumble...Thou hast not permitted that fear should cause me to desert Thy Covenant." The psalmist expects further purification,[255] and echoing the concepts of Ezekiel 36, the writer blesses God for shedding his Holy Spirit upon him. 1QH IV, 25 ("[I thank Thee, O Lord for] Thou didst shed [Thy] Holy Spirit upon Thy Servant") expresses the same idea as 4Q504 V, 15. What

---

knowledge, perception of God and duty" (cf. Isa. 1:1; 56:10) (BDB, pp. 906-9). This is comparable to Ezek. 37:13, 14, which explicitly associate רוּחַ to Israel's "knowing" (ידע): "Then You will know (וִידַעְתֶּם) that I am Yahweh...I will put my Spirit (רוּחִי) in you...then you will know (וִידַעְתֶּם) that I, Yahweh, have spoken."

[252] "It is both the illocution and the perlocution of the Spirit-spoken word to establish the covenant" (Wenk, *Community-Forming Power*, p. 104).

[253] See 1QH VIII, 11-12; XV, 6-7 for the psalmist's idea of the depravity of the human spirit associated with creation.

[254] See 1QS IX, 3, which refers to a community of the Holy Spirit.

[255] "...purifying me by Thy Holy Spirit" (1QH VIII, 11b-12).

is particularly significant is that the context of 4Q504 is preoccupied with the Sinaitic covenant instituted by God through Moses (4Q504 II, 9; III, 10; V, 14). The prayers emphasize obeying the Law ("to plant Thy Law in our heart [that we may never depart from it, straying neither] to right nor to left"[256] cf. "to hearken to Thy voice [according to] all Thou hadst commanded by the hand of Moses Thy servant"[257]). The writer speaks of Israel's sin and distress, and through this, the hope of return to the Sinaitic covenant. He then speaks of the role of the Spirit in this time that becomes a blessing and a source of covenantal renewal ("For Thou hast shed Thy Holy Spirit upon us, bringing upon us Thy blessings, that we might seek Thee in our distress [and whis]per [prayers] in the ordeal of Thy chastisement"[258]). This evidence indicates that the sectarian community conceived of a soteriological pneumatology[259] based upon Ezekiel's promise of the eschatological Spirit. The Spirit's role was to induce behaviour that conformed to the Jewish Law based upon the eschatological promises of Ezek. 36:25-27; 37:5f., which led to a restored relationship with God and covenantal blessings.[260]

3.2 The Two Spirits in 1QS III–IV

The nature and function of the two spirits described in 1QS III-IV has been a source of contention among scholars. P. Wernberg-Moller is representative of those who view the two spirits as simply two human dispositions, which are created by God and are present in every person (cf. 1QS III, 17b-18). It is up to each individual person to choose which spirit to follow.[261] However, there

---

[256] 4Q504 II, 10-15.

[257] 4Q504 V, 14.

[258] 4Q504 V, 15.

[259] "[T]he holy spirit appears several times as an intermediary of salvation...a manifestation of God's saving activity" (H. Ringgren, *The Faith of Qumran: Theology of the Dead Sea Scrolls* [trans. Emilie T. Sander; Philadelphia: Fortress Press, 1963], pp. 87, 89-90).

[260] See also 1QH XXII, 31; XVII, 32; for secondary sources who connect these thoughts to Ezek. 36:25-27 see Johnston, "'Spirit' and 'Holy Spirit' in the Qumran Literature," p. 40; Wenk, *Community-Forming Power*, p. 103; Sekki, *The Meaning of Rua(c)h*, p. 222; Turner, *Power From on High*, p. 127.

[261] "It is significant that our author regards the two 'spirits' as created by God, and that according to IV,23 and our passage (3:18f.) both 'spirits' dwell in man as created by God. We are therefore [dealing]...with the idea that man was created by God with two 'spirits'- the Old Testament term for 'mood' or 'disposition'" (P. Wernberg-Moller, "A Reconsideration of the Two Spirits in the Rule of the Community," *RevQ* 3 [1961], 413-42, quote taken from 422 cf.

are a substantial number of those who believe there is more here than simply a reference to human disposition. Some have emphasized the cosmic dimension of the two spirits, whether the reference is to the Holy Spirit, angels/demons, or more generally, simply to the forces of good and evil.[262] As a cautionary note, it is best not to adopt a rigid "either-or" opinion on the interpretation of the two spirits in 1QS III–IV, since the use of רוח may have multiple meanings within this section.[263] For example, A.E. Sekki, who is inclined to interpret the references to רוח as the various dispositions in humans, admits that there are possible references to the Spirit of God. Commenting on 1QS IV, 18ff., he states, "The author now speaks of rua(c)h not as a spiritual capacity unchangeably conditioning man's religious life from birth but as an eschatological gift of God."[264]

The multiple meanings associated with the use of רוח in 1QS III–IV have been explained in various ways. Matthias Wenk claims the description of רוח in this context is patterned after that of OT pneumatology, which is expressed in descriptive, phenomenological language.[265] The Spirit is communicated as the awareness of God in the manifestation of his power rather than a personal being.[266] Therefore, the emphasis is on God's involvement in human life and a clear distinction cannot always be made between a person's spirit being acted upon by God or God's Spirit (or an evil spirit) acting upon people.[267] Max

---

423); see also M. Treves, who interprets the two spirits as "tendencies or propensities which are implanted in every man's heart" ("The Two Spirits of the Rule of the Community," *RevQ* 3 [1961], 449-52, quote taken from 449); F. Manns, *Le symbole eau-esprit dans le Judaisme ancien* Studium Biblicum Franciscanum 19 (Jerusalem: Franciscan Printing Press, 1983), p. 88; J. Pryke, "'Spirit' and 'Flesh' in the Qumran Documents and some New Testament Texts," *RevQ* 5 (1965), 345-60, particularly 345; Menzies, *The Development of Early Christian Pneumatology*, p.80.

[262] H.G. May, "Cosmological Reference in the Qumran Doctrine of the Two Spirits and in Old Testament Imagery," *JBL* 82 (1963), 1-14; M. Burrows, *More Light on the Dead Sea Scrolls* (New York: Viking Press, 1958), p. 279; E. Schweizer, "πνεῦμα, κτλ.," *TDNT* Vol. VI, p. 390; K.G. Kuhn, "πειρασμός-ἁμαρτία-σάρξ im Neuen Testament und die damit zusammenhängenden Vorstellungen," *ZTK* 49 (1952), 200-22, esp. 206.

[263] This is the case with Menzies who makes a rigid generalization of the use of the word רוח in 1QS III–IV: "I conclude that the two spirits in 1QS are human dispositions" (*The Development of Early Christian Pneumatology*, p. 80).

[264] Sekki, *The Meaning of Rua(c)h at Qumran*, p. 208.

[265] Wenk, *Community-Forming Power*, pp. 100-1.

[266] See Exod. 14:21; 15:8-10; Num. 11:31; Ezek. 13:11; 2 Sam. 22:16.

[267] "Qumran's language of the Spirit does not differ from the Old Testament's in being descriptive and phenomenological; therefore, a certain ambiguity exists in the scrolls between God's Spirit acting upon humanity and a person's spirit being acted upon by God...this same

Turner convincingly explains the various meanings of רוּחַ in 1QS III-IV as "conflicting powers or spheres of influence at play in man."[268] For example, the "spirit of error" is the totality of evil influences (seen as a unity, cf. 1QS III, 20-21 [angel of darkness]; CD XII, 2; 11QMelch XII-XIII [spirits of Belial]) and the "spirit of truth" is not to be read restrictively as a reference simply to human disposition but also includes the influence of the Prince of Lights (1QS III, 20), God, the Angel of Truth (1QS III, 24), and the divine Spirit (1QS IV, 21, 22).

The teaching of the "two spirits" in 1QS III-IV coincides with the comprehensive theme of the Community Rule that those who are admitted into the covenant have devoted themselves wholeheartedly to the observance of the Law.[269] 1QS I serves as an important introduction to the Rule and sets out the main tenets of the Qumran community in general terms.[270] As part of the duties of the members of the community, it states:

> He (the Master) shall admit into the Covenant of Grace all those who have freely devoted themselves to the observance of God's precepts...They shall not depart from any command of God...they shall stray neither to the right nor to the left of any of His true precepts. All those who embrace the Community Rule shall enter into the Covenant before God to obey all His commandments...[271]

Set within this context is the claim that through the Spirit, members are led into truth, cleansing, uprightness, and atonement: "For it is *through the spirit of true counsel* (בְּרוּחַ עֲצַת אֱמֶת) concerning the ways of man that all his sins shall be expiated...He shall be cleansed from all his sins *by the spirit of holiness* (וּבְרוּחַ קְדוֹשָׁה) uniting him to His truth, and his iniquity shall be expiated *by the spirit of uprightness and humility* (וּבְרוּחַ יוֹשֶׁר וַעֲנָוָה)."[272] The use of רוּחַ here cannot refer to an inherent inner quality, since it is impossible for

---

[268] ambiguity between an anthropological and a divine spirit is also present in 1QS 3-4" (*Ibid.*, pp. 100-1).

[268] Turner, *Power From on High*, pp. 128-9.

[269] The author of the Community Rule uses תּוֹרָה 13 times: 1QS V, 2, 3, 8, 16, 21; VI, 6, 18, 22; VIII, 2, 15, 22; IX, 9, 17. It is always referred to positively either as the basis for making decisions or as the basis for codes of conduct within the community. This makes it clear that the Law occupied a central place for the sectarians at Qumran.

[270] Michael A. Knibb, *The Qumran Community* (Cambridge: Cambridge University Press, 1987), p. 79.

[271] 1QS I, 5-20.

[272] 1QS III, 6-8.

members to be cleansed and expiated by their own spirits.[273] The context makes it clear that God is the author of such functions.[274] Significant for our purpose is the notion of cleansing attributed to the Spirit; it is the cleansing that coincides with humble submission "to all the precepts of God" (חֻקֵּי אֵל, 1QS III, 8). These are the characteristics of the members of the covenant who will constitute the eschatological community (1QS III, 12).

In 1QS IV, 20-23, the author celebrates the eschatological promise of Ezek. 36:25-27. The majority of scholars[275] understand רוּחַ קוֹדֶשׁ in 1QS IV, 21 as a reference to the Spirit of God, equating it with "spirit of truth,"[276] "Prince of Lights,"[277] and "the Angel of Truth."[278] The singular form of רוּחַ in the DSS in construct with any form of קודשׁ always refers to God's Spirit.[279] From 1QS IV, 18, the author speaks of רוּחַ not as the disposition of humans deposited in them at birth, but as an eschatological gift of God.[280] The reference in 1QS IV, 21 claims that רוּחַ קוֹדֶשׁ "cleanses" (טהר) humans from sin, which implies that it has an ethical function. This kind of cleansing is never attributed in the DSS to a human spirit but is always the work of God or his Spirit.[281] The "holy Spirit" with which God will sprinkle his people and thus purify them appears to be an intentional association with Ezek. 36:25

---

[273] Contra Knibb, who contends that the "spirit of true counsel" is used in lines 6,7, and 8 to refer to the disposition of the individual (*The Qumran Community*, p. 92); see Wenk for the idea that this cannot refer to an inherent inner quality but is rather a clear statement of the external performance of God (i.e., the Spirit) (*Community-Forming Power*, p. 101).

[274] 1QS III, 9 makes it clear that cleansing comes from the "precepts of God"; reference is made to "all the ways commanded by God" (III, 10); it is "His (God's) truth" that is involved in the process of expiation (III, 7).

[275] See Montague, *The Holy Spirit*, p. 118; Foerster, "Der Heilige Geist im Spätjudentum," 131; O. Seitz, "Two Spirits in Man: An Essay in Biblical Exegesis," *NTS* 6 (1959-60), 82-95, esp. 93;

[276] 1QS IV, 21; it is significant that both the "spirit of holiness" and the "spirit of truth" are similarly associated with the function of "cleansing/ purification" ("He will *cleanse* him of all wicked deeds with *the spirit of holiness*; like *purifying* waters He will shed upon him *the spirit of truth* [to cleanse him] of all abomination and injustice").

[277] 1QS III, 20: as "the Prince of Lights" is said to be associated with righteousness and cannot tolerate injustice, so "the spirit of holiness" cleanses from injustice.

[278] 1QS III, 24: as "the Angel of Truth" succours the "sons of light," so does "the spirit of holiness" assists the "sons of heaven."

[279] Sekki, *The Meaning of Rua(c)h at Qumran*, pp. 72-77.

[280] In 1QS IV, 18ff., the author speaks of "an end for injustice...*at the time of visitation* he will destroy it forever"; "*the appointed time of judgement* shall arise in the world forever"; "God will then *purify every deed* of man with His truth."

[281] Sekki, *The Meaning of Rua(c)h at Qumran*, p. 208.

(זרק), where the same idea is found. God's Spirit cleanses from "all abomination and injustice" and effects a radical change in human disposition.[282] As in Ezek. 36:27, the Spirit is instrumental in establishing renewed covenantal relationship, expressed in a tangible way by inducing obedience to the precepts of the Jewish Law: e.g., "teach...the perfect of way," "there shall be no more lies and all the works of injustice shall be put to shame."[283]

3.3 Summary

Qumran pneumatology demonstrates consistency with OT traditions. 1QH V, 19; VIII, 11; XX, 11, 12, are deliberately patterned upon the new covenant promises of Jer. 31:31-34 and Ezek. 36:25-27. In these hymns, the psalmist indicates how initiates who had entered the community had experienced a new disposition, which led to a renewed covenant relationship with Yahweh. This then was expressed in a tangible way by their obedience of the Jewish Law. But the role of the Spirit did not cease once the initiate entered the sect. The Spirit was continually instrumental in sustaining members of the community within the covenant relationship ("Thou hast shed Thy Holy Spirit upon me that I may not stumble...Thou hast not permitted that fear should cause me to desert Thy Covenant," [1QH XV, 6-7]) by empowering them to observe the Law. The discourse on the two spirits in 1QS III-IV (III, 6-8; IV, 20-23) communicates a central characteristic of the community; each of its members had experienced the eschatological Spirit's cleansing/purification from iniquitous practices associated with failure to observe the Torah. In sum, the Spirit was perceived to take on a comprehensive soteriological role; it was the agent of establishing and maintaining covenant relationship with God. As such, it induced behaviour corresponding to the teachings of the Jewish Law.

---

[282] See Turner (*Power From on High*, p. 129), Sekki (*The Meaning of Rua(c)h at Qumran*, p. 208), and Johnston ("'Spirit' and 'Holy Spirit' in the Qumran Literature," p. 31) who all hold that 1QS IV, 21 is based upon the traditional biblical concept patterned after Ezek. 36:25-27.

[283] 1QS IV, 23.

Conclusion

The literature of Ancient and Second Temple Judaism identifies the Spirit as the agent of covenant renewal whose specific function was to firmly establish a Torah-based ethic. Ancient Judaism provides the framework for the eschatological promise of a new covenant relationship in Israel's restoration. This can be represented pictorially in the following diagram:

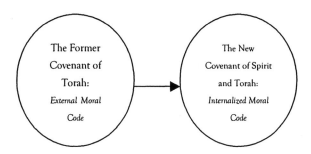

The Former Covenant of Torah: *External Moral Code*

The New Covenant of Spirit and Torah: *Internalized Moral Code*

Diagram 1

New Covenant Expectation in Ancient and Second Temple Judaism

Central to this promise was the belief that Israel will experience a change in inward disposition through the agency of the Spirit. There is widespread attestation to the Spirit as the source of inner transformation, equipping individuals to observe the moral and religious codes of conduct stated in the Jewish Torah. As a result, the Torah is no longer simply an external written code; it will be internalized and received and honoured to become the motive and power of mind and will and consequently, will be obeyed willingly. Correspondingly, even though Second Temple Judaism (Diaspora, Palestinian, and Qumran Literature) exhibited diversity with respect to language, geography, and ideology, there was unanimous belief in the congruent relationship between the roles of the Spirit and the Law; the Spirit was always perceived to act in a complementary way to the Jewish Law in that its primary function was to induce behaviour that was specifically fashioned upon the moral code of the Law.

Because of this survey we are now in a better position to understand how Paul's view of the relationship between Spirit and Law in Rom. 8:1-16 compares with Second Temple Judaism. Paul explicitly stated he was a Jew by birth and continued to promulgate the distinctive teachings of his Jewish beliefs in a positive way, even after his encounter with Christ. Since Second Temple Judaism provided the conceptual framework for Paul's pneumatological reflection, it would have exerted a formidable amount of influence upon the apostle's thinking. However, as we shall see, in Part Two (The Spirit Displaces the Law as the Principle of New Life: Romans 7-8), even though there was significant social pressure to conform to current first century C.E. Jewish thinking on these matters, the apostle Paul makes a rather unprecedented move, challenging the Roman believers that there was a disjunctive relationship between the Spirit and the Jewish Law. Paul's convictions on the Spirit's relationship to the Law invariably were in a perplexing state of tension with his native Jewish convictions.

PART TWO

The Spirit Displaces the Law as the Principle of New Life: Romans 7–8

Introduction

In Part One (Pauline Antecedents: Spirit and Law in Ethical Renewal and Jewish Eschatology), our survey revealed that in spite of the diversity in language, geographical location, and ideological emphases, the various literature representative of Ancient and Second Temple Judaism exhibited unanimous belief in a harmonious relationship between the roles of the Spirit and Law. In particular, central to Jewish eschatology was the expectation of the new covenant, which described the Spirit's primary role in supporting a Torah-based ethic; i.e., the Spirit enabled individuals to observe the Torah. Paul himself was fully knowledgeable of this scriptural tradition and alludes to it[1] in Gal. 4:23-29,[2] Rom. 2:29,[3] 7:6,[4] and more directly in 2 Cor. 3:1-18.[5] However, as we shall see, even though he was fully cognizant of this tradition,

---

[1] See Fee, *God's Empowering Presence*, p. 812, footnote 18.

[2] The mention of "two covenants" in Gal. 4:24 and its association with v. 29 ("according to the Spirit") alludes to the new-covenant promise of Jeremiah read in conjunction with Ezekiel.

[3] Rom. 2:29 combines the idea of "circumcised hearts" with the "Spirit" and thus recalls Deut. 30:6 and the promise of the new covenant.

[4] In Rom. 7:6, "newness of Spirit/ oldness of letter" implies the old and new covenants.

[5] Paul's argument in 2 Cor. 3 corresponds to Jeremiah in that it associates the idea of writing on "hearts" (v.3) with the distinctive phrase "new covenant" (v. 6), which is combined only in Jeremiah in the OT (Jer. 38 [LXX]:31, 33) (Hays, *Echoes of Scripture in the Letters of Paul*, p. 128; Wright, *The Climax of the Covenant*, p. 176, note 7). Also, the contrast between "stony tablets" and "tablets of fleshly hearts" (v.3), in association with the Spirit (vv. 3, 6), no doubt recalls the distinction between "heart of stone" and "heart of flesh" and the work of the Spirit in Ezek 11:19-20; 36:26-27. Paul suspends his normal negative use of σάρξ (see for example, Rom. 6:19; 7:5, 18, 25; 8:3, 6; 1 Cor. 15:50; 2 Cor. 4:11; 7:5; 12:7-9; Gal. 2:20; 3:3; 4:13-14; 5:16-17 cf. vv. 19-23; Phil. 3:3) for the positive reference to ἐν πλαξὶν καρδίαις σαρκίναις (v. 3), paralleled in Ezek. 11:19; 36:26 (Dunn, *The Theology of Paul the Apostle*, p. 147, footnote 103). He has re-created the tradition in a unique way by assimilating "heart of stone" to "tablets of stone" and thus connected it with the Mosaic Law (Martin, *2 Corinthians*, p. 52).

Paul's convictions appear quite contrary to the ideas of Jewish covenant renewal and eschatological beliefs.[6] Paul demonstrates how the Spirit's role in ethics displaces Law observance as the principle of new life in the present age. Law observance was part of the previous age of God's salvific plan, which has been displaced by the soteriological work of the Spirit.

In order to appreciate Paul's explication on the relationship between the Spirit and the Law we shall have to go back to Rom. 7, since the antithesis between Spirit and Law begins here and carries over to Rom. 8. This can be depicted pictorially in the following diagram[7]:

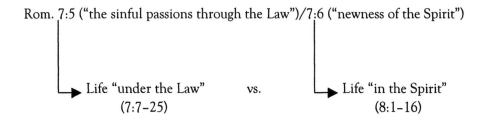

Rom. 7:5 ("the sinful passions through the Law")/7:6 ("newness of the Spirit")

Life "under the Law"   vs.   Life "in the Spirit"
(7:7-25)   (8:1-16)

---

[6] Ironically, even Fee, who interprets Paul contending for a "Torah-less" position, can still claim that his thoughts in Rom. 7-8 coincide with Jewish eschatological expectation based upon the promises in Ezek. 36:26-27; Jer. 31:31-33 (Fee, *God's Empowering Presence*, pp. 813-16); see also Brendan Byrne who communicates the same idea (*Romans*, Sacra Pagina Series Vol. 6 [Collegeville, MN: The Liturgical Press, 1996], p. 212). Certainly, a disjunctive relationship between Spirit and Law (cf. Rom. 7:6; 8:2) is an indication that Paul's thoughts do not conform to contemporary Jewish eschatological expectation. Even if we posit that Paul made a distinction between the Spirit's work in creating the "righteousness" the Law called for and the Law itself, this would still counter the claim of Ezek. 36:25-27 and Jer. 31:31-34, which made no such distinction. The fact remains that it would have been inconceivable for Jews contemporary with Paul to advocate a position that the Law actually resulted in "death" (cf. Rom. 7:5, 9, 11; 8:2) or even promote any form of "Torah-less" position as Paul does. This means that we are faced with the stark reality that Paul's thoughts in Rom. 7-8 on the relationship between the Spirit and Law are possibly in a state of tension with Jewish eschatological expectation. It is the purpose of this part of our investigation to examine whether Paul did in fact conceive of a disjunction between the Spirit and Law.

[7] "Romans 7:5-6 are therefore programmatic for the discussion that follows...Structurally, 7:6d's 'oldness of letter' is taken up in 7:7-25, even as 7:6c's 'newness of the Spirit' acts as a heading for Rom 8. Romans 7 is clearly discussing existence under the law apart from the Spirit" (A. Andrew Das, *Paul, the Law and the Covenant* [Peabody, MA: Hendrickson Publishers, 2001], p. 224, main text and footnote 33).

The subject of Rom. 7:5—"the sinful passions, which were aroused by the Law" (τὰ παθήματα τῶν ἁμαρτιῶν τὰ διὰ τοῦ νόμου)—is taken up in 7:7-25[8] and that of Rom. 7:6—"we serve in newness of the Spirit" (δουλεύειν ἡμᾶς ἐν καινότητι πνεύματος)—is taken up in 8:1-16.[9] These two blocks then function as "panels of a diptych,"[10] each representative of two successive phases in Heilsgeschichte.[11] It is no coincidence that in Rom. 7:7-25, where Paul speaks from the perspective of the former phase of Heilsgeschichte, he suspends all talk of the Spirit, picking it up again only in Rom. 8:1f, where he resumes his description of the eschatological present.[12] Even though in 7:14 the Law is described as πνευματικός, the Spirit is nevertheless external to the "I".[13] When we compare this with 8:2ff, where Paul is describing the new era of the Spirit, the Spirit is said to be "residing" within the believer (8:9, 11). This indicates that for Paul the Spirit was the missing variable in the previous age, when one's relationship with God was entirely dependent upon the Law as the principle of life (cf. Rom. 7:10). This is consistent with the character of

---

[8] See particularly Rom. 7:9-11; the statement "the commandment intended for life, resulted in death" (v.10) is comparable to "sinful passions, which were aroused by the Law...to bear fruit for death" (7:5).

[9] See particularly Rom. 8:2; the statement "the law of the Spirit of life" is reminiscent of "the newness of the Spirit" (7:6).

[10] This is Byrne's manner of describing the phenomenon in Rom. 7-8 (Romans, p. 213).

[11] The ὅτε and νυνί signal the contrast between νόμος and πνεῦμα in Rom. 7:5-6 and correspond to the παλαι-/ καινο- contrast in Rom. 7:6, which is always a salvation-historical description in the Pauline corpus (2 Cor. 3:6, 14; 5:17 cf. Eph. 4:22-24) (Moo, Romans 1-8, pp. 439, 446); Dunn readily admits that Rom. 7:5 and 7:6 are descriptive of two separate phases in salvation-history (Romans 1-8, see comment, "This [7:5] is clearly a description of their preChristian position and experience" [p. 363] / "Once again the eschatological and conversion-initiation νυνί [7:6]..." [p. 365]). Yet, at the same time, he claims that Paul is speaking from the perspective of the present eschatological aeon in Rom. 7:7-25, even though there is sufficient association made between Rom. 7:5 and 7:7-25 ("...[Rom. 7:7-25] are sufficient indication that Paul has in view the eschatological tension of the present stage of salvation history [emphasis added]..." [p. 377]).

[12] "[In Rom. 8:1] again Paul introduces the eschatological 'now'...It picks up immediately on 6:21 and 7:6...[where] the Christian is alive in a new aeon" (Fitzmyer, Romans, p. 481); the ἄρα νῦν in Rom. 8:1 is resumptive of the νυνὶ δέ in Rom. 7:6.

[13] Rom. 7:14 reads, "The Law is spiritual, but I am fleshly, having been sold under sin." Paul describes the Mosaic Law as "spiritual" because he wants to identify its divine origin. There are references to the Law being spoken "through the Holy Spirit" (e.g., tr. Yad. 2:14). It is not uncommon for Paul to use πνευματικός to describe phenomena associated with a pre-Christ time period: e.g., πνευματικὸν βρῶμα ("spiritual food") and πνευματικὸν πόμα ("spiritual drink") describe the children of Israel in the desert, a time prior to Christ (1 Cor. 10:3, 4).

vv. 7–25, where the emphasis is on observing the Law. Paul forms an *inclusio* between v. 7 and v. 25 with the words, δουλεύειν ἡμᾶς...οὐ παλαιότητι γράμματος and δουλεύω νόμῳ θεοῦ respectively, where this whole section is focused around the "I"'s striving to "observe/ practice" (note the use of ποιέω and πράσσω in vv. 15, 16, 19, 20, 21) the "good," where the "good" is said to be associated with the Mosaic Law as the basis of ethics (vv. 14, 16, 22).

CHAPTER THREE

Discharged from the Law to Serve in Newness of the Spirit: Rom. 7:1–6

Rom. 7:1–6 has been characterized as "a specimen of Paul at his worst" or "an embarrassing manifestation of Paul's argumentative inadequacy."[1] C.H. Dodd contends that his "illustration…is confused from the outset," observing that while in Rom. 7:1 the principle states that the *dead* person is released from the Law's dominion, in Rom. 7:2–3 it is the *living* wife who is freed from the Law.[2] Also bemused by Paul's logic is C.K. Barrett who states, "The analogy is imperfect. In marriage, the husband dies and the wife is free. In Christian life, the law does not die (as analogy would require); Christ dies, and by faith Christians die with him."[3] However, it is by no means a consensus that Paul's argumentative logic is confusing. For example Keith Burton states, "Through a

---

[1] This is how various interpreters have characterized Paul's logic in Rom. 7:1–6 (Keith A. Burton, *Rhetoric, Law, and the Mystery of Salvation in Romans 7:1–6*, Studies in the Bible and Early Christianity Vol. 44 [Lewiston: The Edwin Mellen Press, 2001], p. xiii).

[2] C.H. Dodd, *The Epistle of Paul to the Romans* (New York: Harper & Brothers, 1932), pp. 100–1.

[3] C.K. Barrett, *The Epistle to the Romans*, BNTC, Second Edition (London: A & C Black, 1991), p. 128; see also F.F. Bruce who states, "When Paul applies the analogy, we are conscious of a reversal of the situation. The believer in Christ is compared to the wife, and the law to her husband, but whereas in the illustration it was the husband that died, in the application it is not the law that has died, but the believer; the believer has died with Christ— and yet it is still the believer who, no longer bound to the law, is free to be united with Christ" (*The Letter of Paul to the Romans*, TNTC, Revised Edition [Leicester, England: Inter-Varsity Press, 1985], p. 137); "Probably we should accept the fact that the analogy is inexact without trying to find a more obscure level on which it does operate well" (Ziesler, *Paul's Letter to the Romans*, p. 172); "The simile is faulty in that first of all one person is set free by the death of the other, here, however, by his own death; and then, also, in so far as there the dying person and the survivor are always different persons, here they are the same" (Emil Brunner, *The Letter to the Romans: A Commentary* [Philadelphia: Westminster, 1959], p. 57).

careful analysis of rhetorical argumentation and an examination of semantic theory, Paul has been exonerated and Romans 7:1-6 stands as a fine specimen of his rhetorical acumen."[4] Some give him the benefit of the doubt and caution that Paul's illustrations cannot be pressed too far, since they better qualify as parables rather than strict analogy and exist to concentrate on a single point in the argument.[5]

Previous to Rom. 7, the Law loomed in the background,[6] but now in open view Paul provides extensive treatment and explanation of the Law's nexus with sin. Rom. 7:1-6 repeats similar points already made in Rom. 6 with respect to sin: the believer has "died to sin" (v.2) and is thus "freed from it" (vv. 18, 22), so that it no longer "rules" (v. 14a). Correspondingly, in Rom. 7:1-6, the believer has been "put to death to the Law" (v.4) and, thus been "freed from it" (v.6), so that it no longer "rules" (v.1). The most significant correlation between Rom. 6 and 7 is 6:14 ("For sin will not have dominion over[7] you, for you are not under Law but under grace") and 7:6 ("But now we have been discharged from the Law, having died to that with which we were restrained...").[8] The revolutionary implications of Rom. 6:14 run as follows: because you are "not under the Law but under grace" and "sin will have no dominion over you," then to be "under the Law" is to be dominated by sin, and to be "under grace" is to be liberated not only from the dominion of sin but also from the regime of the Law (7:1-6).[9]

---

[4] Burton, *Rhetoric, Law, and the Mystery of Salvation in Romans 7:1-6*, p. 99.

[5] "Paul's illustrations usually resist being pressed too far, and we probably ought to think here more in terms of parable than strict analogy, let alone allegory" (Ziesler, *Paul's Letter to the Romans*, p. 173); "Paul is affirming *only one thing*, just what verse 1 says..." (Anders Nygren, *Commentary on Romans* [trans. Carl C. Rasmussen; Philadelphia: Fortress Press, 1949], p. 270); "He [Paul] uses the illustration for one point only" (Fitzmyer, *Romans*, p. 455); "However, it is not necessary to push for further points of contact with the illustration (vv 2-3)" (Dunn, *Romans 1-8*, p. 369).

[6] See Rom. 3:20 ("through the Law comes knowledge of sin"); 4:5 ("the Law...brings wrath"); 5:20 ("the Law came in only to multiply trespass").

[7] Paul associated "sin" with the verb κυριεύσει in Rom. 6:14. This parallels his association of the "Law" with the identical verb in 7:1.

[8] John Murray, *The Epistle to the Romans: The English Text with Introduction, Exposition and Notes* NICNT (Grand Rapids: William B. Eerdmans Publishing Company, 1968), p. 239; see also Dunn, *Romans 1-8*, p. 357; Byrne, *Romans*, p. 209; Moo, *Romans 1-8*, pp. 433-4; Barrett, *The Epistle to the Romans*, p. 126; Bruce, *Romans*, p. 135.

[9] Commenting on Paul's logic regarding the association between Rom. 6:14 and 7:1-6, Nygren writes, "He who stands under the law also stands under sin...If we continue in bondage to the

With the words γινώσκουσιν νόμον in Rom. 7:1, Paul indicates that some measure of understanding the Law is meant, not just a mere acquaintance with it. This does not imply that all his readers in Rome are Jewish Christians. Many of the Gentile believers in Rome were probably "God-worshippers," or had significant contact with the Jewish synagogue.[10] Current interpretations of the word νόμος in vv. 1-6 include: generic law[11] (because of its anarthrous state), Roman law (because Paul is writing to Romans who were noted for their famous law),[12] and Mosaic Law.[13] Robert Funk notes, "While the article may make a substantive definite, that is not to say that when the article is absent the substantive may not be definite...In each case the context must decide."[14] It is also a fact that in Romans Paul demonstrates no consistency in the relationship between the meaning of νόμος and his use of its articular state,[15] apart from the tendency to exclude the article in the accusative case when νόμος appears as the object of the verb, even when he intends a reference to the Mosaic Law.[16] Nowhere does Paul use νόμος as a reference to Roman secular law, particularly in light of the fact that

law, we are still under the wrath of God and belong to the old aeon...We are not under the law, but under grace. Paul has certified that again and again, in what has gone before (especially in 6:14) and now he turns to make that clearer, and to reinforce it" (*Commentary on Romans*, p. 267).

[10] Walter Schmithals, *Die theologische Anthropologie des Paulus: Auslegung von Röm 7,17–8,39* (Stuttgart: Kohlhammer, 1980), p. 24; Thomas M. Finn, "The God-fearers Reconsidered," *CBQ* 47 (1985), 75-84.

[11] "...it does not have to remind us of the Torah...νόμος here [Rom. 7:1-6] is simply the legal order" (Käsemann, *Commentary on Romans*, p. 187); Vincent Taylor, *The Epistle to the Romans* Epworth's Preacher's Commentaries. Second Edition (London: Epworth Press, 1962), p. 45.

[12] E. Kühl, *Der Brief des Paulus an die Römer* (Leipzig: Quelle & Meyer, 1913), p. 224; Bruce, *Romans*, p.138.

[13] The majority of commentators believe νόμος refers to the Mosaic Law (e.g., Fitzmyer, *Romans*, p. 455; Byrne, *Romans*, p.210); Barrett proposes that it refers to the Old Testament Law "preserved and developed in Judaism" (*Romans*, p. 126); "It is clear that the Decalogue is the only alternative referent of the two occurrences of νόμος in Romans 7:1" (Burton, *Rhetoric, Law, and the Mystery of Salvation in Romans 7:1-6*, p. 72).

[14] R. Funk, "The Syntax of the Article: Its Importance for Critical Pauline Problems," (Ph.D. diss., Vanderbilt University, 1953), pp. 32-3.

[15] With the presence of the article referring to the Mosaic Law: Rom. 2:14; 2:15; 2:18; 2:20; 2:23; 2:26; 2:27; 3:19 (2x); 3:21; 4:15; 4:16, etc.; in anarthrous state referring to the Mosaic Law: Rom. 2:12 (2x); 2:13 (2x); 2:14; 2:17; 2:23; 2:25; 3:20; 3:21; 3:27; 3:28; 4:13, etc. (Kurt Aland, ed., *Computer-Konkordanz zum Novum Testamentum Graece* [Berlin: de Gruyter, 1980]).

[16] Rom. 2:14 (2x); 2:25; 2:27; 3:31 (2x); 7:1; possibly 7:23; 9:31; 10:5; 13:8.

at this point in time he had never visited Rome to address the residents of this capital city in such terms.[17] Furthermore, it is inconceivable that Paul would build the basis of his argument upon a pagan juridical principle such as generic or Roman law.[18] In light of the use of νόμος in Rom. 7:2,3, where reference is made to the marriage relationship, it is clear that Paul was referring to the prohibition in the Mosaic Law, οὐ μοιχεύσεις (Ex. 20:13 [LXX]; Deut. 5:17 [LXX]; 24:2ff [LXX]).[19] His general use of νόμος in Rom. 7:1-6 means that the most likely referent is Mosaic Law *in toto*.[20]

In Rom. 7:1b-6, Paul's logic revolves around two basic arguments. The first is that the Law is "the power which rules human life"[21] and is applicable only to those who are *living* (7:1, ὁ νόμος κυριεύει τοῦ ἀνθρώπου ἐφ' ὅσον χρόνον ζῇ). Consequently, Christians who have *died* through the body of Christ are no longer obligated to observe the Law (7:4a, καὶ ὑμεῖς ἐθανατώθητε τῷ νόμῳ διὰ τοῦ σώματος τοῦ Χριστοῦ). The second is that as a wife is freed only by the death of husband from the stipulation in the Law binding her to him, so the Christian is freed from the Law by dying through the body of Christ (7:2, 3, 4b) to serve in "newness of the Spirit" (7:6). Therefore, Paul is affirming only one thing; death ends the dominion of the Law.[22]

---

[17] See Dunn, *Romans 1-8*, p. 359.

[18] F.J. Leenhardt, *The Epistle to the Romans: A Commentary* (London: Lutterworth, 1961), p. 177.

[19] See the parallels in the Jewish Rabbinic system (*m.Qidd* 1:1; *m.Git* 9:3; *b.Sabb* 30a) (see P.J. Tomson, *Paul and the Jewish Law: Halakha in the Letters of the Apostle to the Gentiles* [Assen/Maastricht: Van Gorcum, 1990], pp. 120-21); the very idea of μοιχαλίς is written from a Jewish perspective since the word is not attested outside of Judeo-Christian tradition prior to this period but appears numerous times in the LXX (Prov. 18:22; 24:55; Ezek. 16:38; 23:45; Hos. 3:1; Mal. 3:5; *T. Lev.* 14:6) and in Matt. 12:39; 16:4; Mk. 8:38; 2 Pet. 2:14; James 4:4.

[20] Burton's claim that νόμος in Rom. 7:1-6 refers restrictively to a specific stipulation of the Decalogue seems improbable (*Rhetoric, Law and the Mystery of Salvation*, p. 75). If Paul had a single precept of the Law in mind he would have used a term such as ἐντολή (cf. Rom. 7:8-9, "You shall not covet [Ex. 20:17]...But sin seizing the opportunity in the commandment [ἐντολή]..."). By νόμος Paul does not mean the OT as a whole but the Mosaic Law as a code or system of ethics (Moo, *Romans 1-8*, p. 440).

[21] W. Foerster, "Κυριεύω," *TDNT* Vol. III, p. 1097; there is no doubt that with the use of κυριεύω in Rom. 7:1, Paul sets up the real κύριος of the believer (cf. Rom. 14:9) and demonstrates how there is a transferal of Lordship from the Law to Christ (Spirit cf. Rom. 7:6).

[22] Joyce A. Little, "Paul's Use of Analogy: A Structural Analysis of Romans 7:1-6," *CBQ* 46 (1984), 82-90; Fitzmyer, *Romans*, p. 455; Byrne, *Romans*, pp. 210-11; Nygren, *Commentary on Romans*, pp. 270-71.

Some commentators interpret the words ὁ νόμος κυριεύει τοῦ ἀνθρώπου ἐφ' ὅσον χρόνον ζῆ in Rom.7:1b as a statement that communicates Paul's dictum of the persistent obligatory force of the Law.[23] The literal translation is: "The Law rules a person *for as long a time as* (ἐφ' ὅσον χρόνον ζῆ) s/he may live."[24] Consequently, the guiding principle throughout the analogy in Rom. 7:1-6 and throughout chapters 7-8 is not that death frees a person from νόμος (i.e., the Mosaic Law) but rather that every living person is under the domain of νόμος. However, Paul's point in Rom. 7:1b is not focused upon the relationship of the Law to those who are *living*, but rather to those who have *died*. This is a logical deduction from the guiding principle, ὁ νόμος κυριεύει τοῦ ἀνθρώπου ἐφ' ὅσον χρόνον ζῆ in Rom.7:1b. It is no coincidence that Paul uses the verb θανατόω four times in 7:1-6 and each time it is equated with being "released/ discharged/ freed" from the Mosaic Law.[25] This, in fact, is the principle that brings cohesion to the entire passage. All that follows in Rom. 7:2-6 is an illustration and an application of this principle.

In Rom. 7:2-3, Paul illustrates this theory using the marriage analogy. The words ἡ ὕπανδρος γυνὴ τῷ ζῶντι ἀνδρὶ δέδεται νόμῳ in 7:2 reiterate the claim that the *living* are bound to the Law. In this case the woman is described as being ὕπανδρος. This is a *hapax legomenon* in the NT. It has the connotation of being "under the power of or subject to a man" (ὑπό ["under"] + ἀνήρ ["man"]= בַּעַל אִישׁ‎ תַּחַת).[26] In the OT, a wife was considered the property

---

[23] "The common element that sustains the analogy— and reveals its inseparability from 6:15-23- is the obligatory force of law *in both situations,* an insight missed when Law (Torah) is aligned with the 'dead husband' in 7:1-6...The binding quality of the divine Law, like that of marriage law in the analogy, remains valid and effectual..." (Elliot, *The Rhetoric of Romans,* pp.242-43).

[24] Burton, *Rhetoric, Law, and the Mystery of Salvation in Romans 7:1-6,* p. 71-72; Robert A.J. Gagnon, "'Should We Sin?' The Romans Debate and Romans 6:1-7:6" (Ph.D. diss., Princeton Theological Seminary, 1993), pp. 235-36. This principle is not mentioned in the OT but is enunciated in rabbinic literature (e.g., "if a person is dead, he is free from the Torah and the fulfilling of the commandments" [*b. Sabb.* 30a; *Sabb.* 151b *bar.*]; see U. Wilckens, *Der Brief an die Römer,* EKKNT Vol. 2 [Neukirchen/Vluyn: Neukirchener and Zürich: Benziger, 1978-82], p. 64, footnote 241). .

[25] In Rom. 7:2, it reads, ἀποθάνῃ ὁ ἀνήρ κατήργηται ἀπὸ *τοῦ νόμου*; (7:3) ἀποθάνῃ ὁ ἀνήρ ἐλευθέρα ἐστὶν ἀπὸ *τοῦ νόμου*; (7:4) ἐθανατώθητε *τῷ νόμῳ*; (7:6) κατηργήθημεν ἀπὸ *τοῦ νόμου* ἀποθανόντες ἐν ᾧ κατειχόμεθα.

[26] BDAG, p.1029; also Dunn, *Romans 1-8,* p. 360; Barrett, *The Epistle to the Romans,* p. 127. John D. Earnshaw contends that ὕπανδρος modifying γυνή does imply the husband's

of her husband, who had full authority over her (cf. Gen. 20:3, בָּעַל means "to marry, rule over = own, possess, esp. a wife or concubine").[27] Νόμος in the phrase, ἡ ὕπανδρος γυνὴ τῷ ζῶντι ἀνδρὶ δέδεται νόμῳ is used as an instrumental dative indicating the instrument by which the wife is "bound" to her living husband. Paul's thinking here is motivated by the Mosaic Law, in particular, Deut. 24:2ff (LXX), where the Law stipulates that a wife is obligated to her husband as long as he lived and only he had the exclusive right to divorce.[28] In the second half of Rom. 7:2, Paul changes one of the variables and describes its consequences: ἐὰν δὲ ἀποθάνῃ ὁ ἀνήρ κατήργηται ἀπὸ τοῦ νόμου τοῦ ἀνδρός. In this clause κατήργηται with the preposition ἀπὸ means "to cause the release of someone from an obligation (one has nothing more to do with it), *be discharged, be released*."[29] If her husband dies, she is "released from the obligation of the Law of the husband (i.e., 'the Law which has to do with [objective genitive] the husband'—the marriage and the authority of the husband over the wife)."[30]

With the words ἄρα οὖν in Rom. 7:3, Paul draws out the implications of the two situations he describes in 7:2. As long as her husband lives and she marries another man, she will be branded μοιχαλίς.[31] However, if her

---

authority over the wife but connotes nothing more than the marital status of the woman. He cites Num. 5:20, 29; Prov. 6:24, 29; Sir. 9:9; 41:23 (LXX) to support his position ("Reconsidering Paul's Marriage Analogy in Romans 7.1-4," NTS 40 [1994], 69-88, esp. 74-75). However, if we take the MT of Num. 5:20, the words תַּחַת אִישֵׁךְ, upon which the LXX is based, indicates the wife is "under his [husband's] authority" (BDB, p. 1065). That the LXX understood this is made clear in Num. 5:19, where the words ὑπὸ τὸν ἄνδρα τὸν σεαυτῆς are used.

[27] BDB, p. 127.

[28] On the other hand, in Roman law, the marriage could be dissolved by either partner (L. Carcopino, *Daily Life in Ancient Rome* [New Haven, CT: Yale University, 1940], pp. 95-96). In Roman law the woman was obligated to mourn her husband's death for twelve months and thus remain unmarried, otherwise she would forfeit all that she acquired from her husband (P.E. Corbett, *The Roman Law of Marriage* [Oxford: Clarendon, 1969], p. 249). These facts indicate that the Mosaic Law rather than Roman law influenced Paul.

[29] BDAG, p. 526; cf. Gal. 5:4.

[30] N. Turner, *Syntax* Vol. 3 of *A Grammar of New Testament Greek*, by J.H. Moulton (Edinburgh: T & T Clark, 1963), p.212; see also Moo, *Romans 1-8*, p. 437.

[31] The word μοιχαλίς is written from a Jewish perspective; it is not attested outside the Judeo-Christian tradition prior to this period but appears several times in the LXX (Ezek. 16:38; 23:45; Hos. 3:1; Mal. 3:5; Prov. 18:22a) and in the NT (Matt 12:39; 16:4; Mk. 8:38; 2 Pet. 2:14; James 4:4).

husband dies, she is *"free* (ἐλευθέρα) from the Law." The word ἐλευθέρα signifies "being free from control or obligation, *independent, not bound.*"[32] Paul specifically states that freedom is ἀπὸ τοῦ νόμου. The wife's manumission was not from the deceased spouse, but from the νόμος that governed (cf. κυριεύω, Rom. 7:1) the relationship; i.e., there is no longer any obligation to this specific stipulation in the Mosaic Law. Even though the specific referent of νόμος in v. 3 is τοῦ νόμου τοῦ ἀνδρός in v. 2, Paul may have chosen an unqualified reference to νόμος in v. 3 to set up his application more effectively with respect to the Mosaic Law.[33] This means that he is not making a sharp distinction between a specific precept in the Law and the Law itself. Paul reiterates the principle in Rom. 7:1 that the "death" of the husband releases her from the Law. One of the consequences of not being bound to this specific requirement of the Law is that the wife is able to marry another man (cf. 7:3). This complies with the wording of Deut. 24:2 (LXX) (γίνομαι + dative) and denotes belonging to the authority of another husband.[34] In this situation, if she marries another, she will not be labeled an "adulteress."

Thus far in Rom. 7:1-3, Paul has set up the following parallels[35]:

v.1 ὁ νόμος	κυριεύει	ἀνθρώπου	ἐφ' ὅσον χρόνον ζῇ
v.2a νόμῳ	δέδεται	ἡ ὕπανδρος γυνὴ	τῷ ζῶντι ἀνδρὶ
v.2b ἀπὸ τοῦ νόμου τοῦ ἀνδρός	κατήργηται	(ἡ ὕπανδρος γυνὴ)	ἀποθάνῃ ὁ ἀνήρ
v.3a μοιχαλὶς		(ἡ ὕπανδρος γυνὴ)	ζῶντος τοῦ ἀνδρὸς/ἀνδρὶ ἑτέρῳ
v.3b ἀπὸ τοῦ νόμου	ἐλευθέρα ἐστὶν	(ἡ ὕπανδρος γυνὴ)	ἀποθάνῃ ὁ ἀνήρ/ἀνδρὶ ἑτέρῳ

---

[32] "*Free* [from the tax]" (Matt. 17:26); "*independent* as far as righteousness is concerned" (Rom. 6:20); "you will be really *free*" (Jn. 8:36) (BDAG, p. 317).

[33] It appears deliberate that Paul does not specifically use ἐντολή here to refer to a single precept of the Law (cf. Rom. 7:7-8) (see also Moo, *Romans 1-8*, p. 437).

[34] Cranfield, *The Epistle to the Romans*, Vol. 1, p. 333, footnote 5.

[35] I have intentionally altered the Greek word order in Rom. 7:1-3 to demonstrate the parallelism that Paul sets up between the concepts Law, ruling over/ being bound/ being discharged/ being freed, the married woman, and the husband.

These parallels indicate how vv. 2–3 are associated with the proposition of v.1, where it is stated that death frees one from the Law. The first marriage (v.2a, b) is analogous to v.1 in that it illustrates how death severs the wife's obligation to the Law. If the husband is *living*, the Law binds the wife to her husband (v. 2a). However, if the husband *dies*, the wife is released from this stipulation in the Law (v. 2b). In v. 3, Paul employs the same analogy but introduces a different variable – her freedom to enter into a relationship with another man. If she enters a relationship with another man while her husband is *alive*, she will be branded an "adulteress" by the Law (v. 3a). However, if the husband *dies*, she is free to enter into a relationship with another man (v. 3b).

As we shall see, the introduction of this variable in v. 3 functions as a stepping-stone into the application in vv. 4–6 and the concerns for this investigation; believers died to the Mosaic Law in order to "serve in the new life of the Spirit" (v.6). The main difficulty with vv. 1–3 is their relationship with vv. 4–6. Many have made the assumption that the details of vv. 1–3 are parallel to the application in vv. 4–6.[36] If the "first husband" (vv. 2a, 3a) represents the Law and the "second husband" (v. 3b) Christ, and the woman the believer, why does Paul have both the first husband (vv. 2b, 3b) in the illustration and the believer (i.e., the woman, vv. 4a, 6a) in the application dying? Some have resorted to an allegorical interpretation of the illustration. Sanday and Headlam see the wife symbolizing the true self, the husband as the old state before conversion, the law of the husband as the Law which condemned that old state, and the new marriage as the union upon which the convert enters with Christ.[37] F.F. Bruce regards the wife as the believer and the husband as the Law.[38] J.C. O'Neill considers the wife as the believer and the husband as the body.[39] However, the allegorical approach imports foreign

---

[36] This is the deduction of Burton, who claims that "the entire argument is chiastically parallel, and the two major sections of the application [from Rom. 7:4–6] are formally and linguistically linked with the two major sections of the illustration [7:2–3]" (*Rhetoric, Law and the Mystery of Salvation in Romans 7:1–6*, p. 81); see also Earnshaw who posits a direct correspondence between the marriage illustration (vv. 2–3) and the details of v. 4 ("Reconsidering Paul's Marriage Analogy in Romans 7.1–4," 72–73).

[37] Sanday and Headlam, *A Critical and Exegetical Commentary on the Epistle to the Romans*, p. 172; similar to Sanday and Headlam is the interpretation of H.M. Gale, who sees the wife as symbolic of the new self and the husband of the old (*The Use of Analogy in the Letter of Paul* [Philadelphia: Westminster, 1964], p. 195).

[38] Bruce, *An Epistle of Paul to the Romans*, p. 179.

[39] J.C. O'Neill, *Paul's Letter to the Romans* (Baltimore: Penguin Books, 1975), p. 122.

concepts into the text, and even these interpretations cannot be consistently applied throughout the first four verses.

Paul's use of this analogy in Rom. 7:2-3 is best understood in a limited fashion. His argumentation has been characterized as "sequential" rather than "integrative," that is, a forward-moving logic that doesn't integrate the previous strands of the argument with the present ones.[40] Elsewhere, Paul demonstrates that he consistently introduces new elements without stopping and integrating them with the previous pieces of his argument. For example, in Gal. 3:15, Paul sets up a legal analogy comprised of three components: a covenant, its ratification, and its finality. In v. 16, he introduces the concept of God's promise, which he understands as analogous to a covenant in order to make the point that there are actually two heirs (Abraham and Christ) to the promise. In v. 17, Paul elaborates by introducing another element, the Law, which in turn sparks the discussion in vv. 18-20 and includes another new factor, inheritance, and how the Law could be added without nullifying the promise. The two elements (heirs and inheritance) give Paul the opportunity to get to the point that he really wants to make in vv. 21-22, namely, the Law consigns all things to sin but the promise gives righteousness to all who believe in Christ. The original legal analogy in v. 15 has been completely sidetracked in the argument. This example reveals that Paul's argumentative logic is sequential rather than integrative. Consequently, it cautions us not to press the details of the analogy in Rom. 7:2-3 too hard onto the application in vv. 4-6. However, it would be going too far to claim that there is a sharp break after v. 3 and that vv. 1-3 are to be interpreted in complete isolation from vv. 4-6.[41] The expression γίνεται ἑτέρῳ, used twice in v. 3, is also used in v. 4 and suggests that Paul wishes to discuss the implications of v. 1 that death severs one's relationship to the Law in vv. 4-6.[42]

---

[40] See Little's characterization of Paul's argumentation as "sequential" rather than "integrative" (cf. Rom. 5:3—afflictions produce perseverance, perseverance produces character, character produces hope) ("Paul's Use of Analogy," 88-89); Gale sees the illustration in Rom. 7:2-3 as a second step in a syllogism that begins in 7:1 and is continued in 7:4 (*The Use of Analogy in the Letter of Paul*, pp. 192-93).

[41] W.G. Kümmel, *Römer 7 und die Bekehrung des Paulus* (Leipzig: J.d. Hinrichs, 1929), p. 41.

[42] Dunn, *Romans 1-8*, p. 361; Burton, *Rhetoric, Law, and the Mystery of Salvation in Romans 7:1-6*, pp. 81-82; Moo, *Romans 1-8*, pp. 437-38.

Paul's limited use of the analogy in Rom. 7:2-3 need not be interpreted as a failure in his logic.[43] He does give a subtle linguistic indication of a shift in the argument, without completely detaching it from his previous thoughts. In Rom. 7:4, the use of ὥστε ("for this reason, therefore") introduces an independent sentence.[44] The implication is that v. 4 is a conclusion (i.e., inference) drawn from vv. 1-3 as a whole rather than a comparison with vv. 2-3 point-by-point.[45] Had Paul thought of a point-by-point comparison with vv. 2-3, he could have used more precise vocabulary such as οὕτως ("in this manner, thus so"[46]), which is expressive of similarity or correspondence and makes a more direct association with the preceding details.[47]

The words ὑμεῖς ἐθανατώθητε τῷ νόμῳ (Rom. 7:4), which are reminiscent of vv. 2b, 3b, indicate that the believer has been set free from the

---

[43] "The apparent confusion of this passage arises from the apostle's not carrying the figure regularly through" (Dodd, *The Epistle of Paul to the Romans*, p. 101); "The simile is faulty..." (Brunner, *The Letter to the Romans*, p. 57); "The analogy is imperfect" (Barrett, *The Epistle to the Romans*, p. 128).

[44] BDAG, p. 1107; ὥστε introduces independent clauses (i.e., a clause that is not dependent adjectivally or adverbially upon another part of a sentence); e.g., in Rom. 7:12 Paul uses ὥστε signaling a new characterization of the Law. It is not dependent adjectivally or adverbially qualifying something he has said in the immediate sentence regarding the Law ("But when the commandment came, sin became alive, and I died" [v. 9] cf. "So then [ὥστε], the Law is holy..." [v. 12]) and indicates a shift in the discussion at this point cf. Rom. 13:2; 1 Cor. 3:7; 7:38; 11:27; 14:22; 2 Cor. 4:12; 5:16f; Gal. 3:9, 24; 4:7, 16).

[45] Cranfield, *The Epistle to the Romans*, p. 335 *contra* Räisänen, *Paul and the Law*, p. 62, footnote 93 ("But the καί in v. 6 shows anyway that Paul does think of an analogy between the example set forth in vv. 2-3 and the situation of the Christians"); Sanday and Headlam, *A Critical and Exegetical Commentary on the Epistle to the Romans*, p. 173 ("The force of καί here [v. 6] is, 'You, my readers, as well as the wife in the allegory'"); Earnshaw, "Reconsidering Paul's Marriage Analogy in Romans 7:1-4), 71 ("It is hard to deny that in Rom 7.1-4 the καί in v. 4 is functioning in a similar manner, indicating the presence of an analogy"). However, Cranfield would not deny that Paul intended an association between vv. 1-3 and vv. 4-6 (i.e., the use of καί in v. 4 and v. 6). But, he would contend that Paul did not make a point-by-point comparison with the *details of the analogy* in vv. 2-3 ("Paul is drawing his conclusion from the *principle* [emphasis added] stated in v. 1 as clarified by vv. 2 and 3; he is not treating his illustration as an allegory to be interpreted"[*The Epistle to the Romans*, p. 335]).

[46] "Referring to what precedes, *in this manner, thus, so...*with reference to what precedes" (BDAG, pp. 741-42).

[47] See the use of οὕτως as a specific reference to what precedes (cf. Rom. 11:4,5 [οὕτως equates God's choice of the 7000 (v. 4) with the remnant (v. 5)]; 1 Cor. 8:10-12 [οὕτως equates the strong ones participation in a meal set in an idol's temple (v. 10) with sinning against the brothers (v. 12)]).

NEWNESS OF THE SPIRIT

control or obligation of the Mosaic Law and is no longer bound to it. With the use of the passive, ἐθανατώθητε, rather than the active, ἀπεθάνετε, Paul emphasizes divine initiative, meaning "put to death by God" (divine passive).[48] Even though the principle in v. 1 and its application (vv. 2-3) emphasize that *death* ends the dominion of the Law and this is the common denominator in v. 4, the passive voice makes it clear that the death he speaks of here in v. 4 is qualitatively different than the natural death of the husband in vv. 2-3.[49] Paul will spell this out more explicitly in what follows. Furthermore, it is also no coincidence that Paul associates God's initiative to act with a decisive moment instituting a new phase in salvation history.[50] This is nowhere clearer than in the passives he employs in Rom. 6:3-6 (ἐβαπτίσθημεν [2x, v. 3], συνετάφημεν [v. 4], ἠγέρθη [v. 4], συνεσταυρώθη [v. 6]), where believers are joined to Christ through action accomplished by God (διὰ τῆς δόξης τοῦ πατρός [v. 4]).[51]

The prepositional phrase τῷ νόμῳ is taken as a dative of disadvantage (*dativus incommodi*); i.e., "to the disadvantage of the Law."[52] Cranfield interprets the phrase "you were put to death to the Law" in light of the words, οὐ γάρ ἐστε ὑπὸ νόμον in Rom. 6:14. Consequently, Paul makes a distinction between the Law itself and the "condemnation/ misunderstanding" that the Law brings. Thus, in Rom. 7:4, Paul means death to the Law's condemnation/ misunderstanding, not to Law observance

---

[48] "You have been made to die [by God]" (Moo, *Romans 1-8*, p. 438); "We are probably to see an action of God, not death from natural causes" (Leon Morris, *The Epistle to the Romans* [Grand Rapids: William B. Eerdmans Publishing Company, 1988], p. 272, footnote 16); Cranfield suggests the possibility that the passive ἐθανατώθητε refers to Christ being put to death on the cross. However, it is most probable that Paul wants to suggest that this "death in the Christians' past is God's doing" paralleling the passive κατηργήθημεν in v. 6 (*The Epistle to the Romans*, pp. 335-36).

[49] Dunn, *Romans 1-8*, p. 361.

[50] For example, see Rom. 5:17 and 19 where Paul communicates God's abundant provision of grace and the gift of righteousness (v. 17). God accomplishes this righteousness when believers are in solidarity with Christ (διὰ τῆς ὑπακοῆς τοῦ ἑνὸς δίκαιοι *κατασταθήσονται* [divine passive] οἱ πολλοί). The Adam and Christ antithesis signals an epochal shift in God's redemptive plan (5:12-21).

[51] The phrase διὰ τῆς δόξης τοῦ πατρός no doubt alludes to the "power of God" specifically associated with the new era of salvation (Günther Bornkamm, "Baptism and New Life in Paul: Romans 6" in *Early Christian Experience*, pp. 71-86 [London: SCM, 1969], see esp. p. 74).

[52] "The dative noun or pronoun identifies the person (thing) adversely affected by the action of the verb" (Young, *Intermediate New Testament Greek*, p. 44); BDF, pp. 101-2.

altogether.[53] However, if it were simply the misunderstanding of the Law that is dealt with, then why would God resort to so drastic a step as the death both of Christ and of the Christian? A new revelation of its true meaning would have been a sufficient course of action.[54] There is nothing in Rom. 7:1-6 that suggests Paul is speaking about a different attitude toward the Law from that of non-believers.[55] On the other hand, reference to condemnation comes to bear. The context speaks of the Law's nexus with sin and death (7:7-12; 8:1). But it is not simply a matter of obeying the Law and the resultant consequence of death when it is not followed. Paul has more in mind than this. For him, the Law has inherent limitations with regard to sin.[56] In fact, the Law actually stimulated sin in the person who is "bound" to it.[57] Paul will continue and explain that the Law as a system and code of ethics is something that is superseded; it was something associated with the previous era of salvation-history.[58] This is not to say that the Law has no positive value in the life of the believer in the present. For example, Paul speaks of the Law's role as a "witness" to the new salvific work of God in the present.[59]

---

[53] Cranfield, *The Epistle to the Romans*, p. 336; cf. his commentary on Rom. 7:6, where he interprets γράμμα not as the Law itself but the legalist's "misunderstanding and misuse of the law" (p. 340); see also his "St. Paul and the Law," *SJT* 17 (1964), 43-68, esp. 56; "Likewise, the passage in Romans 7 that utilizes the 'letter/Spirit' dichotomy is contrasting those who have been released from the condemnation of the Torah (those who have come to true faith in Messiah and therefore are indwelt by the Spirit), with those who are still under its condemnation" (Tim Hegg, *The Letter Writer: Paul's Background and Torah Perspective* [Tacoma, WA: First Fruits of Zion, 2002], p. 224); similar opinions exist in the thoughts of Richard N. Longenecker (*Paul, Apostle of Liberty: The Origin and Nature of Paul's Christianity* [Grand Rapids: Baker, 1976], p. 145), Patrick Fairbairn (*The Revelation of the Law in Scripture* [Grand Rapids: Zondervan, 1957], pp. 429-30), and P.W. Meyer, ("Romans 10.4 and the 'End' of the Law," in *The Divine Helmsman: Studies in God's Control of Humans Events, Presented to Lou H. Silberman*, pp. 59-78 [ed. James L. Crenshaw and Samuel Sandmel; New York: KTAV Publishing House, Inc., 1980], p. 73).

[54] Räisänen, *Paul and the Law*, p. 46;

[55] Sanders, *Paul, the Law, and the Jewish People*, p. 99.

[56] See Rom. 8:3a ("the inability of the Law")

[57] See Rom. 7:5 ("the passions of sin operated through the Law in my members"); 7:11 ("For sin, taking the opportunity through the commandment, deceived me and through it [the commandment] killed [me]").

[58] Moo, *Romans 1-8*, p. 439.

[59] Rom. 3:21 ("But now, without the Law, a righteousness of God has been manifested, being witnessed by the Law and the Prophets").

With the words διὰ τοῦ σώματος τοῦ Χριστοῦ Paul initiates his explanation of the *agency*[60] by which believers have died to the control of or obligation to the Mosaic Law. There is no need to interpret "body" here in an ecclesial sense; i.e., as the "Church," the "body of Christ."[61] These words demonstrate a strong resemblance to the thoughts of Rom. 6:3-6, where Paul teaches that in baptism the believer identifies with Christ, sharing in his death ("baptized into his [Christ Jesus] death," v.3), burial, and resurrection. Other parallels include 1 Cor. 10:16 ("Is not the bread which we break a sharing in *the body of Christ* [τοῦ σώματος τοῦ Χριστοῦ]?"); 11:24 ("This is my body [μού τὸ σῶμα]") cf. v. 27.[62] These parallels do not mean that in Rom. 7:4 Paul is referring specifically to baptism or the Eucharist but, more simply, the common element in both believers' baptism and the Eucharistic celebration, namely, Christ's physical death on the cross and believers' identification with him.[63] So, Paul's referent for σῶμα is the physical body of Christ and thus his death on the cross.[64] In Rom. 7:4, the use of the plural personal pronoun ὑμεῖς with the second person plural form ἐθανατώθητε makes it clear that Paul wishes to emphasize Christ's death as a corporate event in which believers share. Christ's death on the cross was also believers' death.[65] In this case it is death "to the Law" (ὑμεῖς ἐθανατώθητε τῷ νόμῳ).

The phrase εἰς τὸ γενέσθαι ὑμᾶς ἑτέρῳ expresses the reason for which believers were put to death to the Mosaic Law. The use of εἰς with the infinitive here denotes purpose.[66] This phrase echoes the preceding illustration in v. 3, where death separated the woman from her first husband so that she could be "joined to another" (γενομένην...ἑτέρῳ). "To another" is used as a

---

[60] Διά is a "marker of instrumentality, or circumstance whereby someth[ing] is accomplished or effected, *by, via, through*" (BDAG, p. 224).

[61] J.A.T. Robinson, *The Body: A Study in Pauline Theology* SBT 5 (London: SCM, 1952), p. 47; Robert C. Tannehill, *Dying and Rising with Christ: A Study in Pauline Theology* BZNW 32 (Berlin: Töpelmann, 1966), p. 46.

[62] Cf. Gal. 2:19-20 ("I died to the Law in order that I might live to God. I have been crucified with Christ..."); the context of Rom. 7:4 makes it clear that Jesus' physicality and his death are the basis of the argument ("in the likeness of sinful flesh" [8:3]; "He who raised Christ Jesus from the dead" [8:11] cf. Col. 1:22 ("in the body [σώματι] of his flesh through death..."); Heb. 10:5, 10; 1 Pet. 2:24.

[63] Both Dunn (*Romans 1-8*, p. 362) and Moo (*Romans 1-8*, p. 441) emphasize this distinction.

[64] Robert Jewett, *Paul's Anthropological Terms: A Study of Their Use in Conflict Settings* AGJU 10 (Leiden: Brill, 1971), pp. 299-300; Fitzmyer, *Romans*, p. 458.

[65] "Christ dies, and by faith Christians die with him" (Barrett, *The Epistle to the Romans*, p. 128).

[66] See also Rom. 1:11; 3:26; 4:11, 16, 18.

dative of possession[67] picking up the LXX version of Deut. 24:2 referring to a second husband. The words τῷ ἐκ νεκρῶν ἐγερθέντι are in apposition to ἑτέρῳ,[68] clarifying that this is a reference to the risen Christ. These words are a well-established formulaic mode of referring to Christ's resurrection.[69]

Sanders reminds us that the *modus operandi* of salvation for Paul is participatory union.[70] For example, in 1 Cor. 6:13b-18a, Paul speaks of two mutually exclusive unions; union with a prostitute threatens to sever one from union with Christ.[71] Likewise in 1 Cor. 10, he instructs believers that their participation in the body and blood of Christ will not save them if they commit idolatry; that is, idolatry is a participatory union that threatens union with Christ.[72] Paul does not argue that idolatry is a transgression against the commandments of God (e.g., Exod. 20:3-6 [LXX]) but rather that it is a union that excludes one from participation in the body of Christ. When he thinks in terms of Christ's death as in Rom. 7:4, Paul had a change of lordship in mind. By sharing corporately in Christ's death, believers die to the power (i.e., the lordship [ὁ νόμος κυριεύει τοῦ ἀνθρώπου, 7:1; δέδεται νόμῳ/ κατήργηται ἀπὸ τοῦ νόμου, 7:2; ἐλευθέρα ἀπό τοῦ νόμου, 7:3; ἐθανατώθητε τῷ νόμῳ, 7:4]) of the Mosaic Law in order that they might be united with Christ (εἰς τὸ γενέσθαι ὑμᾶς ἑτέρῳ, 7:4).[73] Here in Rom. 7:1-4, as in his thoughts in 1 Cor. 6 and 10 mentioned above, Paul is speaking of two mutually exclusive unions; believers cannot be bound to the Law while they are united with Christ.[74] Thus, believers have been separated corporately

---

[67] "A dative of possession modifies another noun by indicating the person who owns it" (Young, *Intermediate New Testament Greek*, p. 52); BDF, p.102.

[68] Paul demonstrates that the words τῷ ἐγερθέντι are directly associated with ἑτέρῳ by using the dative case as if to say, "to another, that is, the one who was raised..."

[69] See Rom. 4:24; 6:4, 9; 8:11, 34; 10:9; 1 Cor. 6:14; 15:12, 15, 20; Gal. 1:1.

[70] Sanders, *Paul and Palestinian Judaism*, pp. 453-474,

[71] Schweitzer, *The Mysticism of Paul the Apostle*, p. 128.

[72] Cf. κοινωνία τοῦ αἵματος τοῦ Χριστοῦ (1 Cor. 10:16) and κοινωνοὺς τῶν δαιμονίων (10:20).

[73] Cf. Gal. 2:19f, "For I through the Law died to the Law, that I might live to God. I have been crucified with Christ..."; 4:5, "in order that he might redeem those under the Law that we might receive the adoption of sons" (Gal. 4:5); Rom. 8:2, "The law of the Spirit of life in Christ Jesus has set you free from the Law of sin and death."

[74] "The old relation to law has been supplanted by a new relation to Christ" (Barrett, *The Epistle to the Romans*, p. 128); "Paul is happy to pick up part of its imagery (illustration in Rom. 7:2-3) and language since it expresses so well the idea of transfer of lordship" (Dunn, *Romans 1-8*, p. 362); "Christ, who as *Kyrios* becomes a sort of 'second husband' and is the master of the

by death from the Law through the death of Christ in order to be joined to the risen Christ. Since Christ will die no more (cf. Rom. 6:9), the implication is that this new relationship between Christ and believer will never be broken by death, as the old one was, and they should never revert back to their previous relationship with the Law.[75]

Rom. 7:4 ends with another purpose clause using the metaphor of fruit bearing (ἵνα καρποφορήσωμεν τῷ θεῷ),[76] indicating a tangible consequence of believers' union with Christ.[77] It echoes not only the righteousness described in Rom. 6:15-20 (e.g., ἐλευθερωθέντες δὲ ἀπὸ τῆς ἁμαρτίας ἐδουλώθητε τῇ δικαιοσύνῃ, v. 18) cf. vv. 21-22 (τὸν καρπὸν ὑμῶν εἰς ἁγιασμόν) but Gal. 5:22 as well, described as "the fruit (καρπός) of the Spirit."[78] The two purpose clauses in Rom. 7:4 correspond to the two major concerns in Paul's argument. The first is that the death of Christ severed believers' relationship to the Mosaic Law and consequently brought them into a new relationship with Christ. The second and ultimate aim of this new

---

Christian henceforth" (Fitzmyer, *Romans*, p. 459); even though he misconstrues the details of the marriage analogy in Rom. 7:2-3 and forces its details upon Paul's application in v. 4, Earnshaw has grasped Paul's emphasis on the mutually exclusive types of union between the Mosaic Law and Christ ("Reconsidering Paul's Marriage Analogy in Romans 7.1-4," 72).

[75] Bruce, *Romans*, p. 138.

[76] In Rom. 7:4, there are two purpose clauses. The second (ἵνα καρποφορήσωμεν τῷ θεῷ) depends upon the first (εἰς τὸ γενέσθαι ὑμᾶς ἑτέρῳ). Thus the construction εἰς τό expresses the penultimate purpose and the ἵνα the ultimate purpose (Fee, *God's Empowering Presence*, p. 505, footnote 94).

[77] "[T]o cause the inner life to be productive, *bear fruit*" (BDAG, p. 510) cf. "bear fruit in all kinds of good deeds" (Col. 1:10); "Paul wishes to stress that in those who have been received into the body of Christ, in whom the Spirit of Christ is active and who have a share in the gifts of this living fellowship, the outworking- the fruit- appears naturally, because it is not something manufactured" (R. Hensel, "καρπός, κτλ.," *NIDNTT* Vol. 1, pp. 721-23, quote taken from p. 723).

[78] This makes it highly unlikely that the idea of "fruitbearing" is simply an extension of the marriage analogy in Rom. 7:2-3 and thus refers to the "offspring" from the union between Christ and believers ("The believer is free to contract a new union with his Risen Lord, and obtain new progeny through this fresh marriage" [M. Black, *Romans* NCBC (Grand Rapids: Eerdmans Publishing Co., 1989), p. 94]; see also W. Thüsing, *Per Christum in Deum: Studien zum Verhältnis von Christozentrik und Theozentrik in den paulinischen Hauptbriefen*, NTAbh n.s. 1 [Münster in Westfalen: Aschendorff, 1965], pp. 93-101). Paul's specific referent is the moral character (i.e., "righteousness") of the believer who has been united with Christ. This discussion is sparked by the interlocutor's question in Rom. 6:1 ("May we continue in sin, in order that grace may abound?").

relationship is that it anticipates Paul's discussion on the Spirit's role in fashioning the proper moral character, which he will explain more fully in the following verses.

The use of γάρ in Rom. 7:5 indicates the relationship of vv. 5-6 to v. 4 by elaborating on the concept of "fruit bearing." The phrase, "when we were in the flesh" (ὅτε ἦμεν ἐν τῇ σαρκί), is a description of the pre-Christian state written from the perspective of the former age. This is evident by Paul's use of ὅτε (v. 5)...νυνὶ δέ (v. 6), where δέ functions as an adversative to the statements introduced by ὅτε, and νυνί acts as the temporal marker whose focus is on the current moment.[79] Additionally, the use of the imperfect ἦμεν in v. 5 suggests that he is accentuating the past, that is, pre-Christian position and experience.

Out of the 147 instances of σάρξ in the NT,[80] 72 are found in the undisputed Pauline writings, particularly in Romans (26x) and Galatians (18x). The word "flesh" (σάρξ) occupies a spectrum of meaning for Paul. Rarely does he use σάρξ in its simplest meaning as the Hebrew בָּשָׂר to refer to the flesh (skin) of bodies.[81] The word is often used to refer to the human body as a functioning entity[82] or as a designation for humanity in the general and neutral sense.[83] These do not carry any morally pejorative overtones.[84] However, σάρξ can be used in a more discriminating manner that is theologically laden. It can take on an ethical meaning to describe human life, which is independent of, and even in opposition to, God.[85] Paul ultimately

---

[79] BDAG, p. 682.

[80] A.C. Thiselton, "Flesh (σάρξ)," *NIDNTT* Vol. 1, pp. 671-82.

[81] See "flesh" (בָּשָׂר) *of animals* (Gen. 41:2-19; Exod. 21:28; 22:30, etc.); *of humans* (Gen. 40:19; Exod. 4:7; Lev. 12:3; 13:2; Ps. 27:2; Jer. 19:9, etc.) (BDB, p. 142) cf. 1 Cor. 15:39 ("All flesh is not the same: humans have one kind of flesh, animals have another, birds another and fish another") (BDAG, pp. 914-15).

[82] E.g. 1 Cor. 5:5 ("destruction of the flesh"); 6:16 ("The two will become one flesh"); 2 Cor. 7:1 ("from all pollution of the flesh"); Gal. 4:13 ("weakness of the flesh").

[83] E.g. 1 Cor. 10:18 ("Israel according to the flesh"); Rom. 1:3 (Jesus as a descendent of David "according to the flesh"); 4:1 (Abraham "according to the flesh").

[84] *Contra* James D.G. Dunn, "Jesus-Flesh and Spirit: An Exposition of Romans 1:3-4," *JTS* 24 (1973), 40-68, esp. 44-47. With minor exceptions (1 Cor. 10:18), Dunn advocates the view that σάρξ is *always* pejorative in Paul. He attempts to demonstrate how in Rom. 1:3 Paul's mention of Jesus' Davidic lineage "according to the flesh" makes an association with something *sinful.*

[85] T. Laato, *Paulus und das Judentum: Anthropologische Erwägungen* (Abo: Abo Academy, 1991), p. 95; R. Meyer and E. Schweizer, "σάρξ, κτλ.," *TDNT* Vol. VII, pp. 98-151, esp. pp. 125-35;

derives this idea from Second Temple Judaism, which conceives of a cosmological and anthropological dualism between "flesh" and "Spirit."[86] But Fee demonstrates that Paul puts his own particular spin on this and takes it one step further to show how he understands σάρξ in an eschatological sense.[87] With the coming of Christ and the Spirit, God has ushered in the messianic age. The main evidence of this reality was the gift of the Spirit. Paul's frequent contrast between κατὰ πνεῦμα and κατὰ σάρκα was his manner of distinguishing between the present aeon ("in keeping with/ according to the Spirit") versus the former aeon ("in keeping with the flesh"). Thus, for Paul σάρξ not only denotes humans independent of, and even in opposition to, God/Spirit, but also a contrast of phases in salvation-history; life according to the "flesh" (the former age) has been replaced by life according to the "Spirit" (the present age). This is evident in 1 Cor. 3:1; 2 Cor. 1:12, 17; 5:16; 10:2-3; 11:18; Phil. 3:3; Gal. 5:17; Rom. 7:5-6, 14-23.

For example, in 1 Cor. 3:1 the issue is between πνευματικοί and σαρκίνοι. Paul characterizes the Corinthians with the parallel terms σαρκίνοι and νήπιοι. The word νήπιοι in Paul is almost always used pejoratively in contexts to describe the action or thinking of adults that is not commensurate with their being an adult (cf. 1 Cor. 13:12; 14:20). The πνευματικοί are those who have entered the new aeon and have their existence determined by the Spirit and the σαρκίνοι are those whose existence is determined by the former aeon, still habitually indulging in sins and displaying pre-Christian values.[88] Thus, the Corinthians, who claimed to

---

W.D. Stacey, *The Pauline View of Man in Relation to Its Judaic and Hellenistic Background* (London: Macmillan, 1956), pp. 154-80).

[86] This is particularly highlighted by Meyer and Schweizer when they trace the meaning of "flesh" in the DSS (1QH IV, 29-30; VII, 17; IX, 16; XV, 12, 21; 1QS XI, 7, 9, 12; 1QM IV, 3), the Apocrypha and Pseudepigrapha (*Eth. En.* 1:9; *Jub.* 2:2, 11, 30) ("σάρξ, κτλ.," esp. pp. 110-24).

[87] Fee, *God's Empowering Presence*, p. 819; see also Moo who states, "In this ethical sense *sarx* denotes that which is 'this worldly.' Continuing with his salvation-historical framework, Paul pictures *sarx* as another 'power' of the old era, set in opposition to the Spirit, with which *sarx* is always contrasted in chaps. 7-8" (*Romans 1-8*, p. 442); "According to R. 7:5; 8:8f.; Gl. 5:24 the believer no longer lives in the σάρξ; he has crucified it. This message is new and typical of Paul. It stands behind all the formulations in which there is reference to the victory of God and of His promise and Spirit" (Meyer and Schweizer, "σάρξ, κτλ.," p. 134).

[88] Cf. 1 Cor. 2:14-15 (in this context Paul distinguishes between two ages; "this age" [vv. 6, 8] and the future age realized in the present ["a wisdom that has been hidden and that God destined for our glory before time began," v. 7; "we have not received the spirit of the world but

be Spirit-people, did not live up to the characteristics of their claim to be individuals of the present eschatological age of the Spirit.[89] The eschatological context of Paul's use of σάρξ comes out more explicitly in 2 Cor. 5:14-17. Having identified the decisiveness of Christ's death (vv. 14-15), Paul proceeds to explicate the epochal ramifications this has: "we recognize no person according to the *flesh* (σάρξ)" (v. 16), "anyone in Christ is a new creation; *old things* (ἀρχαῖα) passed away; behold, *new things* (καινά) have come" (v. 17). Paul equates σάρξ with ἀρχαῖα and contrasts them with καινά. The language of the "new" and "old" is reminiscent of Paul's discussion of the *old* covenant, which is obsolete because the *new* covenant of the Spirit has been implemented (2 Cor. 3:6). Christ's death has ushered in a new era of salvation, i.e., there is a new manner of "seeing" things (cf. "So, we from *now* on" ['Ωστε ἡμεῖς ἀπὸ τοῦ νῦν], 2 Cor. 5:16).[90] The adverb νῦν is used with the same nuance in 2 Cor. 6:2: "*now* (νῦν) is the acceptable time, behold *now* (νῦν) is the day of salvation." This means that Paul's use of σάρξ signifies pre-Christian values (i.e., the *old*, which is passing away) and must be interpreted from the eschatological perspective of God's salvific work accomplished through the death of Christ and the subsequent realization of this new age with the outpouring of the Spirit.[91]

Coming closer to the point of Rom. 7:5, Gal. 5:17 is similarly set within a discussion of the relationship between the "flesh," "Spirit," and the "Law." In this context σάρξ characterizes a former way of life (vv. 19-21), being descriptive of those who are destined not to be a part of the eschatological kingdom of God (v. 21). Paul emphatically states that such "works of the flesh" (v. 19) are a thing of the past: "But those who belong to Christ Jesus *have crucified the flesh* (τὴν σάρκα ἐσταύρωσαν) with the passions and desires[92]" (v. 24). The use of the aorist tense ἐσταύρωσαν indicates a past

---

the Spirit who is from God," v. 12]); see also the comments of C.K. Barrett, *The First Epistle to the Corinthians* BNTC (Peabody, MA: Hendrickson Publishers, 1968), p. 78.

[89] It is no coincidence that Paul does not call the Corinthian believers ψυχικοί, which would be an indication that he thought them completely devoid of the Spirit (cf. 1 Cor. 2:14).

[90] The use of ἀπὸ τοῦ νῦν signals "the decisive event through which the believer has entered the new life, i.e., the fact that 'one died for all; therefore, all died'...[It is] the time of God's decisive act which changed the situation of men in the world" (Tannehill, *Dying and Rising*, p. 67).

[91] Martin, *2 Corinthians*, pp. 151-52.

[92] The use of the Greek word ἐπιθυμία itself in Gal. 5:24 (cf. 5:16) need not have a negative connotation (cf. 1 Thess. 2:17; Phil. 1:23). It takes on a morally pejorative overtone only when it

accomplishment.[93] This means that the translation "sinful nature" in Gal. 5:17 used to describe the internal and present tension-filled life of the believer is erroneous.[94] When Paul speaks of the "flesh" ("works of the flesh"/ "life according to the flesh") he is referring to life prior to Christ and how it compares to the present experience of the Spirit. This does not rule out the possibility that believers can be in danger of reverting back to a pre-Christian manner of life if they do not keep in step with the Spirit (cf. Gal. 5:16). Significant for our purposes here is that Paul equates the incompatibility between the "flesh" and the "Spirit" with the incompatibility between the "Law" and the "Spirit." As the "Spirit is against the flesh" (τὸ δὲ πνεῦμα κατὰ τῆς σαρκός, v. 17), so those who are "being led by the Spirit are not under the Law" (εἰ δὲ πνεύματι ἄγεσθε οὐκ ἐστὲ ὑπὸ νόμον, v. 18).[95] Paul places both the "flesh" and "Law" over against the Spirit not because the Law

---

is qualified with particular adjectives; e.g. "evil" (1 Cor. 10:6). Therefore, the word does not refer to an inherent human "lust" in and of itself being equivalent to the "sinful nature." Rather, when used in conjunction with "flesh" it signifies the kind of "desire" that one has who lives from the perspective of the flesh (i.e., "the desire *of the flesh*"); see the discussion in Fee, *God's Empowering Presence*, p. 432, esp. footnote 224; Ernest de Witt Burton, A *Critical and Exegetical Commentary on the Epistle to the Galatians* ICC (Edinburgh: T & T Clark, 1921), pp. 199-200.

[93] "Equally significant is the use of the aorist tense at this point, in contrast to the perfect tense of ii.19. What is being emphasized here is the decisive act taken at the beginning of their Christian experience (not subsequent moral decision...)..." (James D.G. Dunn, *The Epistle to the Galatians* BNTC [Peabody, MA: Hendrickson Publishers, 1993], p. 315); J.M. Boice's interpretation is overly creative and farfetched. He contends that Paul's use of the active voice (ἐσταύρωσαν) rather than the passive voice (συνεσταύρωμαι, [Gal. 2:19] cf. Rom. 6:6) signifies what the believer has himself done and must continue to regard as being done. This is the continual act of repentance. Even though the believer has already repented and actually executed the old nature, as in an actual crucifixion, life lingers even though the criminal has been nailed to the cross (*Romans-Galatians* EBC, Vol. 10 [Grand Rapids: Zondervan Publishing House, 1976], p. 500).

[94] This interpretation is the common error of many; Boice, *Romans-Galatians*, pp. 494-95; John R.W. Stott, *The Message of Galatians* BST (Downers Grove: Inter-Varsity Press, 1968), pp. 146-48; James D.G. Dunn, "Romans 7:14-25 in the Theology of Paul," *Essays on Apostolic Themes: Studies in Honor of Howard M. Ervin*, (ed. P. Elbert; Peabody, MA: Hendrickson, 1985), pp. 49-70, esp. p. 63; note also the NIV's translation as "sinful nature." There is no clear and unambiguous text in the Pauline corpus where Paul even hints at Christian life being a struggle between two conflicting internal natures.

[95] "The law and the flesh belong to the same pre-Christian order" (F.F. Bruce, *The Epistle to the Galatians* NIGTC [Grand Rapids: Eerdmans, 1982], p. 256).

is inherently evil but because both "flesh" and "Law" belong to a previous sphere of existence, that is, a pre-Christian disposition associated with a previous phase of salvation-history. Paul uses the phrase ὑπὸ νόμον earlier in his letter as a way to describe life without Christ[96] and concomitantly, equates being led by the Spirit with being a child of God.[97] Gal.5:18 is simply a reiteration of his point in 3:2-5 and 4:29 that "flesh" and "Law," and their relationship with the "Spirit," are mutually exclusive spheres of existence.[98]

When we compare Paul's words, τὴν σάρκα ἐσταύρωσαν in Gal. 5:24, to the words, ἦμεν ἐν τῇ σαρκί in Rom. 7:5 and their respective contexts, we notice some striking similarities. Speaking from the perspective of a salvation-historical framework, the "flesh," and the "Law" are understood to be a part of the previous aeon (aorist tense in Gal. 5:24 cf. imperfect tense in Rom. 7:5). Both passages associate the "flesh" with "the passions" of sin (Gal. 5:19-21, 24 cf. Rom. 7:5); i.e., τὰ παθήματα τῶν ἁμαρτιῶν (Rom. 7:5) most likely understood as a genitive of quality: "sinful passions."[99] While in Gal. 5:18 and its context Paul implies a relationship between the Law and sin, in Rom. 7:5 he is explicit[100] that the Law is the means by which the "sinful passions" were actually aroused (διὰ τοῦ νόμου).[101] It is the relationship of "sin" and "Law" that was active in our cognitive and physical faculties (ἐν τοῖς μέλεσιν

---

[96] See Gal. 3:23 ("Before faith came we were kept in custody under the Law [ὑπὸ νόμον], being shut up to the faith which was later to be revealed"); 4:5 ("in order that he might redeem those who were under the Law [ὑπὸ νόμον] that we might receive the adoption as sons").

[97] See Rom. 8:14-16.

[98] "This means that everything before Christ, which was fundamentally eliminated by his death and resurrection and the gift of the eschatological Spirit, belongs to the same 'old age' sphere of existence. In that sense the Spirit stands over against both the flesh and the Law, in that he replaces the latter and stands in opposition to the former" (Fee, God's Empowering Presence, p. 438); see also J.L. Martyn, "Apocalyptic Antinomies in Paul's Letter to the Galatians," NTS 31 (1985), 410-24, esp. 416.

[99] Murray, The Epistle to the Romans, p. 245; however, some interpret this as an objective genitive (i.e., "the passions that produce sins"), distinguishing between "passions" and "sins" as two separate stages (J.A. Bandstra, The Law and the Elements of the World: An Exegetical Study in Aspects of Paul's Teaching [Kampen: Kok, 1964], p.127).

[100] In Rom. 3:20, the Law is said to reveal sin (διὰ γὰρ νόμου ἐπίγνωσις ἁμαρτίας); in Rom. 5:20, the Law is said to turn sin into transgression (νόμος δὲ παρεισῆλθεν, ἵνα πλεονάσῃ τὸ παράπτωμα).

[101] Διά functions as the "marker of instrumentality or circumstance whereby someth. is accomplished or effected, by, via, through" (BDAG, p. 224).

ἡμῶν)[102] to "bear fruit for death" (εἰς τὸ καρποφορῆσαι τῷ θανάτῳ cf. οἱ τὰ τοιαῦτα πράσσοντες βασιλείαν θεοῦ οὐ κληρονομήσουσιν, [Gal. 5:21]). Paul will spell out more explicitly how the Law actually leads to death in Rom. 7:9-11.[103]

The words "but now" (νυνὶ δέ) in Rom. 7:6 are a characteristic feature of Paul's style, sometimes simply denoting a logical contrast[104] but usually with a distinctive temporal force.[105] Here, used with the aorist it marks a transition point,[106] the beginning of the present in contrast[107] with a previous state of affairs. These words do not simply signal the contrast between the before and after of individual conversion but are descriptive of how individual believers together have been incorporated into a new dispensation.[108] The words are used in an eschatological sense; i.e., they refer to the "eschatological *now*."[109]

Καταργέω used with ἀπό is an active verb that can mean "to cause the release of someone from an obligation (one has nothing more to do with it)." However, in the NT this verb is used with the passive voice meaning to "*be discharged, be released*" as in 7:2.[110] This verb appears in the NT almost exclusively in the undisputed Pauline letters (22 out of the 27 occurrences in the NT). Paul uses the verb καταργέω particularly in salvation-historical

---

[102] Moo, *Romans 1-8*, p. 444.

[103] We will address the relationship between "Law" and "death" more fully under the discussion in Rom. 7:9-11.

[104] See Rom. 7:17; 1 Cor. 12:18; 13:13.

[105] Rom. 3:21; 6:22; 7:6; 15:23, 25; 1 Cor. 15:20; 2 Cor. 8:11, 22; Phil 9, 11.

[106] See the use of νῦν with the aorist in Rom. 5:11; 11:30, 31.

[107] Thus, the adversative δέ. The conjunction δέ is usually considered a weaker adversative than ἀλλά, yet the contrast can still be rather pronounced (cf. Matt. 3:11) (Young, *Intermediate New Testament Greek*, p. 183); BDF, pp. 231-32.

[108] The use of the first person plural in Rom. 7:5-6 (ἦμεν [v. 5], ἡμῶν [v. 5], κατηργήθημεν [v. 6], κατειχόμεθα [v. 6], ἡμᾶς [v. 6]) is a strong indication that Paul was describing the corporate unity among believers who have all entered into a new epoch. A similar use of the "eschatological *now*" is evident in Rom. 3:21 (the context similarly includes a discussion of the place and purpose of the Law) and 6:22 (the context includes a discussion of past bondage to "sin" contrasted with the current freedom culminating with "eternal life").

[109] "The new aeon of the Christian dispensation...this eschatological 'now'" (Fitzmyer, *Romans*, p. 459); "Once again the eschatological and conversion-initiation νυνί" (Dunn, *Romans 1-8*, p. 365); Sanday and Headlam's interpretation, "as it is," doesn't capture the full force of meaning in this context (*The Epistle to the Romans*, p. 175)

[110] BDAG, p. 526.

contexts.[111] In each case it suggests the connotation of a power whose influence is removed.[112] In Rom. 7:6, the words κατηργήθημεν ἀπό are associated with the Mosaic Law (τοῦ νόμου). Cranfield interprets νόμος in a restricted sense as the "Law's condemnation" or "humans' misuse of it" because of the positive statements Paul makes with respect to νόμος in 7:25b (cf. vv. 12, 14a; also 3:31; 8:4; 13:8-10).[113] In a similar manner, although he characterizes Cranfield's interpretation as "narrow," Dunn views the reference to the Law in a double sense: life as regulated by the Law as a description of covenant status, and life dominated by sinful passions destined for death as determined by the Law.[114] Most see Paul's reference to νόμος as the Mosaic Law *simpliciter* and *in toto*,[115] and with the words, ἀποθανόντες[116] ἐν ᾧ κατειχόμεθα that follow, understand him as saying that believers are not obligated to the Law whatsoever. The antecedent of ᾧ in the phrase, ἀποθανόντες ἐν ᾧ κατειχόμεθα, is naturally the Mosaic Law, as the parallel use of verb θανατόω in the phrase, ἐθανατώθητε τῷ νόμῳ in 7:4 suggests.[117] Paul may have simply attempted to avoid tautology and elided the dative following ἀποθανόντες.[118] Given the context, ᾧ is most likely masculine whose antecedent is the Law rather than neuter referring generically to all that has held one captive.[119] Elsewhere, Paul describes the Law's role in

---

[111] See Rom. 3:31; 4:14; 6:6; 7:2, 6; Gal. 3:17; 5:4.

[112] G. Delling, "ἀργός, ἀργέω, καταργέω," *TDNT* Vol. 1, pp. 452-54, esp. p. 453; Bandstra, *The Law and the Elements of the World*, pp. 77-81.

[113] In Rom. 7:4, Cranfield interprets τῷ νόμῳ as the "law's condemnation" (*The Epistle to the Romans*, p. 336) but in 7:6 he speaks of "men's misuse of it [the Mosaic Law]" (*Ibid.*, p. 338); see also his "St. Paul and the Law,"*SJT* 17 (1964), 43-68, esp. 56; K. Stalder interprets this as the curse of the Law (*Das Werk des Geistes in der Heiligung bei Paulus* [Zurich: EVZ, 1962], p. 288f.).

[114] Dunn, *Romans 1-8*, p. 365.

[115] "It is the Torah itself" (Käsemann, *Commentary on Romans*, p. 189); see also Byrne, *Romans*, p. 212; Fitzmyer, *Romans*, pp. 459-60.

[116] Most manuscripts (ℵ, A, B, C, K, P, Ψ) read ἀποθανόντες ("dying") but the Western text-tradition (D, G) read τοῦ θανάτου ("of death"). The latter reading ("of death") is a copyist's attempt to harmonize with Rom. 8:2 (ἀπὸ τοῦ νόμου...τοῦ θανάτου).

[117] Kümmel, *Römer 7 und die Bekehrung des Paulus*, p. 42; .

[118] Dunn, *Romans 1-8*, p. 365.

[119] Fitzmyer, *Romans*, p. 459; Sanday and Headlam believe the antecedent is the "old state" or "old man" which dies, suggested by the isolated use of ἀποθανόντες (*The Epistle to the Romans*, p. 175).

"restraining" individuals.[120] The driving principle that death severs one's obligation to observe the Law in 7:4 is thus affirmed in 7:6. Up to this point in his argument, this proposition, the marriage analogy, and the application (7:1-6a), give no indication of the Law understood in a restrictive sense such as the "condemnation" or "misuse of the Law" or one particular sense of the Law's nexus with sinful passions. The proposition, the marriage analogy, and its application communicate one point: the Law in toto is characteristic of the previous phase of salvation-history.[121] Leon Morris states this succinctly in the following words: "There is no link between the believer and law. Our salvation is not due to the law. We are delivered from the law because we have died to that by which we were held down."[122]

The reason for[123] this release from the Mosaic Law is that believers are now free to "serve in newness of Spirit and not in oldness of letter." The double antithesis (γράμμα/ πνεῦμα; παλαιότης/ καινότης) in Rom. 7:6 is reminiscent of 2:29 (περιτομὴ καρδίας ἐν πνεύματι οὐ γράμματι) and 6:4, 6 (οὕτως καὶ ἡμεῖς ἐν καινότητι ζωῆς περιπατήσωμεν…τοῦτο γινώσκοντες ὅτι ὁ παλαιὸς ἡμῶν ἄνθρωπος συνεσταυρώθη). Paul picks up the language of 2:29 (πνεύματι οὐ γράμματι), but expresses it in the words of 6:4 (καινότητι ζωῆς). In 1:18-3:20 Paul's point is that both Gentile and Jew are related to God by faith in Christ and are equally disadvantaged through sin. With respect to the Jew, he has no prior advantage for possessing or keeping the Mosaic Law or in being circumcised. Paul makes this point by defining what a "true Jew" is (2:17-29). He defines a Jew with the words ἐν κρυπτῷ (v. 29) associated with "circumcision of the heart" (περιτομὴ καρδίας, v. 29). A Jew is οὐ ἐν τῷ φανερῷ (v. 28) and associated with literal circumcision (ἐν σαρκὶ περιτομή, v. 28). The idea of

---

[120] See Gal. 3:23 ("kept in custody under the Law"). The word φρουρέω ("to hold in custody, detain, confine," Gal. 3:23) comes close to the meaning of κατέχω ("to keep within limits in a confining manner, confine," Rom. 7:6); compare p. 1067 with p. 533 in BDAG.

[121] "There is no law that can give life…The law belongs to the old aeon…it is a foremost mark of the Christian life that we are now 'discharged from the law'" (Nygren, Commentary on Romans, p. 276).

[122] Morris, The Epistle to the Romans, p. 275.

[123] The ὥστε in Rom. 7:6 introduces a dependent clause, meaning "so that" (BDAG, p. 1107); ὥστε with an infinitive often indicates an actual result (e.g., Matt. 13:2, 54; 15:31; Acts 1:19; Rom. 15:19; Phil. 1:13). Here the ὥστε clause is dependent upon the aorist verb (κατηργήθημεν) indicating past action. This makes it is most likely that it denotes actual rather than contemplated result (contra Sanday and Headlam, The Epistle to the Romans, p. 175).

"circumcision of the heart" is a fundamental perspective of Deuteronomy[124] and was familiar in Jewish thought.[125] Literal circumcision in the flesh was based upon the religious view that sin and moral impurity, which the fall of Adam introduced into the human race, had concentrated itself in the sexual organs, because it is in sexual life that it generally manifests itself. For this reason, purification or sanctification of the organ of regeneration is especially required. Consequently, circumcision in the flesh became a symbol of the circumcision, i.e., purification of the heart (cf. Lev. 26: 41; Jer. 4:4; 9:25) and entails obedience that is the result of moral purification.[126] Paul uses it in this manner, claiming that the essence of circumcision is not the outward and physical sign of circumcision but the moral purification that it represents. This idea "of the heart" ("inwardly") corresponds to "by the Spirit" (ἐν πνεύματι). The moral purification of the heart takes place ἐν πνεύματι, where the preposition can be taken instrumentally ("by the Spirit") or locally ("in the sphere of the Spirit").[127] Paul is communicating the idea that becoming a "Jew" (i.e., a member of God's covenant community) is a matter of being created anew and experiencing moral regeneration through the Spirit of God.[128]

Greek-speaking Jews contemporary with Paul used the designation τὰ ἱερὰ γράμματα as a reference to the Hebrew Scriptures.[129] But Paul uses γράμμα in a more restrictive sense, not generally referring to Scripture, since he uses γραφή for this meaning.[130] He uses γράμμα 7 times[131] and all but once it refers to the Mosaic Law, and always in antithesis to πνεῦμα.[132] G. Schrenk defines Paul's use of γράμμα in the following words: "Γράμμα is the Law as what is demonstrably written...it characterizes the Law in its quality of

---

[124] See Deut. 10:16; 30:6.

[125] Jer. 4:4; 9:25-26; Ezek. 44:9; 1QpHab. XI,13; 1QS V, 5; 1QH II, 18; XVIII, 20; Philo, *Spec. Leg.* 1.305 and also the hope of its future realization (Deut. 30:6; *Jub.* 1.23)

[126] Keil and Delitzsch, *Commentary on the Old Testament*, Book 1, Vol. I, p. 227.

[127] Byrne, *Romans*, p. 106; Käsemann, *Commentary on Romans*, p. 75.

[128] Cf. *Odes Sol.* 11:1-3 (late first and early second century C.E. Jewish tradition) ("My heart was circumcised and its blossom appeared; grace grew in it and brought forth fruits to the Lord. For the Most High circumcised me by his Holy Spirit...hence circumcision was for me redemption"); see also Col. 2:11ff.

[129] See Josephus' *Ant.* X, 210; XIII, 167; XX, 264; Philo uses the single word γράμμα to refer to the Scriptures or a single verse of it (*Migr.* XV, 85; XXV, 139; *Congr.* XII, 58).

[130] See for example, Gal. 4:30; Rom. 4:3; 9:17; 10:11; 11:2.

[131] Rom. 2:27; 2:29; 7:6; 2 Cor. 3:6 (2x); 3:7; Gal. 6:11.

[132] The exception is Gal. 6:11.

what is written or prescribed."[133] In the context of Rom. 2:29, Paul's *primary concern* is not specifically with the misuse/misunderstanding of the Law[134] to establish righteousness or specifically the national markers of Jewish covenantal relationship with God (i.e., circumcision)[135] but with the failure of the Jews to measure up to what their outward sign of circumcision requires; observing the Law ("for circumcision is of benefit if you *practice* the Law," [v. 25] cf. "You say that one should not commit adultery, do you commit adultery? You who abhor idols, do you rob temples? You who boast in the Law, through your breaking the Law, do you dishonour God?" [vv. 22-23]).[136] In other words, Paul is claiming that the "outward" sign of literal "circumcision" is just a superficial indication of the true condition of Jewish covenantal status with God. If in fact a Jew *does not obey the Law*,[137] this external sign of circumcision is null and void. The point of v. 27 is decisive in this respect. With the words, διὰ γράμματος καὶ περιτομῆς, Paul typifies the Jew who possesses the Law and has the external sign of covenantal status. He juxtaposes this with the Gentile who does not possess the Law or have the external sign of circumcision. The contrast Paul makes is not on the basis of a "misunderstanding/ misuse of the Law" or on the basis of the "ritual Law" (i.e., circumcision), but on the basis of the Gentile's *observance* of the Law ("Therefore, if the uncircumcised *keeps the Law's requirements* [τὰ δικαιώματα τοῦ νόμου φυλάσσῃ, v. 26]...The one who is physically uncircumcised, if he

---

[133] G. Schrenk, "γράφω, γραφή, γράμμα, κτλ.," *TDNT* Vol. 1, pp. 742-73, esp. pp. 765-69, quote taken from p. 765.

[134] So defined by Cranfield quoted above.

[135] See Dunn, who defines γράμμα restrictively as "circumcision" (i.e., the "ritual Law"), as a mark of covenant loyalty and Jewish national distinctiveness. He associates γράμμα so closely with περιτομή to the point that they are virtually the same (e.g., "whether he refers γράμμα to the law as a written code or intends the phrase ['*who through letter and circumcision are a transgressor of the Law*,' v. 27] to be taken as a *hendiadys*, '*literal circumcision*' [emphasis added], the force is the same") (quote taken from *Romans 1-8*, p. 123; see also Dunn's explanation of Rom. 2:25-29 [esp. p. 124 cf. his forced reading of "circumcision" from 2:29 onto 7:6 [p. 366], even though there is no mention of περιτομή and its association with γράμμα in this context). This is a fatal error in Dunn's definition of γράμμα.

[136] See Westerholm, *Israel's Law and the Church's Faith*, pp. 210-11: "that would seem to fix its meaning as referring to circumcision as a form of *keeping* (emphasis added) the written requirement of Torah" (Fee, *God's Empowering Presence*, p. 493).

[137] Notice Paul's consistent emphasis on practising (i.e., obeying the Law) throughout this section (e.g., πράσσω in Rom. 2:1, 2, 3, 25; ἔργα in 2:6, 7, 9 [κατεργάζομαι], 10 [ἐργάζομαι], 15; ποιέω in 2:13, 14; φυλάσσω in 2:26; τελέω in 2:27).

keeps the Law [τὸν νόμον τελοῦσα] will judge you who, *though provided with the letter and circumcision* [διὰ γράμματος καὶ περιτομῆς],[138] are a transgressor of the Law" [v. 27]). This indicates that γράμμα is an alternate way of referring, not to a limited sense of the misuse/misunderstanding of Law or to the ritual part of the Law, but to the Mosaic Law *in toto* possessed in a written form and thus obligating those associated with it to *observe* its precepts.

The association between νόμος and γράμμα is what Paul takes up in Rom. 7:6. He equates νόμος and γράμμα in the verse:

$$\text{κατηργήθημεν ἀπὸ τοῦ } \textit{νόμου}$$
$$\text{ἀποθανόντες ἐν ᾧ κατειχόμεθα}$$
$$(\text{ὥστε δουλεύειν ἡμᾶς ἐν καινότητι πνεύματος καὶ})$$
$$\text{οὐ παλαιότητι } \textit{γράμματος}$$

The aorist and imperfect tenses (κατηργήθημεν/ κατειχόμεθα) indicate past time, which makes an automatic correspondence with the noun παλαιότης, which qualifies γράμμα. The construction of the verse suggests that νόμος and γράμμα are used interchangeably and are essentially equivalent, both being associated with the past—νόμος with καταργέω (κατηργήθημεν ἀπὸ τοῦ νόμου) and κατέχω (ἐν ᾧ κατειχόμεθα), and γράμμα with παλαιότης (παλαιότητι γράμματος). Furthermore, comparable to the γράμμα/νόμος interplay in the discussion surrounding Rom. 2:29, in the context of 7:1-6, Paul similarly engages in the same type of exchange while accentuating the need to *observe* the written Law.[139] This is a sign that Paul is consistently equating γράμμα with νόμος.

However, his argument is more defined in the context of 7:6. Paul adds another dimension to his line of reasoning by placing his description of γράμμα within a salvation-historical framework. With the use of the καινότης /παλαιότης antithesis he positions γράμμα (i.e., the Mosaic Law) squarely within a previous phase of salvation-history. The noun παλαιότης

---

[138] The genitive with διά, in the words διὰ γράμματος καὶ περιτομῆς, must convey *attendant circumstance*, not instrument. Thus, it is translated, "The one who is physically uncircumcised, if he keeps the Law will judge you who, *though provided with the written code and circumcision*, are a transgression of the Law" (BDAG, p. 224).

[139] See Paul's similar emphasis on practising (i.e., obeying) the Law in Rom. 7: κατεργάζομαι (vv. 15, 17, 18, 20); πράσσω (vv. 15, 19); ποιῶ (vv. 16, 19, 21). The difference between the contexts of Rom. 2:29 and 7:6 is that in ch. 7 Paul is more definitive in describing "sin" as the real culprit (see 7:8, 9, 11, 13, 17, 20, 23, 25).

denotes "the state [*especially with respect to an 'age'*] of being superseded or obsolete," represented as such in the writings of Euripides (480- 406 B.C.E.), Plato (428/7- 348/7 B.C.E.), and Aeschines (390-314 B.C.E.).[140] The word has a cognate relationship with the adjective παλαιός and similarly "pertains to that which is obsolete or inferior because of being old."[141] Set in opposition to the noun καινότης or the adjective καινός (-ή, -όν), παλαιός is consistently used by Paul to denote the condition of life under the age prior to Christ.[142]

In Rom. 6:6, the designation ὁ παλαιὸς ἡμῶν ἄνθρωπος refers to humanity in its Adamic condition. It is the age of Adam, dominated by sin and death (cf. 5:12-21).[143] This cannot be reduced to an anthropological interpretation referring to a constitutive part of a human (i.e., human nature). With the first person plural pronoun (ἡμῶν) Paul indicates corporate solidarity in the previous age associated with Adam. But now the believer identifies with Christ in his crucifixion (συνεσταυρώθη).[144] The old age associated with Adam is contrasted to ἐν καινότητι ζωῆς in Rom. 6:4, which is the result of corporate solidarity with Christ in the new aeon. Paul again describes this using a first person plural pronoun (*ἡμεῖς* ἐν καινότητι ζωῆς περιπατήσωμεν) and the συνφcompound verb (συνετάφημεν).[145] Therefore, behind the contrast between the "old" and "newness" is the contrast between the prototypes "Adam" and "Christ" and the respective solidarity of people with these prototypes of the two contrasting phases of

---

[140] BDAG, p. 751; "age," "what is outdated" (H. Seesemann, "πάλαι, κτλ.," *TDNT* Vol. V, pp. 717-21, esp. p. 720).

[141] BDAG, p. 751.

[142] See Rom. 6:4, 6; 7:6; 2 Cor. 3:6, 14 cf. Eph. 4:22, 24.

[143] See particularly Rom. 5:12 ("Therefore, just as through one human being sin entered into the world, and death through sin, and so death spread to all humans, because all sinned"); 5:14 ("Nevertheless, death reigned from Adam until Moses, even over those who had not sinned in the likeness of the offence of Adam, who is the type of him who was to come").

[144] "The salvation-history dimension here should not be reduced to the pietistic experience of the individual; but the reference is to Christians ('*our*' old man) for whom the domination of sin has been broken by their identification with Christ's death" (Dunn, *Romans 1-8*, p. 318).

[145] The συνφcompound verbs that describe a sharing in Christ's death and life are a distinctive feature of Paul's style. They are used to express the communality of believers to Christ and are set in an eschatological perspective for the purpose of expressing the Christian hope of eternal being with Christ (W. Grundmann, "συνφμετα, κτλ.," *TDNT* Vol. VII, pp. 766-97, esp. pp. 786-92).

salvation-history.[146] The καινότης /παλαιότης antithesis in Rom. 7:6 is commensurate with Paul's earlier usage in his epistle; it qualifies νόμος and γράμμα as being associated with a previous phase of salvation-history. Paul connects the Law with "flesh" (7:5) and this is said to be mutually exclusive with the idea of the believer's present participatory union with Christ (7:4), where each category is descriptive of different phases in time. The use of the eschatological νυνὶ δέ[147] and the use of the past tense to describe the Law are both decisive indicators that he is speaking within a salvation-historical framework and that the Mosaic Law is confined to the previous aeon, before Christ.

For the first time in Rom. 7:1-6, Paul's Christology gives way to his pneumatology in v.6, although it is clear that the two are intimately connected in that the Spirit's role is predicated upon the believer's union with Christ (v. 4).[148] He begins to set up a similar antithesis between the Law and the Spirit as he did between the Law and Christ. He characterizes believers' obligation in the present age with the words, ὥστε δουλεύειν ἡμᾶς ἐν καινότητι πνεύματος. In the LXX, the concept of δουλεύειν/δοῦλος was adopted in the language of worship to God and always implied the exclusive nature of the relationship.[149] This is the reason why those who had satisfied the divine claim on them in an exemplary manner were given the honorary title of δοῦλος (κυρίου, μου, κτλ.) (e.g., Joshua [Judg. 2:8], Abraham [Ps. 104:42], David [Ps. 88:3]).[150] For Paul, it is assumed that humans were "servants" both before and after they became believers: (before) to "sin" (Rom. 6:6ff.), to "uncleanness and further lawlessness" (Rom. 6:19), and to the "Law" (Rom. 7:6; Gal. 4:4f); (after) to "Christ" (1 Cor. 7:22 cf. Rom. 14:18; 16:18), to "God" (1 Thess.1:9). It is no coincidence that whenever Paul speaks of the association between

---

[146] Moo, Romans 1-8, p. 391.

[147] See above discussion of the "eschatological now."

[148] Paul deliberately prefaces the antithesis between "Spirit" and "letter" in Rom. 7:6 with words "we have been discharged from the Law"; "having died to that which we were bound," which recall the opposition between "Christ" and the "Law" in 7:1-4 (cf. "discharged from the Law," [v. 1]; "you were put to death to the Law," [v. 4]). This intentionally places the Spirit and Christ on the same side and creates an inextricable bond between them. Also, as noted above, the words, "that we might bear fruit for God" (v. 4) are an indication that Paul is about to integrate his discussion of the Spirit's role as a logical corollary to the believer's union with Christ.

[149] Compare δουλεύειν τοῖς Βααλίμ (Judg. 10:6, 10) and the words, δουλεύειν τῷ κυρίῳ μόνῳ (Judg.10:16).

[150] K.H. Rengstorf, "δοῦλος, κτλ.," TDNT Vol. II, pp. 261-80, esp. pp. 267-68.

δουλεύειν/δοῦλος and νόμος, it is spoken of in a pejorative sense "to be a slave."[151] However, δουλεύειν/δοῦλος in association with God denotes the positive idea of rendering service to God that is the expression of undivided allegiance to the relationship.[152] Thus, Paul uses the word δουλεύειν to express the key role the Spirit plays in the believer's exclusive relationship with God.

In Rom. 7:6, the genitival use of πνεῦμα in the prepositional phrase, ἐν καινότητι πνεύματος, can be an appositive ("newness, that is, the Spirit")[153] but given the salvation-historical framework in which Paul places his discussion here, it is most likely a qualitative genitive ("newness characterized by the Spirit").[154] Πνεῦμα cannot be a reference to "a renewed spirit"[155] since the contrast with γράμμα (i.e., written Law) in the following clause indicates that Paul is speaking of the eschatological Spirit.[156]

The καινότης/παλαιότης and the πνεῦμα/γράμμα contrasts in Rom. 7:6 have significant parallels with his discussion on the new covenant (καινὴ

---

[151] See Rom. 7:25 ("in my flesh I am *a slave* to the Law of sin" cf. vv. 14-21, 23-24; 6:16, 17, 20); Gal. 4:7 ("Therefore, you are no longer a *slave*" cf. "to redeem those under the Law," [v. 5]); Gal. 4:21ff. (Hagar, the Law, and children of *slavery* contrasted with Sarah and the children of promise). We can legitimately include Rom. 7:6 here because of the manner in which Paul speaks of the written Law ("to *serve*...not in the oldness of letter").

[152] See Rom. 12:11; 14:18; 1 Thess. 1:9 (note the distinction between the positive sense of "serving" and the negative sense "to be enslaved" explained in BDAG, pp. 259-60).

[153] Cranfield, *The Epistle to the Romans*, p. 339; Sanday and Headlam, *The Epistle to the Romans*, p. 176.

[154] Cf. ἐν καινότητι ζωῆς in Rom. 6:4, so with Fee, *God's Empowering Presence*, p. 507, footnote 104; Moo, *Romans 1-8*, p. 445.

[155] "That service is a thing of the *spirit* (emphasis added) and of the Spirit. It demands our *human spirit* (emphasis added), but it cannot be carried out without the help of the Spirit of God" (Morris, *The Epistle to the Romans*, pp. 275-76).

[156] Note especially Fee who is emphatic on this point: "As with 2:29 and 2 Cor. 3:6, the contrast between Spirit and 'letter' has nothing to do with the several popularizations of this language: e.g., between 'the spirit and letter' of the law, or between 'internal and external,' or between 'literal and spiritual'! This is eschatological and covenantal language" (*God's Empowering Presence*, p. 507, footnote 105); see also Jacob Kremer, "'Denn der Buchstabe tötet, der Geist aber macht lebendig,' Methodologische und hermeneutische Erwägungen zu 2 Kor 3, 6b," in *Begegnung mit dem Wort (für Heinrich Zimmermann)*, pp. 219-50, BBB 53 (ed. Josef Zmijewski and Ernst Nellessen; Bonn: Peter Hanstein, 1980), pp. 220-29; Käsemann, *Commentary on Romans*, pp. 190-9; Bruce, *Romans*, p. 139.

διαθήκη) in 2 Cor. 3:6.[157] In 2 Cor. 3:6, the antithesis between "letter" and "Spirit" refers to two different ways of rendering service[158] under the two covenants, where each covenant represents a distinct phase in salvation history.[159] Here, as in Rom. 7:6, this contrast is neither a distinction between the "external" and "internal" reading of Scripture, nor a reference to the "misuse" or "misunderstanding" of the Law. The words, ἐν πλαξὶν λιθίναις in v. 3 and in v. 7, ἐν γράμμασιν ἐντετυπωμένη λίθοις, conform to the LXX's description of the written Law that Moses is said to have received ("the two tablets of testimony, *tablets of stone* [πλάκας λιθίνας] written with the finger of God," [Exod. 31:18][160]). These are references to the concrete demands of the Law, inscribed upon stone tablets and associated with the Mosaic covenant.[161] This is the meaning that Paul applies to γράμμα in 2 Cor. 3:6,7. In v. 6, the description, τὸ γράμμα ἀποκτείνει and v. 7, the designation "the ministry of death" with ἐν γράμμασιν ἐντετυπωμένη indicate that he is referring to the consequences associated with not observing the written Law.[162] Interpreted in light of v. 9 ("the ministry that deals in condemnation") and v. 14 ("the old covenant"), the reference is no doubt to the whole system of the Sinaitic legislation.[163] Paul's use of γράμμα is used consistently in Rom. 2:27; 7:6 and 2 Cor. 3:6 as a reference to the written Law

---

[157] Bernadin Schneider, "The Meaning of St. Paul's Antithesis 'The Letter and the Spirit," *CBQ* 15 (1953), 163-207, see esp. 203.

[158] The use of διάκονος in 2 Cor. 3:6 comes close to the meaning of δουλεύω ("service in undivided allegiance to God") in Rom. 7:6. The διάκονος is "one who serves as an intermediary in a transaction, *agent, intermediary, courier*" (BDAG, p. 230).

[159] Stephen Westerholm, "Letter and Spirit: The Foundation of Pauline Ethics," *NTS* 30 (1984), 229-48, esp. 238-39.

[160] Cf. Exod. 24:12; 34:1; Deut. 9:10-11.

[161] Γράμμα is identified by implication with the Sinaitic covenant (Ulrich Luz, "Der alte und der neue Bund bei Paulus und im Hebräerbrief," *EvT* 27 [1967], 318-36, esp. 325; see also Westerholm, *Israel's Law and the Church's Faith*, p. 213).

[162] Cf. Rom. 7:9-11; "the ministry of death" in 2 Cor. 3:7 most likely alludes to Lev. 18:5, where those who observe the Law are promised "life."

[163] Victor P. Furnish, *II Corinthians: A New Translation with Introduction and Commentary*, AB, Vol. 32A (New York: Doubleday, 1984), p. 202.

whose precepts were to be kept.[164] But in distinction, 2 Cor. 3:6 is more definitive in that it employs a specific reference to the covenant.[165]

Paul's point in both 2 Cor. 3:6 and Rom. 7:6 and their respective contexts is that the Law had a positive role to play in God's salvific plan.[166] However, it had only restrictive value and, furthermore, was limited to the previous epoch. Paul communicates this in a unique manner in the context of 2 Cor. 3:6. In v. 7, the attributive feminine participle τὴν καταργουμένην, which here refers restrictively to the splendour (τὴν δόξαν) of Moses' face, is used also in v. 11 (τὸ καταργούμενον) and v. 13 (τοῦ καταργουμένου). This no doubt refers to Exod. 34:29-30 (LXX), where it is said that Moses came down from Sinai with the two tablets of the Law and he did not know that his countenance had been endowed with splendour. Paul uses καταργέω frequently (22 out of the 27 occurrences in the NT) and consistently with reference to something in some way invalidated or replaced.[167] In contrast to v. 7, where Paul uses the feminine participle τὴν καταργουμένην, he employs a neuter substantive participle in vv. 11, 13, which refers not only to the idea that the splendour of Moses' face was being annulled but, more comprehensively, to the entire ministry of the old covenant (including the Law), which Moses symbolized.[168] And by picking up the point in the story of Exod. 34 that Moses' face had a dazzling splendour to it, he builds an argument for the surpassing splendour of the new covenant through a series of superlatives: "Will not the ministry of the Spirit be *even more glorious*?" (v. 8); "*how much more glorious* is the ministry that brings righteousness" (v. 9); "on account of *the glory that surpasses it*" (v. 10); "For if the thing which was being annulled was through glory, *how much more that which remains is in glory*" (v. 11). Finally, in v. 17, Paul claims, "where the Spirit of the Lord is, there is freedom." In this context the noun

---

[164] See the references to Paul's repeated emphasis on "observing/ practising" the Law quoted above in the contexts of Rom. 2:29 and 7:6.

[165] Paul does not actually use the adjective ἡ παλαιὰ διαθήκη in 2 Cor. 3:6 but it is implied with his use of καινὴ διαθήκη. Furthermore, it is clear that a contrast between the old and new covenants is in his mind since he specifically mentions the "old covenant" in v. 14 (τῆς παλαιᾶς διαθήκης).

[166] In 2 Cor 3:7, 9, 10, 11, Paul describes the covenant associated with Law as one that "came with glory." Likewise, in Rom. 7:14, Paul describes the Law in the former age as "spiritual."

[167] BDAG, pp. 525-26.

[168] H. Windisch, *Der zweite Korintherbrief* (Göttingen: Vandenhoeck & Ruprecht, 1924), p. 117; Morna D. Hooker, "Beyond the Things that are Written? St. Paul's Use of Scripture," *NTS* 27 (1981), 295-309, esp. 299, 303-4.

ἐλευθερία, like the adjective ἐλευθέρα in Rom. 7:3, must refer to "freedom" from the Law.[169] This noun appears nowhere in the rest of 2 Corinthians but in 2 Cor. 3:17. The context assures us that the Law is generally in mind, while there may be a specific link to the παρρησία (v. 12) of "the ministers of the new covenant" (v. 6). This should not be dissociated from Paul's thought expressed in vv. 6-11 that speaks of being "ministers of a new covenant" (v. 6), not "engraved in letters of stone" (v. 7) as was the former covenant of Moses.[170]

In 2 Cor. 3:6, Paul's πνεῦμα/γράμμα antithesis is set within his discussion of καινὴ διαθήκη. This is a sure indication that he is picking up the LXX language of Jer. 38:31-34, since this is the only place where the words καινὴ διαθήκη occur together in the OT.[171] Also, the contrast between "stony tablets" and "tablets of fleshly hearts" (v.3), in association with the Spirit (vv. 3, 6), no doubt recalls the distinction between "heart of stone" and "heart of flesh" and the work of the Spirit in Ezek 11:19-20; 36:26-27; 37:1-14. The expression τὸ πνεῦμα ζῳοποιεῖ in 2 Cor. 3:6 echoes πνεῦμα ζωῆς from Ezek. 37:5-6, which is set within an eschatological context describing a future time when the Spirit would be the agent of renewal in Israel.[172] In light of this it is important to note that Paul understands the Spirit as God's promise for a new epoch, which he believes has already come.[173]

There has been a growing tendency, particularly associated with the interpretation of 2 Cor. 3:1-18 read in conjunction with Rom. 2:29; 7:6, to smooth out the dissonance Paul sets up in his discussion of the relationship between πνεῦμα and γράμμα and its comparison with the type of association the Spirit and Law have in Ancient Judaism's conception of the new

---

[169] See Rom. 6:14, 18, 22; 8:2; Gal. 2:4, 16; 4:22-31; 5:1, 13, 18.

[170] C.K. Barrett, *The Second Epistle to the Corinthians* BNTC (Peabody, Mass.: Hendrickson Publishers, 1973), p. 123; Furnish, *II Corinthians*, p. 237; Martin interprets "freedom" here more restrictively as "access to God" in association with the apostles' boldness to proclaim a message of "freedom in Christ" (*2 Corinthians*, p. 71).

[171] ἡ καινή διαθήκη appears in the traditional eucharistic words in 1 Cor. 11:25, in the Synoptic Gospels (Matt. 26:28; Mk. 14:24; Lk. 22:20), and in a pervasive manner in Heb. 8:8; 9:15 cf. 12:24.

[172] Carol K. Stockhausen, *Moses' Veil and the Glory of the New Covenant: The Exegetical Substructure of II Cor. 3:1-4:6*, AnBib 116 (Rome: Pontifical Biblical Institute, 1989), p. 54; Furnish, *II Corinthians*, pp. 184, 201; Fee, *God's Empowering Presence*, p. 304.

[173] Cf. 1 Cor. 10:11 ("And they were written for our admonition, *upon whom the end of the ages has arrived*").

covenant,[174] and in Second Temple Judaism as well. This is evidently the case with both Scott Hafemann and Gordon Fee.[175] Hafemann argues that Paul's thoughts in 2 Cor. 3:1-18; Rom. 2:29; 7:6 find their basis in the new covenant expectation of Jer. 38:31-34 read in light of Ezek. 11:19; 36:26ff.[176] Thus, Paul's operating assumption is that believers have had their "hearts" transformed by the Spirit so that their response to God's will in the Mosaic Law ought to be one of compliant obedience to the Law itself[177]: "The letter/Spirit contrast is between *the Law itself without the Spirit*, as it was (and is! Cf. 3:14f.) experienced by the majority of Israelites under the Sinai covenant, and *the Law with the Spirit*, as it is now being experienced by those who are under the new covenant in Christ."[178] However, nowhere in the context of 2 Cor. 3 does Paul advocate a new covenant where the Spirit's role in transforming hearts results in compliant obedience to the Mosaic Law.

Fee's understanding is even more perplexing in that on the one hand, he consistently maintains that Paul is promoting a "Torah-less" position,[179] but

---

[174] This is true of Fitzmyer (*Romans*, p. 323), Byrne (*Romans*; pp. 103-4, 212); Moo (*Romans 1-8*, pp. 171-72); Bruce (*Romans*, p. 139).

[175] Hübner is another example of this, who attempts to harmonize Rom. 2:29; 7:6 and 2 Cor. 3 with Jer. 31:31-34 (*Law in Paul's Thought*, p. 147); see also S. Kim, *Paul and the New Perspective: Second Thoughts on the Origin of Paul's Gospel* WUNT140 (Tübingen: J.C.B. Mohr [Paul Siebeck], 2002), pp. 158-63.

[176] "Against the backdrop of Jeremiah 31:31-34, Paul's assertion in 2 Cor. 3:6 that he is a servant of the 'new covenant' both confirms and summarizes the structure of his thought and thrust of his ministry as reflected in the Corinthian correspondence as a whole. From Paul's perspective that which was promised in Jeremiah 31:31-34 is now being fulfilled through his own ministry" (pp. 135-36); cf. "The motif of the new 'fleshly heart' and the explicit reference to the Spirit, which are so central to Paul's thought in 3:3 [2 Cor.], both derive from Ezekiel 11:19 and 36:26f." (p. 140) (see also pp. 177-180, where Hafemann addresses the positive association of Rom. 2:27-29; 7:6; 2 Cor. 3 with Jer. 31:31-34; Ezek. 36:26f) (Hafemann, *Paul, Moses, and the History of Israel*); see also his earlier monograph, *Suffering and the Spirit: An Exegetical Study of II Cor. 2:14-3:3 within the Context of the Corinthian Correspondence* WUNT 19 (Tübingen: J.C.B. Mohr [Paul Siebeck], 1986), pp. 204-18 (Regarding the meaning of 2 Cor. 3:3, he states, "If anything is to be assumed as implicit in Paul's contrast in regard to the law, it is that the law is now being kept by those who have received the Spirit, as Ezekiel prophesied!" [p. 214]).

[177] Hafemann, *Paul, Moses, and the History of Israel*, p. 136.

[178] Ibid., p. 171.

[179] "It is between the Law as demand for obedience but unaccompanied by the empowering of the Spirit and the coming of the Spirit who makes the Law in the former sense obsolete, since what the Law requires is now written on the heart" (in the context of a discussion of 2 Cor. 3:6,

on the other hand, he contends that Paul's thoughts are said to comply with the new covenant teaching of Jeremiah read in conjunction with Ezekiel.[180] Fee states:

> To introduce the old covenant (*whose central requirement is obeying the Law*) in whatever specific form it may take to people who already live by the Spirit is retrogression— because the promised Spirit of the new covenant has come, and he 'writes the Law on the heart' so that God's people will be moved to obey him (Ezek. 36:27).[181]

In Part One of this study it was revealed that the central feature of the new covenant teaching of Jeremiah was not a change in the content of Torah or a shift to an alternate foundation for ethics other than Torah; i.e., God's new covenant people were still obligated to *observe* the Torah. The heart of the new covenant was *the manner in which Torah was to be received*; it was to be internalized (i.e., "I will surely put my laws into their mind, and write them on their hearts," [Jer. 38:33, LXX]). Likewise, Ezek. 36:26-27 (LXX) advocates the Spirit as the agent of renewal, which enables Torah obedience ("And I will give you a new heart, and will put a new spirit in you...And I will put my Spirit within you and make it that you will walk in my statutes; and you shall keep my judgments and do them"). This is clearly the manner in which the new covenant promises are understood in Second Temple Judaism. For example, the Qumran sectarians understood themselves as constituting a "household of the Spirit" and demonstrated utmost devotion to obeying the Law. They had no sense whatsoever of any incompatibility between "life in the Spirit" and "life under the Law."[182] For Paul, on the other hand, these stand over against one another, representing two radically different and mutually exclusive modes of existence. Nowhere in the context of Rom. 2:29; 7:6; 2 Cor. 3:1-18

God's Empowering Presence, pp. 305-6); "But with the Spirit, who in Paul's usage elsewhere is the fulfillment of Torah and therefore the one who brings an end to Torah as 'regulation requiring obedience'" (in the context of a discussion of Rom. 2:29, *Ibid.*, p. 493); "The Spirit is God's effective replacement of Torah observance" (in the context of a discussion of Rom. 7:6, *Ibid.*, p. 507).

[180] In the context of a discussion of 2 Cor. 3:6, Fee states, "This concept of a 'new covenant' as a 'covenant of Spirit' comes from a combination of ideas from Ezek 36:26-27 and Jer 31:31-34 (LXX 38:31-34)"(*God's Empowering Presence*, p. 304); (in a discussion of Rom. 2:29) "It is also clear, from the argument in 2 Corinthians 3, that Paul had read this [*Rom. 2:29*] passage in light of Jeremiah (31:31-34 [LXX 38:31-34]) and Ezekiel (11:19; 36:26-27; 37:1-14)" (*Ibid.*, p. 492).

[181] *Ibid.*, p. 306.

[182] See Davies, "Paul and the Dead Sea Scrolls: Flesh and Spirit," pp. 180-81; Herbert Braun, *Qumran und das Neue Testament* Vol. 1 (Tübingen: Mohr, 1966), p. 198.

does Paul promulgate the idea that the Mosaic Law was to be internalized or the idea that the Spirit as the agent of moral renewal would enable believers to obey the Law.[183] His convictions fall desperately short of what both Jeremiah and Ezekiel envisioned. Rather, in Rom. 2:29; 7:6; 2 Cor. 3:1-18, it is precisely the Spirit that is the ethical norm that *replaces* the Law in the new epoch. Even though he employs the new covenant language of Jeremiah read in light of Ezekiel, Paul's convictions stand in tension with Ancient Judaism on the purpose and place of Torah. This will become more evident as we progress in our investigation of Rom. 7 and 8.

---

[183] "Now that we live in the Spirit, we might think the law is no longer a power of destruction, but a helper by our side; through the Spirit we have received the ability to fulfill the law in a new way, and the law gives us indications how the Christian life ought to be 'the third use of the law'... But this is not what Paul says; he rather says the opposite. Not even in the Christian life is the law able to bring forth fruit for God" (Nygren, *Commentary on Romans*, p. 276).

CHAPTER FOUR

Intended for Life, But Resulted in Death: Rom. 7:9, 10, 11, 13, 24

As was stated above,[1] Rom. 7:7-25 describes the previous phase of *Heilsgeschichte*. The identity of the "I" (ἐγώ)[2] in this section, of which the verses under discussion (vv. 9, 10, 11, 13, 24) are a part, has been the subject of protracted controversy.[3] Four main theories have been propounded, although variations and combinations of these views have also been suggested: (1) The "I" is autobiographical, denoting the experience of the apostle Paul,[4] (2) it designates Adam's experience with God's commandment in the garden of Eden,[5] (3) it designates Israel's experience of receiving the Law at Mount Sinai,[6] and (4) it is an existential representation of everybody in general, but

---

[1] See Introduction (Part Two).

[2] The "I" characterizes the whole of Rom. 7:7-25, being used in vv. 9, 10, 14, 17, 20, 24, 25.

[3] See the helpful survey by J. Lambrecht, *The Wretched "I" and Its Liberation: Paul in Romans 7 and 8*, Louvain Theological and Pastoral Monographs 14 (Louvain: Peters, 1992), pp. 59-91; see also Michael P. Middendorf, *The "I" in the Storm: A Study of Romans 7* (Saint Louis: Concordia Academic Press, 1997).

[4] A.F. Segal, *Paul the Convert: The Apostolate and Apostasy of Saul the Pharisee* (New Haven: Yale University Press, 1990), p. 225; R.H. Gundry, "The Moral Frustration of Paul before His Conversion: Sexual Lust in Romans 7:7-25," in *Pauline Studies: Essays Presented to Professor F.F. Bruce on His Seventieth Birthday* (ed. D.A. Hagner and M.J. Harris; Grand Rapids: Eerdmans, 1980), pp. 228-45, esp. p. 229.

[5] Stuhlmacher, *Paul's Letter to the Romans*, pp. 106-7; Longenecker, *Paul, Apostle of Liberty*, pp. 92-96; B.W. Longenecker, *Eschatology and the Covenant: A Comparison of 4 Ezra and Romans 1-11* JSNTSup 57 (Sheffield: JSOT Press, 1991), pp. 237-39; D.B. Garlington, "Romans 7:14-25 and the Creation Theology of Paul," *TJ* 11(1990), 197-235, esp. 207-10.

[6] P. Trudinger, "An Autobiographical Digression? A Note on Romans 7:7-25," *ExpTim* 107 (1995-6), 173-74; W.B. Russell, "Insights from Postmodernism's Emphasis on Interpretive Communities in the Interpretation of Romans 7," *JETS* 37 (1994), 511-27, esp. 523.

nobody in particular.[7] For our purposes it is not necessary to choose one over the other or to rehearse all the arguments in favour of each theory and get sidetracked into an extended discussion. It is also most probable that each theory has something to commend it and somehow contributes to the apostle's train of thought. This will become clearer as we begin to analyse our passages.

What is of significance for us is Paul's discussion on the Mosaic Law. When we examine Rom. 7:7-25, we notice that νόμος is used 15 times and ἐντολή is used 6 times. Paul's citation in 7:7 is almost certainly an abbreviated version of the tenth commandment of the Decalogue (cf. Exod. 20:17; Deut. 5:21). The words οὐκ ἐπιθυμήσεις in v. 7 correspond exactly to 13:9, which lists several commandments, all from the Decalogue.[8] Furthermore, in Pauline literature ἐντολή is used all but once as a reference to the Mosaic Law.[9] Also significant is Paul's persistent reference to ἁμαρτία in the passage, which is brought into direct relationship to his discussion of the Law.[10] The immediate context gives every indication that νόμος refers either directly or indirectly to the Mosaic Law. In this section Paul addresses how sin uses the Law for its purpose (7:7-9, 11, 13). Rom. 7:7-25 is the first panel of the diptych that expands on 7:5, where Paul declares that the Law stimulated the "sinful passions." More specifically, these verses deal with two specific concerns regarding the relationship between the Law and sin that divide this unit nicely into two sections. Consistent with Paul's dialogical style in Romans,[11] the first section (vv. 7-12) introduces the first proposition, "Is

---

[7] Patte, *Paul's Faith and the Power of the Gospel*, pp. 266-77; Günther Bornkamm, "Sin, Law and Death: An Exegetical Study of Romans 7," in *Early Christian Experience* (London: SCM, 1969), pp. 83-94.

[8] Douglas J. Moo, "Israel and Paul in Romans 7.7-12," *NTS* 32 (1986), 122-35, esp. 123; Gundry's contention that the words οὐκ ἐπιθυμήσεις in v. 7 are to be read restrictively as "You shall not lust" ("Moral Frustration," 232-33) is not convincing, given that in v. 8 Paul qualifies this with the words, πᾶσαν ἐπιθυμίαν, indicating coveting in general is being contemplated. Nowhere is the verb ἐπιθυμέω limited to sexual desire (cf. Rom. 13:9; 1 Cor. 10:6; Gal. 5:17) and only 1 of his 15 uses of ἐπιθυμία outside this context focuses on sexual desire (cf. Rom. 1:24).

[9] For ἐντολή and its association with the Mosaic Law see Rom. 7:8, 9, 10, 11, 12, 13; 13:9; 1 Cor. 7:19. The only exception is 1 Cor. 14:37, where reference is made specifically to the ἐντολή κυρίου.

[10] "Sin" (ἁμαρτία) is used 13 times in Rom. 7:7-25 and is always brought into association with νόμος.

[11] See the dialogical pattern also in Rom. 3:3ff; 6:2ff; 6:15ff.

the Law sin?" in v. 7, which is followed by the words, μὴ γένοιτο, and an explanation. The second section (vv. 13-25) is patterned similarly; it introduces the second proposition, "Did that which is good (the Law) become death for me?" in v. 13, followed by the words, μὴ γένοιτο, and an explanation.

In the first section, Paul is emphatic when he states that the Law is not to be equated with "sin" itself: "Is the Law sin?" "Far from it!" (μὴ γένοιτο ["By no means!" "Far from it!" "God forbid!"], v. 7).[12] But at the same time that Paul exonerates the Law from this charge, he admits to an inextricable relationship between the Law and sin, and proceeds to delineate this in greater detail. First, the Law brings recognition of sin and even stimulates it (vv. 7b-8). In v. 9, Paul states, ἐγὼ δὲ ἔζων χωρὶς νόμου ποτέ. This is the first time ἐγώ is used. Most recognize that Paul is speaking in general terms, using the Adam narrative (Gen. 2:7, 16-17) to typify every human being[13] (cf. the use of אָדָם meaning "humankind"[14]). The sequence in Rom. 7:9-10, characterized by the use of ἔζων ποτέ and the reference to ἀπέθανον, reflect the stages in Adam's fall: "the human became a living soul (ψυχὴν ζῶσαν)...And the Lord God commanded (ἐνετείλατο) Adam, saying, 'Of every tree which is in the garden you may freely eat, but of the tree of the knowledge of good and evil— of it you will not eat, but whenever you eat of it, you will certainly die (θανάτῳ ἀποθανεῖσθε)'" (Gen. 2:7, 16-17 [LXX]). When Paul uses the language of the Genesis story he is indicating a sense of corporate solidarity

---

[12] BDAG, p. 197.

[13] "Paul is using the first person in a general sense, and refers to man's situation before the giving of the law, along with which Paul probably has in mind the state of man pictured in Gen. 1.28ff" (Cranfield, The Epistle to the Romans, p. 351); see also Dunn, Romans 1-8, p. 381; BDF, p. 147; Käsemann takes this too far with his statement, "There is nothing in the passage which does not fit Adam, and everything fits Adam alone" (Commentary on Romans, p. 196); this cannot be interpreted too restrictively as a reference to Paul's pre-teenage experience as a boy, prior to his bar mitzwah (Barrett, The Epistle to the Romans, p. 134), since it is clear that the parents of Jewish boys began emphasizing the importance of the Mosaic Law prior to their teenage years (see Philo, Legat. 210; Josephus, Ag. Ap. 2.178). It is also impossible that a Jewish male in Paul's day could every think of a time when the Jewish Law was not a part of his life. Jewish boys were circumcised even before puberty signifying that they were, from birth, part of the covenantal people of God, and concomitantly, were to live a life devoted to observing the Torah (Kummel, Römer 7 und die Bekehrung des Paulus, p. 81).

[14] "Man, mankind," BDB, p. 9; cf. 2 Apoc. Bar. 54:19 ("Each of us has been the Adam of his own soul").

that every human being has with Adam.[15] In this sense Käsemann's words ring true: "we are implicated in the story of Adam."[16] With the use of "I" (ἐγώ) there is an existential character to the whole section (vv. 7-25), where Paul is also to some extent speaking of his own experience.[17]

In v. 10, Paul uses ἀποθνῄσκω to denote the consequence and punishment for sin as vv. 5 and 13 in Rom. 7 make clear.[18] In view of this contrast with ἀπέθανον ("I died") in v. 10, ζάω in v. 9 cannot be interpreted in the milder sense of ("I was living/ I was existing")[19] but must be understood in the stronger sense of "being alive" in terms of a secured relationship with God that stems from not being morally culpable.[20] Paul uses the verb ζάω with this same theological force elsewhere in the epistle.[21] The referent for this state of being and what transpires next in the verse corresponds to the before and after of the giving of the Mosaic Law at Sinai (χωρὶς νόμου, v. 9) as well.[22] Paul's use of νόμος in the phrase, ἐγώ ἔζων χωρὶς νόμου in v. 9 is consistent with his previous usage in Rom. 5:13, where the Mosaic Law is the point of reference. This phrase describes the period of time prior to the actual giving of the Mosaic Law when "sin" was dead, not in the sense that it did not exist but in the sense that it was not as perceivable and not able to arouse one to activity without the specific regulation as set forth in the Mosaic Law.[23] This

---

[15] Cf. Rom. 5:12-21, where "I"=Adam=humankind ("Just as through one human being sin entered into the world, and death through sin, and so death spread to all human beings..."[v. 12]).

[16] Käsemann, Commentary on Romans, p.196.

[17] "A deletion of all autobiographical inference from Romans 7 makes the chapter theologically unintelligible and fruitless for Paul's encounter with Judaism" (Beker, Paul the Apostle, quote taken from p. 241, but see pp. 240-43 as a whole for the argument that Rom. 7 reflects, in some sense, Paul's own life).

[18] R. Bultmann, "θάνατος, κτλ.," TDNT Vol. III, pp. 7-25, esp. p. 15.

[19] P. Benoit, "La Loi et la Croix d'après Saint Paul (Rom. 7:7-8:4)," RB 47 (1938), 481-509, esp. 487; Moo, Romans 1-8, p. 462.

[20] Paul uses ζάω in contexts that describe the believer's relationship with God and the specific pattern of behaviour that accompanies this status (see under Danker's definition of ζάω as "to live in a transcendent sense, live, of the sanctified life of a child of God...to conduct oneself in a pattern of behaviour" [BDAG, p. 425]).

[21] See Rom. 1:17; 6:13; 8:13; 10:5.

[22] Exod. 20:1ff; (Moo, Romans 1-8, p. 462).

[23] In Rom. 7:7, Paul states, "I should not have known what coveting really was if the Law had not said, 'Do not covet.'" The use of ἔγνων here does not mean that people do not actually sin in the absence of the Law but rather that they do not fully recognize sin for what it is, apart from

is consistent with the words, ἐλθούσης δὲ τῆς ἐντολῆς ἡ ἁμαρτία ἀνέζησεν, that most likely refer to the sequence of the Adam story in Gen. 2-3 read in light of the giving of the Law in Exod. 20: God gives the commandment (2:16-17), sin came to life through the serpent (3:1-5), Adam and Eve sin (3:6), death results (3:19), and God expels Adam and Eve from the Garden and the relationship between God and humans is strained (3:24), when the Mosaic Law was given to the children of Israel, sin "sprang to life again" (ἡ ἁμαρτία ἀνέζησεν) (Exod. 20:1ff.).[24] In this way Paul is conflating the corporate solidarity humans have with Adam and his disobedience of God's commandment, with Israel's experience of the Mosaic Law in Exod. 20. There is evidence that Jewish tradition understood Adam as bound by the Torah. One of the Aramaic paraphrases of the OT, Tg. Neof. I, on Gen. 2:15f reads, "And the Lord God took man and caused him to dwell in the Garden of Eden, in order to keep the Law (emphasis added) and to follow his commandments."[25] Also, Tg. Yer. I on Gen. 2:15; 3:9, 22, reads the Mosaic Law into the Genesis story and through the life of Adam and Eve. Philo, an older contemporary of Paul, also interprets the Genesis story in light of the prohibition of covetousness in Leg. All. 1.90-97.[26] Putting this together, it is very probable that Paul knew this interpretation and in the progression of thought in vv. 9-10a ("I was living without the Law"—"the commandment having come"—"sin came to life"—"I died"), he is tracing "sin's" association with the Mosaic Law back to Adam, and because all people are in solidarity

---

the Law (cf. 3:20). It is only in light of the commandment against coveting that they recognize coveting for what it really is—a deliberate disobeying of God's will (Cranfield, The Epistle to the Romans, p. 348).

[24] The use of ἀναζάω in Rom. 7:9 means "to function after being dormant, spring into life" (BDAG, p. 62). In this case, it means that sin "was alive" in Adam's transgression and it "sprang to life" again in the transgressions of the Mosaic Law. Sin "sprang to life" in the sense that the "Law aroused it to activity" (Fitzmyer, Romans, p. 467).

[25] In the same targum, Gen. 3:22 is interpreted as follows: "If Adam had kept the commandment of the Law (emphasis added) and observed its commandments, he would have lived and, like the tree of life, continued to exist for eternity."

[26] P. Stuhlmacher, "Paul's Understanding of the Law in the Letter to the Romans," SEA 50 (1985), 87-104, esp. 98; S. Lyonnet, "'Tu ne convoiteras pas' (Rom. vii 7)," Neotestamentica et patristica: Eine Freundesgabe, Herrn Professor Dr. Oscar Cullmann...überreicht, NovTSup 6 (ed. W.C. van Unnik; Leiden: Brill, 1962), pp. 157-65.

with Adam, the "I" can typify the experience of everybody (both Jew and Gentile).[27]

In Rom. 7:10 Paul writes, "It was found that the commandment intended for life, actually resulted in death" (εὑρέθη μοι ἡ ἐντολὴ ἡ εἰς ζωήν, αὕτη εἰς θάνατον). In this statement Paul is consistent with the OT and Second Temple Judaism, which attributed a life-giving function to observing the Mosaic Law. In the OT, Torah obedience is said to result in life (e.g. "If you will hear the commandments of the Lord your God...to keep his righteous requirements, and his judgements, then you will live [ζήσεσθε]" [Deut. 30:16 LXX]).[28] In Ancient Judaism the basis of "life" is the covenant relationship with Yahweh expressed tangibly in observing the Torah ("If you will obey the commandments of the Lord you God...you will live...But if your heart changes and you will not obey, and you go astray and worship other gods, and serve them...you will perish" [30:16-18]). The definition of "life" also includes material blessings such as the possession of land ("and the Lord your God will bless you in all the land into which you go to inherit it" [Deut. 30:16 LXX]).[29] In Second Temple Judaism, God's commandments are called the "commandments of life."[30] The wording in Pss. Sol. 14:2 comes remarkably close to Paul's rendering: ἐν νόμῳ, ᾧ ἐνετείλατο ἡμῖν εἰς ζωὴν ἡμῶν. The Law had a mediatorial position between God and humans in that it regulated and maintained the covenantal relationship.[31] When one was in the covenant relationship, one was said to possess "life."[32] Paul himself understood the role

---

[27] See N.T. Wright, who observes that the problem addressed by Paul here is not "the hidden Jew in all of us" (Käsemann) but "the hidden Adam in Israel" ("The Messiah and the People of God: A Study of Pauline Theology with Particular Reference to the Argument of the Epistle to the Romans," [D.Phil., Oxford University, 1980], p. 152); even Moo who strenuously argues that the "I" does not make an allusion to Adam, allows for the idea that "the experience of Israel with the law depicted here is parallel to and, to some extent, recapitulates the experience of Adam with the commandment of God in the Garden" (Romans 1-8, pp. 463-64).

[28] See also Lev. 18:5; Deut. 4:1; 5:33; 6:24-25; Ezek. 18:19 c f. vv. 9, 21; 20:11 cf. vv. 13, 21; Neh. 9:29.

[29] Patrick D. Miller, Deuteronomy Interpretation (Louisville: John Knox Press, 1990), p. 214.

[30] See Bar. 3:9, where the commandments are called, ἐντολαὶ ζωῆς cf. 4:1; see also R. Bultmann, "The Concept of Life in Judaism," p. 855.

[31] This is made clear by Sanders' definition of "covenantal nomism" (Paul and Palestinian Judaism, pp. 422, 426-28).

[32] See Sir. 17:11, 12, where the "Law of life" (v. 11) is said to be equivalent to the God who "established an eternal covenant" (v. 12); see also Deut. 30:15-20, where "life" is promised to those who obey (v. 16) and are in a relationship with God (i.e., "hold fast to him" [v. 20]),

of the Law in Judaism in this manner when he cites Lev. 18:5 in Rom. 10:5: "the person who does these things (*what the Law requires*) shall live by them."[33] Lev. 18:5 can be regarded as the representative expression of Israel's obligation to the covenant. The idea of ζάω here means "living" within the covenant.[34] Paul certainly understood this text as life within the covenant in the same manner as his Jewish contemporaries. This is the meaning apparent in Rom. 7:10.[35] The use of εἰς before ζωήν and θάνατον signifies respectively both "intended result" and "actual consequence,"[36] so the interpretation is, "the commandment that *was intended* to bring life, *actually* brought death."[37] Paul perceived that observing the Law had a life-giving intention, but in reality it resulted in death.

In 7:11, 13, Paul makes it clear that "sin" is the real culprit and the cause of "death," not the Law. However, "sin" forms an inextricable nexus with the Law from the time of Adam, and in effect, he claims that the whole system associated with the Law results in "death." V. 11 recapitulates the idea of v. 8a (note the similar use of ἀφορμή and the prepositional phrase διὰ τῆς ἐντολῆς) that sin used the commandment as a bridgehead to kill. As with v. 8a, the prepositional phase διὰ τῆς ἐντολῆς goes with the principal verb to bring a parallel with the first two clauses:

$$
\begin{array}{ll}
\delta\iota\grave{\alpha}\ \tau\tilde{\eta}\varsigma\ \dot{\epsilon}\nu\tau o\lambda\tilde{\eta}\varsigma & \dot{\epsilon}\xi\eta\pi\acute{\alpha}\tau\eta\sigma\acute{\epsilon}\nu\ \mu\epsilon \\
\kappa\alpha\grave{\iota}\ \ \delta\iota'\ \alpha\dot{\upsilon}\tau\tilde{\eta}\varsigma & \dot{\alpha}\pi\acute{\epsilon}\kappa\tau\epsilon\iota\nu\epsilon\nu
\end{array}
$$

---

whereas "death" (v. 17) is the result of those who sever their relationship with God (i.e., "bow to other gods" [v. 18]).

[33] See also Gal. 3:12, where Paul also has Lev. 18:5 in mind.

[34] Cf. Philo's use of Lev. 18:5 in *Congr.* 86-87.

[35] Stuhlmacher reads Rom. 7:10 in an overly limited fashion as a reference to the commandment of God in the Garden given to Adam to protect life in paradise, which eventually brought about Adam's death when he disobeyed it (*Paul's Letter to the Romans*, p. 108). Nevertheless, it is also evident that when Adam disobeyed God's command he was expelled from God's presence (Gen. 3:23-24).

[36] See A.Oepke, who claims in Rom. 7:10, Paul intends εἰς to denote both "goal" and "consequence" (intended "goal" was to bring "life," but the "consequence" was "death" ["εἰς," *TDNT* Vol. II, pp. 420-34, esp. p. 429]).

[37] NIV, "the very commandment that was intended to bring life, actually brought death"; NRSV, "the very commandment that promised life proved to be death"; NASB, "this commandment which was to result in life, proved to result in death."

The use of ἐξηπάτησέν με here echoes Gen. 3:13 ("the serpent *deceived me* [ἠπάτησέν με] and I ate"). This refers specifically to Eve's deception but ultimately has Adam's confrontation with the divine command in mind (Gen. 2:16, 17).[38] However, in place of the "serpent" Paul places "sin" as the culprit that used the commandment of God to deceive and kill. In both Rom. 7:8, 11, and the Genesis account (i.e., the command of God)[39] the Law is the means (διὰ τῆς ἐντολῆς ["by means of the commandment"]) by which sin operates. In v. 8, Paul spoke of the Law as instrumental in creating sinful impulses but in v. 11 he shows it to have been used to "deceive" and "kill."

In vv. 10-13 Paul wishes to call attention to the paradox between the Law's intention to produce life when it is observed and the actual result of death when it is not observed. God meant the Law for life, but it actually brought death (v.10). Sin used it, it deceived, and it killed (v. 11). Even though God's Law is holy, just, and good (v. 12), and even though it was not itself the cause of death, sin worked through it to produce death (v. 13). In v. 13, using two ἵνα clauses, Paul again reiterates his point that the Law becomes the instrument through which sin operates: "*in order that* it might appear to be sin, *through that which is good* (διὰ τοῦ ἀγαθοῦ; cf. the description of the "commandment" [i.e., Law] as ἀγαθή in v. 12) by working death in me"; "*in order that* sin might become excessively sinful *through the commandment* (διὰ τῆς ἐντολῆς)." But at the same time, the two ἵνα clauses convey a divine purpose in all of this; sin reveals its true colours ("in order that it might appear that sin"/ "in order that sin might become excessively sinful").[40] The severity of the situation paves the way for God's solution. This is somewhat similar to Paul's remarks in Rom. 5:20 that the Law came in "to multiply the trespass; but where sin increased, grace increased all the more."[41] Rom. 7:13 and the

---

[38] See the use of ἐξαπατάω in 2 Cor. 11:13 and 1 Tim. 2:14, where it is used to describe Eve's deception.

[39] Disobeying the command of God would result in death (Gen. 2:17: "...you shall not eat, for in the day that you eat of it you shall die").

[40] "But his main purpose is rather to emphasize that even the law's being used by sin for death is part of God's fuller and deeper strategy to bring out the character of sin and of its end product and payment—only death" (Dunn, *Romans 1-8*, p. 387); "These purposes are God's, though they are neither whole, nor yet the ultimate element" (Cranfield, *The Epistle to the Romans*, p. 354); a similar line of thinking is expressed by Barrett, *The Epistle to the Romans*, p. 134; Fitzmyer, *Romans*, 469; Byrne, *Romans*, p. 223.

[41] Cf. Gal. 3:19, "The Law was given for the sake of transgressions"; Rom. 11:32, "God has imprisoned all in disobedience, in order to have mercy upon all" cf. Gal. 3:22.

following verses appear to accentuate the worst possible scenario, intensifying the gravity of the situation to the point of plunging the reader into the depths of despair. But this rhetorical strategy paves the way for the climactic moment in 7:25 and Paul's explication of the work of the Spirit in 8:2ff. The section describing the previous phase of salvation-history culminates in v. 24, where the "I" cries out, "Who will set me free from the body of this death?" (τίς με ῥύσεται ἐκ τοῦ σώματος τοῦ θανάτου τούτου;). The referent for the words, τοῦ σώματος τοῦ θανάτου τούτου, is found in the content of v. 23, in particular the constriction accomplished by that "other law" (ἕτερον νόμον), which is said to "war against the law of my mind" (ἀντιστρατευόμενον τῷ νόμῳ τοῦ νοός μου) and "make me captive" (αἰχμαλωτίζοντά με). The meaning of the "other law" is the exegetical crux that will help us resolve the interpretation of "the body of this death." Some identify the "other law" as the Mosaic Law. The "Law of God" (τῷ νόμῳ τοῦ θεοῦ, i.e., the Mosaic Law, v. 22) is acknowledged by the mind (τῷ νόμῳ τοῦ νοός μου, v. 23) but is perverted by the "Law of sin" (τῷ νόμῳ τῆς ἁμαρτίας, v. 23). The distinctions then are not between two different laws but between different operations and effects of the same Mosaic Law.[42]

However, there are serious objections to this view. Paul qualifies νόμος with the adjective ἕτερος (v. 23) and this "pertains to being dissimilar in kind or class from all other entities."[43] With the use of ἕτερος he wishes to designate a completely different entity, one that is distinct from the Mosaic Law described in v. 22. Furthermore, if ἕτερος νόμος in v. 23 refers to the Mosaic Law, even if viewed from a different perspective, or having a different

---

[42] See Bo Reicke, "Paulus über das Gesetz," TZ 41 (1985), 237-57, esp. 242-44; Eduard Lohse, "ὁ νόμος τοῦ πνεύματος τῆς ζωῆς. Exegetische Anmerkungen zu Röm. 8.2," in Die Vielfalt des Neuen Testaments, (Göttingen: Vandenhoeck and Ruprecht, 1982), pp. 128-36, esp. pp. 133-36; F. Hahn, "Das Gesetzesverständnis im Römer- und Galaterbrief," ZNW 67 (1976), 29-63, esp. 46; Peter von der Osten-Sacken, Römer 8 als Beispiel paulinischer Soteriologie FRLANT 112 (Göttingen: Vandenhoeck & Ruprecht, 1975), pp. 210-11; Klyne Snodgrass, "Spheres of Influence. A Possible Solution for the Problem of Paul and the Law," JSNT 32 (1988), 93-113, esp. 106-7; Thomas R. Schreiner, Romans (Grand Rapids: Baker Books, 1998), pp. 376-77; Dunn, Romans 1-8, pp. 394-95.

[43] BDAG, pp. 399-40; see for example 1 Cor 14:21 ("in the lips of others [ἑτέρων] I will speak to this people"); 1 Cor. 15:40 ("the glory of the heavenly is one [ἑτέρα], and the glory of the earthly is another [ἑτέρα]"); Gal. 1:6 ("I am amazed that you are so quickly deserting him who called you by the grace of Christ, for a different [ἕτερον] gospel")—Even though there is a sense in which this "other gospel" is related to the one Paul's preaches, it is nevertheless significantly different, to the point that Paul claims they are "deserting" God.

function, this would entail a contradictory shift from the perspective of vv. 15-21. In vv. 18, 20, what is in the "flesh" (i.e., in the "I") is the power of "sin," not the Law. This is the antagonist that works against the protagonist, the Mosaic Law (v. 22). The Law is placed on the same side as the will but always in distinction to the flesh and sin.[44] Thus, if the "other law" is identified as the Mosaic Law (v. 23), then Paul would be contradicting what he was so determined to prove, that sin working within the flesh is the real culprit and not the Law.[45]

While there is no *direct* correlation between the Mosaic Law and the νόμος in vv. 21, 23, Paul is certainly attempting to make a play on the word νόμος.[46] This creates an *indirect* relationship with the Law, given that he chooses to use this word here in the context of his discussion of the Mosaic Law.[47] It is difficult to pinpoint the meaning of this second use of νόμος. It is most likely that Paul simply wanted to create a rhetorical association with the Mosaic Law, where the second use of νόμος had no substantive meaning of its own, except to demonstrate that it functions in tandem with the Mosaic Law within the previous phase of salvation history.[48] Of significance is that this "other law" is similar to the Mosaic Law in that they both focus upon codes of behaviour (i.e., ethics). It is no coincidence that in vv. 15-25, Paul underscores the distinction between the "I"'s objective to *observe* the Law and the "other law," which becomes the controlling force that induces the "I" to *perform* something contrary to the Law's requirements.[49] Thus, what can be said of the "other

---

[44] "So now, no longer am I working it, but sin that lives in me" (v. 17); "For I have the desire to do what is good, but I cannot carry it out" (v. 18); "But if I do what I do not wish, it is no longer I working it but sin living in me" (v. 20); "For I joyfully concur with the Law of God...but I see a different law...making me a prisoner of the law of sin..." (vv. 22-23).

[45] See Moo, *Romans 1-8*, pp. 491-92.

[46] "Paul is really playing games with his language!" (Räisänen, *Jesus, Paul and Torah*, p. 64, but see pp. 63-64 for a more detailed explanation).

[47] See Rom. 7:1-6,7-9,12,14,16, 22; 8:3,4,7. Barrett who rejects that νόμος in Rom. 7:21, 23 is a reference to the Mosaic Law or that it is to be confined to meanings such as "rule" or "principle," opts for the sense of "a law-like rule, which as an evil double of the Mosaic law can bear the same name" (*The Epistle to the Romans*, p. 140).

[48] "Authority," "principle" will not do. Paul could have omitted his use of νόμος altogether in Rom. 7:21,23 if he did not want to associate it with the Mosaic Law: e.g., "But I am a prisoner to sin that lives within my members" (7:23). This will be addressed below in the discussion on Rom. 8:2.

[49] See v. 16 ("But if I do [ποιῶ] what I do not wish for, I agree with the Law that it is good"); v. 21 ("I find then the law that evil is present in me, the one who wishes to do [ποιεῖν] good [i.e.,

law" is that it was the influencing force that thwarted the observance of the codes of conduct associated with the Mosaic Law.

The second use of νόμος is further qualified by the genitive τῆς ἁμαρτίας. In fact, the ἕτερος νόμος is clearly the same entity as ὁ νόμος τῆς ἁμαρτίας since they are both defined similarly as being located "in my members" (ἐν τοῖς μέλεσίν μου, v. 23). The "other law" has an association with "sin" resulting in constricting the "I" (αἰχμαλωτίζονταί με ἐν τῷ νόμῳ τῆς ἁμαρτίας, v. 23). This constitutes "the body of this death" (τοῦ σώματος τοῦ θανάτου τούτου, v. 24) of which Paul speaks. Cranfield believes "the body of this death" describes Paul's failure as a Christian to satisfy God's righteous demands in the present moment. In v. 24 the phrase is used to communicate his cry for help as a response to the claims that the gospel makes upon him (cf. v. 22).[50] Others see the use of "the body of this death" to be a variation of "the body of sin" in 6:6, anticipating eschatological deliverance. At this time the present physical body ("the body of sin," 6:6/ "the body of this death," 7:24) will be replaced with a new spiritual body (cf. 8:13 ["if you put to death the practices of the body, you will live"]).[51] Dunn sees a parallel between the "body of death" and the description of the body of the Christian in Rom. 8:10 as "dead because of sin."[52] It is not to be taken as a simple reference to the physical body, but is to be understood as humanity embodied in the existence associated with this age (i.e., "body of sin" [6:6], "this mortal body" [6:12], "my flesh" [7:18], "my constituent parts" [7:23]). Thus, when the "I" cries out for deliverance from "the body of this death," he is crying out for deliverance from everything that constrains in this life, including physical death as well.[53]

Cranfield and Dunn's interpretation of v. 24, that Paul is speaking of the believer's experience with the Law and sin, appears to be incongruous with the request for a redeemer ("Who will set me free from the body of this death?"). Furthermore, if Paul is speaking of the believer's experience, pulled in two directions between the two epochs of Adam and Christ, this would significantly diminish the summit of his argument (7:25a; 8:1ff), which he

---

the Law cf. the Mosaic Law described as "good" in vv. 12, 16]"); v. 25 ("So then, on the one hand, I myself with my mind am serving [δουλεύω] the Law of God, but on the other, with my flesh [I am serving] the law of sin").

[50] Cranfield, *The Epistle to the Romans*, p. 366.

[51] Robert Banks, "Romans 7:25a: An Eschatological Thanksgiving?" *ABR* 26 (1978), 34–42.

[52] James D.G. Dunn, "Rom 7:14–25 in the Theology of Paul," *TZ* 31 (1975), 257–73, esp. 263–64.

[53] Dunn, *Romans 1–8*, p. 397.

went to great lengths at setting up. From vv. 7–25, all mention of Christ and the Spirit is conspicuously absent and to assume some sense of the operative work of Christ and the Spirit prior to the condition described in 7:25 and 8:1 would introduce a serious glitch in his argument. Also, the emphatic sense of the eschatological νῦν in 8:1 signaling a contrast with the previous condition is significantly diminished, concomitantly introducing a disjunction between 7:25 and 8:1.[54]

The use of the near demonstrative adjective τοῦτος in the phrase ("*this* body of death") indicates a specific reference point in the previous discussion. Throughout Romans 7, especially vv. 10, 11, 13, the use of the aorist tense verbs ἀπέθανον, ἀπέκτεινεν, ἐγένετο cannot be read restrictively as Paul's experience of physical death in the past. These verses function as precursors to the section found in vv. 14–25, where "death" denotes a severed relationship with God characteristic of pre-Christian existence. (i.e., "spiritual death"[55]). In the phrase, "body of death" it is inconceivable that σῶμα refers restrictively to the physical body as though physicality were the source of the problem.

While it is true that "body" can denote the physical part of humans in Pauline literature (e.g., Gal. 6:17), it is also a distinctively Pauline nuance to understand "body" figuratively as that which people are "attached to" or "in touch with" in a particular environment.[56] For example, in Rom. 6:6, the unregenerate human is described as ὁ παλαιὸς ἄνθρωπος, which is equated with τὸ σῶμα τῆς ἁμαρτίας. The designation "body of sin" refers to the whole complex of involvement with the world "under" sin (cf. 3:9), typified by Adam (5:12). Consequently, co-crucifixion with Christ has altered one's "attachment to" this world of sin and Adam (i.e., "the body of sin"). Likewise,

---

[54] Cranfield diminishes the sense of νῦν in 8:1 to mean "*since* (emphasis added) Christ has died and been raised from the dead" (*The Epistle to the Romans*, p. 373); while admitting that the νῦν still retains its eschatological nuance, Dunn posits that Paul intended a pause between 7:25 and 8:1, due to dictation and the need for the Roman congregations' need for time to comprehend the spoken words of the letter (*Romans 1–8*, p. 415).

[55] Some have chosen to use the contemporary label "spiritual death": "Spiritual death is the only outcome of the sinful condition" (Fitzmyer, *Romans*, p. 476); "'death' refers to spiritual death" (Moo, *Romans 1–8*, p. 495); others have understood it in a similar fashion but have chosen to describe it in a milder sense: "Man needs not law but deliverance, a new creation" (Barrett, *The Epistle to the Romans*, p. 142); "The anxiety of the creature in which its need of help comes to expression permits a Christian interpretation of pre-Christian experience" (Käsemann, *Commentary on Romans*, p. 210).

[56] See Byrne, *Romans*, p. 191 (comments on Rom. 6:6) and p. 229 (comments on Rom. 7:24).

in Rom. 7:24, the "body" refers to that environment which one is attached to or in touch with. Here it is called "the body of death." Thus, by the complete phrase Paul means the whole sphere of sin (i.e., "law of sin" [v. 23]), which leads to separation from God ("death" [vv. 5, 9, 10, 11, 13]) in which the unregenerate human is caught up and the compelling force of sin (ὁ νόμος τῆς ἁμαρτίας [v. 23]) makes it impossible for the Mosaic Law to be observed. The designation "body of death" functions as a description for the whole system of Law, sin, and death that characterizes the former aeon.

Both v. 13 and v. 24 anticipate the climactic solution in Rom. 8:1ff, where Paul explicates a new phase in *Heilsgeschichte* and where he articulates the counterpart to the system of the Law, sin, and death. It functions as the second panel of the diptych that corresponds to Rom. 7:6 ("we serve in newness of the Spirit"). It is to this that we now turn our attention. What we shall see is that his description of the solution is not a system that advocates a life-producing role for the Law, which is given new vitality to function in this capacity because of the eschatological Spirit. Instead, Paul advocates a completely new system that replaces the former system of the Mosaic Law. Paul asserts that the eschatological Spirit functions in an exclusive manner that leaves no room for the role of the Law; i.e., the eschatological Spirit displaces the Law as the principle of new life.

.

CHAPTER FIVE

The Spirit Replaces the Law as the Source of Life: Rom. 8:2,6,10,11,13

In Rom. 8:1-16, Paul's pneumatological perspective dominates the discussion, resuming his previous reference to "serving in newness of the Spirit" in 7:6. The γάρ in 8:2 does not relate to 7:14-25, where the "I" is enslaved under the power of sin and unable to observe the Law. Rather, 8:2 forms an association with 7:6 ("to serve in newness of Spirit").[1] The word νῦν ("now") in 8:1 is resumptive of the "eschatological now"[2] in 7:6, signaling that Paul is speaking from the perspective of a new era of salvation history inaugurated by Christ's death and resurrection and introducing a new era of the Spirit. In Rom. 8:1-16, Paul clarifies the Spirit's relationship with the Law[3] and associates this with the central theme of "life" in vv. 1-13.[4] The Spirit conquers the power of flesh (vv. 5b-9 cf. 7:5, 14, 18, 25) and rescues the believer from the snares of the power of sin (vv. 2, 10) and death (vv. 2, 6, 10, 11, 13).

---

[1] Schreiner, *Romans*, p. 398; Cranfield, *The Epistle to the Romans*, pp. 373-74; U. Wilckens, *Der Brief an die Römer*, Vol. 2, p. 118.

[2] Compare the use of νῦν in Rom. 3:21; 5:9; 6:19, 22; 7:6. Normally the apostle uses ἄρα οὖν (5:18; 7:3, 25; 8:12; 9:16, 18; 14:12, 19) to indicate concluding remarks or corollary drawn from what has just been said. This indicates that the use of νῦν was intentional, signaling a new era of salvation history.

[3] Πνεῦμα occurs 31 times in Paul's correspondence to the Romans, and out of these, there are 21 occurrences in chap. 8 alone (vv. 2, 4, 5 [2x], 6, 9 [3x], 10, 11 [2x], 13, 14, 15 [2x], 16 [2x], 23, 26 [2x], 27). Even more telling is that out of the 21 times it is used in chap. 8, 17 occur in vv.1-16. Νόμος is used 5 times in Rom. 8 (vv. 2 [2x], 3, 4, 7) and in all of its occurrences it is either directly or indirectly brought into association with πνεῦμα.

[4] See the use of ζωή (vv. 2, 6, 10) and ζάω (vv. 12, 13 [2x]), ζωοποιέω (v. 11).

1. "By Which 'Law' Does Life Come?": Rom. 8:2

The importance of the words, ὁ νόμος τοῦ πνεύματος τῆς ζωῆς ἐν Χριστῷ ᾽Ιησοῦ and their counterpart, τοῦ νόμου τῆς ἁμαρτίας καὶ τοῦ θανάτου in Rom. 8:2 cannot be underestimated since it is most probable that Paul intended that they function as his proposition, which he will explain more fully vv. 3ff.[5] But at the same time, this verse is one of the thorniest verses in the Pauline corpus. The language of Rom. 8:2 appears to be convoluted and overly complex, giving the impression that Paul was attempting to say too much in too few words. The nominative case noun (ὁ νόμος) has two genitives attached to it (τοῦ πνεύματος τῆς ζωῆς), followed by a prepositional phrase (ἐν Χριστῷ ᾽Ιησοῦ), which is finally followed by a verb (ἠλευθέρωσέν). This is then juxtaposed to a second νόμος that has two genitives of its own (τῆς ἁμαρτίας καί τοῦ θανάτου).[6] Besides the difficulty of isolating the specific subjects of the two phrases, the main interpretive problems we must work through are as follows: What does "the law of the Spirit of life" mean? What does the prepositional phrase "in Christ Jesus" mean and what does it modify? After we have answered these questions we have to address the issue of the relationship between these two phrases.

There is an increasing number of scholars who interpret νόμος in the phrase ὁ νόμος τοῦ πνεύματος τῆς ζωῆς and its counterpart, τοῦ νόμου τῆς ἁμαρτίας καὶ τοῦ θανάτου, literally as a reference to the Mosaic Law.[7] According to these scholars, the expression "the law of the Spirit of life" is *not* a metaphorical way of speaking of the new order of things, but refers to the Law. Paul, it is argued, views the Mosaic Law from two perspectives ("the two-sidedness of the Law"[8]). In the context of the flesh, it functions as γράμμα,

---

[5] "This suggests that v. 2 functions as a topic sentence, and that vv. 3–30 are its exposition" (Keck, "The Law and 'The Law of Sin and Death' (Rom 8:1-4)," p. 46; "Indeed, as suggested above, this sentence serves as the 'lead in,' a sort of 'thesis sentence,' to the whole of vv. 2–30" (Fee, *God's Empowering Presence*, p. 521).

[6] The phrase, ὁ νόμος τοῦ πνεύματος τῆς ζωῆς is antithetically parallel to the words, τοῦ νόμου τῆς ἁμαρτίας καί τοῦ θανάτου. This is made clear by the repetition of the word νόμος in both phrases, the antonyms ζωή and θάνατος, and the verb ἐλευθερόω, which indicates that the first phrase is to be understood as the antithesis of the one that follows.

[7] See the discussion above on the "other law" in Rom. 7:23 and corresponding footnotes for representative opinions of those who believe Paul is referring to the Mosaic Law. These opinions are usually applied to the interpretation of νόμος in Rom. 8:2.

[8] See Dunn, *Romans 1-8*, p. 417.

caught in the former epoch, abused and misunderstood as nothing more than a series of demands, where it becomes an instrument of sin, leading to death (7:5, 7-13). However, in the context of the Spirit and the new epoch, the Law is rightly understood, functioning as the instrument of righteousness leading to life (cf. 7:10), complying with the new covenant promise of Jer. 31:31-34; Ezek. 36:26-27.[9]

Both E. Fuchs and E. Lohse press the point that νόμος in Rom. 8:3-4 clearly means the Mosaic Law and that Paul speaks of the same divine Law in 8:2.[10] The Law, which had previously been confiscated by sin, has now changed ownership (Christ) and its true significance has been rediscovered.[11] But as Räisänen has demonstrated, the use of νόμος in 8:3-4 as the Mosaic Law cannot be the determinative factor since in 7:21-25, νόμος is used with diverse meanings: twice with the meaning of Mosaic Law (vv. 22, 25b) and five times with various other nuances (v. 21= rule, compulsion; v. 23a, b = direction of the will; v. 23c = rule, compulsion; v. 25b = power, control).[12] This variation in usage nullifies any argument based on the idea that νόμος must have a consistent meaning in 8:2. Furthermore, the specific subject of 8:2 is not the proper understanding of the Law; i.e., when humans understand the Law in the right way, they will experience the Law as the "law of the Spirit."[13] Nowhere in this context does Paul postulate the "law of the Spirit"

---

[9] "The contrast between the fatal and liberating spiritual reality of the Law in vv. 2-7 reminds one most strongly of Jer. 31:31-34...In Ezek. 36:27 it is also announced that God will grant his Spirit to the people and through it enable them to fulfill his instructions" (Stuhlmacher, *Paul's Letter to the Romans*, pp. 117-18); see also P. Stuhlmacher, "The Law as a Topic of Biblical Theology" in *Reconciliation, Law and Righteousness: Essays in Biblical Theology* (Philadelphia: Fortress Press, 1986), pp. 110-33, esp. pp. 126-27.

[10] See P. von der Osten-Sacken who states that Rom. 8:2 is associated with vv. 3-4, where Paul is clearly speaking of the Mosaic Law. This requires that νόμος be taken as the Law as well in 8:2. There is an "engste syntaktische Zusammenhänge" (*Die Heiligkeit der Tora: Studien zum Gesetz bei Paulus* [Munich: Chr. Kaiser, 1989], p. 16).

[11] E. Fuchs, *Die Freiheit des Glaubens. Römer 5-8 ausgelegt*, BEvT 14 (Munich: Kaiser, 1949), p. 85; Lohse, "ὁ νόμος τοῦ πνεύματος τῆς ζωῆς," pp. 133-36; see also E. Jüngel, *Paulus und Jesus. Ein Untersuchung zur Präzisierung der Frage nach dem Ursprung der Christologie* (Tübingen: Mohr, 1962), pp. 52, 54-59, 61.

[12] Räisänen, *Jesus, Paul and Torah*, pp. 63-64; see also C.E.B. Cranfield, *On Romans and Other New Testament Essays* (Edinburgh: T&T Clark, 1998), pp. 33-35.

[13] "8.2 can be understood as follows: those *for whom* the nomos is the Law of the spirit, i.e., those who exist in the spirit which is the giver of life (cf. 8.10f) are, when they look at the Law, freed from the perverted Law, that is from the compulsion to misuse the law as the 'Law of works'

as the basis for understanding the Law in its proper role or the Spirit, and for that matter, as the basis of revelation.[14]

Those who argue for the meaning of νόμος as the Mosaic Law in Rom. 8:2 and declare that vv. 3-4 is an explanatory note (cf. the use of γάρ in v. 3) on v. 2, go through a strenuous explanation of how these three verses relate. If in 8:2, the nominative case νόμος refers to the Mosaic Law, then this would automatically mean that under the conventions of Greek grammar, Paul intended to communicate how the focal point of liberation was to be found in the Law itself; i.e., it would be the agent of liberation.[15] For example, regarding Rom. 8:2, Thomas R. Schreiner contends that the *Mosaic Law* in the realm of the Spirit functions *as the instrument* through which one is freed from sin and death (cf. ch. 7).[16] However, in vv. 3-4, Paul stresses that it is precisely the Spirit in distinction from the Law that liberates, not the Law viewed in proper perspective[17]: "For God has done what the *Law...could not do...*in order that the righteous requirement of the Law might be fulfilled in us...*who walk by the Spirit.*" The idea of the Law as liberating agent concomitantly diminishes the

---

under the dominion of *hamartia* and thus from the fate of being abandoned to death" (H. Hübner, *Law in Paul's Thought*, Studies of the New Testament and Its World [ed. J. Riches; trans. J.C.G. Greig; Edinburgh: T & T Clark, 1984], quote taken from p. 145 but see pp. 144-49 as a whole for the complete explanation) (Originally published as *Das Gesetz bei Paulus: Ein Beitrag zum Werden der paulinischen Theologie*, Third edition [Göttingen: Vandenhoeck & Ruprecht, 1982]); "We stand anew at the disposal of the power that truly creates life when we believe that in Christ we must understand 'ourselves anew'" (Fuchs, *Die Freiheit des Glaubens*, p. 87); see also Meyer, "Romans 10:4 and the End of the Law," p. 73.

[14] Cf. "For to us God *revealed* [them] *through the Spirit*" (1 Cor. 2:10). It is not until Rom. 8:16ff, where all mention of the Law ceases that Paul takes up the Spirit's redemptive role in the tension between the "here but not yet," where there may be a vague reference to the Spirit as the agent of revelation (e.g., the Spirit is said to "bear witness" to believers of their status as "children of God" [v. 16]).

[15] Räisänen makes it clear that if one argues for νόμος as the Mosaic Law in Rom. 8:2 then one must take the linguistic structure of Rom. 8:2 seriously; i.e., νόμος takes an active role in that it is the *instrument of liberation* (*Paul and the Law*, p. 51).

[16] Schreiner cites Ps.119 and Ps. 19:7-11 as support for the contention that the Torah restores and revives the godly (*Romans*, p. 400); see U. Wilckens who argues for a literal Torah interpretation but who also distorts the syntax of the sentence by positing that a particular perspective of Torah is in view ("Thus the sentence 8.2 describes the annulment of all condemnation ...as *a turn in the law itself*" [Wilckens, *Der Brief and die Römer*, Vol. 1, p. 245]).

[17] "The subject which, in the light of the context (*Rom.* 8:1-4) seems appropriate to this predicate is not God's law but the new factor in the human situation, namely, the Holy Spirit's presence and exercised authority and constraint" (Cranfield, *The Epistle to the Romans*, p. 376).

soteriological force of Paul's Christological assertions both in 8:2 ("in Christ Jesus") and 8:4 ("God did by sending his own Son...condemned sin in the flesh"). It is also a fact that the Law in the rest of the Pauline literature is never described positively as the agent by which one is released from the constraints of sin (cf. Rom. 5:12; 20; 7:5, 8, 9, 11, 13; 1 Cor. 15:56; Gal. 3:19, 22, 23). Therefore, in 8:2, if we were to translate νόμος as the Mosaic Law in the phrase "the law of the Spirit," then v. 2 not only would be contradicting the claim of vv. 3-4 but also would run counter to the rest of Pauline literature.[18]

Since the phrase ὁ νόμος τοῦ πνεύματος τῆς ζωῆς in Rom. 8:2 is not to be found elsewhere in the Pauline corpus, it is best considered to be an ad hoc creation, given the varied uses of νόμος in the immediate context (cf. 7:21–25). Those who do not consider νόμος to be a reference to the Mosaic Law maintain that Paul intended it to be interpreted in a metaphorical way such as "religion,"[19] "power,"[20] "principle,"[21] "authority,"[22] "aeon" or "sphere."[23] However, to translate it with any of these meanings would suppress the linguistic note it strikes with νόμος as the Mosaic Law in the context (7:22; 25b; 8:3-4). Even though Räisänen has demonstrated that in the classical, and particularly the Hellenistic periods, νόμος can mean "custom " or "rule" in the sense of ethical norm,[24] and Paul most likely implies a meaning close to one of the above figurative meanings, it is best not to translate νόμος as any of these. In our examination of νόμος in 7:21, 23, 25, we concluded that it was the controlling force involved in ethics; i.e., it was force that induces the "I" to act (perform/ do) and is specified by the qualifying genitives (ἁμαρτίας, 7:25). With this in mind, it is most probable that νόμος in 8:2 did not have any

---

[18] See also Moo, Romans 1–8, p. 506.

[19] This is Barrett's view from his 1957 commentary ("the religion which is made possible in Christ Jesus, namely that of the 'life-giving Spirit,' would seem to be based on acceptance of this last alternative" [A Commentary on the Epistle to the Romans, HNTC (New York: Harper & Row, 1957), p. 153]) but has been abandoned for the literal interpretation of Mosaic Law in his 1991 commentary (The Epistle to the Romans, pp. 145–46).

[20] Murray, The Epistle to the Romans, p. 276.

[21] Fitzmyer, Romans, p. 482.

[22] Sanday and Headlam, The Epistle to the Romans, p. 190; Cranfield, The Epistle to the Romans, p. 376 (a change from his previous position where he understood it as the Mosaic Law restored by the Spirit ["St. Paul and the Law," SJT 17 (1964), 43–68, esp. 66]).

[23] A. van Dülmen, Die Theologie des Gesetzes bei Paulus SBM 5 (Stuttgart: Katholisches Bibelwerk, 1968), p. 120.

[24] Räisänen, Jesus, Paul and Torah, pp. 74–88.

substantive meaning by itself.[25] To translate νόμος with any of the above words is to undermine Paul's rhetorical strategy in creating an association with the Mosaic Law (Rom. 7:1-6, 7-9, 12, 14, 16, 22).[26] It is most likely that Paul used νόμος in the phrase "the *law* of the Spirit of life in Christ Jesus" to communicate the idea of a controlling force in ethics as an alternative to the system of the Mosaic Law and its association with "sin" and "death."[27] Otherwise, Paul would have no particular incentive to use νόμος at all in this phrase. This is what we will consider in greater detail as we proceed.

The interpretive key to 8:2 is found in the association it makes with 7:1-6, since all the components of 8:2 have already been mentioned there. This becomes most evident when we analyse 8:2 in its constituent parts:

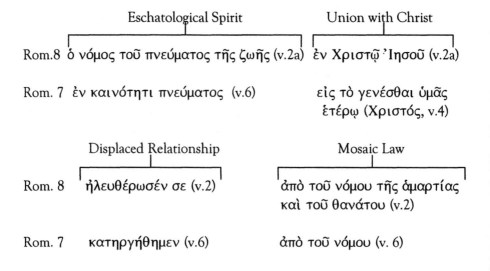

	Eschatological Spirit	Union with Christ
Rom.8	ὁ νόμος τοῦ πνεύματος τῆς ζωῆς (v.2a)	ἐν Χριστῷ ᾿Ιησοῦ (v.2a)
Rom. 7	ἐν καινότητι πνεύματος (v.6)	εἰς τὸ γενέσθαι ὑμᾶς ἑτέρῳ (Χριστός, v.4)

	Displaced Relationship	Mosaic Law
Rom. 8	ἠλευθέρωσέν σε (v.2)	ἀπὸ τοῦ νόμου τῆς ἁμαρτίας καὶ τοῦ θανάτου (v.2)
Rom. 7	κατηργήθημεν (v.6)	ἀπὸ τοῦ νόμου (v. 6)

---

[25] R. Gyllenberg understands νόμος τοῦ πνεύματος in 8:2 as a rhetorical circumlocution for "Spirit" (*Rechtfertigung und Altes Testament bei Paulus* [Stuttgart: Kohlhammer, 1973], p. 20); see also Käsemann who similarly sees a reference to νόμος as "nothing other than the Spirit itself in his ruling function" (*Commentary On Romans*, p. 215); Moo concedes that the use of νόμος in 8:2 "has more rhetorical than material significance" (*Romans 1-8*, p. 508).

[26] Fee, *God's Empowering Presence*, pp. 522-23; see also John A. Bertone, "The Function of the Spirit in the Dialectic Between God's Soteriological Plan Enacted but not yet Culminated: Romans 8.1-27," *JPT* 15 (1999), 75-97, esp. 80; those who translate νόμος in Rom. 8:2 in a figurative sense are quick to qualify this with the idea that Paul intended it to remind his readers of the Mosaic Law ("Undoubtedly a person should thereby be reminded of the Torah" [Käsemann, *Commentary on Romans*, p. 215]); Schweizer, "πνεῦμα, κτλ.," *TDNT* Vol. VI, p. 429.

[27] "The choice of the word (νόμος) has a *polemical* reference to the most common meaning of the word νόμος (Torah)" (Räisänen, *Jesus, Paul and Torah*, p. 64)

In Rom. 7:6, Paul speaks singularly of the "newness of the Spirit" as something that is in disparate relationship with the Law, not as the two working in conjunction with each other. It is with this thought in mind that we are to approach the interpretation of 8:2. As was noted above, the use of νόμος in 8:2 is simply a rhetorical tactic on Paul's part having to do with the controlling force involved in ethics. In this way it is parallel with the Mosaic Law, which also advocates a code of ethics. But at the same time, it is not to be directly identified with the Law. The substantive part of the phrase is to be located in the qualifying genitives (τοῦ πνεύματος τῆς ζωῆς). This is confirmed by that fact that 8:3ff is focused upon the idea of the Spirit as life-giving agent.[28] Moo is quite correct in his comment: "The actor in the situation is, then, the Spirit Himself."[29] The Mosaic Law is not the basis for ethics in the new situation described in 8:2ff.

Paul further defines the Spirit's role with the genitive τῆς ζωῆς. This genitive is to be taken with the "Spirit" rather than "law"; i.e., it is not "the Spirit's life-giving law"[30] but "the law of the life-giving Spirit."[31] In similar syntactical constructions, where there is more than one genitive, the second genitive was clearly dependent on the immediately previous one.[32] The association of the Spirit with "life" has a long-standing tradition in Jewish thought. It connotes humans' complete dependence on God for the breath of life, apart from which existence is impossible.[33] This is particularly true of Paul's understanding of the Spirit's role in producing "life."[34] Furthermore, the formulation "Spirit of life" (MT, חַיִּים רוּחַ cf. LXX, πνεῦμα ζωῆς) is Semitic[35] and he no doubt understood the association of Spirit with "life" as

---

[28] Out of the 31 uses of πνεῦμα in Paul's correspondence to the Romans as a whole, no less than 17 appear in 8:1–16 (vv. 2, 4, 5 [2x], 6, 9 [3x], 10, 11 [2x], 13, 14, 15 [2x], 16 [2x]). More specifically, Paul is consistent in his claim that the "Spirit" is said to be instrumental in producing "life" throughout the chapter (vv. 2, 6, 10, 11, 13).

[29] Moo, Romans 1–8, p. 507;

[30] "It is the 'law of life'..." (Bruce, Romans, p. 151).

[31] "Generally one genitive is dependent on another, whereby an author, particularly Paul, occasionally produces a quite cumbersome accumulation of genitives; to facilitate clarity in such cases, the governing genitive must always precede the dependent genitive" (BDF, p. 93).

[32] See for example, Rom. 2:4; 2 Cor. 7:1; 6:7 cf. 1 Tim. 4:5; Titus 2:13; 3:5; see also Moo, Romans 1–8, p. 530.

[33] See Gen. 2:7; Ezek. 37:5, 6, 8, 10; Job 32:8; 33:4; 34:14; Eccl. 12:7.

[34] Rom. 8:2, 6, 10, 11, 13; 1 Cor. 15:45; 2 Cor. 3:6; Gal. 6:8.

[35] See Gen. 7:15.

part of Israel's hopes for the future,[36] now realized in the present.[37] For example, in 1 Cor. 15:45 the apostle equates the work of Christ, the last Adam, with the "life-giving Spirit." Likewise, in 2 Cor. 3:6, Paul characterizes his whole sense of being a "servant of the new covenant" where the central feature of this covenant was the Spirit as the source of life.[38] But these traditions that Paul picks up really serve as a precursory function to the more immediate concern in this context, which is the juxtaposition Paul sets up in Rom. 8:2 between "the law of the Spirit of life" and "the law of sin and death." The two phrases are parallel to one another.

ὁ νόμος	τοῦ πνεύματος		τῆς ζωῆ
τοῦ νόμου	τῆς ἁμαρτίας	καὶ	τοῦ θανάτου

The "law of the Spirit that produces life"[39] is related to the "the law of sin that produces death." From 7:7-25, we learned how the Mosaic Law in the previous epoch intended to produce "life" when it was observed (v. 10) but fell desperately short of its potential because of its nexus with sin (vv. 7-9, 11, 13); this had the opposite and adverse effect of producing "death" (vv. 9-11, 13). However, as 7:6 indicates, the new era of the Spirit ("newness of the Spirit") has replaced the former era of the Law. This idea is precisely what Paul resumes in 8:2. As an alternative to the old era of the Law with its inextricable association with sin, resulting in death, is the new era of the Spirit, resulting in life. Even though we indicated above that νόμος in 8:2 is not to be identified as the Mosaic Law, it represents an association with the Mosaic Law with respect to ethics. Thus the phrase "the law of the Spirit of life" designates the Spirit's life-giving function in continuity with the Mosaic Law in that the Spirit, like the Law in the previous era, is associated with ethics. But at the

---

[36] See Ezek. 37:5f.; 1 En. 61:7.

[37] However, it must be stated that Paul does not explicitly use the words "new covenant" (καινή διαθήκη) in Rom. 8 and it cannot be said that his thoughts in this chapter comply with the Jewish new covenant expectation (cf. Jer. 38:31-34 [LXX]).

[38] Stuhlmacher, *Paul's Letter to the Romans*, pp. 118-19; Dunn, *Romans 1-8*, p. 418.

[39] I take "life" here to be a "genitive of product" ("the Spirit that produces life" cf. D.B. Wallace, *Greek Grammar Beyond the Basics: An Exegetical Syntax of the New Testament* [Grand Rapids: Zondervan, 1996], p. 106) in light of its use in Rom. 8:6, 10; i.e., the Spirit is the *source* of life. This parallels the following phrase, "the law of sin and death" ("the law of sin that produces death") and is consistent with Paul's use of "death" in Rom. 7:10 ("the commandment...resulted in death").

same time, there is discontinuity between the new era of the Spirit and the old era of the Law in that the Spirit replaces the Law as the basis of ethics.[40] This becomes clear in the corresponding phrase, "has set you free from the law of sin and death." The phraseology that Paul employs in 8:2 (ἠλευθέρωσέν σε[41] ἀπὸ τοῦ νόμου) recalls 7:3 (ἐλευθέρα ἐστὶν ἀπὸ τοῦ νόμου), where the word ἐλευθέρα signifies "being free from control or obligation, *independent, not bound*"[42] to the "law." In 8:2 Paul uses the aorist tense verb ἠλευθέρωσεν to indicate that the liberation has already been accomplished.[43] While in 7:3 νόμος is to be interpreted restrictively as the Mosaic Law, in 8:2 it is more comprehensively "the law of sin and death" that characterizes the whole system and era of the Mosaic Law, sin and death.[44] The collocation of the three words "law" (Mosaic Law [7:7, 8, 9, 12, 14, 16, 22, 25], "law" [7:21, 23, 25]), "sin" (Mosaic Law's nexus with sin [7:9, 11-13]), and "death" (Mosaic Law leads to death [7:9-10, 11, 13]) describes the former era of the Mosaic Law *in toto*.[45] This is parallel to 7:6, where Paul describes release from the Law

---

[40] "The ethical 'possibility' in the Spirit shown up against the 'impossibility' under the law" (Byrne, *Romans*, p. 235); *contra* Moo who believes that Rom. 8:2 does not advocate the idea of a new ethical standard of the Spirit that takes the place of the Mosaic Law ("He does not use it ['law'] to suggest that the Spirit is, or conveys, a norm that functions like, or can be substituted for, the Mosaic law" [*Romans 1-8*, p. 507]). However, 8:2 functions as Paul's proposition that he explains more fully in vv.2ff, and in these verses Paul emphasizes the idea of "walking according to the Spirit"(vv. 4-6, 13, 14) to the exclusion of the Mosaic Law. This is definitive proof that Paul perceives the Spirit as the basis of ethics that displaces the Law in the new era.

[41] The second person singular σε is represented in most of the earliest and best Greek texts (א B F G 1506* 1739* a b). The other less likely reading is με (A D 6 81 104 256 263). This is most likely assimilation to the first person singular used in Rom. 7:7-25. The reading σε is to be preferred because it is the more difficult reading; a scribe would be more likely to conform σε to με than vice versa.

[42] "*Free* from the tax" (Matt. 17:26) cf. Rom. 6:20; Jn. 8:36 (BDAG, p. 317).

[43] "[T]o cause someone to be freed from domination, *free, set free*," (BDAG, p. 317); "This liberation has actually been accomplished" (Cranfield, *The Epistle to the Romans*, p. 376).

[44] In Gal. 3:23, Paul claims, "But before faith came we were *kept in custody* under the Law, being shut up to the faith which was to be revealed."

[45] "This expanded phrase ('*the law of sin and death*') appears to be deliberately chosen to summarize the total situation of the sinner as Paul has described it in chaps. 6 and 7: helpless under sin's power, doomed thereby to death and condemnation" (Moo, *Romans 1-8*, p. 508); "Paul is really referring to the condition dominated by the two powers, sin and death" (Fitzmyer, *Romans*, p. 483 cf. also his "Paul and the Law" in *To Advance the Gospel: New Testament Studies* [New York: Crossroads, 1981], pp. 186-201, esp. p. 193); "It is these negative expressions alone that denote Torah or at least the state of affairs closely associated with the

and "letter." Also in 7:6 is his description of the new era of the Spirit. Thus, Law and Spirit represent two eras in salvation-history. In Rom. 8:2, Paul communicates the same thought; the new era of the Spirit liberates humans from the former era of the Mosaic Law associated with sin and death, and supplies the life that the Mosaic Law could not give.

The association between 7:1–6 and 8:2 is reinforced by the insertion of the prepositional phrase ἐν Χριστῷ 'Ιησοῦ in 8:2, which again conveys participatory union with Christ as a soteriological category that is in disparate relationship with the whole system of the Mosaic Law. It is most likely that it is not linked to τῆς ζωῆς but to the verb ἠλευθέρωσεν[46] for two main reasons: first, there is a propensity on Paul's part to use the verb in contexts where he speaks of the Christ-event[47] and second, there is a parallelism between 8:2 and 7:3–4, where the cognate word ἐλευθέρα is used in connection with Paul's idea that we are "joined to another" (i.e., to Christ). In 7:4, participatory union with Christ is the prerequisite for "bearing fruit for God," which we stated above was a subtle reference to the Spirit.[48] This is

---

reign of the Torah...Rom 3.27 and 8.2 support the conclusion that Paul often speaks of the actual abolition of the Torah" (Räisänen, *Paul and the Law*, p. 52); see also Beker, who points out that Paul uses "liberation symbolism" to communicate a change in power structures (*Paul the Apostle*, p. 256); *contra* Fee, who claims that Paul maintains a consistent distinction between the Mosaic Law ("the first Law") and the "law of sin" ("the second law") in Rom. 7:23, 25, based upon Paul's designation, "a different law" in v. 23 and his attempt to exonerate the Mosaic Law in vv. 13, 14 (*God's Empowering Presence*, pp. 524–25). But this distinction is arbitrary when viewed from the perspective that Paul is describing a pre-Christ situation throughout 7:7–24. He is explicating *a whole era* associated with the Mosaic Law even though sin was the real culprit, not the Law. The point is that this system represented something that simply did not produce life ("This commandment which was to result in life, proved to result in death for me" [7:10]/ "for sin, taking the opportunity through the commandment...killed me" [7:11] cf. "the law of sin and death" [8:2]). Nowhere does Paul advocate the coordinate functions of the Spirit and Law issuing forth in life in his description of the new era (8:1ff). Thus, the whole system of the Mosaic Law associated with the former era has become obsolete in light of the life-giving role of the Spirit in the new era. This means that "the law of sin and death" is to be understood comprehensively as the era of sin and death associated with the Mosaic Law that has been replaced by the new era of the Spirit ("the law of the Spirit of life").

[46] See Sanday and Headlam, *The Epistle to the Romans*, p. 191; Cranfield, *The Epistle to the Romans*, pp. 374–75; Dunn, *Romans 1–8*, p. 418; Fee, *God's Empowering Presence*, pp. 523–24.

[47] See especially Rom. 6:18, 20, 22; 2 Cor. 3:17 cf. Gal. 5:1, 13.

[48] Mehrdad Fatehi, *The Spirit's Relation to the Risen Lord in Paul: An Examination of Its Christological Implications* WUNT 2. Reihe 128 (Tübingen: J.C.B. Mohr [Paul Siebeck], 2000), p. 209, footnote 19.

parallel to 8:2, where the prepositional insertion ἐν Χριστῷ ᾽Ιησοῦ functions as the basis for the Spirit's role in 8:2ff. Thus, the logic of the phrase, "the law of the Spirit of life in Christ Jesus" is that Christ Jesus set us free from sin and death (an accomplished reality), but that the progressive and existing antidote for sin and death is the life-giving Spirit.

In summation, Rom. 8:2 is written from a salvation-historical perspective, one in which a new era of the Spirit ("the law of the Spirit of life") replaces the former era of the Mosaic Law ("the law of sin and death"). The foundation upon which this new era is based is soteriological union with Christ ("in Christ Jesus"); i.e., the Spirit is the source of life through the believer's participatory union with Christ, by which the believer experiences freedom from the former system of the Law, sin, and death. As we proceed further in the chapter Paul will explicate the Spirit as the principle of new life with more clarity and depth. Of particular significance for us is that in this process he never attributes an equal role between the Spirit and Law as the concomitant agents of life, even though he has broached the Jewish belief that the Law had a life-functioning purpose in 7:10. Rather, Paul attributes an exclusive role to the Spirit. Paul spells this out in greater detail in what follows in ch. 8. It is to this that we now turn our attention.

2. The Spirit of Life Versus the Flesh: Rom. 8:6, 10, 11, 13

With the use of γάρ[49] in Rom. 8:3, 4, Paul indicates that he is about to elaborate on the disparate relationship between the Mosaic Law and Christ-Spirit he has just mentioned in 8:2 and reiterates his conviction that the Mosaic Law is part of the former era now obsolete in the new era of the Spirit.[50] This is evident by the opening clause, "what the Law was unable to do

---

[49] The use of γάρ in Rom. 8:3 indicates a connection between vv. 3-4 and v. 2 and is sometimes repeated (vv. 5, 6) to introduce several arguments for the same assertions or to have one clause confirm the other (BDAG, p. 189). It is used in vv. 3, 5, 6 to confirm the statement of v. 2 ("the law of the Spirit of life in Christ Jesus has set you free from the law of sin and death"); v. 3 takes up the issue of the Mosaic Law and its nexus with sin and the flesh and its counterpart, God's redemptive work in Christ, while vv. 5-6 takes up both the issue of the flesh and its association with death and its counterpart, the life-giving Spirit.

[50] "Thus, vs 3a ...dramatically points out that there is no bridge, no line of continuity from the weakened world of the Law to that of the Spirit" (Arthur J. Dewey, *Spirit and Letter in Paul* SBEC Vol. 33 [Lewiston: The Edwin Mellen Press, 1996], p. 189).

in that it was weakened by the flesh," which recapitulates the point of 7:6 ("we serve...not in oldness of letter"), read in conjunction with 7:7-24, that the Law was unable to rescue people from the domain of sin. In Rom. 8:3, the word ἀδύνατος (τὸ...ἀδύνατον τοῦ νόμου) means "the lacking capability in functioning adequately, *powerless, impotent.*"[51] Whether this is to be taken in an active sense ("what the Law was incapable of doing") or in a passive sense ("what was impossible for the Law") makes little difference in the end. Sin and the flesh thwarted the life-giving function of the Law. As a result the Law issued death not life.[52] This confirms our previous contention that the phrase "the law of sin and death" in 8:2 is to be understood comprehensively as the whole system of the Mosaic Law in the previous era, since the topic of Mosaic Law, sin, and death is precisely what Paul takes up in 8:2ff. Thus, the present era of Christ and the Spirit, freedom from the power of sin (flesh), and life ("the law of the Spirit of life in Christ Jesus") is the counterpart to the system in the previous era. Christ became God's way of striking a decisive blow against both sin and the flesh, which the Law was incapable of overcoming, and opened the way for the life-giving role of the Spirit that Paul highlights in 8:4ff.

This brings us to our central interest of the Spirit as the agent of life in v. 4ff. Rom. 8:4 is introduced by the ἵνα clause ("*in order that* the righteous requirement of the Law may be fulfilled in us"[53]) that either points previously to the work of Christ ("God did by sending his own Son...condemned sin in the flesh" [v. 3])[54] or looks forward to the practical and behavioural aspect effected by the Spirit ("walking according to the Spirit" [v. 4]).[55] Given the context, it is most probable that Paul intended a pneumatological emphasis, pointing forward to the appropriation of one's union with Christ in the daily

---

[51] Cf. Rom. 15:1 ("We who are strong ought to bear the weaknesses of *those who are not capable* [τῶν ἀδυνάτων] and not just please ourselves"); see BDAG, p. 22.

[52] Rom. 7:10 cf. Gal. 3:21 ("For if the Law had been given, being able to make alive, then righteousness would indeed have been based on the Law").

[53] We will address Rom. 8:4 in greater detail in the subsequent section (Part Three), where we will consider how Paul describes the Spirit's role in the language of covenantal nomism.

[54] B. Byrne, *"Sons of God"- "Seed of Abraham,"* AnBib 83 (Rom: Pontifical Biblical Institute, 1979), pp. 93-95; see also his commentary (*Romans*, p. 237); M.L. Loane, *The Hope of Glory: An Exposition of the Eighth Chapter in The Epistle to the Romans* (London: Hodder and Stoughton, 1968), pp. 27-28; Schreiner, *Romans*, pp. 404-5.

[55] Paul J. Achtemeier, *Romans* Interpretation (Atlanta: John Knox Press, 1985), p. 134; Bruce, *Romans*, p. 153; Fitzmyer, *Romans*, p. 487 and most commentators.

walk of life. First, even though the foundation upon which Paul builds his argument is Christological, the context clearly indicates that his focus is more on ethics and the behavioural aspects of the believer's life ("according to the Spirit" [vv. 4, 5], "the mind of the Spirit" [v. 6], "in the Spirit" [v. 9], "by the Spirit" [v. 13]). This coincides well with the emphasis on the ethical demand of the Mosaic Law ("the righteous requirement of the Law" [v. 4]). Second, the idea that the Spirit "fulfills" the Law is consistent with Paul's use elsewhere.[56] Thirdly, and most compelling, is the presence of the phrase πληρωθῇ ἐν ἡμῖν. The use of ἐν ἡμῖν is locative[57] (i.e., the location where the activity of fulfillment takes place). Paul consistently describes the Spirit's habitation within the believer in the rest of the chapter ("since the Spirit of God *dwells in you*" [v. 9]; "But if the Spirit of Him who raised Jesus from the dead *dwells in you…*" [v. 11]). With these things in mind, the passive voice verb πληροῦν indicates that it is not Christ nor the individual, but precisely the work of the Spirit that is resident within the believer who does something in and for us.[58] This suggests that while the decisive redemptive work of Christ is foundational, Paul specifically had the ongoing activity of the Spirit in mind as the agent who "fulfills" the intended goal of the Mosaic Law.

One of the most significant descriptions of the Spirit in Rom. 8 is "walking according to the Spirit" (vv. 4, 5) and related designations ("the mindset of the Spirit" [v. 6]; "in [ἐν] the Spirit" [v. 9]; "by the Spirit [πνεύματι]" [v. 13]). Each phrase emphasizes the practical dimension of conformance with the Spirit in the believer's life. The use of the preposition κατά (κατὰ πνεῦμα) designates

---

[56] See Rom. 13:8–10, where "love" is said to "fulfill the Law." In Gal. 5:22, "love" is also said to be a fruit of the Spirit.

[57] The prepositional phrase ἐν ἡμῖν indicates the *location* in which the Spirit has fulfilled the goal of the Law not the instrument (i.e., *believers* fulfill the Law). Had Paul intended the instrumental sense he would have used a prepositional construction with ὑπό and not ἐν with the passive voice.

[58] *Contra* Sanders ("In Rom. 8:3–4 Paul writes that the purpose of God's sending his son was that *Christians* [emphasis added] 'would fulfill the requirement of the law'" [*Paul, the Law and the Jewish People*, p. 98]) and William Hendriksen ("his *people*, by means of the operation of the Holy Spirit in their hearts and lives, *should strive, are striving*, to fulfill the law's righteous requirement" [*Exposition of Paul's Epistle to the Romans* Vol. 1 (Grand Rapids: Baker, 1980), p. 248]); with Schreiner ("The passive πληρωθῇ and the prepositional phrase ἐν ἡμῖν surely signal that the obedience described is the work of God" (*Romans*, p. 405), although he does not rule out cooperative human activity. However, there is no "striving" language in 8:4 (i.e., "fulfillment" takes place in us who walk according to the Spirit); see also Moo, *Romans 1–8*, p. 515; Fee, *God's Empowering Presence*, p. 535.

"a marker of norm of similarity or homogeneity" (e.g., "according to, in accordance with, in conformity with").[59] Thus, the phrase "according to the Spirit" indicates a demonstration of homogeneity and conformity with the Spirit. This is equivalent to Paul's description of having "the mindset (φρόνημα) of the Spirit" [v. 6], which correspondingly means "the faculty of fixing one's mind" on the Spirit.[60] The use of the preposition ἐν in the phrase ἐν πνεύματι (v. 9) fluctuates between the locative and instrumental senses[61] but still conveys the sense of close association to someone.[62] It is not to be interpreted restrictively as an inspired state but is to be understood more comprehensively as the sense of communion with God who enables one in the conduct of daily activity.[63] Likewise the use of the dative πνεύματι (v. 13) denotes the Spirit as the agent ordering the daily conduct of life and overlaps in meaning with the constructions above.[64] Thus, throughout Rom. 8 Paul communicates the prominence of the role of the Spirit in the practical dimensions of the believer's life.

The distinction between "walking according to the flesh" and "walking according to the Spirit" in Rom. 8:4 is one of two separate and mutually exclusive phases of salvation-history. As we stated above in our comments on Rom. 7:5, Paul uses σάρξ over against πνεῦμα not as a description of anthropological dualism (i.e., the internal struggle of the sinful nature with the Spirit) but as a description of one's orientation with respect to God in salvation-history. Thus, "to walk according to the flesh" is to be oriented to the values of this world in rebellion against God.[65] But "to walk according to the Spirit" is to be oriented to the values of the new era of God's Spirit.[66] Therefore, when Paul engages in the dialectical description of "flesh" and

---

[59] BDAG, p. 512 cf. "in keeping with the Spirit" (Fee, God's Empowering Presence, p. 537); "are open to the promptings of the Spirit...take the side of the Spirit" (Fitzmyer, Romans, pp. 488-89).

[60] BDAG, p. 1066.

[61] BDF, p. 118.

[62] BDAG, p. 327; cf. Dunn notes a close connection between Paul's use of κατά and ἐν with respect to the "flesh" and the "Spirit"(Romans 1-8, pp. 427-28).

[63] See Schwweizer, "πνεῦμα, κτλ.," p. 433; so Dunn, Romans 1-8, p. 428..

[64] So Cranfield, The Epistle to the Romans, p. 394 and most other commentators; see also J.D.G. Dunn, "Spirit in the NT," NIDNTT, pp. 693-707, esp. p. 702.

[65] A. Sand, Der Begriff 'Sarx' in den paulinischen Hauptbriefen BU 2 (Regenburg: Pustet, 1967), p. 279.

[66] Fee, God's Empowering Presence, pp. 816-22.

"Spirit" he is explicating the absolutely incompatible nature of the two ways of life, not because believers are caught in the persistent tension between the two but because he wants to demonstrate how believers belong to the new era of the Spirit, which is altogether incompatible with the former era of the flesh. This is why he can state definitively, "but as for you, you are[67] not in the flesh, but in the Spirit" (8:9).

Rom.8:4-8 is neither paraenetic nor argumentative but is descriptive.[68] Paul is neither *warning* believers about two different possibilities of the flesh and the Spirit in order to encourage them to live according to the Spirit[69] nor does he engage in an *argument* on the benefits of living according to the Spirit. Rather, Paul is simply depicting two different groups of people; those oriented towards the "flesh" and those oriented towards the "Spirit." This is evident by Paul's consistent use of the third person plural (οἱ ὄντες [vv. 5, 8]) in the paragraph and the conspicuous absence of imperatives. Thus, Dunn[70] and Cranfield[71] make the error of reading Paul's description as a hortatory injunction to keep on the Spirit side of the conflict with the flesh, even when all the evidence indicates that Paul is simply *describing* the "before and after" of non-believer and believer respectively.

Περιπατεῖν, used in the phrase "*walking* according to the Spirit," is one of Paul's favourite verbs, used 18 times.[72] In the LXX this verb is found in only

---

[67] Paul uses the present tense verb ἐστέ to describe the present status of the Roman believers as oriented to the values of the new era of the Spirit ("you *are in the present moment* not in the flesh, but in the Spirit").

[68] Deidun, *New Covenant Morality*, p. 77; Moo, *Romans 1-8*, pp. 518-19; Fee, *God's Empowering Presence*, p. 540; Schreiner, *Romans*, p. 411; Barrett, *The Epistle to the Romans*, p. 148.

[69] In Gal. 5:16-26, Paul engages in an intense argument and warning concerning the benefits of the Spirit over against the flesh.

[70] "It is much more likely, then, that Paul sharpened up the antitheses for *parenetical reasons* (emphasis added) because he wanted to make clear to his readers that the choice already made in conversion needs to be reaffirmed and renewed in the religious and ethical decisions of daily life. This is probably implicit in his description of the alternatives...as 'taking the side of the flesh' or 'espousing the cause of the Spirit'" (Dunn, *Romans 1-8*, p. 441).

[71] "We take Paul's meaning in this verse (8:5) then to be that those who allow the direction of their lives to be determined by the flesh *are actually taking the flesh's side* (emphasis added) in the conflict between the Spirit of God and the flesh, while those who allow the Spirit to determine the direction of their lives are taking the Spirit's side" (Cranfield, *The Epistle to the Romans*, p. 386).

[72] Rom. 6:4; 8:4; 13:13; 14:15; 1 Cor. 3:3; 7:17; 2 Cor. 4:2; 5:7; 10:2; 10:3; 12:18; Gal. 5:16; Phil. 3:17; 3:18; 1 Thess. 2:12; 4:1 (2x); 4:12.

33 passages and used mostly in a spatial sense of to go or to walk about. It is untypical of Greek thought to use it in a figurative sense of life's conduct.[73] The LXX translates the Hebrew הלך as περιπατεῖν only in 2 Kgs. 20:3; Prov. 8:20; Ecc. 11:9, where it is used to express an individual's religious and ethical walk.[74] In the MT the word הלך is used with some significant frequency as a Hebrew idiom denoting moral and religious life[75] and with particular association with the ethical conduct of Jews according to the Mosaic Law.[76] Paul follows the MT use of the word in a moral sense, rarely using it in spatial sense.[77] As was stated above, "walking according to the Spirit" is equivalent to "the mindset of the Spirit" (v. 6), "in the Spirit" (v. 9), and "by the Spirit" (v. 13), in that each makes the association of the Spirit in the daily walk of life. Furthermore, these designations attribute the believer's behaviour to be in conformity with the Spirit's work in one's life. Nowhere in Rom. 8 does Paul depict the Law as the basis for ethics. Also, after 8:7,[78] all mention of the Law ceases and the Spirit alone is the source for the practical and behavioural dimensions of the believer's life.

In Rom. 8:6 Paul continues[79] the thought of v. 5 ("the ones being according to the flesh...they think on [φρονοῦσιν] the things of the flesh"/ "but the ones according to the Spirit, the things of the Spirit") and is explicit that the "mindset of the flesh" leads to death and the "mindset of the Spirit" leads to life. The respective genitives τῆς σαρκός and τοῦ πνεύματος are descriptive: "the faculty of fixing one's mind, which is characterized by and determined by the flesh/ Spirit."[80] The predicates "death" and "life" typify the mind of the flesh and Spirit in terms of their respective fruits.[81] "Death," as was stated above, is to be interpreted as a state of being in alienation and

---

[73] G. Ebel, "περιπατέω," NIDNTT Vol. 3, pp. 943-45.

[74] G. Bertram, "πατέω, κτλ.," TDNT Vol. V, pp. 940-43, esp. pp. 42-43.

[75] BDB, p. 234.

[76] Lev. 26:3 cf. 1 Kgs. 6:12 ("If you *walk* in my decrees"); Jer. 44:10 ("nor have they *walked* in my Law"); 44:33 ("you did not *walk* in his Law"); see also Exod. 16:4, 14; 2 Kgs. 10:31, etc.

[77] H. Seesemann, "πατέω and Compounds in the NT," TDNT Vol. V, pp. 943-45.

[78] If our description of the "flesh" is correct, Rom. 8:7 conjoins "flesh" with the Law and is part of Paul's description of the former era.

[79] Γάρ, which appears in Rom. 8:6, often occurs to introduce several arguments for the same assertion (BDAG, p. 189).

[80] Moo, *Romans 1-8*, p. 520.

[81] Cranfield, *The Epistle to the Romans*, p. 386.

estrangement from God,[82] which results in condemnation, and in this context functions as one of the components of the tripartite Law, sin, and *death* that Paul uses to depict the former era of the Mosaic Law.[83] This is affirmed in the very next verse (v. 7): "because (διότι)[84] the mindset of the flesh is hostile toward God; for it does not subject itself to the Law of God,[85] neither indeed is it able (to do so)." The idea of the inability of the Mosaic Law is recapitulated here from 8:3 and 7:7–24, where Paul describes the condition of the Law thwarted by sin in the former era. "Life," on the other hand, denotes relationship with God[86] and the objective reality of salvation in the new era of the Spirit.[87]

The theme of the life-giving Spirit continues in 8:10, 11, 13. V. 10 contains the words, "But the Spirit is life because of righteousness." Most agree that this is the main point of the apodosis.[88] Some interpret πνεῦμα in the anthropological sense of "human spirit."[89] This would automatically force the

---

[82] In Rom. 8:6, "peace" is equivalent to "life" in that both are understood to be the result of being in the covenant relationship with God (i.e., "the mind of the Spirit is life *and* peace" [see the discussion of "life" above]). The idea of "peace" does not refer to a subjective state of mind, an inner sense of well-being, or feeling at peace, but is descriptive of an objective reality into which the believer has entered. The "peace" here refers to the outward situation of being in a relationship with God (i.e., "peace with God"). This is contrasted with the non-believer's "enmity toward God" in Rom. 8:7; see Rom. 2:10 and 5:1, where Paul writes εἰρήνην ἔχομεν πρὸς τὸν θεόν. (cf. with the use of πρὸς this denotes being "friendly to, toward, with" [BDAG, p. 874]). This coincides with the use of שָׁלוֹם in the OT which refers to a relationship rather than a state (G. von Rad, "שָׁלוֹם in the OT," *TDNT* Vol.II, pp. 402–6). Paul also refers to the "God of peace" (Rom. 15:33; 16:20; 2 Cor. 13:11; Phil. 4:9; 1 Thess. 5:23).

[83] See Rom. 7:10, 11, 13, 24; 8:2; "The θάνατος...links the description back into the overarching distinction between epochs" (Dunn, *Romans 1–8*, p. 426).

[84] "Διότι" is a "marker used to indicate why something just stated can reasonably be considered valid" (BDAG, p. 251).

[85] The idea that νόμος in Rom. 8:7 does not refer to the Mosaic Law but more generally "the demand of God" (Feuillet, "Loi de Dieu, Loi du Christ et Loi de L'Esprit D'après Les Epîtres Pauliniennes," 42) ignores the parallelism between this verse and 8:3 (i.e., both verses associate the Mosaic Law with "inability" because of the "flesh").

[86] See the above explanation of "peace" and its collocation with "life" in Rom. 8:6.

[87] See Rom. 5:17, 21; 6:22; 11:15 cf. 8:2, 6, 10, 11, 13.

[88] E.g., Moo, *Romans 1–8*, p. 525; Fee, *God's Empowering Presence*, p. 549.

[89] "Clearly the πνεῦμα here meant is the human πνεῦμα which has the properties of life" (Sanday and Headlam, *The Epistle to the Romans*, p. 198); J. Stott, *Romans: God's Good News for the World* (Downers Grove, Ill: InterVarsity, 1994), p.p. 226; Wright, *The Climax of the Covenant*, p. 202; Fitzmyer, *Romans*, p. 491; see also the English versions RSV, NIV, NASB.

noun ζωή to be interpreted as a verb ("but the spirit *is alive*"), something that is never found in the Pauline corpus. If Paul wanted to communicate this he would have used the more precise word ζάω, which specifically means to "be alive, come back to life."[90] Furthermore, the immediate context is permeated with the idea of the Spirit as life-giving agent. Thus, "the Spirit is life" is the more probable translation.[91]

The statement "the Spirit is life" must be understood with the previous clause "the body is dead." Some understand the reference to τὸ σῶμα νεκρὸν διὰ ἁμαρτίαν as the past event of death to sin, which is effected by baptism.[92] However, this is unlikely given that in Rom. 6 Paul uses the dative case (ἀπεθάνομεν τῇ ἁμαρτία, [6:2 cf. v. 10, 11]) to convey this rather than the preposition δία, which normally has a causal meaning ("because of sin"). It is most likely that by the term τὸ σῶμα he meant the physical body, not because the believer is still a sinner,[93] but because the sentence of death has been destined for all people because of Adam's sin.[94] Because we are caught up in the tension between the new era and the old one,[95] physical mortality is still very much a part of the "old era," which is on its way out. The "body is dead"communicates the inevitability that our physical bodies will die. This interpretation is strengthened by the similar phraseology ("your mortal bodies" [τὰ θνητὰ σώματα ὑμῶν]) in the very next verse (v. 11) and the clarification,

---

[90] Paul is prone to using the word ζάω extensively when he wishes (51 times; 23 times in Romans alone [1:17; 6:2, 10, 11, 13; 7:1, 2, 3, 9; 8:12, 13, etc]).

[91] So Byrne, *Romans*, p. 245; Murray, *The Epistle to the Romans*, p. 289; Barrett, *The Epistle to the Romans*, pp. 149-50.

[92] "Baptismal death must be realized" (Barrett, *The Epistle to the Romans*, p. 149); "the death of the body of sin effected in baptism" (Käsemann, *Commentary on Romans*, p. 224); H. Paulsen, *Überlieferung und Auslegung in Römer 8* WUNT 43 (Neukirchen-Vluyn: Neukirchener Verlag, 1974), pp. 69ff.

[93] This is the erroneous deduction of Cranfield ("the Christian must still submit to death as the wages of sin, *because he is a sinner* [emphasis added]" [*The Epistle to the Romans*, p. 389]).

[94] "Through one human sin entered into the world and through sin, death, and thus death came unto all humans" (Rom. 5:12).

[95] The tension between the old era and the new is evident in Rom. 8:10. The protasis, "if Christ is in you" that is indicative of the new era, sets up the condition for the apodosis, "then (μέν) the body is dead because of sin *but* (δέ) the Spirit is life because of righteousness" that is indicative of the tension between old era and the new. The use of the μέν/ δέ is a description of the contrast between the "here" and "not yet" of Christian existence (see Fee, *God's Empowering Presence*, p. 551).

which this verse brings to the meaning of v. 10.[96] Thus, even though the physical body is intended to die, the role of the Spirit as the "Spirit of life" means that we have life presently and in the future. This is what v. 11 will spell out.

The idea of "making alive" in v. 11 refers to resurrection and transformation and is the answer to the "deadness" of the body in v. 10.[97] In v. 11 the use of the future tense ζωοποιήσει speaks of the future resurrection life of believers where the mortal body is given life.[98] There is uncertainty regarding the specific role of the Spirit in the future resurrection of believers. The minor variant textual readings affect the meaning of the text in a significant manner: one textual tradition reads, "the one who raised Christ from the dead will give life also to your mortal bodies *through his Spirit who lives in you* (διὰ τοῦ ἐνοικοῦντος αὐτοῦ πνεύματος[99] ἐν ὑμῖν)" and the other reads, "the one who raised Christ from the dead will give life also to your mortal bodies *because of his Spirit who lives in you* (διὰ τὸ ἐνοικοῦν αὐτοῦ πνεῦμα[100] ἐν ὑμῖν)." Fee argues that the reading with the genitive case makes the Spirit the *agent* of the future resurrection of believers whereas the reading with the accusative makes the Spirit the *guarantor* of the future resurrection of believers. He and others favour the reading with the accusative case.[101] However, both textual traditions have strong and early attestation[102] and even

---

[96] Thus, the δέ in Rom. 8:11 is not an adversative (*contra* Dunn, *Romans 1-8*, p. 432) but resumptive ("And if the Spirit...").

[97] R.H. Gundry, *Sōma in Biblical Theology with Emphasis on Pauline Anthropology* (Grand Rapids: Zondervan, 1987), p. 38.

[98] "The last Adam unto the Spirit *which gives life* [ζωοποιοῦν]" (1 Cor. 15:45 cf. vv. 22, 36; 2 Cor. 3:6).

[99] This reading with the genitive case is attested by ℵ A C 81 104 256 263 436 1319 1506 1573 and is favoured by NA (26)/ UBS (4).

[100] This reading with the accusative case is attested by B D F G Ψ 6 33 424 459 1175 1241 1739 1881 Majority text.

[101] Fee, *God's Empowering Presence*, p. 553; see also Schweizer, "πνεῦμα," TDNT Vol. VI, p. 422; *contra* the genitive reading found in M.M.B. Turner, "The Significance of Spirit Endowment for Paul," *VoxEv* 9 (1975), 58-69, esp. 64, 66; E.F. Scott, *Adoption as Sons of God* WUNT 2/48 (Tübingen: Mohr, 1992), p. 256; B.M.A. Metzger, *A Textual Commentary on the Greek New Testament* (London: United Bible Societies, 1971), p. 517.

[102] The genitive case is read by ℵ A C, which is a fourth and fifth century dating and the accusative read by B D has also a fourth and fifth century dating. Both readings also have a widespread attestation (with the genitive- Alexandrian [ℵ A D 81]; Palestinian [syr (pal) Cyril-

internal evidence is inconclusive.[103] Nevertheless, for our purpose whether the Spirit is specifically the *agent* or *guarantor* of the resurrection, Paul wants to emphasize the idea that the Spirit is the basis for "life." In v. 9, the indwelling Spirit ("since the Spirit of God lives in you") suggests that the Spirit has now made his home in the believer and because the Spirit is life, the presence of the Spirit cannot but result in life for the body of the believer. Thus, there is continuity between the present indwelling of the Spirit and the future resurrection.

The two conditional clauses in Rom. 8:13 are Paul's warnings[104] that correspond to the two possibilities of existence: "*if* you live according to the flesh, you are destined to die"/ "*if* by the Spirit you put to death the practices of the body, you will live." In vv. 5-9, we noted that "flesh" and "Spirit" represented Paul's depiction of two different groups of people, respectively non-believers living in accordance with the previous era and believers living in accordance with the present era of the Spirit. However, here in v. 13, there is indication that liberation in the present from the "flesh" does not preclude warnings against succumbing to the flesh. In the tension between the new era and the old, the believer's decisive break from the Law, sin, and death does not free him from the necessity of mortifying sin in the present; there is a possibility of reverting back to the previous manner of living in the old era of the flesh.[105] As in v. 6 above, the respective fruits of the flesh and the Spirit are described. If one lives "according to the flesh" then death will be the certain outcome. This is the connotation of μέλλετε in the injuction; "*you are destined to die.*"[106] The meaning of "death" must not be eviscerated. In its fullest sense

---

Jerusalem]; Western [it (61) Hippolytus]/ with the accusative- Alexandrian [the combination B 1739]; Palestinian [Methodius, Origen, Theodoret]).

[103] Paul speaks of resurrection "through *his* (God's) *power* (Spirit)" (διὰ τῆς δυνάμεως αὐτοῦ, 1 Cor. 6:14) that indicates the Spirit as the *agent of the resurrection* and likewise of "the first fruits of the Spirit...the redemption of our body" (Rom. 8:23) that indicates the Spirit as *guarantor* of the resurrection.

[104] In Rom. 8:13, Paul intentionally shifts to the second person (ζῆτε, μέλλετε, θανατοῦτε, ζήσεσθε).

[105] "Freed from sin, we are not 'obliged' (ὀφειλέται [v.12]) to 'live according to the flesh' as in the old era; we can sin but we do not *have* to" (Byrne, *Romans*, p. 241); "The believer's once-for-all death to the law and to sin does not free him from the necessity of mortifying sin in his members; it makes it *necessary* and *possible* for him to do so" (Murray, *The Epistle to the Romans*, p. 294); see also Deidun, *New Covenant Morality*, p. 80; Schreiner, *Romans*, p. 420.

[106] "To be inevitable, *be destined, inevitable*" (BDAG, p. 628).

"death" denotes eternal separation from God as the penalty for sin as in Rom. 6:23, which clearly posits "death" as the counterpart to "eternal life."[107] Conversely, it follows that the future verb ζήσεσθε ("you will live") denotes eschatological life.[108] This is achieved through the Spirit, where the dative πνεύματι indicates agency. Rather than simply saying, "live according to the Spirit" in the second protasis and apodosis, Paul strikes an inverse linguistic note with the first protasis and apodosis using the concepts of "living" and "dying" (first protasis and apodosis: "if *you live* [ζῆτε] according to the flesh, you are destined *to die* [ἀποθνήσκειν]" cf. second protasis and apodosis: "if by the Spirit *you put to death* [θανατοῦτε] the practices of the body, *you will live* [ζήσεσθε])."[109] Since he has firmly stated in v. 9 that believers are not in the flesh and the body is destined to die (v. 10), Paul speaks metaphorically by stating that what they are to put to death are "the practices of the body." They are to put to death the "practices" associated with "body," which both belong to the previous age. The meaning is clear enough; they are to have no part with sin associated with "life in the flesh."

Thus, Paul indicates that it is the characteristic work of the Spirit that fashions the behaviour of the believer in the new era. He describes this in various ways: "walking according to the Spirit" (vv. 4, 5); "the mindset of the Spirit" (v. 6); "in the Spirit" (v. 9); "by the Spirit" (v. 13). Each phrase emphasizes the practical dimension of conformance with the Spirit in the believer's life. Nowhere does Paul advocate that the Spirit's role in ethics is compatible with the necessity to observe the Law. In fact, all mention of the Mosaic Law ceased in 8:7, which is a sure indication that the Spirit occupies an exclusive role in this respect. This is consistent with our interpretation of Rom. 8:2 that the new era of the Spirit has displaced the former era of the Law.

---

[107] "᾿Αποθνήσκειν is pregnant...the meaning is not merely that they will die...but that they will die without hope of life with God" (Cranfield, *The Epistle to the Romans*, p. 394); "the sure result will be death at the day of judgment" (Stuhlmacher, *Paul's Letter to the Romans*, p. 130).

[108] Fitzmyer, *Romans*, p. 493; *contra* Stott, who contends that Paul is simply referring to a richer life (*Romans*, pp. 229-30).

[109] Fee recognizes this word play (*God's Empowering Presence*, p. 558).

3. The Spirit and the Experience of Familial Relationship: Rom. 8:14-16

In Rom. 8:2-13, the theme of the Spirit as the agent of life governed the discussion. In vv. 14-16 that follow Paul shifts his discussion to the Spirit's role in establishing familial relationship with God.[110] With the presence of the word γάρ in v. 14 we have a sure indication that Paul intended the closest kind of relationship between these two themes and that what transpires in vv. 14-16 are explanatory remarks not only on v. 13, but on vv. 2-13 as a whole.[111] This suggests that Paul perceived a logical progression between v. 13b and v. 14a; the linguistic similarity between them indicates a certain measure of synthetic parallelism, in particular, the believer's conformance with the life-giving Spirit is said to be directly related to his status of sonship:

εἰ   πνεύματι   τὰς πράξεις τοῦ σώματος θανατοῦτε, ζήσεσθε
ὅσοι πνεύματι θεοῦ ἄγονται,   οὗτοι υἱοὶ θεοῦ εἰσιν

The words, "sons of God" interpret "you will live" and are a sign that Paul equates the idea of "life/ living" with the status of being "sons of God," and both of these are the direct result of the Spirit. Thus, Paul conveys an inextricable relationship between the Spirit's role as life-giving agent, which concerns the practical and ethical dimensions in the believer's life (i.e., "doing"[112]), and the Spirit's role in the believer's familial status with God (i.e., "being").[113] He demonstrates a smooth transition between ethics and familial

---

[110] See the associations made between the Spirit and the idea of "sonship": "For all who are led by the Spirit of God, these are sons of God" (v. 14); "Spirit of adoption" (v. 15); "Spirit by whom we cry, 'Abba, Father'" (v. 15); "the Spirit testifies with our spirit that we are children of God" (v. 16).

[111] Moo, Romans 1-8, p. 533; Scott, Adoption as Sons, p. 260; Bertone, "The Function of the Spirit," 83; Osten-Sacken, Römer 8 als Beispiel paulinischer Soteriologie, pp. 134-36; B. Byrne, "Sons of God" "Seed of Abraham," p. 98.

[112] In Rom. 8:13, the phrase "If by the Spirit you put to death the practices of the body" signifies action and performance ("doing") of behaviour; i.e., the mortification of sin through the agency of the Spirit. As Cranfield puts it, "What is envisaged is an action which is continuous or again and again repeated (emphasis added)" (The Epistle to the Romans, p. 395).

[113] "For all who are being led ('doing') by the Spirit, these are ('being') the sons of God" (Rom. 8:14); see also secondary sources: "Being (emphasis added) sons of God explains why those who are placed under the dominion of the Spirit experience (doing) eschatological life (v. 14, in relation to v. 13)" (Moo, Romans 1-8, p. 532); "The words υἱοί εἰσιν θεοῦ interpret the

status with God, where the believer's behaviour is a tangible expression of his status as son of God. In this sense Rom. 8:14-16 strikes at the very heart of the matter and functions as a climax to the whole section (vv. 1-16), and especially, the designation "the law of the Spirit of life" (v. 2).[114] For Paul ethics is based upon the foundation of a relationship with God and the Spirit functions as the linchpin, which makes the on-going practical and behavioural dimensions of the believer's life operational. Thus, he understands the Spirit to take on a comprehensive role; not only does the Spirit secure relationship with God in the first place (vv. 14-16), but he also is the agent that fosters a tangible expression of this relationship in the daily lives of believers (vv. 2-13). This explains the association of vv. 14-16 with vv. 2-13.

In v. 14, ὅσοι can be interpreted restrictively as "*only those who* are being led by the Spirit of God"[115] or inclusively as "*all those who* are being led by the Spirit of God."[116] Some prefer to keep it ambiguous ("*as many as...*").[117] In any case, Paul communicates the characteristic and unique role of the Spirit in the believer's life. With the passive ἄγονται he defines more precisely the role the Spirit plays. Both de la Potterie and Keesmaat argue that the verb ἄγειν had become the *technicus terminus* for the vocabulary of the Exodus and thus indicates that Paul's thought is patterned upon God leading the people of Israel into the Promised Land.[118] However, apart from Rom. 8:14, Paul uses the verb four times in his writings[119] and in all these contexts there is no association whatsoever with the Exodus event. Of particular importance are 1 Cor. 12:2 and Gal. 5:18, where a similar association is made between the Spirit and the passive form of the verb ἄγειν. In Gal. 5:18 there can be no

---

ζήσεσθε of the previous verse. The life which God promises is not a mere not-dying: it is to be a son of God, to live as a son of God, both now and hereafter" (Cranfield, *The Epistle to the Romans*, pp. 395-96).

[114] J.J.J. van Rensburg, "The Children of God in Romans 8,"*Neot* 15 (1981), 139-79, esp. 159-61.

[115] Taken to be referring to the restrictive group mentioned in Rom. 8:13 (M.-J., Lagrange, *Saint Paul: Epître aux Romains* (Paris: Gabalda, 1950), p. 201.

[116] BDAG, p. 729; Kurt Stalder, *Das Werk des Geistes in des Heiligung bei Paulus*, p. 470.

[117] Dunn, *Romans 1-8*, p. 450.

[118] Ignace de la Potterie, "Le Chrétien conduit par l'esprit dans son cheminement eschatologique," pp. 209-78 in Lorenzo De Lorenzi, *The Law of the Spirit in Rom 7 and 8* (Rome: St. Paul's Abbey, 1976), see esp. p. 221; Sylvia C. Keesmaat, *Paul and his Story: (Re)Intepreting the Exodus Tradition* JSNTSup 181(Sheffield: JSOT Press, 1999), pp. 57-65, 96.

[119] See Rom. 2:4; 8:14; 1 Cor. 12:2; Gal. 5:18; 1 Thes. 4:14.

greater distance between Paul's thought and the Exodus event. Central to the Exodus event was the giving of the Law. But in this context he posits a disparity between "being led by the Spirit" and being "under the Law."[120] This is the case for Rom. 8:14 and its context as well. Paul conveys a mutually exclusive relationship between the former era of the Law and the new era of the Spirit (7:6; 8:2, 3,4). In 1 Cor. 12:2, the use of the passive ἤγεσθε is occasioned by Paul's reference to moments of enthusiasm associated with idol worship. Thus, even if ἄγειν had become a catchword denoting the Exodus, Paul certainly did not use it in this manner.

There is good reason to believe that the use of ἄγειν in Rom. 8:14 is directly associated with and occasioned by Paul's previous descriptions of the Spirit: "walking according to the Spirit" (v. 4); "according to the Spirit" (v. 5); "the mind of the Spirit" (v. 6); "in the Spirit" (v. 10); "Spirit dwells in you" (v. 11).[121] But at the same time, with his use of ἄγειν Paul presses the Spirit's role even further than his previous comments to prepare the reader for the inspirational cry of sonship in v. 15. The concern with ethics ceases after v. 13 and Paul shifts to the experience of sonship from vv. 14-16.[122]

Käsemann makes a compelling case that the passive form ἄγονται is patterned after the vocabulary of the enthusiasts according to 1 Cor. 12:2, meaning to be "driven by the Spirit."[123] The parallels between Rom. 8:14 and 1 Cor. 12:2 are striking: 1. both contexts use the passive form ἄγονται/

---

[120] Keesmaat reasons that the meaning of the Law cannot be understood without its association with the Exodus (p. 35); the giving of the Law was the central aspect of the Exodus event that was retold in the scriptures of Israel (p. 140). At the same time in her discussion of the Law in Galatians, she argues that Paul advocates "radical discontinuity" between the relation of the Law and the new community in Christ (p. 196) (*Paul and his Story*).

[121] Brendan Byrne notes that the clause "led by the Spirit of God catches up beyond this all the various descriptions in the Spirit of the preceding section (vv. 4, 5, 6, 9, 10, 11)" ("*Sons of God*"- "*Seed of Abraham*," p. 98); Dunn, *Romans 1-8*, p. 450; Moo, *Romans 1-8*, p. 534.

[122] If one does not pick up on this subtle shift in Paul's explication of the Spirit, one's interpretation runs amuck. This is the case with most commentators who still see Paul's reference to the Spirit's role in ethics in Rom. 8:14 ("The passive form of the verb is significant, in that it suggests that the Spirit is the *primary agent in Christian obedience* [emphasis added], that it is *his work in believers that accounts for their obedience* [emphasis added]") Schreiner, *Romans*, p. 422; so with Fee, Moo, etc.

[123] "It (ἄγονται) therefore should not be weakened to 'be led by'...in order to preserve the free ethical decision, of which there is no talk here...Paul was not so timid as his expositors. He could appropriate the terms of the enthusiasts because he took 'Christ in us' seriously" (Käsemann, *Commentary on Romans*, p. 226); see also Dunn, *Romans 1-8*, p. 450.

ἤγεσθε, 2. both associate it with Spirit-inspired speech ("Spirit...by whom we cry out" [Rom. 8:15] cf. "no one speaking by the Spirit of God says...no one can say, 'Jesus is Lord' except by the Holy Spirit" [1 Cor. 12:3]). Most agree that in the context of 1 Cor. 12:2, the use of ἤγεσθε refers to the enthusiastic experience associated with idol worship.[124] In v. 3, Paul goes so far as to compare and equate this with the experience of Spirit-inspired speech (ἐν πνεύματι...λαλῶν λέγει). This indicates that he perceived a similarity between the enthusiastic experience associated with idols and Spirit inspiration.[125] At this point it is important to distinguish between ecstatic and enthusiastic experience. "Ecstasy" refers to experiential activity in which the individual loses *complete* control (i.e., if one experiences any one of the following situations: she is forced to speak against her will, she loses self control and raves violently, she speaks things which make no sense to her, she is unaware of her surroundings).[126] But "enthusiasm" *need not imply the complete loss of control*; it refers to inspired activity or speech that is the direct result of being overwhelmed by another presence but not to the point of losing control.[127] Paul makes it clear that in the church Spirit-inspired utterances can and should be controlled by individuals (cf. 1 Cor. 14:30, 31). In the context of Rom. 8:14 as well, Paul advocates the cooperative effort of the Spirit and

---

[124] Aune, *Prophecy in Early Christianity and the Ancient Mediterranean World*, p. 257; E. Schweizer, "πνεῦμα, κτλ.," *TDNT* Vol. VI, p. 423, footnote 603; Barrett, *The First Epistle to the Corinthians*, p. 278; Gordon D. Fee, *The First Epistle to the Corinthians*, NICNT (Grand Rapids: Wm. B. Eerdmans Publishing Co., 1987), pp. 577-78.

[125] "Christian 'enthusiasm' is neither attacked nor defended, but presupposed and analysed...Not the manner but the content of ecstatic speech determines its authenticity" (Barrett, *The First Epistle to the Corinthians*, p. 279).

[126] See T. Callan, "Prophecy and Ecstasy in Greco-Roman Religion and 1 Corinthians," *NovT* 27 (1985), 125-40.

[127] Fee does not make this distinction in his interpretation of Rom. 8:14. He defines it in the extreme sense as "ecstasy" (i.e., "Spirit seizure"); see his quote from Godet, who describes this as "holy violence, the Spirit drags the man where the flesh would fain not go" (*God's Empowering Presence*, p. 563, footnote 263). Certainly if we were to understand Rom. 8:14 in this manner we would oppose the interpretation. But if we were to understand Paul's connotation as "enthusiasm" rather than "ecstasy" it would be more palatable to the interpretation of Rom. 8:14 and better explain the use of the passive and the experience of familial intimacy, which is its primary referent in vv. 14-16, not ethics as Fee intimates by his extensive quotation of the use of ἄγειν in the LXX. Fee makes little use of 1 Cor. 12:2,3, on his comments of Rom. 8:14, where Paul combines his discussion on Spirit-inspired utterance and the use of ἄγειν in the passive voice. This would have been a more fitting comparison.

the individual.[128] Thus, with the phrase πνεύματι θεοῦ ἄγονται, Paul suggests an overwhelming and unique sense of the Spirit, while at the same time the believer is fully aware of what is happening and is engaged in cooperative activity with the Spirit. This is distinctive of Christian experience, as Paul indicates by the following phrase, οὗτοι υἱοὶ θεοῦ εἰσιν.[129]

The plural "sons of God" occurs in the LXX to characterize the intimate relationship Yahweh has with the people of Israel, and is here picked up by Paul to denote the eschatological community of God through Christ.[130] Evident also with this reference to "sonship" is Paul's statement against the Law.[131] This may be the reason for the emphatic use of οὗτοι ("these are sons of God"), which has an excluding and contrasting force.[132] Israel's sonship was grounded in the Law. Israel demonstrated its status of sonship when it obeyed the Law.[133] For example, Jub. 1:24b, 25a, reads, "And they will do my commandments. And I shall be a father to them, and they will be sons to me. And they will all be called 'sons of the living God.'"[134] This idea is further emphasized in Rabbinic literature. In a homiletic midrash on Deut. 29:1 which begins a discussion on Israel's covenant obligations, it reads, "You have the wish to be signaled out, that you are my sons? Busy yourselves with the Torah and observance of the commandments, so all will see that you are my sons."[135] In response, Paul claims that the status of sonship is determined exclusively by the experience of the eschatological Spirit. He will spell this out in more detail in what is to follow in vv. 15-16.

---

[128] "You received the Spirit of adoption, by whom we cry out, 'Abba, Father'"; see also Dunn's cautionary comments (Romans 1-8, p. 450).

[129] "Here again (Rom. 8:14ff.) therefore we have Paul describing an existential experience [the charismatic awareness of sonship], which is the mark of the Spirit of God, and which marks out the Spirit as distinctively the Spirit of sonship, the Spirit of God's Son" (Dunn, Jesus and the Spirit, pp. 319-20).

[130] See Deut. 14:1; Isa. 43:6; Hos. 2:1; Wis. 5:5; see also the OT Pseudepigrapha (T. Mos. 10:3; 2 Bar. 13:9); compare with Byrne, "Sons of God"- "Seed of Abraham," p. 98; G. Fohrer, E. Schweizer, and E. Lohse, "υἱός, κτλ.," TDNT Vol. VIII, pp. 340-92, esp. pp. 354, 391, 392.

[131] Fee, God's Empowering Presence, p. 564.

[132] "Οὗτοι has the emphasis and has the force of 'these and no other'" (Murray, The Epistle to the Romans, p. 295, footnote 15).

[133] Eduard Lohse, "Palestinian Judaism: Israel and the Righteous as Sons of God," TDNT Vol. VIII, pp. 359-40; G. Vermes, Jesus the Jew: A Historian's Reading of the Gospels (Philadelphia: Fortress Press, 1973), p. 195; Dunn, Romans 1-8, pp. 451, 459.

[134] See also T. Jud. 24:3 ("you shall be his sons in truth and walk in his commandments").

[135] Deuteronomium rabba 7; see also Midr. Ps. 2, 9 on 2:7; Sir. 4:10.

In v. 15, Paul states, "For you did not receive a spirit of slavery again unto fear but you received the Spirit of adoption, by whom we cry out, 'Abba, Father'." With another γάρ in v. 15, Paul draws out the connection between the experience of being led or controlled by the Spirit and the status of being sons of God. The presence of the verb λαμβάνειν in association with πνεῦμα by this point in time for believers had become a *technicus terminus* for their initial reception of the Spirit.[136] Written in the aorist tense, ἐλάβετε no doubt signaled the decisive moment in the past of the beginning of their life as believers.[137]

V. 15 draws out an antithesis between πνεῦμα δουλείας εἰς φόβον and πνεῦμα υἱοθεσίας. The use of "spirit" could refer to the human spirit in the sense of human attitude or disposition.[138] Alternatively, it could refer to two kinds of spirits: evil spirits and the Spirit of God respectively as is evidenced in the DSS and the *T. Twelve Patriarchs*.[139] Most believe that Paul uses the word πνεῦμα rhetorically, close to the use in 1 Cor. 2:12.[140] Thus, "the Spirit that you have received is *not* a 'spirit of bondage' (πνεῦμα δουλείας) but a Spirit of adoption (πνεῦμα υἱοθεσίας)."[141]

If Paul intends a rhetorical use of πνεῦμα in Rom. 8:15, it most likely functions like the use of νόμος in 8:2 in that it describes two separate and mutually exclusive phases in salvation-history: πνεῦμα δουλείας εἰς φόβον represents the former era of the Mosaic Law (cf. "the law of sin and death")[142] and πνεῦμα υἱοθεσίας ("the law of the Spirit of life") represents the present era of the Spirit.[143] However, πνεῦμα δουλείας εἰς φόβον cannot refer to the

---

[136] See for example, 2 Cor. 11:4; Gal. 3:2, 14 cf. Jn. 7:39; 14:17; 20:22; 1 Jn. 2:27.

[137] See Dunn, *Romans 1-8*, p. 451; Cranfield, *The Epistle to the Romans*, p. 396; R.H. Stein, *Difficult Passages in the Epistles* (Grand Rapids: Baker, 1988), pp. 116-26.

[138] "A particular state, habit, or temper of the human spirit" (Sandy and Headlam, *The Epistle to the Romans*, p. 202).

[139] Cf. with the DSS (1QS III. 18ff- "Spirit of truth" vs. "spirit of falsehood") and the *T. Twelve Patriarchs* (*T. Reub.* 5:3; *T. Sim.* 2:7; 3:1; 4:7; *T. Lev.* 2:3; 9:9; 18:7, 11; *T. Jud.* 13:3; 14:2, 8; 20:1) cf. 1 Cor. 2:12; 2 Cor. 11:4.

[140] Stalder, *Werk des Geistes*, pp. 480-81; Byrne, *"Sons of God"- "Seed of Abraham,"* p. 99; Scott, *Adoption as Sons*, p. 264.

[141] Moo, *Romans 1-8*, p. 536.

[142] This best explains the use of πάλιν in Rom. 8:15 ("the spirit of slavery *again* unto fear"), which sets up the salvation-historical contrast between "spirit of slavery" and "Spirit of adoption"; "reverting back to the former era of the Law and its association with fear."

[143] Osten-Sacken, *Römer 8 als Beispiel paulinischer Soteriologie*, p. 132; Dunn, *Romans 1-8*, p. 452.

previous role of the Spirit working with God's Law in the previous era,[144] since Paul has gone to great lengths to show that the Spirit was precisely the missing variable in the former era of the Law.[145] The use of πνεῦμα in the phrase "*spirit* of slavery unto fear" may be similar to the use of νόμος in 8:2 in that it did not have any substance of its own and served only to characterize the situation of "bondage unto fear" (δουλείας εἰς φόβον) and demonstrate the liberation and state that exist when the Spirit functions as "the Spirit of adoption" (πνεῦμα υἰοθεσίας). In other words, the word πνεῦμα in the phrase "*the spirit* of slavery unto fear" is used simply to strike a linguistic note with the use of πνεῦμα in the phrase "*the Spirit* of adoption."

The Mosaic Law is frequently spoken of in a pejorative sense as being inextricable from sin; this whole system is said to enslave individuals.[146] The closest parallel to Rom. 8:15 is found in Gal. 4:5, where the parallel ideas of the Mosaic Law, slavery, adoption as sons, and the inspired cry of sonship ("Abba, Father") are found. The role of Christ was to buy out of slavery those who were imprisoned under the Law. Ἐξαγοράσῃ means to "secure deliverance of"[147] (i.e., "that *he might secure deliverance of* those under the Law"). In Gal. 4:3 Paul is explicit that "we were enslaved (δεδουλωμένοι) under the basic principles of the world," where "the basic principles of the world" are defined comprehensively as "the influence or sway of primal and cosmic forces" that includes the elemental substances of which the cosmos is composed, the elementary forms of religion, and the divine powers which influence or determine human destiny.[148] Consequently, Paul equates being under the Law with being enslaved to the "basic principles of the world" and being under the age of majority (νήπιος [vv. 1, 3]).[149] But in vv. 4–5, he indicates that the time-limited purpose of the Law and the enslavement (i.e., the age of minority) had come to an end when God sent his Son; a new period

---

[144] Cambier, "Le liberté du spirituel dans Rom. 8:12–17," p. 212; see also E.F. Kevan who interprets this more in an individualistic manner of the Spirit's work in the heart of a person in conjunction with the Law leading to a state of "bondage," hence, "the Spirit of bondage" (*The Grace of Law: A Study of Puritan Theology* [Grand Rapids: Baker, 1976], pp. 88–89); see also M. Lloyd-Jones, *Romans: An Exposition of Chapter 8:5–17: The Sons of God* (Grand Rapids: Zondervan, 1975), pp. 197–205.

[145] See discussion above on Rom. 7:7–24 and its relationship to Rom. 8:2.

[146] See Rom. 6:16, 17, 20; cf. v. 14; 7:6; Gal. 4:1 cf. v. 5.

[147] BDAG, p. 343.

[148] Dunn, *The Epistle to the Galatians*, pp. 212–13.

[149] L. Ann Jervis, *Galatians* NIBCNT (Peabody, MA: Hendrickson, 1999), p. 109.

had dawned in God's salvific plan (cf. Rom. 8:3). Christ redeemed, bought out of slavery, those imprisoned under the Law (cf. Gal. 3:13). Picking up the theme of inheritance from 4:1, Paul states that they received the "full rights of sons" (ἵνα τὴν υἱοθεσίαν ἀπολάβωμεν [v. 5]). In v. 6 the soteriological linchpin of Paul's argument is the claim that "the Spirit of God's Son" authenticates the full status of adopted sons by the inspired cry of legitimate children, "Abba, Father." He is referring to the Galatians' experience of the Spirit to demonstrate that they have already achieved all they could ever ask for (cf. Gal. 3:2-5).

Thus, Rom. 8:15, following the pattern of Gal. 4:1-5, indicates Paul's description of the two separate phases of salvation-history, where "the spirit of slavery unto fear" refers to the system associated with the Mosaic Law and "the Spirit of adoption" refers to the new era of the Spirit.[150] The association of the former era of the Mosaic Law with "fear" (φόβος) represented the fear of eschatological punishment, since the Law functions to bring awareness of sin and the corresponding penalty of condemnation (cf. Rom. 7:9-11).[151] The association of the Spirit with "adoption" (πνεῦμα υἱοθεσίας) is somewhat surprising because it is not a legal institution among the Jews, which explains its absence in the LXX. However, as a cautionary note, there is some indication of something equivalent to the idea of adoption in the OT.[152] In the Greco-Roman world "adoption" is a technical term that denotes the incorporation of a person into the status of sonship with all legal rights and privileges, into a natural family that is not his own by birth.[153] The metaphor

---

[150] The use of the strong adversative ἀλλά in Rom. 8:15 makes it clear that Paul intends the clearest distinction between the two phases of salvation history ("You did not [οὐ] receive the spirit of slavery unto fear [i.e., the previous system of the Mosaic Law] but [ἀλλά] you received the Spirit of adoption [i.e., the new era of the Spirit]") cf. "ἀλλά appears most frequently as the contrary to a preceding οὐ" (BDF, p. 232, section 448).

[151] See Byrne, "Sons of God". "Seeds of Abraham," p. 99; Moo, Romans 1-8, p. 536; Schreiner, Romans p. 424; contra Cranfield, who believes "fear" refers to the anxiety experienced under paganism or the misunderstanding and misuse of the Law associated with Judaism (The Epistle to the Romans, pp. 398-97, see also footnote 1 on p. 397); see also Dunn who understands "fear" as being associated with the sectarian mentality in Jewish boasting (Romans 1-8, p. 452).

[152] See Gen. 15:2-4; Exod. 2:10; 4:22f; 2 Sam. 7:14; Esther 2:7; 1 Chron. 28:6; Ps. 2:7; 89:26f; Jer. 3:19; Hos. 11:1; for secondary literature see Scott, Adoption as Sons of God, pp. 3-114; Cranfield, The Epistle to the Romans, p. 397.

[153] Francis Lyall, "Roman Law in the Writings of Paul-Adoption," JBL 88 (1969), 458-66; M.W. Schoenberg, "'Huiothesia': The Word and the Institution," Scr 15 (1963), 115-23.

of adoption occurs in the NT only in Pauline literature (Rom. 8:15, 23; 9:4; Gal. 4:5 cf. Eph. 1:5).

It is not certain whether πνεῦμα υἱοθεσίας in Rom. 8:15 denotes the Spirit as the agent who *brings about* adoption or the agent who *affirms* adoption. Barrett interprets this as a reference to a future time of adoption based on v. 23.[154] However, the use of the present tense verbs, εἰσιν (v. 14), κράζομεν (v. 15), and ἐσμέν (v. 16), argues against this interpretation here in v. 15.[155] In Gal. 4:6 it appears that Paul intimates the Spirit's role in affirming the status of adoption. For example, Paul prefaces his statement on the inspired cry of sonship with the words, ὅτι δέ ἐστε υἱοί, which clearly indicates the prior status of adoption as the condition for the filial affirmation induced by the Spirit. However, the precise distinction between the Spirit as the agent who *brings about* adoption or the agent that *affirms* adoption appears to be ambiguous in light of what Paul claims of the role of the Spirit in the decisive point of conversion (cf. Rom. 8:15, "you *received*[156] the Spirit of adoption"), the continuous cry of sonship (κράζομεν, v. 15) and the persistent and confirmatory witness (συμμαρτυρεῖ, v. 16) the Spirit provides for the believer. Because the Spirit is considered the "law of the Spirit of life" (8:2) throughout ch. 8, it is best to interpret the Spirit's role in a comprehensive manner, including all stages of the believer's life both past and present (past [conversion], present [cry of sonship, witness]).[157]

"By means of" (ἐν ᾧ)[158] the Spirit believers "cry out" (κράζομεν), "Abba, Father" (Αββα ὁ πατήρ). The precise meaning of "cry out" is disputed and Pauline usage is diverse. The verb is used 3 times in Paul (Rom. 8:15; 9:27; Gal. 4:6). In Rom. 9:27 he uses it in the sense of inspired, proclamatory speech to introduce a solemn declaration.[159] In the other two occurrences, κράζω is used in association with the Spirit and the words, "Abba, Father" and the idea of adoption. Most agree that the prayer acknowledges confidence

---

[154] Barrett, *The Epistle to the Romans*, p. 153; see also Byrne, *"Sons of God"- "Seeds of Abraham"*, pp. 49–61.

[155] Cranfield, *The Epistle to the Romans*, p. 397.

[156] See the previous discussion of the function of the aorist tense verb ἐλάβετε as a technical term for conversion in Christian circles.

[157] This is recognized by both Moo (*Romans 1–8*, p. 537) and Schreiner (*Romans*, p. 425).

[158] Elsewhere the words ἐν ᾧ mean "in that" or "because" (Rom. 8:3) but here the antecedent is clearly πνεῦμα υἱοθεσίας, which makes the instrumental usage certain (C.F.D. Moule, *An Idiom Book of New Testament Greek* [Cambridge: University, 1971], p. 131).

[159] Käsemann, *Commentary on Romans*, p. 275.

in the adoptive status: "*the Spirit of adoption,* by whom we cry out, 'Abba, Father'" (Rom. 8:15) cf. "that we might receive *the adoption as sons*...God has sent forth the Spirit of his Son...crying, 'Abba, Father'" (Gal. 4:5-6).[160] It is set in contrast to the "fear" associated with the previous era of the Mosaic Law ("the spirit of slavery unto fear").[161] There is a sense that the action of "crying out" is intense and conveys a deep sense of emotion and has an enthusiastic character to it, particularly when associated with demons.[162] It is used in the context of urgent praying, particularly in the LXX.[163] When the word κράζειν is associated with the Spirit as in Rom. 8:15 and Gal. 4:6, it communicates the consciousness of being moved upon by divine power and of words that are given to speak out in the sense of an enthusiastic outcry as in prophetic utterances (see 1 Cor. 14:30-31 ["if a revelation is given...you can all prophesy"]).[164] Ultimately, in this verse Paul is describing a religious experience that is ineffable and mystical in the best sense of the word. The truth of Rom. 8:15 is not simply a statement of fact to be grasped with our intellect. It is more than this; it involves the emotions as well in that it is also a deeply felt and intensely experienced cry of filial relationship with God.[165] If we strip this from the meaning of Rom. 8:15, we will fail to appreciate the profundity of Paul's assertion.

The verb κράζομεν is written in the present tense, using the first person plural to accentuate the perpetual role the Spirit plays in the believer's life in securing and sustaining relationship with God. Paul no doubt juxtaposes the decisive moment of conversion in the past, using the aorist tense ("*you received* the Spirit of adoption" [ἐλάβετε]) and the continuous experience of filial intimacy, using the present tense ("*we continue to cry out*" [κράζομεν]). The use of the first person plural form ("*we cry out*") indicates a subtle shift from the

---

[160] So W. Grundmann, "κράζω, κτλ.," *TDNT* Vol. III, pp. 898-903, see esp. pp. 902-3; G. Schrenk and G. Quell, "πατήρ, κτλ.," *TDNT* Vol. V, pp. 945-1022, esp. p. 1006.

[161] Byrne, *Romans*, p. 252.

[162] See Mk. 5:5; 9:26; Lk. 9:39, where κράζειν is used for the cries of demons; for the idea of the deep sense of emotion see Acts 19:28, 32, 34; 21:28; 21:36, where the word is used for the tumultuous cries of the mob.

[163] Ps. 3:5; 4:4; 17:7; 21:3, 6; 33:7; see also the secondary source U. Wilckens, *Der Breif an die Römer* Vol. 2, p. 137.

[164] Rudolf Bultmann, *Theology of the New Testament* Vol. 1 (New York: Scribner's, 1951), p. 161; Barrett, *The Epistle to the Romans*, p. 164; Dunn, *Romans 1-8*, p. 453; C.H. Dodd, *The Epistle of Paul to the Romans* (London: Hodder & Stoughton, 1932), p. 129.

[165] See Moo, *Romans 1-8*, p. 538; Schreiner, *Romans*, p. 427.

previous second person plural ("you") in the verse.[166] This indicates that the experience of filial relationship with God is the common experience of all believers, including Paul himself.[167]

The use of αββα has been the subject of much discussion.[168] It is a transliteration in the Greek of the Aramaic אַבָּא used in the emphatic vocative ("Father!"). When it was translated in Greek, the words ὁ πατήρ were added to the Aramaic transliteration and became a liturgical formula in Greek-speaking Christian communities.[169] It is generally accepted that "Abba" was characteristic of Jesus' own prayer,[170] and certainly while we should not overplay the issue of intimacy and make over sentimentalized conclusions from the prayer,[171] there is still good reason to believe the term connotes the type of Father-son intimacy Jesus experienced.[172] Thus, Paul intimates that in crying out, "Abba, Father," the believer gives voice to his or her consciousness of intimate relationship with God. Furthermore, it is of comparable quality to the cry associated with Jesus' status as Son of God. These words are not simply a repetition of the tradition of the early Christian movement, but read in this context, they communicate the unique sense of filial relationship with God that believers experience through the Spirit who inspires the cry (πνεῦμα υἱοθεσίας ἐν ᾧ κράζομεν). This is also meant as a contrast to the "fear" associated with the previous era of the Mosaic Law ("the spirit of slavery unto fear").

---

[166] "But *you* did not *receive* (ἐλάβετε) the spirit of slavery unto fear but *you received* (ἐλάβετε) the Spirit of adoption by whom *we cry out* (κράζομεν), 'Abba, Father'" (Rom. 8:15) cf. "The same Spirit testifies with *our spirit* (τῷ πνεύματι ἡμῶν) that *we are* (ἐσμέν) children of God" (Rom. 8:16).

[167] "The one in whom *Christians* (emphasis added) are enabled to cry" (Fitzmyer, *Romans*, p. 501); "That the *community* (emphasis added) is here reminded of its innermost experience of the Spirit..." (Schrenk, "πατήρ, κτλ.," *TDNT* Vol. V, p. 1006).

[168] See J. Jeremias, *The Prayers of Jesus* (London: SCM, 1967), pp. 11–65.

[169] See Gal. 4:6; Mk. 14:36; for secondary literature see J.A. Fitzmyer, "Abba and Jesus' Relation to God" in *A cause de l'Evangile: Etudes sur les Synoptiques et les Actes offertes au P. Jacques Dupont, O.S. B. à son 70e anniversaire*, LD 123, (ed. R. Gantoy; Paris: Cerf, 1985), pp., 15–38; J. Barr, "'Abba, Father' and the Familiarity of Jesus' Speech," *Theology* 91 (1988), 173–79; E. Haenchen, *Der Weg Jesu*, Second Edition (Berline: de Gruyter, 1968), esp. pp. 492–94.

[170] Jeremias, *The Prayers of Jesus*, pp. 11–65.

[171] This is a corrective particularly emphasized by James Barr, "Abba Isn't Daddy," *JTS* 39 (1988), 28–47.

[172] See Dunn, *Jesus and the Spirit*, pp. 21–40.

With the words, "the Spirit himself testifies with our spirit that we are children of God" in v. 16, Paul provides further elaboration on the υἱοθεσίας and the ἐν ᾧ of v. 15. The first instance of πνεῦμα refers to the Spirit and the second to the human spirit. Paul indicates this in two ways: first, with the use of αὐτό with the first πνεῦμα, he wants to stress the activity of the Spirit ("the Spirit himself!") he spoke of in v.15, and second, with the personal pronoun ἡμῶν qualifying the second use of πνεῦμα, he indicates the human spirit. Nowhere in Pauline literature does Paul use a personal pronoun to denote the Holy Spirit, but he does use it with a reference to the human spirit.[173]

The verb συμμαρτυρεῖ (v. 16) is written in the present tense like the verb κράζομεν in v. 15. This is interpreted as "the Spirit *continues to bear witness with* our spirit."[174] Paul intends to demonstrate the continuous act of crying out, which refers to a description of the Spirit's work subsequent to conversion. It is this experience of the Spirit that "bears witness with our spirit" that we are children of God.[175] There is a strong possibility that Paul is adding certainty to the situation by following the principle in Deut. 19:15 and the Roman law that required multiple witnesses for an adoption to be legal.[176] Thus, with the verb συμμαρτυρεῖ Paul is taking things further and stressing how the Spirit concurs with Christians in continually acknowledging this special relation with the Father (i.e., "we are children of God") through the prayer, "Abba, Father."

In Gal. 4:6, Paul gives us more detail on this activity: "God has sent forth the Spirit of his Son into our hearts, crying 'Abba, Father'." The insertion of the words, "into our hearts" (εἰς τὰς καρδίας ἡμῶν) is the missing component that we can legitimately carry over from Gal. 4:6 into our interpretation of Rom. 8:16. The ancient world thought of the human "heart" as that part of the human being that determined action, feeling, and

---

[173] E.g., Rom. 1:9 ("God, whom I serve in *my spirit* [πνεύματί μου]); 1 Cor. 14:14 ("If I pray in a tongue, *my spirit* [πνεῦμα μου] prays"); "my spirit" or "our spirit" can never be identified as the Holy Spirit (Wilckens, *Der Brief an die Römer*, Vol. 2, pp. 137–38).

[174] "To bear witness with" (BDAG, p. 957; so with Fitzmyer, *Romans*, p. 501; Dunn, *Romans 1–8*, p. 454; Stalder, *Die Werk des Geistes*, p. 484; Fee, *God's Empowering Presence*, pp. 568-69).

[175] "I bear witness, 'I am God's child,' because the Spirit has already borne witness, 'You are God's child': and the evidence for this is the cry of 'Abba,' which I make but do so by the Spirit's prompting " (Fee, *God's Empowering Presence*, pp. 568-69).

[176] Bruce, *The Epistle to the Galatians*, pp. 199-200.

thought.[177] Taking this into consideration, it means that Paul envisioned how one's whole being is involved in the process of the affirmation of sonship, including the reality of subjective experience and emotion. In other words, the verification of adoptive sonship involves more than simply the cognition of the status of sonship. For Paul, a vital component of the Spirit's role also includes the experiential appropriation of the status of sonship through inward conviction and the participation of one's whole being (action, feeling, and thought).[178]

In summation, Paul's underscores the central role of the Spirit in the believer's experience of familial relationship with God in Rom. 8:14-16. He advances the argument that the former system and era associated with the Mosaic Law led only to bondage and fear, where fear is the result of estrangement from God. As a mutually exclusive alternative to this former system is the present system and era of the Spirit who not only secures relationship with God but conjointly with believers affirms the status of familial intimacy. Vv. 14-16 function as the foundation upon which Paul's explication of the practical dimensions of the Spirit in the believer's life is based and is thus the climactic conclusion to vv. 1-13. Vv. 14-16 is consistent with vv. 1-13 in depicting the Spirit as the agent of new life that replaces the Mosaic Law.

---

[177] "That the heart is the centre of the inner life of man and the source or seat of all the forces and functions of soul and spirit is attested in many different ways in the NT" (F. Baumgärtel and J. Behm, "καρδία, κτλ.," TDNT Vol. III, pp. 605-14, esp. pp. 611-13, quote taken from p. 611); see also BDAG, pp. 508-9; Jewett, Paul's Anthropolical Terms, pp. 305-33.

[178] Fee underemphasizes the experiential and emotional ground of the cry of sonship (God's Empowering Presence, p. 569), but others see it as a major component of the dynamics of Paul's discussion in Rom. 8:14-16 (see E.F. Harrison, Romans EBC Vol. 10 [Grand Rapids: Zondervan, 1976], p. 93; Schreiner, Romans, p. 427; Dunn, Romans 1-8, p. 454 and The Epistle to the Galatians, p. 219).

Conclusion

In this section of our study we discovered that even though Paul was fully aware of Jewish eschatology and the new covenant expectation, where the Spirit was perceived to be instrumental in the promotion of an internalized moral code fashioned upon the Law (see Diagram 1 and conclusion in Part One), he nevertheless advocates a system that is categorically different from that of Ancient and Second Temple Judaism. The following diagram depicts Paul's system of the new era of the Spirit:

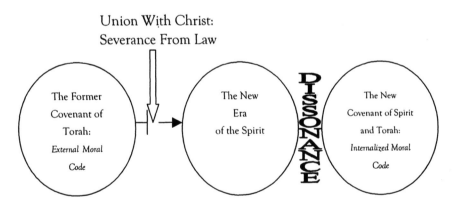

Diagram 2
The New Era of the Spirit: Dissonance with Covenantal Nomism

The coming of Christ and the believer's participatory union with him ushered in a new era of the Spirit. Paul perceived a decisive point of discontinuity between the former covenant and the new era of the Spirit, where the Spirit displaces the Law and functions exclusively as the principle of new life; i.e., the Spirit's role is comprehensive in that he secures familial relationship with God and sustains this relationship by fashioning the practical and behavioural dimensions of the believer's life. Consequently, Paul sets up a tension and dissonant relationship between his conception of the new era of the Spirit, and Ancient and Second Temple Judaism.

At the same time, as we shall see in Part Three (Consonance Between the New Era of the Spirit and Judaism's Covenantal Nomism), Paul does not take an arbitrary leap in an irrational manner from one soteriological system into the other, completely leaving his distinctive Jewish beliefs by the wayside. Rather, in response to this perceived tension, he creates a sense of continuity between them in two ways: first, he employs the characteristic categories inherent to the system of covenantal nomism to describe the role of the Spirit in the new era, and second, he demonstrates how the intended goal of covenantal nomism is actually achieved by the Spirit.

PART THREE

Consonance Between the New Era of the Spirit and Judaism's Covenantal Nomism

Introduction

In Part Two (The Spirit Displaces the Law as the Principle of New Life: Romans 7-8) our investigation revealed how Paul believed that a new era of the Spirit had dawned, which made Law observance obsolete. This was categorically different than covenantal nomism and Jewish eschatological expectation, where the central feature of the new covenant expectation was an internalized moral code based upon the Mosaic Law; i.e., individuals are enabled to observe the Law by the Spirit in their lives. Consequently, there is a tension between Paul's conception of the new era, and Ancient and Second Temple Judaism. As we shall see, this incongruity manifests itself tangibly in an internal textual tension in Rom. 8:1-16, where Paul attempts to negotiate the differences between his present convictions on the Spirit in the new era and his former convictions of the Law in the previous era. Regardless of the fact that the Spirit has replaced the Law as the principle of new life, Paul goes to great lengths to show how the Spirit's role in the present era is analogous to that of the Law.

So often in his writings Paul takes an unambiguous position on an issue but then spoils it with a further remark that apparently confuses it or implies just the opposite. Henry Chadwick characterizes this as Paul's "giving with one hand what he takes away with the other."[1] This is especially true when he relates Judaism to his current Christian convictions, which is his way of saying both "yes" and "no" to Judaism.[2] Interestingly, this is a major rhetorical

---

[1] Henry Chadwick, "'All Things to All Men' (1 Cor.IX.22)," NTS 1 (1955), 261-75, here 271.

[2] For example, on the one hand, Paul asks, "Then what advantage has the Jew? Or what is the value of circumcision? Much in every way" (Rom. 3:1-2a). On the other hand, just a few verses down, Paul asks, "What then? Are we Jews any better off? No, not at all" (Rom. 3:9).

feature of his correspondence to the Roman believers.[3] However, it is not limited to this letter. This type of interchange between covenantal nomism and Christianity appears as a consistent pattern throughout the Pauline corpus.[4]

In an effort to pin Paul's thoughts down, Sanders engages in a discussion on the relationship between Paul's conception of Christianity and covenantal nomism. Using 2 Cor. 3:6-18 and Rom. 7-8, Sanders explains how Paul says both "yes" and "no" to Judaism in the very same context, with these statements standing side-by-side. Even though Paul is advocating a discontinuity between the two, the similarities between Christianity and covenantal nomism are so striking that Sanders is forced to admit, "one can see already in Paul how it is that Christianity is going to become a *new form of covenantal nomism*" (emphasis added).[5] Sanders observes how the type of

---

[3] Johan S. Vos, "To Make the Weaker Argument Defeat the Stronger: Sophistical Argumentation in Paul's Letter to the Romans," in *Rhetorical Argumentation in Biblical Texts* (ed. T.H. Olbricht et al.; Harrisburg, PA: Trinity Press International, 2001); Mark D. Given, *Paul's True Rhetoric: Ambiguity, Cunning, and Deception in Greece and Rome* (Harrisburg, PA: Trinity Press International, 2001), p. 23, footnote 86.

[4] On the one hand, Paul speaks of Law observance as being obsolete (Rom. 7:6; 8:2; 10:4;2 Cor. 3:6; Gal. 5:18, 23 cf. the negative comments on the Law in Rom. 3:20; 5:20; 7:5, 7-12, 14-25; Gal. 2:19; 3:23; 4:1, 21-31; Phil. 3:2). On the other hand, Paul demonstrates a sense of continuity the Law has with faith (Rom. 3:31) and God's redemptive purpose in Christ (Rom. 8:3,4); he exonerates the Law (Rom. 7:12, 14); he praises those who are the recipients of the Law (Rom. 3:2 cf. 9:4). More specific to our purpose, this same type of oscillation occurs when Paul associates the Law with the Spirit. On the one hand, there is discontinuity between the Law and Spirit (Rom. 7:6; 8:2) but at the same time, he advocates a harmonious relationship between them (Rom. 8:4) and takes up various nuances previously associated with the Law and defines them in terms of their association with the Spirit (1 Cor. 6:11 ["you were justified...by the Spirit"]; 2 Cor. 3:6 ["a new covenant...of the Spirit"]; Gal. 3:14 ["the promise of the Spirit"]; 4:24 ["two covenants" cf. v. 29, "according to the Spirit"]; Rom. 2:29 ["circumcision of the heart by the Spirit"]; 14:17 ["the righteousness and peace and joy in the Holy Spirit"]; Phil. 3:3 ["the circumcision...by the Spirit of God"]).

[5] Sanders, *Paul and Palestinian Judaism*, p. 513; compare with the comment of Davies: "It appears that for the Apostle the Christian Faith was the full flowering of Judaism...the application to the Person of Jesus of those concepts which Judaism had reserved for its greatest treasure, the Torah, so that we felt justified in describing the Pauline Christ as a New Torah" (*Paul and Rabbinic Judaism*, p. 323); see also Morna D. Hooker, who notes the overlapping categories Paul exhibits between his notion of participatory union with Christ and the work of the Spirit, and Judaism's covenantal nomism ("Paul and 'Covenatal Nomism'" in *Paul and Paulinism: Essays in Honour of C.K. Barrett* [ed. M.D. Hooker and S.G. Wilson; London: SPCK, 1982], pp. 47-56);

oscillation between the former dispensation of the Mosaic Law and the new dispensation of the Spirit demonstrates the dilemma about the Law which constantly plagued Paul's mind; he was struggling to hold together his native conviction that the Law was given by God and thus had a central function in salvation-history, with his new conviction that life comes only through the Spirit. In 2 Cor. 3:6-18, the era of the Law is called the dispensation of death (3:7) and condemnation (3:9) but the era of the Spirit (3:8) gives life (3:6). Yet at the same time, he describes the former covenant as "glorious" (3:7, 9, 10). Similarly, as we recall in Rom. 7-8, Paul claimed the Law resulted in death (7:10, 11; 8:2), but then in the very same context he exonerates the Law ("the Law is holy and the commandment is holy and righteous and good" [7:12]; "for we know that the Law is spiritual" [7:14]) and still speaks positively of the Law as being analogous to the role of the Spirit the new era ("in order that the righteous requirement of the Law may be fulfilled in us...who walk according to the Spirit" [8:4]). Sanders' concludes, "[Paul] is caught here as elsewhere between two convictions."[6] We concur with Sanders on this point.

Daniel Patte identifies how we can recognize convictions in a written text. They are found within "the cracks," that is, what is odd in the argument, what does not contribute to the unfolding of the argument; e.g., the strange reasonings, the apparent contradictions, and the repetitions.[7] He singles out Paul's contradictory statements about the Law. These were a demonstration of how Paul's own convictions related to other systems of convictions (e.g., Judaism [i.e., the Pharisaic view, which characterized his former convictions on the Mosaic Law]).[8] As we stated previously in the Introduction (4.3.1 Spirit and Law: Conflict Within Paul's Convictional World), since the interchange between the Spirit and Law is not confined to one specific correspondence, or even to one or more correspondence dealing with similar pastoral concerns,

---

Das intimates the continuity between Judaism and Christianity by the use of the term "christological nomism" (*Paul, the Law, and the Covenant*, p. 11); see also Whiteley, *The Theology of St. Paul*, pp. 74-76.

[6] Sanders, *Paul, the Law, and the Jewish People*, p. 138; see also Räisänen, who states, "The tensions are to be acknowledged; they should be accepted as clues to *Paul's internal problems*" (emphasis added) (*Paul and the Law*, p. 83).

[7] Patte, *Paul's Faith and the Power of the Gospel*, pp. 39-40.

[8] "We need to note that a system of convictions can (and usually does) involve convictions about other systems of convictions...we can say that Paul's system of convictions involves convictions about the 'religions' of the Pharisees, of Hellenistic people...as well as convictions about their relationship to his own 'religion' (his faith in the Gospel)" (*Ibid.*, p. 49).

and is of the type that occurs rather offhandedly, where we would not expect Paul to bring up the issue of the Spirit's relationship to the Law in the flow of his argument, we must conclude that we are dealing with the deeper level of Paul's convictional world. These characteristics correspond to the "cracks," the repetitions, the oddities in Paul's reasoning and flow of argument that Patte mentions above. They are good indications that Paul is attempting to reduce the conflicts and tensions among his personal convictions between his Christian present and his Jewish past. In Rom. 8 this interchange between the Spirit and Law is not primarily to provide a rebuttal to the accusation of supporting an antinomian point of view. Rather, he was articulating the components of his own Gospel.[9] The textual tensions in Rom. 8:1-16 are not entirely the result of the external exigencies of his pastoral ministry, though these may have provided him with the stimulus to work out the implications of his basic convictions.

Mistakenly, both Sanders and Räisänen claim that these textual tensions indicate *straightforward contradictions about the Law*.[10] These are the direct result of his struggle to reconcile his Christian present with his Jewish past. On the other hand, Dunn and Thielman deny the existence of these tensions altogether. They find continuity between Paul's Jewish and Christian convictions and explain the textual tension, not as a contradiction on Paul's part, but as his description of *the two-sided perspective of Law observance* operating in two separate epochs: Law observance impeded by the power of sin in the previous epoch and Law observance enabled by the new power of the Spirit in the present epoch.[11]

With the use of Cognitive Dissonance Theory, we will propose that the textual tensions in Rom. 8:1-16 between the Spirit and the Law do not indicate a straightforward contradiction about the Law in Paul's thinking.

---

[9] See L.A. Jervis who, using the approach of epistolography, concludes that Paul's purpose in Romans was to proclaim the Gospel (*The Purpose of Romans: A Comparative Letter Structure Investigation* JSNTSup 55 [Sheffield: JSOT Press, 1991], pp. 163-64). Lauri Thurén offers a cautionary note: it is possible to learn about the convictions of Paul himself only when we take into account that the text of Romans was primarily a means of persuasion, not a neutral presentation, and that it was aimed at the congregation(s) at Rome (*Derhetorizing Paul: A Dynamic Perspective on Pauline Theology and the Law* [Tübingen: J.C.B. Mohr (Paul Siebeck), 2000], pp. 99-101).

[10] See Introduction (2.2) for a more detailed discussion of the positions of Sanders and Räisänen.

[11] See Introduction (2.3) for a more detailed discussion of the positions of Dunn and Thielman.

Rather, the tensions are the result of *a concentrated effort to negotiate the conflict between his native Jewish convictions on the Law and his present Christian convictions on the Spirit.* Paul employs the language of covenantal nomism and attempts to demonstrate cognitive overlap between the Spirit and the Law, and through this, hopes to achieve social validation for his cognitions within his own social group of Roman believers, with whom he identified and had a sense of affinity.

CHAPTER SIX

The Spirit's Identification with Covenantal Nomism

Regarding Rom. 8, N.T. Wright states, "the overtones throughout are *covenantal*" (his emphasis).[1] For example, in vv. 1-16, "law/Law" (vv. 2, 3, 4, 7), "life" (vv. 2, 6, 10, 11, 13), "righteous requirement" (v. 4), "peace" (v. 6), "sonship" (vv. 14-16) are all concepts in Ancient and Second Temple Judaism that are uniquely associated with God's covenant relationship with Israel, and in particular, are directly related to the Mosaic Law. But, despite these covenantal overtones, Paul does not correlate them with the Mosaic Law. Instead, they are exclusively linked to the role of the Spirit in the believer's life. If we are correct in our interpretation of 8:1-16— that the Spirit and Law represented two mutually exclusive eras in salvation-history and that the Spirit replaces the Law as the principle of new life— then the question arises as to why Paul does not simply dismiss these covenantal categories as being irrelevant in light of the new situation of the Spirit. In response to this, we can surmise at this point in our investigation that they still occupy a prominent place in the apostle's mind and he is still very much embedded within a Jewish frame of thinking. He has intentionally chosen to re-orient these concepts around the Spirit in the new epoch. Therefore, it can be said that Paul's Jewish past and his Christian present intersect in a significant manner and are more than "just two ships passing in the night."[2] In keeping with this analogy,

---

[1] Wright, *The Climax of the Covenant*, p. 203; see also his "The Messiah and the People of God," pp. 142-44; Hübner, *Law in Paul's Thought*, pp. 147-48; Stuhlmacher, *Paul's Letter to the Romans*, pp. 117-22.

[2] This is the analogy coined by William Horbury to describe Sanders' disparate depiction of the relationship between Paul's Christian present and his Jewish past (Review of *Paul and Palestinian Judaism*, *ExpTim* 89 [1977-78], 116).

we propose that they can be more appropriately described as one ship intentionally pausing beside the other, taking full stock of the other's inventory, borrowing only what it needs for the journey, and then moving on. We now turn our attention to Paul's use of Judaism's covenantal concepts (i.e., "the other's inventory") and their relationship to the Spirit in Rom. 8:1–16.

1. "The *Law* of the Spirit": Rom. 8:2

It is intriguing that in Rom. 8:2 Paul used the designation, ὁ νόμος τοῦ πνεύματος τῆς ζωῆς instead of simply, τὸ πνεῦμα τῆς ζωῆς. Rafael Gyllenberg states, "In 8.2 the word νόμος could just as well be omitted, since it contributes nothing to the development of thought and has been applied by Paul only for the sake of rhetorical and stylistic balance."[3] However, most interpreters identify νόμος here as either a direct or indirect reference to the Mosaic Law[4] and, furthermore, its meaning specifies the type of relationship the Spirit has with the Law; i.e., either the Spirit's role is harmonious with that of the Law or the Spirit forms a discordant relationship with the Law. The majority who interpret νόμος in a nonliteral or metaphorical way find the expression intentionally paradoxical, having a polemical motivation, used by Paul to draw attention to the *dissimilarity* between the two systems of Spirit and Law. His indirect reference to the Law intimates that he was promoting nothing less than the abolition of the Law.[5] We have already concluded above

---

[3] My translation of "8,2 könnte *nomos* ebensogut fehlen, da es nichts zur Gedankenentwicklung beiträgt und von Paulus nur um des rhetorisch-stilistischen Gleichgewichts willen eingesetzt worden ist" (Gyllenberg, *Rechtfertigung und Altes Testament bei Paulus*, p. 20).

[4] Those who believe Paul made a *direct* reference to the Mosaic Law in Rom. 8:2 usually define this as a two-sided perspective of Law observance (so with Dunn, Thielman, Wright, Hübner, [see discussion above]). On the other hand, those who define νόμος as something other than the Law usually define it something close to "principle," "rule," "authority," etc., but ultimately admit that Paul intended an *indirect* association with the Law, since it is the topic of discussion in close proximity (Rom. 7:6, 7, 9, 12, 14, 16, 21, 22, 25; 8:2, 3, 4, 7) (so with Sanders, Räisänen, Käsemann, [see discussion above]) ("All agree that the choice of the word [νόμος] alludes in some way to the Torah; there has to be some kind of connection between Law and 'law'" [Räisänen, *Jesus, Paul and Torah*, p. 49]).

[5] E.g., "In 8:2 there is 'doubtless' a reminder of Torah, which, however, is intended to point up the *contrast* (emphasis added), not to construct a bridge" (Räisänen, *Jesus, Paul and Torah*, p. 91);

that the use of νόμος in the phrase, "the *law* of the Spirit," is not a direct reference to the Law but is rhetoric that signifies the controlling force in ethics. This indicates how the Spirit is the new basis of ethics that has replaced the former code of ethics based upon the Law.[6] But we have not explored any further connotation of Paul's use of the word in this context. It is also entirely possible that Paul used νόμος because he wanted to communicate some sense of *similarity or continuity* between the Spirit and Law, and thus, convey a more positive parallelization of the new era of the Spirit with the former era of the Law.[7] Thus, those who contend that in the phrase "the *law* of the Spirit" Paul advocates continuity between the Mosaic Law and the Spirit may not be entirely erroneous in their claim, in light of the context in which the phrase is used (cf. Rom. 8:4).[8]

Paul makes a *polysemous* use of the word νόμος in the phrase "the *law* of the Spirit." *Polysemy* refers to the concept of words with multiple meanings.[9] For example, the word *leaf* can refer to the sense of *foliage* but can also refer to *a sheet of paper*. In English dictionaries these meanings are represented as separate acceptations under *one* entry. This is to be distinguished from *homonymy*, where words have the same orthographic or phonetic form but are unrelated in meaning.[10] For example, *ear* can refer to *an organ of hearing in*

"A person should thereby be reminded of the Torah. Yet the *contrast* (emphasis added) is heightened in this way; no bridge is built" (Käsemann, *Commentary on Romans*, p. 215).

[6] See Part Two above.

[7] See for example van Dülmen, *Die Theologie des Gesetzes bei Paulus*, pp. 119-20.

[8] "Paul himself explicitly links the Torah and the Spirit in a wholly positive way in the very next sentence" (Dunn, *Romans 1-8*, p. 416); "In Romans 8:1-4 he moves to a thoroughly positive evaluation of the law in its new role in the eschatological age of the Spirit" (Thielman, *From Plight to Solution*, p. 102); "*Existence in the spirit of God now says what Law is*"(Hübner, *Law in Paul's Thought*, pp. 147-48); "He now once again enhances this positive evaluation of the Law of God as God's goodwill which encounters the Christian in the manner now determined by the Spirit of Christ which makes alive" (Stuhlmacher, *Paul's Letter to the Romans*, p. 119); "Paul is making a positive connection between the Spirit and the Torah" (Wright, *The Climax of the Covenant*, p. 204).

[9] Moisés Silva defines *polysemy* as "the phenomenon of *one* symbol with several senses" (*Biblical Words and Their Meaning: An Introduction to Lexical Semantics* [Grand Rapids: Zondervan Publishing House, 1983], p. 114).

[10] Silva identifies the presence of *homonymy* when there are two words that sound or are spelled the same but have "*two distinct symbols*" with different senses (*Ibid.*, p. 114). In *Rhetoric* 2.24.2, Aristotle (384-322 B.C.E.) addresses the various use of diction and gives three examples of homonymy (τὴν ὁμωνυμίαν) unique to his own historical context: 1. the word μῦς can be

humans and animals or it can refer to *a spike, head of corn*. In English dictionaries these meanings are represented as *two* separate entries. Philologists note that the concept of *polysemy* can be detected when different senses of a single word display a semantic relationship. *Homonymy*, on the other hand, refers to different meanings of a word that correspond to different etymologies and have no semantic relationship whatsoever.[11]

In the Greek and Hellenistic world, the word νόμος had the basic meaning of "existing or accepted norm, order, custom, usage or tradition."[12] This includes the general meaning, *custom, rule, principle, norm, legal system* as well as the more specific meaning, *the legislation of the Sinaitic covenant given by Moses*. Even though these are different senses of νόμος, they nevertheless fall under the same semantic range of meanings associated with this word in the Greek and Hellenistic world.

Some have erroneously described Paul's use of νόμος in Rom. 8:2 as a *homonym*. For example, Johan S. Vos notes how Paul employed the word νόμος as a homonym in order to make dissociations and create persuasive definitions.[13] However, Vos' various definitions of Paul's use of νόμος in Rom. 8:4 ("those parts of the law that are in force for the Gentile Christians"); 7:21-23 ("various anthropological functions of the sinful human being"); 8:2 ("two forms of the law")[14] are all acceptations from the one basic meaning; i.e.,

---

interpreted negatively as a mere rodent, "mouse," and at the same time, be associated with the most honoured of all religious festivals, namely, the mysteries (μυστήρια), 2. the word κύνα can mean "dog" but it also implies the dog in heaven (Sirius), or Pan (called "the dog of Cybele," the great nature-goddess of the Greeks), 3. the designation κοινὸς Ἑρμῆς can have a double meaning: it can imply that Hermes is both "liberal to others" and "sociable." He considers the above words to have "a double meaning" (οὐχ ἁπλῶς λέγεται) (J.H. Freese, *Aristotle with an English Translation: "The Art of Rhetoric"*, LCL [Cambridge, Mass.: Harvard University Press, 1959], pp. 324-27). These examples indicate that Aristotle understood homonymy as we defined it above; i.e., one word with the same sound or spelling but with two very different and unrelated meanings.

[11] Kerstin Fischer, *From Cognitive Semantics to Lexical Pragmatics: The Functional Polysemy of Discourse Particles* (New York: Mouton de Gruyter, 2000), p. 5.

[12] H. Kleinkneckt, "νόμος," *TDNT*, Vol. IV, pp. 1022-35, quote taken from p. 1024; "The primary mng. relates to that which is conceived as standard or generally recognized rules of civilized conduct esp. as sanctioned by tradition" (BDAG, pp. 677-78, quote taken from p. 677).

[13] Vos, "To Make the Weaker Argument Defeat the Stronger," pp. 217-31, esp. pp. 224-25.

[14] *Ibid.*, pp. 224-25.

"existing or accepted norm, order, custom, usage or tradition." This means that the use of νόμος in Rom. 7-8 is an example of polysemy, not homonymy. Mark D. Given contends that in Rom. 7-8 Paul intentionally employed νόμος as a homonym in the manner used by sophists.[15] Sophists used homonyms in their argumentation to send two very different messages to a single audience simultaneously.[16] This was done for various reasons: e.g., it was used to protect oneself from giving the impression of disagreeing with one opinion even though the speaker favoured another, or it was used to intentionally deceive and stir up factions within the audience. Given claims that Paul made a homonymous use of νόμος, indulging in cunning and deception to present his controversial views because he knew that the Gentile congregations in Rome already had a strongly Judaistic character and he suspected that they had already heard of Paul's severe criticisms of the Law.[17] Commenting on Rom.7-8, he states, "What we have here is another example of Paul's tendency to begin, or in this case begin again, by saying what he knows some of the audience wants and expects, but then later to use ambiguity (e.g., the homonym νόμος [emphasis added]) to introduce his own ideas cunningly and deceptively to those with ears to hear."[18] The homonymous use of νόμος made Paul appear as if he was defending the Mosaic Law for those who favoured Law observance, in order to combat charges that he was an antinomian. At the same time, the word νόμος allowed him to maintain his true conviction that the Law was obsolete by insinuating that it was replaced by another law (rule, principle, norm).[19]

However, Given incorrectly understands Paul's use of νόμος as a homonym. This results in a faulty comparison with sophistical trickery. As we stated above, the use of νόμος can be more accurately described as polysemy,

---

[15] Given, *Paul's True Rhetoric*, pp. 145, 155-58.

[16] In *Rhetoric* 3.2.1-7, Aristotle discusses some of the "excesses" of speaking or some of the departures of "suitable language" (τοῦ πρέποντος) such as "strange words/glosses" (γλώτταις), "double words" (διπλοῖς), and "coinages" that are one's own inventions (πεποιημένοις). But the epitome of all excesses was homonymy, typically used by sophists in their manner of argumentation (σοφιστῆ ὁμωνυμίαι) (Freese, *"The Art of Rhetoric"*, pp. 351-55; see also G.A. Kennedy, Aristotle *"On Rhetoric": A Theory of Civic Discourse* [New York/Oxford: Oxford University Press, 1991], p. 223; C. Atherton, *The Stoics on Ambiguity*, CCS [Cambridge: Cambridge University Press, 1993], pp. 273-328).

[17] Given, *Paul's True Rhetoric*, p. 145.

[18] *Ibid.*, p. 158.

[19] *Ibid.*, p. 155.

not homonymy. This means that we cannot make a direct correlation between a sophistical use of homonymy and the intention to deceive the audience through insinuation, and Paul's polysemous use of νόμος in Rom. 7-8. The context makes it clear that Paul did not intend to do this. He did not merely *insinuate* that the Law was obsolete; he was explicit on this point ("But now *we have been discharged from the Law*" [7:6]). He was perfectly frank about his position in this matter, not resorting to the use of deception. He makes it absolutely clear that the Spirit and Law represented two incongruent ways of "serving," corresponding to two mutually exclusive phases in salvation-history (Rom. 7:1-6).

Given exaggerates the claim that every component of the argument in Rom. 7-8 was a carefully crafted effort on Paul's part to present his controversial views less offensively in order to respond to the charges that he was an antinomian and a Jewish apostate. In his view, Paul calculated and planned his every word through cunning and deception to avoid the ire associated with those who disagreed with his Law-free Gospel, while at the same time affirming those who resonated with his true convictions on the Law. Consequently, Paul told the audience what they wanted to hear. However, nowhere in this context does Paul indicate that he is preoccupied with the external claims of those who accused him of advocating an antinomian point of view. He used first and second person plural forms throughout the discourse[20] to invite the audience into his own process of negotiating the tensions between the Spirit and Law in the course of presenting the complications associated with the particulars of his message. He never states as he does in Rom. 3:8 ("Why not say—as we are being slanderously reported as saying and as some claim that we say") that he was addressing specific accusations against him.[21] This means that there is a

---

[20] "Are *you* ignorant" (Rom. 7:1); "*you* were put to death to the Law" (7:4); "for while *we* were in the flesh" (v. 5); "What shall *we* say...?" (7:7); "fulfilled in *us*...who walk according to the Spirit" (8:4); "*you* are not in the flesh but in the Spirit" (8:9), etc.

[21] Mistakenly, Thielman associates Paul's thoughts in Rom. 6:1 ("Are we to continue in sin that grace may abound?") and 6:15 ("Are we to sin because we are not under Law but under grace?") with 8:4. He contends that both chs. 6 and 8 are occupied with Paul's defence against the charge of antinomianism leveled against him (*From Plight to Solution*, pp. 88-89). However, chs. 6 and 8 are dealing with two very separate issues. Rom. 6 relates the concepts of "grace" and "sin" with the Law, while ch. 8 specifically addresses the relationship between the "Spirit" and the "Law" with no mention of "grace." Therefore, in Rom. 8 there is a shift in Paul's thought, not a continuation of his discussion from ch. 6.

possibility that Paul's polysemous use of νόμος in the phrase, "the *law* of the Spirit" is a tangible expression of the ambiguity that existed in his own thinking between the Spirit and the Mosaic Law; he perceived a sense of continuity between the Spirit and Law even though the new "*law* of the Spirit" had replaced the Mosaic *Law* as the principle of new life.

We must take up the possibility that Paul makes *polysemous* use of the word νόμος in Rom. 8:2 as an instrument to clarify the complicated relationship he perceived between the Spirit and the Law. It is entirely possible that he wanted to speak of the Spirit's role as being simultaneously both congruent and incompatible with that of the Law. In order to examine this possibility, first, we must examine whether a polysemous use of νόμος can be found elsewhere in literature contemporary with Paul and the purpose which it served, and second, how this compares with Paul's use in his own writings. This information will enable us to make more accurate conclusions about Paul's use of νόμος in Rom. 8:2.

In Wis. 2:11,[22] the impious can say, "Let our strength be the *law of righteousness* (νόμος τῆς δικαιοσύνης), for what is weak[23] proves itself to be useless." In the verse that follows (2:12) the same group states, "he (the righteous one) denounces us with our *sins of the Law* (ἁμαρτήματα νόμου)." The repetition of νόμος in v. 11 and v. 12 appears to be deliberate. However, there is an interesting shift in the meaning of this word. In 2:12, νόμος clearly refers to the Mosaic Law but in 2:11, νόμος is ambiguous in the sense that it can be interpreted as both the "Law" or as something like "principle, rule, force in ethics."[24] Since it is clear that νόμος refers to the Law in 2:12, those who hear νόμος in 2:11 may simply identify it as the Mosaic Law and understand it in the sense that the impious have a twisted interpretation of its demands of righteousness. However, others may understand νόμος in 2:11 as something like "principle, rule, force" that the impious exhibit, which runs contrary to and takes the place of the Mosaic Law. Putting this together, it is entirely possible that the author made an intentionally polysemous use of νόμος in 2:11 to convey both senses of continuity and discontinuity with the

---

[22] The Wisdom of Solomon is generally dated in the 1st century B.C.E. but possible dates range from mid-2nd century B.C.E. to the mid 1st century C.E.

[23] In the immediate context, the "weak" refers to "the poor righteous man, widow, and the aged" (Wis. 2:10).

[24] See O. Hofius, "Das Gesetz des Mose und das Gesetz Christi," *ZTK* 80 (1983), 262–86, esp. 280, footnote 61.

Mosaic Law; there is continuity when νόμος is understood as the Law because it still functions as the basis of ethics (albeit, a perverted understanding of its demands), but, at the same time, there is discontinuity with the Law when νόμος is interpreted as "principle, rule, basis of ethics," since the impious are understood as having their own system of ethics that functions in place of the Mosaic Law. In the end, both of these interpretations serve the same purpose. It challenges the impious to see who is better off, the righteous ones or the impious.[25]

In the same manner, in certain places Paul is inclined to use νόμος ambiguously, with multiple meanings in the very same context in order to communicate both senses of discontinuity and continuity with respect to the Mosaic Law. For example, in Rom. 3:27,[26] "the *law* of faith" (νόμου πίστεως) is used in close proximity to "works of the *Law*" (ἔργων νόμου [v. 28]). Most identify ἔργων νόμου as an explicit reference to the Mosaic Law, in particular, "the deeds demanded by the Law" (cf. Rom. 3:20; Gal. 2:16; 3:2, 5, 10).[27] This is a reference to the performance and obedience of the Law understood by Jews as the means of preserving their covenantal status before God.[28] The designation νόμου πίστεως has stimulated considerable

---

[25] E.g., "He denounces us with our sins of the *Law* ...He professes to have the knowledge of God...He was made to reprove our thoughts...*Let us see if his words be true and let us prove what shall happen in the end of him*" (emphasis added) (Wis. 2:12–17).

[26] For other polysemous uses of νόμος compare Gal. 6:2 ("*law* of Christ"[τὸν νόμον τοῦ Χριστοῦ]) with 6:13 ("do not keep the *Law* themselves" [νόμον φυλάσσουσιν]) (cf. "under the *law* of Christ" [ἔννομος Χριστοῦ] [1 Cor. 9:21] to "under the *Law*" [ὑπὸ νόμον] [9:20]; "without the *Law*" [ἀνόμους] [9:21]).

[27] Westerholm, *Israel's Law and the Church's Faith*, p. 116; Barrett, *The Epistle to the Romans*, p. 70; Cranfield, *The Epistle to the Romans*, p. 70; *contra* Dunn and Gaston. Dunn understands this as "a mode of existence marked out in its distinctiveness as determined by the law, the religious practices (e.g., *circumcision and food laws* ['*boundary markers*']) which set those 'within the law (v 19)' apart as people of the law" (*Romans 1-8*, p. 154; see also James D.G. Dunn, "The New Perspective on Paul," *BJRL* 65 [1983], 95–122, esp. 107). Lloyd Gaston proposes that ἔργων νόμου be translated as a subjective genitive, "works which the law does" ("Works of the Law as a Subjective Genitive," *SR* 13 [1984], 39–46). However, both Dunn and Gaston's proposals are seriously flawed in light of Paul's distinction between Abraham's faith and that which is "done" (i.e., Abraham's own deeds cf. Rom. 4:1-5). Thus, "works of the Law" cannot refer to the Law's effects (Gaston, "works which the law does") nor be interpreted restrictively as "the Jewish identity markers" (Dunn) but must be read as the deeds demanded by the Law.

[28] Cf. 1QS V, 21, 23; VI, 18, where reference to "deeds of the Law" was understood within the Qumran community in the context of an individual's dedication to the covenant.

discussion. It has been interpreted as the Mosaic Law "as it is fulfilled in faith,"[29] or metaphorically as in Rom. 8:2, as "principle, rule, authority, sphere, etc. of faith."[30] There is lexical support for both interpretations. On the one hand, νόμος can refer to the Mosaic Law as it relates positively to the Christian faith.[31] On the other hand, νόμος can refer to "any kind of existing or accepted norm, order, custom, usage, or tradition,"[32] other than the Mosaic Law, which is well attested in literature contemporary with Paul.[33] Thus, both interpretations can muster lexical support.

The use of ποῖος in the question, διὰ ποίου νόμου ("through *what* law?") does not help in making a decision between the two meanings. Ποῖος can be translated given its full qualitative force ("*what kind of* law?"), suggesting that Paul is inquiring about the nature of one νόμος (i.e., the Mosaic Law) rather than two different laws,[34] or as losing all qualitative force, being equivalent to τί ("what?"),[35] in which case it would most naturally refer to two different laws. Contextual considerations are also inconclusive. Friedrich contends that Rom. 3:21-22 corresponds to vv. 27-28: χωρὶς νόμου (v. 21a) is equivalent to χωρὶς ἔργων νόμου (v. 28), μαρτυρουμένη ὑπὸ τοῦ νόμου (v. 21b) corresponds to νόμου πίστεως (v. 27), and διὰ πίστεως (v. 22) to πίστει (v. 28). This indicates that the νόμου πίστεως must be the Mosaic Law, since the referent for νόμος in v. 21 is clearly the Law.[36] But Räisänen contends that v. 28 presents a closer parallel to v. 27 than v. 21, where in v. 28 πίστις is the

---

[29] Wright, "The Messiah and the People of God," pp. 117-18; Osten-Sacken, *Römer 8 als Beispiel paulinischer Soteriologie*, pp. 245-46; Jüngel, *Paulus und Jesus*, pp. 54-55.

[30] Räisänen, "Das 'Gesetz des Glaubens' (Röm. 3,27) und das 'Gesetz des Geistes' (Röm. 8,2)," 101-17; J. Fitzmyer, "Paul and the Law," in *To Advance the Gospel: New Testament Studies* (New York: Crossroad, 1981), pp. 186-201, esp. pp. 186-87; Gutbrod, "νόμος," p. 1071; F. Watson, *Paul, Judaism, and the Gentiles: A Sociological Approach* SNTSMS 56 (Cambridge: Cambridge University Press, 1986), p. 132; Ziesler, *Paul's Letter to the Romans*, p. 118.

[31] E.g., Rom. 3:31; 4:16; 8:4,7; 10:4; 13:8.

[32] Rom. 3:27b; 7:21, 23, 25; 8:2; Gal. 6:2; Heb. 7:16 (see Kleinknecht, "νόμος," pp. 1023-24; BDAG, p. 677).

[33] E.g., "νόμοι of war" (Josephus, *J.W.* 5.123); "law of historical writing" (Josephus, *J.W.* 5.20); "νόμοι of music" (Philo, *Creation* 70.54); cf. Räisänen, *Jesus, Paul, and Torah*, pp. 69-94.

[34] G. Friedrich, "Das Gesetz des Glaubens Röm. 3, 27," *TZ* (1954), 401-17, esp. 415; BDAG, p. 843; although Räisänen has shown that even if it is given its full qualitative force, two different laws could still be involved (*Jesus, Paul, and Torah*, p. 56).

[35] Danker lists the majority of uses of ποῖος as "which, what?," devoid of qualitative force (BDAG, p. 843).

[36] Friedrich, "Das Gesetz des Glaubens Röm. 3, 27," 415.

antithesis of ἔργων νόμου.[37] But as a retort to Räisänen, in Rom. 3:31, Paul makes the statement, "Do we then, *nullify* the Law by this faith? Not at all! Rather, we *uphold* the Law." He uses the verb καταργέω, which literally means "invalidate, make powerless" ("nullify")[38] and the verb ἵστημι, which means "reinforce validity of, uphold, maintain, validate"[39] to demonstrate continuity between "faith" and "the Law." Paul does not elaborate just how justification by grace through faith "upholds" the Law here in this context. It appears that if we understand the "works of the Law" (vv. 27, 28) as emphasizing the idea that the Law obligates one to keep or observe it, then it could mean that Paul understands how faith in Christ provides for the full satisfaction of the demands of the Law.[40]

Schreiner honestly admits that the meaning of the designation νόμου πίστεως (v. 27) is difficult to determine and while being *slightly* inclined to read this literally as a reference to the Mosaic Law, he is really indecisive on the issue.[41] Perhaps this ambiguity was precisely the manner in which Paul intended νόμος to be understood in the phrase, νόμου πίστεως (Rom. 3:27). The context indicates that both meanings are possible. The polysemous use of νόμος provided him with great utility in saying both "yes" and "no" to the Law and covenantal nomism: "faith" is continuous with the Mosaic Law, while at the same time the use of "law" communicates how "a new principle, rule, authority, sphere, etc. of faith" has replaced the former "Law."

In Rom. 8:2, we must now examine precisely how the phrase, "the *law* of the Spirit" can be interpreted in two very different, but legitimate manners. When Paul states, "the *law* of the Spirit of life in Christ Jesus has set you free

---

[37] "Friedrich thus once again presupposes what must first be demonstrated, that v. 28 offers a closer parallel to v. 27, and a more natural basis for its exposition than v. 21" (Räisänen, *Jesus, Paul, and Torah*, p. 57).

[38] BDAG, p. 525.

[39] *Ibid.*, p. 482; some believe this pair of verbs correspond to the Hebrew world בטל and קום in rabbinic exegetical discussions (Cranfield, *The Epistle to the Romans*, pp. 223-24; Käsemann, *Commentary on Romans*, p. 104). But, this is far from certain.

[40] U. Luz, *Das Geschichtsverständnis des Paulus* BevT 49 (Munich: Chr. Kaiser, 1968), pp. 171-72; Gutbrod, "νόμος," p. 1076.

[41] "A decision here is particularly difficult, but I slightly incline to the literal view (*Mosaic Law*) despite the long-standing popularity of the metaphorical interpretation"; cf. his footnote that he held to a nonliteral interpretation in his previous work (*Romans*, p. 202 and footnote 3); "However, I think the former interpretation ('principle,' 'order,' or 'rule') is slightly stronger" (see Thomas R. Schreiner, *The Law and Its Fulfillment: A Pauline Theology of Law* [Grand Rapids: Baker, 1993], pp. 34-35).

from the *law* of sin and death," it is quite likely that he intended for some of the recipients of his letter to understand him as being consistent with his statement in 7:6 that the Spirit has replaced the Law as the principle of new life in the new era: "the *law* (the new force involved in ethics) of the Spirit has made the former *Law* (the former Mosaic code of ethics) obsolete."[42] However, this does not mean that Dunn and Thielman, who interpret Paul as promoting continuity between the Spirit and Law, are completely wrong. We must consider the possibility that Paul intended to express his opinion in such a way that some others would understand him to be saying that there is a sense of continuity between the Spirit and Law: "'the *law* of the Spirit' is related to the Mosaic Law and demonstrates a sense of continuity with the purpose and function of the Mosaic Law." There is no doubt that, upon hearing the use of νόμος in 8:2, some would naturally associate it with the Mosaic Law, particularly since Paul attempts to demonstrate how the Spirit relates to the Law in the immediate context. Thus, some of the original hearers, in the manner of Dunn and Thielman, would see their interpretation confirmed in 8:4 ("in order that the righteous requirement of the *Law* may be fulfilled in us who do not walk according to the flesh, but according to the *Spirit*" cf. "The *Law* is *spiritual*" [7:14]). The context reveals both senses of νόμος. There is an unequivocal use of νόμος as a reference to the Mosaic Law in Rom. 7:1-6, 7-9, 12, 14, 16, 22, 25; 8:3, 4, 7. But in Rom. 7:21, 23, 25; 8:2, νόμος can be interpreted as something other than the Mosaic Law. This leads to the possibility that in 8:2 Paul intended νόμος to take on a double sense and to function as *polysemy*; some hearers would have understood Paul as saying the new order of the Spirit had replaced the Mosaic Law but others would also legitimately have understood him as saying that the Spirit's role is continuous with the role of the Mosaic Law in the new dispensation. In Part Two (The Spirit Displaces the Law as the Principle of New Life: Romans 7-8) we demonstrated how Paul was convinced that the Spirit had replaced the Law as the principle of new life. But, in what follows, we will examine how the phrase "the *law* of the Spirit" (Rom. 8:2) can also be interpreted as communicating continuity between the Spirit and Law. This sets the tone for vv. 2-16, where Paul intentionally aligns covenantal concepts previously associated with the Law and re-orients them with the Spirit and consequently, demonstrates how the Spirit's role is analogous to the role of the Law. Thus, Paul intended to communicate a sense of continuity even in discontinuity.

---

[42] So Sanders, Räisänen, and others (see above).

2. The Law's Goal of Righteousness Achieved by the Spirit

2.1 "Fulfilling the Law": Rom. 8:4

The meaning of Rom. 8:4 continues to be debated. Paul states, "in order that the righteous requirement of the Law might be fulfilled in us who do not walk according to the flesh, but according to the Spirit." The centre of the debate involves choosing between two main lines of interpretation: first, whether Paul is pointing backward to Jesus' mission and death (v. 3) and therefore is still thinking in more forensic terms of how Christ's substitutionary death (e.g., "God, having sent his own Son...and concerning sin [περὶ ἁμαρτίας],[43] condemned sin in the flesh") becomes effective, or second, whether Paul is anticipating the behavioural aspects of righteousness effected by the Spirit in the participial construction in v. 4 ("who walk not according to the flesh but according to the Spirit" ([κατὰ πνεῦμα]).

It cannot be denied—particularly in light of Paul's reference to the impotence of the Law (τὸ ἀδύνατον τοῦ νόμου), his mention of God sending his Son to condemn sin in 8:3, and his use of ἵνα ("in order that") at the beginning of 8:4—that there is an association and continuity between Jesus' mission and death, and the Law.[44] However, the point of the argument in vv. 2ff emphasizes the work of the Spirit in ethics (cf. περιπατοῦσιν[45] κατὰ πνεῦμα [8:4], κατὰ πνεῦμα [8:5], τὸ φρόνημα τοῦ πνεύματος [8:6],

---

[43] The phrase περὶ ἁμαρτίας is used in the LXX to translate the Hebrew חַטָּאת(לְ) ("as a sin offering") in Lev. 5:6-7, 11; 16:3, 5, 9; Num. 6:16; 7:16; 2 Chron. 29:23-24; Neh. 10:33; Ezek. 42:13; 43:19 cf. Heb. 10:6, 8; 13:11; see also E.Schweizer, "υἱός, κτλ.," *TDNT* Vol. VIII, pp. 383-84; E.H. Riesenfeld, "περί," *TDNT* Vol. VI, p. 55; *contra* Barrett ("to deal with") (*The Epistle to the Romans*, p. 147); Cranfield ("it is better understood in a general sense as indicating that with which the mission of the Son had to do") (*The Epistle to the Romans*, p. 382).

[44] Paul is attempting to communicate the idea that Jesus' death did not simply *result* (one of the surprising or accidental benefits) in fulfilling the Law but was rather God's planned *purpose* in sending his Son in the first place (Dunn, *Romans 1-8*, p. 423). Cranfield implies that the ἵνα clause conveys both purpose and result; all of God's purposes come to fulfillment in the end, but also, v. 4 clarifies the significance of the liberation in v. 2 and is thus the result of the liberation (Cranfield, *The Epistle to the Romans*, p. 383). See also Byrne, *Romans*, pp. 237–38 and his, "*Sons of God*"–"*Seed of Abraham*," pp. 93–95; Reimer Grönemeyer, "Zur Frage nach dem paulinischen Antinomismus: Exegetisch-systematische Überlegungen mit besonderer Berücksichtigung der Forschungsgeschichte im 19. Jahrhundert," Dokotorwürde Diss., University of Hamburg, 1970, pp. 134-40.

[45] "To conduct one's life, *comport oneself, behave, live* as a habit of conduct" (BDAG, p. 803).

τῷ νόμῳ τοῦ θεοῦ οὐχ ὑποτάσσεται, οὐδε γάρ δύναται [8:6]).[46] This appears to be the direction that the purpose clause is moving in 8:4. Paul realizes that the work of Christ, not the Spirit, decisively took care of sin *in the past*; hence the ἐν Χριστῷ insertion in 8:2, the aorist tense κατέκρινεν ("God having sent his own Son...*condemned* sin") and the explanation of Christ's decisive blow against sin in 8:3. The participial construction in 8:4, however, emphasizes the point that Paul has been aiming at from 7:6 and 8:2 ("the law of the *Spirit of life*"); i.e., the *ongoing, after-effects* of the Spirit.[47] This is confirmed by the insertion of ἐν ἡμῖν in 8:4 ("in order that the righteous requirement of the Law may be fulfilled *in us*...who walk according to the Spirit"). The passive use of πληρωθῇ indicates God's work, not the striving of believers.[48] Throughout Rom. 8, Paul consistently emphasizes how the Spirit resides in the believer.[49] The Spirit's role is concentrated on the behavioural dimension of the believer's union with Christ; thus the idea, "the righteous requirement of the Law has been fulfilled *in us*." This is in distinction to the present role of Christ "who was raised and *who is at the right hand of God, who also intercedes on our behalf* " (ὅς ἐστιν ἐν δεξιᾷ τοῦ θεοῦ, ὅς καὶ ἐντυγχάνει ὑπὲρ ἡμῶν [v. 34]).[50] Our interpretation is further confirmed by

---

[46] Thielman, *From Plight to Solution*, pp. 88-89.

[47] It is no coincidence that whenever Paul describes the role of the Spirit in the believer's life it is always using present tense verbs (e.g. "you *are* [ἐστὲ]...in the Spirit" [v.9]; "the Spirit *lives* [οἰκεῖ] in you" [vv. 9,11]; see also vv. 14-16).

[48] R.H. Mounce, *Romans* NAC 27 (Nashville: Broadman and Holman, 1995), p. 176; P.Melanchthon, *Commmentary on Romans* (trans. F. Kramer; St. Louis: Concordia Publishing House, 1992), pp. 166-67; Keck, "The Law and 'the Law of Sin and Death,'" pp. 51-53.

[49] E.g., πνεῦμα οἰκεῖ ἐν ὑμῖν (v. 9) and in the phrase, τις πνεῦμα Χριστοῦ ἔχει (v. 11). The use of ἐν ἡμῖν/ὑμῖν cannot be understood as being instrumental ("the Spirit resides *by* you") but locative ("the Spirit resides *within* you"). Had Paul intended an instrumental sense he would have used the preposition ὑπό with the genitive case.

[50] The only exception is found in Rom. 8:10, where Paul writes, "If *Christ is in you*" (Χριστὸς ἐν ὑμῖν). However, this is simply Paul's way of demonstrating the closest possible relationship between the Spirit and Christ; i.e., to have the Spirit residing in the believer is to have Christ residing in the believer since the Spirit's work is predicated upon the work of Christ (thus, "the law of the *Spirit* of life in *Christ Jesus*" [8:2]). This is why Paul can use the words, "Spirit of Christ"(πνεῦμα Χριστοῦ, v. 9) interchangeably with the "Spirit." It is as if Paul were saying, "Christ is in you by his Spirit" ("the indwelling of the Spirit being 'the manner of Christ's dwelling in us'" [Cranfield, *The Epistle to the Romans*, p. 389]). Barrett opposes the opinion of those who see the interchange between "the Spirit in you" and "Christ in you" as Paul's inability to distinguish between the identity of the Spirit and the identity of Christ. Rather, he states, "What Paul means is that 'Spirit in you' is impossible apart from 'Christ in you.' Union

Paul's use of πληροῦν and its association with the Spirit in similar contexts: Gal. 5:14-16 (cf. 6:2), and later in Rom. 13:8-10. In Rom. 13:8-10 the Law is "fulfilled" by "loving one's neighbour." This is linked to the Spirit in that one of the fruits of the Spirit is "love" (cf. Gal. 5:22). Thus one can conclude that Paul's primary concern in Rom. 8:4 is with the Spirit's role in the believer's behaviour and how it lines up with the demands advocated in the Mosaic Law.

Outside the NT, the word δικαίωμα can mean: legal ground or claim, written proof, document, validation, statute, decree or ordinance, or punishment, sentence.[51] The plural form δικαιώματα in papyri from 300 B.C.E. to 100 C.E. is used to refer to documents of proof in a court of justice, conveying the idea of the claim, for example, that the master has upon his slave, the privileges of a city, or deeds of conveyance proving possession purchased by a father or forefather.[52] In non-biblical Greek δικαίωμα is used to mean "punishment, sentence." For example, in Plato's *Leg.* IX, 864e, there is a reference to "other punishments" (τῶν δὲ ἄλλων δικαιωμάτων) as well as "harm" (βλάβη). Δικαίωμα is used in the sense of legal claim in 2 Ki. 19:28, where Mephibosheth asks David, "What *legal claim* (δικαίωμα) do I have any longer even to cry to the king?" The word δικαίωμα is used frequently in the LXX for חֹק and חֻקָּה (70 times) for prescribed statutes of the Mosaic Law (Ex. 15:25; Deut. 4:1, 5, 8, 40; Ezek. 11:12; 36:27).[53] It is directly associated with the Mosaic Law when the LXX translates the word מִשְׁפָּט (40 times) as δικαίωμα (*ordinance* of the Law) in Exod. 21:1, 9; Num. 36:13.[54] When associated with the Mosaic Law it means "statute, righteous requirement, or ordinance" of the Law.[55]

The noun δικαίωμα is found ten times in the NT, five of which are in Romans, the only occurrences in Pauline literature.[56] When the δικαι-root is associated with a legal code it means "that which is legally and ethically right

---

with Christ is the only way into the life of the Age to Come, of which the distinguishing mark is the Spirit" (*The Epistle to the Romans*, p. 149).

[51] G. Schrenk, "δικαίωμα," *TDNT* Vol. II, pp. 219-20.

[52] H.W.M. van de Sandt, "Research into Rom. 8.4a: The Legal Claim of the Law," *Bijdr* 37 (1976), 252-69, esp. 256-60.

[53] BDB, p. 349.

[54] BDB, p. 1048.

[55] Schrenk, "δικαίωμα," p. 221.

[56] Lk. 1:6; Heb. 9:1, 10; Rev. 15:4; 19:8; Rom. 1:32; 2:26; 5:16, 18; 8:4.

(i.e., *righteousness*)."[57] With the use of the -μα suffix, it signifies the concretization of righteousness. The NT follows the LXX in using it to refer to the "righteous requirement" of the Law (e.g., Lk 1:6, ταῖς ἐντολαῖς καὶ δικαιώμασιν; Heb. 9:1, εἶχε...ἡ πρώτη ["the first covenant"] δικαιώματα; Rev.15:4, τὰ δικαιώματα σου; cf. v. 3, "And they sang the song *of Moses*").

When in Rom. 1:32 Paul uses the phrase, τὸ δικαίωμα τοῦ θεοῦ in reference to Gentiles (cf. v. 23 [idol worship], vv. 26-27 [homosexuality]), he does so not to denote the "requirement of the Law" but more generally to speak of something recognized as being right in the divine will (cf. singular use of τὸ δικαίωμα).[58] In v. 32, the ὅτι clause—"that the ones practising such things" (ὅτι οἱ τὰ τοιαῦτα πράσσοντες)—ties the specific content of τὸ δικαίωμα τοῦ θεου to the sins depicted in vv. 29-31. These ones are said to be "worthy of death." Thus, δικαίωμα can concomitantly imply an indictment of punishment or sentence as well.[59]

In 5:16, δικαίωμα is the antithesis of κατάκριμα ("condemnation").[60] Consequently, δικαίωμα is equivalent to the meaning of "justification."[61] This is parallel to its usage in v. 18. Here δικαιώματος is explicitly associated with δικαίωσιν: "so one human's *righteous act* (*of Christ* [δικαιώματος] cf. v. 15 [τοῦ ἑνὸς ἀνθρώπου 'Ιησοῦ Χριστοῦ]) resulted in *righteousness* (δικαίωσιν) that brings life for all human beings."[62] The meaning, "righteous act" is a more fitting translation here than "justification" as in v. 16, since it forms a better parallelism with the "offence" (παραπτωμάτος) committed by

---

[57] C. Brown, "Righteousness, Justification," *NIDNTT* Vol. 3, pp. 352-77, quote taken from p. 353.

[58] "What is required by what is right" (Fitzmyer, *Romans*, p. 290); "knowledge which is obviously part of man's knowledge of God" (Dunn, *Romans 1-8*, p. 69); "a recognizable divine order which is to be embraced...as the one divine will" (Schrenk, "δικαιωμα," p. 221).

[59] Bienert, "The Apostle Paul's View of the Law According to Romans 8.1-17," p. 51.

[60] "Judicial pronouncement upon a guilty person" (BDAG, p. 518).

[61] "It is equivalent in meaning to δικαίωσις (*justification, vindication, acquittal*)" (BDAG, pp. 249-50); "It provides rhetorical balance to κατάκριμα" (Dunn, *Romans 1-8*, p. 281); "the antonyms [δικαίωμα and κατάκριμα] make it plain what is the meaning at each point [in Rom. 5:16, 18])" (Schrenk, "δικαιωμα," pp. 222-23).

[62] Cf. LXX 2 Ki. 19:28 where δικαίωμα translates צְדָקָה (2 Sam. 19:29, "righteousness" [BDB, p. 843]) in the MT.

Adam. Also, it is rather awkward to speak of "justification" as being "of Christurchnull."[63]

The closest parallel to the use of δικαίωμα in 8:4 (τὸ δικαίωμα τοῦ νόμου) is found in 2:26 (τὰ δικαιώματα τοῦ νόμου), where both refer to the "*righteous requirement(s)* of the Law" following the usual LXX meaning.[64] Variations of the phrase, τὰ δικαιώματα τοῦ νόμου are used in Deuteronomy (4:40 [φυλάξασθε τὰς ἐντολὰς καὶ τὰ δικαιώματα αὐτοῦ]; 6:2; 7:11, 17:19; 28:45; 30:10, 16) and Ezekiel (11:20 [τὰ δικαιώματά μου φυλάσσωνται]; 18:9; 20:18) as an injunction to Israel for her to observe the Mosaic Law as part of her covenant obligations.[65] Both Rom. 8:4 and 2:26 are directly associated with the Mosaic Law. In 2:26 Paul poses the question, "If therefore the uncircumcised *keeps* (φυλάσσῃ) the *righteous requirements* (δικαιώματα) of the Law will his uncircumcision not be regarded as circumcision?" However, there is a significant difference between the two. In 8:4 Paul uses the singular δικαίωμα (cf. the plural δικαιώματα in 2:26). This indicates that he does not have *all* the specific "requirements" of the Law in mind. Various interpretations have been proposed to explain this: Paul is denoting the Law as "unity,"[66] the "summary of what the Law demands"[67] or "what the Law ideally required...the goal or purpose of the law."[68] Sanders[69]

---

[63] See Moo, *Romans 1-8*, pp. 354-55; "the focus is on the act of Christ rather than its outcome" (Dunn, *Romans 1-8*, p. 283); "'act of righteousness' as in 5.18" (Cranfield, *Epistle to the Romans*, p. 384).

[64] "*Just requirement(s)/ordinance(s)* of the Law" (Schreiner, *Romans*, pp. 140, 404); Cranfield, *The Epistle to the Romans*, p. 384; Barrett, *The Epistle to the Romans*, p. 148; Moo, *Romans 1-8*, pp. 166, 514.

[65] "Δικαίωμα can perfectly properly (*sic*) bear the meaning 'the covenant decree', i.e., the decree according to which one who does these things shall live (e.g. Deuteronomy 30.6-20)" (Wright, *The Climax of the Covenant*, p. 203); G. Bertram, "φυλάσσω, φυλακή," *TDNT* Vol. IX, pp. 236-44, esp. pp. 237, 240-41.

[66] Schrenk, "δικαιωμα," p. 221; "The use of the singular is significant. It brings out the fact that the law's requirements are essentially a unity, the plurality of commandments being not a confused and confusing conglomeration but a recognizable and intelligible whole" (Cranfield, *The Epistle to the Romans*, p. 384).

[67] J.A.T. Robinson, *Wrestling with Romans* (Philadelphia: Westminster, 1979), p. 95; Wilckens, *Der Breif an die Römer*, Vol. 2, pp. 128-30; Moo, *Romans 1-8*, p. 515; Fee, *God's Empowering Presence*, p. 535.

[68] Fitzmyer, *Romans*, p. 487; K. Kertelge, "Righteousness, etc." *EDNT* Vol. 1, p. 335.

[69] Sanders, *Paul, the Law, and the Jewish People*, pp. 100, 102.

and Dunn[70] detect an implicit reduction of the Law, focusing on the moral norms, excluding circumcision (cf. Gal. 6:15; Rom. 2:26), Sabbath observance (cf. Rom. 14:5), and the food laws (cf. Rom. 14:2; Gal. 2:11-14), since Paul addresses the statement in 8:4 to believers, including Gentile converts as well. Occasionally, Paul quotes the Law and demonstrates how its behavioural aspects are analogous to the ethics required of believers.[71] He offers no theoretical basis for this dichotomy within the Law but nevertheless makes a distinction between the Law's ethical and cultic parts.[72]

Thompson understands the singular use of δικαίωμα in 8:4 to be the Law and its relationship to love, gaining support from Gal. 5:14 and Rom. 13:8-10.[73] Ziesler contends that in both the NT and the LXX the singular δικαίωμα never refers to the Law as a whole. He suggests that the tenth commandment is the referent for δικαίωμα in Rom. 8:4, since the violation of the prohibition against coveting dominates 7:7-25.[74] However, both Thompson and Ziesler's solutions are overly restrictive, since Paul does not adequately prepare the reader for such applications in the immediate context. The use of δικαίωμα in 8:4 suggests a reference to the intended goal of righteousness as stipulated in the moral Law for God's covenant people. This reading of the

---

[70] "He [Paul] has in mind something more or other than the requirements his fellow Jews would normally focus on as part of their distinctive self-definition (circumcision, Sabbath, food laws, etc.)" (Dunn, Romans 1-8, p. 423).

[71] See Rom. 13:8-10; however, it must be emphasized here that Paul is careful to say that the Law "has been fulfilled" (πεπλήρωκεν [v. 8]) or "it is summed up" (ἀνακεφαλαιοῦται [v. 9]) but never encourages believers to actually observe or keep the Law (see discussion below on Paul's use of πληροῦν). Paul's point here is that these are considered sins against the Spirit just as they once were considered breaking the Mosaic Law.

[72] Besides Sanders and Dunn, see also Eckert, who notes that Paul views the "ceremonial" Law to be invalid (Die urchristliche Verkündigung im Streit zwischen Paulus und seinen Gegnern nach dem Galaterbrief, p. 159).

[73] Thompson, "How is the Law Fulfilled in Us?" 31-40; see also S. Lyonnet, "Le Nouveau Testament à lumière de l'Ancien," 582-84; van de Sandt, "Research into Rom. 8,4a: The Legal Claim of the Law," 252-69 and "An Explanation of Rom. 8,4a," Bijdr 37 (1976), 361-78; Osten-Sacken, Die Heiligkeit der Tora, p. 45; Bandstra, The Law and the Elements of the World, pp. 107-8.

[74] J.A. Ziesler, "The Just Requirement of the Law (Romans 8.4)," ABR 35 (1987), 77-82, esp. 78-79; also his Paul's Letter to the Romans, p. 207; see also Watson, Paul, Judaism, and the Gentiles, pp. 156ff, though he understands the tenth commandment strictly as referring to coveting sexually; see also Schreiner, The Law and Its Fulfillment, pp. 153-54.

text will become clearer as we now turn to the meaning of the word πληροῦν in Rom. 8:4.

Paul's phraseology in 8:4 ("in order that the righteous requirement of the Law might be fulfilled in us who walk...according to the Spirit") has been mistakenly interpreted as his promotion of Law observance for believers. For example, Räisänen, who candidly admits that Paul rejects the Law, writes the following words: "Taken together, verses 8.4 and 8.7 very much suggests that *the law 'remains the norm of the Christian's existence'* (emphasis added)."[75] Likewise Sanders, who previously interprets Rom. 7:1-6, as Paul's admonition that believers are no longer obligated to observe the Law ("Paul views all Christians, whether Jew or Gentile, as having died to the law. It is part of the old world order...Christians die to the law or are freed from it, Rom. 6:14f: 7:4, 6"),[76] writes: "The distinction in Rom. 8:1-4 is not that Christians take a different attitude toward the law from that of non-Christians...The question is about ability. Those in the flesh, despite their best efforts...cannot do what the law requires; *those in the Spirit can and do* (emphasis added)."[77] This has led to the erroneous conclusion that Paul's convictions on the Law are riddled with contradictions.[78]

The *crux interpretum* of Rom. 8:4 is the meaning conveyed by the verb πληροῦν. When Paul uses this verb is he claiming that believers are to *observe* or *keep* the Mosaic Law, in which case the Law functions as the norm of Christian behaviour, or is there a subtle distinction between *observing* or *keeping* the Law, and *fulfilling* the Law, whereby the behaviour induced by the Spirit in the believer's life achieves the *intended goal* of the Law? If this distinction is valid, it would maintain the idea that the Spirit, not the Law, is the basis for Christian behaviour, but, at the same time, provides the means by

---

[75] Räisänen, *Paul and the Law*, p. 67.

[76] Sanders, *Paul, the Law, and the Jewish People*, p. 83.

[77] *Ibid.*, p. 99.

[78] "I suggest that Paul's theology of the law can only be understood if the tensions and self-contradictions in it are taken seriously"(p. 83) cf. "Paul states in unambiguous terms that the law has been abolished...Paul also makes positive statements which imply that the law is still valid. The claim it justly puts on men is fulfilled by Christians" (p. 199) (Räisänen, *Paul and the Law*); "The important point to observe is that what Paul said about the law depends on the problem which he was addressing. His answers to questions of behaviour have a logic of their own. There is no systematic explanation of how those who have died to the law obey it" (Sanders, *Paul, the Law, and the Jewish People*, p. 114).

which Paul could express continuity between the role of the Spirit in the present era and the role of Law in covenantal nomism in the previous era.

The verb πληρόω has the following possible lexical range of meanings: (1) *non-biblical* — to fill (e.g., a bottle of water [Philo, *Post.* [Cain] 130), figuratively to satisfy a demand, to fulfill an ethical requirement (e.g., Philo, *Praem.* 83.3), to make complete, to run its course, to fulfill promises, to come to fulfillment (of an oracular saying), (2) *LXX*—(literally), to make full (e.g., with intoxicating drink [Jer. 13:13]), (figuratively) to fill someone with something (with confusion [3 Macc. 6:19]), to satisfy (divine commission [1 Macc. 2:55]), to fulfill the divine promises which God has spoken (3 Ki. 8:15, 24), (3) *NT* — to fulfill a norm, a measure, a promise (cf. Phil. 4:18), to fulfill a demand or claim (always in the NT with reference to the will of God: e.g. a total legal demand [Rom. 8:4; 13:8; Gal. 5:14]), to complete or fulfill a prophetic saying (Acts 3:18; 13:27), to complete (Lk 7:1).[79]

Paul uses the verb πληρόω 13 times,[80] but only three of these are explicitly associated with the Mosaic Law and are relevant to our investigation (Rom. 8:4; Gal. 5:14; Rom. 13:8). In Rom. 8:4, the "fulfilling" is to take place in believers ("in us" [ἐν ἡμῖν]) and the subject who performs the action is the Spirit ("walking according to the *Spirit*"; note references to the Spirit residing within the believer [vv. 9, 11]). The immediate context of Gal. 5:14 indicates that the believer "fulfills" the Law when he or she "loves one's neighbour" ("through love you serve one another. For the whole Law has been fulfilled..." [vv. 13-14]). However, in v. 16, Paul commands believers to "walk *by the Spirit*." This is to be read in conjunction in v. 22, where Paul explicitly states that *love* is a fruit of the Spirit ("the fruit of the Spirit is *love*"). This means that even though believers actively determine to "love one's neighbour," this conduct is the result of yielding to the promptings of the Spirit. When πληρόω is used in the active voice in Rom. 13:8 (believer "fulfills" the Law), the act of "fulfilling" is also to be understood in association with the Spirit ("*he who loves* his neighbour has fulfilled the Law" [cf. Gal. 5:22-"love" as a fruit of the Spirit]). We can confidently state that even in Rom. 13:8, when the believer "fulfills" the Law by making a conscious choice to love his or her neighbour, Paul perceives the Spirit as the agent or prime motivator who

---

[79] G. Delling, "πληρόω, κτλ.," pp. 286-298.

[80] Rom. 1:29; 8:4; 13:8; 15:13, 14, 19; 2 Cor. 7:4; 10:6; Gal. 5:14; Phil. 1:11; 2:2; 4:18, 19.

initiates such action. Thus, the Spirit "fulfills" the Law in all three of these examples cited above, particularly in Rom. 8:4.[81]

It is important to isolate just what Paul expects to be "fulfilled" and what he expects believers to "observe." In Gal. 5:14 Paul states, "*the whole Law* (ὁ πᾶς νόμος) has been fulfilled *in one word* (ἐν ἑνὶ λόγῳ): 'you will love your neighbour as yourself.'" The adjective πᾶς signifies "a high degree of completeness or wholeness" and can be translated "the *whole or entire* Law."[82] The words ἐν ἑνὶ λόγῳ can be rendered as "in one commandment" reflecting the traditional reference to the Ten Commandments as "the ten words."[83] Here Paul cites the specific commandment in Lev. 19:18. Rom. 13:8-10 is similar to Gal. 5:14 in that he quotes the identical commandment: the one "who loves his neighbour has fulfilled the Law" (v. 8). However, further to Gal. 5:14, in Rom. 13:9 Paul lists the commandments of prohibitions against adultery, murder, theft, and coveting from the Decalogue.[84] It is clear from this list that when he speaks in the context of "fulfilling" the Law with respect to believers, he intentionally excludes the cultic requirements of the Law (circumcision, food regulations, Sabbath day) and has only the ethical dimensions of the Law in mind.[85] As we have demonstrated above, this is the sense in which our text in Rom. 8:4 is to be interpreted. When Paul mentions the "righteous requirement of the Law" he has in mind the moral and ethical demand for "righteousness" as stipulated in the Mosaic Law. Our interpretation of Gal. 5:14, Rom. 13:8-10, and 8:4 is consistent with what Paul states elsewhere. Paul sees no practical use for the cultic sense of the Law for Christians. When he speaks of the behavioural dimension in the believer's

---

[81] Commenting on the meaning of πληρωθῇ in Rom. 8:4, Fitzmyer states, "This is a theological passive...It is God himself who brings about the fulfillment of the law through...the Spirit" (*Romans*, pp. 487-88); "The striking thing here is the passive, the *passivum divinum* of grammarians...it is something which God...works in us through the Spirit" (B. Byrne, "Living out the Righteousness of God: The Contribution of Rom. 6:1-8:13 to an Understanding of Paul's Ethical Presuppositions,"p. 569); see also Zerwick, *Biblical Greek*, section 236.

[82] BDAG, pp. 783-84; "the entire law" (Jervis, *Galatians*, p. 141); "all the law" (Sanders, *Paul, the Law, and the Jewish People*, p. 96); "the law seen as a whole" (Dunn, *The Epistle to the Galatians*, p. 288)

[83] See for example, Exod. 34:28; Deut. 10:4; Philo, *Quis Her.* 168; Josephus, *Ant.* III, 138.

[84] See Exod. 20:13-15, 17; Deut. 5:17-19, 21; Paul follows the order of Deuteronomy in listing the commandments here (C.D. Stanley, *Paul and the Language of Scripture: Citation Technique in the Pauline Epistles and Contemporary Literature* SNTSMS 69 [Cambridge: Cambridge University Press, 1992], pp. 174-75).

[85] See discussion above; see also Hübner, *Law in Paul's Thought*, pp. 84-87.

life it is always related in a restrictive sense to the moral requirement of the Mosaic Law. This is specifically what Paul says is "fulfilled" within believers.

The perfect tense verbs πεπλήρωται (Gal. 5:14) or πεπλήρωκεν (Rom. 13:8) are probably gnomic, that is, they do not refer to a specific point in the past when the action took place but denote a descriptive truth with no particular reference to time.[86] In these contexts they are both associated with the love commandment in Lev. 19:18 to communicate the idea that the *designed goal, end, or destiny* of the Law has been achieved.[87] In Rom. 13:9, the verb ἀνακεφαλαιοῦται is most likely meant to convey a parallel nuance to the verb πεπλήρωκεν in 13:8, since Paul cites Lev. 19:18[88] in v. 9 as well. V. 9 reads, "In this word *it is summed up*, 'You will love your neighbour as yourself.'" The verb ἀνακεφαλαιόω literally means "to bring everything to a head,"[89] thus, to "sum up."[90] Related in meaning to the verbs "to fulfill" or "sum up" the Law in Rom. 13:8,9 is the thought of Matt. 22:40. Here, the words, "the whole Law" (ὅλος ὁ νόμος), found on the lips of Jesus in Matt. 22:40, are said to "depend"[91] (κρέμαται) upon the dual commandments, "you will love the Lord God with all your heart, soul, and understanding" (Deut. 6:5) and "you will love your neighbour as yourself" (Lev. 19:18). So, in Rom. 13:8, 9 we can say that Paul understood the prohibitions of adultery, murder, theft, and coveting as being both "fulfilled" (bringing the Law to its intended goal) and "summarized" in the single love commandment (v. 8).

---

[86] Matt. 4:4, 7, 10; 13:46 (see BDF, p. 177; "a timeless truth" [Young, *Intermediate New Testament Greek*, pp. 128-29]; Käsemann, *Commentary on Romans*, p. 361).

[87] "The whole law *has found its full expression*"(of Gal. 5:14 in BDAG, p. 828); "to bring [the Law] to a designed end" (of Rom. 13:8 in BDAG, p. 829).

[88] There is no precedent in Jewish texts prior to Paul for giving the love commandment in Lev. 19:18 any particular prominence, especially using the verb πληροῦν and expressing the sense of achieving the goal of the Mosaic Law (cf. Sir. 13:15; Jub. 7:20; 20:2; 36:4, 8; T. Reub. 6:9; T. Iss. 5:2; T. Gad 4:2; T. Ben. 3:3-4; 1QS V, 25; VIII, 2). However, this is not the case after Paul's time. For example, Rabbi Akiba (early second century) describes Lev. 19:18 as "the *encompassing principle* of the Torah" (*Gen. Rab.* 24.7 on *Gen. 5.1* quoted from J. Neusner, *Genesis Rabbah* Vol. 1 [Atlanta: Scholars Press, 1985], p. 270); see also secondary sources, J.M.G. Barclay, *Obeying the Truth: A Study of Paul's Ethics in Galatians* (Edinburgh: T & T Clark, 1988), p. 138; Jervis, *Galatians*, p. 142; see also Str-B, Vol. I., pp. 353-64; Thielman, *From Plight to Solution*, pp. 50-54.

[89] H. Schlier, "κεφαλή, ἀνακεφαλαιόομαι," *TDNT* Vol. III, pp. 673-682, esp. pp. 681-82.

[90] BDAG, p. 65.

[91] Κρεμάννυμι literally means "to cause to hang," thus "all the Law...*hangs (depends)* on these two commandments" (BDAG, p. 566).

It is important to note that in the contexts of both Gal. 5:14 and Rom. 13:8-10, Paul does not say that believers are to "observe, keep, or perform" the Law. Instead, believers are simply given the directives to "*serve* one another through love" (διὰ τῆς ἀγάπης δουλεύετε ἀλλήλοις [Gal. 5:13]) and "*to love* one another" (τὸ ἀλλήλους ἀγαπᾶν) as an expression of their union with Christ and the manifestation of the Spirit in their lives (cf. Gal. 5:5, 6, 16-18, 22-23, 25). The Spirit is the basis of ethics for the believer, not the Law. However, at the same time Paul expresses continuity between the work of the Spirit in believers' lives, and the Mosaic Law; i.e., Paul understands believers' acts of love towards one another as achieving the designed goal of the Mosaic Law or even the summary of the Decalogue ("love your neighbour").[92]

As with Rom. 8:4, some have erroneously interpreted both Gal. 5:14 and Rom. 13:8-10 as an admonition that believers are under obligation to observe the Law. For example, Dunn contends that Paul's use of the verb "fulfill" entails obedience to the Law conditioned by one's love for his or her neighbour, where the relative importance of the other laws is determined by this one commandment.[93] Thielman believes that Paul's use of the verb "fulfill" is to be understood in an eschatological sense. With the mention of the Spirit in Gal. 5:16-18, 22, 25, he believes Paul is imploring believers to obey the Law.[94] Räisänen interprets the sense of the verb "fulfill" and Paul's emphasis on loving one neighbour in Gal. 5:14 and Rom. 13:8-10 as a reduction of the Law to the love command, but nevertheless as his way of communicating the idea that believers are still obligated to observe the Law.[95]

However, such readings of Rom. 8:4; 13:8-10 and Gal. 5:14 would clearly imply that there is a contradiction between these verses and Paul's statement in Gal. 5:3,4 ("every one who lets himself be circumcised is required to do the whole Law[96]...You have been severed from Christ who are seeking to be

---

[92] See the distinction made between "fulfilling" and "doing" the Law by H.D. Betz, *Galatians* Hermeneia (Philadelphia: Fortress Press, 1979), p. 275; R.N. Longenecker, *Galatians* WBC 41 (Dallas: Word, 1990), pp. 242-43.

[93] Dunn, *Epistle to the Galatians*, pp. 290-91; see also van Dülmen, *Die Theologie des Gesetzes bei Paulus*, p. 60; Hübner, *Law in Paul's Thought*, pp. 36-42.

[94] Thielman, *From Plight to Solution*, p. 53.

[95] Räisänen, *Paul and the Law*, p. 27; see also V.P. Furnish, *The Love Command in the New Testament* (Nashville, Tenn.: Abingdon, 1972), pp. 97, 108-11.

[96] The proselyte's act of circumcision entailed commitment to adopt the Jewish way of life as a whole, which included observing the Mosaic Law (see for example, Esther 8:17 [LXX]; Eusebius, *Praep. Evang.* 9.22.5; Josephus, *Ant.* XIII,257).

justified by the Law") and Rom 7:1-6. In Gal. 5:2 Paul is stating that to undergo circumcision after conversion to Christ was to deny the sufficiency of Christ ("Christ will be of no benefit to you"). Indeed, "circumcision" was an external sign of a comprehensive commitment and obligation to live within Judaism's covenant, of which obeying the Law was a central part (cf. Paul's reasoning "one who receives circumcision is obligated to observe the whole Law [Gal. 5:3]").[97] Consequently, the Law represented an alternate means of justification contrary to Paul's gospel ("you have been severed from Christ you who are seeking to be justified by the Law; you have fallen from grace" [v. 4]; "if righteousness comes through the Law, then Christ died needlessly" [2:21]; cf. "You were made to die to the Law through the body of Christ" [Rom. 7:4]). If Dunn, Thielman, and Räisänen are correct in their interpretations, then there is an unmistakable contradiction in Paul's position on the Law. Such a conclusion, however, should be accepted only as a last resort. We have to take up the possibility that Paul intended a sharp distinction between "fulfilling" and "doing" the Law and investigate the purpose that this serves. This is preferable in that it leaves open the possibility of more consistent reading of Paul's thoughts on the Law.

It is no coincidence that when Paul refers to the believer's relationship with the Mosaic Law he conveniently avoids the verbs ποιεῖν, πράσσειν, ὑποτάσσειν, which all communicate one of the following meanings: "to do, practice, perform, observe, submit to, subject oneself to, be under the authority of"[98] the Mosaic Law. The use of these verbs would give the impression that the Law still functions as the basis of Christian ethics and believers are still obligated to observe it. Paul is not unaccustomed to using these verbs in contexts where Christian behaviour is being contemplated. However, they are never used with reference to Christians observing the Law. For example, Paul encourages believers to "*do* (ποίει) what is good" (Rom. 13:3).[99] In 1 Cor. 16:16, Christians are required to be "*in subjection* (ὑποτάσσησθε) to such ones (those devoted to ministry)."[100] In 2 Cor. 5:10,

---

[97] "'To do the whole law' was 'to abide by everything which has been written in the book of the law to do them' (iii.10- Deut. xxvii.26)...to adopt a Jewish way of life through and through" (Dunn, *The Epistle to the Galatians*, p. 266).

[98] BDAG, pp. 839-42, 860, 1042.

[99] See also 1 Cor. 10:31; Gal. 6:9, 10, where Paul uses the verb ποιεῖν in the context of Christian ethics.

[100] Cf. Rom. 13:1.

Paul refers to "the things *one practised* (ἔπαξεν), either good or worthless."
However, when Paul describes the Jewish non-believer's relationship to the
Law or the previous era of covenantal nomism, he is prone to using ποιεῖν,
πράσσειν, or ὑποτάσσειν to describe the necessity of "doing, practising, or
being subjected under" the Mosaic Law.[101] For example, in Rom. 7:16, Paul
writes, "For if what I do not wish, is what *I do* (ποιῶ), I agree with the Law."[102]
In Rom 2:25, Paul states, "For indeed circumcision is of value, if *you practise*
(πράσσῃς) the Law."[103] Similarly, in Rom. 8:7, he claims that the mind set on
the flesh "does not *subject itself* (ὑποτάσσεται) to the Law of God."[104] Paul

---

[101] In 1 Cor. 7:19, Paul implores believers "to keep" the commandments of God (τήρησις
ἐντολῶν θεοῦ). These are not a reference to the Mosaic Law but are the commandments of
Paul and the Lord ("But to the rest I say, not the Lord" [v. 12]/ "To the married I give this
command [not I, but the Lord]" [v. 10]).

[102] See also Gal. 5:3 and Rom. 2:14. Räisänen contends that Rom. 2 renders an intentional
terminological distinction between ποιεῖν and πληροῦν to be dubious. The "doing" credited
to the Gentiles in 2:14f cannot refer to the individual precepts of the Law that must be "done."
The Gentiles Paul had in mind could not "do" the Law in any other sense than the Christians
"fulfill" the Law by living according to its principles (*Paul and the Law*, p. 64, footnote 104).
Firstly, the "Gentiles" Paul speaks of in Rom. 2:13-14 are not necessarily believing Gentiles.
Normally when Paul makes a reference to ἔθνη as Gentile believers it is clear that this is what is
meant (cf. Rom. 11:13; 15:9). The context demands that it simply be understood as "some
Gentiles" in general (note the absence of the definite article in v. 14 [simply ἔθνη]). This
coincides with Paul's view that only those apart from Christ are obligated "to do" the Law.
Secondly, while Räisänen's point may be true in principle, Paul's emphasis seems to be driven
by the need to show how Jewish non-believers, not Christians (there is no mention of believers
in this context), act with respect to the requirements of the Law, thus, the emphasis on "doing"
the Law. Consequently, Jews who claim to possess the Law are no better off if they do not "do"
the Law (v. 13, "not the hearers of the Law are just before God, but the *doers* of the Law will be
justified"). This means that the point still stands; those who are "under the Law" must "do" it.

[103] See also Rom. 7:15, 19.

[104] In the context of his discussion on how prophecy is to function in the church (a group of
believers), Paul commands that women "*subject themselves* (ὑποτασσέσθωσαν) just as the Law
says" (1 Cor. 14:34). It is not known where this particular reference is found in the "Law."
Some commentators think of Gen. 3:16 (P. Bläser, *Das Gesetz bei Paulus* [Münster: Aschendorff,
1941], p. 36). There is considerable doubt concerning the authenticity of I Cor 14:34-35 based
upon both transcriptional and intrinsic probability. It is believed that these verses were part of a
marginal gloss which was included to quell the rise of a feminist movement at the end of the
first century or the beginning of the second (cf. 1 Tim. 2:9-15; 5:11-15) and to reconcile 1 Cor.
14 with 1 Tim. 2. Furthermore, Paul's argument makes better sense when one excludes these
verses; i.e., the guidelines for tongues with interpretation and prophecy with discernment are

intentionally avoids using these verbs in the contexts where he relates Christian behaviour to the Law. Instead, he uses the verb πληροῦν when he wants to mention the Mosaic Law positively in his discussion of Christian ethics.[105] This indicates that he perceives the believer's relationship with the Law in a distinctive manner, which is expressed definitively in this verb. However, he avoids using the verbs ποιεῖν, πράσσειν, or ὑποτάσσειν because they do not appropriately communicate the distinct type of relationship he perceives between Christian existence and the Law, which is categorically different than that of the non-believing Jew.

Our analysis reveals that this sharp difference in vocabulary is intentional. When Paul addresses non-believers' relationship to the Law, he uses the verbs ποιεῖν, πράσσειν, or ὑποτάσσειν, indicating how the Law prescribes their behaviour. However, when Paul speaks of the believers' relationship to the Law, he uses the verb πληρόω, intentionally avoiding the use of ποιεῖν, πράσσειν, or ὑποτάσσειν. This indicates that he is not giving directives to obey the Law like he did when he was describing non-believers' obligation to observe the Law. Rather, Paul is simply describing how Christian behaviour compares to the Law. At the same time, we notice that Paul uses the verbs ποιεῖν, πράσσειν, or ὑποτάσσειν when his gives directives on Christian behaviour, but in these contexts there is no reference to the Mosaic Law whatsoever. These distinctions indicate Paul is careful to demonstrate that the Law does not *prescribe* Christian behaviour, but that he simply wants to *describe* the relationship between Christian behaviour and the Law.

When Paul speaks of believers "fulfilling" the Law, the view is retrospective, that is, he is contemplating the specific requirements of the Mosaic Law in the previous era and he is comparing them to Christian ethics in the present. Thus, his primary purpose was not to delineate the specific precepts in the Law and explicate the believer's obligation to observe them, but rather, to demonstrate how the quality of Christian conduct fares with respect to the Law.[106] This is the reason for Paul's enumeration of some of the specific commandments in the Decalogue (e.g., Rom. 13:9); he wants to show how Christian behaviour compares with the ethics advocated in the Law.

---

better concluded with the notes on vv. 32–33 (See Fee, *The First Epistle to the Corinthians*, pp. 699–702).

[105] Cf. Rom. 8:4; 13:8–10; Gal. 5:14.

[106] See Westerholm, *Israel's Law and the Church's Faith*, p. 202; Betz, *Galatians*, p. 275; van Dülmen, *Die Theologie des Gesetzes bei Paulus*, pp. 229–30.

So, how does Christian conduct fare with the Law? In our discussion above on Rom. 8:4 we concluded that τὸ δικαίωμα τοῦ νόμου refers to the righteous requirement demanded of the moral Law, which was the Law's intended goal or purpose for God's covenant people. However, the Mosaic Law was an insufficient system to bring the goal of righteousness to fruition. When we understand Paul's purpose for using the verb πληροῦν ("to fill completely [completely satisfy]"), we can confidently conclude that he wanted to convey the idea that the righteous requirement of the moral Law was completely filled and satisfied by the Spirit in the believer's life. The verb expresses the precise nuance that Paul intended; it was not encumbered with extreme specificity, giving the impression that believers were obligated to actually observe the Law; but, at the same time, it allowed for the interpretation that the Law's righteous requirement was fully met. In the end, the righteous requirement of the Law was achieved, not by obeying the Law but by yielding to the Spirit.

This is analogous to the genius teenager (e.g., the Doogie Howser [M.D.] type) who finds himself in Medical School, not following the normal paces associated with the steady and yearly progression from High School, University, on to Medical School, and not having to experience the daily routine and requirements of attending classes, writing papers and passing exams associated with each of those years and levels of study. The course on the intricate functioning of the human body in an advanced anatomy class in University is better suited to his level of intelligence than a High School course in general Physiology dealing with the rudimentary principles of the functioning of living organisms. The genius teenager fully recognizes the importance of the general principles of how organisms survive but nevertheless feels compelled to by-pass this level of learning and the daily routine associated with it since it would be retrogression into knowledge he had already mastered and would do more to impede than to advance his progression. Even though he accepts the pedagogic importance of the content of knowledge gained through the class lectures, exams, and disciplined study during those years, his situation makes it inevitable that he take an alternate route. In the end, at age 19, he reached his intended goal and is a fully licensed M.D. He "fulfilled" the requirements necessary for practising medicine without actually following ("doing") the prescribed course of study required of a medical doctor, while the student of normal intelligence is still obligated to "observe" and follow all the regular requirements.[107]

With the Spirit's assistance, Paul believes the righteous requirements of the Law are adequately "fulfilled" (cf. the genius teenager's alternate route rather than follow "the prescribed course of study" in the analogy above), even though the actual specific requirements of the Law have not been actually "done". However, at the same time, the righteous requirement of the Law is not ignored (cf. the genius teenager's recognition of the pedagogic importance of the regular student's "prescribed course of study") in that it has been realized and reached its intended goal. This means that Paul perceived a sense of cognitive overlap between the righteous requirement demanded by the moral Law, which was the Law's intended goal for God's covenant people ("covenantal nomism"), and Christian behaviour induced by the Spirit, which actually achieved the goal of righteousness.

Various explanations have been posed as to why Paul was so preoccupied with the sense of "fulfilling the Law" and demonstrating continuity between the Law and the Spirit, between covenantal nomism, associated with Paul's past, and Christianity, associated with Paul's present. Some claim it is possible that Paul forgot what he wrote in Rom. 7:1-6 and occasionally lapsed into a Jewish mode of thinking (see also Rom. 10:4 cf. 13:8-10; Gal. 5:3-4 cf. 5:14).[108] This is not probable since Paul intentionally takes over the specific subjects in 7:1-6 and revisits them in 8:2ff.[109] In Rom. 8:4, perhaps Paul utilized a piece of Jewish-Christian tradition, disturbing his logic and tacitly twisting the meaning of νόμος to mean God's will in distinction with the Mosaic Law.[110] Even if Paul is patterning the verse on a traditional formula,

---

[107] This analogy is somewhat similar to that of Westerholm's consummate musician, demonstrating the difference between the concert pianist, who is granted advanced status and "fulfills" the requirements for the music course but who does not actually "do" the specified work for the course, and the novice music student who is required to submit to the necessary requirements of study ("do") in the course but refuses to comply. The consummate musician "fulfilled" the intention of the rules without actually observing them, but the novice neither "did" nor "fulfilled" the "law" of the musical trade (*Israel's Law and the Church's Faith*, p. 203).

[108] P. Feine, *Das gesetzesfreie Evangelium des Paulus nach seinem Werdegang dargestellt* (Leipzig: J.C. Hinrichs, 1899), p. 73; J. Knox, *The Ethic of Jesus in the Teaching of the Church: Its Authority and Its Relevance* (London: SCM, 1961), p. 103.

[109] See Part Two (Chapter Five, Section 1. "By Which 'Law' Does Life Come?": Rom. 8:2).

[110] "We have an anacolouthon which obviously disturbs the logic of the train of thought...pre-Pauline tradition is fragmentarily cited" (Käsemann, *Commentary on Romans*, p. 218); see also

there is no break in the flow of thought; it allows for a smooth transition to the following discussion on the distinction between walking according to the flesh or according to the Spirit, which is characteristically Pauline.[111] Also, his readers would most likely understand νόμος in Rom. 8:4 as a reference to the Mosaic Law, particularly in light of its meaning in v. 3, where it undoubtedly refers to the Law. Most claim that the use of πληροῦν in Rom. 8:4 and elsewhere in its association with the Law is polemically motivated; Paul is defending his views of the Law against alternate and opposing viewpoints. In other words, the reasons are entirely the result of external circumstances occasioned by his pastoral ministry. For example, Westerholm states, "When Paul describes the results (emphasis removed) of a life lived in conformity with Christian principles, it is, *for polemical reasons* (emphasis added), important for him to say that Christian behavior is condemned by no law...that love which is the hallmark of Christian conduct in fact fulfills the law."[112] Likewise, Räisänen claims, "8.4 is intended as the climax of his *'apology of the law'* (or *rather 'apology of his theology of the law'!*) (emphasis added)...it was important for Paul to stress his 'conservatism,' at least before the Romans audience."[113] Thielman writes, "Beginning with 6:1, Paul has been *defending himself against the charges of antinomianism* (emphasis added) and insisting on righteous behavior within the believing community...8.4 fits snugly into this context."[114]

However, the contention that Paul's "fulfillment" language is polemically motivated, responding to charges that he advocated both libertarian and antinomian points of view, does not fully explain its usage in the respective contexts. The impetus behind the use of this language appears to be more complex. Paul was not simply correcting the impression that he was promoting a position to do all that Moses prohibited. In fact, this language of "fulfilling the Law" appears to be rather intrusive in contexts and also runs contrary to the general tenor of his argument in his correspondence. This is particularly the case with Gal. 5:14. Generally speaking, if the Jewish "troublemakers" or

---

Betz, *Galatians*, p. 275; some regard the tradition to be fragmentary, limited to the phrase, "God, having sent his own Son" (Osten-Sacken, *Römer 8 als Beispiel paulinischer Soteriologie*, p. 145); Keck allows for the possibility that Paul may have followed a tradition pattern but the purpose clause was his own ("The Law and 'The Law of Sin and Death' [Rom. 8:1-4]," p. 44).

[111] "The tradition serves his argument beautifully; there can be no talk of an unassimilated fragment" (Räisänen, *Paul and the Law*, p. 66).

[112] Westerholm, *Israel's Law and the Church's Faith*, p. 201.

[113] Räisänen, *Paul and the Law*, p. 67.

[114] Thielman, *From Plight to Solution*, pp. 88–89.

"agitators" (Gal. 1:7; 5:10, 12) had infiltrated the ranks of the Galatian believers, emphasizing the necessity of circumcision (5:2; 6:12–13) and the Law, and Paul's purpose was to correct this aberrant belief, it would run counter to his argument if in his defence he affirmed rather than challenged the place and purpose of the Law. Furthermore, in light of Paul's forceful argument, the intensity in which he approaches this matter, and the impatience that bursts forth (e.g., 1:8–9 ["let him be eternally condemned" v. 9]; 2:12–14 [Paul's public confrontation with Peter]; 3:1 ["You foolish[115] Galatians! Who has bewitched you?"), it is highly unlikely that his sensitivity to what others thought about his Law-free Gospel was foremost in his mind. Instead, Paul approaches this situation as a roaring lion ready to devour its prey.

More specifically, in Gal. 5:14, it is surprising and odd in the argument for Paul to emphasize the necessity of love by way of reference to the very Law he has been so determined to dispute previous to this in both the broader and immediate contexts.[116] In v. 15, he is describing the essence of love tangibly expressed in the Christian community: "But if you bite and devour one another, watch out or you will be destroyed by each other." Most agree that this is a generalized statement, rather than a description of the actual situation in Galatia (cf. v. 19).[117] He could have made an appeal to mutual love without

---

[115] Paul's language (ἀνόητος: "unintelligent, foolish, dull-witted" [BDAG, p. 84]) is vitriolic, both underscoring his sense of the severity of the situation at Galatia and demonstrating his bewilderment at how the Galatians, who previously accepted Christ and experienced the Spirit, could resort to such an erroneous belief regarding the Law.

[116] Gal. 2:16 ("knowing that one is not justified by works of the Law"); 2:19 ("For through the Law, I died to the Law"); 2:21 ("if righteousness comes through the Law, then Christ died needlessly"); see also 3:2, 5, 10 ("As many as are of the works of the Law are under a curse"), 11–13, 19–29; 4:5, 21–31. This is especially true in the immediate context ("If you receive circumcision, Christ will be of no benefit to you" [5:2]). Note also his forceful degradation of his opponents in 5:12 ("Would that those who are troubling you would even castrate themselves").

[117] The exhortations of vv. 16–21 indicate a danger to be avoided rather than a situation to be rebuked (Dunn, The Epistle to the Galatians, p. 293). V. 15 can also be a logical corollary of the nature of Christian freedom in v. 1 approached from the negative point of view (Jervis, Galatians, p. 142). However, it should be emphasized that in v. 1 Paul expresses a discordant relationship ("do not be subject again to a yoke of slavery") between freedom (associated with Christ) and slavery (associated with the Law), yet in v. 15 ("the whole Law is fulfilled") he expresses a concordant relationship between the believer (one associated with Christ and the Spirit) and the Law.

any reference to the Law whatsoever if love was his primary concern. But it is obvious in his logic that he is attempting to place a favourable spin on the Law and uses Christian love as a means to do this. He is attempting to demonstrate how Christian love is harmonious with the love commandment. In a similar manner in v. 23b ("against such things there is no Law [νόμος]"), he both affirms and devalues the Law in this phrase. He affirms the Law in the sense that life in the Spirit results in producing behaviour that would be in accordance with what is advocated in the Law and its responsibility to restrain evil. But, at the same time, he devalues the Law in that these qualities do not need to be controlled by the Law since they are the fruit of the Spirit.[118] Paul consistently attempts to describe the Law in a favourable manner when the opportunity presents itself, even when the circumstances of the letter militate against it. In sum, the more temperate statement in Gal. 5:14 appears to be Paul's personal choice, not necessarily a logical corollary to his Law-free Gospel and not out of his concern for what others might say about his convictions on the Law, but because of his Jewish past that continually played upon his current convictions, even as a believer in Christ. Thus, the roaring lion stops and composes himself because he comes to the stark realization that he is about to devour something which he himself as a Jew was previously a part of and which continues to be part of his life in the present, albeit in a limited sense.

When we turn to Rom. 13:8-10, where the Law is similarly described in association with the love command, we notice that there are no seeds of antinomianism being intimated in the context whatsoever.[119] In this context, Paul treats the Law in a congenial manner. It can be considered a summary of the whole discussion of social relationships beginning with the rule of love in 12:1 ("Love must be sincere" [12:9]).[120] It is Christian love (i.e., love between believers) that is the primary subject in this section, not the Law. The mention of the Mosaic Law in 13:8-10 appears rather abruptly; there is no explicit mention of νόμος in the whole section up to this point (12:1-13:7) and it is

---

[118] Boice, *Galatians*, p. 499; H.N. Ridderbos, *The Epistle of Paul to the Churches of Galatia* NICNT (Grand Rapids: Wm. B. Eerdmans Publishing Co., 1953), p. 208.

[119] Räisänen, *Paul and the Law*, p. 64; C.F.D. Moule, "Obligation in the Ethic of Paul," in *Christian History and Interpretation: Studies Presented to John Knox* (ed. W.R. Farmer, C.F.D. Moule, and R.H. Niebuhr; Cambridge: Cambridge University Press, 1967), pp. 389-406.

[120] Rom. 13:8-10 appears to prepare the reader for the discussion in 14:1-15:13 (on the weak and the strong) based on the verbal similarities: "walking according to *love*" (14:15); "please one's *neighbour*"(15:2).

disjunctive with what Paul has previously stated regarding the Law (e.g., "we have been discharged from the Law...we serve in newness of the Spirit" [7:6] and "Christ is the end of the Law" [10:4]).[121] As with Gal. 5:14, Paul again unexpectedly brings up the Law, in a way that jolts with the context, in order to convey a sense of continuity between Christian love and the love commandment in the Mosaic Law.

Similarly when we analyse our passage in Rom. 8:4, even though the discussion is centred upon the relationship between the Law and the Spirit, we find that the motivation for the language of *"fulfilling the Law"* is not that Paul anticipated objections to his stance on the Law.[122] There is nothing similar to the statement in 3:8 ("And why not say [as we are slanderously reported and some affirm that we say], 'Let us do evil that good may come'"), or even the presence of the dialogical style (question and answer) that Paul employs in 7:7-25, characteristics that would indicate that Paul perceived potential objections or weaknesses in his argument that needed to be addressed. Furthermore, Paul's statement in 8:4 is intrusive in this context. In 8:3 Paul communicates discontinuity between the Law and Christ: "For what the Law was incapable of doing...God did by sending His own Son." However, in 8:4 Paul attempts to show how the role of the Spirit is harmonious with the role of the Law: "In order that the righteous requirement of the Law may be fulfilled in us...who walk according to the Spirit." This communicates continuity between the Spirit and the Law. If Paul wanted to convey a parallelism between 8:3 and 8:4 he would have used καθάπερ ("as") and the adverb οὕτως ("in this manner")[123] and expressed the Law's inability to achieve "righteousness." On the contrary, in 8:4 Paul expresses the Spirit's relationship with the Law in a positive manner. Therefore, the thought of a harmonious relationship between the Spirit and the Law in 8:4 is disjunctive with 8:3. In 8:4, these facts indicate that we are dealing with Paul's personal convictions. He is preoccupied with expressing his own opinions of the Law;

---

[121] Contra Dunn, who claims Paul neatly pulls things together from scattered references on the themes of "love" (Rom. 5:5; 8:28; 12:9) and "fulfillment" (8:4) (*Romans 1-8*, p. 775), even though Paul makes no association between "love" and the Law in 5:5; 8:28; 12:9 and he makes no association between "fulfillment" and "love" in 8:4. This indicates that Paul's thoughts on the relationship between "love," "fulfillment," and the Law are not as carefully thought out and calculated as Dunn proposes.

[122] Paul wanted to "blunt the force of the objection that certain individual requirements (*of the Law*)...have not been 'done'" (Westerholm, *Israel's Law and the Church's Faith*, p. 205).

[123] Cf. Rom. 12:4, 5; 1 Cor. 12:12; 2 Cor. 8:11.

he is not encumbered with what others thought or engaging in a disputation, where he argues from various perspectives to advance his own position on the matter. His own conviction on the Spirit's harmonious relationship with the Law appears abruptly in 8:4. This is consistent with the other contexts where the same wording occurs. Räisänen's position is that Paul's oscillating language on the Law, especially his use of the phrase "fulfilling the Law," was motivated by polemical reasons. However, he allows for the possibility that Paul was attempting to reconcile his Christian present with his Jewish past. He states, "This can hardly be just missionary strategy...It is difficult not to detect *a deeply felt personal urge* (emphasis added) as well, a 'nostalgic' longing for a harmony with his own past."[124]

2.2 The Spirit Fashions Righteous Behaviour Patterned Upon the Law: Rom. 8:10

In our previous discussion of Rom. 8:10 we interpreted the phrase "the body is dead because of sin" to signify the sentence of death destined for all people because of Adam's sin.[125] As a counterpart to this Paul claims, "the Spirit is life *because of righteousness*" (διὰ δικαιοσύνην). The referent for "righteousness" in the prepositional phrase has been identified either as the gift of righteousness that Christ's death and resurrection have provided for the believer, understood in a forensic sense,[126] or as the behavioural righteousness effected by the Spirit, understood in an ethical sense.[127] The unusual shift to Χριστὸς ἐν ὑμῖν in the *protasis* ("If Christ is in you") has erroneously been taken to suggest the possibility that Christ functions as the conceptual subject of the action in the verse and indicates Paul had a forensic use of

---

[124] Räisänen, *Paul and the Law*, p. 71.

[125] See Part Two (Chapter Five, Section 2, The Spirit of Life Versus the Flesh: Rom. 8:6, 10, 11, 13) above.

[126] Schmithals, *Die theologische Anthropologie des Paulus*, pp. 110–12; Cranfield, *The Epistle to the Romans*, p. 390; Dunn, *Romans 1–8*, p. 432; Schreiner, *Romans*, p. 415.

[127] J.A. Ziesler, *The Meaning of Righteousness in Paul: A Linguistic and Theological Enquiry* SNTSMS 20 (Cambridge: Cambridge University Press, 1972), pp. 168, 204; Ziesler, *Paul's Letter to the Romans*, p. 212; M.J. Lagrange, *Saint Paul Épitre aux Romains* (Paris: Gabalda, 1950), p. 199; H. Lietzmann, *Einführung in die Textgeschichte des Paulusbriefes an die Römer* HNT (Tübingen: J.C.B. Mohr [Paul Siebeck], 1933), p. 80; Käsemann, *Commentary on Romans*, p. 224.

righteousness in mind, not behavioural righteousness.[128] However, πνεῦμα is the subject in the *apodosis* ("the *Spirit*[129] is life for the sake of [goal] of righteousness"), emphasizing the Spirit's life-giving role and how this relates to righteousness. This is consistent with Rom. 8, where Paul underscores the role of the Spirit in the behavioural aspects of the believer's life.[130] The designation "Christ is in you" (v. 10) in the protasis is simply his way of communicating the idea that the Spirit's work is predicated upon the work of Christ in the past and the believer's present participatory union with Christ (cf. Rom. 8:1,2 ["in Christ Jesus"]; 7:3,4 ["having become joined to another"]). This conveys the closest possible association between Christ's work in the past and the Spirit's work in the present[131]; it is not a shift in emphasis from the Spirit to Christ, or even a shift from the behavioural aspects in the believer's life to an emphasis on eschatological existence, for that matter.[132] In Rom. 8, and specifically in the immediate context, Paul is preoccupied with the Spirit and the on-going effects of the Spirit in the believer's life, not with justification or righteousness associated with Christ in the past. For example, in vv. 11–13 he repeats the same concepts conveyed in v. 10. In v. 11 Paul communicates how the presence of the Spirit in the present functions as the guarantee for future bodily resurrection ("If the Spirit resides in you...the one who raised Christ from the dead will also give life to your mortal bodies" cf. "the Spirit is life" [v. 10]). In v. 13 he takes up the idea of the Spirit's current role in fashioning behaviour that results in life ("If by the Spirit, you put to death the practices of the body, you will live" cf. "the Spirit is life for the purpose of righteousness"

---

[128] "'Imputed righteousness' that leads to life" (Moo, *Romans 1–8*, p. 525); "Christ in you means life in the Spirit precisely *because of the righteousness that he [Christ] has brought to you*" (Fee, *God's Empowering Presence*, p. 551).

[129] The words τὸ πνεῦμα are written in the nominative case in v. 10.

[130] *Contra* Cranfield who states, "It is not till v. 12 that Paul explicitly *returns* (emphasis added) to the subject of the Christian's ethical obligation" (*The Epistle to the Romans*, p. 390, footnote 4). However, this distinction is arbitrary since the words "the Spirit is life" (v. 10) and "the Spirit...resides in you" (v. 11), which are directly associated with our prepositional phrase, are implicit references to the Spirit's role in Christian behaviour, running parallel to "walking according to the Spirit" (vv. 4–5); "the mindset of the Spirit" (v. 6).

[131] Cf. "Union with Christ is the only way into the life of the Age to Come, of which the distinguishing mark is the Spirit" (Barrett, *The Epistle to the Romans*, p. 149); note also Rom. 8:34 ("And he [Christ] is at the right hand of God"); 8:2-3 ("The law of the Spirit *in Christ Jesus* has set you free"; "God, having sent his own Son...condemned sin...so that the righteous requirement of the Law may be fulfilled in us...who walk...according to the Spirit").

[132] *Contra* Fee, *God's Empowering Presence*, p. 552.

[v. 10]). Both of these verses associate the Spirit with future life, and concomitantly indicate that this life is dependent upon the Spirit's role in ethics in the present. V. 13 is more explicit on this in that it clearly identifies the Spirit's role in the believer's conduct, which is the prerequisite for future life. This corresponds precisely with the words "the Spirit is life for the sake of righteousness" in 8:10.

This reading of "righteousness" in 8:10 is consistent with our conclusion above that "the *righteous requirement* of the Law" (8:4) refers specifically to the behavioural dimension in the believer's life where the Spirit achieves the goal "righteousness."[133] The prepositional phrase διὰ δικαιοσύνην is interpreted in a purposive or telic sense (*"for the sake of [for the goal of]* righteousness"), used similarly in 1 Cor. 11:9: "neither was man created *for the sake of* woman (διὰ τὴν γυναῖκα) but woman *for the sake of* man (διὰ τὸν ἄνδρα)," and Mk. 2:27: "the Sabbath was made *for the sake of humans* (διὰ τὸν ἄνθρωπον)."[134] Thus, "the Spirit is life for the sake of (for the goal of) righteousness" in Rom. 8:10 expresses the idea that the intention or goal of the Spirit acting as the agent of life is to produce righteous behaviour.

In Rom. 14:17,[135] Paul relates the Spirit to "righteousness": "For the kingdom of God is not eating and drinking but *righteousness* (δικαιοσύνη) and peace and joy in the *Holy Spirit* (πνεύματι ἁγίῳ)." The collocation "the Spirit," "the kingdom," and "righteousness" suggests that "righteousness" is to be understood more than simply in a forensic sense. The context emphasizes believers' life-conduct (cf. "walking according to love" [v. 15]). "Righteousness" is a quality of those who are transformed and is reflected in one's behaviour.[136]

---

[133] This is Fee's interpretation of Rom. 8:4 as well (*God's Empowering Presence*, pp. 535-36). Consequently, it is somewhat confusing why Fee would choose to interpret Paul suddenly shifting to a forensic use of righteousness in 8:10 (*Ibid.*, pp. 551-52), even though there is no explicit reference to this understanding of righteousness at all in the immediate verses and in the chapter as a whole.

[134] BDF, section 222, p. 119.

[135] See also Gal. 5:5, where δικαιοσύνη is described not simply as an initial act in conversion, but related to the Spirit, refers to a sustained relationship with God through correct behaviour (cf. its counterpart, "keeping the whole Law" [v. 3]), culminating in the ultimate goal of "righteousness."

[136] P. Stuhlmacher, "The Apostle Paul's View of Righteousness," in *Reconciliation, Law and Righteousness*, (trans. Everett R. Kalin; Philadelphia: Fortress, 1986), pp. 68-93; "The focus is on divine enabling which comes to expression in conduct" (Dunn, *Romans 1-8*, p. 823); commenting on Rom. 14:17, Fitzmyer states, "Uprightness and peace proceed from the Spirit's promptings and are conditions of Christian conduct in the kingdom" (*Romans*, p. 697).

In 1 Cor. 6:11, Paul's emphasis is on the believer's behaviour (vv. 1-8). He contrasts the behaviour of the "unrighteous ones" (v. 9) with that of believers because God has both removed the stains of their past sins and has begun the work of ethical transformation. The words *"you were made righteous* (ἐδικαιώθητε) in the name of the Lord Jesus Christ and *by the Spirit* (ἐν τῷ πνεύματι) of our God" describe Paul's understanding of the work of Christ in the past effected by the Spirit in the present, who functions as the agent of ethical transformation.[137] This is similar to the thought of 2 Cor. 3:8-9, where he characterizes the Spirit's role as "the ministry of righteousness" (ἡ διακονία τῆς δικαιοσύνης).[138] In this context, "the ministry of righteousness" is associated with the Spirit (ἡ διακονία τοῦ πνεύματος [v. 8]) and is contrasted with "the ministry of condemnation," which is identified as the Mosaic Law (τὸ γράμμα ἀποκτείνει [v. 6]). The Mosaic Law is unable to effect life because one is not able to keep it. On the other hand, the Spirit achieves the righteous behaviour as required by the Law and consequently effects life (τὸ πνεῦμα ζωοποιεῖ [v. 6]).

Putting this together, Paul is not unaccustomed to understanding δικαιοσύνη in an ethical sense referring to the Spirit's role in effecting righteous behaviour. The context in Rom. 8:10 seems better suited to this interpretation. Thus, Paul is saying, "If Christ by his Spirit resides in you, even though your bodies are destined for death because of Adam's sin, the presence of the Spirit destines you for life because the Spirit achieves the goal of righteous behaviour."

Most of the occurrences of δικαιοσύνη in the LXX are translated from the Hebrew words צֶדֶק (81 times), צְדָקָה (134 times), and צַדִּיק (6 times); only rarely is δικαιοσύνη translated from other terms (חֶסֶד [8 times- e.g., Gen. 19:19; Exod. 15:13]; אֱמֶת [6 times- e.g., Gen. 24:49; Jos. 24:14]; מֵשָׁרִים [1 Chron. 29:17]; טוֹב [Ps. 37:21]; מָדוֹן [Prov. 17:14]; נִקָּיוֹן [Gen. 20:5]; פֶּתִי [Prov. 1:22]; זָכוּ [Dan. 6:23]; הַשְׂכִּיל [Prov. 21:16]).[139] In most instances the words צֶדֶק, צְדָקָה, and צַדִּיק are contrasted with "wickedness, evil, wicked";

---

[137] "The presupposition is again the relation between indicative and imperative, holiness and active sanctification" (H. Conzelmann, *1 Corinthians: A Commentary on the First Epistle to the Corinthians* Hermeneia [Philadelphia: Fortress Press, 1975], p. 107; see also Barrett, *The First Epistle to the Corinthians*, p. 143).

[138] "*Spirit* points to the subjective apprehension of it [*Gospel*] in the re-creation of man" (Barrett, *The Second Epistle to the Corinthians*, p. 117).

[139] G. Quell, "δίκη, κτλ.," *TDNT* Vol. II, pp. 174-75.

they involve doing right in God's eyes, being faithful to him in the conduct of life and society.[140] "Righteousness" is not necessarily thought of as perfect moral uprightness, but is essentially a relational concept. It is understood as "right" conduct, that is, behaviour that is in keeping with the covenant relationship.[141] The basis for this "right" conduct is the Law. This is the whole purpose of the Law; it was given for the goal of producing "righteousness" ("right" conduct) in order to maintain the covenant relationship Israel had with Yahweh.[142] For example, the psalmist exclaims: "But I shall appear in righteousness (δικαιοσύνη) before your face: I shall be satisfied when your glory appears" (Ps. 16:15). In this context he appeals to Yahweh because he has obeyed the Law (cf. "not spoken with deceitful lips" [v. 1]; "unrighteousness has not been found in me" [v. 3]). Now in v. 15, he comforts himself with the fact that his "righteousness" is the basis for a secure sense of relationship he has with Yahweh ("I shall appear in righteousness *before your face*").[143]

This notion of "righteousness" understood as covenant faithfulness, tangibly expressed by observing the Law in Ancient Judaism, is to be found in Second Temple Judaism as well. For example, in 1 Macc. 2:50-52, Mattathias implores his sons to consider Abraham as an example of one who observed the Law, and consequently, was said to exhibit covenantal faithfulness: "My children, *be zealous for the Law* (ζηλώσατε τῷ νόμῳ) and give your lives *for the covenant* (ὑπὲρ διαθήκης) of your fathers...Was not Abraham found faithful and it was considered unto him as *righteousness* (δικαιοσύνην)?"[144] In the *Book of Jubilees* individuals such as Enoch,[145] Noah,[146] Abraham,[147] and above all,

---

[140] See for example, Isa. 1:21, 26; Jer. 22:13; Ezek. 3:20 (צֶדֶק), Deut. 9:4, 5, 6; 1Sam. 26:23 (צִדְקָה), Isa. 57:1; Ezek. 18:5, 9, 20, 24, 26 (צַדִּיק).

[141] See Ziesler, *The Meaning of Righteousness in Paul*, pp. 25, 39, 40; D. Hill, *Greek Words and Hebrew Meanings: Studies in the Semantics of Soteriological Terms* SNTSMS 5 (Cambridge: Cambridge University Press, 1967), pp. 85-86; G. von Rad, *Old Testament Theology* Vol. 1 (London: Oliver and Boyd, 1975), p. 373; C. Brown, "Righteousness," *NIDNTT* Vol. 3, pp. 356-58.

[142] "A man is righteous when he meets certain claims which another has on him in virtue of relationship" (G. Schrenk, "δικαιοσύνη, κτλ.," *TDNT* Vol. II, p. 195).

[143] For example, Isa. 26:9 states, "My spirit seeks you very early in the morning, O God, for your commandments (τὰ προστάγματά σου) are a light on the earth; learn *righteousness* (δικαιοσύνην), you that live upon the earth"; see also Ezek. 18:19, 21.

[144] See also Tob. 14:7, 9; *T. Lev.* 8:2; *T. Ash.* 6:4.

[145] *Jub.* 10:17.

[146] *Jub.* 5:19; 10:17.

[147] *Jub.* 11:5-12, 17; 17:15-18; 18:16; 23:10.

Jacob,[148] are clearly understood to be within the covenantal relationship because of their "righteousness." These figures are all considered prototypes for observing the Law.[149] Even though the members of the Qumran community considered themselves ethically upright, the Damascus Document indicates how their behaviour was motivated out of their covenantal relationship with Yahweh. For example, in CD I, 15-20, the righteous are compared to the wicked in terms of covenant faithfulness: "Abolishing the ways of *righteousness*...he might call down on them the curses of His Covenant and deliver them up to the avenging sword of the Covenant...they justified the wicked and condemned the just, and they transgressed the Covenant and violated the Precept. They banded together against the life of the *righteous*..."[150] The title, "Teacher of *Righteousness*," refers to the one who teaches righteousness, that is, teaches and encourages behaviour as stipulated by the Law in keeping with the covenant.[151] In *4 Ezra* the wicked do not follow the commandments and thus forsake the covenant (7:22-24), but the "righteous" keep the commandments and live according to the covenant (7:45, 51).

Paul was certainly cognizant of this understanding of "righteousness" associated with the Law and covenantal faithfulness. In Rom. 9:31 he writes, "But Israel, pursuing *a Law of righteousness* (νόμον δικαιοσύνης), did not arrive at that *Law* (νόμον) (cf. "Israelites, to whom belongs the adoption as sons and glory and the covenants and the giving of the Law" [9:4])." In this verse the verb "to pursue" (διώκων) describes the type of commitment contemporary Jews had to the covenant relationship and how the Mosaic Law articulated the goal of righteousness, which Yahweh required of his covenant people.[152] In Rom. 10:5 Paul states, "For Moses writes with reference to *the*

---

[148] *Jub.* 27:17; 35:12; Jacob is given the epithet "plant of righteousness" (*Jub.* 16:26; 21:24; 22:11; 33:19-20; 36:6), which is applicable to all Israel (Sanders, *Paul and Palestinian Judaism*, p. 363).

[149] Ellen Juhl Christiansen, *The Covenant in Judaism and Paul: A Study of Ritual Boundaries as Identity Markers* (New York: E.J. Brill, 1995), p. 93.

[150] צֶדֶק is used in this sense in 1QS III, 20, 22; IV, 2; CD I, 1, 16; 1QM III, 6; XIII, 3; XVII, 8; 1QH XIV, 19; VIII, 5; 1QSb V, 26; צְדָקָה in 1QS V, 4; VIII, 2; 1QH XV, 14; צַדִּיק in CD I, 19, 20; XI, 21; XX, 20; 1QH VII, 15; IX, 36.

[151] See CD VI, 11.

[152] James D.G. Dunn, *Romans 9-16* Vol. 38b (Dallas, TX: Word Books, Publisher, 1988), p. 581; "the Law that promises uprightness"/ "the Law that would lead Israel to uprightness," see H. Schlier, *Der Römerbrief Kommentar* HTKNT (Freiburg im Breisgau: Herder, 1977), p. 307; P.W. Meyer, "Romans 10:4 and the 'End' of the Law," in *The Divine Helmsman: Studies on God's*

righteousness of the Law (τὴν δικαιοσύνη τὴν ἐκ νόμου): the one who observes these things will live in them." He uses Moses to characterize the previous epoch of the Law.[153] Paul's wording, τὴν δικαιοσύνην τὴν ἐκ νόμου instead of simply νόμος δικαιοσύνης, refers more restrictively to those who observe the Law[154] and derive their sense of appropriate behaviour from the Law and the covenant relationship. This coincides with the use of τὴν ἰδίαν ("seeking to establish *their own* righteousness") in v. 3 and the specific reference to the Jewish understanding of "righteousness." Paul is intentionally associating "righteousness" in this verse with the thought of Lev. 18:5, where the Law is said to be the source of life.[155] The wording between Rom. 10:5 and Lev. 18:5 is too close to be simply coincidental:

Lev. 18:5:   καὶ ποιήσετε αὐτά, ἃ ποιήσας ἄνθρωπος ζήσεται ἐν αὐτοῖς
Rom. 10:5: ὁ ποιήσας   αὐτὰ   ἄνθρωπος ζήσεται ἐν αὐτοῖς

Lev. 18:5 was regarded as a typical expression of Israel's obligation to the Law and promise under the covenant.[156]

However, δικαιοσύνη in Rom. 8:10 is not associated with the Mosaic Law but has been wholly re-oriented with the role of the Spirit. As we concluded above, the concept of righteousness is best understood as behavioural righteousness effected by the Spirit ("the Spirit... achieves the goal of righteous behaviour"). The concept of "righteousness" in both Ancient and Second Temple Judaism was defined as behaviour befitting the covenant relationship, which was articulated in the Law. Consequently, in Rom. 8:10, Paul has

---

Control of Human Events, Presented to Lou H. Silberman (ed. J.L. Crenshaw and S. Sandmel; New York: KTAV, 1980), pp. 59–78, esp. p. 62; Cranfield, *The Epistle to the Romans*, p. 508, footnote 1; Käsemann, *Commentary on Romans*, p. 277; Fitzmyer, *Romans*, p. 578.

[153] Cf. Rom. 5:14; 1 Cor. 10:2; 2 Cor. 3:7–15.

[154] "A righteousness delimited by the law, restricted to those who observe the law, the covenant people" (Dunn, *Romans 9–16*, p. 600).

[155] H. Hübner, *Gottes Ich und Israel: Zum Schriftgebrauch des Paulus in Römer 9–11* FRLANT 136 (Göttengen: Vandenhoeck & Ruprecht, 1984), p. 93; M. Silva, "Is the Law against the Promises? The Significance of Gal. 3:21 for Covenant Continuity," in *Theonomy: A Reformed Critique* (ed. W.S. Barker and W.R. Godfrey; Grand Rapids: Zondervan, 1990), pp. 153–67, esp. pp. 163–66; B.W. Longenecker, *Eschatology and the Covenant: A Comparison of 4 Ezra and Romans 1–11* JSNTSup 57 (Sheffield: JSOT Press, 1991), pp. 222–24; Fitzmyer, *Romans*, p. 589; Schreiner, *Romans*, p. 552.

[156] E.g., Deut. 4:1; 5:32–33; 8:1; 16:20; Ezek. 18:9, 17, 19, 21; 20:11, 13, 21; *Pss. Sol.* 14:2–3.

patterned, to some extent, the covenantal understanding of righteousness with the role of the Spirit and the believer's participatory union with Christ. This indicates that he perceives continuity between the Spirit and the Law regarding the concept of "righteousness."

3. "The Commandment Intended for Life" Realized in "The Spirit of Life"

In Part Two we concluded that one of the key concepts in Rom. 8:1–16 is "life" (vv. 2, 6, 10, 13) and furthermore, that life was the exclusive result of the Spirit in the believer and not the result of observing the Law. Our analysis also revealed that Paul's thoughts were categorically different than both Ancient and Second Temple Judaism, each of which advocated a harmonious relationship between the Spirit and Law in eschatological expectation. Thus, Paul's explication of the Spirit as the agent of life in Rom. 8 is not predicated upon any form of Jewish "new covenant" expectation. It is rather an expression of his personal conviction on the Spirit's relationship to the Mosaic Law and comes as a reactionary response to his Jewish understanding of the Law (i.e., covenantal nomism) in the previous epoch (ch. 7).[157] In Rom. 7:10 he broaches the idea that the Law intended to give "life" but immediately qualifies this by saying that the previous system associated with Law actually resulted in "death" (7:11, 13). As a response to this, Paul perceives the Spirit as the agent of "life" and communicates this in Rom. 8. In other words, "life," which was the goal of the Mosaic Law in the previous epoch, becomes realized through the work of the Spirit in the present epoch.

Our previous analysis of the designation "the law of the Spirit of life" in 8:2 suggested that, in some sense, Paul wanted to communicate a positive parallelization between the Spirit, Mosaic Law, and life. "Life" was the intended goal of the Mosaic Law in the previous era (Rom. 7:10) and the word νόμος in the phrase in 8:2 reminds his readers of the Mosaic Law. This indicates that Paul wanted to convey an analogous sense of "life" between the

---

[157] This may be the reason why the designation, "new covenant" (καινή διαθήκη), is conspicuously absent in Rom. 8. This is significant in light of the fact that elsewhere Paul indicates his full awareness of this Jewish eschatological expectation (e.g., 2 Cor. 3:6 [καινή διαθήκη] cf. 3:14 [παλαιά διαθήκη]). Some have mistakenly and intrusively read this into Rom. 8 and see it as the motivation for Paul's explication of the Spirit in Rom. 8, particularly the relationship between the Spirit and life (so with Fee, Moo, Schreiner, etc.).

former era of the Law and the Spirit's life-giving role in the new era (Rom. 8:2, 6, 10, 11, 13). The purpose in this section will not be to repeat our analysis of the Spirit as the principle of new life (Part Two), but more specifically, to demonstrate how Paul perceives a sense of continuity between the Law and the Spirit with respect to the concept of "life."

In Ancient Judaism, Law obedience is said to result in life: "And now, Israel, hear the righteous requirements and the judgments, all that I teach you this day *to do* [ποιεῖν] in order that *you may live* [ζῆτε]...*keep the commandments* [φυλάσσεσθε τὰς ἐντολάς] of the Lord our God [Deut. 4:1,2 (LXX)]."[158] The use of ποιεῖν and φυλάσσειν indicates that the writer had the performance of the commandments in mind, where obedience to the commandments leads to the possession of life (ζῆτε) and the enjoyment of God's blessings (cf. Deut. 27-28 [blessings and curses]). For Israel, the basis of "life" was their covenant relationship with Yahweh tangibly expressed in observing the Mosaic Law. Conversely, those who disobey the commandments are condemned as wicked and said to be subject to a divine curse and the sentence of "death," standing in danger of severing their relationship with Yahweh.[159]

In Lev. 18:5 we read the words, "And you will keep all my ordinances, and all my judgments, and observe them; if one observes them, *he will live by them* (ζήσεται ἐν αὐτοῖς)." The thought of this chapter is driven by the exhortation to obey the Mosaic Law: Israel is to follow the Law rather than the customs and practices of Egypt (vv. 1-5); various aspects of the Law are specified (vv. 6-23); the chapter concludes with an exhortation to obey the Law and a warning of judgment if it is not observed (vv. 24-30). In this context, Lev. 18:5 is not simply saying that one who does the commandments will live out his life in the "sphere of the Law" ("will live *in* them"), taking the ἐν of the LXX as a locative of sphere.[160] "Living" ("life") is understood more comprehensively as the result of being a member of Israel (cf. disobedience

---

[158] See also Deut. 5:33; 6:24-25; 8:1; 30:15-18; Ezek. 18:19 cf. vv. 9, 21; 20:11 cf. vv. 13, 21; Neh. 9:29.

[159] Deut. 6: 15; 7:4, 10; 8:19; 28:20, 22, 45.

[160] This is the view taken by W.C. Kaiser, Jr., "Leviticus and Paul: 'Do this and you shall live (eternally?)," *JETS* 14 (1971), 19-28; B.A. Levine, *Leviticus* JPS Torah Commentary (Philadelphia: Jewish Publication Society, 1989), p. 119.

results in expulsion from Israel [vv. 28, 29])[161] and entails covenantal relationship with Yahweh, which in turn includes material prosperity, fruitful harvest, peace, and longevity of life (cf. Lev. 26:3-13; Deut. 28:1-14). Lev. 18:5 is a warning that the continuance of "life" is dependent upon Israel's faithful observance of the Law.[162]

In Second Temple Judaism, God's commandments are called the "commandments of life"[163] and the Torah is called the "Law of life."[164] The wording in *Pss. Sol.* 14:2 comes close to Paul's rendering in Rom. 7:10: ἐν νόμῳ ᾧ ἐντείλατο ἡμῖν εἰς ζωὴν ἡμῶν (*Pss. Sol.* 14:2) cf. ἡ ἐντολὴ ἡ εἰς ζωήν (Rom. 7:10). The Law had a mediatorial function between Yahweh and Israel, regulating and maintaining the covenant relationship. When one was in the covenant relationship, one was said to possess "life." In Sir. 17:11-12, "law of life" (νόμον ζωῆς, v. 11) is said to be equivalent to the "eternal covenant" (διαθήκην αἰῶνος, v. 12).[165] This description of the Law reflects the purpose that it was considered to have among many of Paul's Jewish contemporaries. *4 Ezra*, which was composed about 100 C.E., indicates how those who are on the earth have been ordained to obey the Law (cf. 7:20 ["Law of God"]), which is a condition to be met so that they could "live" ("what they should do *to live*" [4 Ezra 7:21]). Commenting on Lev. 18:5, *t. Sabb.* 15:17 reads, "The commands were given only that humans should *live through them*, not that

---

[161] R.K. Harrison, *Leviticus* TOTC (Grand Rapids: Wm. B. Eerdmans Publishing Co., 1980), p. 185; G. Wenham, *A Commentary on Leviticus* NICOT (Grand Rapids: Wm. B. Eerdmans Publishing Co., 1979), p. 253.

[162] D. Moo, *Epistle to the Romans* NICNT (Grand Rapids: Wm. B. Eerdmans Publishing Co., 1996), p. 648, footnote 13.

[163] See Bar. 3:9, where the commandments are called ἐντολὰς ζωῆς; cf. "This is the book of the commandments of God, and the Law that endures forever: all they that keep it *shall come to life* (εἰς ζωήν)"(4:1). See also R. Bultmann, "The Concept of Life in Judaism," *TDNT* Vol. II, pp. 855-61, esp. p. 855.

[164] Sir. 17:11 reads, "He bestowed knowledge upon them, and allotted to them the *Law of life* (νόμον ζωῆς)"; see also *m. Abot* 6:7.

[165] Cf. Deut. 30:15-20, where "life" is promised to those who obey (v.16) and are in a relationship with God ("hold fast to him" [v. 20]), whereas "death" (v. 17) is the result of those who sever their relationship with God ("bow to other gods" [v. 18]).

humans should die through them."[166] Rabbinical teaching understood the Law as a means of choosing life and banishing death from the world.[167]

Paul himself understood the role of the Law in Judaism in this manner when he cites Lev. 18:5 in Gal. 3:12[168]: "The one who observes the Law will live by them."[169] Lev. 18:5 is also the basis for Rom. 10:5 ("the person who does these things [*what the Law requires*] shall live by them")[170] and Rom. 7:10 ("the commandment that was intended to bring life").[171] Paul concedes, in principle, that observing the Law was a path to eternal life. Even though Lev. 18:5 does not address the attainment of eternal life, Paul nevertheless understands it in this manner as did some Jewish authors.[172] In Rom. 7:10, Paul is simply stating a common Jewish rule or fact without giving a definite purpose or intention explaining his reason for doing so.[173] This indicates that we are dealing with his personal conviction, which he shares with his Jewish contemporaries.[174] Nowhere in the Pauline corpus is this idea ever contradicted or even questioned.[175] Paul's point is simply that it was a system

---

[166] See the discussion of H.J. Schoeps, *Paul: The Theology of the Apostle in Light of Jewish Religious History* (Philadelphia: Westminster, 1961), p. 175; Str-B, Vol. 3, p. 237; G.F. Moore, *Judaism in the First Centuries of the Christian Era* Vol. 1 (New York: Schocken, 1971), p. 491.

[167] E.E. Urbach, *The Sages: Their Concepts and Beliefs* Vol. 1 (Jerusalem: Magnes, 1979), p. 426.

[168] In Gal. 1:13 Paul describes his knowledge and personal association with Judaism: "my previous way of life in Judaism."

[169] Ronald Y.K. Fung, *The Epistle to the Galatians* NICNT (Grand Rapids: William B. Eerdmans Publishing Co., 1988), p. 145.

[170] See Dunn who demonstrates how Paul's wording in Rom. 10:5 is linguistically parallel with Lev. 18:5 (LXX) and notes how Lev. 18:5 is a typical expression of what Israel saw as its obligation under the covenant (*Romans 9–16*, p. 601).

[171] Byrne, *Romans*, p. 223; Fitzmyer, *Romans*, p. 468; Schreiner, *Romans*, p. 359.

[172] See *Tg. Onq.* and *Tg. Ps.-J; b. Sanh.* 58b; *Sipra Lev.* 337a; Str.-B, Vol. 3, p. 278.

[173] Thurén, *Derhetorizing Paul*, p. 113.

[174] "This doctrine-a thoroughly Jewish doctrine...finds its echo occasionally in Paul (Rom. 2.7-13; 10:5; Gal. 3.12)" (S. Kim, *The Origin of Paul's Gospel* WUNT 2. Reiche 4 [Tübingen: J.C.B. Mohr (Paul Siebeck), 1984], p. 281); "That the law promises life is thus Paul's own conviction, though one which [he believes] he shares with the 'Israel' of his day" (Westerholm, *Israel's Law and the Church's Faith*, p. 146).

[175] *Contra* Dunn, who, commenting on Rom. 7:10, states Paul "implied [a] sharp reverse to and rebuttal of the traditional Jewish assumption that the law/commandment produced life" (*Romans 1–8*, p. 384); see also H.D. Betz, who contends Paul is arguing against Jewish tradition and the idea that the Law was never given for the purpose of bestowing life (*Galatians*, p. 174); see also E. De Witt Burton, *A Critical and Exegetical Commentary on the Epistle to the Galatians* ICC (Edinburgh: T & T Clark, 1921), p. 167.

that did not work.[176] He falls short of denying the validity of the principle or deeming it to be erroneous. For example, when Paul claims that the Law promises life to its adherents, he cites Moses in a favourable manner in Rom. 10:5.[177] In the juxtaposition between the Law (Lev. 18:5) and faith (Hab. 2:4) in Gal. 3:12, he is not denying the principle, "the one who observes these things (in the Law) will live by them" in Lev. 18:5, but rather, is focusing more restrictively on the notion of *doing* the Law.[178] He is using Lev. 18:5 to summarize what for him is the essence of the Mosaic Law: life is contingent on obedience. This is contrasted with the relationship lived out on the basis of *faith* advocated in Hab. 2:4. Paul confirms this reading of the text in the immediate context:

> Is the Law opposed to the promises of God? Certainly not! For if the Law had been given that was able to impart life, then righteousness would indeed have been based on the Law. But the scripture has imprisoned all things under the power of sin, in order that the promise given through faith in Jesus might be given to those who believe" (vv. 21-22).[179]

Likewise, in Rom. 10:5, Paul is not specifically objecting to the principle that the Law can confer life if it is observed.[180] He speaks positively of how the Law can bestow life if it is obeyed.[181] Paul is conveying the idea that the Mosaic Law

---

[176] Paul uses the following words to describe the role of the Law: "resulted in death" (Rom. 7:1); was not accompanied "by faith" (Rom. 10:6, 10; Gal. 3:12); was not observed (Rom. 7:8, 9, 11, 13-17, 19-21). This communicates Paul's understanding of a system that did not function adequately.

[177] Paul always cites Moses in a positive manner; see Rom. 9:15; 10:19; 1 Cor. 9:9; *contra* Sanders who claims Paul's point in Rom. 10:5-8 is that "Moses was incorrect" and "that Scripture itself shows that real righteousness is by faith" (*Paul, the Law, and the Jewish People*, p. 41); in Rom. 10:4, 5, (as in Rom. 7:10) Paul is speaking in the context of salvation history and simply states the fact that the former age associated with the Law has been superseded by the new age associated with Christ ("Christ is the end/goal of the Law"). Thus, he is not stating that Moses was "incorrect" but rather the Law, given through Moses, was not able to deliver on its promise of life and was replaced in this new epoch by Christ.

[178] "The more limited purview of *doing the Law* (emphasis added)" (Dunn, *The Epistle to the Galatians*, p. 175); Longenecker, *Galatians*, p. 120.

[179] "Paul understands the law as adequate for the role it was intended to play but regards that role as limited in both duration and function" (Jervis, *Galatians*, p. 99).

[180] Das, *Paul, the Law, and the Covenant*, pp. 262-65.

[181] *Contra* Käsemann, who contends that Paul objects that "no one...should achieve salvation in this way" (*Commentary on Romans*, p. 285); "Paul indicts works in the context of *the law*" (Beker,

has been brought to its culmination in Christ (v. 4 "Christ is the goal of the law") and in seeking to establish a relationship with God through the Law, one is seeking a relationship through *doing* rather than through *faith*.[182]

When we turn to Rom. 7:10, Paul is intimating the same type of principle; the Law bestows eternal life if it is observed. It is no coincidence that throughout 7:7-25[183] Paul portrays the "I" as striving to *do/ practice* the "good thing" (see the use of ποιεῖν or πράσσειν in vv. 15, 16, 19, 20, 21 cf. the use of τὸ ἀγαθόν in vv. 13, 18, 19). In v. 12, he describes the commandment as "good" (ἀγαθή), which inevitably makes an association with τὸ ἀγαθόν in vv. 13, 18, 19. This indicates that he understands the Law as the object which the "I" is striving to *do/ practice*. The phrase, ἡ ἐντολὴ ἡ εἰς ζωήν has a telic force: "the commandment *intended to bring* (for the goal/ purpose of) life."[184] From this it seems fair to conclude that Paul believed the Law had the capability of giving life had it been observed.

From the perspective of the new era in Rom. 8:2ff, Paul picks up the theme of "life," previously associated with the Mosaic Law in the former era articulated in 7:10, and demonstrates how the goal of "life" is realized through the Spirit (vv. 2, 6, 10, 11, 13). This means that his description of the Spirit's role in 8:2ff is occasioned by his description of the Law in 7:10ff. We can surmise this from the manner in which he formulates his explication of the new era of the Spirit. First, in 7:7-25 the Law occupied a central and active role, but in 8:2ff, it is described passively, always in comparison with and subordinated to work of Christ or the role of the Spirit (e.g., "the *law of the Spirit* of life *in Christ Jesus* has set you free from the *law* of sin and death" [v. 2]; "God has done what the *Law* was unable to do...by sending his own *Son*" [v. 3]; "the righteous requirement of the *Law* has been fulfilled in us...who walk

---

Paul the Apostle, p. 246); R. Bultmann, *Theology of the New Testament* Vol. 1 (New York: Charles Scribner's Sons, 1951), p. 264.

[182] A. Lindemann, "Die Gerechtigkeit aus dem Gesetz: Erwägungen zur Auslegung und zur Textgeschichte von Römer 10.5," ZNW 73 (1982), 231-50, esp. 242-46; J.-N. Aletti, *Comment Dieu est-il juste? Clefs pour interpréter l'épître aux Romains* (Rome: Editions du Seuil, 1991), pp. 124-27; B.L. Martin, *Christ and the Law in Paul* NovTSup 62 (Leiden: Brill, 1989), pp. 139-40; Fairbairn, *The Revelation of the Law in Scripture*, p. 446; Moo, *The Epistle to the Romans*, p. 649.

[183] The words, δουλεύειν...οὐ παλαιότητι γράμματος in Rom. 7:6 are parallel to the words, δουλεύω νόμῳ θεοῦ in 7:25, forming an *inclusio*, where Paul is preoccupied with the description of the Law in the former era.

[184] Hofius, "Das Gesetz des Mose und das Gesetz Christi," 270; Stuhlmacher, "Paul's Understanding of the Law in the Letter to the Romans," 98-99.

according to the *Spirit*" [v. 4]; "the mind set on the flesh...does not subject itself to the *Law* of God, for it is not even able to do so...But you are not in the flesh but in the *Spirit*" [vv. 8-9]). This demonstrates that Paul's thoughts are preoccupied with how the Law compares with the roles of Christ and the Spirit in the new era. That is, his argument in 8:2ff is specifically motivated by his perception of the place and purpose of Law in the previous era described in 7:10ff. Put another way, the Law is no longer the lead actor in the scene as it was in 7:10ff, but, instead, occupies the role of supporting actor in 8:2ff. In this new role it serves to enhance the leading role (Christ and the Spirit) by demonstrating a limited sense of harmony and continuity with it.

Second, and more specific to our concern in this section, Paul intentionally patterns his description of the Spirit as the agent of "life" in 8:2ff upon his previous discussion of the Law and its relationship to "life" in 7:10ff. In doing this he sets the stage for a positive relationship between the Spirit and Law with respect to the concept of "life" in 8:2 ("the *law*" [related to the Mosaic Law] + "of the *Spirit of life*" [i.e., continuity between the Mosaic Law and the Spirit with respect to the concept of life]) and the following verses. One element of this pattern has to do with sin. While in 7:7-25, the Law's inability to give life was the result of "sin"[185] and the "flesh,"[186] in 8:2-13 the Spirit is life because he delivers from "sin"[187] and believers are not to live according to the "flesh"[188] but the Spirit. Another element of the pattern involves the antithesis between "life" and "death," which appears in 7:7-25 in association with the Law but in 8:2-16 in association with the Spirit.[189]

---

[185] Note the comments on "sin" in Rom. 7:7-25: "For *sin*, seizing the opportunity afforded by the *commandment*" (v. 11); "*sin* through the *commandment*" (v. 13); "having been sold under *sin*" (v. 14); "*sin* living in me" (vv. 17, 20).

[186] See Paul's comments on the "flesh" in Rom. 7:7-25: "I am *fleshly*" (v. 14); "in my *flesh*" (v. 18); "with the *flesh*" (v. 25).

[187] Note Paul's descriptions of the Spirit in Rom. 8:2ff: "*Spirit of life*...sets you free from the law of *sin* and death" (v. 2); "body is dead because of *sin* but the *Spirit* is life"([v. 10).

[188] See Paul's comments on the relationship between the Spirit and "flesh" in Rom. 8:2ff: "not walking according to the *flesh* but the *Spirit*" (v. 4); "according to the *flesh*, the mind of the *flesh* is death, but the mind of the *Spirit* is life" (v. 6); "you are not in the *flesh* but in the *Spirit*" (v. 9); "if you live according to the *flesh*, you will die, but if by the *Spirit*...you will live" (v. 13).

[189] With respect to the Law, see Rom. 7:7-25: "when the *commandment* came, I *died*" (v. 9); "this *commandment* intended for *life*, actually brought *death*" (v. 10); "through the *commandment*...*killed* me" (v. 11); "this body of *death*" (v. 24); with respect to the Spirit, see Rom. 8:2ff: "*Spirit of life* has set you free from the law of sin and *death*" (v. 2); "mind set on the flesh is *death*, but the mind set on the *Spirit* is *life*" (v. 6); "body is *dead*...but the Spirit is *life*" (v. 10); "if the *Spirit*

Putting these things together we are now in a better position to state more confidently that Paul's explication of the Spirit as the agent of life in Rom. 8:2-13 was conditioned to a significant degree by covenantal nomism and the Jewish belief that observing the Law was a path to life. The shape of the argument in 8:2ff is intentionally patterned upon his explication of the Law in 7:10ff. This is a sign that Paul perceives that the goal of the Mosaic Law, which was to confer life, is realized in the Spirit, who is the exclusive agent of life in the new era.

4. The Spirit Ensures Covenantal "Peace" with God

In most cases the LXX uses εἰρήνη to translate the Hebrew word שָׁלוֹם, which carries a very comprehensive meaning in the MT, including an individual's well-being, material prosperity, bodily health, and stability of relationship.[190] Thus, in the LXX the word εἰρήνη came to denote more than simply a "state of peace" (i.e., a cessation or absence of hostilities in the state of war), as it was understood in secular Greek.[191] The word שָׁלוֹם was understood as a social concept concerning the relationship between two parties.[192] This kind of alliance between two parties was equivalent to בְּרִית. Consequently, it is not surprising that שָׁלוֹם frequently becomes associated with a "covenant," so much so that it becomes a catchword intimating covenantal relationship.[193] For example, in Josh. 9:15, it is said that Joshua made both "peace" (שָׁלוֹם) and "a covenant" (בְּרִית) with the people. The relationship of "peace" to the covenant can be understood in two ways: 1. it

---

...resides in you, He who raised Christ from the *dead* will also give *life* through his *Spirit*" (v. 11); "you *die*, but if by the *Spirit*...you will *live*" (v. 13).

[190] W. Foerster and G. Von Rad, "εἰρήνη, κτλ.," *TDNT* Vol. II, pp. 400-20, esp. pp. 402, 406-8; there are exceptions in the LXX where εἰρήνη translates something other than שָׁלוֹם in the MT. For example in Gen. 26:31, שָׁלוֹם is translated as σωτηρία ("salvation"); in Isa. 48:22 it is rendered as χαρά ("joy", "gladness"); see also Gen. 28:21; 29:6; 37:14; 41:16; 43:23, 27; Exod. 18:7; Josh. 10:21; Jer. 20:10; Isa. 55:12; 57:21; Job 21:9 for other variances in the LXX; Foerster concludes that שָׁלוֹם is consistently translated εἰρήνη only when it refers to the prosperity which comes to a human from God (*Ibid.*, p. 408).

[191] *Ibid.*, p. 401.

[192] See, for example, the use of שָׁלוֹם to describe "the peaceful relations" between Hiram and Solomon (1 Ki. 5:26); see also Jud. 4:17; 1 Ki. 5:4; Gen. 34:21; 1 Chron. 12:18.

[193] See for example 1 Ki. 5:26; Obad. 7.

may convey the idea that "peace" is *sealed* by both parties in a covenant or, 2. it may be taken that the covenant *inaugurates* a relationship of "peace."[194]

The OT prophets used the term שָׁלוֹם to characterize Israel's covenant relationship with Yahweh. Ezekiel claims that Yahweh makes a בְּרִית שָׁלוֹם (Ezek. 34:25; 37:26) and in the context makes it clear that the relationship of "peace" is the result.[195] "Peace" is often used interchangeably with "salvation."[196] In Isa. 52:7 we read the following words: "How beautiful on the mountains are the feet of him who brings good news, who announces *peace* (שָׁלוֹם) and brings good news of happiness, who announces *salvation* (יְשׁוּעָה) and says to Zion, 'Your God reigns!'"[197] The covenants with Phinehas (Num. 25:12; Sir. 45:24) and with Levi (Mal. 2:5) are covenants of peace. One of the characteristic qualities of those who entered this covenant was their commitment to observe the Law. The eschatological "covenant of peace" will be established with a Davidic King, and furthermore, Yahweh proclaims, "They (children of Israel [v. 21]) will follow *my Laws* and be careful to keep *my decrees*" (Ezek. 37:24-26).[198] In the LXX the concept of "peace" (εἰρήνη) is likewise associated with the covenant, salvation, and the Law. For example εἰρήνη and σωτήριον are linked in a positive way in Ps. 84:8,9: "For he (the Lord God) will speak *peace* to his people...Moreover his *salvation* is near them that fear him." In Ps. 118:165 *peace* is said to be the possession of "those who love your *Law*" (τοῖς ἀγαπῶσι τὸν νόμον σου).

In the NT, εἰρήνη can be understood in one of three ways: 1. generally, order or harmony,[199] 2. the comprehensive salvation of human beings in an eschatological sense,[200] or 3. a state of reconciliation with God.[201] It is this last conception of "peace" that will occupy our attention, and in particular, we shall examine whether Paul used and understood the meaning of this word in

---

[194] Von Rad, "εἰρήνη, κτλ.," *TDNT*, Vol. II, p. 403.

[195] See also Isa. 54:10, which also mentions a "covenant of peace."

[196] Dunn defines the Jewish concept of "peace" as "all that makes for the total well-being and harmony" (*Romans 1-8*, p. 262); "the well-being, prosperity, or *salvation* (emphasis added) of the godly person" (Moo, *The Epistle to the Romans*, p. 299).

[197] Isa. 52:7 is quoted by Paul in Rom. 10:15.

[198] See Mal. 3:7

[199] Cf. "For God is not a God of disorder but of *peace*" (1 Cor. 14:33).

[200] Cf. "To guide our feet into the path of *peace*" (Lk. 1:79 cf. vv. 68-79 [God's final day of redemption]; see also Lk. 2:14; 19:42).

[201] Foerster, "εἰρήνη, κτλ.," *TDNT* Vol. II, p. 412.

the same manner as the MT and LXX, that is, in a relational and covenantal sense.

In Rom. 5:1, Paul writes, "Therefore, having been justified by faith, we have[202] peace with God through our Lord Jesus Christ." The use of the phrase "peace with God" (εἰρήνην...πρὸς τὸν θεόν) indicates that Paul does not understand this "peace" as simply an internal equanimity of mind ("peace of mind") but as a reference to the external situation of being in a relationship with God.[203] Even though εἰρήνη is not used again in this paragraph, the language of "reconciliation" (καταλλάσσειν) in vv. 10-11 picks up this concept.

In v. 1, "peace with God" is made possible by Christ ("peace with God *through our Lord Jesus Christ*"), but the activity of the Spirit in 5:5 ("because the love of God has been poured out in our hearts through the *Holy Spirit* who was given to us") should not be distinguished too sharply from the work of Christ in this context, since the role of the Spirit is to bring to fruition the work of Christ in the life of the believer.[204] For example, Paul associates the Spirit with "peace" in Rom. 14:17. Even though the context indicates that it refers

---

[202] Even though the reading ἔχωμεν πρὸς τὸν θεόν ("*Let us have* peace with God"[the subjunctive use ἔχωμεν]) is represented in the most reliable Greek sources (א*, A, B*, C, D, 33, 81, 1175), most commentators prefer the reading ἔχομεν πρὸς τὸν θεόν ("*We have* peace with God"[the indicative use ἔχομεν]) (א1, B2, F, G, ψ, 0220), contending that auditory confusion between ο and ω took place on the part of the copyist (A.R. Crabtree, "Translation of Romans 5:1 in the Revised Standard Version of the New Testament" *RevExp* [1946], 436-39; M. Wolter, *Rechtfertigung und zukünftiges Heil: Untersuchungen zu Röm 5:1-11* BZNW 43 [Berlin: de Gruyter, 1978], pp. 89-95; Byrne, *Romans*, p. 170; Cranfield, *The Epistle to the Romans*, p. 257, footnote 1). Also, the indicative use of ἔχομεν fits better with the other indicatives in the context (ἐσχήκαμεν, καυχώμεθα [v. 2], κατεργάζεται [v. 3]) and is better suited to express the *effect* of justification. V. 1 is part of vv. 1-5 that emphasizes the basis of hope (indicative use) that believers have in Christ rather than their responsibility to enjoy that hope (subjunctive use).

[203] In a construction where friendly (or hostile) relationships are part of the context, πρός can be used with a noun to designate a friend (or enemy) and can mean "friendly to, toward, with" (BDAG, p. 874). This coincides with the use of שָׁלוֹם in the OT which refers to a relationship rather than a state (Von Rad, "εἰρήνη, κτλ.," *TDNT*, Vol. II, pp. 402-6). Paul also refers to the "God of peace" (Rom. 15:33; 16:20; 2 Cor. 13:11; Phil. 4:9; 1 Thess. 5:23), which may make some association with this concept; see also Käsemann, *Commentary on Romans*, p. 132; Fitzmyer, *Romans*, p. 395; Foerster, "εἰρήνη, κτλ.," p. 415.

[204] "The Spirit denotes par excellence the divine presence to the justified Christian" (Fitzmyer, *Romans*, p. 398); "Much of what is said in vv. 1-5 appears elsewhere in Paul as the effectual working of the Spirit in Christian life, not in the sense of securing such life but of realizing or experiencing it" (Fee, *God's Empowering Presence*, p. 495, footnote 63).

specifically to the horizontal dimension of the believer's reconciliation with other believers over the issue of "kosher" meat,[205] the manner in which Paul associates it with "the kingdom of God" implies that it is to be understood comprehensively, including the vertical sense of the believer's "peace with God." The relationship between the believer and God is indicated in the following verse: "for the one who serves Christ in this[206] is well-pleasing to God" (14:18). Paul underscores the point that "peace" is central in the kingdom and this is what "pleases/ is acceptable" to God. To be "pleasing/ acceptable" to God means that those who exhibit "peace" with other believers are also found to have "peace" with God, that is, to be in a favourable relationship with God (before the judgment throne of God).[207] This is the induction of eschatological peace (both vertical and horizontal dimensions) that translates itself into a present-day reality.[208] Likewise, the meaning of "peace" in Rom. 5:1 (εἰρήνην ἔχομεν πρὸς τὸν θεόν) is understood in the OT covenantal sense, denoting the relationship of peace with God.[209]

Paul annunciates the same understanding of "peace" in Rom. 8:6: "the mindset of the Spirit is life and *peace* (εἰρήνη)." In the following verse he explicates the inverse situation of a relationship of "peace" with God, where the mindset of the flesh leads to enmity (ἔχθρα) with God. The use of διότι to introduce v. 7 ("*because* the mind of the flesh is enmity with God") has a causal force, explaining the content of v. 6 ("the mindset on the flesh is death").[210] In the LXX, the word ἐχθρός was used to describe the enemies of

---

[205] Rom. 14:2 ("even though one person's faith allows him to *eat* everything") cf. 14:17 ("For the kingdom of God is not *eating* and drinking"); see also M. Thompson, *Clothed with Christ: The Example and Teaching of Jesus in Romans 12.1–15.13* JSNTSup 59 (Sheffield: JSOT Press, 1991), p. 204; Moo, *The Epistle to the Romans*, p. 857; Barrett, *The Epistle to the Romans*, p. 243; Fee, *God's Empowering Presence*, p. 495, footnote 63.

[206] The referent of the words, γὰρ ἐν τούτῳ in Rom. 14:18 includes all of verse 17 (Fitzmyer, *Romans*, p. 697; Schreiner, *Romans*, p. 741), where the use of γάρ indicates a "marker of clarification" (BDAG, p. 189).

[207] Cf. 2 Cor. 5:9–10, where Paul understands the concept of εὐάρεστος within the context of relationship with God before the judgment seat of Christ (see Stuhlmacher, *Paul's Letter to the Romans*, p. 228).

[208] Schreiner, *Romans*, p. 741.

[209] The comments of Dunn on Rom. 5:1 ring true: "It is important to remember the extent to which, in Jewish thought, God-given peace was bound up with the covenant" (*Romans 1–8*, p. 247).

[210] "Marker used to indicate why something just stated can reasonably be considered valid" (BDAG, p. 251).

God, in particular, those who were considered ungodly and did not observe the Law.[211] For example, in Ps. 36:20, the psalmist writes, "For the sinners will perish; and *the enemies of the Lord* (οἱ ἐχθροὶ τοῦ Κυρίου) at the moment of their being honoured and exalted have utterly vanished like smoke." The "enemy of the Lord" in this psalm is also described as the one who performs "unlawful deeds" (ποιοῦντι παρανομίας) and is contrasted with "the righteous" (δίκαιος, vv. 12, 16, 17, 25, 29, 31, 32, 39) who has "the Law of God" (ὁ νόμος τοῦ θεοῦ) in his heart (v. 31).[212] This equates precisely with the thought of Rom. 8:7, where it is stated that "enmity against God" is the result of those who live according to the flesh and do not observe the Law[213] ("the mindset on the flesh...does not submit to the Law of God"). This demonstrates that Paul perceives the concept of "peace" here in Rom. 8:6 in a covenantal sense, as a favourable relationship with God.[214]

5. "Sons/Children of God": The Status of Covenant Faithfulness

In the LXX, υἱός, τέκνον, and παιδίον usually translate the Hebrew word בֵּן in the MT.[215] In most occurrences בֵּן is a patronymic term[216] used to denote

---

[211] W. Foerster, "ἐχθρός, ἔχθρα," *TDNT* Vol. II, pp. 811–15, esp. p. 812.

[212] See also Isa. 63:10, where it is said that the disobedience of Israel resulted in making God her *enemy* (ἐστράφη αὐτοῖς εἰς ἔχθραν).

[213] Moo's suggestion that νόμος in Rom. 8:7 depicts the "demand of God" (*The Epistle to the Romans*, p. 488) does not hold much conviction since it is clear that Paul's thought here is intentionally patterned upon his discussion in 7:14-25, particularly the idea that those who are fleshly are sold under sin (7:14) and do not obey the Mosaic Law.

[214] "Friendship with God" (Fitzmyer, *Romans*, p. 489); "To be determined by that which is God and not oneself means life and peace, not only as subjective experiences but *as objective relationship with God* (emphasis added)" (Barrett, *The Epistle to the Romans*, p. 148); "the objective reality of the salvation into which the believer, 'who has the mind of the Spirit,' has entered" (Moo, *The Epistle to the Romans*, p. 488); *contra* Foerster, who states, "He is not thinking in terms either of a harmonious disposition of soul or *of peace with God* (emphasis added)" ("εἰρήνη, κτλ.," p. 414).

[215] The only exceptions where υἱός is used for other Hebrew words are: 14 times each for אִישׁ and בַּיִת, 4 times for יֶלֶד or וָלָד, once each for זֶרַע and מִשְׁפָּחָה, and once each for 6 names of origin ending in "i" (P. Wülfing von Martitz, G. Fohrer, E. Schweizer, E. Lohse, W. Schneemelcher, "υἱός, υἱοθεσία," *TDNT* Vol. VIII, pp. 334–399, esp. p. 353).

[216] There is a widespread practice of appending appositionally to a male's name, the name of his father: e.g., "Ishmael, son of Abraham" (Gen. 25:12).

the status of an individual in the organic context of one's family; e.g., used in the genealogies (cf. "the sons of Abraham" [בְּנֵי אַבְרָהָם, Gen. 10:1-32]; "the sons of Jacob" [בְּנֵי יַעֲקֹב, Gen. 46:19]). But often the term is used to express formal relationship to a member of society, group, or fellowship.[217] The father-son relation is used to describe the relation of Yahweh to Israel or the Israelites. For example, Yahweh speaks of Israel as his firstborn son whom he has given a special place among the nations.[218] Yahweh is similarly called the Father of Israel[219] and addressed as "our Father."[220] It is a natural consequence that the idea of "sonship" denotes the status of Israel's covenant relationship with Yahweh. The Israelites are considered "sons of the covenant" (בְּנֵי בְרִית) and are distinguished as such from all Gentiles (cf. 1QM XVII,8 ["sons of his [God's] covenant"]).[221] The psalmist addresses Israel with the designation, "the children of the covenant" (*Pss. Sol.* 17:15), emphasizing her unique status. In 2 Sam. 7:14, Yahweh's promise, "I will be a father for him and he will be a son for me," applies to the anointed son of David. In Ps. 88:20-38 (LXX) this promise is presented as an eternally valid covenant arrangement ("and *my covenant* [ἡ διαθήκη μου] will be firm with him" [v. 29]), which cannot be broken by God. Since Israel is also called Yahweh's son in Exod. 4:22f; Hos. 11:1; Jer. 31:9, 20, the covenant which holds true for David's household is applied to all of Israel in Isa. 55:3 ("I will make with you *an everlasting covenant, the sure mercies of David*") and subsequently in Second Temple Judaism. For example, in *Jub.* 1, both the Mosaic[222] and Davidic covenants are amalgamated and applied to Israel, where Yahweh communicates the intimate relationship he will have with Israel: "And I shall be a father to them, and they will be sons

---

[217] Fohrer, "υἱός, υἱοθεσία," pp. 342, 345-6.

[218] Exod. 4:22; Jer. 31:9.

[219] Deut. 32:6, 18; Jer. 3:4.

[220] Isa. 63:16; 64:8; Mal. 2:10.

[221] Str-B, II, pp. 627ff.

[222] Cf. The Lord spoke to Moses, "Set your mind on every thing which I shall tell you on this mountain, and write it in a book so that their descendants might see that I have not abandoned them on account of all of the evil which they have done to instigate transgression *of the covenant* which I am establishing between me and you today on Mount Sinai for their descendants" (*Jub.* 1:5).

to me.[223] And they will be called 'sons of the living God'...they are my sons and I am their father" (v. 25).[224]

As good children, the people of Israel will naturally be submissive and obedient to Yahweh, their Father. For example, in Deut. 14:1ff, Yahweh stipulates some of the cultic, dietary, and behavioural requirements that are an expression of their status as "sons of Yahweh."[225] In Hos. 1 the Israelites are described as God's sons or children ("sons of the living God" [1:10][226]) and were marked out by a particular code of conduct. Israel's sonship is grounded in the Torah and demonstrates its faithfulness to this relationship when it obeys the Torah.[227] For example, in *Test. Jud.* 24:3, we read how Judah predicts the arrival of a sinless, eschatological king who will pour out the spirit of grace upon his sons, which will have a profound effect upon his children: "you will be his (God's) sons in truth and walk in his commandments."[228] This idea is further emphasized in Rabbinic literature. In a homiletic midrash on Deut. 29:1 which begins a discussion on Israel's covenant obligations, it reads, "You have the wish to be signaled out, that you are my sons? Busy yourselves with the Torah and observance of the commandments, so all will see that you are my sons."[229]

In our previous analysis of Rom. 8:14-16, we concluded that for Paul, the Spirit conferred the status of sonship. This was not contingent upon observing the Law whatsoever. However, his association between the Spirit and sonship is strikingly similar to Judaism's designation of the people of Israel and their covenantal status as "sons/children of God." This becomes particularly evident in Paul's understanding of Christian obedience. In Rom. 8:14, he writes, "For all who are being led by the Spirit of God, these are the sons of God." The passive form ἄγονται signifies "being controlled/ determined by/ governed by" the Spirit. This suggests that the Spirit is the primary agent in Christian ethics. Furthermore, the words "these are the sons of God" indicate that this is a distinguishing sign of being "sons of God." Correspondingly,

---

[223] Cf. "I will be his father, and he will be my son" (2 Sam. 7:14).

[224] "The promises of Ps. 2:7 and 2 S. 7:14 are applied to the whole people in *Jub.* 1:24f." (Lohse, "υἱός, υἱοθεσία," p. 359).

[225] See also Deut. 32:6, 18; Isa. 1:2; 30:1, 9; 45:9-11; 64:7.

[226] Paul indicates his knowledge of Hos. 1:10 when he quotes it in Rom. 9:26.

[227] Lohse, "υἱός, υἱοθεσία," pp. 359-40; Vermes, *Jesus the Jew*, p. 195.

[228] Cf. Philo's statement that not every Israelite is considered God's son but only the doer of the Law (*Spec. Leg.* I, 318; *Quaest. in Gn.* I, 92).

[229] *Deut. Rab* 7 on Deut. 29:1; cf. Str-B, I, pp. 17-19, 220

Paul appears to equate the Jewish understanding of the Israelites as sons/children of God,[230] whose lives were marked by faithfulness to the covenant, with believers as sons/children of God, whose lives were distinguished by faithfulness to their relationship with God by yielding to the inward impulses of the Spirit. He has intentionally re-oriented the status of sonship depicting covenantal faithfulness around the role of the Spirit conferring the status of sonship upon believers.[231]

6. Conclusion

In Rom. 8:1-16, even though Paul communicates his conviction that the Spirit has replaced the Law as the principle of new life, he nevertheless goes to great lengths to show how the Spirit's role in the present era is analogous to that of the Law; i.e., he demonstrates the Spirit's association with the constituent elements of covenantal nomism. He has intentionally chosen to re-orient covenantal concepts around the Spirit in the new epoch. Therefore, it can be said that Paul's Jewish past and his Christian present intersect in a significant and positive manner. We can depict this phenomenon in the following diagram:

---

[230] "The notion of human beings as 'children of God' is not simply an apt image plucked out of Paul's imagination at this point (Rom. 8:14). It is part of the technical language in which the Jewish apocalyptic tradition expressed its hopes for the future...it came to be associated particularly with the eschatological Israel, God's people destined to 'inherit' the promises of salvation" (Byrne, *Romans*, pp. 248-49; see also Byrne, *"Sons of God"-"Seed of Abraham"*, pp. 9-70, 98).

[231] "The divine sonship of individuals is determined by the Spirit of God, the power of God as understood within Jewish tradition, now experienced in eschatological outpouring, but defined in terms of the *Spirit*; not in terms of the law or of faithfulness to the law" (Dunn, *Romans 1-8*, p. 451); "The source for the term υἱοί should be located in the OT and other Jewish literature, for Israel is quite frequently identified in both the singular and plural as God's son" (Schreiner, *Romans*, p. 423); Scott claims Rom. 8:15 is influenced by the 2 Sam. 7:14 tradition in connection with Ezek. 36:26-28 and the idea of divine adoption (*Adoption as Sons of God*, pp. 263-63); see also Stuhlmacher's comments on the influence of Jewish traditions on Rom. 8:12-17 (*Paul's Letter to the Romans*, p. 129).

Union With Christ:
Severance From Law

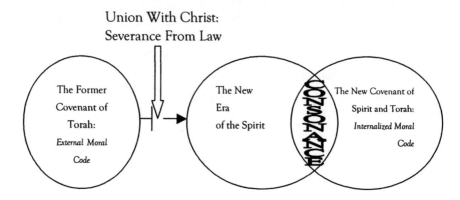

Diagram 3
The New Era of the Spirit: Consonance with Covenantal Nomism

In Diagram 2 (Part Two) we illustrated how Paul perceived a decisive point of discontinuity and dissonance between covenantal nomism in Judaism and the new era of the Spirit, where the Spirit displaces the Law and functions exclusively as the principle of new life. The central feature of Judaism's new covenant expectation was the idea that the Spirit would empower individuals to obey the Torah (e.g., Ezek. 36:25-37:14; Jer. 31:31-34 cf. *Jub.* 1:23-24). However, Paul makes an unprecedented break with covenantal nomism. He advocates that the eschatological Spirit makes Law observance obsolete: "But now we have been discharged from the Law...to serve in newness of the Spirit not in oldness of the letter" (Rom. 7:6); "For the law of the Spirit of life in Christ Jesus has set you free from the law of sin and death" (8:2). Paul claims that the Spirit alone achieves life (8:2, 6, 10, 13). At the same time, in this section of our investigation we discovered that Paul perceived a sense of consonance between the roles of the Spirit and covenantal nomism (i.e., new covenant expectation). Paul explicates the Spirit's role using covenantal concepts that were previously associated with the Law ("the law of the Spirit" [8:2]; "the Law may be fulfilled ...according to the Spirit" [8:4]; "the Spirit is life because of righteousness" [8:10]; the Spirit and life [8:2, 6, 10, 13]; the Spirit and "peace" with God [8:6]; the Spirit and familial relationship [8:14-16]). This serves to align the Spirit positively with the Law and communicates a sense of continuity between them. As a result, the dissonance between the Spirit and Law is softened and the break with covenantal nomism is masked.

This is represented by the space labeled "CONSONANCE" in Diagram 3 above.

In the following chapter we will utilize Cognitive Dissonance Theory to elucidate and provide an understanding of this phenomenon. We will propose that in Rom. 8:1-16, Paul engaged in a concentrated effort to assuage the tensions between his native Jewish convictions on the Law and his present convictions on the Spirit by employing the language of covenantal nomism. He demonstrates cognitive overlap between the Spirit and the Law, and through this, also hopes to achieve social validation for his cognitions within his own social group of Roman believers, with whom he identified and had a sense of affinity.

CHAPTER SEVEN

Cognitive Dissonance and the Quest for Consonance

1. A Definition of Cognitive Dissonance Theory

Cognitive Dissonance Theory is based on the assumption that individuals who encounter contradictions in their lives strive towards consistency, harmony, and equilibrium between cognitions.[1] For example, if a father believes that a college education is important (cognition 1) he will very likely encourage his children to go to college. However, he may discover that his daughter does not want to go to college but wants to pursue an acting career in Hollywood right after high school. His daughter points out that her father has always said that it was important for them to make their own decisions (cognition 2). Consequently, the father encounters inconsistency between these two cognitions. Individuals who encounter such circumstances exhibit predictable behavioural patterns; i.e., they attempt to reconcile these inconsistencies. There are also many scenarios where persons may not always be successful in explaining away or in rationalizing inconsistencies to themselves and attempts to achieve consistency may fail. Leon Festinger's Cognitive Dissonance Theory addresses the behaviour of individuals encountering persistent inconsistencies in their lives. In place of the concept of "inconsistency," he uses the term "dissonance" and in place of "consistency" he uses the term "consonance."[2]

---

[1] Social scientists are aware of exceptions to this rule, where individuals do not always seek to reconcile discrepancies or resolve conflicts and tensions. Many belief systems do not require consistency (Snow and Machalek, "On the Presumed Fragility of Unconventional Beliefs," 22–23). There is also the possibility that conflicts and tension may be ubiquitous and can be counteracted by more powerful drives such as learning potential and experience (Aronson, "Dissonance Theory: Progress and Problems" in *Theories of Cognitive Consistency*, p. 26).

[2] Festinger, A *Theory of Cognitive Dissonance*, pp. 1–3.

The term "cognition" (or "cognitive element") is used loosely, referring to knowledge, opinion, belief about the environment, about oneself, or about one's behaviour.[3] Thus, Cognitive Dissonance Theory serves as a heuristic tool in order to comprehend the behavioural patterns of individuals when they encounter inconsistency between two cognitions.

In particular, Festinger's formulation of cognitive dissonance relates to explaining problems in post-decisional conflict and circumstances; i.e., when individuals have made firm commitments to beliefs ("cognitions") but find that the expectations associated with these beliefs are inconsistent with reality and experience.[4] This is to be distinguished from theories explaining conflicts and dilemmas faced when first encountering commitments to be made between alternatives. Cognitive Dissonance Theory is concerned with the relationship between expectation and experience. The new cognitions formed in the experiences of life will exert pressure in the direction of bringing the appropriate cognition into correspondence with that reality. Cognitions formed by what one experiences daily are an unequivocal reality for which the possibilities of change are virtually impossible.[5] If a commitment to a certain belief is inconsistent with reality and experience, this gives rise to the experience of cognitive dissonance and the need to reduce it. Festinger proposes that individuals faced with such circumstances exhibit a drive to bring all cognitions into a consistent relationship with one another, that is, there is a drive that seeks to resolve dissonance and restore a sense of equilibrium: "Cognitive dissonance can be seen as an antecedent condition which leads to activity oriented toward dissonance reduction."[6] This disequilibrium motivates a person to reduce or eliminate the perceived dissonance and achieve more consistency ("consonance").[7]

There are at least three possible types of relationship between different cognitions: 1. they may be *irrelevant* and be cognitively neutral in relationship to one another, 2. they may be *relevant* and *consonant* with each other, where they function harmoniously together, or 3. they may be *relevant* and *dissonant*

---

[3] *Ibid.*, pp. 3, 9–11.

[4] Festinger makes it clear that his theory involves "the consequences of decisions": "One of the major *consequences of having made a decision* (emphasis added) is the existence of dissonance" (*Ibid.*, quote taken from p. 32 but see pp. 32–47 inclusive).

[5] *Ibid.*, pp. 10–11; see also Wicklund and Brehm, *Perspectives on Cognitive Dissonance*, p. 125.

[6] Festinger, *A Theory of Cognitive Dissonance*, p. 3.

[7] Jack W. Brehm and Arthur R. Cohen, *Explorations in Cognitive Dissonance* (New York: John Wiley and Sons, Inc., 1962), pp. 11–17.

with each other, where they do not fit together, in which case they may be inconsistent or contradictory and the culture or group values dictate that they do not fit. Regarding the third type of relationship, Festinger further defines it as follows: "two elements (cognitions) are in a dissonant relation if, considering these two alone, the obverse of one element would follow from the other."[8] To put it in more formal terms x and y are dissonant if not-x follows from y.[9] Cognitive Dissonance Theory deals with cognitively relevant, dissonant relationships.

There are different degrees of dissonance. The more important the decision that has been made, the stronger will be the dissonance. The magnitude of the dissonance will depend upon the importance and function of the two cognitions to the individual. The more value the cognitions have for a person, the greater the magnitude of dissonance.[10] The central feature in Festinger's theory is the claim that "the presence of dissonance gives rise to pressure to reduce and eliminate the dissonance. The strength of the pressure to reduce the dissonance is a function of the magnitude of the dissonance."[11] Therefore, the greater the magnitude of dissonance, the greater the motivation to reduce it. However, there are limits to the magnitude of dissonance: "the maximum dissonance that can possibly exist between any two elements (cognitions) is equal to the total resistance to change of the less resistant element (cognition)."[12] The magnitude of dissonance cannot exceed this amount because the less resistant cognition would change and consequently eliminate the dissonance.

As we stated above, the existence of dissonance will give rise to pressures to reduce it. Post-decisional dissonance can be reduced in three main ways: 1. changing or revoking the decision made, 2. changing the attractiveness of the alternatives involved in the choice, or 3. establishing cognitive overlap among

---

[8] Festinger, A *Theory of Cognitive Dissonance*, p. 13.

[9] Non-fitting relationships (inconsistencies) that have the potential to lead to a dissonant relationship can be of different types. Festinger lists four: 1. dissonance could arise from logical inconsistencies, 2. dissonance could arise because of cultural mores, where the culture defines what is consonant and what is not, 3. dissonance may arise because one specific opinion is sometimes included, by definition, in a more general opinion, 4. dissonance may arise because current experience does not coincide with past experience (A *Theory of Cognitive Dissonance*, p. 14).

[10] *Ibid.*, p. 37.

[11] *Ibid.*, p. 18.

[12] *Ibid.*, p. 28.

the dissonant cognitions.[13] An individual could simply change her decision and admit that she made the wrong choice or deny that a responsible decision was made in the first place. However, the case often arises where one's decision was well thought out and intentional and is now very resistant to change. If one's beliefs are such that they are both reasonable and self-evident then change will be very difficult. If change involves pain and loss and the current behaviour gives meaning to life there will be little incentive to change. Many times the choices are irrevocable, e.g., having a baby or purchasing an automobile. In these cases 2 or 3 are the most likely course of action.

The most common manner of reducing post-decision dissonance is to alter the perception of some of the cognitive elements associated with the alternate choice. This can be accomplished by reducing the favourable cognitive elements of the *unchosen* alternative and adding new ones that are consonant with the cognitions of the *chosen* one. For example, if a contract has been signed to build a new home with Builder A instead of Builder B, and in the process of building the home there are disagreements over the quality of construction between Builder A and the homeowner, the homeowner may experience post-decisional dissonance with his choice of Builder A over Builder B. In order to reduce this dissonance he may reason that the better quality of construction Builder B could have given him would have incurred an unaffordable expense (eliminating favourable cognitive elements of the unchosen alternative). Furthermore, the homeowner might seek evidence that the quality of construction Builder A brings to the home exceeds the quality required in the buildings codes and is in fact affirmed by other reputable builders in the area (adding new cognitive elements consonant with the decision made).

Another manner of reducing the magnitude of dissonance is by establishing or inventing cognitive overlap. This involves adding new cognitive elements that are in consonant relationship with the opposing cognition; e.g., noticing similar characteristics, having the same desired result or achieving the same goal.[14] Taking the above example further, if the homeowner learns that Builder A uses the same tradesmen to build the home as Builder B and

---

[13] *Ibid.*, pp. 42–47.

[14] "The more the cognitive elements corresponding to the different alternatives involved in a decision are alike, the less is the resulting dissonance...one way of establishing cognitive overlap is to take elements corresponding to each of the alternatives and [to] put them in a context where they lead to the same end result" (*Ibid.*, pp. 45–46).

similarly purchases identical building supplies from the same vendors, he could reason that Builder A's construction of his home would be comparable to the home that Builder B would have constructed (similar characteristics, achieving the same goal). It is important to indicate that the locus of the dissonance between alternatives is between the unfavourable cognitive elements of the choice made and the corresponding favourable cognitive elements of the unchosen alternative. Thus, the greater the cognitive overlap between the corresponding cognitive elements of the two alternatives, the less the qualitative distinction between them and consequently, the less dissonance that would exist after the choice has been made.[15]

Thus far we have limited our discussion regarding the reduction of post-decisional dissonance to explanatory schemes but we have not addressed the role of the social group. Festinger's theory properly belongs to the field of study called social psychology, which attempts to ascertain behavioural patterns within a given social setting.[16] Humans are social beings whose needs and desires can only be satisfied in community with other people. We know persons by the society or the company we keep: "Human behaviour, social scientists inform us, follows paths marked off by the major structures of the society in which persons have been socialized...there is a close relationship among values, self-interests, and social structures."[17]

The social group is the pivot of one's response to dissonance in that it can be either a major cause of cognitive dissonance for the individual or a major vehicle for eliminating and reducing the dissonance that may exist in her. This means that the processes of social interaction are inextricably woven with the processes of the creation and reduction of dissonance.[18] The existence of disagreement among members of a group regarding a belief produces a certain degree of cognitive dissonance. The larger the number of people that one knows who disagree with a given belief which one holds, the greater will be the

---

[15] *Ibid.*, p. 41.

[16] Festinger dedicates a whole chapter to the function of social support and its relationship to Cognitive Dissonance Theory ("The Role of Social Support: Theory" [Chapter 8], *Ibid.*, pp. 177-202); "Dissonance theory...suggests that man is a rationalizing animal—that he attempts to appear rational, *both to others and himself* (emphasis added)" (R.P. Abelson, *et al.*, *Theories of Cognitive Consistency: A Sourcebook* [Chicago: Rand McNally, 1968], p. 6).

[17] Malina and Neyrey, *Portraits of Paul*, p. 10.

[18] Festinger, *A Theory of Cognitive Dissonance*, p. 177.

magnitude of dissonance.[19] Inversely, the major method of reducing dissonance within the group setting is by achieving social support for one's beliefs and influencing people to change their opinion to agree with one's own belief[20]:

> Another way of reducing the dissonance would be to influence those persons who disagree to change their opinion so that it more closely corresponds to one's own. This is, of course, analogous to changing the environment and thereby changing the cognitive elements reflecting that environment.[21]

In this process one achieves social validation for one's beliefs. The logical corollary is that if a large number of people share these beliefs there must be something right or influential about them.[22] This is clearly evident in religious and political systems. For example, large-scale proselytizing could undoubtedly render dissonance negligible, where an individual finds himself in a group whose cognitive holdings constitute a dissonance-free environment.

We can be more specific on the dynamics of how dissonance is reduced in a group setting. If an individual experiences dissonance, she will naturally communicate with those who share similar cognitions. She might attempt to obtain knowledge that others agree with her opinion, consequently adding new consonant cognitive elements.[23] For example, if there is a situation where a person has recently purchased a new convertible and she then discovers that mechanical problems with the automatic top are common with this vehicle, this individual may experience qualms about having bought it (cognitive dissonance). One would expect her to communicate with someone she knows who owns a similar convertible and gather some new information affirming that there have been significant improvements made to the mechanisms that manoeuvre the tops of convertibles. However, if she is not successful in obtaining social support, dissonance may persist and even be increased. This individual may then engage in a social influence process. For example, she may

---

[19] Festinger lists other variables that impact the degree of dissonance one experiences in the group dynamic. For example, the extent that the evidence to support one's cognition is objective and verifiable, the relevance or importance of the disagreeing individual to the group in which the disagreement is voiced, the extent of the disagreement itself (complete disagreement or qualified disagreement) (*Ibid.*, pp. 178–81).

[20] See especially *Ibid.*, pp. 189, 191.

[21] *Ibid.*, p. 182.

[22] Festinger, Riecken and Schachter, *When Prophecy Fails*, p. 28.

[23] Festinger, *A Theory of Cognitive Dissonance*, p. 189.

encounter some friends who claim the automobile she just purchased was mechanically flawed and subsequently begin to persuade her friends that the model she purchased is equipped with a new and improved mechanical device that guarantees breakdown will never occur. If she achieves social support for her cognitions the dissonance will be materially reduced.

Social support is particularly easy to obtain when a large number of people in the group are found to be in the same situation, where they all come to recognize that they share common experiences and find themselves in similar circumstances; i.e., the possibility of dissonance is evident and the potential to reduce it in the same manner exists for all the members.[24] New and incontrovertible information gained by these experiences in life may be dissonant with a very widely held belief. If this circumstance arises, there will be a large number of people having almost the same type of cognitive dissonance and the possibility of social support would be increased. For example, members of the religious group who believed that the year 2000 C.E. would usher in the millennium would most likely experience uniform cognitive dissonance when the year proved to be uneventful.[25]

Having outlined the core components of Cognitive Dissonance Theory, we will now use it as an explanatory mechanism to explicate the apparent tension between the Spirit and Law in Rom. 8:1–16 and the broader issue of the tension between Paul's Jewish past as a covenantal nomist and his understanding of participatory union with Christ and the role of the Spirit in his Christian present.

2. Paul's Commitment to Judaism: Zealot for the Jewish Law

Festinger's theory stresses the importance of commitment as a necessary condition for the arousal of dissonance.[26] Commitment to a set of cognitions

---

[24] Ibid., pp. 192–96.

[25] Carroll addresses a similar situation in his monograph (When Prophecy Failed, pp. 111ff.). The focus of his analysis is on the predictions set up by the prophetic traditions of the OT and the community's reaction and explanations necessary for its survival in light of disconfirming information.

[26] One of the distinctive features of Cognitive Dissonance Theory is that it explains problems arising in post-decisional conflict and circumstances (see above); see also Brehm and Cohen, Explorations in Cognitive Dissonance, esp. pp. 7–11.

facilitates the specification of what is consonant and what is dissonant. The level of commitment will also indicate the potential magnitude of dissonance. When a high level of commitment is made to a set of cognitions that is important and valued and an individual perceives cognitions that are dissonant with this commitment, there will be a high magnitude of dissonance. If the previous commitment is irrevocable or there is the threat of serious repercussions if the commitment is revoked, dissonance cannot be eliminated. In this case, there will be the motivation to reduce the dissonance.[27] This means that in order to make this theory applicable to the dynamics of Rom. 8:1-16 we will have to isolate precisely the level of Paul's previous commitment to covenantal nomism when he wrote this part of his correspondence to the Roman believers.

It is important to note at the outset of this section that when Paul wrote his epistle to the Romans he was still very much imbedded in a Jewish frame of thinking. Most New Testament scholars recognize that it is inappropriate to speak of Paul as having experienced a "conversion" at Damascus. Paul did not change religions but experienced a "calling," an assignment to a new task.[28] "Christianity" was not a new religion in Paul's time but was rather a sect within Judaism. Generally speaking, this means that his Jewish identity and his continuing commitment to the constituent elements of Judaism remain intact.

---

[27] Festinger, A Theory of Cognitive Dissonance, p. 16.

[28] This was the specific contribution of K. Stendahl (Paul Among the Jews and Gentiles and Other Essays, pp. 7-23); Paul understands the Damascus experience "as the commission to proclaim the gospel, that is, to serve Christ among the Gentiles" (Beker, Paul the Apostle, p. 6); Beverly Gaventa claims the term "call" does not sufficiently encompass Paul's recognition of Jesus as Messiah or his radical change in values. She prefers the term "transformation," that is, Paul had a transformed understanding of God and God's action in the world (From Darkness to Light: Aspects of Conversion in the New Testament [Philadelphia: Fortress Press, 1986], p. 40). However, Alan F. Segal offers a cautionary note. Even though Paul's language invokes the concept of prophetic commissioning, his commissioning clearly presents a religious conversion; i.e., Paul did not follow the norms of those who came from Judaism and who became involved in the early Christian movement. His authority is not derived through ordinary apostolic traditions but was said to come by a direct and ecstatic revelation of Christ. Paul's message was controversial even to the early Christianity movement (e.g., his message of a Torahless Christianity). Segal states, "He (Paul) is no Pharisee whose faith in Christ confirms his Judaism; rather, his conversion makes a palpable difference in his Christianity" (Paul the Convert: The Apostolate and Apostasy of Saul the Pharisee [New Haven: Yale University Press, 1990], quote from p. 71, but see also pp. 34-71 inclusive).

Paul still speaks positively of his current Jewish pedigree: "*I am*[29] an Israelite, of the seed of Abraham, of the tribe of Benjamin" (Rom. 11:1). Thus, there is a sense in which Paul identified with Judaism even after his Damascus experience. He did not automatically replace one set of Jewish cognitions for a new set of Christian ones, severing all former ties with his Jewish past. Indeed, this would be an erroneous characterization of Paul and one that he would vigorously oppose. Paul's continued commitment to the constituent elements of Judaism means that Cognitive Dissonance Theory is appropriate for our analysis of Rom. 8. The applicability of the theory depends upon whether one can demonstrate that an individual is simultaneously holding on to two opposing sets of cognitions and the newly acquired cognitions are in tension with the social group with whom one identifies.[30] In this case, Paul is simultaneously clinging to the convictions related to his Jewish past and the new convictions formed in the present as a believer in whom the Spirit resides.

More specific to our concern in this section is Paul's self-description of his pre-Damascus commitment to the Jewish Law. Sociological analyses indicate that those who have experienced dramatic cognitive shifts in their religious convictions tend to construe both their former life and the moment when the shift occurred using the norms and expectations of their current self-understanding and convictions. This means that autobiographical information about one's former beliefs and experience cannot provide accurate information about the past.[31] However, while it is generally true that there is a tendency to reconstruct the past on the basis of a present new self-understanding in such circumstances, much of Paul's descriptions of his former beliefs and lifestyle were public knowledge, information that could well be confirmed by others. For example, in Gal. 1:13 Paul writes, "*You have heard*

---

[29] Paul uses the present tense verb εἰμί here in Rom. 11:1 to describe his *current* claim to the covenant name of his people ("Paul speaks from within 'Israel'" [Dunn, *Romans 9–16*, p. 635]); "*As a Jew who still identified with his people* (emphasis added), he could hardly countenance God's abandonment of Israel...He probably mentions his tribal ancestry simply to reinforce his *Jewishness* (emphasis added)" (Moo, *The Epistle to the Romans*, p. 673).

[30] Festinger plainly states that dissonance may be reduced or even eliminated completely by changing one's own opinion so that it corresponds more closely with one's knowledge of what others believe (*A Theory of Cognitive Dissonance*, p. 182).

[31] "Paul's rejection of the things that he once regarded as important stems from his conversion...Paul's own convictions are again called into question" (Gaventa, *From Darkness to Light*, p. 39); see also Paula Fredriksen, "Paul and Augustine: Conversion Narratives, Orthodox Traditions and the Retrospective Self," *JTS* 37 (1986), 3–34.

of my former manner of life in Judaism." Others were circulating disparaging reports insinuating that Paul was a doubtful character who could not be fully trusted[32] (cf. v. 20, "I assure you before God that what I am writing you is no lie"; v. 23, "They only heard the report; 'the one who formerly persecuted us is now preaching the faith he once tried to destroy'"[33]). In this situation Paul is appealing to widespread information provided by individuals who were highly suspicious of him and were attempting to get at the truth. Furthermore, Paul's self-description includes his association with very public and familiar groups such as the Pharisees (Phil. 3:5) and well-established religious tendencies such as zeal and zealotry (Phil. 3:6). The interpretations of the characteristics of these groups are subjected to the constraints imposed by the historical circumstances of the first-century world.[34] Therefore, despite the tendency of individuals who experience dramatic cognitive shifts to misconstrue the facts of the past, much of the information Paul conveys in description of his pre-Damascus associations and convictions can be verified by other pieces of historical documentation.

In Gal. 1:14 Paul describes his former life in Judaism by presenting himself as one who is "to the extreme, a zealot (περισσοτέρως ζηλωτής) for the traditions of my fathers." He repeats the same idea in Phil. 3:6: "By way of zeal (κατὰ ζῆλος), persecuting the church." The words ζηλωτής and ζῆλος generally refer to "one who is earnestly committed to a side or cause" and one who has "an intense positive interest in something,"[35] but also includes a sense of both "jealousy" and "zeal."[36] The LXX uses ζηλωτής with the meaning of "jealous One" associated with God.[37] In the NT it can be used in a general sense of those who have an intense interest ("eagerness") for something: e.g., manifestations of the Spirit (1 Cor. 14:12), to perform good deeds (Tit. 2:14), for what is right (1 Pet. 3:13). It is also used in a restrictively Jewish sense for one who is "zealous" for the Torah and the traditions of Judaism: "They are all zealous for the Law (ζηλωταὶ τοῦ νόμου)" (Acts 21:20 cf. Gal. 1:14).[38]

---

[32] F.F. Bruce, *The Epistle to the Galatians*, p. 90.

[33] "Paul was evidently able to quote, or effectively summarize as a quotation what was said of him in the Judean churches during this period" (Dunn, *The Epistle to the Galatians*, p. 83).

[34] See A.E. Harvey, *Jesus and the Constraints of History* (Philadelphia: Westminster, 1982).

[35] BDAG, p. 427.

[36] Terence L. Donaldson, "Zealot," *ISBE* Vol. IV (Grand Rapids: Wm. B. Eerdmans Publishing Co., 1988), pp. 1175-79.

[37] "I am your Lord God, a *jealous* (ζηλωτής) God" (Exod. 20:5).

[38] See also Acts 22:3.

The designation "zealot" was the name taken by some who led the revolt against Rome (66-70 C.E.).[39] However, the term only referred to one of several rebel factions and there is no evidence of an actual organized Zealot party in the pre-war period.[40] The idea of zealotry most likely developed from OT prototypes. For example Phinehas gained a reputation for demonstrating zeal for the Torah with his violent opposition to Baal worship (Num. 25). He slew Zimri the Israelite for his sexual union with Cozbi the Midianite woman (vv. 6-13).[41] Phinehas' zeal was commemorated in future generations.[42] It is clear from this example that zealotry included a fervent commitment to the Torah and when individuals were contravening, opposing, or subverting the Law, a zealot was prepared to use violence against these individuals. Furthermore, zealots were willing to suffer and die for the sake of the Torah,[43] even to die at their own hand.[44] In the Maccabean revolt, Mattathias and his sons were said to possess zeal for the Law. Mattathias' rallying cry was, "*Whoever is zealous for the Law* (πᾶς ὁ ζηλῶν τῷ νόμῳ) and supports the covenant come out with me" (1 Macc. 2:27). Later on when he was at the point of death he urged his sons to "*be zealous for the Law* (ζηλώσατε τῷ νόμῳ) and *give your lives* for the covenant of our father" (2:50). Philo conveys the same attitude when he warns that "there are thousands, who are *zealots for the laws*, strictest guardians of the ancestral traditions, merciless to those who do anything to subvert them" (*Spec.* 2.253). The texts cited above illustrate that the idea of zealotry was widespread in Second Temple Judaism.[45]

This is precisely the attitude to which Paul refers, when he describes himself as being, "to the extreme, a zealot for the traditions of my fathers" in Gal. 1:14 (cf. Phil. 3:6). Paul uses the word περισσοτέρως, meaning "to a

---

[39] E. Schürer, *The History of the Jewish People in the Age of Jesus Christ*, 4 Volumes (ed. G. Vermes and F. Millar; Edinburgh: T & T Clark, 1973-87), see Vol. II, pp. 598-606.

[40] Donaldson, "Zealot," p. 1176.

[41] See also Elijah's zeal for the Torah when he slaughtered the prophets of Baal and Asherah, who had induced Israel to forsake the covenant (1 Ki. 19:10, 14 cf. Sir. 48:1f.); in Second Temple Judaism, Simeon and Levi's slaughter of the Shechemites in retaliation for the rape of their sister Dinah (Gen. 34) is understood as zeal in *Jub.* 30:18; *T. Levi* 6:3; Jdt. 9:2-4.

[42] See Sir. 45:23-24 ("Phinehas...had *zeal* [ζηλῶσαι] in the fear of the Lord," v. 23); 1 Macc. 2:26 ("And he *was zealous for the Law* [ἐζήλωσε τῷ νόμῳ] just as Phinehas did to Zimri son of Salmon").

[43] 2 Macc. 7:2; 8:21; 4 Macc. 18; Josephus, *Ant.* 18.51.

[44] 2 Macc. 14:37-46; Josephus, *J.W.* 7.320-401.

[45] See also 1QS IX, 23; *m. Sanh.* 9.6.

much greater degree, far more, far greater"[46] to emphasize the fact that he displayed zeal in a much greater degree than many of his Jewish contemporaries ("I progressed in Judaism beyond many contemporaries among those of my same age").[47] His zeal was for "the traditions of my fathers." F. Büchsel understands this as "Jewish tradition generally, both written and verbal"[48] but in this context it most likely has a more specific referent.[49] Paul makes a similar but more amplified claim in Phil. 3:5-6. Here he describes himself as a "Hebrew of Hebrews; as to the Law, a Pharisee; as to zeal, a persecutor of the church; as to the righteousness which is in the Law, faultless." In this context the idea of zeal is explicitly associated with the Pharisaical party to which Paul belonged and the traditions associated with this group.[50] The Pharisaic concern was to live in accord with and defend as necessary both the written and the oral Law (*halakhah*), which is drawn from the Torah. In Phil. 3:5, Paul defines his association with the Pharisaical party in a very specific manner, in relationship to the Law ("*as to the Law,* a Pharisee"). He identified himself with members of the Jewish sect who had given themselves wholly to the study of the Law and its codification. This coincides with the information about Paul provided in Acts: "instructed in accordance with the strictness *of the ancestral Law* (τοῦ πατρῴου νόμου), being a zealot (ζηλωτὴς) for God" (22:3).[51]

The magnitude of Paul's commitment to the Law in Phil. 3:5-6 is demonstrated tangibly in his unrelenting devotion to stamping out the Christian movement: "As for zeal, persecuting the church." His zeal for the Law is the point of emphasis in these two verses and the motivation for his persecution of the church. This is made plain by the structure of the verses (preposition + a reference to the Mosaic Law):

κατὰ   νόμον Φαρισαῖος
κατὰ   ζῆλος διώκων τὴν ἐκκλησίαν
κατὰ   δικαιοσύνην τὴν ἐν νόμῳ γενόμενος ἄμεμπτος

---

[46] BDAG, p. 806.

[47] "He (Paul) far surpassed his contemporaries in his zeal" (F. Hauck, "περισσεύω, κτλ.," *TDNT* Vol. VI, pp. 58-63, quote taken from p. 62).

[48] F. Büchsel, "παράδοσις," *TDNT* Vol. II, pp. 172-73.

[49] Fung, *The Epistle to the Galatians,* p. 57.

[50] H.F. Weiss, "Φαρισαῖος," *TDNT* Vol. IX, pp. 35-48, esp. p. 46.

[51] Cf. "Regulations which the Pharisees introduced in accordance with the ancestral tradition" (Josephus, *Ant.* 13.408); "the Pharisees had passed on to the people certain regulations handed down from the fathers" (Josephus, *Ant.* 13.297).

The phrases each make a statement about Paul's status (Pharisee) or achievement (persecuting the church/ being faultless). In the first and third phrases he explicitly states how the Law serves as the basis for these assertions. If the second phrase follows the same pattern, it indicates that when Paul mentions "zeal" (ζῆλος) he is referring to the zeal he had for the Law, just as his status as a Pharisee and his achievements were both mentioned in their association to the Law.[52] The final prepositional phrase brings these assertions to a climax: "as to righteousness in the Law, being faultless."[53] As far as Law observance is concerned Paul had no blemishes. This was no casual commitment. He scrupulously adhered to the Pharisaic interpretation of the Law to the point that he was prepared to do harm to those who contravened, opposed, or subverted the Law. The Law defined the very essence of Paul's existence. His persecution of the church was a tangible expression of his firm dedication to observe the Law.[54]

Even though after Paul's Damascus experience he no longer persecuted the Christian movement,[55] he nevertheless maintained a significant level of commitment to his Jewish roots, and in a qualified sense, to covenantal nomism as well. Our analysis in the previous section revealed that in Rom. 8 Paul intentionally demonstrated how the Spirit's role in the present era is analogous to that of the Law and that these statements reflected his personal convictions.[56] Rom. 8:4 ("in order that the righteous requirement of the Law may be fulfilled in us...who walk according to the Spirit") typifies his tendency to demonstrate how his convictions on the Spirit compared to his convictions

---

[52] Gordon D. Fee, *Paul's Letter to the Philippians* NICNT (Grand Rapids: William B. Eerdmans Publishing Co., 1995), pp. 305, 308 (footnote 17).

[53] ῎Αμεμπτος means "blameless, faultless" and can be associated with the Mosaic covenant (BDAG, p. 52).

[54] "There is a link between his (Paul's) passion to keep the law in an irreproachable way and the ardour with which he opposed primitive Christianity...One can see in his activity as persecutor the display and proof of his 'zeal'" (J. Dupont, "The Conversion of Paul and its Influence on His Understanding of Salvation by Faith," in *Apostolic History and the Gospel: Biblical and Historical Essays Presented to F.F. Bruce on his 60th Birthday* [ed. W.W. Gasque and R.P. Martin; Grand Rapids: Wm. B. Eerdmans Publishing Company, 1970], pp. 176-94, quote taken from p. 183); "This κατὰ ζῆλος in Phil. 3:6 is framed by two references to the law. It does not mean so much individual emotion as the concrete fact of 'zeal for the law'" (M. Hengel, *The Pre-Christian Paul* [London: SCM Press, 1991], p. 70).

[55] "But whatever was to my profit I now consider loss for the sake of Christ...I consider them refuse in order that I may gain Christ" (Phil. 3:7-8).

[56] See Chapter Six (The Spirit's Identification with Covenantal Nomism).

on the Mosaic Law, even from the current perspective of his relationship to Christ. This indicates that Paul's ties with Judaism and covenantal nomism were not completely severed and there still existed a substantial level of commitment to the Mosaic Law in his post-Damascus frame of thinking.

3. A State of Dissonance Between Judaism's Covenantal Nomism and Paul

As we noted above, Paul still considers himself embedded in the thinking of both Ancient and Second Temple Judaism. He currently believes he is a member of Israel, with generational ties to both Abraham and the tribe of Benjamin.[57] His persistent positive references throughout his letters to categories characteristic of covenantal nomism[58] are certain signs that he is significantly influenced by Jewish traditions. In Part One[59] of our study we concluded that the literature of Ancient and Second Temple Judaism identified the Spirit as the agent of covenant renewal whose specific function was to establish a Torah-based ethic. In particular, Judaism looked forward to the implementation of a new covenant, where the Spirit would enable individuals to keep the Law fully. Paul himself was knowledgeable of this scriptural tradition and alludes to it in Gal. 4:23–29,[60] Rom. 2:29,[61] 7:6,[62] and more directly in 2 Cor. 3:1–18.[63] There are signs that Paul's discussion in

---

[57] See Rom. 11:1.

[58] For example, Paul affirms covenantal nomism in the following passages: the Law is said to be an advantage of the Jews in that they have "been entrusted with the very words of God" (Rom. 3:2 cf. 9:4); "faith does not nullify the Law" rather, it "establishes or upholds it" (Rom. 3:31); "the Law has become our tutor to lead us to Christ"(Gal. 3:24); "Is the Law sin? May it never be"(Rom. 7:7); "the Law is holy, and the commandment is holy and righteous and good"(Rom. 7:12); "did that which is good (Law) become death for me? May it never be"(Rom. 7:13).

[59] Part One (Pauline Antecedents: Spirit and Law in Ethical Renewal and Jewish Eschatology); see also the Conclusion in Part Two (The Spirit Displaces the Law as the Principle of New Life: Romans 7–8).

[60] The mention of "two covenants" in Gal. 4:24 and its association with v. 29 ("according to the Spirit") alludes to the new-covenant promise of Jeremiah read in conjunction with Ezekiel.

[61] Rom. 2:29 combines the idea of "circumcised hearts" with the "Spirit" and thus recalls Deut. 30:6 and the promise of the new covenant.

[62] In Rom. 7:6, "newness of Spirit/ oldness of letter," implies the old and new covenants.

[63] Paul's argument in 2 Cor. 3 corresponds to Jeremiah in that it associates the idea of writing on "hearts" (v.3) with the distinctive phrase "new covenant" (v. 6), which is combined only in

Rom. 8:1–16 is most likely conditioned by this Jewish scriptural tradition. For example, these verses explicate the Spirit's relationship to the Law in the context of eschatology, where Paul attempts to align their respective roles ("the righteous requirement of the Law may be fulfilled in us...who walk...according to the Spirit" [8:4]). In addition, Paul's discourse is oriented around the terms and concepts associated with covenantal nomism. These features make it highly probable that his comments in the chapter are a response to Judaism's new covenant expectation.

With these things in mind we can confidently state that there was a *cognitively relevant* relationship between covenantal nomsim and Paul's current cognition on the association between the Spirit and the Law; i.e., when Paul speaks about the Spirit's association with the Law, the new covenant expectation from covenantal nomism is brought into the discussion either explicitly or implicitly as a logical corollary.[64] Festinger makes it clear that cognitive dissonance can *only* occur between cognitions that form a *relevant relationship*.[65] Consequently, this sets up the potential for Paul to perceive either a consonant or dissonant relationship between covenantal nomism and his own current cognition. Festinger defines a state of dissonance between two cognitions in the following manner: "two elements (cognitions) are in a dissonant relation if, considering these two alone, the obverse of one element would follow from the other."[66] In other words, x and y are dissonant if not-x follows from y. A brief summary of the main points of our previous analysis is

---

Jeremiah in the OT (Jer. 38 [LXX]: 31, 33). Also, the contrast between "stony tablets" and "tablets of fleshly hearts" (v.3) in association with the Spirit (vv. 3, 6) no doubt recalls the distinction between "heart of stone" and "heart of flesh" and the work of the Spirit in Ezek 11:19-20; 36:26-27. Paul suspends his normal negative use of σάρξ (see for example, Rom. 6:19; 7:5, 18, 25; 8:3, 6; 1 Cor. 15:50; 2 Cor. 4:11; 7:5; 12:7-9; Gal. 2:20; 3:3; 4:13-14; 5:16-17 cf. vv. 19-23; Phil. 3:3) for the positive reference to ἐν πλαξὶν καρδίαις σαρκίναις (v. 3), paralleled in Ezek. 11:19; 36:26. He has re-created the tradition in a unique way by assimilating "heart of stone" to "tablets of stone" and thus connected it with the Mosaic Law.

[64] A *cognitively relevant* relationship is to be distinguished from a *cognitively neutral* relationship. A *neutral* relationship between two cognitions means that two cognitions have nothing to do with one another, whereas a *relevant* relationship means that the one cognition directly impinges upon the other. Therefore, when we say that covenantal nomism's new covenant expectation forms a *cognitively relevant* relationship with Paul's current cognition on the association between the Spirit and the Law, we are saying that the cognition from covenantal nomism impinges upon Paul's cognition on the Spirit and the Law.

[65] Festinger, *A Theory of Cognitive Dissonance*, pp. 12-13.

[66] *Ibid.*, p. 13.

in order here to see if Festinger's formula applies to the phenomenon in Rom. 8:1–16.

Ancient Judaism provided the framework for the eschatological promise of a new covenant relationship in Israel's restoration. Central to this promise was the belief that Israel will experience a change in inward disposition through the agency of the Spirit. There is widespread attestation to the Spirit as the source of inner transformation, equipping individuals to observe the moral and religious codes of conduct stated in the Jewish Torah. For example, beginning with Ezekiel, there is consistent attestation to the divine Spirit as the agent of inner transformation.[67] The Spirit was the principal feature in the coming age.[68] In Ezekiel, it is said that the Spirit would enable Israel to observe the Torah and, subsequently, would also be the means by which ratification of the new covenant would be achieved (36:25–27; 37:1–14). Even though Jer. 31:31–34 makes no mention of the Spirit, vv. 33–34 are comparable to Ezek. 36:27 in that both passages advocate Torah obedience as the central component of the new covenant relationship. The Spirit, which leads to this radically different type of relationship, was, in effect, the indication that a new dispensation had dawned.

Various other passages in Ancient Judaism identify the core of Jewish eschatological expectation as the outpouring of the Spirit, whereby Israel would experience ethical and covenant renewal that would ensue in unprecedented Torah obedience.[69] Furthermore, God would provide Spirit-anointed leaders that would be instrumental in fulfilling this promise for the future.[70] As a result, the Torah is no longer simply an external written code; it will be internalized and received and honoured to become the motive and power of mind and will and consequently, will be obeyed willingly.

Correspondingly, even though Second Temple Judaism (Diaspora, Palestinian, and Qumran Literature) exhibited diversity with respect to language, geography, and ideology, there was unanimous belief in the congruent relationship between the roles of the Spirit and the Law; the Spirit was always perceived to act in a complementary way to the Jewish Law in that its primary function was to induce behaviour that was specifically fashioned upon the moral code of the Law. There are specific examples where the

---

[67] See Ezek. 39:29; Isa. 44:3; 59:21; Joel 2:28, 29.
[68] See Ezek. 37:14; 39:29; Is. 42:1; 44:3; 59:21; Hag. 2:5; Joel 3:1–2.
[69] See Isa. 40:1–14; 44:3; Joel 3:1; Zech. 4:6.
[70] See Isa. 11:2; 42:1–4; 61:1–2.

eschatological promises of Ezek. 36:25-27; 37:14; Jer. 31: 31-34 are taken up in Second Temple Judaism: *Jub*. 1:23-24; 1QH V, 19; VIII, 11; XX, 11, 12; 1QS IV, 20-23. One central feature remains intact in both Ancient and Second Temple Judaism; the Spirit's distinctive role was to motivate individuals to observe the Torah.

Judaism's new covenant expectation is fundamentally different than Paul's conception of the relationship between the Spirit and the Law articulated in Rom. 7:6 and 8:2. In Rom. 7:6 Paul states, "But now *we have been discharged from* the Law...so that we may serve in newness of the Spirit and not in oldness of letter." In both 7:6 and 7:2 the use of καταργειν means to "*be discharged, be released.*"[71] This verb appears in the NT almost exclusively in the undisputed Pauline letters (22 out of the 27 occurrences in the NT). Paul uses the verb particularly in salvation-historical contexts.[72] In each case it suggests the connotation of a power whose influence is removed.[73] Elsewhere, Paul describes the Law's role in "restraining" individuals.[74] With the words "having died to that by which we were bound" that follow in v. 6, we understand him as saying that believers are not obligated to the Law whatsoever. The driving principle that death severs one's obligation to observe the Law in 7:4 is thus affirmed in 7:6. The proposition (death severs one from the Law, v.1), the marriage analogy (vv. 2-3) and its application (v. 4) communicate one point: the Law *in toto* is characteristic of previous phase of salvation-history; to be joined to Christ is to be released from the Law (v. 4). The logical consequence of being discharged from the Law[75] is that we are able to "serve in newness of the Spirit and not in oldness of the letter" (v. 6c). Paul understood that service in the Spirit implies disassociation from the Law.

Paul conveys the same message in Rom. 8:2ff. In v. 2 he resumes his previous reference to "serving in newness of the Spirit" in 7:6. The word νῦν

---

[71] BDAG, p. 526.

[72] See Rom. 3:31; 4:14; 6:6; 7:2, 6; Gal. 3:17; 5:4.

[73] Delling, "ἀργός, ἀργέω, καταργέω," TDNT Vol. 1, pp. 452-54, esp. p. 453; Bandstra, *The Law and the Elements of the World*, pp. 77-81.

[74] See Gal. 3:23 ("kept in custody under the Law"). The word φρουρέω ("to hold in custody, detain, confine," Gal. 3:23) comes close to the meaning of κατέχω ("to keep within limits in a confining manner, confine," Rom. 7:6); compare p. 1067 with p. 533 in BDAG.

[75] Note the use of ὥστε ("But now we have been released from the Law, having died to that by which we were bound, *so that* we may serve in newness of the Spirit and not in oldness of the letter"); ὥστε introduces dependent clauses—"of the actual result *so that*" (BDAG, p. 1107).

("now") in 8:1 is resumptive of the "eschatological *now*"[76] in 7:6, signaling that Paul is again speaking from the perspective of a new era of salvation history inaugurated by Christ's death and resurrection and introducing a new era of the Spirit. In Rom. 8:1–16, Paul clarifies the Spirit's relationship with the Law[77] and associates this with the central theme of "life" in vv. 1–13.[78] In 8:2, Paul pits the Spirit against the Law, where the phrase, "the law of the Spirit of life" is contrasted with the subsequent phrase, "the law of sin and death." He communicates discontinuity between the new era of the Spirit and the old era of the Law. With the words, "has set you free from the law of sin and death," Paul indicates how the Spirit replaces the Law as the basis of ethics in the new era. The phraseology, ἠλευθέρωσέν σε ἀπὸ τοῦ νόμου in 8:2 recalls 7:3 (ἐλευθέρα ἐστὶν ἀπὸ τοῦ νόμου), where the word ἐλευθέρα signifies "being free from control or obligation, *independent, not bound*"[79] to the "Law." In 8:2 Paul uses the aorist tense verb ἠλευθέρωσέν to indicate that the liberation has already been accomplished.[80] While in 7:3 νόμος is to be interpreted restrictively as the Mosaic Law, in 8:2 it is more comprehensively "the law of sin and death" that characterizes the whole system and era of the Mosaic Law, sin and death.[81] Thus, in 8:2 Paul understood the Law and Spirit as representing two eras in salvation-history, where the Spirit liberates humans

---

[76] Compare the use of νῦν in Rom. 3:21; 5:9; 6:19, 22; 7:6. Normally the apostle uses ἄρα οὖν (5:18; 7:3, 25; 8:12; 9:16, 18; 14:12, 19) to indicate concluding remarks or corollary drawn from what has just been said. This indicates that the use of νῦν was intentional, signaling a new era of salvation history.

[77] Πνεῦμα occurs 31 times in Paul's correspondence to the Romans, and out of these, there are 21 occurrences in chap. 8 alone (vv. 2, 4, 5 [2x], 6, 9 [3x], 10, 11 [2x], 13, 14, 15 [2x], 16 [2x], 23, 26 [2x], 27). Even more telling is that out of the 21 times it is used in chap. 8, 17 occur in vv.1–16. Νόμος is used 5 times in Rom. 8 (vv. 2 [2x], 3, 4, 7) and in all of its occurrences it is either directly or indirectly brought into association with πνεῦμα.

[78] See the use of ζωή (vv. 2, 6, 10) and ζάω (vv. 12, 13 [2x]), ζωοποιέω (v. 11).

[79] "*Free* from the tax" (Matt. 17:26); "*independent as far as righteousness is concerned*" (Rom. 6:20); "of the *freedom* of one *set free* by Christ" (Jn. 8:36) (BDAG, p. 317).

[80] "To cause someone to be freed from domination, *free, set free*," (BDAG, p. 317); "This liberation has actually been accomplished" (Cranfield, *The Epistle to the Romans*, p. 376).

[81] The collocation of the three words "law" (Mosaic Law [7:7, 8, 9, 12, 14, 16, 22, 25], "law" [7:21, 23, 25]), "sin" (Mosaic Law's nexus with sin [7:9, 11–13]), and "death" (Mosaic Law leads to death [7:9–10, 11, 13]) describes the former era of the Mosaic Law *in toto*; see Moo, *Romans 1–8*, p. 508; Fitzmyer, *Romans*, p. 483 cf. also his "Paul and the Law," p. 193; Räisänen, *Paul and the Law*, p. 52; Beker, *Paul the Apostle*, p. 256.

from the former era of the Mosaic Law associated with sin and death, and supplies the life that the Mosaic Law could not give (cf. 7:10-11).

This summary indicates that Paul's cognition on the relationship between the Spirit and Law conflicts with the new covenant expectation widely held in Judaism. He claims that the Spirit has displaced the Law. We pointed out above that Paul still considers himself embedded in the thinking of both Ancient and Second Temple Judaism, yet at the same time, he makes a distinct break with this Jewish scriptural tradition. Consequently, the new covenant expectation of covenantal nomism would have exerted a formidable amount of pressure upon him to conform to its central cognition that in the future the Spirit and the Law would co-exist harmoniously; i.e., the Spirit would enable individuals to keep the Law fully. However, Paul maintained his cognition that there was a disparity between the Spirit and Law. Therefore, we can confidently state that he is caught between two cognitions that are in a state of tension with one another. The expectation in covenantal nomism that in the future the Spirit would enable people to keep the Law fully conflicts with Paul's cognition that the Spirit displaces the Law as the principle of new life.

Furthermore, this tension between covenantal nomism and Paul's post-Damascus belief is not confined to his discussion on the Spirit. It surfaces elsewhere in the Pauline corpus. Multiple facets of the believer's relationship with Christ and the implications these have with respect to the Law are brought into discussions where the tension appears. On the one hand, he affirms the Law,[82] but on the other hand, he describes the Law in a depreciatory manner.[83] Throughout this study we have underscored the point that the interplay between these statements cannot be fully explained as simply a situational response to the pastoral concerns of the early Christian movement. It is better understood as stemming from a deeper convictional level and is indicative of a conflict within Paul's own convictional world. The even distribution of these conflicting statements on the Law throughout his

---

[82] See footnote above.

[83] For example, the Law is said to lead to condemnation (2 Cor. 3:9); the Law leads to death (2 Cor. 3:6; Gal. 2:19; Rom. 7:5,9); those who promote the Law belong to "the mutilation" (Phil. 3:2) and are enemies of Christ (Gal. 5:12); with the coming of Christ the time of the Law has come to an end (Rom. 10:4; Gal. 5:18, 23); the Law brings knowledge of sin (Rom. 3:20; 7:7-12); it was "added so that the trespass might increase" (Rom. 5:20); to be under the Law is to be "kept in custody" (Gal. 3:23; 4:1); the Law means one is a descendant of Hagar (slavery) rather than of Sarah (freedom) (Gal. 4:21-31).

letters and their presence in his correspondence to the Roman believers particularly[84] indicate that he was not successful in explaining away or rationalizing the inconsistencies he perceived between covenantal nomism and his post-Damascus beliefs. These were persistent inconsistencies that he grappled with throughout his apostolic career.

Festinger's Cognitive Dissonance Theory is especially suited to explain the behaviour of individuals encountering persistent inconsistencies in their lives. Above we noted the formula that would assist us in detecting a state of dissonance: if "not-x follows from y" it can be said that a state of dissonance exists between the two cognitions x and y. We can apply this to the phenomenon in Rom 8:1-16. If x represents the new covenant teaching in covenantal nomism and y represents Paul's current cognition on the Spirit and Law, then we can express it as follows: "The new covenant teaching in covenantal nomism does not follow from Paul's current cognition on the relationship between the Spirit and Law." Therefore, his cognition of the Spirit's association with the Law is in a dissonant relationship with covenantal nomism.

4. Paul's Search for Consonance with Covenantal Nomism

Festinger proposes that individuals encountering a dissonant relationship between cognitive elements exhibit a drive to bring all cognitions into a consistent relationship with one another, that is, there is a drive that seeks to resolve dissonance and restore a sense of equilibrium: "Cognitive dissonance can be seen as an antecedent condition which leads to activity oriented toward dissonance reduction."[85] This disequilibrium motivates a person to reduce or

---

[84] The significance of this tension in Paul's correspondence to the Romans cannot be overstated. This is a letter written at the end of a major phase of Paul's missionary work (Rom. 15:18-24), which no doubt came after the period in which he wrote most of his other letters. Therefore, it can be said that this correspondence communicated a mature understanding of his Gospel (Rom. 1:16-17). It was written under the most congenial circumstances of his mission with time for careful reflection and composition, where Paul was not encumbered by the pastoral concerns that took priority in his other letters. Of all the letters written by Paul, his letter to the Roman believers qualifies as the most sustained and reflective statement communicating Paul's personal convictions (compare with Dunn, *The Theology of Paul the Apostle*, p. 25).

[85] Festinger, *A Theory of Cognitive Dissonance*, p. 3.

eliminate the perceived dissonance and achieve more consistency ("consonance").[86] Post-decisional dissonance can be reduced in three main ways: 1. changing or revoking the decision made, 2. changing the attractiveness of the alternatives involved in the choice, or 3. establishing cognitive overlap among the dissonant cognitions.[87]

In Rom. 7:6 Paul gives expression to one of his fundamental Christian cognitions: the Spirit has displaced the Law as the principle of new life. He communicates this elsewhere in his letters.[88] Yet at the same time, he describes the Spirit's role using terms and concepts drawn from Judaism's understanding of the covenant and the Law. For example, he associates the Law and Spirit in a positive manner in Rom. 8:4: "In order that the righteous requirement of the Law may be fulfilled in us who walk...according to the Spirit." This tendency is also evident throughout his letters[89] and is definitive proof that he is still struggling to reconcile the Law's relationship to the Spirit no matter what pastoral concerns prompted the discussion in the first place. Even though the roles of the Spirit and Law represent two very different alternative cognitions, Paul still demonstrates a very real commitment to the Law and simply does not dismiss it, but attempts to align it positively with his conception of the role of the Spirit. More comprehensively, there is a state of dissonance between his current cognitions and those of covenantal nomism. He still continues to negotiate his cognitions between his Jewish past and his current ones. This indicates that Paul has not fully relinquished his commitment to the Law and Judaism. In other words, he does not adopt the first of Festinger's options, i.e., changing or revoking the decision made.

---

[86] Brehm and Cohen, *Explorations in Cognitive Dissonance*, pp. 11–17.

[87] Festinger, *A Theory of Cognitive Dissonance*, pp. 42–47.

[88] E.g., "Circumcision is that which is of the heart, by the Spirit, not by the letter" (Rom. 2:29); "Not of letter but of the Spirit; for the letter kills but the Spirit gives life" (2 Cor. 3:6); "Does God supply you with the Spirit and work miracles among you by doing the works of the Law, or by believing what you heard?" (Gal. 3:5); "But if you are led by the Spirit, you are not under the Law" (Gal. 5:18); "But the fruit of the Spirit is love...against such things there is no Law" (Gal. 5:22–23).

[89] E.g., "Circumcision...by the Spirit" (Rom. 2:29); "For we know that the Law is Spirit-ual" (Rom. 7:14); "the law of the Spirit" (Rom. 8:2); "the Spirit is life and peace" (Rom. 8:6); "Spirit is life because of righteousness" (Rom. 8:10); "Spirit of adoption by which we cry out, 'Abba, Father'" (Rom. 8:15); "new covenant...of the Spirit" (2 Cor. 3:6); "Having the same Spirit of faith" (2 Cor. 4:13); "But the fruit of the Spirit is...peace...faithfulness" (Gal. 5:22).

In Rom. 7:12, 13, Paul exonerates the Law: "So the Law is holy and the commandment is holy and righteous and good. Therefore, did that which is good be death to me? By no means!"[90] At the same time, Paul believes the Spirit is the long-awaited agent of new life in the new aeon.[91] Thus, Paul does not reduce the dissonance according to Festinger's second option by changing the attractiveness of the alternatives involved in the choice. We are left with further exploring Festinger's third option of "establishing cognitive overlap among the dissonant cognitions."

Establishing cognitive overlap involves adding new cognitive elements that form a consonant relationship with the opposing cognition. This is accomplished by taking characteristics corresponding to each of the alternatives and putting them in a context where they lead to the same end result.[92] The greater the cognitive overlap between the corresponding cognitive elements of the two alternatives, the less the qualitative distinction between them. Consequently, reducing the qualitative distinction between two opposing cognitions would result in the reduction of dissonance between them.[93]

The character of Paul's discussion on the Spirit in Rom. 8:1-16 can be interpreted as an attempt to establish cognitive overlap between covenantal nomism and his post-Damascus beliefs. The interpretation of the designation "the *law* of the Spirit" in 8:2 is pivotal because it specifies the type of relationship the Spirit has with the Mosaic Law and is a vital part of Paul's proposition that he takes up in his discourse that follows. The context allows for νόμος to make an indirect association with the Mosaic Law[94] and be interpreted something to the effect of the controlling force in ethics.[95] Our previous analysis revealed that νόμος in 8:2 cannot be interpreted restrictively as the Mosaic Law. At the same time it does not mean simply "principle, authority, rule." It is better to take νόμος as an example of *polysemy*, conveying the simultaneous meanings of both the Spirit's continuity and discontinuity with the Mosaic Law. Some would naturally understand Paul as communicating the idea that the new order of the Spirit had replaced the

---

[90] See also Rom. 7:14: "For we know that the Law is spiritual."

[91] Rom. 8:2, 6, 10, 11, 13.

[92] Festinger, A *Theory of Cognitive Dissonance*, pp. 45–46.

[93] Ibid., p. 41.

[94] Rom. 7:1–6, 7–9, 12, 14, 16, 22, 25; 8:3, 4, 7.

[95] Rom. 7:21, 23, 25.

Mosaic Law ("'the *law* of the Spirit' has replaced the Mosaic Law") but others would understand him as saying that the Spirit's role is continuous with the role of the Mosaic Law in the new dispensation ("'the *law* of the Spirit' is analogous to the Mosaic Law"). Paul most likely intended both meanings. He carefully chooses his words in 8:2 so he could articulate a sense of continuity between the Law and the Spirit, and more specifically, represent a positive parallelization between them. This sets the tone for vv. 3-16, where Paul goes into more detail as to how this plays out in the believer's behaviour and status. Furthermore, it corresponds to Festinger's idea that individuals caught between two opposing cognitions demonstrate a propensity to lessen the dissonance by underscoring the common characteristics between them ("cognitive overlap"). It is to this idea that we now turn our attention.

In Rom. 8:4 Paul makes the statement, "in order that the righteous requirement of the Law may be fulfilled in us who walk...according to the Spirit." The use of the verb πληρωθῆ ("it may be fulfilled") is specifically suited for this context in that it conveys the unique nuance of the Law's potential to reach *its designed goal, end, or destiny*[96] without giving the impression that believers are obligated to observe the Law. This verb is to be distinguished from ποιεῖν, πράσσειν, or ὑποτάσσειν. If Paul had used any of these three verbs in 8:4 it would have been a clear injunction for believers to observe the Law.[97] However, he intentionally avoids using these verbs in association with the Law when he is prescribing Christian behaviour. When he speaks of

---

[96] "To bring to a designed end" (BDAG, pp. 828-29) cf. "the whole law *has found its full expression*"(of Gal. 5:14); see also Rom. 13:8.

[97] Paul uses ποιεῖν, πράσσειν, or ὑποτάσσειν in contexts where Christian behaviour is being contemplated. However, they are never used with reference to Christians observing the Law. For example, Paul encourages believers to "*do* (ποίει) what is good" (Rom. 13:3). In 1 Cor. 16:16, Christians are required to be "*in subjection* (ὑποτάσσησθε) to such ones (those devoted to ministry)." In 2 Cor. 5:10, Paul refers to "the things one *practised* (ἔπαξεν), either good or worthless." However, when Paul describes the Jewish non-believer's relationship to the Law or the previous era of covenantal nomism, he is prone to using ποιεῖν, πράσσειν, or ὑποτάσσειν to describe the necessity of "doing, practising, or being subjected under" the Mosaic Law. For example, in Rom. 7:16, Paul writes, "For if what I do not wish, is what I *do* (ποιῶ), I agree with the Law." In Rom 2:25, Paul states, "For indeed circumcision is of value, if *you practise* (πράσσῃς) the Law." Similarly, in Rom. 8:7, he claims that the mind set on the flesh "*does not subject itself* (ὑποτάσσεται) to the Law of God." Paul intentionally avoids using these terms in contexts where he relates Christian behaviour to the Law. When Christian behaviour is related positively to the Mosaic Law, the verb πληροῦν is used (Rom. 8:4; 13:8-10; Gal. 5:14).

believers *fulfilling* the Law, the view is retrospective, that is, he is contemplating the requirements of the Mosaic Law in the previous era and compares them to Christian ethics in the present, which simply functions as a statement of resultant fact. His primary purpose was not to delineate the specific precepts in the Law and explicate the believer's obligation to observe them, but rather, to demonstrate how the quality of Christian conduct fares with respect to the Law.[98]

The "righteous requirement of the Law" is that which is fulfilled in believers. The word δικαίωμα in 8:4 suggests a reference to the righteousness called for in the moral Law and the intended goal or purpose for God's covenant people. Paul intends an implicit reduction of the Law in this verse, focusing on the moral norms, excluding circumcision,[99] Sabbath observance,[100] and the food laws.[101] This suits the context of his correspondence to the Romans in light of the fact that he addresses this thought in 8:4 to Gentile converts as well. Occasionally, Paul quotes the Law and demonstrates how its behavioural aspects are analogous to the ethics required of believers.[102] He offers no theoretical basis for this dichotomy within the Law but nevertheless makes a distinction between the Law's ethical and cultic parts. This is a new cognition that shapes Paul's thinking in Rom. 8:4.

So, the believer's conduct is comparable with the moral requirements of Law in that they have been fully satisfied through the Spirit. We could re-state Paul's thought in 8:4 in the following manner: "If we yield to the Spirit in our lives and do not revert back to our pre-Christian disposition and values, the moral requirement of the Law will reach its intended goal." When we analyse this verse it is clear that Paul's intent was to reduce the qualitative distinction between the Law and the Spirit ("the righteous requirement of the Law may be fulfilled in us who walk...according to the Spirit"). He has taken a positive characteristic of the Law ("the righteous requirement") and re-oriented it

---

[98] See Westerholm, *Israel's Law and the Church's Faith*, p. 202; Betz, *Galatians*, p. 275; van Dülmen, *Die Theologie des Gesetzes bei Paulus*, pp. 229–30.

[99] See Gal. 6:15; Rom. 2:26.

[100] See Rom. 14:5.

[101] See Rom. 14:2; Gal. 2:11–14.

[102] See Rom. 13:8–10; however, it must be emphasized here that Paul is careful to say that the Law "has been fulfilled" (πεπλήρωκεν [v. 8]) or "it is summed up" (ἀνακεφαλαιοῦται [v. 9]) but never encourages believers to actually *observe* or *keep* the Law. Paul's point here is that these commandments are considered sins against the Spirit just as they once were considered breaking the Mosaic Law.

around its alternative, the Spirit. Furthermore, he demonstrates how the Spirit's role in the believer actually takes up and achieves the same end result as the Law ("the righteous requirement of the Law *may be fulfilled* [i.e., *may reach its designed goal, end, or destiny*]"). This equates precisely to Festinger's definition of cognitive overlap, where dissonance is reduced when one takes characteristics corresponding to each of the alternatives and places them in a context where they lead to the same end result. If one reduces the qualitative distinction that exists between the alternatives, it follows that the dissonance between them will also be reduced.

In our analysis above[103] we demonstrated how Rom. 8:2ff is replete with covenantal terms and concepts drawn from Ancient and Second Temple Judaism. However, Paul does not correlate these with the Mosaic Law. Instead, they are exclusively linked to the role of the Spirit in the believer's life. Nevertheless, their presence in Rom. 8 indicate that they still occupy a prominent place in the apostle's mind and he is still very much embedded within a Jewish frame of thinking. He has intentionally chosen to re-orient concepts that were uniquely associated with the Jewish Law around his conception of the role of the Spirit in the new epoch. We will briefly rehearse these to show how this plays out in Rom. 8:1–16 and how they relate to Festinger's idea of reducing dissonance between two opposing cognitions by establishing cognitive overlap.

Paul's understanding of "righteous requirement (δικαίωμα)" (Rom. 8:4) and "righteousness (δικαιοσύνην)" (Rom. 8:10) derives from the LXX and in particular its association with the Law and the covenant. The word δικαίωμα is used frequently in the LXX referring to the prescribed statutes of the Mosaic Law.[104] When associated with the Mosaic Law it means "statute, righteous requirement, or ordinance" of the Law."[105] It is clear that Paul takes up this understanding of δικαίωμα in Rom. 8:4 when he qualifies it as "the righteous requirement *of the Law* (τοῦ νόμου)."

The word δικαιοσύνη occurs frequently in the LXX.[106] "Righteousness" is not necessarily thought of as perfect moral uprightness, but is essentially a relational concept. It is understood as "right" conduct, that is, behaviour that

---

[103] See Chapter Six (The Spirit's Identification with Covenantal Nomism).

[104] Ex. 15:25; 21:1, 9; Num. 36:13; Deut. 4:1, 5, 8, 40; Ezek. 11:12; 36:27.

[105] Schrenk, "δικαίωμα," *TDNT* Vol. II, p. 221.

[106] See for example, Isa. 1:21, 26; Jer. 22:13; Ezek. 3:20 (צֶדֶק), Deut. 9:4, 5, 6; 1Sam. 26:23 (צְדָקָה), Isa. 57:1; Ezek. 18:5, 9, 20, 24, 26 (צַדִּיק).

is in keeping with the covenant relationship.[107] The basis for this "right" conduct is the Law. This is the whole purpose of the Law; it was given for the goal of producing "righteousness" ("right" conduct) in order to maintain the covenant relationship Israel had with Yahweh.[108]

Paul was certainly cognizant of this understanding of "righteousness" associated with the Law and covenantal faithfulness. In Rom. 9:31 he writes, "But Israel, pursuing *a Law of righteousness* (νόμον δικαιοσύνης), did not arrive at that *Law* (νόμον)" (cf. "Israelites, to whom belongs the adoption as sons and glory and the covenants and the giving of the Law" [9:4]). The verb "to pursue" (διώκων) indicates the commitment contemporary Jews had to the covenantal relationship and how the Mosaic Law articulated the goal of righteousness, which Yahweh required of his covenant people. In Rom. 10:5 Paul states, "For Moses writes with reference to *the righteousness of the Law* (τὴν δικαιοσύνη τὴν ἐκ νόμου): the one who observes these things will live in them." He uses Moses to characterize the previous epoch of the Law.[109] Paul's wording, τὴν δικαιοσύνην τὴν ἐκ νόμου instead of simply νόμος δικαιοσύνης, refers more restrictively to those who observe the Law and derive their sense of behaviour from the Law and the covenant relationship. This coincides with the use of τὴν ἰδίαν ("seeking to establish *their own* righteousness") in v. 3 and the specific reference to the Jewish understanding of "righteousness." Paul is intentionally associating "righteousness" in this verse with the thought of Lev. 18:5, where the Law is said to be the source of

---

[107] See Ziesler, *The Meaning of Righteousness in Paul*, pp. 25, 39, 40; Hill, *Greek Words and Hebrew Meanings*, pp. 85–86; von Rad, *Old Testament Theology* Vol. 1, p. 373; Brown, "Righteousness," pp. 356–58.

[108] See Schrenk, "δικαιοσύνη, κτλ.," *TDNT* Vol. II, p. 195; e.g., Ps. 16:15: "But I shall appear in righteousness (δικαιοσύνη) before your face: I shall be satisfied when your glory appears (Ps. 16:15)." In this context he appeals to Yahweh because he has obeyed the Law (cf. "not spoken with deceitful lips" [v. 1]; "unrighteousness has not been found in me" [v. 3]). Now in v. 15, he comforts himself upon the fact that his "righteousness" is the basis for a secure sense of relationship he has with Yahweh ("I shall appear in righteousness *before your face*") cf. Isa. 26:9: "My spirit seeks you very early in the morning, O God, for your *commandments* (τὰ προστάηματά σου) are a light on the earth; learn *righteousness* (δικαιοσύνην), you that live upon the earth"; see also Ezek. 18:19, 21; this idea is also found in Second Temple Judaism, e.g., 1 Macc. 2:50–52; Tob. 14:7, 9; *T. Lev.* 8:2; *T. Ash.* 6:4; 1 QS III, 20, 22; IV, 2; CD I, 1, 16; 1QM III, 6; XIII, 3; XVII, 8; 1QH XIV, 19; VIII, 5; 1QSb V, 26; 1QS V, 4; VIII, 2; 1QH XV, 14; CD I, 19, 20; XI, 21; XX, 20; 1QH VII, 15; IX, 36.

[109] Cf. Rom. 5:14; 1 Cor. 10:2; 2 Cor. 3:7–15.

life. Lev. 18:5 was regarded as a typical expression of Israel's obligation to the
Law and promise under the covenant.[110]

However, δικαιοσύνη in Rom. 8:10 is not associated with the Mosaic Law
but has been wholly re-oriented with the role of the Spirit. As we concluded
above, the concept of righteousness is best understood as behavioural
righteousness effected by the Spirit ("the Spirit... achieves the goal of righteous
behaviour"). The concept of "righteousness" in both Ancient and Second
Temple Judaism was defined as behaviour befitting the covenant relationship,
which was articulated in the Law. But in Rom. 8:10, Paul has re-interpreted
the covenantal understanding of righteousness around the role of the Spirit,
not the Law.

One of the key concepts in Rom. 8:1-16 is "life" (vv. 2, 6, 10, 13). Ancient
Judaism understood "life" to be associated with the Law: "And now, Israel,
hear the righteous requirements and the judgments, all that I teach you this
day to do in order that you may live...keep the commandments of the Lord
our God [Deut. 4:1,2 (LXX)]."[111] For Israel, the basis of "life" was their
covenant relationship with Yahweh tangibly expressed in observing the Mosaic
Law. Conversely, those who disobey the commandments are condemned as
wicked and said to be subject to a divine curse and the sentence of "death,"
standing in danger of severing their relationship with Yahweh.[112] In Lev. 18:5
we read the words, "And you will keep all my ordinances, and all my
judgments, and observe them; if one observes them, he will live by them."
"Living" ("life") is understood comprehensively. It entails covenantal
relationship, which in turn includes material prosperity, fruitful harvest,
peace, and longevity of life (cf. Lev. 26:3-13; Deut. 28:1-14). Lev. 18:5 is a
warning that the continuance of "life" is dependent upon Israel's faithful
observance of the Law.

In Second Temple Judaism, God's commandments are called the
"commandments of life"[113] and the Torah is called the "Law of life."[114] The

---

[110] E.g., Deut. 4:1; 5:32-33; 8:1; 16:20; Ezek. 18:9, 17, 19, 21; 20:11, 13, 21; *Pss. Sol.* 14:2-3.

[111] See also Deut. 5:33; 6:24-25; 8:1; 30:15-18; Ezek. 18:19 cf. vv. 9, 21; 20:11 cf. vv. 13, 21;
Neh. 9:29.

[112] Deut. 6: 15; 7:4, 10; 8:19; 28:20, 22, 45.

[113] See Bar. 3:9, where the commandments are called ἐντολὰς ζωῆς; cf. "This is the book of
the commandments of God, and the Law that endures forever: all they that keep it *shall come to
life* (εἰς ζωήν)"(4:1).

[114] Sir. 17:11 reads, "He bestowed knowledge upon them, and allotted to them the *Law of life*
(νόμον ζωῆς)." See also *m. Abot* 6:7.

Law had a mediatorial function between Yahweh and Israel, regulating and maintaining the covenant relationship. When one was in the covenant relationship, one was said to possess "life."[115] This description of the Law reflects the purpose that it was considered to have among many of Paul's Jewish contemporaries. 4 Ezra, which was composed about 100 C.E., indicates how those who are on the earth have been ordained to obey the Law (cf. 7:20 ["Law of God"]), which is a condition to be met so that they could "live" ("what they should do to live" [4 Ezra 7:21]).

In Rom. 7:10, Paul himself understood the role of the Law in Judaism in this manner ("the commandment that was intended to bring life").[116] The phrase, ἡ ἐντολὴ ἡ εἰς ζωήν has a telic force: "the commandment *intended to bring* (for the goal/ purpose of) life."[117] He concedes, in principle, that observing the Law was a path to eternal life, something that he shares with his Jewish contemporaries. He is simply stating a common Jewish rule or fact without giving a definite purpose or reason for doing so. This indicates the presence of a personal conviction that he shares with his Jewish contemporaries.[118] Nowhere in the Pauline corpus is this idea ever contradicted or even questioned.[119] Paul's point is simply that it was a system that did not work.[120]

---

[115] Cf. Sir. 17:11-12, where "law of life" (νόμον ζωῆς, v. 11) is said to be equivalent to the God, who established "an eternal covenant" [διαθήκην αἰῶνος, v. 12]).

[116] Paul cites Lev. 18:5 in Gal. 3:12: "The one who observes the Law will live by them." Lev. 18:5 is also the basis for Rom. 10:5 ("the person who does these things [*what the Law requires*] shall live by them").

[117] Hofius, "Das Gesetz des Mose und das Gesetz Christi," 270; Stuhlmacher, "Paul's Understanding of the Law in the Letter to the Romans," pp. 98-99.

[118] "That the law promises life is thus Paul's own conviction, though one which [he believes] he shares with the 'Israel' of his day" (Westerholm, *Israel's Law and the Church's Faith*, p. 146).

[119] For example, when Paul claims that the Law promises life to its adherents, he cites Moses in a favourable manner in Rom. 10:5 (cf. Rom. 9:15; 10:19; 1 Cor. 9:9). In Rom. 10:4, 5, (as in Rom. 7:10) Paul is speaking in the context of salvation history and simply states the fact that the former age associated with the Law has been superseded by the new age associated with Christ ("Christ is the end/goal of the Law"). Thus, he is not stating that Moses was "incorrect" but rather that the Law, given through Moses, was not able to deliver on its promise of life and was replaced in this new epoch by Christ.

[120] Paul uses the following words to describe the role of the Law: "resulted in death" (Rom. 7:1); was not accompanied "by faith" (Rom. 10:6, 10; Gal. 3:12); was not observed (Rom. 7:8, 9, 11, 13-17, 19-21). This communicates Paul's understanding of a system that did not function adequately.

Paul picks up the theme of "life" in Rom. 8:2ff from the perspective of the new era and demonstrates how the Law's goal of "life" is realized through the Spirit (vv. 2, 6, 10, 11, 13). It is most probable that his description of the Spirit's role in 8:2ff is occasioned by his description of the Law in 7:10ff. We can surmise this from the manner in which he formulates his explication of the new era of the Spirit. Paul's thoughts are preoccupied with how the Law compares with the roles of Christ and the Spirit in the new era. That is, his argument in 8:2ff is specifically motivated by his perception of the place and purpose of Law in the previous era described in 7:10ff. Paul intentionally patterns his description of the Spirit as the agent of "life" in 8:2ff upon his previous discussion of the Law and its relationship to "life" in 7:10ff. In doing this he presents a parallelism between the Spirit's role in granting life and the intent of the Law to give life.[121] Therefore, we can confidently state that Paul's explication of the Spirit as the agent of life in Rom. 8:2ff was conditioned to a significant degree by covenantal nomism and the Jewish belief that observing the Law was a path to life. The shape of the argument in 8:2ff is intentionally patterned upon his explication of the Law in 7:10ff. This is a sure sign that Paul perceives the goal of the Mosaic Law to confer life expressed in 7:10 ("the commandment *intended to bring* [for the goal/ purpose of] life") is realized in the Spirit, the agent of life. Once again we have further evidence that Paul attempts to bridge the gap between the Law and the Spirit and reduce the qualitative distinction between them. He shows how his new Christian cognition ("so that we may serve in newness of the *Spirit*" [7:6]) is, in fact, consonant with his native Jewish cognition that the Law was given by God for the purpose of life ("this *commandment* intended for life" [7:10]); i.e., the Law's intent to bring "life" was brought to fruition by the Spirit (8:2, 6, 10, 11, 13).

In Rom. 8:6, Paul states, "the mindset of the Spirit is life and *peace* (εἰρήνη)." The LXX translators most often use εἰρήνη to render the Hebrew word שָׁלוֹם. The word שָׁלוֹם frequently becomes associated with a "covenant."[122] The OT prophets used the term שָׁלוֹם to characterize Israel's covenant relationship with Yahweh. Ezekiel claims that Yahweh makes a

---

[121] In Rom. 7:7-25, the Law's inability to give life was the result of "sin" (7:11, 13, 14, 17, 20) and the "flesh" (7:14, 18, 25). Correspondingly, in 8:2ff the Spirit is life because he delivers from "sin" (8:2, 10) and believers are not to live according to the "flesh" but the Spirit (8:4, 6, 9, 13). Paul sets up the same "life" and "death" antithesis associated with the Spirit in 8:2-16 as he did with the Law in 7:7-25 (see 7:9, 10, 11, 24 cf. 8:2, 6, 10, 11, 13).

[122] E.g., 1 Ki. 5:26; Obad. 7.

בְּרִית שָׁלוֹם (Ezek. 34:25; 37:26) and in the context makes it clear that the relationship of "peace" is the result.[123] One of the characteristic qualities of those who entered this covenant was their commitment to observe the Law. The eschatological "covenant of peace" will be established with a Davidic King, and furthermore, Yahweh proclaims, "They will follow *my Laws* and be careful to keep *my decrees*" (Ezek. 37:24-26).[124] In the LXX the concept of "peace" (εἰρήνη) is associated with the covenant, salvation, and the Law. For example εἰρήνη and σωτήριον are linked in a positive way in Ps. 84:8,9: "For he (the Lord God) will speak *peace* to his people...Moreover his *salvation* is near them that fear him." In Ps. 118:165 *peace* is said to be the possession of "those who love your *Law*" (τοῖς ἀγαπῶσι τὸν νόμον σου).

Paul presents the concept of "peace" in Rom. 8:6 in a manner similar to both the MT and the LXX, in a covenantal sense, as a favourable relationship with God.[125] In v.7 he describes an inverse situation, where the mindset of the flesh leads to enmity (ἔχθρα) with God. The use of διότι to introduce v. 7 ("*because* the mind of the flesh is enmity with God") has a causal force, explaining the content of v. 6 ("the mindset on the flesh is death").[126] In the LXX, the word ἐχθρός was used to describe the enemies of God, in particular, those who were considered ungodly and did not observe the Law.[127] For example, in Ps. 36:20, the psalmist writes, "For the sinners will perish; and *the enemies of the Lord* (οἱ ἐχθροὶ τοῦ Κυρίου) at the moment of their being honoured and exalted have utterly vanished like smoke." The "enemy of the Lord" in this psalm is also described as the one who performs "unlawful deeds" (ποιοῦντι παρανόμιας) and is contrasted with "the righteous" (δίκαιος, vv. 12, 16, 17, 25, 29, 31, 32, 39) who has "the Law of God" (ὁ νόμος τοῦ θεοῦ) in his heart (v. 31).[128] This equates precisely with the thought of Rom. 8:7, where it is stated that "enmity against God" is the result of living according to the flesh and not observing the Law ("the mindset on the flesh...does not submit to the Law of God"). This demonstrates that Paul

---

[123] See also Isa. 54:10, which also mentions a "covenant of peace."

[124] See Mal. 3:7

[125] Cf., Fitzmyer, *Romans*, p. 489; Barrett, *The Epistle to the Romans*, p. 148; Moo, *The Epistle to the Romans*, p. 488.

[126] "Marker used to indicate why something just stated can reasonably be considered valid" (BDAG, p. 251).

[127] Foerster, "ἐχθρός, ἔχθρα," *TDNT* Vol. II, p. 812.

[128] See also Isa. 63:10, where it is said that the disobedience of Israel resulted in making God her *enemy* (ἐστράφη αὐτοῖς εἰς ἔχθραν).

understands the Spirit's association with "peace" in Rom. 8:6 in a covenantal sense, describing the relationship between the believer and God. He has re-oriented the concept of peace, previously the result of observing the Law in Judaism, with the Spirit. This serves to convey a positive parallelization between the Law and the Spirit; i.e., the Spirit secures a relationship of peace between the believer and God just as the Law intended to secure peace between Israel and Yahweh in the covenant relationship.

In Rom. 8:14-16, Paul explicates the Spirit's role in the believer's familial status with God. Israel is called Yahweh's son/ child in Ex. 4:22f; Hos. 11:1; Jer. 31:9, 20. As good children, the people of Israel will naturally be submissive and obedient to Yahweh, their Father. For example, in Deut. 14:1ff, Yahweh stipulates some of the cultic, dietary, and behavioural requirements that are an expression of their status as "sons of Yahweh."[129] Hos. 1-2 demonstrates that individual Israelites as God's sons or children ("sons of the living God" [1:10][130]) were marked out by a particular code of conduct. Yahweh declares, "I will take you for my wife in righteousness and in judgment, in mercy, and in tender compassion. I will take you for my wife in faithfulness" (2:19-20). Israel's sonship is grounded in the Torah and demonstrates its faithfulness to this relationship when it obeys the Torah. For example, in Test. Jud. 24:3, we read how Judah predicts the arrival of a sinless, eschatological king who will pour out the spirit of grace upon his sons, which will have a profound effect upon his children: "you will be his (God's) sons in truth and walk in his commandments."[131]

In Rom. 8:14-16, Paul's description of the Spirit and the status of sonship is strikingly similar to Israel's covenantal status as "sons/ children of God" and their obligation to abide by the Torah. This becomes particularly evident in Paul's understanding of the believer's behaviour. In Rom. 8:14, he writes, "For all who are being led by the Spirit of God, these are the sons of God." The passive form ἄγονται signifies "being controlled/ determined by/ governed by" the Spirit. This suggests that the Spirit is the primary agent in Christian

---

[129] See also Deut. 32:6, 18; Isa. 1:2; 30:1, 9; 45:9-11; 64:7.

[130] Paul indicates his knowledge of Hos. 1:10 when he quotes it in Rom. 9:26.

[131] Cf. Philo's statement that not every Israelite is considered God's son but the one who observes the Law can claim this special status (Spec. I, 318; QG I, 92). This idea is further emphasized in Rabbinic literature. In a homiletic midrash on Deut. 29:1 which begins a discussion on Israel's covenant obligations, it reads, "You have the wish to be signaled out, that you are my sons? Busy yourselves with the Torah and observance of the commandments, so all will see that you are my sons" (Deut. Rab 7 on Deut. 29:1; cf. Str-B, I, pp. 17-19, 220).

ethics. Furthermore, the words, "these are the sons of God" indicates that this is a distinguishing sign of being "sons of God." Correspondingly, Paul appears to equate the Jewish understanding of the Israelites as sons/children of God, whose lives were marked by faithfulness to the covenant and the Law, with a Christian idea of believers as sons/children of God, whose lives were distinguished by faithfulness to their relationship with God by yielding to the inward impulses of the Spirit. He has intentionally re-oriented the status of sonship depicting covenantal faithfulness around the role of the Spirit and the believer's status of sonship.[132] Once again Paul defines the role of the Spirit in covenantal terms, corresponding to the role of the Law.

In Rom. 8:1–16, Paul demonstrates a propensity to lessen the dissonance between the Spirit and the Law. Even though the Spirit and Law represented two alternative ways of serving (7:6), and more comprehensively, his post-Damascus beliefs were in a state of tension with those he inherited from his Jewish past, he attempts to establish cognitive overlap between these conflicting cognitions. Festinger propounded that dissonance is significantly reduced when one takes characteristics corresponding to each of the alternatives and puts them in a context where they lead to the same end result. The greater the cognitive overlap ("consonance") between the corresponding cognitive elements of the two alternatives, the less the qualitative distinction between them, which in turn, results in the reduction of dissonance. In 8:1–16 Paul attempts to convey a positive parallelization between the Spirit and the Law, and more particularly, to show how the Spirit brings to fruition all that the Law attempted to accomplish. To be more specific, the covenantal terms and concepts "righteousness," "life," "peace," and "sonship," concepts that were specifically associated with the Torah in both Ancient and Second Temple Judaism, are re-oriented around the role of the Spirit in the new aeon. In this manner Paul decreases the qualitative distinction between the Spirit and Law and reduces the dissonance between them and furthermore, decreases the dissonance between his post-Damascus beliefs and his

---

[132] "The divine sonship of individuals is determined by the Spirit of God, the power of God as understood within Jewish tradition, now experienced in eschatological outpouring, but defined in terms of the Spirit; not in terms of the law or of faithfulness to the law" (Dunn, Romans 1–8, p. 451); "The source for the term υἱοί should be located in the OT and other Jewish literature, for Israel is quite frequently identified in both the singular and plural as God's son" (Schreiner, Romans, p. 423); Scott, Adoption as Sons of God, pp. 262–63; Stuhlmacher, Paul's Letter to the Romans, p. 129.

convictions he inherited from his Jewish past. Therefore, we can characterize Rom. 8:1-16 as Paul's search for consonance with covenantal nomism.

5. Paul's Appeal for Support from the Community of the Spirit

Festinger's Cognitive Dissonance Theory was originally developed to analyse the behavioural patterns of individuals in a North American twentieth century society. However, this theory has been applied to cultural matrices different from that in which Festinger originally developed the theory.[133] We wish to use it in the cultural matrix of the first century Mediterranean world of which Paul was a part.[134] This was a collectivist society where people assessed themselves in terms of stereotypes often explained as deriving from family:

> What characterized first-century Mediterranean people was not individualistic, but 'dyadic' or group-oriented personality...the basic, most elementary unit of social analysis is not the individual person but the dyad, a person in relations with and connected to at least one other social unit, in particular, the family.[135]

In a collectivist, first century context individuals are embedded with various other persons with whom they shared common characteristics and perspectives. This means that they derive a sense of loyalty and solidarity to their "in-group." These "in-groups" could be the polis (a "citizen" of a geographical location [e.g., "Philo of Alexandria"]), a patron-client relationship ("Jesus is Lord" [Rom. 10:9; 1 Cor. 12:3; Phil. 2:11]), work groups ("Zacchaeus, tax collector" [Lk. 19:2]), family ("James and John, sons of Zebedee" [Matt. 4:21]) or fictive family (Paul was a disciple of Gamaliel [Acts 22:3]).[136]

---

[133] See Carroll, *When Prophecy Failed*; "Prophecy, Dissonance and Jeremiah XXVI," 12-23; "Ancient Israelite Prophecy and Dissonance Theory," 135-51; Gager, *Kingdom and Community*, pp. 37-49; Jackson, "The Resurrection Belief of the Earliest Church: A Response to the Failure of Prophecy?," 414-25; Wernik, "Frustrated Beliefs and Early Christianity," 96-130; Collins, *Between Athens and Jerusalem*.

[134] For a discussion on the applicability of Cognitive Dissonance Theory in a first century Mediterranean context see the Introduction (4.3.3 Criticisms and Developments) above.

[135] Malina and Neyrey, "First-Century Personality: Dyadic, Not Individualistic," pp. 72-73; see also Bruce J. Malina, *The New Testament World: Insights from Cultural Anthropology* (Atlanta: John Knox Press, 1981), p. 55.

[136] See Malina and Neyrey, *Portraits of Paul*, pp. 158-164.

First century Christian groups constituted a fictive family. They considered themselves the "household of faith"[137] and addressed one another as "sister" or "brother."[138] Along this line of thinking, in Rom. 8:1-16, Paul addresses the Roman believers as a distinct community. They were the community of the Spirit and consequently, had the status of "sons of God" or "children of God." In Rom. 8, Paul underscores tangible experiences of the Spirit in the lives of believers: "walking according to the Spirit" (v. 4), "you are...in the Spirit" (v. 9), "the Spirit of God dwells in you" (vv. 9, 11), "but if by the Spirit you put to death..." (v. 13), "for those who are being led by the Spirit" (v. 14), "the Spirit of adoption, by whom we cry out..." (v. 15), "the same Spirit testifies with our spirit..." (v. 16). In all of these statements the Spirit is described as an experienced and present reality for the community of faith.[139] A significant shift takes place in vv. 15-16; Paul switches from the second person plural,[140] where he specifically addresses the believers in Rome, to the first person plural,[141] indicating that he includes himself in the community of believers who have the benefit of the Spirit in their lives.

Above[142] we indicated how Paul makes a smooth transition between ethics and familial status with God, where the believers' behaviour is a tangible expression of their status as children of God. Rom. 8:14-16 functions as a climax to the whole section (vv. 1-16). For Paul ethics is based upon the foundation of a relationship with God, where the Spirit is understood as the linchpin, which makes these operational. He understands the Spirit to take on a comprehensive role in securing relationship with God (vv. 14-16) and also as the agent whereby the on-going practical and behavioural dimensions of the relationship are tangibly expressed (vv. 2-13). This best explains the transition from vv. 2-13 to vv. 14-16. Putting this together from a sociological perspective, we can confidently state that Paul understood the experience of

---

[137] Gal. 6:10.

[138] Mk. 3:31-35.

[139] In Rom. 8, whenever Paul describes the work of the Spirit in believers' lives he uses present tense verbs (see vv. 4, 9, 11, 13, 14, 15).

[140] For example, Paul uses the second person plural form in the following phrases: "If by the Spirit...*you put to death* (θανατοῦτε), *"you will live* (ζήσεσθε) (v. 13) and *"you received* (ἐλάβετε) the Spirit" (v. 15).

[141] In v. 15, Paul writes, "by whom *we cry out* (κράζομεν)" and in v. 16, "the Spirit testifies with *our spirit* (συμμαρτυρεῖ τῷ πνεύματι ἡμῶν) that *we are* (ἐσμὲν) children of God."

[142] See Chapter Five (3. The Spirit and the Experience of Familial Relationship: Rom. 8:14-16) in Part Two.

the Spirit as the definitive mark of the fictive family in which he was embedded.[143]

In his correspondence with the community of believers in Rome, Paul reveals his impending plans to visit them via his travels to Spain.[144] We stated above[145] that one of Paul's main purposes in writing this letter was to receive support for his plans to go to Jerusalem because he is aware that he may encounter opposition there.[146] The manner in which he hopes to gain their support is by introducing himself by way of communicating the components of his gospel message.[147] In the process of conveying the intricacies of his gospel message, he reflected upon the various subjects addressed in his previous preaching and correspondence. This is particularly true of his discourse on the Law and the Spirit in Rom. 8:1-16.[148] But in his reflections on the distinctions between the respective roles of the Law and the Spirit (e.g., 7:1-6), he attempts to reconcile the tensions between covenantal nomism and his own cognition on the association between the Spirit and the Law (e.g., 8:4). Furthermore, we can surmise that ch. 8 coincides with the general tendency of Paul's letter as a whole; he was attempting to receive validation for both his convictions and his role as an apostle from the community of believers in Rome, and consequently, count on them as a centre of support for his missionary exploits.

With these things in mind we can utilize Festinger's theory to understand the motivation behind Paul's discourse in Rom. 8 and the role of social validation. Festinger reasoned that the process of social interaction is

---

[143] Cf. "If therefore there is any encouragement in Christ, if there is any consolation of love, if there is any *fellowship of the Spirit*, if any affection and compassion..." (Phil. 2:1).

[144] Cf. Rom. 15:23-24, 28.

[145] See Introduction (4.3.1 Spirit and Law: Conflict Within Paul's Convictional World).

[146] Cf. Rom. 15:30-31.

[147] "In setting out such a full statement of his understanding of the gospel...Paul surely wished to gain acceptance for that understanding among the believers" (Dunn, *Romans 1-8*, p. lvi); Paul demonstrated "the need to unify the Romans around 'his' gospel to support his work in Spain...[which] forced Paul to write a letter in which he carefully rehearsed his understanding of the gospel" (Moo, *The Epistle to the Romans* p. 20); "We see that Paul...propounds his understanding of the gospel not only to get across to them his important missionary reflections on it...but also to win support for it from the Roman Christian community" (Fitzmyer, *Romans*, p. 79).

[148] For example, Rom. 7:25; 8:1-2 (through Christ/ Spirit one is freed from the Law, sin, and death) demonstrates some parallel to 1 Cor. 15:57; 2 Cor. 3:17; Gal. 5:18. Also Rom. 8:14-15 (those who are led by the Spirit; adoptive sonship, "Abba, Father") is comparable to Gal. 4:5-6.

inextricably woven with the process of reducing dissonance.[149] The major method of reducing dissonance involves influencing people to comply with one's cognitions.[150] The logical corollary is that if a large number of people share these beliefs there must be something right or influential about them.[151]

We can be more specific on the dynamics of how this plays out in Rom. 8. Paul perceived a state of dissonance between Judaism's covenantal nomism and its expectation that in the future the Spirit would enable people to keep the Law fully, and his own cognition that the Spirit displaced the Law as the principle of new life. According to Festinger's theory, if such a state of dissonance arises, an individual will naturally communicate with those who share similar experiences and cognitions and attempt to influence them to agree with the perceived cognitions in order to receive affirmation. This leads to the reduction of dissonance.[152] This also coincides with our understanding of first century Mediterranean people as a collectivist society, that is, individuals being embedded with various other persons with whom they shared common characteristics and perspectives from whom they derive a sense of loyalty and solidarity. In Rom. 8:1–16 Paul seeks corroboration for his cognitions from the community of faith because they all share the experience of the Spirit and have acquired the identical status as children of God just as he has ("the Spirit of adoption, by which *we cry out* 'Abba, Father'...the Spirit testifies with *our* spirit that *we are* children of God" [vv. 15–16]). This is the common bond between believers and the group of people with whom he can make his appeal for understanding and support.

An individual in this situation, such as Paul, may engage in a social influence process. By attempting to obtain social support an individual concomitantly increases the potential to add new cognitions that are consonant with his current cognition, which will in turn reduce the total magnitude of dissonance.[153] Applying this to Rom. 8, when Paul states, "the righteous requirement of the Law has been fulfilled in us...who walk according to the Spirit" (i.e., "the moral requirement of the Law has reached its intended

---

[149] "Processes of social communication and social influence are...inextricably interwoven with processes of creation and reduction of dissonance" (Festinger, A *Theory of Cognitive Dissonance*, p. 177).

[150] See especially *Ibid.*, pp. 182, 189, 191.

[151] Festinger, Riecken, and Schachter, *When Prophecy Fails*, p. 28.

[152] Festinger, A *Theory of Cognitive Dissonance*, p. 189.

[153] *Ibid.*, p. 188.

goal in us who walk according to the Spirit" [v. 4]), he is attempting to influence the community of faith in Rome that his perception of the relationship between covenantal nomism and his current cognition on the Spirit is accurate. He is hoping that other believers who have experienced the Spirit (the "fictive group" with whom he associates) can identify with this claim and affirm this statement. In turn, if Paul acquires corroboration from the community of faith in Rome of the positive parallelization between covenantal nomism and his cognition on the Spirit, then, he in fact achieves social validation for his cognition. He will have succeeded in achieving group consensus and backing from the social group in which he is embedded. Using Festinger's terminology, Paul would have acquired a "consonant new cognition" that confirms that there is "something right or influential " about his statement in Rom. 8:4 if the social group whom he identifies with shares the same cognition. If this transpires Paul would have succeeded in significantly reducing the magnitude of dissonance between covenantal nomism and his current cognition on the Spirit.

Paul's tendency to re-orient terms and concepts specifically associated with covenantal nomism around the Spirit in Rom. 1–16 is part of his attempt at influencing believers in Rome to comply with his line of reasoning that there is a positive parallelization between covenantal nomism and his post-Damascus beliefs. The concepts of "righteousness," "life," "peace," and "sonship," that were specifically associated with the Torah in both Ancient and Second Temple Judaism, are re-oriented around the role of the Spirit in the new aeon; i.e., the Spirit brings to fruition all that the Torah hoped to accomplish. Members in the community of faith, especially those in Rome who are familiar with and support the major tenets of Judaism,[154] and who likewise experience the Spirit as he does, can affirm that the Spirit is the basis of ethics and are in the position to verify Paul's cognition. Festinger reasoned that if an individual experiences dissonance, he will naturally communicate with those who share similar cognitions. He might attempt to obtain knowledge that others agree

---

[154] The letter to the Romans is dominated by the issue of Jew/Gentile relationships ("to the Jew first and also to the Greek" [1:16]; definition of a "Jew" [2:25-29]; the identification of the elect of God [1:7; 8:33; 9:6-13; 11:5-7, 28-32]; the gospel as no longer limited to Jews [chs. 2-5] but still with Jews in view [chs. 9-11]; Jew and Gentile worship God together [15:8-12]). This indicates that the community in Rome is most likely composed of both Gentiles (11:13-32; 15:7-12 cf. 1:6, 13; 15:15-16) and Jews, and more precisely, it indicates how Gentile and Jewish Christians should understand their relationship to each other (11:17-24).

with his opinion, consequently adding new consonant cognitive elements.[155] An individual in this situation will gravitate to a social group whose cognitive holdings constitute a dissonance-free environment. If Paul receives validation from believers on these convictions, there will be an appreciable reduction of dissonance between the two clusters of cognitions represented by covenantal nomism and his post-Damascus beliefs.[156] He would have formed a new consonant cognition that others affirm his understanding of the intersection between Judaism and his post-Damascus beliefs and would have succeeded in producing a dissonant free environment among the community of the Spirit in Rome.

6. Conclusion

It was noted above[157] that Paul often takes an unambiguous position on an issue but then spoils it with a further remark that apparently confuses it or implies just the opposite. This is especially true in Rom. 7-8 when he relates Judaism to his post-Damascus convictions, which is his way of saying both "yes" and "no" to Judaism. On the one hand, he writes, "But now we have been discharged from the Law, having died to that by which we were restrained, so that we serve in newness of the Spirit not in oldness of the letter" (7:6). On the other hand, he states, "In order that the righteous requirement of the Law may be fulfilled in us...who walk according to the Spirit" (8:4). Sanders observes how the type of oscillation between the Mosaic Law and the Spirit demonstrates the dilemma about the Law which constantly plagued Paul's mind; he was struggling to hold together his native conviction that the Law was given by God, with his new conviction that life comes only through the Spirit. We concur with Sanders that this textual tension is evidence of Paul's struggle to hold on to two sets of convictions: one from his previous commitment to covenantal nomism and the other from his current convictions on the Spirit. However, mistakenly, both Sanders and Räisänen have taken an extreme position on this and explain the textual tensions as

---

[155] Festinger, A Theory of Cognitive Dissonance, p. 189.

[156] "One would consequently expect that if a person has appreciable dissonance between two clusters of cognitive elements, he would initiate communication and influence processes with other persons in an attempt to reduce this dissonance. He might attempt to obtain knowledge that others agree with his opinion." (Ibid., p. 189).

[157] See Part Three (Introduction).

straightforward contradictions, the direct result of a conflict between Paul's Christian present with his Jewish past.[158] On the other hand, Dunn and Thielman deny the existence of these tensions altogether. They find continuity between Paul's Jewish and Christian convictions and explain the textual tension not as a contradiction on Paul's part, but as a description of the two-sided perspective of Law observance operating in two separate epochs: Law observance impeded by the power of sin in the previous epoch and Law observance enabled by the new power of the Spirit in the present epoch.[159]

With the use of Cognitive Dissonance Theory, we propose that in Rom. 8:1-16 Paul perceived a state of dissonance between covenantal nomism and its expectation that in the future the Spirit would enable individuals to keep the Law fully, and his post-Damascus cognition that the Spirit displaced the Law as the principle of new life. As a result, he engaged in a concentrated effort to reduce this dissonance by re-orienting the role of the Spirit around terms and concepts taken from Judaism's covenantal nomism. He was attempting to bridge the gap between his cognition from his Jewish past and the one from his Christian present by reducing the qualitative distinction between them. Using Festinger's terminology, Paul attempted to reduce the dissonance between covenantal nomism and his current cognition on the Spirit in Rom. 8:1-16. He did this in two ways: 1. by establishing cognitive overlap between them, and 2. by striving to achieve social validation for his cognitions within his own social group of Roman believers with whom he shared the experience of the Spirit and with whom he had a sense of affinity.

---

[158] See Introduction (2.2 A Christological Solution that Precedes Plight: Paul's Contradictory Thoughts on the Law) for a more detailed discussion of the positions of Sanders and Räisänen.

[159] See Introduction (2.3 Continuity Between Jewish and Christian Convictions: Two-Sided Perspective of Law Observance) for a more detailed discussion of the positions of Dunn and Thielman.

Conclusion

1. Summary

Two tensions are apparent in Rom. 8:1-16. The first is internal, between Rom. 8:2,4, ("the law of the Spirit" [8:2]; "in order that the righteous requirement of the Law may be fulfilled in us...who walk according to the Spirit" [8:4]) where the Spirit and Law are complementary, and its surrounding context, where the Spirit and Law are set in opposition ("But now we have been discharged from the Law...to serve in newness of Spirit and not in oldness of letter" [7:6]; "...the Spirit of life in Christ Jesus has set you free from the Law of sin and death" [8:2]) or where the Law is eclipsed by the Spirit (8:5-16), particularly as the principle of new life. But this brings a second tension to light, between Paul's view of the Spirit and Law, and Jewish eschatology, which expected Spirit and Law to co-exist in a harmonious manner.

In Part One our investigation revealed how the literature of Ancient and Second Temple Judaism identifies the Spirit as the agent of covenant renewal whose specific function was to establish a Torah-based ethic. Ancient Judaism provided the framework for the eschatological promise of a new covenant relationship in Israel's restoration. Central to this promise was the belief that Israel would experience a change in inward disposition through the agency of the Spirit. There was widespread attestation to the Spirit as the source of inner transformation, equipping individuals to observe the moral and religious codes of conduct stated in the Jewish Torah. As a result, the Torah was no longer simply an external written code; it would be internalized and received and honoured to become the motive and power of mind and consequently, obeyed willingly. Correspondingly, even though Second Temple Judaism (Diaspora, Palestinian, and Qumran Literature) exhibited diversity with respect to language, geography, and ideology, there was unanimous belief in the congruent relationship between the roles of the Spirit and the Law; the Spirit was always perceived to act in a complementary way to the Jewish Law in that its primary function was to induce behaviour that was specifically fashioned upon the moral code of the Law.

In Part Two we discovered that even though Paul was fully aware of Jewish eschatology and the new covenant expectation, where the Spirit was perceived to be instrumental in the promotion of an internalized moral code fashioned upon the Law, he nevertheless advocated a system that was categorically different from that of Ancient and Second Temple Judaism. The coming of Christ and the believer's participatory union with him ushered in a new era of the Spirit. Paul perceived a decisive point of discontinuity between the former covenant and the new era of the Spirit, where the Spirit displaced the Law and functioned exclusively as the principle of new life; i.e., the Spirit's role was comprehensive, securing familial relationship with God and sustaining this relationship by fashioning the practical and behavioural dimensions of the believer's life. Consequently, Paul sets up a tension and perceived a dissonant relationship between his conception of the new era of the Spirit, and Ancient and Second Temple Judaism.

The phenomenon observed in Rom. 8:2,4, where Paul aligns Spirit and Law, is part of a larger phenomenon apparent in Rom. 8:5-16, where Paul consistently describes the role of the Spirit using terms and concepts drawn from Judaism's covenantal nomism. This trend stands in contrast with Paul's more fundamental conviction, that the Spirit has displaced the Law as the principle of life for the believer. In Part Three we noted how the overtones throughout Rom. 8 are covenantal. For example, in vv. 1-16, "law/Law" (vv. 2, 3, 4, 7), "life" (vv. 2, 6, 10, 11, 13), "righteous requirement" (v. 4), "peace" (v. 6), "sonship" (vv. 14-16) are all concepts in Ancient and Second Temple Judaism that are uniquely associated with God's covenant relationship with Israel, and in particular, are directly related to the Mosaic Law. But, to the contrary, Paul does not correlate these with the Mosaic Law. Instead, they are exclusively linked to the role of the Spirit in the believer's life. If we are correct in our interpretation of 8:1-16—that the Spirit and Law represented two mutually exclusive eras in salvation-history and that the Spirit replaces the Law as the principle of new life—then the question arises as to why Paul does not simply dismiss these covenantal categories as being irrelevant in light of the new situation of the Spirit. In response to this, we posit that they still occupy a prominent place in the apostle's mind and he is still very much embedded within a Jewish frame of thinking. He has intentionally chosen to re-orient these concepts around the Spirit in the new epoch. Therefore, it can be said that Paul's Jewish past and his Christian present intersect in a significant manner and are more than "just two ships passing in the night." They can be more appropriately described as "one ship intentionally pausing beside the other, taking full stock of the other's inventory, borrowing only what it needs for the journey, and then moving on."

With the use of Cognitive Dissonance Theory, we propose that in Rom. 8:1-16 Paul perceived a state of dissonance between covenantal nomism and his post-Damascus cognition on the relationship between the Spirit and Law. As a result, he engaged in a concentrated effort to reconcile this tension by re-orienting the role of the Spirit around terms and concepts taken from Judaism's covenantal nomism. He was attempting to bridge the gap between the Law and the Spirit by reducing the qualitative distinction between them. Using Festinger's terminology, in Rom. 8:1-16 Paul attempted to reduce the dissonance between covenantal nomism and his current cognition by emphasizing the consonance between them. He did this by establishing cognitive overlap, and by striving to achieve social validation for his cognitions within his own social group of Roman believers with whom he shared the experience of the Spirit and with whom he had a sense of affinity.

2. Implications for Pauline Scholarship

Paul's explication of the Law has been a persistent thorn in the flesh for Pauline scholarship. On the one hand, many have shown how his thoughts on the Law are inconsistent, irreconcilable, and unintelligible. On the other hand, some have tried to deny the inconsistencies altogether and forced them to comply with a Jewish eschatological grid. These extreme positions are the result of employing a faulty methodology and one that does not adequately isolate the core issues. Consequently, the continuity/discontinuity interplay between Spirit and Law in Rom. 8:1-16 has been erroneously dismissed as being prompted by nothing more than the situational context in which Paul finds himself with respect to the believers in Rome; i.e., Paul was responding to allegations that he was advocating an antinomian point of view.

Significant advances have been made by noting a distinction between the surface elements of the text and an underlying set of basic convictions. A conviction-centred approach attempts to ascertain the core level of Paul's thinking about the Law, that is, a commitment of beliefs about the Law that are undisturbed by the external situation in which Paul finds himself. Since the continuity/discontinuity interplay on the Law surfaces frequently and occurs rather offhandedly throughout most of Paul's written correspondences regardless of the circumstances, it is most likely that we have isolated underlying convictions. Furthermore, they can be characterized as two separate and competing clusters of convictions, which we contend is the issue in Rom. 8; Paul attempts to negotiate the tensions between his convictions from his Jewish past and those from his Christian present. Consequently, if we are to comprehend Paul's understanding of the relationship between the Spirit and the Law in Rom. 8 we must distinguish between the situational context of the letter and the level of Paul's convictional core to which these ideas belong. The continuity/discontinuity interplay with respect to the Law is evidence of a conflict within Paul's convictional world and evidence that he is attempting to reconcile these two sets of convictions.

In addition to this, further advance has been made in the field of social psychology, which examines the behavioural patterns of individuals of the first-century Mediterranean world of which Paul was a part. The society during this time and in this geographical location was considered a "collectivist culture," where individuals' self-interests are embedded with the interests of groups with whom they share a common bond. This brings a new dynamic to Rom. 8 and one that has significant ramifications for understanding Paul's thoughts on the Spirit and Law. Therefore, we are compelled to approach the interpretation of this chapter from a social-scientific perspective. This is particularly true in light of Paul's use of familial language to describe the social group with whom he had an affinity. He makes an appeal to the community of faith for support by seeking corroboration for his thoughts on the Law. The members of the community of faith represented his own "in-group" who have similarly experienced the sense of familial relationship with God through the Spirit in their lives and were in the position of affirming his perceptions.

In our Introduction[1] above we indicated that the best way to understand the tension in Paul's discourse about the Law is to posit a new set of convictions and a new perspective on Judaism, which resulted from Paul's transformative experiences. We noted how Pauline scholarship would affirm that the catalyst for Paul's new perspective on the Law and Judaism was the result of a one-time Damascus experience and one that is principally

---

[1] See Introduction (3. The Aims of This Study).

Christological in emphasis.[2] However, Paul's explication of the place and purpose of the Law for believers in Rom. 8 is described in pneumacentric not Christocentric language. The frequency with which he refers to the Spirit in Rom. 8 is a *prima facie* indication that the interpretive key is his pneumatology. Consequently, if our aim is to understand Paul's statements on the Law in this chapter, his pneumatology should not be absorbed by his Christology to the extent that it is interpreted through a restrictive Christological funnel.

There is a consistent pattern in Paul's writings regarding his understanding of the Spirit. Whenever he reminds his readers of the decisive moment of their conversion he invariably refers to the role played by the Spirit.[3] Numerous confessional texts within the Pauline corpus allude to some decisive moment in believers' lives, where Paul includes himself together with his readers as recipients of the Spirit.[4] For example in Rom. 5:5 Paul writes, "the love of God has been poured out in *our* hearts through the Holy Spirit who has been given to us." Fee comments, "[This] almost certainly reflect[s]...[Paul's] experience of the Spirit at the time of his own conversion."[5] This coincides with our comments on Rom. 8. In vv. 15-16, Paul intentionally switches from second to first person plural, indicating that he includes himself among the community of faith who shares the decisive, on-going experience of the Spirit's inspirational cry of familial relationship with God: "*You* received the Spirit of adoption by whom *we* cry: 'Abba, Father'. The Spirit testifies with *our* spirit that *we* are children of God." We indicated that the use of the aorist verb in phrase, "the law of the Spirit of life in Christ Jesus *has set* you *free* (ἠλευθέρωσεν) from the Law of sin and death" (8:2) forms an association with 7:3-4, where the cognate word ἐλευθέρα is used in connection with Paul's idea that we are "joined to another" (i.e., to Christ). Paul pinpoints the decisive time of the believer's change in status as that time

---

[2] In particular, we have Sanders' *Christological* "solution that precedes plight" in mind ("God intended that salvation be by faith; thus be definition it is not by law. Further, this discussion is connected with faith in Christ, so that one may equally well call the principle that of Christology" [*Paul, the Law, and the Jewish People*, p. 47]).

[3] It is no coincidence that whenever Paul reminds his readers of their decisive point of transformation, he mentions the Spirit (in a presuppositional manner [1 Cor. 2:4-5; 6:11; 1 Thess. 1:5-6, 9-10; or where the Spirit is central to the argument [2 Cor. 3:3; Gal. 3:1-5]).

[4] See for example, Gal. 3:13-14; 4:4-7; 2 Cor. 1:21-22.

[5] Gordon D. Fee, "Paul's Conversion as Key to His Understanding of the Spirit," in *The Road from Damascus* (ed. R.N. Longenecker; Grand Rapids: Wm. B. Eerdmans Publishing Co., 1997), pp. 167-83, quote taken from p. 180.

when he is joined to Christ. In 7:4, participatory union with Christ is the prerequisite for "bearing fruit for God," which we claimed was a subtle reference to the Spirit. This is parallel to 8:2, where the prepositional insertion ἐν Χριστῷ ʼΙησοῦ functions as the basis for the Spirit's role in 8:2ff and the decisive point at which the believer was set free from the power of sin and death. We can surmise from this that Paul's cognitions on the Spirit in Rom. 8 were not the recitation of a detached piece of Jewish tradition. Rather, with Fee we can state that his perceptions were ones fashioned to a significant degree by the experiences of his own life, particularly his own decisive experience of the Spirit at Damascus, the point of his own transformation.[6]

Given this presupposition, we can legitimately look beyond Paul's rhetoric in Rom. 8 and can state with a degree of confidence that his experience of the Spirit at Damascus was also a catalyst for his perception of the place and purpose of the Law for believers. In Rom. 7:1-6, we have demonstrated how Paul's understanding of participatory union with Christ is aligned positively with and is inextricable from his statements on the Spirit in the new era, against the former era of the Law: "You also were made to *die to the Law through the body of Christ*, that you might be joined to another, to him who was raised from the dead...*we were discharged from the Law...so that we may serve in newness of the Spirit*" (vv. 4-6). Therefore, Paul's thoughts on the Law are not simply the result of a one-time Damascus experience described in Christocentric language, but are also the result of Paul's decisive and on-going experience of the Spirit begun at Damascus described in pneumacentric language in Rom. 8. If we are to understand Paul's perception of the place and purpose of the Law for believers, Pauline scholarship must give pneumatology an equal place of prominence with Christology. It cannot simply be considered an appendage or a shadow of Paul's Christology. Paul's pneumatology deserves its own unique place and one that will make its own significant contribution in the discussion of Paul's view of the Law.

In summation, Pauline scholarship can be assured that the apparent textual conflicts in Rom. 8 are not "signs of falsity" but are a demonstration of Paul's attempt at "bending the contradictions with gentleness and time."[7] His thoughts on the Spirit and Law still vie as a climactic moment in Pauline soteriology and ones that will continue to challenge inquisitive minds that

---

[6] *Ibid.*, p. 167.

[7] See opening quotes from Blaise Pascal and Saint Frances de Sales (Introduction).

strive to understand one of the most enigmatic, yet influential authors in the first century C.E.

Bibliography

Primary Sources

Texts and Translations

The Apocrypha and Pseudepigrapha of the Old Testament. Edited by R.H. Charles. 2 Vols. Oxford:Clarendon Press, 1912-1913.

Aristotle with an English Translation: "The 'Art' of Rhetoric." Translated by J.H. Freese. LCL. Cambridge, Mass: Harvard University Press, 1959.

Biblia Hebraica Stuttgartensia. Edited by K. Elliger and W. Rudolph. New Ed. Stuttgart: Deutsche Bibelgesellschaft, 1977.

The Complete Dead Sea Scrolls in English. Translated by Geza Vermes. Fourth Edition. New York: Penguin Books, 1997.

The Complete Works of Josephus. Translated by W. Whiston. Grand Rapids: Kregel Publications, 1981.

Genesis Rabbah, Vol. 1. Translated by Jacob Neusner. Atlanta: Scholars Press, 1985.

The Greek New Testament. Edited by B. Aland, K. Aland, J. Karavidopoulous, C.M. Martini, B.M. Metzger. Fourth Revised Edition. Stuttgart: Deutsche Bibelgesellschaft, 1983.

The Greek Versions of the Testaments of the Twelve Patriarchs. Edited by R.H. Charles. Oxford: Clarendon Press, 1966.

Josephus with an English Translation. Edited by H.J. Thackeray and R. Marcus. 9 Vols, LCL. London: W. Heinemann, 1926-65.

The Mishna: A New Translation. Translated by Jacob Neusner. London: Yale University Press, 1988.

The Old Testament Pseudepigrapha. Edited by J.H. Charlesworth. 2 Vols. Garden City: Doubleday, 1983-1985.

Philo. Edited by F.H. Colson, G.H. Whitaker, R. Marcus. 12 Vols., LCL. London: Heinemann; Cambridge, MA: Harvard University Press, 1929-1962.

Septuaginta: Id est Vetus Testamentum graece iuxta LXX interpretes. Edited by A. Rahlfs. 2 Vols. in 1. Stuttgart: Deutsche Bibelgesellschaft, c1935.

Die Texte aus Qumran: Hebräisch und Deutsch mit Masoretischer Punktuation, Übersetzung, Einführung und Anmerkungen. Edited by E. Lohse. Second Edition. München: Kösel Verlag, 1971.

The Thanksgiving Hymns: Translated and Annotated with an Introduction. Translated by M. Monsoor. Grand Rapids: Wm. B. Eerdmans Publishing Co., 1961.

The Wisdom of Ben Sira: A New Translation with Notes. Translated by P.W. Skehan and A.A. DiLella. AB Vol. 39. New York: Doubleday, 1987.

The Works of Philo: Complete and Unabridged. Translated by C.D. Yonge. Peabody, MA: Hendrickson Publishers, 1993.

Concordances and Lexica

Aland, K., ed. *Computer-Konkordanz zum Novum Testamentum Graece.* Berlin: de Gruyter, 1980.

Borgen, P.; Fuglseth, K.; Skarsten, R. *The Philo Index: A Complete Greek Word Index of the Writings of Philo of Alexandria.* Grand Rapids: Wm. B. Eerdmans Publishing Company, 2000.

Danker, Frederick W. Ed. *A Greek-English Lexicon of the New Testament and Other Early Christian Literature,* Third Edition, Based on the 6th rev. ed. of Walter Bauer's *Griechisch-deutsches Worterbuch zu den Schriften des Neuen Testaments und der übrigen urchristlichen Literatur.* Chicago and London: The University of Chicago Press, 2000.

Hatch, E.; Redpath, H.A. *A Concordance to the Septuagint and other Greek Versions of the Old Testament (including the Apochryphal Books),* Vol. II. Oxford: Clarendon Press, 1897.

Kuhn, K.G. *Kondordanz zu den Qumrantexten.* Göttingen: Vandenhoeck & Ruprecht, 1960.

Rengstorf, K.H. *A Complete Concordance to Flavius Josephus,* Vol. III (Λ-Π). Leiden: E.J. Brill, 1979.

Secondary Literature

Abelson, R.P. et al. *Theories of Cognitive Consistency: A Sourcebook.* Chicago: Rand McNally, 1968.

Achtemeier, Paul J. *Romans.* Atlanta: John Knox Press, 1985.

Aletti, J.-N. *Comment Dieu est-il juste? Clefs pour interpréter l'épître aux Romains.* Rome: Editions du Seuil, 1991.

Allen, L.C. *Ezekiel 20-48,* Vol. 29, WBC. Dallas: Word Books, Publisher, 1990.

——.*The Books of Joel, Obadiah, Jonah and Micah,* NICOT. Grand Rapids: Wm. B. Eerdmans Publishing Company, 1976.

Anderson, A.A. "The Use of 'Rua(c)h' in 1QS, 1QH and 1QM,"*JSS* 7 (1962), 293-303.

Aronson, E. "Dissonance Theory, Progress, and Problems." Pages 5-27 in *Theories of Cognitive Consistency: A Sourcebook.* Edited by R.P. Abelson et al. Chicago: Rand McNally and Co., 1968.

Aronson, E; Carlsmith, J.M. "Effect of the Severity of Threat on the Violation of Forbidden Behavior," *JASP* 66 (1963), 584-88.

Atherton, C. *The Stoics on Ambiguity,* CCS. Cambridge: Cambridge University Press, 1993.

Aune, D.E. *Prophecy in Early Christianity and the Ancient Mediterranean World.* Grand Rapids: Wm. B. Eerdmans Publishing Co., 1983.

——. "The Use of ΠΡΟΦΗΤΗΣ in Josephus," *JBL* 101/3 (1982), 419-21.

Bandstra, Andrew J. *The Law and the Elements of the World: An Exegetical Study in Aspects of Paul's Teaching.* Kampen: J.H. Kok N.V., 1964.

Banks, R. "Romans 7:25a: An Eschatological Thanksgiving?" *ABR* 26 (1978), 34-42.

Barclay, J.M.G. *Obeying the Truth: A Study of Paul's Ethics in Galatians.* Edinburgh: T & T Clark, 1988.

Barker, K.L. *Daniel-Minor Prophets,* Vol. 7, EBC. Grand Rapids: Zondervan Publishing House, 1985.

Barr, J. "'Abba Father' and the Familiarity of Jesus' Speech," *Theology* 91 (1988), 173-79.

———. "'Abba Isn't 'Daddy'," *JTS* 39 (1988), 28-47.

Barrett, C.K. *The First Epistle to the Corinthians,* BNTC. Peabody, MA: Hendrickson Publishers, 1968.

———. *The Second Epistle to the Corinthians,* BNTC. Peabody, MA: Hendrickson Publishers, 1973.

———. *A Commentary on the Epistle to the Romans,* BNTC/ HNTC. London: Black/ New York: Harper & Row, 1957, 1975, 1991.

Barth, C. *God With Us: A Theological Introduction to the Old Testament.* Grand Rapids: Wm B. Eerdmans Publishing Company, 1991.

Baumgärtel, F. "Flesh in the Old Testament," *TDNT,* Vol. VII, pp. 105-8.

Baumgärtel, F.; Behm, J. "καρδία, κτλ.," *TDNT,* Vol. III., pp. 605-14.

Becker, J. *Untersuchungen zur Entstehungsgeschichte der Testamente der Zwölf Patriarchen.* Leiden: E.J. Brill, 1970.

———. *Das Heil Gottes: Heils- und Sündenbegriffe in den Qumrantexten und im Neuen Testament,* SUNT 3. Göttingen: Vandenhoeck & Ruprecht, 1964.

Beker, J.C. *Paul the Apostle: The Triumph of God in Life and Thought.* Philadelphia: Fortress, 1980.

———. "Suffering and Triumph in Paul's Letter to the Romans," *HBT* 2 (1985), 105-19.

Benoit, P. "La Loi et la Croix d'après Saint Paul (Rom. 7:7-8:4)," *RB* 47 (1938), 481-509.

Bertone, John A. "The Function of the Spirit in the Dialectic between God's Soteriological Plan Enacted But Not Yet Culminated: Romans 8.1-27," *JPT* 15 (1999), 75-97.

Bertram, G. "παιδεύω, κτλ.," *TDNT,* Vol. V, pp. 596-625.

———. "θεοσεβής, θεοσέβεια," *TDNT,* Vol. III, pp. 123-8.

———. "ὁρμή, κτλ.," *TDNT,* Vol. V, pp. 467-74.

———. "πατέω, κτλ.," *TDNT,* Vol. V, pp. 940-43.

———. "φυλάσσω, φυλακή," *TDNT,* Vol. IX, pp. 236-44.

Best, E. "The Use and Non-Use of Pneuma by Josephus," *NovT* 3 (1959), 218-25.

Betz, H.D. *Galatians,* Hermeneia. Philadelphia: Fortress Press, 1979.

Bienert, K.D. "The Apostle Paul's View of the Law According to Romans 8.1-17," Doct. Diss., São Leopoldo, 2001.

Black, M. *Romans,* NCBC. London: Oliphants/Grand Rapids: Eerdmans, 1989.

Bläser, Peter. *Das Gesetz bei Paulus.* Munster: Aschendorffsche Verlagsbuchhandlung, 1941.

Blenkinsopp, J. *Ezekiel,* Interpretation. Louisville: John Knox Press, 1990.

———. "Prophecy and Priesthood," *JJS* 25 (1974), 241-2.

Boice, J.M. *Romans-Galatians,* EBC, Vol. 10. Grand Rapids: Zondervan Publishing House, 1976.

Bornkamm, G. "The Letter to the Romans as Paul's Last Will and Testament," *ABR* 11 (1963-64), 2-14.

——. "Baptism and New Life in Paul: Romans 6," Pages 71-86 in *Early Christian Experience*. London: SCM, 1969.

——. "Sin, Law and Death: An Exegetical Study of Romans 7," Pages 83-94 in *Early Christian Experience*. London: SCM, 1969.

Braun, H. *Qumran und das Neue Testament*, Vol. 1. Tübingen: Mohr, 1966.

Brehm, Jack W.; Cohen, Arthur R. *Explorations in Cognitive Dissonance*. New York: John Wiley and Sons, Inc., 1962.

Brehm, M.L.; Back, K.W.; Bogdonoff, M.D. "A Physiological Effect of Cognitive Dissonance under Stress and Deprivation," *JASP* 69 (1964), 303-10.

Brown, C. "Righteousness, Justification," *NIDNTT*, Vol. 3, pp. 352-77.

Brown, R. *Social Psychology*. Glencoe, Illinois: The Free Press, 1965.

Bruce, F.F. *Paul, Apostle of the Heart Set Free*. Grand Rapids: Wm. B. Eerdmans Publishing Co., 1977.

——. "Holy Spirit in the Qumran Texts," *The Annual of Leeds University Oriental Society* 6 (1966-68), 49-55.

——. *The Epistle to the Galatians*, NIGTC. Grand Rapids: Wm. B. Eerdmans Publishing Co., 1982.

——. *The Letter of Paul to the Romans*, TNTC, Revised Edition. Leicester: Inter-Varsity Press, 1985.

Brueggemann, W. *The Land: Place as Gift, Promise and Challenge in Biblical Faith*. Philadelphia: Fortress Press, 1977.

Brunner, Emil. *The Letter to the Romans*. Philadelphia: Westminster Press, 1959.

Büchsel, F. *Der Geist Gottes im Neuen Testament*. Gütersloh: C. Bertelsmann, 1926.

——. "παράδοσις," *TDNT*, Vol. II, pp. 172-73.

Bultmann, R. *Theology of the New Testament*, Vol. 1. New York: Charles Scribner's Sons, 1951.

——. "Weissagung and Erfüllung," *ST* 2 (1949), 21-44.

——. "γινώσκω, κτλ.," *TDNT*, Vol.I, pp. 696-701.

——. "The Concept of Life in Judaism," *TDNT*, Vol. II, pp. 855-61.

——. "καυχάομαι, κτλ.," *TDNT*, Vol. III, pp. 645-54.

——. "θάνατος, κτλ.," *TDNT*, Vol. III, pp. 7-25.

Burrows, M. *More Light on the Dead Sea Scrolls*. New York: Viking Press, 1958.

Burton, E. De Witt. *A Critical and Exegetical Commentary on the Epistle to the Galatians*, ICC. Edinburgh: T & T Clark, 1921.

Burton, K.A. *Rhetoric, Law, and the Mystery of Salvation in Romans 7:1-6*, Studies in the Bible and Early Christianity, Vol. 44. Lewiston: The Edwin Mellen Press, 2001.

Byrne, B. *Romans*, SP, Vol. 6. Collegeville, MN: The Liturgical Press, 1996.

——. "Sons of God"- "Seed of Abraham", AnBib 83. Rome: Pontifical Biblical Institute, 1979.

——. "Living out the Righteousness of God: The Contribution of Rom. 6:1-8:13 to an Understanding of Paul's Ethical Presuppositions," *CBQ* 43 (1981), 557-81.

Callan, T. "Prophecy and Ecstasy in Greco-Roman Religion and 1 Corinthians," *NovT* 27 (1985), 125-40.

Carcopino, L. *Daily Life in Ancient Rome*. New Haven, CT: Yale University, 1940.

Carroll, Robert P. *When Prophecy Failed: Cognitive Dissonance in the Prophetic Traditions of the Old Testament.* New York: The Seabury Press, 1979.

———. "Prophecy, Dissonance and Jeremiah XXVI," *Transactions of the Glasgow University Oriental Society* 25 (1976), 12-23.

———. "Ancient Israelite Prophecy and Dissonance Theory," *Numen* 24 (1977), 135-51.

———. *From Chaos to Covenant: Use of Prophecy in the Book of Jeremiah.* London: SCM Press Ltd., 1981.

Chadwick, H. "'All Things to All Men' (1 Cor.IX.22)," *NTS* 1 (1955), 261-75.

Charlesworth, J.H. "The Origin and Subsequent History of the Authors of the Dead Sea Scrolls: Four Transitional Phases Among the Qumran Essenes," *RevQ* 10 (1980), 213-33.

Chevallier, M.A. *Souffle de dieu: Le Saint-Esprit dans le Nouveau Testament,* Le Point Théologique 26. Paris: Éditions Beauchesne, 1978.

———. *L'Espirit et le Messie dans le Bas-Judaïsme et le Nouveau Testament.* Paris: Presses Universitaires de France, 1958.

Christiansen, E.J *The Covenant in Judaism and Paul: A Study of Ritual Boundaries as Identity Markers.* Leiden/ New York/ Köln: E.J. Brill, 1995.

Clarke, E.G. *The Wisdom of Solomon.* London: Cambridge University Press, 1973.

Cohen, N.G. *Philo Judaeus: His Universe of Discourse.* New York: Peter Lang, 1995.

Collins, J.J. *Between Athens and Jerusalem.* New York: Crossroad, 1983.

Conybeare, F.C.; Stock, G. *Grammar of Septuagint Greek: With Selected Readings, Vocabularies, and Updated Indexes.* Peabody, MA: Hendrickson, 1995.

Conzelmann, H. *1 Corinthians: A Commentary on the First Epistle to the Corinthians,* Hermeneia. Philadelphia: Fortress Press, 1975.

Cooke, G.A. *A Critical and Exegetical Commentary on The Book of Ezekiel,* ICC. Edinburgh: T & T Clark, 1936.

Corbett, P.E. *The Roman Law of Marriage.* Oxford: Clarendon Press, 1969.

Crabtree, A.R. "Translation of Romans 5:1 in the Revised Standard Version of the New Testament," *RevExp* (1946), 436-39.

Craigie, P.C. *The Old Testament: Its Background, Growth and Content.* Burlington, ON: Welch Publishing Company Inc., 1986.

Cranfield, C.E.B. *On Romans and Other New Testament Essays.* Edinburgh: T&T Clark, 1998.

———. *A Critical and Exegetical Commentary on the Epistle to the Romans,* ICC, 2 Vols. Edinburgh: T&T Clark, 1975, 1979.

Crogan, G.W. *Isaiah, Jeremiah, Lamentations, Ezekiel,* EBC, Vol. 6. Grand Rapids: Zondervan Publishing House, 1986.

Das, A.A. *Paul, the Law and the Covenant.* Peabody, MA: Hendrickson Publishers, 2001.

Davenport, G.L. *The Eschatology of the Book of Jubilees.* Leiden: E.J. Brill, 1971.

Davies, W.D. "Paul and the Dead Sea Scrolls: Flesh and Spirit." Pages 157-82 in *The Scrolls and the New Testament.* Edited by Krister Stendahl. London: SCM Press Ltd., 1957.

———. *Paul and Rabbinic Judaism: Some Rabbinic Elements in Pauline Theology* Fourth Edition. Philadelphia: Fortress, 1980.

———. *Invitation to the New Testament.* Garden City, NY: Doubleday & Co., 1966.

Davis, J.A. *Wisdom and Spirit: An Investigation of 1 Corinthians 1.18–3.20 against the Background of Jewish Sapiential Tradition in the Greco-Roman Period.* Lanham, MD: University Press of America, 1984.

De Jonge, M. "Christian Influence in the Testament of the Twelve Patriarchs," *NovT* (1960), 182–235.

De la Potterie, I; Lyonnet, S. "Le Chrétien conduit par l'esprit dans son cheminement Eschatologique." Pages 209–78 in Lorenzo De Lorenzi, *The Law of the Spirit in Rom 7 and 8.* Rome: St. Paul's Abbey, 1976, pp. 209–78.

Delling, G. "ἀργός, ἀργέω, καταργέω," *TDNT*, Vol. 1, pp. 452–54.

——. "πληρόω, κτλ.," *TDNT*, Vol.VI, pp. 283–311.

Dewey, Arthur J. *Spirit and Letter in Paul*, Studies in the Bible and Early Christianity Vol.33. Lewiston/ Queenston/ Lampeter: The Edwin Mellen Press, 1996.

Dibelius, Martin. *Paul.* Edited by W.G. Kümmel. Translated by F. Clarke. Philadelphia: Westminster Press, 1953.

Dodd, C.H. *The Epistle of Paul to the Romans.* New York: Harper & Brothers, 1932.

Donaldson, Terence L. *Paul and the Gentiles: Remapping the Apostle's Convictional World.* Minneapolis: Fortress Press, 1997.

——. "Zealot," *ISBE*, Vol. IV. Grand Rapids: Wm. B. Eerdmans Publishing Co., 1988, pp. 1175–79.

Donfried, Karl P., ed. *The Romans Debate: Revised and Expanded Edition.* Peabody, MA: Hendrickson, 1991.

van Dülmen, A. *Die Theologie des Gesetzes bei Paulus*, SBM 5. Stuttgart: Katholisches Bibelwerk, 1968.

Dumbrell, W.J. *The Faith of Israel: Its Expression in the Books of the Old Testament.* Grand Rapids: Baker Book House, 1988.

Dunn, J.D.G. "'A Light to the Gentiles': The Significance of the Damascus Road Christophany for Paul." Pages 251–66 in *The Glory of Christ in the New Testament.* Edited by L.D. Hurst and N.T. Wright. Oxford: Clarendon Press, 1987.

——. *Romans*, WBC 38 A/B. Dallas: Word Books, 1988.

——. *The Theology of Paul the Apostle.* Grand Rapids, Michigan/Cambridge, U.K.: Wm. B. Eerdmans Publishing Co., 1998.

——. "The New Perspective on Paul," *BJRL* 65 (1983), 95–122. Later published Pages 183–214 in *Jesus, Paul, and the Law: Studies in Mark and Galatians.* Louisville, KY: Westminster/ John Knox Press, 1990.

——. *Baptism in the Holy Spirit: A Re-examination of the New Testament Teaching on the Gift of the Spirit in Relation to Pentecostalism Today*, SBT, Second Series, no. 15. London: SCM Press Ltd., 1970.

——. *Jesus and the Spirit: A Study of the Religious and Charismatic Experience of Jesus and the First Christians as Reflected in the New Testament.* Grand Rapids: Wm. B. Eerdmans Publishing Co., 1997.

——. "Spirit, Holy Spirit (NT)," *NIDNTT*, Vol. 3. Grand Rapids: Zondervan Publishing House, 1986, pp. 693–707.

———. "Spirit Speech: Reflections on Romans 8:12-27." Pages 82-91 in *Romans and the People of God: Essays in Honor of Gordon D. Fee on the Occasion of His 65ᵗʰ Birthday.* Edited by Sven K. Soderlund and N.T. Wright. Grand Rapids: Wm. B. Eerdmans Publishing Co., 1999.

———. "Jesus-Flesh and Spirit: An Exposition of Romans 1:3-4," *JTS* 24 (1973), 40-68.

———. *The Epistle to the Galatians*, BNTC. Peabody, MA: Hendrickson Publishers, 1993.

———. "Romans 7:14-25 in the Theology of Paul," *Essays on Apostolic Themes: Studies in Honor of Howard M. Ervin.* Edited by P. Elbert. Peabody, MA: Hendrickson, 1985.

Dupont, J. "The Conversion of Paul, and Its Influence on His Understanding of Salvation by Faith." Pages 176-94 in *Apostolic History and the Gospel.* Edited by W.W. Gasque and R.P. Martin. Grand Rapids: Wm. B. Eerdmans Publishing Co., 1970.

Dupont-Sommer, A. *The Essene Writings From Qumran.* Translated by G. Vermes. Oxford: Basil Blackwell, 1961.

Earnshaw, J.D. "Reconsidering Paul's Marriage Analogy in Romans 7.1-4," *NTS* 40 (1994), 69-88.

Ebel, G. "περιπατέω," *NIDNTT*, Vol. 3, pp. 943-45.

Eckert, J. *Die urchristliche Verkündigung im Streit zwischen Paulus und seinen Gegnern nach dem Galaterbrief*, BU 6. Regensburg: F. Pustet, 1971.

Eichholz, G. *Die Theologie des Paulus im Umriss.* Neukirchen-Vlugn: Neukirchen-Verlag, 1972.

Eissfeldt, O. *Einleitung in das Alte Testament unter Einschluss der Apokryphen und Pseudepigraphen sowie der apokryphen- und pseudepigraphenartigen Qumran-Schriften*, Fourth Edition. Tübingen: J.C.B. Mohr (Paul Siebeck), 1976.

Elliott, M.A. *The Survivors of Israel: A Reconsideration of the Theology of Pre-Christian Judaism.* Grand Rapids: Wm. B. Eerdmans Publishing Co., 2000.

Elliott, Neil. *The Rhetoric of Romans: Argumentative Constraint and Strategy and Paul's Dialogue with Judaism.* JSNTSup 45. Sheffield: JSOT Press, 1990.

Enslin, M.S. *Reapproaching Paul.* Philadelphia: Westminster Press, 1972.

Fairbairn, P. *The Revelation of the Law in Scripture.* Grand Rapids: Zondervan, 1957.

Fatehi, M. *The Spirit's Relation to the Risen Lord in Paul: An Examination of Its Christological Implications*, WUNT 2. Reihe 128. Tübingen: J.C.B. Mohr (Paul Siebeck), 2000.

Fee, G.D. *God's Empowering Presence: The Holy Spirit in the Letters of Paul.* Peabody, MA: Hendrickson, 1994.

———. *The First Epistle to the Corinthians*, NICNT. Grand Rapids: Wm. B. Eerdmans Publishing Co., 1987.

———. *Paul's Letter to the Philippians*, NICNT. Grand Rapids: William B. Eerdmans Publishing Co., 1995.

———. "Paul's Conversion as Key to His Understanding of the Spirit." Pages 167-83 in *The Road from Damascus.* Edited by R.N. Longenecker. Grand Rapids: Wm. B. Eerdmans Publishing Co., 1997.

Feine, P. *Das gesetzesfreie Evangelium des Paulus nach seinem Werdegang dargestellt.* Leipzig: J.C. Hinrichs, 1899.

Feldman, L.H. *Josephus's Interpretation of the Bible.* Berkeley: University of California Press, 1998.

———. "Prophets and Prophecy in Josephus," *JTS* 41 (1990), 388-422.

Ferguson, E. *Backgrounds of Early Christianity*. Grand Rapids: Wm. B. Eerdmans Publishing Co., 1987.

Festinger, Leon. *A Theory of Cognitive Dissonance*. Stanford, CA: Stanford University Press, 1962.

Festinger, L.; Riecken, H.W.; Schachter, S. *When Prophecy Fails: A Social and Psychological Study of a Modern Group that Predicted the Destruction of the World*. Minneapolis: University of Minnesota, 1956.

Feuillet, A. "Loi de Dieu, loi du Christ et loi de l'Esprit d'après les épitres pauliniennes: Les rapports de ces trois lois avec la Loi Mosaique," *NovT* 22 (1980), 29-65.

Finn, T.M. "The God-fearers Reconsidered," *CBQ* 47 (1985), 75-84.

Fischer, K. *From Cognitive Semantics to Lexical Pragmatics: The Functional Polysemy of Discourse Particles*. New York: Mouton de Gruyter, 2000.

Fitzmyer, J.A. "Paul and the Law." Pages 186-201 in *To Advance the Gospel: New Testament Studies*. New York: Crossroads, 1981.

——. "Abba and Jesus' Relation to God." Pages 15-38 in *A cause de l'Evangile: Etudes sur les Synoptiques et les Actes offertes au P. Jacques Dupont, O.S. B. à son 70e anniversaire*, LD 123. Edited by R. Gantoy. Paris: Cerf, 1985.

——. *Romans: A New Translation with Introduction and Commentary*, AB 33. New York: Doubleday, 1993.

Foerster, W. "Der Heilige Geist im Spätjudentum," *NTS* 8 (1961-62), 117-34.

——. "κληρονόμος," *TDNT*, Vol. III, pp. 776-81.

——. "Κυριεύω," *TDNT*, Vol. III, p. 1097.

——. "ἐχθρός, ἐχθρα," *TDNT*, Vol. II, pp. 811-15

Foerster, W; Von Rad, G. "εἰρήνη, κτλ.," *TDNT*, Vol. II, pp. 400-20.

Fohrer, G. "σοφία-The Old Testament," *TDNT*, Vol. VII, pp. 476-96.

Fohrer, G.; Schweizer, E.; Lohse, E. "υἱός, κτλ.," *TDNT*, Vol. VIII, pp. 340-92.

Fredriksen, P. "Paul and Augustine: Conversion Narratives, Orthodox Traditions and the Retrospective Self," *JTS* (1986), 3-34.

Friedrich, G. "Das Gesetz des Glaubens Röm. 3, 27," *TZ* (1954), 401-17.

Fuchs, E. *Die Freiheit des Glaubens. Römer 5-8 ausgelegt*, BEvT 14. Munich: Kaiser, 1949.

Fung, R.Y.K. *The Epistle to the Galatians*, NICNT. Grand Rapids: Wm. B. Eerdmans Publishing Co., 1988.

Funk, R. "The Syntax of the Article: Its Importance for Critical Pauline Problems". Ph.D. diss., Vanderbilt University, 1953.

Furnish, V.P. *Theology and Ethics in Paul*. Nashville: Abingdon, 1968.

——. *II Corinthians: A New Translation with Introduction and Commentary*, AB, Vol. 32A. New York: Doubleday, 1984.

——. *The Love Command in the New Testament*. Nashville, Tenn.: Abingdom, 1972.

Gager, John G. *Kingdom and Community: The Social World of Early Christianity*. Englewood Cliffs: Prentice-Hall, 1975.

Gagnon, R.A. "'Should We Sin?' The Romans Debate and Romans 6:1-7:6." Ph.D. dissertation, Princeton Theological Seminary, 1993.

Gale, H.M. *The Use of Analogy in the Letter of Paul*. Philadelphia: Westminster, 1964.

Gamson, W.A. "The Social Psychology of Collective Action." Pages 53-76 in *Frontiers in Social Management Theory*. Edited by A.D. Morris and C. McClurg Mueller. New Haven, CT: Yale University Press, 1992, pp. 53-76.

Garlington, D.B. "Romans 7:14-25 and the Creation Theology of Paul," *TJ* 11(1990), 197-235.

Gaston, L. *Paul and the Torah*. Vancouver: University of British Columbia, 1987.

———. "Works of the Law as a Subjective Genitive," *SR* 13 (1984), 39-46.

Gaventa, Beverly Roberts. *From Darkness to Light: Aspects of Conversion in the New Testament*. Philadelphia: Fortress Press, 1986.

Given, M.D. *Paul's True Rhetoric: Ambiguity, Cunning, and Deception in Greece and Rome*. Harrisburg, PA: Trinity Press International, 2001.

Grabbe, L.L. *Wisdom of Solomon*. Sheffield: Sheffield Academic Press, 1997.

Greenberg, M. *Ezekiel 21-37: A New Translation with Introduction and Commentary* AB. New York: Doubleday, 1997.

Grogan, G.W. "Isaiah," *Isaiah-Ezekiel*, EBC, Vol. 6. Grand Rapids: Zondervan Publishing House, 1986.

Grönemeyer, R. "Zur Frage nach dem paulinischen Antinomismus: Exegetisch-systematische Uberlegungen mit besonderer Berücksichtigung der Forschungsgeschichte im 19. Jahrhundert," Dokotorwürde Diss., University of Hamburg, 1970.

Grundmann, W. "συν-μετα, κτλ.," *TDNT*, Vol. VII, pp. 766-97.

———. "κράζω, κτλ.," *TDNT*, Vol. III, pp. 898-903.

Gundry, R.H. "The Moral Frustration of Paul before His Conversion: Sexual Lust in Romans 7:7-25." Pages 228-45 in *Pauline Studies: Essays Presented to Professor F.F. Bruce on His Seventieth Birthday*. Edited by D.A. Hagner and M.J. Harris. Grand Rapids: Wm. B. Eerdmans Publishing Co., 1980.

———. *Sōma in Biblical Theology with Emphasis on Pauline Anthropology*. Grand Rapids: Zondervan, 1987.

Gunkel, H. *The Influence of the Holy Spirit: The Popular View of the Apostolic Age and the Teaching of the Apostle Paul*. Philadelphia: Fortress Press, 1979. Originally published as *Die Wirkungen des Heilgen Geistes nach der populären Anschauung der apostolischen Zeit und der Lehre des Apostles Paulus*. Göttingen: Vandenhoeck & Ruprecht, 1888.

Gutbrod, W.; Kleinknecht, H. "νόμος," *TDNT*, Vol. IV, pp. 1022-91.

Gyllenberg, R. *Rechtfertigung und Altes Testament bei Paulus*. Stuttgart: Kohlhammer, 1973.

Haenchen, E. *Der Weg Jesu*, Second Ed. Berline: de Gruyter, 1968.

Hafemann, S.J. *Paul, Moses and the History of Israel: The Letter/Spirit Contrast and the Argument from Scripture in 2 Corinthians 3*, WUNT 81. Tübingen: J.C.B. Mohr (Paul Siebeck), 1995.

———. *Suffering and the Spirit: An Exegetical Study of II Cor. 2:14-3:3 within the Context of the Corinthian Correspondence*, WUNT 19. Tübingen: J.C.B. Mohr (Paul Siebeck), 1986.

Hahn, F. "Das Gesetzesverständnis im Römer—und Galaterbrief," *ZNW* 67 (1976), 29-63.

Hamilton, N.Q. *The Holy Spirit and Eschatology in Paul*, SJTOP 6. Edinburgh: Oliver and Boyd, 1957.

Harder, G. "Reason, Mind, Understanding," *NIDNTT*, Vol. 3, pp. 122-30.

Harrington, D.J. "Pseudo-Philo: A New Translation and Introduction," *OTP*, Vol. 2, pp. 297-378.

Harrison, E.F. *Romans*, EBC,Vol. 10. Grand Rapids: Zondervan, 1976.

Harrison, R.K. *Leviticus*, TOTC. Grand Rapids: Wm. B. Eerdmans Publishing Co., 1980.

Harvey, A.E. *Jesus and the Constraints of History*. London: Duckworth, 1982.

Hauck, F. "περισσεύω, κτλ.," *TDNT*, Vol. VI, pp. 58–63.

Hays, Richard B. *Echoes of Scripture in the Letters of Paul*. New Haven, Conn.: Yale University Press, 1989.

Hegg, T. *The Letter Writer: Paul's Background and Torah Perspective*. Tacoma, WA: First Fruits of Zion, 2002.

Hehn, J. "Zum Problem des Geistes im alten Orient und im alten Testament," *ZAW* 43 (1925), 210–25.

Hendriksen, W. *Exposition of Paul's Epistle to the Romans*, Vol. 1. Grand Rapids: Baker, 1980.

Hengel, Martin. *The Pre-Christian Paul*. London: SCM/Philadelphia: Trinity, 1991.

———. *Judaism and Hellenism: Studies in their Encounter in Palestine During the Early Hellenistic Period*, Vol. 1. Translated by J. Bowden. London: SCM Press, 1974.

Hensel, R. "καρπός, κτλ.," *NIDNTT* Vol. 1, pp. 721–23.

Heron, A.I.C. *The Holy Spirit*. Philadelphia: Westminster Press, 1987.

Hildebrandt, W. *An Old Testament Theology of the Spirit of God*. Peabody, MA: Hendrickson, 1995.

Hill, D. *Greek Words with Hebrew Meanings: Studies in the Semantics of Soteriological Terms*, SNTSMS 5. Cambridge: Cambridge University Press, 1967.

Hofius, O. "Das Gesetz des Mose und das Gesetz Christi," *ZTK* 80 (1983), 262–86.

Holladay, W.L. *Jeremiah*, Vol. 2, Hermeneia. Minneapolis: Fortress Press, 1989.

Hollander, H.W.; De Jonge, M. *The Testament of the Twelve Patriarchs: A Commentary*. Leiden: E.J. Brill, 1985.

Holm-Nielsen, S. *Hodayot: Psalms From Qumran*. Aarhus: Universitetsforlaget I Aarhus, 1960.

Holtz, T. "Christliche Interpolationen in 'Joseph and Aseneth,'" *NTS* 14 (1967/68), 482–97.

Hooker, Marna D. "Paul and 'Covenantal Nomism.'" Pages 47–56 in *Paul and Paulinism: Essays in Honour of C.K. Barrett*. Edited by Morna Hooker and S.G. Wilson. London: SPCK, 1982.

———. "Beyond the Things that are Written? St. Paul's Use of Scripture," *NTS* 27 (1981), 295–309.

Hopkins, K. *Conquerors and Slaves, Sociological Studies in Roman History*, Vol. 1. Cambridge: Cambridge University Press, 1978.

Horbury, W. Review of *Paul and Palestinian Judaism* by E.P. Sanders, *ExpTim* 89 (1977–78), 116–18.

Hübner, Hans. *Law in Paul's Thought*. Translated by James C.G. Greig. Edinburgh: T. & T. Clark, 1984.

———. *Gottes Ich und Israel: Zum Schriftgebrauch des Paulus in Römer 9–11*, FRLANT 136. Göttengen: Vandenhoeck & Ruprecht, 1984.

Humphrey, E.M. *Joseph and Aseneth*. Sheffield: Sheffield Academic Press, 2000.

van Imschoot, P. "L'Esprit de Jahvé et l'alliance nouvelle dans l'Ancien Testament," *ETL* 22 (1936), 201–26.

———. "Sagesse et Esprit dans l'Ancien Testament," *RB* 47 (1938), 23–49.

Isaacs, M.E. *The Concept of the Spirit: A Study of Pneuma in Hellenistic Judaism and its Bearing on the New Testament*, Heythrop Monographs 1. London: Heythrop College, 1976.

———. "1 (Ethiopic Apocalypse of) Enoch: A New Translation and Introduction," *OTP*, Vol.1., pp. 5-90.

Jackson, H. "The Resurrection Belief of the Earliest Church: A Response to the Failure of Prophecy?" *JR* 55 (1975), 414-25.

Jeremias, J. *The Prayers of Jesus*. London: SCM, 1967.

Jervell, J. "Ein Interpolator interpretiert: Zu der christlichen Bearbeitung der Testamente der zwölf Patriarchen," in *Studien ze den Testamenten der zwölf Patriarchen*. Edited by W. Eltester. Berlin: Alfred Töpelmann, 1969.

Jervis, L. Ann. *The Purpose of Romans: A Comparative Letter Structure Investigation*. JSNTSup 55. Sheffield: JSOT Press, 1991.

———. *Galatians*, NIBCNT. Peabody, MA: Hendrickson, 1999.

Jewett, R. *Paul's Anthropological Terms: A Study of Their Use in Conflict Settings*, AGJU 10. Leiden: Brill, 1971.

Johnston, G. "'Spirit' and 'Holy Spirit' in the Qumran Literature." Pages 27-42 in *New Testament Sidelights: Essays in Honor of A.C. Purdy*. Edited by H.K. McArthur. Hartford, Conn.: Hartford Seminary Foundation Press, 1960.

Jones, D.R. *Jeremiah*, NCB. Grand Rapids: Wm. B. Eerdmans Publishing Co., 1992.

Jüngel, E. *Paulus und Jesus. Ein Untersuchung zur Präzisierung der Frage nach dem Ursprung der Christologie*. Tübingen: Mohr, 1962.

Kaiser, Jr., W.C. "Leviticus and Paul: 'Do this and you shall live (eternally?)'," *JETS* 14 (1971), 19-28.

Käsemann, E. *Commentary on Romans*. Translated by Geoffrey W. Bromiley. Grand Rapids: Eerdmans/London: SCM, 1980.

Keck, L.E. "The Law of 'The Law of Sin and Death' (Romans 8:1-4): Reflections on the Spirit and Ethics in Paul." Pages 41-57 in *The Divine Helmsman: Studies on God's Control of Human Events, presented to Lou H. Silberman*. Edited by J.L. Crenshaw and S. Sandmel. New York: KTAV, 1980.

Kee, H.C. "Membership in the Covenant People at Qumran and in the Teaching of Jesus." Pages 104-22 in *Jesus and the Dead Sea Scrolls*. Edited by James H. Charlesworth. New York: Doubleday, 1992.

———. "Testament of the Twelve Patriarchs: A New Translation and Introduction," *OTP* Vol.1, pp. 775-828.

Keesmaat, Sylvia C. *Paul and his Story: (Re)Intepreting the Exodus Tradition*, JSNTSup 181. Sheffield: JSOT Press, 1999.

Keil, C.F.; Delitzsch, F. *Biblical Commentary on the Old Testament*, Vols. 1-10. Translated by James Martin. Grand Rapids: Wm. B. Eerdman's Publishing Co., 1985.

Kennedy, G.A. *Aristotle 'On Rhetoric': A Theory of Civic Discourse*. New York/Oxford: Oxford University Press, 1991.

Kerrigan, A. "The 'Sensus Plenior' of Joel III, 1-5 in Act., II, 14-36," in *SP Volumen Alterum*. Paris: Gabalda, 1959.

Kertelge, K. "Righteousness, etc." *EDNT*, Vol. 1, p. 335.

Kevan, E.F. *The Grace of Law: A Study of Puritan Theology*. Grand Rapids: Baker, 1976.

Kim, S. *The Origin of Paul's Gospel*, WUNT 2. Reiche 4. Tübingen: J.C.B. Mohr (Paul Siebeck), 1984.

———. *Paul and the New Perspective: Second Thoughts on the Origin of Paul's Gospel* WUNT 140. Tübingen: J.C.B. Mohr (Paul Siebeck), 2002.

Kleinknecht, H.; Baumgärtel, F.; Bieder, W.; Sjöboerg, E.; Schweizer, E. "πνεῦμα, πνευματικός, πνέω, ἐμπνέω, πνοή, ἐκπνέω, θεόπνευστος," *TDNT*, Vol. VI, pp. 332–455.

Kloppenborg, J.S. "Isis and Sophia in the Book of Wisdom," *HTR* 75 (1982), 57–84.

Knibb, M.A. *The Qumran Community*. Cambridge: Cambridge University Press, 1987.

Knox, J. *Chapters in the Life of Paul*. London: A & C Black, 1974.

———. *The Ethic of Jesus in the Teaching of the Church: Its Authority and Its Relevance*. London: SCM, 1961.

Koch, Dietrich-Alex. *Die Schrift als Zeuge des Evangeliums: Untersuchungen zur Verwendung und zum Verständnis der Schrift bei Paulus*, BHT 69. Tübingen: J.C.B. Mohr (Paul Siebeck), 1986.

Koester, H. *History and Literature of Early Christianity: Introduction to the New Testament*, Vol. 2. Philadelphia: Fortress Press, 1982.

Kremer, J. *Begegnung mit dem Wort (für Heinrich Zimmermann)*. Pages 219–50. Edited by Josef Zmijewski and Ernst Nellessen, BBB 53. Bonn: Peter Hanstein, 1980.

Kugler, R.A. *The Testaments of the Twelve Patriarchs*. Sheffield: Sheffield Academic Press, 2001.

Kühl, E. *Der Brief des Paulus an die Römer*. Leipzig: Quelle & Meyer, 1913.

Kuhn, H,W. *Enderwartung und gegenwärtiges Heil: Untersuchungen zu den Gemeindeliedern von Qumran*, SUNT 4. Göttingen: Vandenhoeck & Ruprecht, 1966.

Kuhn, K.G. "πειρασμός-ἁμαρτία-σάρξ im Neuen Testament und die damit zusammenhängenden Vorstellungen," *ZTK* 49 (1952), 200–22.

Kuhn, Thomas S. *The Structure of Scientific Revolutions*, Second Edition. Chicago: University of Chicago Press, 1970.

Kümmel, W.G. *Römer 7 und die Bekehrung des Paulus*. Leipzig: J.d. Hinrichs, 1929.

Laato, T. *Paulus und das Judentum: Anthropologische Erwägungen*. Abo: Abo Academy, 1991.

Lagrange, M.-J. *Saint Paul: Epître aux Romains*. Paris: Gabalda, 1950.

Lambrecht, J. *The Wretched "I" and Its Liberation: Paul in Romans 7 and 8*, Louvain Theological and Pastoral Monographs 14. Louvain: Peters, 1992.

Lawrence, D.H.; Festinger, L. *Deterrants and Reinforcement*. Stanford: Stanford University Press, 1962.

Leenhardt, F.J. *The Epistle to the Romans: A Commentary*. London: Lutterworth, 1961.

Leven, C. *Die Verheissung des neuen Bundes in ihrem theologiegeschichtlichen Zusammenhang ausgelegt*, FRLANT 137. Göttingen: Vandenhoeck & Ruprecht, 1985.

Levine, B.A. *Leviticus*, JPS Torah Commentary. Philadelphia: Jewish Publication Society, 1989.

Levison, J.R. "Inspiration and the Divine Spirit in the Writings of Philo Judaeus," *Journal for the Study of Judaism in the Persian, Hellenistic, and Roman Period* 26 (1995), 271–323.

Lietzmann, H. *Einführung in die Textgeschichte des Paulusbriefe an die Römer*, HNT. Tübingen: J.C.B. Mohr (Paul Siebeck), 1933.

Lindemann, A. "Die Gerechtigkeit aus dem Gesetz: Erwägungen zur Auslegung und zur Textgeschichte von Römer 10.5," *ZNW* 73 (1982), 231–50.

Little, J.A. "Paul's Use of Analogy: A Structural Analysis of Romans 7:1-6," *CBQ* 46 (1984), 82-90.

Lloyd-Jones, M. *Romans: An Exposition of Chapter 8:5-17: The Sons of God.* Grand Rapids: Zondervan, 1975.

Loane, M.L. *The Hope of Glory: An Exposition of the Eighth Chapter of the Epistle to the Romans.* London: Hodder and Stoughton, 1968.

Lohse, E. "ὁ νόμος τοῦ πνεύματος τῆς ζωῆς: Exegetische Anmerkungen zu Röm 8:2." Pages 128-36 in *Die Vielfalt des Neuen Testaments.* Göttingen: Vandenhoeck and Ruprecht, 1982.

——. "Palestinian Judaism: Israel and the Righteous as Sons of God," *TDNT*, Vol. VIII, pp. 359-40.

Longenecker, B.W. *Eschatology and the Covenant: A Comparison of 4 Ezra and Romans 1-11,* JSNTSup 57. Sheffield: JSOT Press, 1991.

Longenecker, R.N. *Paul, Apostle of Liberty: The Origin and Nature of Paul's Christianity.* Grand Rapids: Baker, 1976.

——. *Galatians,* WBC 41. Dallas: Word, 1990.

Luz, U. "Der alte und der neue Bund bei Paulus und im Hebräerbrief," *EvT* 27 (1967), 318-36.

——. *Das Geschichtsverständnis des Paulus,* BevT 49. Munich: Chr. Kaiser, 1968.

Lyall, F. "Roman Law in the Writings of Paul- Adoption," *JBL* 88 (1969), 458-66.

Lyonnet, S. "Le Nouveau Testament à la lumière de l'Ancien, à propos de Rom 8,2-4," *NRTh* 87 (1965), 561-87.

——. "'Tu ne convoiteras pas' (Rom. vii 7)." Pages 157-65 in *Neotestamentica et patristica: Eine Freundesgabe, Herrn Professor Dr. Oscar Cullmann...überreicht,* NovTSup 6. Edited by W.C. van Unnik. Leiden: Brill, 1962.

Ma, W. *Until the Spirit Comes: The Spirit of God in the Book of Isaiah,* JSOTSup 271. Sheffield: Sheffield Academic Press, 1999.

MacMullen, R. *Roman Social Relations: 50 B.C. to A.D. 284.* New Haven, CT: Yale University Press, 1974.

Maier, G. *Mensch und freier Wille: Nach den jüdischen Religionsparteien zwischen Ben Sira und Paulus,* WUNT 12. Tübingen: J.C.B. Mohr (Paul Siebeck), 1971.

Malina, B.J. "Normative Dissonance and Christian Origins," *Semeia* 35 (1986), 35-59.

——. "Jesus as Charismatic Leader?" *BTB* 14 (1984), 55-62.

——. "The Individual and the Community- Personality in the Social World of Early Christianity," *BTB* 9 (1979), 126-38.

——. "Is There a Circum Mediterranean Person? Looking for Stereotypes," *BTB* 22 (1992), 66-87.

——. *The New Testament World: Insights from Cultural Anthropology.* Atlanta: John Knox Press, 1981.

Malina, B.J.; Neyrey, J.H. "First Century Personality: Dyadic, not Individual." Pages 67-96 in *The Social World of Luke-Acts.* Edited by J.H. Neyrey. Peabody, MA: Hendrickson Publishers, 1991.

——. *Portraits of Paul: An Archaeology of Ancient Personality.* Louisville, KY: Westminster- John Knox Press, 1996.

Manns, F. *Le symbole eau-esprit dans le Judaïsme ancien*, SBF no 19. Jerusalem: Franciscan Printing Press, 1983.

Martin, Brice L. *Christ and the Law in Paul*. Leiden: E.J. Brill, 1989.

Martin, R.P. *2 Corinthians*, WBC 40. Waco, TX: Word Books, Publisher, 1986.

Martyn, J.L. "Apocalyptic Antinomies in Paul's Letter to the Galatians," *NTS* 31 (1985), 410-24.

Mauss, M. "A Category of the Human Mind: The Notion of Personhood; the Notion of Self." Pages 1-25 in *The Category of the Person: Anthropology, Philosophy, History*. Edited by M. Carrithers, S. Collins, and S. Lukes. Translated by W.D. Halls. Cambridge: Cambridge Unversity Press, 1985.

May, H.G. "Cosmological Reference in the Qumran Doctrine of the Two Spirits and in Old Testament Imagery," *JBL* 82 (1963), 1-14

McComiskey, T.E. "Micah," *EBC*, Vol. 7. Grand Rapids: Zondervan Publishing House, 1985.

McDonagh, E.L. "Attitude Changes and Paradigm Shifts: Social Psychological Foundations of the Kuhnian Thesis," *SSS* 6 (1976), 51-76.

Melanchthon, P. *Commmentary on Romans*. Translated by F. Kramer. St. Louis: Concordia Publishing House, 1992.

Menzies, Robert P. *The Development of Early Christian Pneumatology with Special Reference to Luke-Acts*, JSNTSup 54. Sheffield: JSOT Press, 1991.

Metzger, B.M. *A Textual Commentary on the Greek New Testament*. London: United Bible Societies, 1971.

Meyer, P.W. "Romans 10.4 and the 'End' of the Law." Pages 59-78 in *The Divine Helmsman: Studies in God's Control of Humans Events, Presented to Lou H. Silberman*. Edited by James L. Crenshaw and Samuel Sandmel. New York: KTAV Publishing House, Inc., 1980.

Meyer, R.; Schweizer, E. "σάρξ, κτλ.," *TDNT*, Vol. VII, pp. 98-151.

Middendorf, M.P. *The "I" in the Storm: A Study of Romans 7*. Saint Louis: Concordia Academic Press, 1997.

Miller, P.D. *Deuteronomy*, Interpretation. Louisville: John Knox Press, 1990.

Montague, G.T. *The Holy Spirit: Growth of a Biblical Tradition*. New York: Paulist Press, 1976.

Montefiore, Claude G. "Rabbinic Judaism and the Epistles of Paul," *JQR* 13 (1900-1901), 161-217.

Moo, D.J. "Israel and Paul in Romans 7.7-12," *NTS* 32 (1986), 122-35.

——. *Epistle to the Romans*, NICNT. Grand Rapids: Wm. B. Eerdmans Publishing Co., 1996.

——. *Romans 1-8*, The Wycliffe Exegetical Commentary. Chicago: Moody Press, 1991.

Moore, G.F.. "Christian Writers on Judaism," *HTR* 14 (1921), 197-254.

——. *Judaism in the First Centuries of the Christian Era*, Vol. 1. New York: Schocken, 1971.

Morris, L. *The Epistle to the Romans*. Grand Rapids: Wm. B. Eerdmans Publishing Co. / Leicester: Inter-Varsity, 1988.

Moule, C.F.D. *An Idiom Book of New Testament Greek*. Cambridge: University, 1971.

——. "Obligation in the Ethic of Paul." Pages 389-406 in *Christian History and Interpretation: Studies Presented to John Knox*. Edited by W.R. Farmer, C.F.D. Moule, and R.H. Niebuhr. Cambridge: Cambridge University Press, 1967.

Mounce, R.H. *Romans*, NAC 27. Nashville: Broadman and Holman, 1995.

Munck, J. *Paul and the Salvation of Mankind*. London: SCM, 1959.

Murphy-O'Connor, J.; Charlesworth, J.H., eds. *Paul and the Dead Sea Scrolls*. New York: Crossroads, 1990.

Murray, John. *The Epistle to the Romans*, NICNT. Grand Rapids: Wm. B. Eerdmans Publishing Co., 1968.

Neuss, W. *Das Buch Ezechiel in Theologie und Kunst bis zum Ende des XII. Jahrhunderts: Beiträge zur Geschichte des Alten Mönchtumus und des Benediktinerordens*, Vols. 1-2. Münster: Aschendorff, 1912.

Neve, L. *The Spirit of God in the Old Testament*. Tokyo: Seibunsha, 1972.

Nickelsburg, George W.E. *Jewish Literature Between the Bible and the Mishnah: A Historical and Literary Introduction*. London: SCM Press, 1981.

Nicholson, Ernest W. *The Book of the Prophet Jeremiah: Chapters 26-52*. Cambridge: Cambridge University Press, 1975.

North, C.R. *Isaiah 40-55* Torch Bible Commentary, Second Edition. London: SCM Press, 1964.

Nötscher, F. "Heiligkeit in den Qumranschriften," *RevQ* 2 (1960), 333-44.

Nygren, A. *Commentary on Romans*. London: SCM/Philadelphia: Muhlenberg, 1949.

Oepke, A. "λάμπω, κτλ.," *TDNT*, Vol. IV, pp. 16-28.

———. "εἰς," *TDNT*, Vol. II, pp. 420-34.

O'Neill, J.C. *Paul's Letter to the Romans*. Baltimore: Penguin Books, 1975.

Osten- Sacken, P. von der. *Römer 8 als Beispiel paulinischer Soteriologie*, FRLANT 112. Göttingen: Vandenhoeck & Ruprecht, 1975.

———. *Gott und Belial: Traditionsgeschichtliche Untersuchungen zum Dualismus in den Texten aus Qumran*. Göttingen: Vandenhoeck & Ruprecht, 1969.

———. *Die Heiligkeit der Tora: Studien zum Gesetz bei Paulus*. Munich: Chr. Kaiser, 1989.

Paulsen, H. *Überlieferung und Auslegung in Römer 8*, WUNT 43. Neukirchen-Vluyn: Neukirchener Verlag, 1974.

Patte, Daniel. *Paul's Faith and the Power of the Gospel*. Philadelphia: Fortress Press, 1983.

Pearson, B.A. "Hellenistic-Jewish Wisdom Speculation and Paul," Pages 43-66 in *Aspects of Wisdom in Judaism and Early Christianity*, UNDCSJCA, 1. Edited by R.L. Wilken Notre Dame, IN: University of Notre Dame Press, 1975.

Perowne, T.T. *The Books of Haggai and Zechariah*. Cambridge: Cambridge University Press, 1886.

Pinnock, Clark H. "The Concept of Spirit in the Epistles of Paul," Ph.D. diss., Manchester, 1963.

Pryke, J. "'Spirit' and 'Flesh' in the Qumran Documents and some New Testament Texts," *RevQ* 5 (1965), 345-60.

Quell, G. "ἀλήθεια, κτλ.," *TDNT*, Vol. I, pp. 232-7.

———. "δίκη, κτλ.," *TDNT*, Vol. II, pp. 174-75.

Quell, G.; Behm, J. "διατίθημι, διαθήκη," *TDNT*, Vol. II, pp. 104-34.

von Rad, G. *Wisdom in Israel*. Translated by J.D. Martine. London: SCM, 1972.

———. "שָׁלוֹם in the OT," *TDNT*, Vol.II, pp. 402-6.

Räisänen, Heikki. *Paul and the Law*, Second Edition, WUNT no. 29. Tübingen: J.C.B. Mohr (Paul Siebeck), 1987.

——. "The 'Law' of Faith and the Spirit." Pages 63-68 in *Jesus, Paul and Torah: Collected Essays*, JSNT no. 43. Translated by David E. Orton. Sheffield: JSOT Press, 1992.

——. "Das 'Gesetz des Glauben' (Röm 3:27) und das 'Gesetz des Geistes' (Röm 8:2)," *NTS* 26 (1979/80), 101-17.

Reicke, B. "Paulus über das Gesetz," *TZ* 41 (1985), 237-57.

Rengstorf, K.H. "δοῦλος, κτλ.," *TDNT*, Vol. II, pp. 261-80.

van Rensburg, J.J.J. "The Children of God in Romans 8," *Neot* (1981), 139-79.

Ridderbos, H.N. *The Epistle of Paul to the Churches of Galatia*, NICNT. Grand Rapids: Wm. B. Eerdmans Publishing Co., 1953.

Riesenfeld, E.H. "περί," *TDNT*, Vol. VI, p. 55.

Ringgren, H. *The Faith of Qumran: Theology of the Dead Sea Scrolls*. Translated by Emilie T. Sander. Philadelphia: Fortress Press, 1963.

Robinson, J.A.T. *The Body: A Study in Pauline Theology*, SBT 5. London: SCM, 1952.

——. *Wrestling with Romans*. Philadelphia: Westminster, 1979.

Russell, W.B. "Insights from Postmodernism's Emphasis on Interpretive Communities in the Interpretation of Romans 7," *JETS* 37 (1994), 511-27.

Sand, A. *Der Begriff 'Sarx' in den paulinischen Hauptbriefen*, BU 2. Regenburg: Pustet, 1967.

Sanday, W.; Headlam, A.C. *The Epistle to the Romans* ICC. Edinburgh: T & T Clark, 1896, 1906, 1958.

Sanders, E.P. *Paul and Palestinian Judaism: A Comparison of Patterns of Religion*. Philadelphia: Fortress Press, 1983.

——. *Paul, the Law, and the Jewish People*. Philadelphia: Fortress Press, 1983.

Sandmel, Samuel. *Philo's Place in Judaism: A Study of Conceptions of Abraham in Jewish Literature*. New York: Ktav Publishing House, Inc., 1971.

van de Sandt, H.W.M. "Research into Rom. 8.4a: The Legal Claim of the Law," *Bijdr* 37 (1976), 252-69.

——. "An Explanation of Rom. 8,4a," *Bijdr* 37 (1976), 361-78.

Sänger, D. *Antikes Judentum und die Mysterien: Religonsgeschichtliche Untersuchungen zu Joseph und Aseneth*. Tübingen: J.C.B. Mohr (Paul Siebeck), 1980.

Schiffman, Lawrence H. *Reclaiming the Dead Sea Scrolls: The History of Judaism, the Background of Christianity, the Lost Library of Qumran*. New York: Doubleday, 1995.

Schlier, H. "κεφαλή, ἀνακεφαλαιόομαι," *TDNT*, Vol. III, pp. 673-682.

——. *Der Römerbrief Kommentar*, HTKNT. Freiburg im Breisgau: Herder, 1977.

Schmithals, W. *Die theologische Anthropologie des Paulus: Auslegung von Röm 7,17-8,39*. Stuttgart: Kohlhammer, 1980.

Schnabel, E.J. *Law and Wisdom from Ben Sira to Paul*. Tübingen: J.C.B. Mohr, 1985.

Schneider, B. "The Meaning of St. Paul's Antithesis 'The Letter and the Spirit," *CBQ* 15 (1953), 163-207.

Schoemaker, W.R. "The Use of Ruach in the Old Testament and πνεῦμα in the New Testament," *JBL* 23 (1904), 13-67.

Schoenberg, M.W. "Huiothesia: The Word and the Institution," *Scr* 15 (1963), 115-23.

Schoeps, H.J. *Paul: The Theology of the Apostle in the Light of Jewish Religious History*. Philadelphia: Westminster, 1961.

Scholer, D.M. "An Introduction to Philo" in *The Works of Philo: Complete and Unabridged.* Translated by C.D. Yonge. Peabody, MA: Hendrickson Publishers, 1993.

Schrage, W. "τυφλός, κτλ.," *TDNT*, Vol. VIII, pp. 270-94.

Schreiner, T.R. *The Law and Its Fulfillment: A Pauline Theology of Law.* Grand Rapids: Baker, 1993.

———. *Romans.* Grand Rapids: Baker Books, 1998.

Schrenk, G. "δικαίωμα," *TDNT*, Vol. II, pp. 219-20.

———. "δίκη, κτλ.," *TDNT*, Vol. II, pp. 179-225.

———. "γράφω, γραφή, γράμμα, κτλ.," *TDNT*, Vol. 1, pp. 742-73.

Schrenk, G.; Quell, G. "πατήρ, κτλ.," *TDNT*, Vol. V, pp. 945-1022.

Schürer, E. *The History of the Jewish People in the Age of Jesus Christ,* Vols. I-III. Edited by G. Vermes and F. Millar. Edinburgh: T & T Clark, 1973-87.

Schweitzer, Albert. *The Mysticism of Paul the Apostle.* Translated by W. Montgomery. New York: Seabury, 1968.

Schweizer, E. "υἱός, κτλ.," *TDNT*, Vol. VIII, pp. 383-84.

Scott, J.M. *Adoption as Sons of God,* WUNT 2.48. Tübingen: J.C.B. Mohr (Paul Siebeck), 1992.

Seesemann, H. "πάλαι, κτλ.," *TDNT*, Vol. V, pp. 717-21.

———. "πατέω and Compounds in the NT," *TDNT*, Vol. V, pp. 943-45.

Segal, Alan F. *Paul the Convert: The Apostolate and Apostasy of Saul the Pharisee.* New Haven/London: Yale University Press, 1990.

Seitz, C.R. "Expository Articles: Ezekiel 37:1-14," *Inter* 46 (Jan., 1992), 53-56.

Seitz, O. "Two Spirits in Man: An Essay in Biblical Exegesis," *NTS* 6 (1959-60), 82-95.

Sekki, A. *The Meaning of Rua(c)h at Qumran.* Atlanta: Scholars Press, 1989.

Seow, C.L. *A Grammar for Biblical Hebrew.* Nashville: Abingdon Press, 1987.

Silva, M. *Biblical Words and Their Meaning: An Introduction to Lexical Semantics.* Grand Rapids: Zondervan Publishing House, 1983.

———. "Is the Law against the Promises? The Significance of Gal. 3:21 for Covenant Continuity." Pages 153-67 in *Theonomy: A Reformed Critique.* Edited by W.S. Barker and W.R. Godfrey. Grand Rapids: Zondervan, 1990.

Snodgrass, K. "Spheres of Influence. A Possible Solution for the Problem of Paul and the Law," *JSNT* 32 (1988), 93-113.

Snow, D.A.; Machalek, R. "On the Presumed Fragility of Unconventional Beliefs," *JSSR* 21 (1982), 15-26.

Stacey, W.D. *The Pauline View of Man in Relation to Its Judaic and Hellenistic Background.* London: Macmillan, 1956.

Stadelmann, H. *Ben Sira als Schriftgelehrter: Eine Untersuchung zum Berufsbild des vormakkabäischen Sofer unter Berücksichtigung seines Verhältnisses zu Priester-Propheten- und Weisheitslehrertum,* WUNT 2.6. Tübingen: J.C.B. Mohr (Paul Siebeck), 1980.

Stählin, G. "φιλέω, κτλ.," *TDNT*, Vol. IX, pp. 113-71.

Stalder, K. *Das Werk des Geistes in der Heilgung bei Paulus.* Zurich: EVZ, 1962.

Stanley, C.D. *Paul and the Language of Scripture: Citation Technique in the Pauline Epistles and Contemporary Literature,* SNTSMS 69. Cambridge: Cambridge University Press, 1992.

Stein, R.H. *Difficult Passages in the Epistles.* Grand Rapids: Baker, 1988.

Stendahl, K. *Paul among Jews and Gentiles.* Philadelphia: Fortress, 1976.

———. "The Scrolls and the New Testament: An Introduction and a Perspective." Pages 1-17 in *The Scrolls and the New Testament.* Edited by Krister Stendahl. London: SCM Press Ltd., 1957.

Stockhausen, C.K. *Moses' Veil and the Glory of the New Covenant: The Exegetical Substructure of II Cor. 3:1-4:6,* AnBib 116. Rome: Pontifical Biblical Institute, 1989.

Stott, J.R.W. *The Message of Galatians,* BST. Downers Grove: Inter-Varsity Press, 1968.

———. *Romans: God's Good News for the World.* Downers Grove, Ill: InterVarsity, 1994.

Strathmann, H. "μάρτυς, κτλ.," *TDNT,* Vol. IV, pp. 474-514.

Stuhlmacher, P. "Paul's Understanding of the Law in the Letter to the Romans," *SEA* 50 (1985), 87-104.

———. "The Apostle Paul's View of Righteousness," in *Reconciliation, Law and Righteousness,* Translated by Everett R. Kalin. Philadelphia: Fortress, 1986, pp. 68-93.

———. "The Law as a Topic of Biblical Theology." Pages 110-33 in *Reconciliation, Law and Righteousness: Essays in Biblical Theology.* Philadelphia: Fortress Press, 1986.

———. *Paul's Letter to the Romans: A Commentary.* Translated by Scott J. Hafemann. Louisville, Westminster/ John Knox Press, 1994.

Talmon, S. "The Community of the Renewed Covenant: Between Judaism and Christianity." Pages 3-24 in *The Community of the Renewed Covenant.* Edited by Eugene Ulrich and James Vanderkam. Notre Dame: University of Notre Dame Press, 1994.

Tannehill, R.C. *Dying and Rising with Christ: A Study in Pauline Theology,* BZNW 32. Berlin: Töpelmann, 1966.

Taylor, V. *The Epistle to the Romans,* Epworth's Preacher's Commentaries, Second Edition. London: Epworth Press, 1962.

Thielman, Frank. *From Plight to Solution: A Jewish Framework for Understanding Paul's View of the Law in Galatians and Romans.* Leiden/ New York: E.J. Brill, 1989.

———. *Paul and the Law: A Contextual Approach.* Downers Grove, Illinois: InterVarsity Press, 1994.

———. *The Law and the New Testament: The Question of Continuity.* New York: The Crossroad Publishing Company, 1999.

Thiselton, A.C. "Flesh (σάρξ)," *NIDNTT,* Vol. 1, pp. 671-82.

Thompson, J.A. *The Book of Jeremiah,* NICOT. Grand Rapids: Wm. B. Eerdmans Publishing Co., 1980.

Thompson, M. *Clothed with Christ: The Example and Teaching of Jesus in Romans 12.1-15.13,* JSNTSup 59. Sheffield: JSOT Press, 1991.

Thompson, R.W. "How is the Law Fulfilled in Us? An Interpretation of Rom 8:4," *LS* 11 (1986), 31-40.

Thurén, L. *Derhetorizing Paul: A Dynamic Perspective on Pauline Theology and the Law.* Tübingen: J.C.B. Mohr (Paul Siebeck), 2000.

Thüsing, W. *Per Christum in Deum: Studien zum Verhältnis von Christozentrik und Theozentrik in den paulinischen Hauptbriefen,* NTAbh n.s. 1. Münster in Westfalen: Aschendorff, 1965.

Tomson, Peter. *Paul and the Jewish Law: Halakha in the Letters of the Apostle to the Gentiles.* Assen: Van Gorcum and Minneapolis: Fortress Press, 1990.

Treves, M. "The Two Spirits of the Rule of the Community," *RevQ* 3 (1961), 449-52.

Triandis, H.C. "The Self and Social Behaviour in Differing Cultural Contexts," *PR* 98 (1989), 506-20.

——. "Cross-Cultural Studies of Individualism and Collectivism." Pages 41-133 in *Cross-Cultural Perspectives*. Edited by J.J. Berman. Lincoln, Nebraska: University of Nebraska Press, 1990.

Trudinger, P. "An Autobiographical Digression? A Note on Romans 7:7-25," *ExpTim* 107 (1995-6), 173-74.

Turner, M.M.B. *Power From On High: The Spirit in Israel's Restoration and Witness in Luke-Acts*, JPTSup. 9. Sheffield: Sheffield Academic Press, 1996.

——. "The Significance of Spirit Endowment for Paul," *VoxEv* 9 (1975), 58-69.

Turner, N. Syntax, Vol. 3 of *A Grammar of New Testament Greek*. Edinburgh: T & T Clark, 1963.

Ulrichsen, J.H. *Die Grundschrift der Testamente der Zwölf Patriarchen: Eine Untersuchung zu Umfang, Inhalt und Eigenart der ursprünglichen Schrift*, Acta Universitatis Upsaliensis, Historia Religionum, 10. Uppsala: Almqvist & Wiksell, 1991.

Urbach, E.E. *The Sages: Their Concepts and Beliefs*, Vol. 1. Jerusalem: Magnes, 1979.

VanderKam, J.C. *Textual and Historical Studies in the Book of Jubilees Harvard Semitic Museum*, Harvard Semitic Monograph 14. Missoula, Montana: Scholars Press, 1977.

——. "The Book of Jubilees," in *Outside the Old Testament*. Edited by M. De Jonge. Cambridge: Cambridge University Press, 1985.

Verbeke, G. *L'évolution de la doctrine du Pneuma du Stoicisme à S. Augustin*. Paris:Desclée de Brouwer, 1945.

——. "Le pneuma dans la doctrine de Philon," *ETL* 27 (1951), 390-437.

Vermes, Geza. *Jesus the Jew: A Historian's Reading of the Gospels*. Philadelphia: Fortress Press, 1973.

——. *An Introduction to the Complete Dead Sea Scrolls*. Minneapolis: Fortress Press, 2000.

——. "The Qumran Interpretation of Scripture in its Historical Setting." Pages 84-97 in *The Annual Leeds University Oriental Society*, Vol VI. Edited by John McDonald. Leiden: E.J. Brill, 1969.

Vos, G. "The Eschatological Aspect of the Pauline Conception of the Spirit." Pages 211-59 in *Bulletin and Theological Studies*. New York: Charles Scribner's Sons, 1912.

Vos, J. *Traditionsgeschichtliche Untersuchungen zur paulinischen Pneumatologie*. Assen: Van Gorcum, 1973.

Vos, J.S. "To Make the Weaker Argument Defeat the Stronger: Sophistical Argumentation in Paul's Letter to the Romans." Pages 217-31 in *Rhetorical Argumentation in Biblical Texts*. Edited by T.H. Olbricht, W. Ubelacker, and A. Eriksson. Harrisburg, PA: Trinity Press International, 2001.

Wallace, D.B. *Greek Grammar Beyond the Basics: An Exegetical Syntax of the New Testament*. Grand Rapids: Zondervan, 1996.

Walton, D. *Fallacies Arising from Ambiguity*, ALS 1. Boston, London: Kluwer Academic Publishers, 1996.

Wanke, G. "φόβος, κτλ.," *TDNT*, Vol. IX, pp. 197-219.

Watson, F. *Paul, Judaism, and the Gentiles: A Sociological Approach*, SNTSMS 56. Cambridge: Cambridge University Press, 1986.

Webb, R.L. *John the Baptizer and Prophet: A Socio-Historical Study.* Sheffield: JSOT Press, 1991.

Weber, Ferdinand. *Jüdische Theologie auf Grund des Talmud und verwandter Schriften*, Second Edition. Edited by Franz Delitzsch and George Schnedermann. Leipzig: Dörffling Franke, 1897.

Wedderburn, A.J.M. *Baptism and Resurrection: Studies in Pauline Theology against Its Graeco-Roman Background*, WUNT 44. Tübingen: J.C.B. Mohr, 1987.

Weippert, H. "Das Wort vom Neuen Bund in Jeremia xxxi 31-34," *VT* 29 (1979), 336-51.

Weiss, H.F. "Φαρισαῖος," *TDNT*, Vol. IX, pp. 35-48.

Wenham, G. *A Commentary on Leviticus*, NICOT. Grand Rapids: Wm. B. Eerdmans Publishing Co., 1979.

Wenk, M. *Community-Forming Power: The Socio-Ethical Role of the Spirit in Luke Acts*, JPT Supp. 19. Sheffield: Sheffield Academic Press, 2000.

Wernberg-Moller, P. "A Reconsideration of the Two Spirits in the Rule of the Community," *RevQ* 3 (1961), 413-42.

Wernik, U. "Frustrated Beliefs and Early Christianity," *Numen* 22 (1975), 96-130.

Westerholm, Stephen. *Israel's Law and the Church's Faith: Paul and His Recent Interpreters.* Grand Rapids: Wm. B. Eerdmans Publishing Co., 1988.

——. "On Fulfilling the Whole Law (Gal. 5.14)," *SEA* 51 (1985-87), 229-37.

——. "Letter and Spirit: The Foundation of Pauline Ethics," *NTS* 30 (1984), 229-48.

Westermann, Claus. *Isaiah 40-66: A Commentary.* Translated by David M.G. Stalker. Philadelphia: Westminster Press, 1969.

Whiteley, D.E.H. *The Theology of St. Paul*, Second Edition. Oxford: Basil Blackwell, 1974.

Whybray, R.N. *The Heavenly Counsellor in Isaiah XI. 13-14.* Cambridge: Cambridge University Press, 1971.

Wicklund, Robert A.; Brehm, Jack W. *Perspectives on Cognitive Dissonance.* Hillsdale, NJ: Lawrence Erlbaum Associates, Publishers, 1976.

Wilckens, Ulrich. "Die Bekehrung des Paulus als religionsgeschichtliches Problem." Pages 11-32 in *Rechtfertigung als Freiheit: Paulusstudien.* Neukirchen-Vluyn: Neukirchener, 1974.

——. "Uber Abassungszweck und Aufbau des Römerbriefs." Pages 110-70 in *Rechtfertigung als Freiheit: Paulusstudien.* Neukircken-Vlugn: Neukircken-Verlag, 1974.

——. *Der Brief an die Römer*, EKKNT 6. 3 Vols. Zürich: Benziger/ Neukirchen-Vluyn: Neukirchener Verlag, 1982.

Williams, R.J. *Hebrew Syntax: An Outline.* Toronto: University of Toronto Press, 1967.

Williamson, R. *Jews in the Hellenistic World: Philo.* Cambridge: Cambridge University Press, 1989.

Windisch, H. *Der zweite Korintherbrief.* Göttingen: Vandenhoeck & Ruprecht, 1924.

Winston, D. *The Wisdom of Solomon*, AB 43. New York: Doubleday, 1979.

Wintermute, O.S. "Jubilees: A New Translation and Introduction," *OTP*, Vol. II, pp. 35-142.

Wise, M.O. *The Temple Scroll: Its Composition, Date, Purpose and Provenance.* Ph.D. dissertation, University of Chicago, 1988.

Wolff, Hans Walter. *Anthropologie des Alten Testaments*, Fifth Edition. Munich: Chr. Kaiser Verlag, 1990.

Wolter, M. *Rechtfertigung und zukünftiges Heil: Untersuchungen zu Röm 5:1-11*, BZNW 43. Berlin: de Gruyter, 1978.

Wright, N.T. *The Climax of the Covenant: Christ and the Law in Pauline Theology*. Edinburgh: T & T Clark, 1991.

————. "The Messiah and the People of God: A Study of Pauline Theology with Particular Reference to the Argument of the Epistle to the Romans," D.Phil., Oxford University, 1980.

Wright, R.B. "Psalms of Solomon: A New Translation and Introduction," *OTP*, Vol. 2, pp. 639-670.

Wülfing von Martitz, P.; Fohrer, G.; Schweizer, E.; Lohse, E.; Schneemelcher, W. "υἱός, υἱοθεσία," *TDNT*, Vol. VIII, pp. 334-399.

Young, E.J. *The Book of Isaiah: The English Text, with Introduction, Exposition,and Notes*, Vol. III. Grand Rapids: Wm. B. Eerdmans Publishing Co., 1972.

Young, R.A. *Intermediate New Testament Greek: A Linguistic and Exegetical Approach*. Nashville, TN: Broadman and Holman Publishers, 1994.

Zerwick, M. *Biblical Greek*. Translated by J. Smith. Rome: Biblical Institute, 1963.

Ziesler, J.A. *The Meaning of Righteousness in Paul: A Linguistic and Theological Enquiry*, SNTSMS 20. Cambridge: Cambridge University Press, 1972.

————. "The Just Requirement of the Law (Romans 8.4)," *ABR* 35 (1987), 77-82.

————. *Paul's Letter to the Romans* TPI New Testament Commentaries. London: SCM Press/ Philadelphia: Trinity Press International, 1989.

Zimmerli, W. *Ezekiel*, Vol. 2, Hermeneia. Translated by James D. Martin. Philadelphia: Fortress Press, 1983.

Index

Studies in Biblical Literature

This series invites manuscripts from scholars in any area of biblical literature. Both established and innovative methodologies, covering general and particular areas in biblical study, are welcome. The series seeks to make available studies that will make a significant contribution to the ongoing biblical discourse. Scholars who have interests in gender and sociocultural hermeneutics are particularly encouraged to consider this series.

For further information about the series and for the submission of manuscripts, contact:

Peter Lang Publishing
Acquisitions Department
P.O. Box 1246
Bel Air, Maryland 21014-1246

To order other books in this series, please contact our Customer Service Department:

(800) 770-LANG (within the U.S.)
(212) 647-7706 (outside the U.S.)
(212) 647-7707 FAX

or browse online by series at:

WWW.PETERLANG.COM